Each year Americans spend at least 120 billion hours and over $150 billion on legal forms of entertainment. In this newly revised book, Harold Vogel, managing director and senior entertainment industry analyst at Cowen & Co. (and formerly at Merrill Lynch), examines the business economics of the major entertainment enterprises: movies and television programming, music, broadcasting, cable television, casino gambling and wagering, sports, performing arts, theme parks, and toys. The fourth edition adds a key chapter on publishing and the Internet and integrates international dimensions of the broadcasting, cable, film, and music industries in particular. The result is a comprehensive, up-to-date reference guide to the economics, financing, production, and marketing of entertainment-related goods and services in the United States and overseas.

The books brings together valuable data from a wide variety of sources to provide a detailed analysis of changes over time of each of the industry segments discussed. After a general introduction to the economic factors affecting leisure and entertainment, the book considers each major segment separately, providing a brief historical overview and a systematic discussion of the production, distribution, and financial accounting procedures. Periodic examples illustrate the actual methods used by the businesses. The book's usefulness as a reference is further enhanced by timeliness and the expanded glossary and appendices of the fourth edition.

Investors, executives, lawyers, arts administrators, accountants, M.B.A.s, journalists, and general readers will find that *Entertainment Industry Economics* provides a strong foundation for understanding how the various entertainment industries operate, and how entertainment relates to the economy as a whole. The book is unique in taking a fully integrated approach to the business of entertainment.

Entertainment industry economics

Entertainment industry economics

A guide for financial analysis

FOURTH EDITION

HAROLD L. VOGEL

CAMBRIDGE
UNIVERSITY PRESS

PUBLISHED BY THE PRESS SYNDICATE OF THE UNIVERSITY OF CAMBRIDGE
The Pitt Building, Trumpington Street, Cambridge, CB2 1RP, United Kingdom

CAMBRIDGE UNIVERSITY PRESS
The Edinburgh Building, Cambridge CB2 2RU, United Kingdom
40 West 20th Street, New York, NY 10011-4211, USA
10 Stamford Road, Oakleigh, Melbourne 3166, Australia

First published 1998

Printed in the United State of America

Typeset in Times Roman

Library of Congress Cataloging-in-Publication Data
Vogel, Harold L., 1946–
    Entertainment industry economics : a guide for financial analysis
  / Harold L. Vogel. — 4th ed.
        p.   cm.
    Includes bibliographical references (p.   ) and index.
    ISBN 0-521-59438-3 (hard)
    1. Performing arts—Finance.   I. Title.
  PN1590.F55V6   1997
  338.4'7791—dc21   97-13160
                                                                          CIP

A catalog record for this book is available from the British Library

ISBN 0 521 59438 3 hardback

TO MY DEAR FATHER
—WHO WOULD HAVE BEEN SO PROUD

Contents

Preface

en·ter·tain·ment — the act of diverting, amusing, or causing someone's time to pass agreeably; something that diverts, amuses, or occupies the attention agreeably.

in·dus·try — a department or branch of a craft, art, business, or manufacture: a division of productive or profit-making labor; especially one that employs a large personnel and capital; a group of productive or profit-making enterprises or organizations that have a similar technological structure of production and that produce or supply technically substitutable goods, services, or sources of income.

ec·o·nom·ics — a social science that studies the production, distribution, and consumption of commodities; considerations of cost and return.

Webster's Third New Unabridged International Dictionary, G. & C. Merriam Company, Springfield, Massachusetts, 1967.

Each year Americans cumulatively spend at least 120 billion hours and more than $150 billion on legal forms of entertainment. So we might begin by asking: What is entertainment, why is there so much interest in it, and what do its many forms have in common?

At the most fundamental level, anything that stimulates, encourages, or otherwise generates a condition of pleasurable diversion could be called entertainment. The French word, *divertissement,* perhaps best captures this essence.

Yet entertainment can be much more than a mere diversion. It is something that is so universally interesting and appealing because, when it is effective, it moves you emotionally. As the Latin root verb *tenare* suggests, it grabs you: it touches your soul.

Although life is full of constraints and disciplines, responsibilities and chores, and a host of things disagreeable, entertainment, in contrast, encompasses activities that people enjoy and look forward to doing, hearing, or seeing. This is the basis of the demand for – or the consumption of – entertainment products and services; this is the primary attribute shared by the many distinct topics – from cinema to sports, from theme parks to theater – that are discussed in the pages that follow.

Entertainment – the cause – is thus obversely defined through its effect: a satisfied and happy psychological state. Yet, somehow, it matters not whether the effect is achieved through active or passive means. Playing the piano can be just as pleasurable as playing the stereo.

Entertainment indeed means so many different things to so many people that a manageable analysis requires sharper boundaries to be drawn. Such boundaries are here established by classifying entertainment activities into industry segments – that is, enterprises or organizations of significant size that have similar technological structures of production and that produce or supply goods, services, or sources of income that are substitutable.

Classification along those lines facilitates contiguous discussion of entertainment *software,* as we might more generically label films, records, and video games, and of *hardware* – the physical appurtenances and equipment on which or in which software, the instruction sets, are executed. Such classification also allows us to more easily trace the effects of technological developments in this field.

In fact, so accustomed are we now to continuous improvements in the performance of entertainment hardware and software, that we have trouble remembering that early in the twentieth century, moving pictures and music recordings were novelties, radio was regarded as a modern-day miracle, and television was a laboratory curiosity. Simple transistors and lasers had yet to be invented and electronic computers and earth-orbiting communications satellites were still in the realm of science fiction.

These fruits of applied technology have nevertheless spawned new art forms and vistas of human expression and have brought to millions of people around the world, at virtually the flick of a switch, a much more varied and higher-quality mix of entertainment than has ever before been imagined feasible.

Little or none of this, however, has happened because of *ars gratia artis* (art for art's sake) – in itself a noble but ineffectual stimulus for technological development. It is *economic forces* – profit motives, if you will – that are always behind the scenes, regulating the flows and rates of implementation. Those are the forces that shape the relative popularity and growth patterns of competing, usually interdependent, entertainment activities and products. And those are the forces that ultimately make available to the masses what was previously affordable only by upper-income classes.

It is therefore somewhat surprising to find that most serious examinations of the economics of entertainment are desultorily scattered among various pamphlets, trade publications and journals, stockbrokers' reports, and incidental chapters in books on other topics. The widely available popular magazines and newspapers, biographies, histories, and technical manuals do not generally provide in-depth treatments of the subject.

This book, then, is a direct outgrowth of my search for a single comprehensive source. It attempts to present information in a style accessible and interesting to general readers. Yet it can be used as a text for graduate or advanced undergraduate students in applied economics and management/administration courses in film, music, communications, professional sports, performing arts, and hotel-casino operations. And it should also prove a handy reference for executives, financial analysts and investors, agents and legal advisors, accountants, economists, and journalists. To that end, extensive supplementary data are presented in Appendix C, following the Notes.

The selected topics have been chosen on the basis of industry size measured in terms of consumer spending and employment, length of time in existence as a distinct subset, and availability of reliable data. In a larger sense, however, topics have been selected with the aim of providing no more and no less than would be required by a ''compleat'' entertainment industry investor. Thus, inevitably, the perspectives are those of an investment analyst, portfolio manager, and economist.

Whereas this decision-oriented background leads naturally to an approach that is more practical and factual than highly theoretical, it nevertheless assumes some familiarity with the language of economics and finance. For the assistance of readers without fluency in those areas, a Glossary has been appended.

This fourth edition has been further revised and broadened and differs from its predecessors by the inclusion of a new chapter covering aspects of publishing and new media. Also, to provide greater historical perspective, time-line presentations have been added.

I am especially grateful to Elizabeth Maguire, former editor at Cambridge University Press, for her early interest and confidence in this project. Thanks, too, to Cambridge's Rhona Johnson and production editor Michael Gnat, who worked on the first edition, to Matthew N. Hendryx, who worked on the second, and to Scott Parris for the third and fourth.

I am further indebted to those writers who earlier cut a path through the statistical forests and made the task of exposition easier than it would otherwise have been. Particularly noteworthy are the books of John Owen on demand for leisure, Paul Baumgarten and Donald Farber on the contractual aspects of filmmaking (first edition; and second with Mark Fleischer), David Leedy on movie industry accounting, David Baskerville and Sidney Shemel/M. William Krasilovsky on the music business, John Scarne and Bill Friedman on the gaming field, Gerald W. Scully on sports, and William Baumol/William Bowen on the performing arts. Extensive film industry commentaries and data collections by A. D. Murphy of *Variety* (and later, *The Hollywood Reporter* and the University of Southern California) were important additional sources.

My thanks also to the following present and former senior industry executives who generously took time from their busy schedules to review and to advise on sections of the first edition draft. They and their company affiliations, as of that time, were: Michael L. Bagnall (The Walt Disney Company), Jeffrey Barbakow (Merrill Lynch), J. Garrett Blowers (CBS Inc.), Erroll M. Cook (Arthur Young & Co.), Michael E. Garstin (Orion Pictures Corp.), Kenneth F. Gorman (Viacom), Harold M. Haas (MCA Inc.), Howard J. Klein (Caesars New Jersey), Donald B. Romans (Bally Mfg.), and James R. Wolford (The Walt Disney Company). Greatly appreciated, too, was the comprehensive critique provided by my sister, Gloria. Acknowledgments for data in the second edition are also owed to Arnold W. Messer (Columbia Pictures Entertainment) and Angela B. Gerken (Viacom).

Although every possible precaution against error has been taken, for any mistakes that may inadvertently remain, the responsibility is, of course, mine alone.

I've been most gratified by the success of the previous editions and, as before, my hope and expectation remains that this work will provide valuable insights and a thoroughly enjoyable adventure.

Now, on with the show.

New York City   Harold L. Vogel

Part I
Introduction

1
Economic perspectives

To everything there is a season, and a time to every purpose under the heaven.
– Ecclesiastes

Extending this famous verse, we can also say that there is a time for work and a time for play. There is a time for leisure.

An important distinction, however, is to be made between the precise concept of a time for leisure and the semantically different and much fuzzier notion of *leisure time,* our initial topic. In the course of exploring this subject, the fundamental economic forces that affect spending on all forms of entertainment will be revealed, and our understanding of what motivates expenditures for such goods and services will be enhanced. Moreover, the perspectives provided by this approach will enable us to see how entertainment is defined and how it fits into the larger economic picture.

1.1 Time concepts

Leisure and work

Philosophers and sociologists have long wrestled with the problem of defining *leisure* – the English word derived from the Latin *licere,* which means "to be

3

permitted" or "to be free." In fact, as Kraus (1978, p. 38) and Neulinger (1981, pp. 17–33) have noted, leisure has usually been described in terms of its sociological and psychological (state-of-mind) characteristics.[1]

The classical attitude was epitomized in the work of Aristotle, for whom the term *leisure* implied both availability of time and absence of the necessity of being occupied (DeGrazia, 1962, p. 19). According to Aristotle, that very absence is what leads to a life of contemplation and true happiness – yet only for an elite few, who would not have to provide for their daily needs. Veblen (1899) similarly saw leisure as a symbol of social class. To him, however, it was associated not with a life of contemplation, but with the "idle rich," who identified themselves through its possession and its use.

Leisure has more recently been conceptualized either as a form of activity engaged in by people in their free time or, preferably, as time free from any sense of obligation or compulsion.[2] As such, the term *leisure* is now broadly used to characterize time not spent at work (where there is an obligation to perform). Naturally, in so defining leisure by what it is not, metaphysical issues remain largely unresolved. There is, for instance, a question of how to categorize work-related time such as that consumed in preparation for, and in transit to and from, the workplace. And sometimes the distinctions between one person's vocation and another's avocation are difficult to draw: People have been known to "work" pretty hard at their hobbies.

Although such problems of definition appear quite often, they fortunately do not affect analysis of the underlying concepts.

Recreation and entertainment

In stark contrast to the impressions of Aristotle or Veblen, today we rarely, if ever, think of leisure as contemplation or as something to be enjoyed only by the privileged. Instead, "free" time is used for doing things and going places, and the emphasis on activity more closely corresponds to the notion of recreation – refreshment of strength or spirit after toil – than to the views of the classicists.

The availability of time is, of course, a precondition for recreation, which can be taken literally as meaning re-creation of body and soul. But because such active re-creation can be achieved in many different ways – by playing tennis, or by going fishing, for example – it encompasses aspects of both physical and mental well-being. As such, recreation may or may not contain significant elements of amusement and diversion or occupy the attention agreeably. For instance, amateurs training to run a marathon might arguably be involved in a form of recreation. But if so, the entertainment aspect here would be rather minimal.

On the other hand, as noted in the Preface, entertainment is defined as that which produces a pleasurable and satisfying experience. The concept of entertainment is thus subordinate to that of recreation: It is more specifically defined through its direct and primarily psychological and emotional effects.

Time

Most people have some hours left over – "free time," so to speak – after subtracting the hours and minutes needed for subsistence (mainly eating and sleep-
ing), for work, and for related activities. But this remaining time has a cost in
terms of alternative opportunities forgone.

Because time is needed to use or to consume goods and services as well as
produce them, economists have attempted to develop theories that treat it as a
commodity with varying qualitative and quantitative cost features. However, as
Sharp (1981) notes in his comprehensive coverage of this subject, economists
have been only partially successful in this attempt:

> Although time is commonly described as a scarce resource in economic literature, it is
> still often treated rather differently from the more familiar inputs of labor and materials
> and outputs of goods and services. The problems of its allocation have not yet been fully
> or consistently integrated into economic analysis (Sharp, 1981, p. 210).

Nevertheless, investigations into the economics of time, including those of
Becker (1965) and DeSerpa (1971), have suggested that the demand for leisure
is affected in a complicated way by the cost of time to both produce and consume.
For instance, according to Becker (see also Ghez and Becker 1975),

> The two determinants of the importance of forgone earnings are the amount of time
> used per dollar of goods and the cost per unit of time. Reading a book, getting a haircut,
> or commuting use more time per dollar of goods than eating dinner, frequenting a night-
> club, or sending children to private summer camps. Other things being equal, forgone
> earnings would be more important for the former set of commodities than the latter.
>
> The importance of forgone earnings would be determined solely by time intensity only
> if the cost of time were the same for all commodities. Presumably, however, it varies
> considerably among commodities and at different periods. For example, the cost of time
> is often less on week-ends and in the evenings (Becker, 1965, p. 503).

From this it can be seen that the cost of time and the consumption-time intensity
of goods and services are significant factors when selecting from among entertainment alternatives.

Expansion of leisure time

Most of us do not normally experience sharp changes in our availability of leisure
time (except on retirement or loss of job). But there is nevertheless a fairly widespread impression that leisure time has been trending steadily higher ever since
the Industrial Revolution of more than a century ago. Still, the evidence on this
is mixed. In examining the length of an average workweek for agricultural and
nonagricultural industries, we can see that significant increases in leisure time
(workweek reductions) were achieved prior to 1940 (Figure 1.1); more recently,
however, the lengths of average workweeks, as adjusted for increases in holidays
and vacations, have scarcely changed for the manufacturing sector and have also

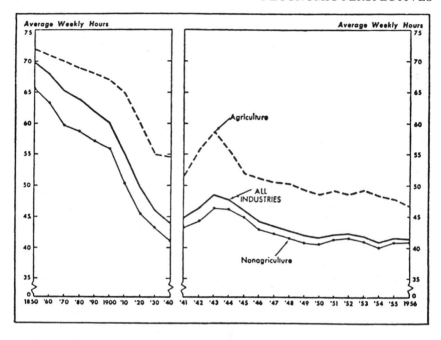

Figure 1.1. Estimated average weekly hours for all persons employed in agricultural and nonagricultural industries, 1850–1940 (10-year intervals) and 1941–56 (annual averages for all employed persons, including the self-employed and unpaid family workers). *Source:* Zeisel (1958).

Table 1.1. *Average weekly hours at work, 1948–1995,[a] and median weekly hours at work for selected years[b]*

Average hours at work			Median hours at work	
Year	Unadjusted	Adjusted[c]	Year	Hours
1948	42.7	41.6	1973	40.6
1956	43.0	41.8	1975	43.1
1962	43.1	41.7	1980	46.9
1969	43.5	42.0	1984	47.3
1975	42.2	40.9	1987	46.8
1986	42.8		1995	50.6

[a]Nonstudent men in nonagricultural industries. *Source:* Owen (1976, 1988).
[b]*Source:* Harris (1995).
[c]Adjusted for growth in vacations and holidays.

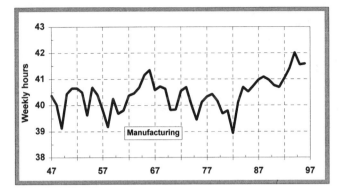

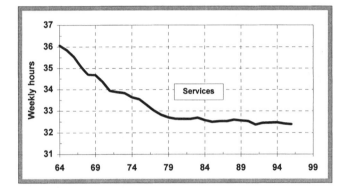

Figure 1.2. Average weekly hours worked by production workers in: (a) manufacturing, 1947–96; and (b) service industries, 1964–96. *Source:* U.S. Department of Commerce.

stopped declining in the services sector (Table 1.1 and Figure 1.2). A related comparison of trends in average annual hours worked in the United States versus other major countries appears in Figure 1.3.

Although this indeed suggests that there has been little, if any, expansion of leisure time in most years, Hedges and Taylor (1980), with a more detailed break-down of labor force statistics, were able to show that between 1968 and 1979, work time for wage and salary employees tended to decline. This decline was attributed to changes in industry and occupation structures, in federal laws, and in collective-bargaining agreements. In fact, weekly hours worked in private in-dustry as a whole have declined modestly since 1965 – remaining fairly constant in the manufacturing segments, but falling sharply in services (Supplementary Table S1.2).

Yet data from so-called Area Wage Surveys conducted by the Bureau of Labor Statistics (BLS) suggest that the average workweek has not shrunk at all in re-cent years. What has apparently happened instead is that work schedules now

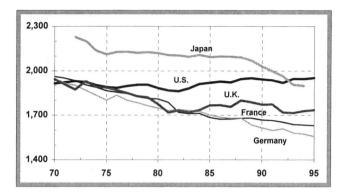

Figure 1.3. Average annual hours worked in the U.S. versus other countries, 1970–1995. *Source: OECD Employment Outlook.*

provide greater diversity: "A larger percentage of people worked under 35 hours or over 49 hours a week in 1985 than in 1973, yet the mean and median hours (38.4 and 40.4, respectively, in 1985) remained virtually unchanged."[3]

And indeed, if findings from public-opinion surveys of Americans and the arts conducted in 1995 and earlier years by Louis Harris and Associates, Inc., are to be believed, the number of hours available for leisure may actually be declining.[4] This view has also been supported by Schor (1991, p. 29), with an estimate that between 1969 and 1987, "the average employed person is now on the job an additional 163 hours, or the equivalent of an extra month a year . . . and that hours have risen across a wide spectrum of Americans and in all income categories."[5]

Still, these data also appear suspect, and some evidence to the contrary is provided by Robinson (1989, p. 34), who has measured free time by age categories and found that "most gains in free time have occurred between 1965 and 1975 [but] since then, the amount of free time people have has remained fairly stable." By adjusting for age categories, the case for an increase in total leisure hours available becomes much more persuasive.[6] In addition, Roberts and Rupert (1995) found that total hours of annual work have not changed by much, but that the *composition* of labor has shifted from home work to market work with nearly all of the difference attributable to changes in the total hours worked by women.[7]

In all, it seems safe to say that for most middle-aged and middle-income Americans, leisure time is not expanding. However, no matter what the actual rate of expansion or contraction of leisure time may be, there has been a natural evolution toward repackaging the time set aside for leisure into more long holiday weekends and extra vacation days, rather than in reducing the minutes worked each and every week.[8] Particularly for those in the higher-income categories – conspicuous consumers, as Veblen would say – the result is that personal-consumption expenditures (PCEs) for leisure activities are likely to be intense, frenzied, and compressed instead of evenly metered throughout the year. Estimated apportion-

Table 1.2. *Time spent by adults on selected leisure activities, 1970 and 1995 estimates*

Leisure activity	Hours per person per year[a]		% of total time accounted for by each activity	
	1970	1995	1970	1995
Television	1,226	1,575	46.5	46.2
Network affiliates		836		24.5
Independent stations		183		5.4
Basic cable programs		468		13.7
Pay cable programs		88		2.6
Radio	872	1,091	33.1	32.0
Home		442		13.0
Out of home		649		19.0
Newspapers	218	165	8.3	4.8
Records & tapes	68	289	2.6	8.5
Magazines	170	84	6.5	2.5
Leisure books	65	99	2.5	2.9
Movies: theaters	10	12	0.4	0.4
home video		45		1.3
Spectator sports	3	14	0.1	0.4
Video games: arcade		4		0.1
home		24		0.7
Cultural events	3	5	0.1	0.1
Total	2,635	3,407	100.0[b]	100.0[b]
Hours per adult per week	50.7	65.5		
Hours per adult per day	7.2	9.3		

[a]Averaged over participants and nonparticipants.
[b]Totals not exact due to rounding.
Source: CBS office of Economic Analysis, Wilkofsky Gruen Associates, Inc.

ments of leisure hours among various activities, and the changes in such apportionments between 1970 and 1995, are indicated in Table 1.2.[9]

1.2 Supply and demand factors

Productivity

Ultimately, however, more leisure time availability is not a function of government decree, labor union activism, or factory-owner altruism. It is a function of the rising trend in output per person-hour – in brief, rising productivity of the economy. Quite simply, technological advances embodied in new capital equipment and in the training of a more skilled labor pool enable more goods and

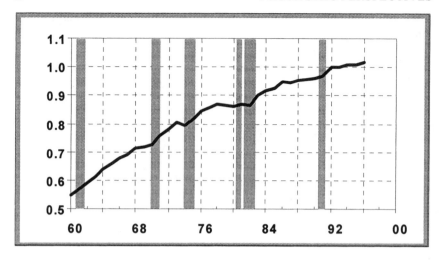

Figure 1.4. Nonfarm business productivity in the U.S., 1960–96, shown by output per hour. Index 1992 = 100. Bars indicate periods of recession. *Source:* U.S. Department of Labor.

services to be produced in less time or by fewer workers. Thus, it happens that long-term growth in leisure-time-related industries depends on the rate of technological development throughout the economy.

Information concerning trends in productivity and other aspects of economic activity is provided by the National Income and Product Accounting (NIPA) figures of the U.S. Department of Commerce. According to those figures, overall productivity during the 1970s and 1980s rose at an average annual rate of 1.2%, as compared with rates averaging 2.9% during the 20 years immediately following World War II.[10] The apparently reduced rate of improvement in this later period may have been caused by unexpected sharp cost increases for energy and capital (interest rates), by high corporate debt levels, or perhaps by the burgeoning "underground" (off-the-books) economy not directly captured in (and therefore distorting) the NIPA numbers. But whatever the reasons, the potential for leisure-time expansion seems to have remained fairly steady in the last third of the twentieth century (Figure 1.4).

Demand for leisure

All of us can choose to either fully utilize our free time for recreational purposes (defined here and in NIPA data as being inclusive of entertainment activities) or use some of this time to generate additional income. How we allocate free time between the conflicting desires for more leisure and for additional income then becomes a subject that economists investigate with standard analytical tools.[11] In effect, economists can treat demand for leisure as if it were, say, demand for gold,

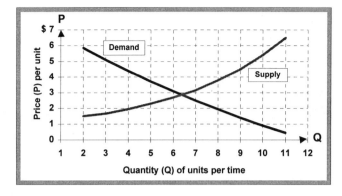

Figure 1.5. Supply and demand schedules.

or for wheat, or for housing. And they often estimate and depict the schedules for supply and demand with curves of the type that are shown in Figure 1.5. Here, in simplified form, it can be seen that as the price of a unit rises, the supply of it will normally increase and the demand for it decrease so that, over time, price and quantity equilibrium in an openly competitive market will be achieved at the intersection of the curves.[12]

It is also important to note that consumers normally tend to substitute less expensive goods and services for more expensive ones and that the total amounts they can spend – their budgets – are limited or constrained by income. The effects of such substitutions and changes in income as related to demand for leisure have been extensively studied by Owen (1970), who observed:

> An increase in property income will, if we assume leisure is a superior good, reduce hours of work. A higher wage rate also brings higher income which, in itself, may incline the individual to increase his leisure. But at the same time the higher wage rate makes leisure time more expensive in terms of forgone goods and services, so that the individual may decide instead to purchase less leisure. The net effect will depend then on the relative strengths of the income and price elasticities . . . It would seem that for the average worker the income effect of a rise in the wage rate is in fact stronger than the substitution effect (Owen, 1970, p. 18).

In other words, as wage rates continue rising, up to point A in Figure 1.6, people will choose to work more hours to increase their income (income effect). But they eventually begin to favor more leisure over more income (substitution effect, between points A and B), with the result of a backward-bending labor-supply curve.[13] Although renowned economists, including Adam Smith, Alfred Marshall, Frank Knight, A. C. Pigou, and Lionel Robbins have substantially differed in their assessments of the net effect of wage-rate changes on the demand for leisure, it is clear that "leisure does have a price, and changes in its price will affect the demand for it" (Owen, 1970, p. 19). Indeed, results from a Bureau of Labor Statistics survey of some 60,000 households in 1986 suggest that about

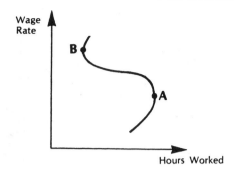

Figure 1.6. Backward-bending labor-supply curve.

two-thirds of those surveyed do not want to work fewer hours if it means earning less money.[14]

As Owen (1970) has demonstrated, estimation of the demand for leisure requires consideration of many complex issues including the nature of "working conditions," the effects of increasing worker fatigue on production rates as work hours lengthen, the greater availability of educational opportunities that affect the desirability of certain kinds of work, government taxation and spending policies, market unemployment rates, and several other variables.[15]

Expected-utility comparisons

Individuals differ in terms of the sense of psychic gratification experienced from consumption of different goods and services. And so it is difficult to measure and compare the degrees of satisfaction derived from, say, eating dinner as opposed to buying a new car. To facilitate comparability, economists have adapted an old philosophical concept known as utility.[16] As Barrett (1974, p. 79) has noted, utility "is not a measure of usefulness or need but a measure of the desirability of a commodity from the psychological viewpoint of the consumer."

Of course, rational individuals try to maximize utility – in other words, make decisions that provide them with the most satisfaction. But they are hampered in this regard because decisions are normally made under conditions of uncertainty, with incomplete information, and therefore with risk of an undesired outcome. People thus tend to implicitly include a probabilistic component in their decision-making processes – and they end up maximizing *expected utility* rather than utility itself.

The notion of expected utility is especially well applied in thinking about demand for entertainment goods and services. It helps, for example, to explain why people may be attracted to gambling, or why they are sometimes willing to pay scalpers enormous premiums for theater tickets. The application of expected utility also sheds light on how various entertainment activities compete for the limited time and funds of consumers.

To illustrate, assume for a moment that the cost of an activity per unit of time is somewhat representative of its expected utility. If the admission price to a two-hour movie is $6, and if the purchase of video-game software for $25 provides six hours of play before the onset of boredom, then the cost per minute for the movie is 5 cents, and that for the game is 6.9 cents. Now, obviously, no one decides to see a movie or buy a game based on explicit comparisons of cost per minute. Indeed, for an individual, many qualitative (nonmonetary) factors, especially fashions and fads, may affect the perception of an item's expected utility. But, in the aggregate and over time, such implicit comparisons do have a significant cumulative influence on relative demand for entertainment (and other) products and services.

Demographics and debts

Over the longer term, the demand for leisure goods and services can also be significantly affected by changes in the relative growth of different age cohorts. For instance, teenagers tend to be important purchasers of recorded music; people under the age of 30 are the most avid moviegoers. Accordingly, a large increase in births following World War II created, in the 1960s and 1970s, a market highly receptive to movie and music products. As this postwar generation matures past its years of family formation and into years of peak earnings power and then retirement, spending interests may be naturally expected to shift to areas such as amusement/theme parks, casinos, and tourism and travel, and relatively away from areas of interest to people in their teens or early twenties.

The broad demographic shifts most important to entertainment industry prospects in the United States include (1) a projected shrinkage of the numbers of 18- to 34-year-olds during the 1990s (6.4 million fewer in 2000 than in 1990), (2) a projected rapid growth in the large group of 35- to 64-year-olds (up from 84 million in 1990 to 106 million in 1995), and (3) a significant expansion of the population over age 65 (Table 1.3).

That the number of people in the 45 to 64 age group will be gaining rapidly in proportion to the number of people in the 18 to 34 age group is of particular importance given that those in the younger category are generally apt to spend much of their income when they enter the labor force and form households. Those in the older category, however, are already established and are thus more likely to be in a savings mode, perhaps to finance college educations for their children or to prepare for retirement, when earnings are lower. A ratio of people in the younger group to those in the older group, in effect, the spenders versus the savers, is illustrated in Figure 1.7(a), and suggests that expenditures on lower-priced nondurables and services might be relatively more favored than expenditures on high-priced durables until well past the turn of the century.

Depending on the specific industry component to be analyzed, proper interpretation of long-term changes in population characteristics may also require that consideration be given to several additional factors, including dependency ratios,

Table 1.3. *U.S. population by age bracket, components of change and trends by life stage, 1970–2010*

Components of population change

Age	Percentage distribution					Change (millions)		
	1970	1980	1990	2000[a]	2010[a]	1980–90	1990–2000[a]	2000–2010[a]
Under 5	8.4	7.2	7.6	6.9	6.6	2.4	0.0	0.8
5–17	29.3	24.6	18.2	18.8	17.6	– 1.9	6.5	0.5
18–34	15.1	18.2	28.1	23.1	23.0	2.0	– 6.4	4.8
35–65	33.2	34.3	33.6	38.5	39.5	13.7	21.7	12.3
65 and over	14.0	15.7	12.5	12.7	13.3	5.5	3.7	4.8
Total	100.0	100.0	100.0	100.0	100.0	21.7	25.5	23.2

Population trends by life stage (millions)

Life stage	1970	1980	1990	2000[a]	2010[a]
0–13 Children	53.8	47.6	50.9	55.0	55.2
14–24 Young adults	40.6	46.5	40.1	41.9	46.9
25–34 Peak family formation	25.3	37.6	43.1	37.4	38.4
35–44 Family maturation	23.1	25.9	37.8	44.7	38.9
45–54 Peak earning power	23.3	22.8	46.3	37.1	43.7
55–64 Childless parents	18.7	21.8	21.1	24.0	35.4
65 and retirement	20.1	25.7	31.2	34.9	39.7
Total	204.9	227.9	249.4	275.0	298.1

[a]Forecast.
Source: U.S. Department of Commerce, series P25.

14

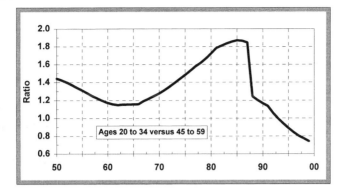

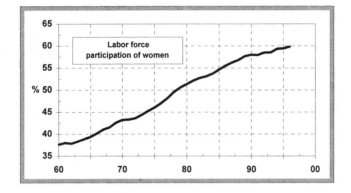

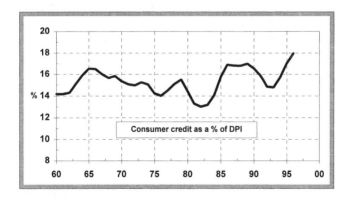

Figure 1.7. (a) Ratio of spenders to savers, 1950–99. (b) Labor force participation rate for women, 1960–96. (c) Consumer credit as a percentage of personal income, 1960–96.

fertility rates, number of first births, number of families with two earners, and trends in labor-force participation rates for women.[17] (Figure 1.7b).

Indeed, two paychecks have become an absolute necessity for many families as they have attempted to service relatively high (in proportion to income) installment and mortgage debt obligations that have been incurred in the household-formative years. As such, elements of consumer debt (Figure 1.7c), weighted by the aforementioned demographic factors, probably explain why, according to the Louis Harris surveys previously cited, leisure hours per week seem to have declined noticeably since the early 1970s. However, in the next decade, these very same elements may combine to abate recent pressures on time availability.

Barriers to entry

The supply of entertainment products and services offered will also depend on how readily prospective new businesses can overcome barriers to entry and thereby *contest* the market. Barriers to entry restrict supply and fit broadly into the following categories, listed in order of importance to entertainment industries:

Capital
Know-how
Regulations
Price competition

To compete effectively, large corporations must, of course, invest considerable time and capital to acquire technical knowledge and experience. But the same goes for individual artists seeking to develop commercially desirable products in the form of plays, books, films, or songs. Government regulations such as those applying to the broadcasting, cable, and casino businesses often present additional hurdles for potential new entrants to surmount. And, in most industries, established firms would ordinarily have some ability to protect their positions through price competition.

1.3 Primary principles

Marginal matters Microeconomics provides a descriptive framework in which to analyze the effects of incremental changes in the quantities of goods and services supplied or demanded over time. A standard diagram of this type, Figure 1.8, shows an idealized version of a firm that maximizes its profits by pricing its products at the point where marginal revenue (MR) – the extra revenue gained by selling an additional unit – equals marginal cost (MC), the cost of supplying an extra unit. Here, the average cost (AC), which includes both fixed and variable components, first declines and is then pulled up by rising marginal cost. Profit for the firm is represented by the shaded rectangle (price [p] times quantity [q] minus cost [c] times quantity [q]).

Given that popular entertainment products feature one-of-a-kind talent (e.g., Elvis or Sinatra recordings) or brand name services (e.g., MTV, Disney theme

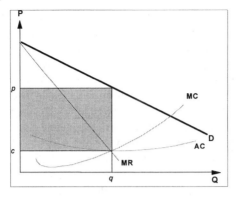

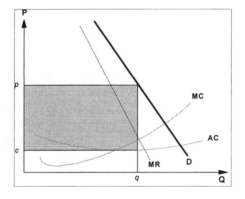

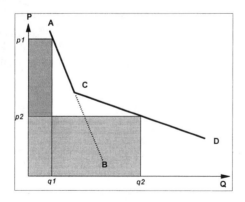

Figure 1.8. Marginal costs and revenues.

parks), the so-called competitive-monopolistic model of Figure 1.8(a), in which many firms produce slightly differentiated products, is not far-fetched. The objective for such profit maximizing firms is to both rightward-shift and also steepen the demand schedule idealized by line D. By thus making the schedule of demand more vertical – that is, quantity demanded becomes less sensitive to change in price (i.e., more price-inelastic) through promotional and advertising efforts – a firm would be able to reap a potentially large proportionate increase in profits as long as marginal costs are held relatively flat (Figure 1.8b).

Look, for example, at what happens when a movie is made. The initial capital investment in production and marketing is risked without knowing how many units – including theater tickets, home video sales and rentals, television viewings, and the like – will ultimately be demanded. The possibilities range from practically zero to practically infinite.

Yet, whatever the ultimate demand turns out to be, the costs of production and marketing, which are large compared to other, later costs, are mostly borne up front. Come what may, the costs here are *sunk*, whereas in many other manufacturing processes, the costs of raw materials and labor embedded in each unit produced (variable and marginal) may be relatively high and continuous over time. In entertainment, the cost of producing an incremental unit is normally quite small as compared to sunk costs and, accordingly, it often makes sense for a distributor to take a chance on spending a little more on marketing and promotion in an attempt to shift the demand schedule into a more price-inelastic and rightward position.

Price discrimination If, moreover, a market for, say, airline or theater seats (see Chapter 12) can be segmented into first and economy classes, profits can be further enhanced by capturing what is known in economics as the *consumers' surplus* – the price difference between what consumers actually pay and what they would be willing to pay. Such a price discrimination model extracts, without adding much to costs, the additional revenues shown in the cross-hatched rectangular area of Figure 1.8c.

Public good characteristics Public goods are those that can be enjoyed by more than one person without reducing the amount available to any other person. Spending on national defense or on programs to reduce air pollution provide examples. In entertainment, also, it is not unusual to find goods that have near public good characteristics. The marginal cost of adding one viewer to a television network program, or of allowing an extra visitor to a theme park is not measurable.

1.4 Personal-consumption expenditure relationships

Recreational goods and services are those used or consumed during leisure time. As a result, there is a close relationship between demand for leisure and demand for recreational products and services.

Table 1.4. *PCEs for recreation in real (1992) dollars, 1970 to 1995[a]*

Type of product or service	1970	1980	1985	1990	1995
Total recreation expenditures	93.8	189.7	215.8	291.8	395.5
Percentage of total personal consumption	4.3	5.3	6.1	7.1	8.6
Books and maps	12.8	12.5	13.9	17.6	19.4
Magazines, newspapers, sheet music	16.7	23.3	21.7	23.8	23.0
Nondurable toys and sport supplies	10.8	20.1	25.7	32.6	41.8
Wheel goods, durable toys, sports equipment[b]	11.7	21.4	25.2	31.2	42.1
Radio and TV receivers, records, musical instruments	6.2	12.7	24.7	47.9	106.0
Radio and television repair	3.2	4.1	4.0	4.6	4.6
Flowers, seeds and potted plants	4.8	7.0	8.7	12.5	13.5
Admissions to specified spectator amusements	10.9	13.1	14.2	16.5	18.0
Motion picture theaters	5.5	5.1	4.7	5.6	5.1
Legitimate theaters and opera, and entertainments of nonprofit institutions[c]	1.7	3.5	4.7	6.1	8.1
Spectator sports	3.7	4.5	4.8	4.8	4.8
Clubs and fraternal organizations[d]	4.5	4.8	7.5	9.5	11.7
Commercial participant amusements[e]	7.7	15.3	20.0	24.9	33.9
Pari-mutuel net receipts	3.8	4.8	4.1	3.7	3.0
Other[f]	14.2	32.2	52.7	68.3	82.1

[a]In millions of dollars, except percentages. Represents market value of purchases of goods and services by individuals and nonprofit institutions. See *Historical Statistics, Colonial Times to 1970*, series H 878–893, for figures issued prior to 1981 revisions.
[b]Includes boats and pleasures aircraft.
[c]Except athletic.
[d]Consists of dues and fees excluding insurance premiums.
[e]Consists of billiard parlors; bowling alleys, dancing, riding, shooting, skating, and swimming places; amusement devices and parks; golf courses; sightseeing buses and guides; private flying operations and other commercial participant amusements.
[f]Consists of net receipts of lotteries and expenditures for purchase of pets and pet care services, cable TV, film processing, photographic studios, sporting and recreation camps, and recreational services, not elsewhere classified.
Source: U.S. Bureau of Economic Analysis. *The National Income and Product Accounts of the United States, 1929–1976;* and *Survery of Current Business,* July issues.

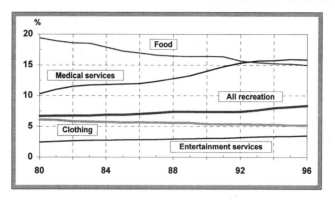

Figure 1.9. Trends in percent of total personal consumption expenditures in selected categories, 1980–96.

As may be inferred from Table 1.4, NIPA data classify spending on recreation as a subset of total personal-consumption expenditures (PCEs). This table is particularly important because it allows comparison of the amount of leisure-related spending to the amount of spending for shelter, transportation, food, clothing, national defense, and other items.[18] For example, the percent of all PCEs allocated to selected major categories in 1996 was as follows:

Medical care services	*15.8%*
Housing	*15.1*
Food	*15.0*
Transportation	*11.2*
All recreation	*8.3*
Clothing	*6.5*

Also, as may be seen in Figure 1.9, spending on entertainment services has held to a fairly stable percentage of all PCEs, whereas the percentage spent on medical services has risen and on clothing and food declined.

That spending on total recreational goods and services responds to prevalent economic forces with a degree of predictability can be seen in Figure 1.10 and in Supplementary Table S1.1.[19] Figure 1.10 illustrates that PCEs for recreation as a percentage of total disposable personal incomes (DPI) have held in a band of roughly 4.0% to 6.5% for most of the 60 years beginning in 1929. It is only since the late 1980s that new heights have been achieved as a result of a relatively lengthy business cycle expansion, increased consumer borrowing ratios, demographic and household formation influences, and the proliferation of leisure-related goods and services utilizing new technologies.

Measuring real (adjusted for inflation) per capita spending on total recreation and on recreation *services* provides yet another long-term view of how Americans have allocated their leisure-related dollars. Although the services subsegment ex-

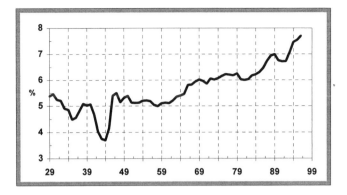

Figure 1.10. PCE for recreation as percentage of disposable income, 1929–96.

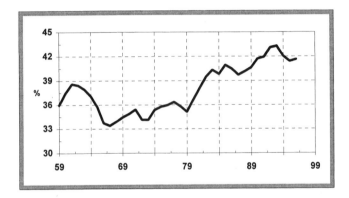

Figure 1.11. PCE on recreation *services* as percentage of total PCE on recreation, 1959–96.

cludes spending on durable products such as television sets, it includes movies, cable TV, sports, theater, commercial participant amusements, lotteries, and pari-mutuel betting – areas in which most of the largest growth has been recently seen. The percentage of recreation services spending is now above 40% of the total spent for all recreation (Figure 1.11). And a steeper uptrend in real per capita PCEs on total recreation and on recreation services beginning around 1960 is suggested by Figure 1.12.[20]

This apparent shift toward services, which is also being experienced in other economically advanced nations, is a reflection of relative market saturation for durables, relative price-change patterns, and changes in consumer preferences that follow from the development of new goods and services. As such, even small percentage shifts of spending may represent billions of dollars flowing into or out of entertainment businesses. And for many firms, the direction of these flows may make the difference between prosperous growth or struggle and decay.

Because various entertainment sectors have markedly different responses

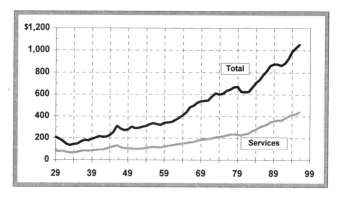

Figure 1.12. Real per capita spending on total recreation and on recreation services, 1929–96.

to changing conditions, the degree of recession resistance, or cyclicity of the entertainment industry relative to that of the economy at large, is unfortunately not well depicted by such time series. For example, broadcasting revenue trends are dependent on advertising expenditures which are in turn related to total corporate profits. But the movie and theater segments often exhibit contracyclical tendencies. In order to effectively study these business cycle relationships, data at a less aggregated level must therefore be used. In other words, measures of what is known as the Gross National Product (GNP), or of the more recent standard of Gross Domestic Product (GDP), can provide only a starting point for further investigations.[21]

1.5 Overview of industry segments

The relative economic importance of various industry segments is illustrated in Figure 1.13, from which it is possible to conclude that the amount of news coverage that a segment receives is not necessarily in proportion to its size.

These trendlines provide important long-range macroeconomic perspectives of entertainment industry growth patterns. But over a shorter period, financial operating performances are better revealed by Table 1.5, where revenues, pretax operating incomes, assets, and cash flows for a selected sample of major public companies are presented. This sample includes an estimated 80% of the transactions volume in entertainment-related industries and provides a means of comparing efficiencies in various segments. We can learn a lot by analyzing it closely.

For example, cash flow is important because it can be used to service debt, acquire assets, or pay dividends. Representing the difference between cash receipts from the sale of goods or services and cash outlays required in production of the same, operating cash flow is usually understood to be operating income before deductions for interest, depreciation, and amortization. Cash flow, so de-

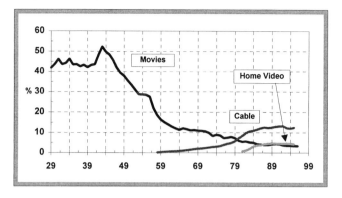

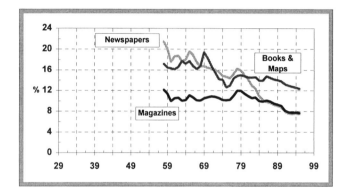

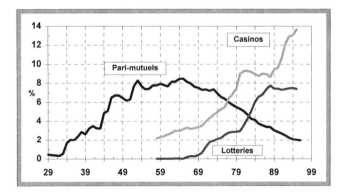

Figure 1.13. PCEs of selected entertainment categories as percentages of total PCE on recreation, 1929–96.

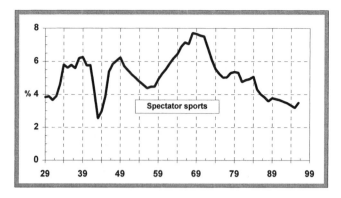

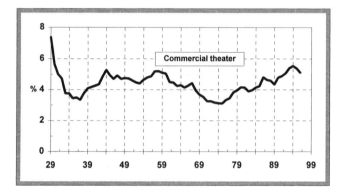

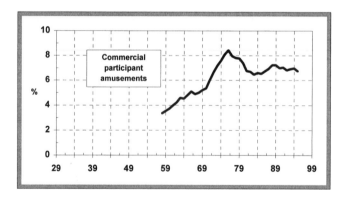

Figure 1.13. *(cont.)*

Table 1.5. *Entertainment industry composite, 1992–96*

Compound annual growth rates (%): 1992–96

Industry segment	No. companies in sample	Revenues	Operating income	Assets	Operating cash flow
Broadcasting	76	8	15	19	16
Cable	35	12	1	17	8
Filmed entertainment	7	9	8	10	8
Gaming (casinos)	39	11	9	15	10
Publishing (books, cons. mag., newsp.)	75	5	7	7	7
Recorded music	5	6	7	1	9
Theatrical exhibition	9	6	15	8	12
Theme parks	5	8	10	8	10
Toys	8	5	4	5	5
Total	259				

Total composite

	Pretax return on		Revenues	Operating income ($ million)	Assets	Operating cash flow
	Revenues	Assets				
1996	13.4%	11.5%	$171,222	$22,983	$200,708	$36,766
1995	13.7	13.6	153,917	21,067	155,002	31,318
1994	13.9	14.0	140,600	19,501	139,123	28,820
1993	13.6	13.4	126,754	17,241	128,401	24,968
1992	13.3	13.5	118,422	15,750	116,937	23,802
CAGR:[a]			7.7	7.9	11.4	9.1

[a]Compound annual growth rate (%).
[b]Not meaningful.
[c]Not available.
Sources: Company reports, Veronis, Suhler & Associates, Inc., Wilkofsky Gruen Associates, Inc.

fined, is the basis for valuing all kinds of media and entertainment properties because the distortionary effects of differing tax and financial structure considerations are stripped away: A business property can thus be more easily evaluated from the standpoint of what it might be worth to potential buyers.

More immediately, we can further see that entertainment industries generated revenues (on the wholesale level) of about $125 billion (excluding publishing) in 1996, and that annual growth between 1992 and 1996 averaged approximately 7.7%. Over the same span, operating income rose at a compound rate of 7.9%, whereas assets have increased at a rate of 11.4%. Clearly then, operating cash flows, rising at a rate of 9.1%, have not kept pace with the growth of assets. And

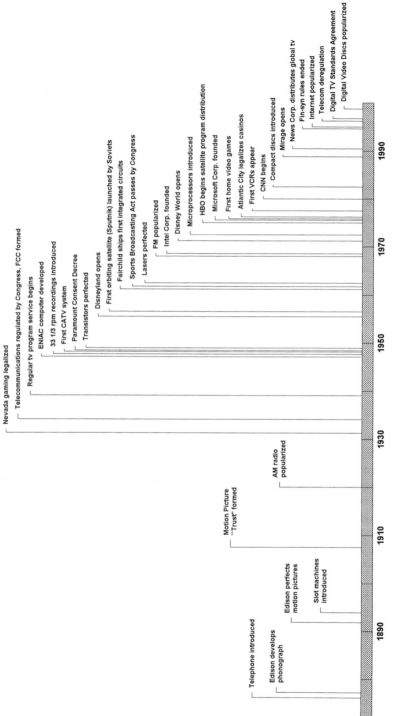

Figure 1.14. Entertainment industry milestones, 1870–2000.

additions to assets have thus, of necessity, been financed by borrowings and/or by sales of equity (i.e., shares of stock).[22]

More worrisome still is that the return on composite industry assets has declined from an average of 13.5% in the early 1990s to 11.5% in 1996. However, a thorough analysis of the composites shown in Table 1.5 would further require consideration of many business-environmental features, including interest rates, antitrust policy attitudes, and the trend of dollar exchange rates.

1.6 Concluding remarks

This chapter has sketched the economic landscape in which all entertainment industries operate. It has indicated how hours at work, productivity trends, expected utility functions, demographics, and other factors can affect the amounts of time and money we spend on leisure-related goods and services. And it has also provided benchmarks against which the relative growth rates and sizes of different industry segments or composites can be measured. We can see, for example, that as a percentage of disposable income, United States PCEs for recreation – encompassing spending on entertainment as well as other leisure-time pursuits – first rose to well over 6% in the 1980s. And we can see that entertainment is big business: At the wholesale level it is now generating annual revenues exceeding $100 billion. Moreover, as measured in dollar value terms, entertainment has consistently been one of the largest net export categories (estimated to be at least $5 billion in 1997) for the United States.[23]

Technological development has obviously played an important role too. It, of course, underlies the very growth of productivity and thus of the relative supply of leisure time. But just as significantly, technological development, represented by the timeline of Figure 1.14, has changed the way in which we think of entertainment products. Such products – whether movies, music, TV shows, video games, or words – must now be regarded as composite bits of "information" that can be produced and processed and distributed as a series of digits – coded bursts of zeros and ones that can represent sounds and pictures and texts. Already, this has greatly altered the entertainment industry's economic landscape.

Past, then, is clearly not prologue – especially in a field where creative people are constantly finding new ways to turn a profit. The broad economic perspectives discussed in this chapter, however, provide a common background for all that follows.

Selected additional reading

Cutler, B. (1990). "Where Does the Free Time Go?" *American Demographics* 12(11)(November).

"The Determinants of Working Hours," *OECD Employment Outlook,* September 1983.

Deutschman, A. (1994). "Scramble on the Information Highway," *Fortune,* 129(3)(February 7).

"The Entertainment Economy" *Business Week,* No. 3362 (March 14, 1994):58.

Epstein, G. (1995). "Myth: Americans Are Working More. Fact: More Women Are Working," *Barron's,* April 3.

Frank, A. D. (1987). "The Fault Is Not in Our Stars," *Forbes* 140(6)(September 21):120.

Fuchsberg, G. (1994). "Four-day Workweek Has Become a Stretch for Some Employees," *Wall Street Journal,* August 3.

Gabriel, T. (1995). "A Generation's Heritage: After the Boom, a Boomlet," *New York Times,* February 12.

Gray, M. B. (1992). "Consumer Spending on Durables and Services in the 1980s," *Monthly Labor Review* 115(5)(May).

Hedges, J. N. (1980). "The Workweek in 1979: Fewer but Longer Workdays," *Monthly Labor Review* 103(8)(August):31.

———— (1973). "New Patterns for Working Time," *Monthly Labor Review* 96(2)(February):3.

Jablonski, M., Kunze, K., and Otto, P. (1990). "Hours At Work: A New Base for BLS Productivity Statistics," *Monthly Labor Review* 113(2)(February).

Kilborn, P. T. (1996). "Factories That Never Close Are Scrapping 5–Day Week," *New York Times,* June 4.

Malabre, A. L., Jr., and Clark, L. H., Jr. (1992). "Productivity Statistics for the Service Sector May Understate Gains," *Wall Street Journal,* August 12.

Meyersohn, R., and Larrabee, E. (1958). "A Comprehensive Bibliography on Leisure, 1900–1958," in *Mass Leisure.* Glencoe, Ill.: The Free Press; also in *American Journal of Sociology* 62(6)(May 1957):602–15.

Moore, G. H., and Hedges, J. N. (1971). "Trends in Labor and Leisure," *Monthly Labor Review* 94(2)(February):3.

Oi, W. (1971). "A Disneyland Dilemma: Two-Part Tariffs for a Mickey Mouse Monopoly," *Quarterly Journal of Economics,* vol. 85 (February).

Owen, J. D. (1971). "The Demand for Leisure," *Journal of Political Economy* 79(1)(January/February):56–75.

Pollak, R. A., and Wachter, M. L. (1975). "The Relevance of the Household Production Function and Its Implications for the Allocation of Time," *Journal of Political Economy* 83(2).

"The Productivity Paradox," *Business Week,* No. 3055 (June 6, 1988):100.

"The Revival of Productivity," *Business Week* No. 2828 (February 13, 1984):92.

"Riding High: The Productivity Bonanza,"*Business Week,* No. 3445 (October 9, 1995):134.

Rifkin, J. (1995). *The End of Work.* New York: Putman.

Robinson, J. P., and Godbey, G. (1996). "The Great American Slowdown," *American Demographics,* June.

Staines, G. L., and O'Connor, P. (1980). "Conflicts among Work, Leisure, and Family Roles," *Monthly Labor Review* 103(8)(August):35.

"The 21st Century Family," *Newsweek,* special edition, 1989.

Part II
Media-dependent entertainment

2
Movie macroeconomics

You oughta be in pictures!

A more appealing pitch to investors would be hard to find. Many people imagine that nothing could be more fun, and potentially more lucrative, than making movies. After all, in its first four years, *Star Wars* returned profits of over $150 million on an initial investment of $11 million (and many millions more on re-release twenty years later). Yet, ego gratification rather than money may often be the only return on an investment in film. As in other endeavors, what you see is not always what you get. And, in fact, of any 10 major theatrical films produced, on the average, six or seven may be broadly characterized as unprofitable. Still, as we shall soon discover, there are many reasons why such characterizations must be applied with care and why the success ratio for studio/distributors is considerably better than for individual participants.

Be that as it may, moviemaking is still truly entrepreneurial: It is often a triumph of hope over reality, where defeat can easily be snatched from the jaws of victory. But its magical, mystical elements notwithstanding, it is also a business, affected as any other by basic economic principles.

This chapter is concerned with macroeconomic trends and movie asset valuations; the next two chapters deal with issues of operational structure, accounting, and television-related microeconomics.

2.1 Flickering images

Snuggled comfortably in the seat of your local theater or, as is increasingly likely, in front of the screen attached to your home video-exhibition device, you are transported far away by your imagination as you watch – a movie. Of course, not all movies have the substance and style to accomplish this incredible feat of emotional transportation, but a surprising number of them do. In any case, what is seen on the screen is there because of a remarkable history of tumultuous development that is still largely in process.

Putting pictures on a strip of film that moved was not a unique or new idea among photographers of the late nineteenth century. As noted by Margolies and Gwathmey (1991, p. 9), it was by then already known that the way we see film move is an optical illusion based upon the eye's persistence of vision; an image is retained for a fraction of a second longer than it actually appears. But the man who synthesized it all into a workable invention was Thomas Edison. By the early 1890s, Edison and his assistant, William Dickson, had succeeded in perfecting a camera ("Kinetograph") that was capable of photographing objects in motion. Soon thereafter, the first motion picture studio was formed to manufacture "Kinetoscopes" at Edison's laboratory in West Orange, New Jersey. These first primitive movies – filmstrips viewed through a peephole machine – were then shown at a "Kinetoscope Parlor" on lower Broadway in New York, where crowds formed to see this most amazing novelty.

The technological development of cameras, films, and projection equipment accelerated considerably at this stage, and the most astute of the business were quick to understand the money-making potential in showing films to the public. The early years, though, were marked by a series of patent infringement suits and attempts at monopolization that were to characterize the industry's internal relations for a long time. As Stanley (1978, p. 10) notes:

movies were being shown in thousands of theaters around the country, . . . After years of patent disputes, the major movie companies realized it was to their mutual advantage to cooperate . . . A complex natural monopoly over almost all phases of the nascent motion picture industry was organized in December 1908. It was called the Motion Picture Patents Company.

This company held pooled patents for films, cameras, and projectors, and apportioned royalties on the patents. It also attempted to control the industry by buying up most of the major film exchanges (distributors) then in existence, with the goal of organizing them into a massive rental exchange, the General Film Company.

The Patents Company and its distribution subsidiary (together known as the "Trust") often engaged in crude and oppressive business practices that fostered great resentment and discontent. But eventually the Trust was overwhelmed by the growing numbers, and by the increasing market power, of the independents that sprang up in all areas of production, distribution, and exhibition (i.e., theaters). The Trust's control of the industry, for example, was undermined by the many "independent" producers who would use the Patent Company's machines, without authorization, on film stock that was imported. Yet more significantly, it was from within the ranks of these very independents that there emerged the founders of companies that were later to become Hollywood's giants: Carl Laemmle, credited with starting the star system and founder of Universal; William Fox, founder of the Fox Film Company, which was combined in 1935 with Twentieth Century Pictures; Adolph Zukor, who came to dominate Paramount Pictures; and Marcus Loew, who in the early 1920s assembled two failing companies (Metro Pictures and Goldwyn Pictures) to form the core of MGM.

At around the same time, there began a distinct movement of production activity to the West Coast. Southern California was not only far for the Trust enforcers to reach, but it could also provide low-cost nonunion labor and advantageous climate and geography for filming. Thus, by the mid-1920s, most production had shifted to the West, although New York retained its importance as the industry's financial seat.

However, not long after, the industry was shaken by the introduction of motion pictures with sound, and by the onset of the Great Depression. In that time of economic collapse, the large amounts of capital required to convert to sound equipment could only be provided by the Eastern banking firms — who refinanced and reorganized the major companies. Ultimately, it was those companies with the most vertical integration – controlling production, distribution, and exhibition – that survived this period intact. Those companies were Warner Brothers, RKO, Twentieth Century–Fox, Paramount, and MGM. On a lesser scale were Universal and Columbia, who were only producer–distributors, and United Artists, essentially a distributor. The Depression, moreover, also led to the formation of powerful unions of skilled craftsmen, talent guilds, and other institutions that now play an important role in the economics of filmmaking.

Except for their sometimes strained relations with the unions, the eight major companies came out of this period of restructuring with a degree of control over the business that the early Patents Company founders could envy, and the complaints of those harmed in such an environment began to be heard by the Justice Department. After five years of intensive investigation, the government filed suit in 1938 against the eight companies and charged them with illegally conspiring to restrain trade by, among other things, causing an exhibitor who wanted any of a distributor's pictures to take all of them (i.e., block booking them). Yet, by agreeing to a few relatively minor restrictions in a consent decree signed in 1940, the majors were able to settle the case without having to sever the link between distribution and exhibition. Because of this, five majors retained dominance in about 70% of the first-run theaters in the country.

Not surprisingly, complaints persisted, and the Justice Department found it necessary to reactivate its suit against Paramount in 1944. After several more years of legal wrangling, the defendants finally agreed in 1948 to sign a decree that separated production and distribution from exhibition. It was this decree – combined with the contemporaneous emergence of television – that ushered the movie business into the modern era (Table 2.1 and Figure 2.1).

Table 2.1. *Chronology of antitrust actions in the motion-picture industry*

1908	Motion Picture Patents Co. established; horizontal combination of 10 major companies that held most of the patents in the industry; cross-licensing arrangement
1910	General Films Co. purchased 68 film exchanges (local distribution companies) (vertical integration)
1914	Five film exchanges combined as Paramount to distribute films (vertical integration)
1916	Famous Players merged with Lasky to form major studio (horizontal integration)
1917	Famous Players–Lasky acquired 12 small producers and Paramount (vertical and horizontal integration)
1917	Motion Picture Patents Co. and General Films Co. dissolved as a result of judicial decisions and innovations by independents
1917	3,500 exhibitors became part of First National Exhibitors Circuit; financed independents, built studios (vertical and horizontal integration)
1918	Exhibitor combination formed in 1912 partially enjoined
1925	Series of federal suits brought against large chains of exhibitors for coercing distributors
1927	Paramount ordered to cease and desist anticompetitive practices
1929	Standard exhibition contract struck down as restraint of trade
1929	Exhibitor suit resulted in injunction against restrictive practices of sound manufacturers (talkies)
1930	Full vertical integration established as norm (production/ distribution/exhibition); major exhibitor circuits given special treatment such as formula deals, advantageous clearances; studios owned supply of natural resources (stars)
1932	Uniform zoning and protection plan for the Omaha distributing territory enjoined
1938	Start of a series of Justice Department antitrust actions against the industry (Paramount case I)
1940	Major studios entered into a series of consent decrees
1944	Justice Department brought Paramount case II, asked for divestiture of exhibition segment of major studios; District Court stopped short of divestiture, but ordered other practices to cease; both parties appealed
1948–49	Supreme Court (in effect) ordered divestiture
	Under jurisdiction of District Court, major studios divested themselves of their theaters and entered into consent decrees in other areas
1950–96	Series of antitrust actions (private and federal) against various segments of the industry for past practices, violations of the consent decree, price fixing, block booking, product splitting, and other anticompetitive activities

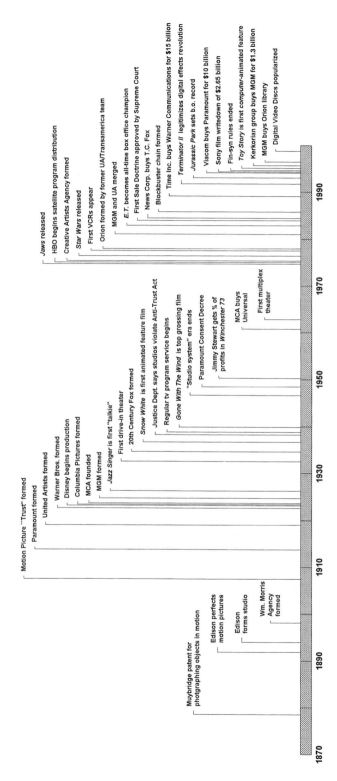

Figure 2.1. Film industry milestones.

2.2 May the forces be with you

Evolutionary elements

The major forces shaping the structure of the movie industry have included (1) technological advances in the filmmaking process itself, in marketing and audience sampling methods, and in the development of television, cable, satellites, video recorders, computers, and laser discs; (2) the need for ever-larger pools of capital in order to launch motion-picture projects; (3) the 1948 consent decree separating distribution from exhibition; (4) the emergence of large multiplex theater chains in new suburban locations; and (5) the constant evolution and growth of independent production and service organizations. Each of these items will be discussed in the context of a gradually unfolding larger story.

Technology Unquestionably the most potent impetus for change over the long term has been, and will continue to be, the development of technology. As Fielding has observed:

> If the artistic and historical development of film and television are to be understood, then so must the peculiar marriage of art and technology which prevails in their operation. It is the involvement of twentieth-century technology which renders these media so unlike the other, older arts. (Fielding 1967, p. iv)

In the filmmaking process itself, for instance, the impact of technological improvements has been phenomenal. To see how far we have come, we need only remember that "talkies" were the special-effects movies of the late 1920s; indeed, it was not until the 1970s that special effects began to be created with the help of advanced computer-aided designs and electronic editing and composition devices. *Terminator 2, Top Gun,* and *Independence Day* are examples of films that would not and could not have been made without the new machines and methods.

In addition, technological developments have enabled distributors to launch international marketing campaigns with much more speed and complexity than could have been imagined in the early years of the industry. And distributors and exhibitors now have the ability – using sophisticated sampling techniques and forecasting models – to closely estimate audience size and demographic responsiveness to a picture within a day or two of its release, and to therefore quickly make adjustments.

Of course, the ready availability of television, cable, and other home video displays has also been important in changing the movie industry's economic and physical structure; film presentations on any of these media are competitive as well as supplementary to theatrical exhibitions – historically the core business. Indeed, advancements in program distribution and storage capabilities have made it possible to see a wide variety of films in the comfort of our homes and at our own discretion. Such unprecedented access to filmed entertainment – enabling viewers to control the time and place of viewing – has redirected the economic power of studios and distributors and opened the way for new enterprises to flourish. As the rate of change in signal distribution technology begins to outpace the rate of change in production technology, filmed-entertainment products and services are sure to become ever more personalized and adaptable.[1]

Capital After technology, the second most important long-term force for change has been the packaging and application of relatively large amounts of capital to the total process of production, distribution, and marketing. In this regard, financing innovations (as discussed in the next chapter) have played a leading role. Without the development of sophisticated financing methods and access to a broad and deep capital market, it is doubtful that the movie industry could have arrived at the position it occupies today.

From an economist's standpoint, it is also interesting to observe further that the feature-film business does not easily fit the usual molds. Industries requiring sizable capital investments can normally be expected to evolve into purely oligopolistic forms: steel and automobile manufacturing, for example. But because movies – each uniquely designed and packaged – are not stamped out on cookie–cutter assembly lines, the economic structure is somewhat different. Here, instead, we find a combination of large oligopolistic production/distribution/financing organizations regularly interfacing with and being highly dependent on a fragmented assortment of small, specialized service and production firms.

At least in Hollywood, energetic little fish often can swim with great agility and success among the giant whales, assorted sharks, and hungry piranha.

Pecking orders

Exhibition Back in the 1920s, a 65-cent movie ticket would buy a comfortable seat in the grandeur of a marbled and gilded theater palace in which complimentary coffee was graciously served while a string quartet played softly in the background. But those were the good old days.

The aforementioned 1948 antitrust consent decree had considerable impact on movie industry structure because it disallowed control of the retail exhibition side of the business (local movie theaters) by the major production/distribution entities of that time. Disgruntled independent theater owners had initiated the action leading to issuance of the decree because they felt that studios were discriminating against them: Studios would book pictures into their captive outlets without public bidding.

However, the divestitures – ordered in the name of preserving competition – turned out to be a hollow victory for those independents. Soon after the distribution-exhibition split had been effected, studios realized that it was no longer necessary to supply a new picture every week, and they proceeded to substantially reduce production schedules. Competition for the best pictures out of a diminished supply then raised prices beyond what many owners of small theaters could afford. And by that time, television had begun to wean audiences away from big-screen entertainment; the number of movie admissions had begun a steep down-

Table 2.2. *Exhibition industry composite, nine companies, 1992–96*

	Revenues	Operating income	Operating[a] margin (%)	Assets	Operating cash flow
CAGR(%)[b] 1992–96	6.3	15.3	NM[c]	8.4	11.9

[a]Average margin 1992–96 = 5.6%.
[b]Compound annual growth rate.
[c]Not meaningful.

ward slide. The 1948 decree thus triggered and also hastened the arrival of a major structural change that would have eventually happened anyway.[2]

In the United States, exhibition is dominated by several major theater chains, including those operated by GC Companies (formerly General Cinema), UA Communications (formerly UA Theater Circuit), Cineplex Odeon (Plitt, Walter Reade, and RKO), AMC Entertainment (American Multi-Cinema), Carmike Cinemas, Redstone (National Amusements, Inc.), Commonwealth, Sony (Loews), and Marcus Corp. In aggregate, these companies operate approximately 14,000 of the best-located and most modern urban and suburban (e.g., shopping mall) movie screens, with most of the other 16,000 or so older theaters still owned by individuals and small private companies. As such, the chains control 45% of the screens, but probably account for at least 80% of the total exhibition revenues generated.

In Canada, however, two chains, Cineplex Odeon and Famous Players Ltd. (owned by Viacom Inc.), are estimated to control about 65% of annual theatrical revenues, which are roughly 10% of those in the United States.

In both the United States and Canada, construction of conveniently located multiple-screen (i.e., multiplexed) theaters in suburban areas by these large chains has more than offset the decline of older drive-in and inner-city locations and has accordingly helped to stave off competition from other forms of entertainment, including home video. The chains, moreover, have brought economies of scale to a business that used to be notoriously inefficient in its operating practices and procedures. As a result, control of exhibition is gradually being consolidated into fewer and financially stronger hands.[3] Indeed, the seven companies aggregated in Table 2.2 together account for over 50% of total industry dollar volume.

Production and distribution Theatrical film production and distribution have evolved into a multifaceted business, with many different sizes and types of organizations participating in some or all parts of the project development and marketing processes. However, companies with important and long-standing presences in both production and distribution, with substantial library assets, and with some studio production facilities (although nowadays this is not a necessity) have been collectively and historically known as the ''Majors.''

As of the late-1990s, subsequent to many mergers and restructurings, there were six major theatrical-film distributors (studios): The Walt Disney Company (Buena Vista, Touchstone, and Hollywood Pictures), Sony Pictures (formerly Columbia Pictures Entertainment, wholly owned by Sony and distributor of Columbia and TriStar films), Paramount (Viacom Inc.), Twentieth Century Fox (News Corp.), Warner Bros. (Time Warner Inc.), and Universal (80%-owned by Seagram Co. as of 1995 and formerly MCA, Inc.).[4] These companies produce, finance, and distribute their own films, but also finance and distribute pictures initiated by so-called independent filmmakers who either work directly for them or have projects "picked up" after progress toward completion has already been made.[5]

Of considerably lesser size and scope in production and distribution activities are Metro-Goldwyn-Mayer Inc. (an oft-restructured, erstwhile major), and so-called "mini-majors" such as New Line Cinema (Time Warner) and the defunct Orion Pictures (whose library was bought by MGM). Many smaller production companies will also often have significant distribution capabilities in specialized market segments. Generally, such smaller companies would not handle theatrical product lines that are as broad as those of the majors, nor would they have the considerable access to capital that a major would have. Nevertheless, these smaller companies can occasionally produce and nationally distribute pictures that attract audiences large enough to attract media attention.[6]

Several smaller, "independent" producers also either feed their production into the established distribution pipelines of the larger companies or have mini-distribution organizations of their own. Many of these newer independents, formed in the late 1980s, largely finance their productions away from the majors and then, in effect, merely make distribution agreements with the larger studios (i.e., they "rent" the studio's distribution apparatus). They thus retain much more control over a film's rights and can build a library of such rights. In addition, there are many executive project development firms that themselves do not produce, but that option existing literary properties and/or develop new properties for others to produce.

Moreover, small independent firms, sometimes called 'states-righters', handle distributions in local and regional markets not well covered by the majors or submajors.[7] They have counterparts in overseas markets, where distributors of various sizes operate.

Although at first it may be a bit startling to learn of the existence of so many different production and service organizations, their enduring presence underscores the entrepreneurial qualities of this business. The many "independents" have been a structural fact of life since the industry began; they add considerable variety and spice to the filmmaking process; and they help prevent stagnation.

2.3 Ups and downs

Admission cycles

There has long been a notion, derived from the depression-resistant performance of motion-picture ticket sales, that the movie business has somewhat contracy-

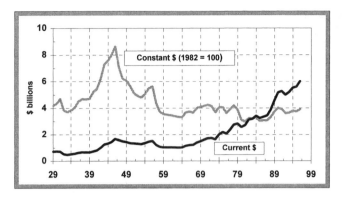

Figure 2.2. PCEs on movies, 1929–96.

clical characteristics (Figure 2.2). Indeed, it may be theorized that as the economy enters a recessionary phase, the leisure-time spending preferences of consumers shift more toward lower-cost, closer-to-home entertainment activities than when the economy is robust and expansionary. If so, this would explain why ticket sales often remain steady during early to middle stages of a recession, faltering only near the recession's end. By that stage, many people's budgets are apt to be severely stretched and long-postponed purchases of essential goods (e.g., new cars) and services (e.g., fixing leaky ceilings) will naturally take priority over spending on entertainment. The performance of movie-ticket sales vis-à-vis the economy during recessionary episodes since 1929 is illustrated in Figure 2.3.

In fact, an important study of cycles in ticket demand (Nardone (1982)) has indicated that the motion-picture industry acts contracyclically to the economy 87.5% of the time in peaks and 69.3% of the time in troughs. Also, there are suggestions that both a 4-year and a 10-year cycle in movie admissions may be present, but the statistical evidence in this regard is inconclusive.[8] Ticket sales peaked in 1946 and troughed in 1971 – a time when the economic survival of several major distributors was seriously in question.

Seasonal demand patterns are, fortunately, much easier to discern and to interpret than are the long-wave cycles. Families find it most convenient to see films during vacation periods such as Thanksgiving, Christmas, and Easter, and children out of school during the summer months have time to frequent the box office.[9] Contrariwise, in the fall, school begins again, new television programs are introduced, and elections are held; people are busy with activities other than moviegoing. And in the period just prior to Christmas, shopping takes precedence. Thus the industry tends to concentrate most of its important film releases within just a few weeks of the year. This makes the competition for moviegoers' attention and time more expensive than it would be if audience attendance patterns were not as seasonally skewed (see section 3.4 on marketing costs). Normalized seasonal patterns are illustrated in Figure 2.4.

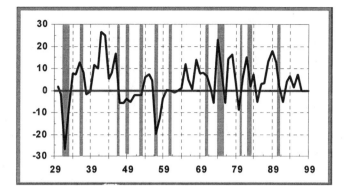

Figure 2.3. Motion-picture receipts: percentage change over previous year's receipts, 1929–96. Bars indicate periods of recession.

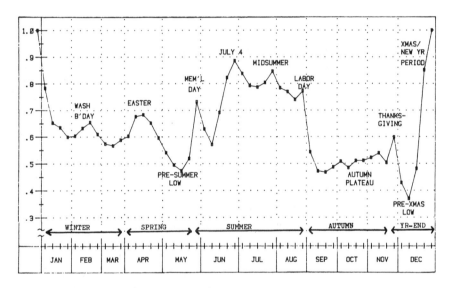

Figure 2.4. Normalized weekly fluctuations in U.S. film attendance, 1969–84.
Source: Variety, copyright 1984 by A. D. Murphy.

Prices and elasticities

Ticket sales for new film releases normally are not very responsive to changes in box-office prices per se, but there may be sensitivity to the total cost of movie-going, which can include fees for baby-sitters, restaurant meals, and parking. Although demand for major-event movies, backed by strong word-of-mouth advertising and reviewer support, is essentially price-inelastic, exhibitors are often able to stimulate admissions by showing somewhat older features at very low prices during off-peak times (e.g., Tuesday noon screenings when schools are in session). Many retired and unemployed people, and probably bored housewives

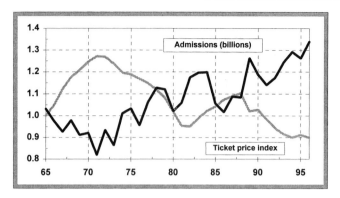

Figure 2.5. Motion-picture admissions in billions and average real ticket-price index, 1965–96.

and truants, like to take advantage of such bargains. There is, moreover, a widespread impression that ticket prices have risen inordinately. Yet, as Figure 2.5 indicates, movie-ticket prices, as deflated by the consumer price index, remain below the peak of the early 1970s.

Production starts and capital

In at least one respect, the movie industry is no different from the housing construction industry. The crucial initial ingredient is capital. Without access to it, no project can get off the ground. It should thus come as no surprise to find that the number of movies started in any year may be sensitive to changes in interest rates and in the availability of credit. To illustrate this relationship, a statistical experiment was conducted using the *Daily Variety* end-of-quarter production-start figures from 1969 to 1980, the quarterly average bank prime interest rate adjusted by the implicit gross-national-product (GNP) deflator for the same period, and the banking system's borrowed reserves (also deflated) as a proxy for the availability of capital. The results were as follows:

1. There may be a moderate, statistically significant inverse correlation, with at least a one-quarter lag, betweeen real interest rates and the number of production starts.
2. There probably exists, with a six-quarter lag, an inverse relationship between production starts and borrowed reserves (credit availability) (Figure 2.6).

That production starts should lag behind changes in the availability of capital by as much as six quarters should not be unexpected in view of the long lead time usually needed to assemble the many diverse components required for motion-picture productions. Beginning with a rudimentary outline or treatment of a story idea, it can often take over a year to arrange financing, final scripts, cast,

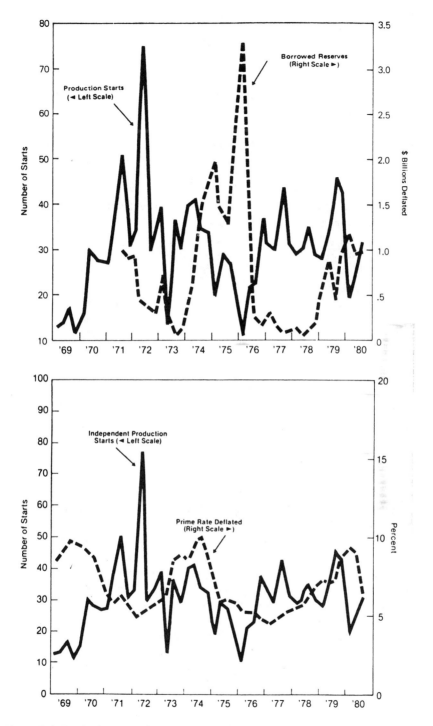

Figure 2.6. Production starts, interest rates, and borrowed reserves lagged six quarters, 1969–80.

and crew. And, in total, it normally requires at least 18 months to bring a movie project from conception to the answer-print stage – the point at which all editing, mixing, and dubbing work has been completed.

Moreover, because the industry ordinarily depends on a continuous flow of cash, when credit is restricted by the Federal Reserve Bank, sources of funding for movie projects rapidly dry up: Everyone in the long chain of revenue disbursement slows payments on bills, and it becomes more difficult to effectively attract relatively scarce capital flows away from alternative uses that promise higher returns for less risk. Thus, especially for independent filmmakers, the cost and availability of credit with which to finance a project are often the most important variables affecting the time that elapses from start to finish.

No matter what the monetary environment, however, in theory (but not always in practice) only the worthiest of projects are supported – with the best concepts presumably first being offered to, and sometimes erroneously rejected by, the large studios/financiers/distributors. In this respect, it is significant that the number of potential film projects on Hollywood's drawing boards always far exceeds the number that can actually be financed. Parkinson's Law applies here: The number of projects will always expand to fully absorb the capital available, regardless of quality, and virtually without regard to the quantity of other films scheduled for completion and release at around the same time.

Releases and inventories

Variations in production starts are eventually reflected in the number of films released (supplied) to theaters. In turn, the number of releases and the rate of theater admissions influence industry operating profits. But it is difficult to estimate (using regression models) how large this effect may be; variations in the numbers of releases and admissions are not independent of each other, and aggregate profits are also influenced by the demand for filmed entertainment products in television, cable, and other markets.[10]

Sometimes, a more practical way to view the effects of changes in supply is through comparison of total dollar investments in film inventories against sales (i.e., film rentals). As in other industries, such comparisons often lead to the discovery of important economic relationships. For instance, a falling ratio of inventory to sales may be a manifestation of improving demand and/or of declining investments in production; either way, inventories become less financially burdensome to carry as cash is being recycled relatively rapidly.

Estimated inventory-to-sales figures for the major studios are shown in Table 2.3, where proper interpretation requires recognition that *many independently produced projects are carried off-balance-sheet* until release impends. The visible ratios – generally around 0.6 or higher since the early 1980s – are consequently somewhat akin to the tip of an iceberg, the size of which is often more easily gauged from the number of films rated each year by the Motion Picture Association of America (MPAA).[11] Additional industry data is shown in Table 2.4.

Table 2.3. *Filmed entertainment industry operating performance, major theatrical distributors, 1973–96*

	Revenues ($ millions)	Oper. income ($ million)	Margin (%)	Film inventory ($ million)	Invent/ revenue ($ million)
1996	24,679	1,870	7.6	16,850	0.68
1995	22,073	1,831	8.3	12,361	0.56
1994	19,710	967	4.9	12,288	0.62
1993	17,583	733	4.2	11,598	0.66
1992	16,147	1,302	8.1	10,374	0.64
1991	14,128	941	6.7	9,663	0.68
1990	12,676	1,103	8.7	8,127	0.64
1989	11,571	1,130	9.8	7,242	0.63
1988	9,121	1,151	12.6	5,089	0.56
1987	8,251	928	11.2	4,710	0.57
1986	6,839	799	11.7	4,458	0.65
1985	6,359	465	7.3	4,216	0.66
1984	5,839	516	8.8	3,370	0.58
1983	5,324	590	11.1	2,980	0.56
1982	4,548	565	12.4	2,729	0.60
1981	3,749	301	8.0	2,267	0.60
1980	3,997	489	12.2	1,423	0.36
1979	4,009	661	16.5	1,538	0.38
1978	3,498	606	17.3	1,212	0.35
1977	2,739	406	14.8	973	0.36
1976	2,336	336	14.4	936	0.40
1975	2,078	353	17.0	822	0.40
1974	1,803	259	14.4	862	0.48
1973	1,485	109	7.3	840	0.57

Five-, ten-, and twenty-year compound annual growth rates

1992–96	11.8	14.7		11.8	
1987–96	13.7	8.9		14.2	
1977–96	12.5	9.0		15.5	

Market-share factors

Many consumer-product industries rely on market-share information to evaluate the relative positions of major participants. However, because consumers have little, if any, brand identification with movie distributors (or most producers), and because market share tends to fluctuate considerably from year to year for any one distributor, such data generally have limited applicability and relevance. In the picture business, the approach is of necessity far different than in market-share research for soaps, or cigarettes, or beverages.

This kind of information therefore seems best suited for contrasting the effec-

Table 2.4 (cont.).

	U.S. number of admissions (billion)	Avg. ticket price ($)	Total number of MPAA releases	Number of domestic screens			Average per screen		Screens per MPAA release
				Total	Indoor	Drive-in	Dom. B.O ($)	Admissions	
1996	1.339	4.42	240	29,690	28,864	826	199,107	45,086	123.7
1995	1.263	4.35	234	27,805	26,958	847	197,572	45,409	118.8
1994	1.292	4.18	183	26,586	25,701	885	202,971	48,586	145.3
1993	1.244	4.14	161	25,737	24,887	850	200,256	48,335	159.9
1992	1.173	4.15	150	25,105	24,233	872	194,025	46,732	167.4
1991	1.141	4.21	164	24,570	23,662	908	195,490	46,422	149.8
1990	1.189	4.23	169	23,689	22,774	915	211,989	50,175	140.2
1989	1.263	3.99	169	23,132	22,029	1,103	217,595	54,591	136.9
1988	1.085	4.11	160	23,234	21,689	1,545	191,891	46,690	145.2
1987	1.089	3.91	129	23,555	21,048	2,507	180,552	46,211	182.6
1986	1.017	3.71	139	22,765	19,947	2,818	165,957	44,683	163.8
1985	1.056	3.55	153	21,147	18,327	2,820	177,302	49,941	138.2
1984	1.199	3.36	167	20,200	17,368	2,832	199,535	59,361	121.0
1983	1.197	3.15	190	18,884	16,032	2,852	199,428	63,382	99.4
1982	1.175	2.94	173	18,020	14,977	3,043	191,604	65,228	104.2
1981	1.060	2.78	173	18,040	14,732	3,308	164,390	58,758	104.3

Year									
1980	1.022	2.69	161	17,590	14,029	3,561	156,254	58,073	109.3
1979	1.121	2.52	138	16,901	13,331	3,570	166,913	66,327	122.5
1978	1.128	2.34	114	16,251	12,671	3,580	162,636	69,411	142.6
1977	1.063	2.23	110	16,041	12,434	3,607	147,871	66,268	145.8
1976	0.957	2.13	133	15,832	12,197	3,635	128,600	60,447	119.0
1975	1.033	2.05	138	15,030	11,402	3,628	140,719	68,729	108.9
1974	1.011	1.89	155	14,417	10,839	3,578	132,413	70,126	93.0
1973	0.865	1.76	163	14,420	10,765	3,655	105,687	59,986	88.5
1972	0.934	1.70	193	14,428	10,694	3,734	109,717	64,735	74.8
1971	0.820	1.65	183	14,055	10,335	3,720	96,051	58,342	76.8
1970	0.921	1.55	185	13,750	10,000	3,750	103,927	66,982	74.3
1969	0.912	1.42	183	13,480	9,750	3,730	95,994	67,656	73.7
1968	0.979	1.31	196	13,190	9,500	3,690	97,195	74,223	67.3
1967	0.927	1.20	199	13,000	9,330	3,670	85,385	71,308	65.3
1966	0.975	1.09	181	12,930	9,290	3,640	82,521	75,406	71.4
1965	1.032	1.01	210	12,825	9,240	3,585	81,248	80,468	61.1
CAGR:									
1965-95	0.7%	5.0%		2.6	3.6	-4.7	3.0	-1.9	
1980-96	1.7	3.1		3.3	4.6	-8.7	1.5	-1.6	

Note: In traditional industry parlance, the term *domestic* includes U.S. and Canadian rentals. In this table, *foreign* includes Canada.
Source: Variety and *Daily Variety* as based on MPAA-MPEAA data.

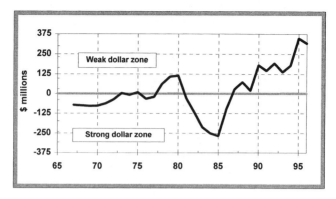

Figure 2.7. Film industry foreign theatrical rentals, estimated differentials for dollar exchange rate effects, 1965–96.

tiveness of major distributor organizations over the long-term or for comparing a film's short-term rental performance in one region against that for another film in the same region. In long-term analysis, for example, averaging of Disney's share and those of other distributors over the dozen years beginning in 1970 would quantify that company's significant erosion of market presence in the 1970s and rebound into the 1990s (Supplementary Table S2.4).

Exchange-rate effects

Between 30% and 45% of gross rentals earned by the majors usually are generated outside the so-called domestic market, which includes both the United States and Canada (about 10% of the U.S. total). Swings in foreign-currency exchange rates may therefore substantially affect the profitability of U.S. studio/distribution organizations.

For instance, during most of the 1970s and after 1985, with the U.S. dollar relatively weak against major export-market currencies (Japanese yen, British pound sterling, Deutsche mark, French franc, and Swiss franc), studio profitability was significantly enhanced as movie tickets purchased in those currencies translated into more dollars. Contrariwise, in the late 1970s and early 1980s, a strengthening dollar probably reduced the industry's operating profits by some 10%–15% ($100 million or so) under what would otherwise have been generated. In other words, although there is some countervailing effect from the higher costs of shooting pictures in strong-currency countries and from maintaining foreign-territory distribution and sales facilities in such locations, a weakening dollar exchange rate will, on-balance, noticeably improve movie industry profitability.

Estimates of the importance of foreign-currency translation rates on industry profits are shown in Figure 2.7, from which it can be seen that a weakening dollar results in significant net benefit. Aggregate theatrical admissions in five developed countries are shown in Figure 2.8(a), with theatrical admissions on a per capita basis and screen availability comparisons shown in Figure 2.8(b) and (c).[12]

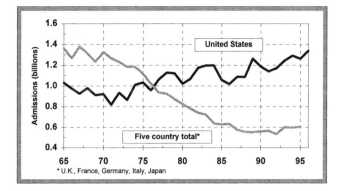

Figure 2.8(a). Theatrical admissions in the United States and in five major developed countries, 1965–96. *Source:* Country statistical abstracts and MPAA data.

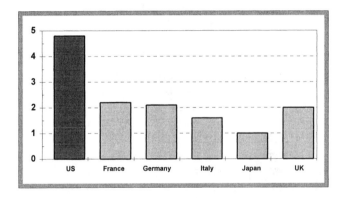

Figure 2.8(b). Admissions per capita, selected countries, 1995.

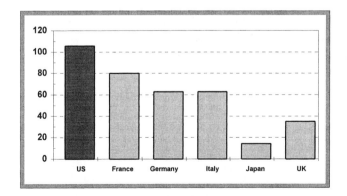

Figure 2.8(c). Screens per 1 million population, selected countries, 1995.

Table 2.5. *Estimated ancillary revenues for an "average" MPAA-member film*[a]
1997 ($ million)

Typical license fees or revenues per film[b]	
Pay cable	8.5
Home video (cassettes and discs)	10.0
Network TV licenses	2.5
Syndication	1.5
Foreign TV	2.0
Total	24.5

[a]Per-film figures for ancillary markets represent the approximate going rate for representative pictures. However, they are not derived by dividing total ancillary-market revenues by an exact number of releases. Averages would, of course, be much lower if non-MPAA member films were to be included.

[b]Also see section 3.5, where it is explained why averages such as those used here require careful interpretation. Examples of wide positive and negative deviations from these approximate averages are shown in Table 4.8.

Financial aggregates

As we have already seen, for all its purported sophistication and glamor, the movie industry remains fragmented in its organizational structure: especially on the creative ends it is very much still a cottage industry, and there are good economic reasons to believe that it will remain so, if only because many small service firms and production units are efficiently scaled.

The majors, though, still consistently generate the bulk of industry revenues (an estimated 90% of gross domestic film rentals), and when they have problems, so does everyone else in the business. The financial statements of these large companies accordingly provide, in the aggregate, a useful overall representation of the industry's financial performance trends (Table 2.3). But because entertainment companies find it well-nigh impossible to systematically match overhead and financing costs against revenues from specific sources, these data do not normally allow us to analyze whether profit potential is greater in theatrical, television, or ancillary-market sales. Such issues are best addressed through an understanding of the microeconomic aspects of the business, which are discussed in the chapters that follow.[13]

2.4 Markets primary and secondary

Theaters have historically been the primary retail outlet for movies; that is where most of the revenues have been collected and where most of the viewing has occurred. But since the mid-1980s, fees from the licensing of films for use in ancillary markets – network and syndicated television, pay cable, and home video – have in the aggregate begun to far overshadow revenues derived from theatrical release. Table 2.5 illustrates what an "average" feature film released through a

Table 2.6. *Approximate cost of movie viewing per person-hour, 1997*[a]

Theater (first-run big cities)	$4.50
Pay cable channel	0.50
Home video	0.60
''Free'' commercial television[b]	0.06

[a]Assumes 2-hour movie, and 2 person household.
[b]Calculated by assuming $30 billion in TV advertising, divided by 2,555 (7 hours a day average viewing time × 365 days) × 100 million households.

major distributor might garner from each of the ancillary markets as of the mid-1990s.

Yet, technological development, the driving force behind the transition to dominance by so-called ancillary markets, has led to sharp decreases in the costs of distributing and storing the bits of information that are contained in entertainment software. Whether such unit-cost decreases are in themselves sufficient to sustain the industry's profitability is still an open question.

An individual seeing a newly released feature film in a theater would, for example, ordinarily generate revenue (rental or gross) to the distributor of anywhere between $1.50 and $4.00. However, viewing on pay television, or from a rented prerecorded disc or cassette, sometimes results in revenue per person-view of as little as 20 to 30 cents (Table 2.6). That happens when several people in a household watch a film at the same time, or when an individual watches several times without incurring additional charges.

It may, of course, be argued that in recent years, declining average unit costs at home have had no discernible effect on theater admissions and that, indeed, markets for filmed entertainment products have been broadened by attracting, at the margin, viewers who would not pay the price of a ticket in any case. In addition, it seems that, no matter how low the price at home, people still enjoy going out to the movies.

But as sensible as this line of reasoning appears to be – it is platitudinous within the industry – there are several problems in accepting it without challenge. One of the most noticeable tendencies, for instance, has been the virtual dichotomization of the theatrical market into a relative handful of ''hits'' and a mass of also-rans. This can be seen from several recent peak-season box-office experiences, in which four out of perhaps a dozen major releases have generated as much as 80% of total revenues.

Although ''must-see'' media-event films are as much in demand as ever, such dichotomization suggests that admissions to pictures requiring less immediate responsiveness are probably being replaced by home screenings that on average generate much less revenue per view. The new home-video options obviously allow people to become much more discriminating as to when and where they spend an evening out.[14]

In other words, what is gained in one market may be at least partially lost in

Table 2.7. *Filmed entertainment industry operating performance: composite of 7 companies, 1992–96*

	Revenues	Operating income	Operating margin[a] (%)	Assets	Operating cash flow
CAGR(%)[b]	8.9	7.5	NM[c]	10.2	8.1

[a]Average margin 1992–96 = 6.6%.
[b]Compound annual growth rate.
[c]Not meaningful.

another. Indeed, in the aggregate, ancillary-market cash flow is often largely substitutional and thus not necessarily a net increment to total revenues. To wit: Extensive exposures on pay-cable prior to showings on network television have sharply reduced network ratings garnered by feature film broadcasts. And the networks now generally pay much less than they used to for feature-film exhibition rights.

The development of ancillary markets has also been widely heralded as a boon to movie industry profitability. Yet contributions from new revenue sources, especially those from pay cable and home video, have not been sufficient to offset the sharply diminished profitability of theatrical production and release. Between 1980 and 1996, for example, the cost of the average picture made by a major studio rose from $9.4 million to $39.8 million, and marketing costs more than quadrupled: Returns on revenues (operating margins) have meanwhile fallen by at least one-third and have remained well below the peaks of the late 1970s (see Table 2.3). And aggregate industry profit growth, as seen in Table 2.7, has not been accelerating.

Just as significantly, however, the existence of ancillary markets has enabled many independent producers to finance their films through so-called *presales* of rights. Presales – which may be in the form of funds, guarantees, or commitments that may be used to obtain funds – often support projects that perhaps could not and should not have otherwise been made. Indeed, many projects financed in this manner, typically through sale of foreign rights, are unable to generate cash flows in excess of the amounts required to cover the costs of both production *and* release (marketing and prints).[15]

Companies generally relying on presale strategies manage to cushion, but not eliminate, their downside risks while giving away much of the substantial upside profit and cash flow potential from hits. Such companies will also inevitably have a relatively high cost of capital as compared to that of a major studio, if only because presale cash commitments (from downstream distributors) are generally relayed to the producer in installments. The producer will still usually need interim (and relatively costly) loans to cover cash outlays during the period of production and perhaps up until well after theatrical release. Thus, over the longer run, the relatively few hits such firms might produce are often insufficient in number or in degree of success to cover their many losing or break-even projects.[16]

Table 2.8. *Film industry sources of revenue estimated, 1980 and 1995*[a]

	1980		1995	
	$ millions	%	$ millions	%
Theatrical:				
Domestic	1,183	29.6	2,600	14.4
Foreign	911	22.8	2,300	12.8
Home video	280	7.0	7,300	40.6
Pay cable	240	6.0	1,400	7.8
Network TV	430	10.8	250	1.4
Syndication	150	3.8	750	4.2
Foreign TV	100	2.5	1,200	6.7
Made for TV films	700	17.5	2,200	12.2
Total	3,994	100.0[b]	18,000	100.0[b]

[a]Major filmed entertainment companies in the United States.
[b]Total not exact due to rounding.

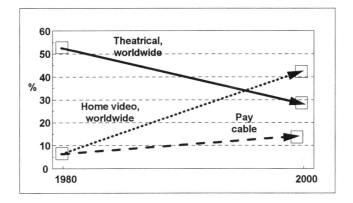

Figure 2.9. Estimated percentage of film industry revenue derived from feature film exploitation in theatrical, home video, and pay cable markets, 1980 and 2000.

As we can see from the data, ancillary market development has not as yet been (and may never be) fully translated into enhanced industry profitability. In essence, weak cost constraints, fragmentation of markets and audiences, and increased competition for talent resources have capped profit margins.[17]

It is somewhat simplistic and unpopular, but nonetheless accurate, to thus portray new-media revenues as having so far been more important as a prop for, than as a source of, improved profitability. Yet there is no denying that the new media have forever changed the income structure of the film business at large. As Table 2.8 illustrates, as recently as 1980, theatrical sources accounted for over half of all industry revenues. Fifteen years later, theatrical sources accounted for only a fourth of all such revenues (Figure 2.9).

Although a distinct shift of preference away from "free" advertiser-supported programming and toward the direct-purchase of entertainment in the form of movie tickets, pay-cable services, and home-video units (through either sales or rentals) would lead to a significant improvement in profitability, such a shift appears to be happening only gradually.[18] For the most part, the inherent uncertainties have instead created a constantly shifting jumble of corporate cross-ownership and joint-venture arrangements (Figure 2.10) that – in a scramble for control of "content" and distribution power – more often resemble hedged bets than bold and insightful strategic maneuvers.[19]

New technology – emerging in the form of what has come to be broadly known as interactive multimedia – will indeed provide the viewer with unprecedented control over when and where entertainment may be enjoyed. Technology has already also significantly lowered the price per view and established important new revenue sources, thus generally diffusing the economic power of the more traditional suppliers of programming. Still, new viewing options almost invariably displace older ones. And marketing costs rise as both the old and the new compete for the attention of wide-ranging, yet finicky, audiences.

2.5 Assets

Film libraries

More guesswork and ambiguity appears in the valuation of film library assets than in perhaps any other area relating to the financial economics of the movie business. Yet this topic is of prime concern to investors who, over the years, have staked billions of dollars on actual and rumored studio takeovers. Twentieth Century Fox, United Artists, Columbia Pictures, and MCA Inc. have been among the many major acquisitions in an industry long rife with buy-out attempts. Still, factors that might not at first glance be considered significant – technological advances, interest rates, legislative developments, recent utilization (depletion) rates, and prevailing social temper – all affect a library's perceived value.

Technology Of all these factors, technological advances have been by far the most important and have generated the most controversy. On the one hand, the flourishing new electronic media have increased the demand for programming, effectively providing opportunities to sell a lot of old wine (software) in a wide variety of new bottles. On the other hand, new entertainment delivery and storage technologies have made it possible for practically anyone to record programming conveniently and inexpensively. This common capability has probably adversely affected library values, given that millions of copies of once-scarce products are now controlled by consumers, and that such programming may thus be no longer able to command substantial licensing fees or, for that matter, warrant the expense of theatrical reissuance.[20]

Utilization rates The prior degree of public exposure (i.e., the utilization rate) of major features is a key element in valuation. Utilization-rate considerations, in

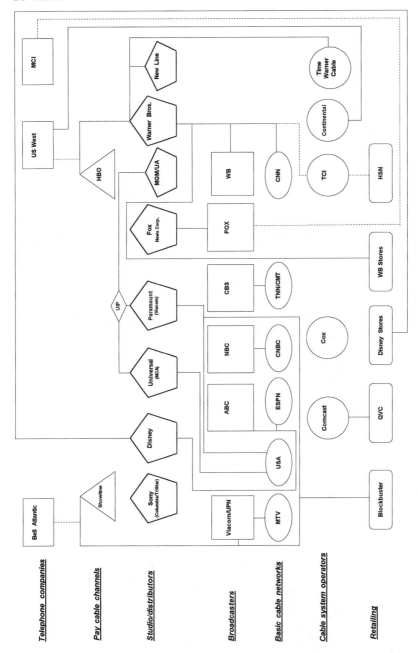

Figure 2.10. Significant entertainment company interrelationships, 1997. Dashed lines indicate indirect relationships.

Table 2.9. *Approximate number of majors' feature titles as of 1997[a]*

Studio	Approximate no. of titles
Sony (Columbia/TriStar)	2,400
Disney	600
Paramount	950
Twentieth Century Fox	2,000
MGM (including Orion)	1,800
Universal	3,200
Warner Bros. (including New Line, pre-1987 MGM)	4,500
Total	15,450

[a]Universal owns 1,000 pre-1948 Paramount features, and UA owns 745 pre-1950 Warner Bros. films. UA also owns free-TV rights to 700 pre-1950 RKO pictures. Also see chapter note 21.

particular, involve some interesting economic (and philosophical) trade-offs: For a library to be worth a lot, it cannot be exposed (i.e., exhibited) too frequently. But in order to generate cash, and to thereby reflect its latent or inherent worth, it either must be licensed for exhibition or must be sold outright.

Moreover, because the most recent pictures generally arouse the greatest audience interest, and thus at the margin garner the greatest amount of revenue, there is usually — except for those rare features deemed classics — a time-decay (perishability) factor involved. In this regard, changes in social temperament may be important. A vault full of war epics, for instance, might be very popular with the public during certain periods, but very unpopular during others. Some humor in films is timeless, some so terribly topical that within a few years audiences may not understand it. And because everything from hair and clothing styles to cars and moral attitudes changes gradually over time, the cumulative effects of these changes can make movies from only two decades ago seem rather quaint.

Of the more than 15,000 features in the vaults of Hollywood's majors (Table 2.9), it is therefore difficult to imagine – after considering the cost of prints and advertising (p & a) – that more than 50 or so per annum could be profitably reissued to theaters. Demand for older movies is not much greater on pay-cable channels, which generally thrive on new materials. And although home video has also become an important avenue for exploitation of libraries, the major studios would normally find it difficult to promote effectively an average of much more than one new title per week. Moreover, syndicated television – long the main market for older features – also relies heavily on the relative handful of titles that have consistently proved strong enough to attract audiences.

In all, then, the structural constraints are such that the industry probably cannot in the aggregate regularly deploy in the domestic and foreign markets more than about 1,000 or so items (7%) a year from its full catalog of features.

Interest and inflation rates The effect of interest rates, the single most important external variable in valuation, can be best understood by visualizing a portfolio of film-licensing contracts (lasting for, say, the typical three to five years) as entitling the holder to an income stream similar to that derived from an intermediate-maturity bond or annuity. As in the bond market, rising interest rates diminish a portfolio's value, and vice versa. In other words, the net present value (NPV) of a library is the sum of all discounted cash flows, risk-adjusted for uncertainties, that are estimated to be derived from the future licensing of rights or from outright sales of films in the group. A discounted cashflow concept of this kind may be mathematically presented in its most elementary form as

$$\text{NPV}_a = \sum_{t=0}^{n} A_t/(1 + r)^t$$

where r is the risk-adjusted required rate of return (which is linked to interest rates), A_t is the estimated cash to be received in period t for film a, and n is the number of future periods over which the cash stream is to be received. Because it is often procedurally difficult to make precise estimates of revenues and net residuals and other participant costs more than a few years into the future, relatively large adjustments for risk must normally be assumed either directly in the formula (by raising the assumed r) or by further trimming of the calculated NPVs.

Inflation is, of course, one of many possible reasons for license fees to rise over time. But to the extent that license fees reflect general inflationary pressures, there is merely an illusion of enhanced worth. Another inflation illusion appears when people speak of "priceless" assets that are often priceless primarily in an artistic sense. Many animated Disney classics, for example, could not be made today at less than astronomical cost, and these pictures are widely considered to be "priceless." However, that does not necessarily mean that these films can consistently generate high license fees or box-office grosses every year. Most of them, in fact, cannot.

Collections and contracts Other factors entering into an evaluation process include questions of rights ownership and completeness. As in philately or numismatics, a complete collection of a series (e.g., all *Rocky* or James Bond or Marx Brothers films) is obviously more valuable than an incomplete set. Control over a complete series of related films (and their elements such as original negatives and soundtracks, stills, one-sheets, and TV commercials) makes full marketing exploitation much more efficient.

In addition, rights-ownership splits can present especially nettlesome problems. To fully assess a library, many hundreds of detailed contracts signed over the span of many years must be reviewed to determine the sizes of participations and residual payments, the licensability of rights (including copyright protections), and also any potential restrictions as to transferability. But because such contract stipulations are never well documented (or, for that matter, made available to outsiders), most evaluations must be made at a distance from extrapolations of what is known about available rights to a few key properties. The

Table 2.10. *Selected film library transfers, 1957–97*[a]

Year	Assets transferred	Sold by	Bought by	Approximate price
1957	700 Warner Bros. features, shorts, cartoons	Associated Artists	United Artists	$30 million
1958	750 pre-1948 features	Paramount	MCA	$50 million
1979	500 features	American International Pictures	Filmways	$25 million
1981	2,200 features, shorts, studio, and distribution system	Transamerica	MGM	$380 million
1981	1,400 features, Aspen Skiing, Coke Bottling, Deluxe Film Labs, 5 TV stations, Intl Theater Chain, studio real estate	Twentieth Century Fox	Marvin Davis, private investor	$722 million
1982	1,800 features, studio property, TV stations, arcade games manufacturing	Columbia Pictures	Coca-Cola	$750 million
1982	500 features	Filmways	Orion Pictures	$26 million
1985	4,600 features, 800 cartoons, shorts, Metrocolor Lab, studio property	MGM/UA Entertainment (K. Kerkorian)	Turner Broadcasting (T. Turner)	$1.5 billion
1985	950 features, distribution system, and other rights to MGM library	Turner Broadcasting	United Artists (K. Kerkorian)	$480 million

60

Year	Assets	Seller	Buyer	Price
1989	2,400 features and 20,000 TV episodes plus distribution system, 800 screens, and other rights	Columbia Pictures Entertainment and Coca-Cola	Sony Corp	$4.8 billion[b]
1990	3,100 features, 14,000 TV episodes	MCA Inc.	Matsushita Electric	$6.1 billion[c]
1993	200 features	New Line	Turner Broadcasting	$500 million
1994	900 features, 4,000 TV episodes, ½ USA network, teams, TV stations, publishing	Paramount	Viacom Inc.	$9.6 billion
1995	3,200 features, 14,000 TV episodes	Matsushita[d]	Seagram Co., Ltd.	$5.7 billion
1996	1,500 features and 4,100 TV episodes	Credit/Lyonnais	K. Kerkorian/Seven Network	$1.3 billion
1997	2,000 features	Orion/Samuel Goldwyn	Metro-Goldwyn-Mayer	$573 million

[a]Several other transactions or proposed transactions reflect library values. In 1985, a half interest in Twentieth Century Fox was obtained by magnate Rupert Murdoch for $162 million in cash and an $88 million loan, equivalent to about $180,000 a title if real estate, studio assets, and distribution are assumed to comprise half of the asset valuation.
In 1982, the pre-1948 Warner Bros. library including 745 features, 327 cartoons, all the outstanding syndication rights, and the MGM/UA music publishing business was almost sold to Warner Communications for around $100 million. Adjusting for the non-film assets in the proposed sale would indicate a per title average of somewhat under $100,000 a title.
[b]Includes assumption of debt of $1.4 billion. In addition, subsequent buyout of Guber-Peters Entertainment assets required several hundred million dollars more.
[c]Includes recorded music, theme parks, publishing.
[d]Matsushita retained 20% equity interest.

total number of films in a library may thus provide only a rough measure of its potential value.

Library transfers From the outside, the most obvious method of determining what a library might be worth is to study previous asset–transfer prices for comparable film portfolios. After all, what people actually pay is more significant than what they say. This approach, however, may be difficult to implement because library sales are fairly infrequent and because the conditions under which such trades take place may differ significantly. The motives for transfer and the prevailing market sentiment for entertainment products at the time of transfer often carry great weight in establishing a transfer price. Consequently, even for two libraries of substantially the same size and quality, the prices may be greatly dissimilar.[21]

From the information in Table 2.10, we can estimate that as of the mid 1990s, the going rate for a major feature film might, on the average, be about $1 million. We can also say that the film-asset evaluation process is neither simple nor precise. As with assessments of beauty, value is often only a function of the beholder's imagination.

Real estate

For a long time, the Hollywood majors neglected and underutilized their real-estate assets. But that is no longer the case.[22] By the early 1980s, studio real-estate assets were in the middle of a steep valuation uptrend as proximity to major urban growth areas, inflation, and the numbers of made-for-television movies, theatrical features, and cable productions rose to new heights.[23]

Compared with the neglect and downsizing of a generation ago, it is clear that movie-company real-estate assets are now being actively managed and are becoming more impressive all the time. The scope of those assets and development plans is revealed in Table 2.11.

As always, real-estate values in Hollywood or elsewhere will be sensitive to changes in interest rates and to the growth rates of the economy as a whole. But anticipated rising demand for new entertainment software-production facilities and completion of ambitious property-development plans suggest that these assets have become significant in the financial analysis of film companies and their corporate parents.

2.6 Concluding remarks

This chapter has taken a macroeconomic view of the movie industry. As we have seen, many of the things that affect other industries – economic cycles, foreign exchange rates, antitrust actions, technological advances, and interest rates – also affect profits and valuations here. From this angle, moviemaking is a business like any other. How the film business differs from other businesses will more

Table 2.11. *Major studio real-estate assets, 1995*

Studio	Assets
Columbia Pictures (Sony Corp.)	44 acres in Culver City, near Los Angeles (formerly MGM)
Walt Disney Company	27,500 acres, Disney World, Florida 160 acres, Disneyland, California 44 acres, Burbank, California headquarters 691-acre ranch outside Los Angeles
Fox (News Corp.)	63 acres, studio and headquarters, Los Angeles
Universal (MCA) (Seagram Co.)	420 acres, Los Angeles headquarters and studio-tour 444 acres, Orlando, Florida, studio-tour
Paramount (Viacom, Inc.)	50 acres, studio, Los Angeles
Warner Bros. (Time Warner, Inc.)	140 acres, Burbank studios

easily be seen from the microeconomic and accounting perspectives that are presented in the next two chapters.

Selected additional reading

Altman, D. (1992). *Hollywood East: Louis B. Mayer and the Origins of the Studio System.* New York: Carol Publishing (Birch Lane).

Balio, T. (1987). *United Artists: The Company That Changed the Film Industry.* Madison, Wis.: University of Wisconsin Press.

Brownstein, R. (1990). *The Power and the Glitter: The Hollywood–Washington Connection.* New York: Pantheon Books, and 1992 Vintage paperback.

Cieply, M. (1984). "Movie Classics Transformed to Color Films," *Wall Street Journal,* September 11.

Egan, J. (1983). "HBO Takes on Hollywood," *New York* 17(24)(June 13):40.

Friedrich, O. (1986). *City of Nets: A Portrait of Hollywood in the 1940s.* New York: Harper & Row.

Izod, J. (1988). *Hollywood and the Box Office, 1895–1986.* New York: Columbia University Press.

Klein, E. (1991). "A Yen For Hollywood: Hollywood vs. Japan," *Vanity Fair* 54(6)(September).

Landro, L. (1995). "Ego and Inexperience Among Studio Buyers Add Up to Big Losses, *Wall Street Journal,* April 10.

Sherman, S. P. (1984). "Coming Soon: Hollywood's Epic Shakeout," *Fortune* 109(9)(April 30):204–16.

 (1986). "Movie Theaters Head Back to the Future," *Fortune* 113(2)(January 20).

 (1986). "Ted Turner: Back from the Brink," *Fortune,* 114(1)(July 7).

Smith, P. A. (1987). "Film Colorists Forecast Royalty Payoff," *Wall Street Journal,* May 15.

Steinberg, C. (1980). *Reel Facts.* New York: Vintage Books (Random House).

Thompson, K. (1986). *Exporting Entertainment: America in the World Film Market, 1907–1934.* London: British Film Institute.

Turner, R., and King, T. R. (1993). "Disney Stands Aside as Rivals Stampede to Digital Alliances," *Wall Street Journal,* September 24.

Twitchell, J. B. (1992). *Carnival Culture: The Trashing of Taste in America.* New York: Columbia University Press.

3
Making and marketing movies

Dough makes bread and dough makes deals.

Some people would argue that deals, not movies, are Hollywood's major product. ''Contract-driven'' is a handy way to describe the business.

Yet, although we frequently think of studios as monolithic enterprises, in actuality they are simultaneously engaged in four distinct business functions: financing, producing, distributing, and marketing/advertising movies. Each function requires the application of highly specialized skills that include raising and investing money, assessing and insuring production costs and risks, and planning and executing marketing and advertising campaigns. This chapter describes the framework in which these functions are performed.

3.1 Properties physical and mental

A movie screenplay begins with a story concept based on a literary property already in existence, a new idea, or a true event. It then normally proceeds in stages from outline to treatment, to draft, and finally to polished form.[1]

Prior to the outline, however, enter the literary agent, familiar with the latest novels and writers and always primed to make a deal on the client's behalf. Normally, unsolicited manuscripts make little or no progress when submitted directly to studio editorial departments. But with an introduction from an experienced agent – who must have a refined sense of the possibility of success for the client's work and of the changing moods of potential producers – a property can be submitted for review by independent and/or studio-affiliated producers. Expenditures to this stage usually involve only telephone calls and some travel, reading, and writing time.

However, should the property attract the interest of a potential producer (or perhaps someone capable of influencing a potential producer), an option agreement will ordinarily be signed. Just as in the stock or real-estate markets, such options provide, for a small fraction of the total underlying value, the right to purchase the property in full. Options have fixed expiration dates and negotiated prices and, depending on the fine print, they can sometimes be resold. Literary agents, moreover, usually begin to collect at least 10% of the proceeds at this point.

Now assuming, against considerable odds, that a film producer decides to adapt one of the many properties offered, the real fund-raising effort begins. And this effort is legalistically based on what is known as a Literary Property Agreement (LPA), a contract describing the conveyance of various rights by the author and/or other rights-owners to the producer. To a great extent, the depth and complexity of the LPA will be shaped by the type of financing available to the producer of this project.

For example, if the producer is affiliated with a major studio, the studio will normally (in the LPA) insist on retaining a broad array of rights so that a project can be fully exploited in terms of its potential for sequels, television series spin-offs, merchandising, and other opportunities. Such an affiliation will often significantly diminish, if not totally relieve, the producers' financing problems because a studio distribution contract can be used to secure bank loans. Better yet, a studio may also invest its own capital. But more commonly, "independent" producers will have to obtain the initial financing from other sources – which means that they are thus not fully independent. In the pursuit of such start-up capital many innovative, if not truly ingenious, financing structures have been devised.

Even so, funding decisions are normally highly subjective, and mistakes are often made: Promising projects are rejected or aborted, and whimsical ones accepted (i.e., "green-lighted" in industry jargon). The highly successful features *Star Wars* and *Raiders of the Lost Ark,* for instance, were shopped around to several studios before Twentieth Century Fox and Paramount, respectively, agreed to finance and distribute them. *Jaws* was, moreover, nearly canceled midway in production because of heavy cost overruns, *Home Alone* was placed in turnaround well after its preparation had started, and the script for *Back to the Future* was initially rejected by every studio.[2]

Of course, in order for funding to be obtained, a project must already be outlined in terms of story line, director, producer, location, cast, and estimated budget. To reach this point, enter the talent agents or, pejoratively, the "flesh peddlers.'' Agents play an important role in obtaining work for their clients, sometimes by assembling into ''packages'' the diverse but hopefully compatible human elements that go into the making of good feature films or television programs.[3]

The largest multidivision talent agencies are the William Morris Agency, International Creative Management (ICM), and The Creative Artists Agency (CAA) – which became a Hollywood powerhouse in the 1980s.[4] But, in addition, there are also many smaller and highly specialized firms, among which are ''discount'' agencies that place talent for fees of less than the standard 10% of income.

In the aggregate, agents perform a vital function by generally lowering the cost of searching for key components of a film project and by relaying and replenishing that constant and necessary industry data base known as gossip. As such, gossip is a natural offshoot of an agent's primary purpose, which is to advance the careers of clients at whatever price the talent market will bear. The use of agents also permits talent employers to confine their work relations to artistic matters and to delegate business topics to expert handling by the artists' representatives.

3.2 Financial foundations

Some of the most creative work in the entire movie industry is reflected not on the screen, but in the financial offering prospectuses that are circulated in attempts to fund film projects. As we shall see, financing for films can be arranged in many different ways, including the formation of limited partnerships and the direct sale of common stock to the public. However, financing sources fall generally into three distinct classes:

1. *Industry sources,* which include studio development and in-house production deals, and financings by independent distributors, talent agencies, laboratories, completion funds, and other end-users such as television networks, pay cable, and home video distributors.
2. *Lenders,* including banks, insurance companies, and distributors.
3. *Investors,* including public and private funding pools arranged in a variety of organizational patterns.

The most common financing variations available from investors and lenders are discussed in the following section. Industry sources are discussed in Chapter 4.

Common-stock offerings

Common-stock offerings are structurally the simplest of all to understand. A producer hopes to raise large amounts of capital by selling a relatively small percentage of equity interest in potential profits.

However, as historical experience has shown, common-stock–based offerings do not, on the average, stand out as a particularly easy method of raising production money for movies. Unless speculative fervor in the stock market is running high, movie-company start-ups usually encounter a long, tortuous, and expensive obstacle course.

The main difficulty is that a return on investment from pictures produced with seed money may take years to materialize, if it ever does, and underlying assets initially have little or no worth. Hope that substantial values will be created in the not too distant future is usually the principal ingredient in these offerings. In contrast to boring but safe investments in Treasury bills and money-market funds, new movie-company issues promise excitement, glamor, and risk. The following examples of common-stock offerings in the 1980s are illustrative.

In the case of a Kings Road Productions offering in the early summer of 1981, rapidly deteriorating market conditions caused withdrawal of the proposed sale of 1.8 million shares at prices between $10 and $12 per share through a large managing underwriter. Experienced producer Stephen Friedman contributed as a core of assets his previously released theatrical features – *Slapshot, Blood Brothers, Fast Break, Hero at Large,* and *Little Darlings* – several of which had already been profitable. United Artists, moreover, was at that time about to distribute Friedman's *Eye of the Needle,* a $15 million picture based on the best-selling novel of the same title.[5] Options on several promising literary properties were also among the Kings Road assets.

It was not until 1985, however, that Kings Road Entertainment finally raised capital from the public in an offering, led by two small underwriters, of 1.5 million shares at $10 a share. The assets included profit participations in the aforementioned pictures and in five others, the most prominent of which was *All of Me.* At the time of the offering, MCA Universal had been granted domestic theatrical and most other distribution rights (except for home video) in most of the company's upcoming productions. MCA, in turn, had agreed to provide material cash advances for the production of those films.

In the 1980s, many other new companies raised or attempted to raise public capital through common stock offerings at low prices. Although most of these small companies began with an intention to eventually produce films on their own, some of them were organized solely for the purpose of developing and arranging financing, production, and distribution for others; that is, they functioned as executive production outfits.

Thus, in general, straight common-stock offerings of unknown new companies are difficult to launch except in all but the frothiest of speculative market environments.[6] And, strictly from the stock market investor's viewpoint, experience has shown that most of the small initial common stock movie offerings have in recent years provided at least as many investment nightmares as tangible returns.

Combination deals

Common stock is often sold in combination with other securities so as to appeal to a wider investor spectrum or to more closely fit the financing requirements of the issuing company. This is illustrated by the Telepictures equity offering of the early 1980s. At that time, Telepictures was primarily a syndicator of television series and feature films and a packager and marketer of made-for-television movies and news.

As of its initial 1980 offering by a small New York firm, Telepictures had distribution rights to over 30 feature films and to about 200 hours of television programming in Latin American territories. The underwriting was in the form of 7,000 units, each composed of 350,000 common shares, warrants to purchase 350,000 common shares, and $7 million in 20-year 13% convertible subordinated debentures. In total, Telepictures raised $6.4 million in equity capital.

Another illustration of a combination offering was that of DeLaurentiis Entertainment Group Inc., which in 1986 separately but simultaneously sold 1.85 million shares of common stock and $65 million in 12.5% senior subordinated 15-year notes through a large New York underwriting firm. In this instance, the well-known producer Dino DeLaurentiis contributed his previously acquired rights in the 245-title Embassy Films library and in an operational film studio in North Carolina to provide an asset base for the new public entity. Among the several major films in the library were *The Graduate, Carnal Knowledge,* and *Romeo and Juliet.*

The underlying concept for this company, as well as for many other similar issues brought public at around the same time, was that presales of rights to pay cable, home video, and foreign theatrical distributors could be used to cover, or perhaps more than cover, direct production expenses on low-budget pictures. The subsequent difficulties experienced by this company and several others applying the same approach, however, proved that the concept most often works better in theory than in practice. The reason is that companies in the production start-up phase of development normally encounter severe cash-flow pressures unless they are fortunate enough to have a big box-office hit early on.[7]

Limited partnerships and tax shelters

Limited partnerships have in the past generally provided the opportunity to invest in movies, but with the government sharing some of the risk. In fact, before extensive tax-law adjustments in 1976, movie investments were among the most interesting tax-shelter vehicles ever devised. Prior to that revision, limited partners holding limited recourse or nonrecourse loans (i.e., loans without personal liability exposure) could write down losses against income several times the original amount invested; they could experience the fun and ego gratification of sponsoring movies and receive a tax benefit to boot.

Such agreements were in the form of either purchases or service partnerships. In a purchase, the investor would buy the picture (usually at an inflated price) with, say, a $1 down payment and promise to pay another $3 with a nonrecourse loan secured by anticipated receipts from the movie. Although the risk was only $1, there was a $4 base to depreciate and on which to charge investment tax credits.

In the service arrangement, an investor would become a partner in owning the physical production entity rather than the movie itself. Using a promissory note, deductions in the year of expenditure would again be a multiple of the actual amount invested – an attractive situation to individuals in federal tax brackets of over 50%.

Tax-code changes applicable between 1976 and 1986 permitted only the amount at risk to be written off against income by film "owners" (within a strict definition). The code also specified that investment tax credits (equivalent to 6⅔% of the total investment in the negative, assuming that more than 80% of the picture had been produced in the United States) were to be accrued from the date of initial release.[8] Revised tax treatment also required investments to be capitalized – a stipulation that disallowed the service-partnership form.

Beginning with the Tax Reform Act of 1986, however, the investment tax credit that many entertainment companies had found so beneficial because it had helped them to conserve cash was repealed. And significantly, so-called "passive losses" from tax shelters could no longer be used to offset income from wages, salaries, interest, and dividends. Such passive losses became deductible only against other passive activity income. Accordingly, since 1986, there have been notably fewer and differently structured movie partnerships offered to the public.[9]

More prototypical of the partnership structures of the 1980s, though, was the first (1983) offering of Silver Screen Partners. Strictly speaking, it was not a tax-sheltered deal. Here, Home Box Office (HBO, the Time Inc. wholesale distributor of pay-cable programs) guaranteed – no matter what the degree of box-office success, if any – return of full production costs on each of at least 10 films included in the financing package.

However, because only 50% of a film's budget was due on completion, with five years to meet the remaining obligations, HBO in effect received a sizable interest-free loan, while benefiting from a steady flow of fresh product.[10] For its 50% investment, HBO also retained exclusive pay-television and television syndication rights and 25% of network TV sales. This meant that partners were largely relying on strong theatrical results, which, if they occurred, would entitle them to "performance bonuses."[11] Subsequent Silver Screen offerings of substantially the same structure, but of larger size (up to $400 million), had also been used to finance Disney's films (see Table 3.1).[12]

Such partnership units, though, are not the only types available. Quasi-public offerings that fall under the Securities and Exchange Commission's Regulation D may still, for example, be used by independent filmmakers in structuring so-called Regulation D financings for small corporations or limited partnerships. Regulation D offerings allow up to 35 private investors to buy units in a corporation or a partnership without registration under the Securities Act of 1933.[13]

Limited-partnership financing appeals to studios because the attracted incremental capital permits greater diversification of film-production portfolios: Cash resources are stretched, and there are then more films with which to feed ever-hungry distribution pipelines.[14] Also, a feature may not provide any return to

Table 3.1. *Movie partnership financing: a selected sample, 1981–7*

Partnership	Total amount sought ($ million)	Minimum investment ($ thousand)	Management fee as % of funds raised	Limited partners' share of profits
Delphi III (January 1984)	60	5	1.16% for 1985–9, then 0.67% for 1990–4	99% to limited partners, 1% to general partners until 100% capital return; then general partners entitled to 20% of all further cash distribution
SLM Entertainment Ltd. (October 1981)	40	10	2.5% of capitalization in 1982, 3% in 1983–7, and 1% in 1988–94	99% until 100% returned, then 80% until 200% returned, and 70% afterward
Silver Screen Partners (April 1983)	75	15	4% of budgeted film costs + 10% per year to the extent payment is deferred	99% until limited partners have received 100% plus 10% per annum on adjusted capital contribution, then 85%
Silver Screen Partners III (October 1986)	200	5	4% of budgeted film cost + 10% per year on overhead paid to partnership	99% to investors until they have received an amount equal to their modified capital contribution plus 8% priority return

Source: Partnership prospectus materials.

investors owning a percentage of the negative yet, depending on the partnership structure, may contribute to coverage of studio fixed costs (overhead) via earn-out of distribution fees that are taken as a percentage of rentals.[15]

From the standpoint of the individual investor, most movie partnerships cannot be expected to provide especially high returns on invested capital. Few of them have historically returned better than 10% to 15% annually. But such partnerships occasionally generate significant profits, and they have provided small investors with opportunities to participate in major studio-packaged financings of pictures like *Annie, Poltergeist, Rocky III, Flashdance,* and *Who Framed Roger Rabbit.* More often than not, however, when the pictures in such packages succeed at the box office, most investors would probably find that they could have done at least as well by investing directly in the common stocks of the production and/or distribution companies (if for no other reason than considerations of liquidity) than in the related partnerships.

Bank loans

Established studios will normally be able to raise capital for general corporate purposes through debt or equity financings, or through commercial bank loans. In these situations, there is a considerable amount of flexibility as to the terms and types of financings that may be structured; a wide variety of corporate assets may be used as collateral.

Production loans to an independent producer are, however, quite another story: An independent producer may have little or no collateral backing except for presale contracts and other rights agreements relating directly to the production that is to be financed. As a practical matter, then, the bank must actually look to the creditworthiness of the various licensees for repayment of not only the loan itself, but also of the interest on the loan. This accordingly makes a production loan more akin to an accounts receivable financing than to a standard term loan on the corporate assets of an ongoing business.[16]

From the producer's standpoint, such bank loan financing may be attractive in that it can provide a means of circumventing the high costs and the rigidities, both financial and artistic, that normally come with a studio's distribution and financing deal. On the other hand, the fractionalization of distribution rights across many borders and across many different media absorbs time and effort that the producer might better apply to a project's creative aspects.

3.3 Production preliminaries

The big picture

Data from the Motion Picture Association of America (Table 3.2) indicate that between 1980 and 1996, the average cost of production, or *negative cost*, for features produced by the majors rose at a compound annual rate of 9.5% – thereby far exceeding the rate of inflation over that span. And indeed, by 1996, the average cost of producing an MPAA-member film had risen to approximately $40 million.[17]

Costs in this industry always tend to rise faster than in many other sectors of the economy because moviemaking procedures, although largely standardized, must be uniquely applied to each project and because efficiencies of scale are not easily attained. But other factors also pertain.

For example, during the 1970s, fiscal sloppiness pervaded the industry as soon as it became relatively easy to finance using other people's tax-sheltered money. Indulgence of "auteurs," who demanded unrestricted funding in the name of creative genius, further contributed to budget bloating. And "bankable" actors and directors (popular personalities expected to draw an audience by virtue of their mere presence) came to command millions of dollars for relatively little expenditure of time and effort. It was only a short while before everyone else involved in a production also demanded more.[18]

Of course, by the early 1980s, the burgeoning of new media revenue sources,

Table 3.2. Marketing and negative cost expenditures for major film releases, 1980–96

Year	MPAA releases (Total)	Average cost per film ($ million) Negatives[b]	Ads	Prints	Total releasing
1996	240	39.8	17.2	2.6	59.7
1995	234	36.4	15.4	2.4	54.1
1994	183	34.3	13.9	2.2	50.3
1993	161	29.9	12.1	1.9	44.0
1992	150	28.9	11.5	2.0	42.3
1991	164	26.1	10.4	1.7	38.2
1990	169	26.8	10.2	1.7	38.8
1989	169	23.5	7.8	1.4	32.7
1988	160	18.1	7.1	1.4	26.6
1987	129	20.1	6.9	1.4	28.3
1986	139	17.5	5.4	1.2	24.1
1985	153	16.8	5.2	1.2	23.2
1984	167	14.4	5.4	1.3	21.1
1983	190	11.9	4.2	1.0	17.1
1982	173	11.8	4.1	0.9	16.8
1981	173	11.3	3.5	0.9	15.7
1980	161	9.4	3.5	0.8	13.7
CAGR[a] (%): 1980–96		9.3	9.9	7.2	9.4

[a]Compound annual growth rate.
[b]Negative costs for the years 1975 to 1979 were $3.1, $4.2, $5.6, $5.7, and $8.9 respectively.
Source: MPAA

primarily in cable and home video, also naturally attracted (until the 1986 tax code changes) relatively large and eager capital funding commitments for investments in movie and television projects. But none of this could have gone quite so far without the ready availability of funds from so-called junk-bond financings, an upward-trending domestic stock market, and the spill-over of wealth and easy credit from Japan's "bubble" economy.[19] In fact, it was not until the early 1990s, when more stringent limitations on access to bank financing were imposed, and when movie stock takeover speculation was cooled by the onset of an economic recession, that cost pressures were somewhat abated.

Even under the best of circumstances, though, production budgets – in which there are thousands of expense items to be tracked – are not easy to control.[20] The basic cost components that go into the making of a film negative are, for example, illustrated in Figure 3.1.

In the category of *above-the-line costs* – that is, the costs of a film's creative

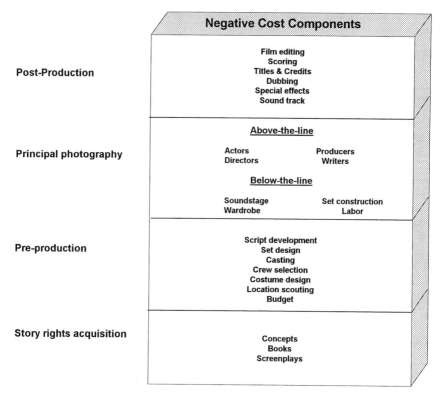

Figure 3.1. Negative cost components.

elements including cast and literary-property acquisition – contracts are signed and benefits and payments administered for sometimes hundreds of people.

But good coordination is also required when budgeting *below-the-line costs* – the costs of crews and vehicles, transportation, shelter, and props.[21] For each film, wardrobes and props must be made or otherwise acquired, locations must be scouted and leases arranged, and scene production and travel schedules must be meticulously planned. Yet should any one of those elements fall significantly out of step – as happens when the weather on location is unexpectedly bad, or when a major actor takes ill or is injured – expenses skyrocket. At such points of distress, a film's completion bond insurance arrangements become significant.[22] Also, additional below-the-line costs would be incurred in post-production activities.[23]

Labor unions

Unions have a significant influence on the economics of filmmaking, beginning with the very first phase of production. Indeed, union guidelines for compensation at each defined level of trade skill allow preliminary below-the-line production cost estimates to be determined with a fair degree of accuracy. The major unions in Hollywood include:

American Federation of Television and Radio Artists (AFTRA)
Directors Guild of America
International Alliance of Theatrical and Stage Employees (IATSE).
Producers Guild of America
Screen Actors Guild (SAG)
Writers Guild of America

Individuals belonging to these unions will normally be employed in the production of all significant motion pictures. And the unions, in turn, will negotiate for contract terms with the studios' bargaining organization, the Alliance of Motion Picture and Television Producers (AMPTP).[24]

Still, it is possible to produce a film with no noticeable qualitative differences for up to 40% less in nonunion or flexible-union territories outside of Hollywood, and independent producers may sometimes attempt to reduce below-the-line costs by filming in such territories.[25] Studios may sometimes also make use of an IATSE contract provision (Article 20) that allows the financing of low-budget nonunion movies and television shows if the studio claims to have no creative control.[26]

In any case, however, it is important to early–on develop realistic budget estimates, if only to assure that the whole production can be financed.

3.4 Marketing matters

Distributors and exhibitors

Sequencing After the principal production phase has been completed, thousands of details still remain to be monitored and administered. Scoring, editing, mixing sound and color, and making prints at the film laboratory are but a few of the essential steps. Once in the postproduction stages, however, perhaps the most critical preparations are those for distribution and marketing.

Sequential distribution patterns are determined by the principle of the second-best alternative. That is, films are normally first distributed to the market that generates the highest marginal revenue over the least amount of time. They then "cascade" in order of marginal-revenue contribution down to markets that return the lowest revenues per unit time. This has historically meant theatrical release, followed by licensing to pay-cable program distributors, home video, television networks, and finally local television syndicators. Yet because the amounts of capital invested in features have become so large, and the pressures for faster recoupment so great, there appears to be a gradual trend toward earlier opening of all windows (Figure 3.2).

Sequencing is always a marketing decision that attempts to maximize income, and it is generally sensible for profit-maximizing distributors to price-discriminate

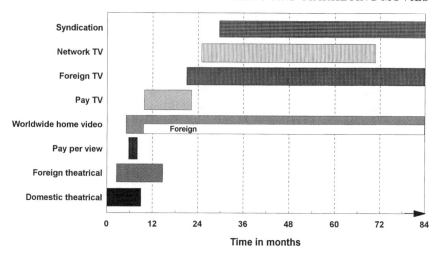

Figure 3.2. Market windows from release date, circa 1996.

in different markets or "windows" by selling the same product at different prices to different buyers.[27] It should not be surprising to thus find that, as new distribution technologies take hold and as older ones fade in relative importance, shifts in sequencing strategies will occur.[28] Such "windowing" is also a way in which the public-good characteristics of movies used as television programs can be fully exploited.[29]

All this, of course, threatens exhibitors, who – if they were to lose first-play rights on important films – would find it difficult, if not impossible, to survive on just leftovers. The resulting shrinkage of the theatrical-distribution pipeline obviously would then also make it more difficult to nurture lightly marketed but nonetheless promising releases to the point at which such releases could attract enough attention to be profitable.

Distributor-exhibitor contracts   Distributors normally design their marketing campaigns with certain target audiences in mind, and they are always interested in efficiently reaching those audiences. Distributors will thus typically attempt to align their releases with the most demographically suitable theaters, subject to availabilities of screens and to previously established relationships with the exhibition chains. They accomplish this by analyzing how similar films have previously performed in each potential location and by then developing a releasing strategy that provides the best possible marketing mix, or platform, for the picture. Sometimes the plan may involve a slow build-up through limited local or regional release; at other times it may involve a broad national release on literally thousands of screens simultaneously.

Of course, no amount of marketing savvy can make a really bad picture play well, but an intelligent strategy can almost certainly help to make the box office (and ultimately the home video and cable) performance of a mediocre picture better. It has thus now become most common for distributors to negotiate arrangements with exhibitors for specific theater sites.

Nevertheless, instead of negotiating, distributors may also sometimes elect, several months in advance of release, to send so-called bid letters to theaters located in regions in which they expect (because of demographic or income characteristics) to find audiences most responsive to a specific film's theme and genre.[30] This would normally be the preferred method of maximizing distributor revenues at times when the relative supply of pictures (to screens) is limited, as had happened in the late 1970s (Figure 3.3a). Theaters that express interest in showing a picture then usually accept the *terms* (i.e., the implied cost of film rental and the playing times) suggested by the distributor's regional branch exchange (sales office).

Such contracts between distributors and exhibitors are usually of the boilerplate variety (fairly standard from picture to picture), and are arranged for large theater chains by experienced film bookers who bid for simultaneous runs in several theaters in a territory. Smaller chains or individual theaters might also use a professional agency for this purpose.

Still, there can be variations. For example, in the early 1970s the film *Billy Jack* received wide publicity for its distribution through "four-wall" contracts. Here the distributor in effect rents the theater (four walls) for a fixed weekly fee, pays all operating expenses, and then mounts an advertising blitz on local television to attract the maximum audience in a minimum of time. Yet another simple occasional arrangement is flat rental: The exhibitor (usually in a small, late-run situation) pays a fixed fee to the distributor for the right to show the film during a specified period.

Most contracts between distributors and exhibitors, however, would almost always call for a sliding percentage of the box-office gross after allowance for the exhibitor's "nut" (house expenses, which include location rents and telephone, electricity, insurance, and mortgage payments). But whether assumed or negotiated, it is generally conceded that the nut will normally provide exhibitors with an additional cushion of profit.

For a major release, sliding-scale agreements may stipulate that 70% or more of the first week or two of box-office receipts after subtraction of the nut are to be remitted to the distributor, with the exhibitor retaining 30% or less. Every two weeks thereafter, the split may then be adjusted by 10% as 60:40, then 50:50, and so forth in the exhibitor's favor.

Thus, the distributor's gross (otherwise known as "rentals") is in effect received for a carefully defined conditional lease of a film over a specified period. Lease terms may include bid or negotiated "clearances," which provide time and territorial exclusivity for a theater.[31] No exhibitor would want to meet high terms for a film that would soon (or, even worse, simultaneously) be playing in a competitor's theater down the block.

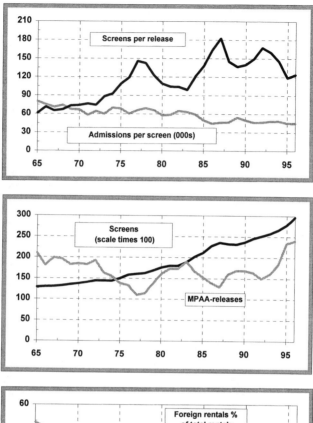

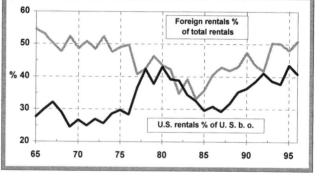

Figure 3.3. Exhibition industry trends, 1965–96. (a) Screens per release and admissions per screen; (b) Number of screens and number of MPAA-member releases; (c) Rentals percentages: foreign vs. total, and as a percentage of U.S. box-office receipts.

Should a picture not perform up to expectations, the distributor also usually has the right to a certain minimum or ''floor'' payment. These minimums are direct percentages (often more than half) of box-office receipts prior to subtraction of house expenses, but any previously advanced (or guaranteed) exhibitor monies can be used to cover floor payments owed. For a film that is a total flop, though, the distributor may reduce (in a nonbid situation) the exhibitor's burden through a quietly arranged settlement.[32]

Consequently, it often happens that the largest profit source for many exhibitors is not the box office, but the candy, popcorn, and soda counter – where the operating margin may exceed 50%. Theater owners have full control of proceeds from such sales; they can either operate food and beverage stands (and, increasingly, video games) themselves or lease to outside concessionaires. The importance of these concession profits to an exhibitor can be seen in the numerical example in Table 4.7.

Given the high percentage normally taken by the distributor, it is in the distributor's interest to maintain firm ticket pricing, whereas it may be in the exhibitor's interest to set low ticket prices to attract high-margin candy-stand patronage. In most instances, ticket prices are set by exhibitors, and the potential for a conflict of interest does not present any difficulty to either party. But there have been situations (for example, the releases of *Superman, Annie,* and a few Disney films) in which minimum per-capita admission prices have been suggested by the distributor to protect against children's prices that are too low. What distributors fear is that low ticket prices will divert spending from ticket sales (where they get a significant cut) to the exhibitor's high-margin concessions sales.

Release strategies, bidding, and other related practices Large production budgets, high interest rates, and the need to spend substantial sums on marketing provide strong incentives for distributors to release pictures as broadly and as soon as possible (while also, incidentally, reducing the exhibitor's risk). A film's topicality and anticipated breadth of audience appeal will then influence the choice of marketing strategies that might be employed to bring the largest return to the distributor over the shortest time.

Many alternatives are available to distributors. Some films are supported with national network-television campaigns arranged months in advance; others with only a few carefully selected local spots, from which it is hoped that strong word-of-mouth advertising will build. Sometimes a picture will be opened in one or two theaters in New York or Los Angeles (at a cost of perhaps half a million dollars) the last week of the year in order to qualify for that year's Academy Award nominations, and then be broken wide the following spring. Or there may be massive simultaneous release on more than 2,500 screens around the country at the beginning of summer. Regional or highly specialized release is, of course, appropriate if a picture does not appear to contain elements of interest to a broad national audience.

In any case, different anti–blind-bidding laws (laws that prohibit completion of contracts before exhibitors have had an opportunity to view the movies on which they are bidding) are effective in at least 23 states. This legal mosaic tends to make the release strategies of distributors more complicated than they would otherwise be.

Anti–blind-bidding statutes were passed by state legislatures in response to exhibitor complaints that distributors were forcing them to bid on and pledge (guarantee) substantial sums for pictures they had not been given an opportunity to evaluate in a screening: in other words, buying the picture sight unseen. Distributors now generally screen their products well in advance of release, but large pledges are still required to obtain important pictures in the most desirable playing times, such as the week of Christmas through New Year's. For these seasonal high periods, the terms at many major-city theaters may require that upward of $125,000 in nonrefundable cash advance against future rentals owed (i.e., guarantees) be paid 10 days prior to issuance.

Whereas in theory, movie releases from all studios can be expected to play in different houses depending only on the previously mentioned factors, in reality, some theaters, mostly in major cities, more often than not end up consistently showing the products of one particular distributor. Industry jargon denotes these as theater "tracks" or "circuits." Tracks can evolve from long-standing personal relationships (many going back to before the Paramount Consent Decree) that are reflected in negotiated rather than bid licenses, or they may indicate de facto *product-splitting* or *block-booking* practices.

Product splitting occurs when several theaters in a territory tacitly agree not to bid aggressively against each other for certain films – the intention being to reduce average distributor terms. Each theater in the territory then has the opportunity, on a regular rotating basis, to obtain major new films for relatively low rentals percentages.[33]

In block booking, on the other hand, a distributor will accept a theater's bid on desirable films contingent on the theater's commitment that it will also run the distributor's less popular pictures.

As may be readily inferred, symbiosis between the exhibitor and distributor segments of the industry has not led to mutual affection. The growth of pay-per-view cable and the possibility of simultaneous releases (known as day and date in the industry) in home-video formats may further strain their relations.

Exhibition industry characteristics: (a) Capacity and competition The long-run success of an exhibition organization is highly dependent on its skill in evaluating and arranging real-estate transactions. Competition for good locations (which raises lease payment costs), as well as too many screens in a small territory, can significantly reduce overall returns.

To achieve economies of scale, since the 1960s exhibitors have tended to consolidate into large chains operating multiple screens located near or in shopping-center malls. Meanwhile, older movie houses in decaying center-city locations have encountered financial hardships as the relatively affluent consumers born after World War II have grown to maturity in the suburbs, and as rising crime rates and scarcity of parking spaces have become deterrents to regular moviegoing by city residents. (Ironically, the very same social pressures contributed to the disappearance of many drive-in theaters situated on real estate too valuable to be used only for evening movies.[34])

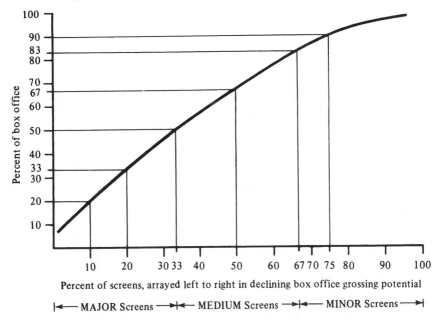

Figure 3.4. Domination of box-office performance by key U.S. movie theaters. *Source: Variety,* July 7, 1982. Copyright 1982 by A. D. Murphy.

In 1996 there were approximately 29,700 screens, a diminishing proportion of which were drive-ins. The total has been increasing since 1965 at an average rate of 2.7%, with box-office gross per screen rising an average 2.9% per year (see Table 2.4). During this time, operating incomes and market shares for large, publicly owned theater chains (especially regionals) have obviously gained rapidly at the expense of single-theater operators. For example, as of 1982, the top-grossing one-third of screens generated half of the box office, with the bottom third generating about one-sixth of the box office ((Murphy, 1983) and Figure 3.4). Currently, the top one-third of screens probably account for 65% of all theater grosses.

In effect, over the last decade, the number of screens has increased substantially (Figure 3.3b), while the number of separate theater locations has stayed about the same: Many locations have simply been "multiplexed." Moreover, it is now more difficult to "platform" a film because there are essentially only first-run multiple-screen houses, and all others. Previously, there had been at least three tiers of theater quality ranging from first-run fancy to last-run, small, neighborhood "dumps."

Whether or not a film has "legs" (i.e., strong popular appeal so that it runs a long time), the maximum theoretical revenue R is a function of the average length of playing time P, the number of showings per day N, the average number of seats per screen A, the number of screens S, the average ticket price T, and audience suitability ratings (G, PG, PG-13, R, NC-17/X). Exclusive of the ratings factor,

$$R = N \times S \times T \times A$$

where $N = f(P)$.

For example, if the average ticket price is \$4, the average number of showings per day is four, the average seats per theater are 300, and the number of screens is 500, the picture can theoretically gross no more than \$2.4 million (4 × 4 × 300 × 500) per day, or \$16.8 million per week. This type of analysis will be of increasing interest to distributors as comparisons are made to the potential of pay-per-view cable release, from which there is the potential to earn, on a \$4 per-view charge, at least \$20 million overnight.[35]

Because the preceding figures used in calculating a theoretical weekly total gross for a single picture are about average for the whole industry, they can also be used to estimate an aggregate for all exhibitors. Following this line, we can determine that in 1996, the maximum theoretical annual gross, based on 29,690 screens, was about \$143 million per day or about \$52.0 billion per year. The industry obviously operates well below its theoretical capacity because there are many parts of the week and many weeks of the year during which people do not have the time or inclination to fill empty theater seats: In 1996, the industry's average occupancy rate per seat per week was roughly 2.9 times, and box-office receipts of around \$5.9 billion in 1996 were thus only a bit above 10% of theoretical capacity.

Actually, for the major film releases most likely to be opened during peak seasons, calculations of this kind do not have much relevance because there are no more than about 8,000 quality first-run screens, of which perhaps only 3,000 can normally be simultaneously booked. But the most important effect of competition for quality play dates in peak seasons is that the competition places severe upward pressure on marketing budgets. As a result, modestly promoted films, even those of high artistic merit, may have little time to build audience favor before they are "pulled" from circulation.[36]

In comparing the popularities of different films in different years, most newspaper accounts merely show the box-office grosses: Film A did \$10, and film B did \$11; therefore B did better than A. In addition, a deeper, but still often misleading, comparison is sometimes derived by calculating an average gross per screen. However, as can be seen from the preceding discussion, close analysis and comparison of box-office figures requires that variables such as ticket-price inflation, film running time, season, weather conditions, number and quality of theaters, average seats per theater, and types of competing releases be considered.[37]

(b) Rentals percentages All other things being equal, when the supply of films is small compared with exhibitor capacity, the percentage of box office reverting to distributors (the rentals percentage) rises.[38] Faced with a relatively limited

selection of potentially popular pictures, theater owners tend to bid more aggressively and to accede to stiffer terms than they otherwise would. To some extent, however, the rentals percentage also depends on ticket prices and on how moviegoers respond to a year's crop of releases. A poorly received crop tends to reduce the average distributor rentals percentage as "floor" (minimum) clauses on contracts with exhibitors are activated, as advances and guarantees are reduced in size and number, and as "settlements" are more often required.

Especially in the late 1970s, for example, there were loud complaints by exhibitors of "product shortage" as the total number of new releases and reissues declined by 43% to 110 in 1978 from the preceding 1972 peak of 193. As might be expected, distributor rental percentages (and thus profit margins) were high in the late 1970s (Table 2.4 and Figure 3.3c).

Home video and merchandising

Home video Until the 1980s, moviemakers both large and small were primarily concerned with marketing their pictures in theaters. But starting in 1986, distributors generated more in domestic wholesale gross revenues from home video (about $2 billion) than from theatrical ($1.6 billion) sources. Home video has thus forever altered the fundamental structure of the business and changed the ways in which marketing strategies are pursued.[39]

With cumulative unit sales to date exceeding 650 million, videocassette recorders (VCRs) have by now become a familiar item in households around the world. Indeed, in most developed nations, including the United States, Japan, Britain, France, Germany, Italy, Holland, and Scandinavia, VCRs are already found in over two-thirds of the television households. This enormous installed base has, in fact, become an incredibly powerful funds-flow engine for filmmakers: The machines, it seems, have evinced a voracious appetite for entertainment software products of all kinds.[40]

As a result, from virtually zero in 1980, prerecorded home-video software sales (Figure 3.5) have grown, in the space of just over a dozen years, into a business that now generates more than $16 billion in domestic retail revenues. As it happens, the bulk of those revenues (two-thirds or so) are consistently derived from sales or rentals (to the consumer) of feature films.[41] Given, also, that some 30% to 40% of Hollywood's aggregate production costs are covered by domestic home video receipts, it is easy to see why filmmakers and distributors cannot afford to treat video marketing-campaign strategies lightly.

Perhaps the most important decision for the home-video divisions of the major studios concerns pricing. The decision is to either price high for the video store *rental* market or to price low for what is known as the *sell-through* (consumers') market. But since the cost of manufacturing and marketing a cassette or digital video disk is about the same (under $4 a unit) for all regular feature films, the decision always comes down to whether the distributor can earn more from rentals or from sell-through to individuals.[42] As of the mid-1990s, a growing share, some

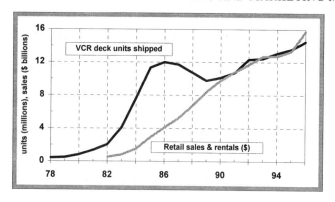

Figure 3.5. Hardware and software trends in the home video-market, 1978–96.

35%–40% of total U.S. consumer spending on video, has been for sell-through products, with roughly 45% of this total generated by feature films.[43]

For "evergreen" titles, such as many of the Disney animations, the decision is almost always to go for sell-through because the arithmetic can be so compelling. With, say, a suggested retail price of $24.95 and a wholesale price of about $13.50, six million units would generate an impressive $81 million in revenues and perhaps $57 million of gross profit to the distributor.

The much likelier alternative, however, is to set the suggested retail price of the cassette much higher, so that it becomes primarily a rental item. Most such "A"-title releases, as films with the potentially widest appeal are known, would list for $89.95 or above, and of this price the distributor would probably retain around $56.57 (i.e., 63%) from the initial sale.[44] But the distributor would, of course *not* normally participate further in the cash flow that is derived from retailers' rentals of the cassette.[45]

All other things being equal, then, the studio-distributor – in effect, the home video's publisher – would select the larger of the following options:

Expected number of rental units times 63% of rental unit retail price

or

Expected number of sell-through units times wholesale unit price[46]

But because marketing costs figure prominently in the success of sell-through titles, the distributor must generally be able to project sales of at least seven to eight times as many copies of a sell-through than a rental title in order to justify the decision. Such projections would be made, for example, on a typical fitted curve (Figure 3.6), off which the number of home-video units demanded might be estimated as a function of the domestic box-office performance of recent titles.[47]

Independent filmmakers would, of course, face a different set of problems. Indies will typically be most interested in preselling (or fractionalizing) rights to their pictures in order to finance production. For this purpose, they can approach

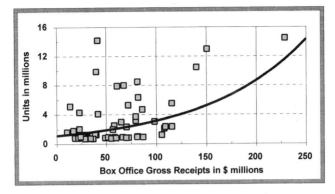

Figure 3.6. An example of box office grosses versus video unit sales circa 1990.

one of the majors or submajors, or go to an independent home video distributor.[48] But rights fractionalization is not normally welcomed.[49]

So-called direct-to-video features, which are designed to entirely skip a theatrical release phase and go directly to the home-video market, are also becoming more prominent, especially in the family film genre. Elimination of relatively high theatrical releasing costs here enhances the profit potential of such titles.[50]

Moreover, of necessity, all film distributors must now take the projected rapid growth of pay-per-view (PPV) cable into consideration. At a minimum, the rise of PPV technology appears likely to dampen the growth of home-video unit demand, and to also alter the sequential release patterns for certain types of films.[51]

Merchandising Product merchandising opportunities relating to film characters and concepts have increased noticeably in recent years, and marketing activities have become highly sophisticated. The best examples of this have been seen in Disney's recent animated features such as *Beauty and the Beast, Aladdin,* and *The Lion King,* and in Universal's (MCA) *Jurassic Park,* which have each been able to generate merchandise license profits exceeding $50 million. Multimedia products that include samples of a film's sights and sounds are now also readily marketed in CD-ROM, DVD, and other interactive formats (Chapter 8). And in the action and children's film genres, licensing opportunities in music, books, comics, and toys abound.[52] An important product license to a major toy manufacturing company might, for instance, return at least 6% to 7% of wholesale merchandise revenues to the studio.[53]

Marketing costs

In recent years, expenditures on the marketing of films have tended to rise considerably faster than the overall rate of inflation. But the likelihood of any significant reductions in this rate of increase are relatively slight given that the more "megabudget" pictures in simultaneous release, the more intensive are the marketing efforts required for each: Capital turnover must usually be maximized at times when quality, peak-season exhibitor play-dates are at a premium.

In theory, studios have much greater cost-control potential in a film's marketing phase than in its production and financing phases. Yet in practice, restraint in marketing expenditures is rarely seen; studios will often add 50% to a picture's production budget just for advertising and publicity. And, as already noted, seasonal, cyclical, and other factors contribute to the bunching of important releases and therefore to the necessity of spending a lot in order to attract attention.[54]

Still, no matter which media prevail in the future, the importance of marketing decisions in filmmaking and distribution cannot be underestimated. Marketing decisions made prior to theatrical release can critically affect the income-generating potential of a film in all subsequent markets, including those abroad. As De Vany and Walls (1996) note, "the opening performance is statistically a dominant factor in revenue generation."[55]

3.5 Profitability synopsis

That a person can drown in a river of an average depth of six inches underscores the difficulty in analyzing data by means of averages alone. Many, if not most, films do not earn any return, even after taking account of new-media revenue sources; it is the few big winners that pay for the many losers. This is especially true for outside investors, who, in terms of the funds-flow sequence, are usually among the first to pay in and the last to be paid out.

Also, because pictures are financed largely with other people's money, there is an almost unavoidable bias for costs to rise (Parkinson's law again) at least as fast as anticipated revenues. This implies that much of the incremental income expected to be derived from growth of the new-media sources is likely to be absorbed, dissipated, and diverted as cost – an especially daunting consideration if, as is now common for a film released by a major studio, only a much diminished 50% or so share of such costs are recovered directly from domestic theatrical rentals (Figure 3.7a). As Figure 3.7b illustrates, costs have often grown faster than revenues. And industry operating margins have been erratic (Figure 3.7c).[56]

Using data on the number of releases, the effects of ancillary-market revenue growth (sections 2.4 and 3.4), average negative costs, average marketing costs, and aggregate rentals (section 2.3), there emerges a profile suggesting that, in a statistical sense, most major-distributed films do no better than to financially break – even – with deviations from this mean (Table 4.8) extreme in both directions.[57]

Yet, remarkably, and despite the potential for loss on an "average" picture, most major studios, bolstered by distribution revenues related to library titles and television programs, have long been successfully engaged in this business.[58]

The existence of profitable studio enterprises in the face of apparent losses for the "average" picture can be reconciled only when it is realized that the heart of

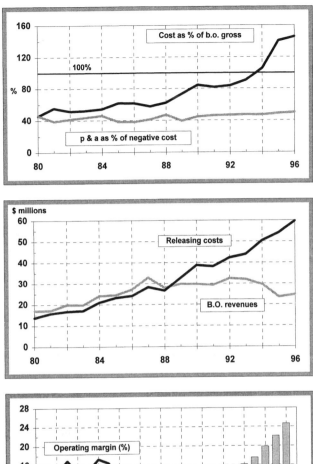

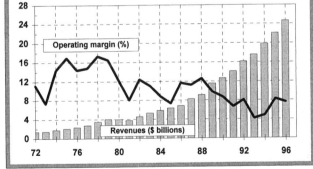

Figure 3.7. Film industry revenue and cost trends: (a) MPAA-member production (negative) costs as a percentage of domestic box-office gross receipts and p & a as a percent of production costs, 1980–96 MPAA films.

(b) Average per MPAA film: Releasing cost (including negative plus p & a), and domestic box office revenue, 1980–96.

(c) Revenues and operating margins for major studios, 1972–96.

a studio's business is distribution and financing and that, therefore, the brunt of marketing and production-cost risk is often deflected and/or transferred to (sometimes tax-sheltered) outside investors and producers. As the following chapter will indicate, studio profits are highly dependent on distribution and other fee income.

3.6 Concluding remarks

Since the mid-1970s, the movie industry has been in a transition phase characterized by a shift to electronic/optic distribution and storage methods, and by declining control of distribution and product pricing through traditional organizational arrangements. Although this transition has already provided consumers with an increasingly varied selection of easily accessed, low-cost entertainment, it has not been beneficial to all industry segments. In fact, technology has made it possible for more content to be created by more people, and to be distributed more widely and at lower cost (e.g., via the Internet), than ever before.

Yet the movie business remains as fascinating as it is unique. That feeling has been summarized by veteran movie writer A. D. Murphy (1982), who has made the following observations:

Even after a history of over 100 years, the business remains entrepreneurial and capitalistic.

Films are by nature research-and-development products; they are perishable and cannot be test marketed in the usual sense.

The film industry manufactures an art form for the masses.

Seasonal changes in theatrical attendance are radical, but domestic attendance over two decades has fluctuated within a fairly narrow range.

Despite long-standing trade restrictions, a fairly stable domestic market is reinforced by a strong export market.

From acquisitions of literary properties to final theater bookings, virtually every phase of the industry's operations is negotiated, and this, contrary to widespread opinion, implies that personal trust and high standards of professional integrity largely prevail.

As Squire (1992, p. 23) further said:

In no other business is a single example of product fully created at an investment of millions of dollars with no real assurance that the public will buy it. In no other business does the public "use" the product and then take away with them [as Marx (1975) observed] merely the memory of it.

Selected additional reading

Akst, D. (1987). "Directors and Producers Face Showdown Over Residuals," *Wall Street Journal,* June 11.

Attanasio, P. (1983). "The Heady Heyday of a Hollywood Lawyer," *Esquire* 99(4)(April):91.

Bach, S. (1985). *Final Cut: Dreams and Disaster in the Making of "Heaven's Gate."* New York: William Morrow.

Bart, P. (1990). *Fade Out: The Calamitous Final Days of MGM.* New York: William Morrow.

Bonnell, R. (1989). *La Vingt-Cinquième Image: Une Économie de l'Audiovisuel.* Paris: Gallimard/FEMIS.

Brown, G. (1995). *Movie Time: A Chronology of Hollywood and the Movie Industry.* New York: Macmillan.

Canby, V. (1990). "A Revolution Reshapes Movies," *New York Times,* January 7.

Cassidy, J. (1997). "Chaos in Hollywood," *The New Yorker,* March 31.

Cieply, M. (1986). "An Agent Dominates Film and TV Studios with Package Deals," *Wall Street Journal,* December 19.

Cooper, M. (1987). "Concession Stand: Can the Hollywood Unions Survive?" *American Film* XIII(3)(December):33.

Cox, M. (1984). "A First Feature Film Is Made on the Cheap, Not Hollywood's Way," *Wall Street Journal,* May 14.

Daly, M. (1984). "The Making of *The Cotton Club:* A True Tale of Hollywood," *New York* 17(19)(May 7):40.

DeGeorge, G. (1996). *The Making of a Blockbuster: How Wayne Huizenga Built a Sports and Entertainment Empire.* New York: John Wiley & Sons.

Denby, D. (1986). "Can the Movies Be Saved?" *New York* 19(28)(July 21).

Evans, D. A. (1984). "Reel Risk: Movie Tax Shelters Aren't Box-Office Boffo," *Barron's,* January 9.

Finler, J. W. (1988). *The Hollywood Story.* New York: Crown Publishers.

Fleming, C. (1995). "$200 Million Under the Sea: The Inside Story of Kevin Costner's Disaster-Prone *WaterWorld,"Vanity Fair,* August.

Garcia, B. (1989). "Who Ya Gonna Call If a Ghostbuster's Proton Pack Breaks?: Insurance Helps Hollywood Survive Almost Anything," *Wall Street Journal,* August 24.

Goldman, W. (1983). *Adventures in the Screentrade: A Personal View of Hollywood and Screenwriting.* New York: Warner Books.

Gregory, M. (1979). *Making Films Your Business.* New York: Schocken Books.

Griffin, N. (1993). "How They Built the Bomb: Inside the Last Seven Weeks of 'Last Action Hero',"*Premiere,* September.

Gubernick, L. (1988). "Miss Jones, Get Me Film Finances," *Forbes* 142(14)(December 26).

Gubernick, L., and Lane, R. (1993). "I Can Get It For You Retail," *Forbes* 151(12)(June 7).

Harmetz, A. (1987). "Hollywood Battles Killer Budgets," *New York Times,* May 31.

——— (1993). "Five Writers + One Star = A Hit?" *New York Times,* May 30.

Hirschberg, L. (1995). "Winning the TV Season," *New York Magazine* 28(27)(July 10).

Hirschhorn, C. (1979). *The Warner Bros. Story.* New York: Crown Publishers.

Horn, J. (1997). "Can Anyone Dethrone Disney?" *Los Angeles Times,* June 1.

Kenney, R. W., and Klein, B. (1983). "The Economics of Block Booking," *Journal of Law and Economics,* vol. 26.

King, T. R. (1993). "*Jurassic Park* Offers a High-Stakes Test of Hollywood Synergy,"*Wall Street Journal,* February 10.

——— (1995). "Why 'Waterworld,' With Costner in Fins, Is Costliest Film Ever," *Wall Street Journal,* January 31.

King, T. R., and Bannon, L. (1995). "No Longer Bit Players, Animators Draw Fame as Hollywood Stars," *Wall Street Journal*, October 6.

Knowlton, C. (1988). "Lessons from Hollywood Hit Men," *Fortune* 118(5)(August 29):78.

Koch, N. (1992). "She Lives! She Dies! Let the Audience Decide."*New York Times*, April 19.

Landro, L. (1983). "If You Have Always Wanted to Be in Pictures, Partnerships Offer the Chance, but With Risks," *Wall Street Journal*, May 23.

——— (1984). "Frank Mancuso's Marketing Savvy Paves Ways for Paramount Hits," *Wall Street Journal*, June 27.

——— (1985). "Movie Partnerships Offer a Little Glitz, Some Risk – and Maybe a Decent Return," *Wall Street Journal*, May 20.

——— (1989). "Sequels and Stars Help Top Movie Studios Avoid Major Risks," *Wall Street Journal*, June 6.

——— (1990a). "'Godfather III' Filming Begins After 15 Years And 3 Studio Regimes," *Wall Street Journal*, February 9.

——— (1990b). "Hollywood in Action: Making a Star," *Wall Street Journal*, February 16.

Lane, R. (1996). "The Magician," *Forbes*,157(5)(March 11).

Lees, D., and Berkowitz, S. (1981). *The Movie Business*. New York: Vintage Books (Random House).

Lippman, J. (1995). "How a Red-Hot Script That Made a Fortune Never Became a Movie," *Wall Street Journal*," June 13.

Magnet, M. (1983). "Coke Tries Selling Movies Like Soda Pop," *Fortune* 108(13)(December 26):119–26 (also see counterpoint by A. D. Murphy, "In Defining 'Hit Film' Economics, 'Fortune' Looks in Wrong Eyes," *Variety*, December 14, 1983).

Mayer, M. F. (1978). *The Film Industries: Practical Business/Legal Problems in Production, Distribution, and Exhibition*, 2d ed., New York: Hastings House.

McClintick, D. (1982). *Indecent Exposure: A True Story of Hollywood and Wall Street*, New York: William Morrow.

Moldea, D. (1986). *Dark Victory*, New York: Viking.

Noglows, P. (1990). "Newcomers Turn Completion Game into Risky Business,"*Variety*, August 8.

O'Neill, K. (1995). "Gumption," *Premiere*, 8(8)(April).

Rose, F. (1996). "This Is Only a Test," *Premiere*, August.

Rosen, D., and Hamilton, P. (1987). *Off-Hollywood: The Making and Marketing of American Specialty Films*, New York and Colorado: The Independent Feature Project and The Sundance Institute, and New York: Grove Weidenfeld (1990).

Rudell, M. I. (1984). *Behind the Scenes: Practical Entertainment Law*, New York: Harcourt Brace Jovanovich.

Salamon, J. (1991). *The Devil's Candy: The Bonfire of the Vanities Goes to Hollywood*. Boston: Houghton Mifflin.

Salmans, S. (1984). "A Nose for Talent – and for Tradition," *New York Times*, May 20.

Sansweet, S. J. (1982). "Who Does What Film? It Depends on Who Talks to What Agent," *Wall Street Journal*, June 23.

Sansweet, S., and Landro, L. (1983). "As the Money Rolls in, Movie Makers Discover It Is a Mixed Blessing," *Wall Street Journal*, September 1.

Schlender, B. (1995). "Steve Jobs' Amazing Movie Adventure," *Fortune*, 132(6)(September 18).

Sharpe, A. (1995). ''Small-Town Audience Is Ticket to Success of Movie-House Chain,'' *Wall Street Journal*, July 12.

Sherman, S. P. (1986). ''A TV Titan Wagers a Wad on Movies,'' *Fortune* 113(10)(May 12).

Singular, S. (1996). *Power to Burn: Michael Ovitz and the New Business of Show Business.* Secaucus, N.J.: Birch Lane (Carol Publishing).

Slater, R. (1997). *Ovitz. The Inside Story of Hollywood's Most Controversial Power Broker.* New York: McGraw-Hill.

Spragins, E. (1983). ''Son of Delphi,'' *Forbes* 132(2)(July 18).

Sterngold, J. (1997). ''The Return of the Merchandiser,'' *New York Times*, January 30.

Tromberg, S. (1980). *Making Money Making Movies: The Independent Moviemaker's Handbook*, New York, New Viewpoints/Vision Books (Division of Franklin Watts).

Turner, R. (1989a). ''A Showdown for Discount Movie Houses,'' *Wall Street Journal*, July 18.

——— (1989b). ''A Hot Movie Studio Gobbles Up the Cash but Produces No Hits,'' *Wall Street Journal*, June 14.

——— (1994). ''Disney, Using Cash and Claw, Stays King of Animated Movies,'' *Wall Street Journal*, May 16.

Welkos, R. W. (1996). ''Starring in the Biggest Deals in Hollywood: Top Lawyers Rival Agents as Power Brokers,'' *Los Angeles Times*, January 12.

Wiese, M. (1986). *Home Video: Producing for the Home Market.* Stoneham, Mass.: Butterworth.

Zweig, P. L. (1987). ''Lights! Camera! Pinstripes!'' *Institutional Investor* XXI(9) (September).

4

Financial accounting in movies and television

Happy trails to you, until we meet again. – Dale Evans.[1]

This song is perhaps more appropriately sung by Hollywood accountants than by cowboys. But, as this chapter indicates, the problems that arise in accounting for motion-picture and ancillary-market income are more often due to differing viewpoints and interpretations than to intended deceits.

4.1 Dollars and sense

Contract clout

No major actor, director, writer, or other participant in an entertainment project makes a deal without beforehand receiving some kind of high-powered help, be it from an agent, personal manager, lawyer, accountant, or tax expert. In some cases, platoons of advisors are consulted; in others, all functions may be performed by only one person or a few individuals. Thus an image of naive, impressionable artists negotiating out of their league with large, powerful, and knowledgeable producer or distributor organizations is most often not accurate.

As in all loosely structured private-market negotiations, bargaining power (in the industry's jargon, ''clout'') is the only thing that matters. A new, unknown talent who happens on the scene will have little if any clout with anyone. Top stars, by definition, have enough clout to command the attention of just about everyone.

By hiring people whose ability to attract large audiences has already been proved, a producer can gain considerable financial leverage. It may be less risky to pay a star $1.5 million than to pay an unknown $100,000; the presence of the star may easily increase the value of the property by several times that $1.5 million salary through increased sales in theatrical and other markets, whereas the unknown may contribute nothing from the standpoint of return on investment. Clout, it seems, is best measured on a logarithmic scale.[2]

Contracts are usually initially agreed on in outline (a deal memo), with the innumerable details being structured later by professionals representing both sides. But final contracts normally are complex documents, and those with imprecisely drawn clauses that are open to different interpretations can lead to disputes. It is, of course, in the nature of this industry to attract a disproportionate amount of publicity when such disputes arise.

Orchestrating the numbers

Accounting principles provide a framework in which the financial operating performance of a business can be observed and compared with the performance of other businesses. But it was not until 1973 that the American Institute of Certified Public Accountants (AICPA) published an accounting guide, *Accounting for Motion Picture Films,* that pragmatically resolved many (but far from all) controversial issues. Publication of that guide significantly diminished the number of interpretations used in describing film industry transactions and thus made comparisons of one company's statements with those of another considerably easier and more meaningful than before.

The AICPA guide, however, has not prevented accountants from tailoring financial reports, starting with a set of base figures, to suit the needs and purposes of the users and providers of funds. Just as there are different angles from which to photograph an object to illustrate different facets, there are different perspectives from which to examine the data derived from the same base. In fact, given the complexity of many contracts, it is an absolute necessity to view financial performance from the angle that suits the needs of the viewer.

For example, outside shareholders generally need to know only the aggregate financial position of the company, not the intricate details of each participant's contract. Those participants, by the same token, usually will care only about their own share statements, from which the aggregates are constructed. In the sections that follow, the two different accounting perspectives are more fully described.

4.2 Corporate overview

Because this is not strictly an accounting text, no attempt will be made to describe the full terminology used by CPAs. However, it will be useful to note instances in which movie business definitions are different from those used in other industries.

Revenue-recognition factors

Industry practice with regard to recognition of revenues from theatrical exhibition is fairly straightforward. With either percentage or flat-rent contracts, revenues from exhibitors are accrued and recognized by distributors when receivable, which, because of cash intake at the box office, is almost immediately. Contrariwise, ancillary-market revenue recognition is potentially much more complex. Prior to the issuance of the aforementioned accounting guide, four methods existed:

1. Contract method: All revenue is recognized on contract execution.
2. Billing method: Revenue is recognized as installment payments become due.
3. Delivery method: Revenue is recognized on delivery to the licensee.
4. Deferral or apportionment method: Revenue is recognized evenly over the whole license period.

To place the entire industry on a uniform basis, the AICPA guide indicated that television license revenues for feature films should not be recognized until all the following conditions are met:

1. The license fee (sales price) for each film is known.
2. The cost of each film is known or reasonably determinable.
3. Collectibility of the full license fee is reasonably assured.
4. The film is accepted by the licensee in accordance with the conditions of the license agreement.
5. The film is available; that is, the right is deliverable by the licensor and exercisable by the licensee.

Although there are many further complicating elements – discounting for the time value of money on long-term receivables or the possibly different methods used for tax-reporting purposes as compared with those (as described earlier) used for shareholder reports – for most analytical purposes only a few points need be noted.

Availability (item 5) is most important with regard to television or other ancillary-market licenses. Even when contract-specified sequencing to downstream markets restricts a distributor from making films available at certain times, the distributor often retains great discretion as to when product is to be made available. For example, television networks interested in obtaining a movie may be totally indifferent as to whether the picture is available on September 30 or on October 1. But to a distributor company trying to smooth its reported quarterly earnings results, the difference of one day could be substantial.

Another sensitive and potentially litigious area concerns fees allocated to films in a package of features that might be sold to a network.[3] Packages usually contain a dozen or so films, with, of course, some titles much stronger than others. Theoretically, each film is individually negotiated, but in practice the package is offered as whole. The problem is then to allocate the total-package revenues among all the films according to a proportion formula based on relative theatrical grosses. Previously, a rule of thumb was that the strongest film in a package might be worth 2.5 times the value of the weakest, with strength being defined by box-office performance figures. Allocation procedures are further discussed in section 4.4.

Of further significance are "backlogs" – the accumulation of contracts from which future license fees will be derived. Important contracts for ancillary-market exhibition are often written far in advance, sometimes even before the film is produced or released in theaters. Such backlogs generally do not appear directly anywhere on the balance sheet as contra to inventories, except when there are amounts received prior to revenue recognition. In those cases, the amounts are carried as advance payments and are included in current liabilities.

It has with some justification thus been argued that film company financial statements only partially reflect true corporate assets. However, companies ordinarily will indicate in balance sheet footnotes or other reports, such as annuals and 10-K filings with the Securities and Exchange Commission, the extent to which backlogs have changed during the reporting period.

Inventories

Perhaps the greatest conceptual difference between the movie industry and other industries is in the definition of inventory, which is normally taken to be a current asset – i.e., an asset that is used for production of goods or services in a single accounting period. Because the life cycles of filmed entertainment products (from beginning idea or property to final distribution) are measured in years, entertainment company inventories are categorized, in balance sheets that are classified, into current-period and noncurrent-period components. Included as inventories are the costs of options, screenplays, and projects in the preproduction, current-production, and postproduction phases awaiting release.

More formally, according to the accounting guide, inventories classified as current assets include the following:

1. For films in release, unamortized film costs allocated to the primary market.
2. Film costs applicable to completed films not released, net of the portion allocable to secondary markets.
3. Television films in production that are under contract of sale.

Costs allocated to secondary markets and that are not expected to be realized within 12 months, and all other costs related to film production, are classified as noncurrent. Typically, a film company will include the following captions:

Film productions:
    Released, less amortization
    Completed, not released

In process
Story rights and scenarios

Amortization of inventory

Inventories are matched in a "cost-of-goods-sold" sense against a *forecasted* schedule of receipt of income. Of course, forecasts of film receipts are mostly best guesses, although in the aggregate it is fairly certain that, on the average, perhaps 80% of all theater-exhibition revenues will be generated in the first nine months of release and almost all the remainder by the end of the second year.

Rather than using a cost-recovery theory, in which no gross profit is recognized until all costs and expenses have been recovered, the film industry's theoretical approach is based on a system in which costs are amortized in a pattern that parallels income flows. With this flow-of-income approach, gross profit is recognized as a standard portion of every dollar of gross revenue recorded.

Prior to implementation in 1981 of statement 53 of the Financial Accounting Standards Board (FASB), which essentially formalized the aforementioned AICPA guidelines, there were two amortization approaches generally applied. A company could use separate estimates of gross revenue for each film or it could use average tables (as in Supplementary Table S4.1 in Appendix C) based on the combined experience for many films. The use of such tables is, however, no longer practicable.[4]

With costs in the industry now reported according to FASB statement 53 at the lower of unamortized cost or net realizable value on a film-by-film basis (i.e., on an individual rather than group average), accountants' procedures require that estimates be reviewed periodically (at least quarterly and at the end of each year) to be sure that the best available data are being used (Table 4.1). If there are material revisions in gross-revenue estimates, amortization schedules must be recomputed, but previously reported interim-period results are not to be restated. For this reason, films performing very poorly in early release are quickly written down. Moreover, a write-down before release will be required in the rare situations in which the cost of a production obviously exceeds expected gross revenues.

The rules also presume that if story rights have been held for three years and not been set for production, those story costs will be charged to production overhead. Properties are to be reviewed periodically, and if it is determined that they will not be adapted for film projects, their costs are to be charged to current-period overhead.

Unamortized residuals

Before the days of television, pay-cable, and home video, theatrical exhibition was practically the only source of income for a film.[5] But that gradually began to change as television's appetite for movies increased and as receipts grew with

Table 4.1. *Individual-film-forecast-computation method of amortization:*
an example

Assumptions:	
Film cost	$10,000,000
Actual gross revenues:	
First year	12,000,000
Second year	3,000,000
Third year	1,000,000
Anticipated total gross revenues:	
At end of first year	24,000,000
At end of second and third years	20,000,000

Amortization   *Amount of*
                                          amortization

First-year amortization

$$\frac{\$12,000,000}{\$24,000,000} \times \$10,000,000 = \$5,000,000$$

Second-year amortization (anticipated total gross revenues reduced from
$24,000,000 to $20,000,000)[a]

$$\frac{\$3,000,000}{\$8,000,000^b} \times \$5,000,000^c = \$1,875,000$$

Third-year amortization

$$\frac{\$1,000,000}{\$8,000,000^d} \times \$5,000,000^d = \$\ \ 625,000$$

[a]If there were no change in anticipated gross revenues, the second-year amortization would
be as follows:

$$\frac{\$3,000,000}{\$24,000,000} \times \$10,000,000 = \$1,250,000$$

[b]$20,000,000 minus $12,000,000 or anticipated total gross revenues from beginning of
period.
[c]$10,000,000 minus $5,000,000 or cost less accumulated amortization at beginning of
period.
[d]The $8,000,000 and $5,000,000 need not be reduced by the second-year gross revenue
($3,000,000) and second-year amortization ($1,875,000), respectively, because anticipated
gross revenues did not change from the second to the third year. If such reduction were
made, the amount of amortization would be as follows:

$$\frac{\$1,000,000}{\$5,000,000} \times \$3,125,000 = \$625,000$$

Source: Appendix to FASB statement 53. © Financial Accounting Standards Board, High
Ridge Park, Stamford, CT 06905, USA. Reprinted with permission. Copies of the complete
document are available from the FASB.

audience size. In order to more closely match revenue and cost, a portion of a production's cost known as an *unamortized residual* was therefore set aside to be written down against expected future income from television.[6] For a major feature in the 1970s, an unamortized residual of $750,000 or so was typical.

But as income "ultimates" – revenues ultimately receivable from pay-cable, home video, and syndication – have become proportionally more significant in comparison with those derived from theatrical exhibition, unamortized residuals have also been set aside, pro rata, for those markets. Accordingly, such residuals have, on the average, become much larger than in the past and may lead to instances in which the bulk of a picture's cost will be written down against future revenues from nontheatrical sources.

In the late 1970s and early 1980s, unanticipated rapid growth of revenues from the new media sources did, in fact, upwardly bias reported industry profits. At the time, amortization was primarily against income derived from initial theatrical release, so that there was little if any cost left over to match against windfall receipts from burgeoning pay-cable and home-video markets. The industry, moreover, had also experienced a spate of unusual write-downs in those years. The Securities and Exchange Commission (SEC) reacted to such inconsistencies by expressing concern that investors did not have enough information about the timing and recoverability of film costs.

In response to those concerns, the AICPA appointed a task force to study these matters and to arrive at recommended disclosures that would better explain cost-recoverability methods without unduly burdening the industry. As a result, companies now disclose information about (a) their assumed revenue cycles and the composition of their film costs and (b) the expected timing of future amortization of the unamortized costs of released films.[7]

Interest expense and other costs

As interest rates and average production budgets have soared, interest expense has become a proportionally more important component of feature filmmaking. Until 1980, when FASB statement 34 concerning treatment (capitalization) of interest was issued, such costs were written off as incurred. Under the new standard, interest costs are capitalized and then charged as part of the negative cost.

Although studio period outlays, including those for rents and salaries, fall into a normal-expense category, studios also incur other costs of distribution (exploitation) that are capitalized. These may include, but are not limited to, prints and advertising and payments of subdistribution fees. For example, prints typically cost over $2,000 each (for five reels), and because simultaneous saturation booking is now common and often requires that well over 1,000 copies be made, this can add up to a substantial investment. Print costs are usually amortized according to a formula similar to that used for amortization of the negative.

Also, according to FASB statement 53, all exploitation costs (for prints, advertising, rents, salaries, and other distribution expenses) that are clearly to benefit future periods, should be capitalized as film-cost inventory and amortized over a period in which the major portion of gross revenue from the picture is recorded. This method especially pertains to national advertising, in which expenses before release can be considerable. Local and cooperative advertising expenditures, however, are generally closely related to local grosses and are normally expensed as incurred because they usually do not provide any benefits in future periods.

Calculation controversies

For sure, FASB statement 53 has contributed to a much improved basis for comparison of film and television company financial data versus the relatively amorphous conditions that had prevailed prior to its issuance.

Yet the statement has nevertheless drawn criticism for allowing considerable discretionary variation in the treatment of marketing and inventory cost amortizations in particular. With marketing costs often accounting for more than 35% of inventory, and overhead for another 10%, the recoupment of such costs is proportionally far more important to earnings reports in films and television programming than in other, say, manufactured-products industries. In most other industries, such cost amortizations are a relatively smaller percentage of total expenses and are much more closely related to the projected useful lives of assets based on prior experiences with other similar assets.

Instead, according to the rules for movies and television, the rate of amortization depends on *management's* projections (market-by-market and media-by-media) of often uncertain *revenue* streams that are expected to be received sometime in the possibly distant future. Moreover, because income recognition is generally unrelated to cash collections, it is entirely possible to report earnings and yet to be insolvent at the same time. It is thus often argued that the accounting picture rendered by application of FASB statement 53 may not accurately reflect the true earnings power, cash-flow potential, or asset value of a company.

Some companies, for example, might assume that all advertising costs incurred during theatrical release create values in the ancillary markets. As such, they will capitalize some of the costs despite the fact that local advertising in Tampa will ordinarily have no effect on video market sales in Toronto or Tanzania. In addition, some companies will amortize prints over estimated revenues from all markets rather than against revenues generated in specific markets, for instance, domestic versus foreign.

Other companies may assume long lives for their films and television series and thus include second- or third-cycle syndication sales even though such syndication sale events may not be known in terms of precise timing or pricing. Yet still others may differ on how long, or through what means, development project costs from in-house independent producers are capitalized and then written off as studio overhead; the costs of abandoned properties should be amortized as soon as it is clear that the properties will not be produced, but it is not unusual for many projects to be lost in creative limbo for relatively long periods. Even

Table 4.2. *Accounting ratio benchmarks for major film studio/distributors 1982–1996*

| | Film cost amortization as % of | | | Unamortized film costs of released films as a % of inventories | Additions to film costs as a % of film cost amortization |
	Revenues	Inventories	Operating cash flow		
1996	53.8	72.3	100.5	69.0	77.5
1995	51.9	80.9	92.5	61.7	63.2
1994	46.0	74.1	100.5	59.9	66.9
1993	60.5	71.8	109.0	53.5	95.6
1992	50.6	74.4	84.4	52.4	84.2
1991	43.8	75.4	77.4	58.0	83.7
1990	41.8	69.0	70.0	50.0	104.9
1989	38.4	69.2	66.0	54.4	104.0
1988	46.2	91.4	76.0	56.3	112.9
1987	46.1	95.3	80.6	61.9	113.3
1986	47.8	69.7	85.1	51.5	112.2
1985	52.6	80.9	88.8	65.4	128.3
1984	46.4	77.1	87.7	66.6	131.2
1983	44.8	78.9	92.6	52.8	122.6
1982	38.6	65.2	71.0	42.7	107.7
Mean:	47.3	80.8	85.5	57.1	100.6

Source: Company reports.

receivables under FASB statement 53 present problems: Receivables, according to the rules, are shown on the balance sheet as *discounted* to present value, whereas estimates of far more uncertain revenue ultimates are not.

Thus, under FASB statement 53, there is ample room for substantial variations in earnings reporting practices to appear, and it is essential for the analyst comparing one company to another to understand such differences.[8] The mean values for several commonly computed financial statement ratios that are presented in Table 4.2 should prove useful in this regard at least until modified standards currently being discussed by AICPA and FASB committees are implemented.

Finally, it helps to remember that at the core of many accounting problems and controversies between studio corporations and individuals are differences in assumptions about the timing of receipts and subsequent disbursements to participants. For example, distributors would normally use accrual accounting methods (booking income when *billed*) for their own financial-statement reporting purposes, and they would use cash accounting methods (based on revenues when *collected* and out-of-pocket expenses when incurred) for tracking disbursements to producers and others.[9]

Because of this, all levels of the industry are extremely sensitive to cash-flow considerations, and delays of payments tend to compound rapidly on the way to downstream receivers. Although the financial performance of a film company can sometimes be disguised by accounting treatments, the true condition becomes evident once the flow of new investment stops.

Merger and acquisition issues

Although the most frequently encountered aspects of corporate accounting for filmed entertainment products have already been outlined, several additional points are worthy of note.

In business combinations or reorganizations, for example, two different methods can be used to integrate the balance sheets of separate corporate entities. As described by Accounting Principles Board opinion 16, the "purchase" method accounts for business combinations as the acquisition of one company by another, with the acquiring corporation recording as its cost the assets less liabilities assumed. Under this method, goodwill (generally to be amortized in equal annual amounts over a period not to exceed 40 years) is a difference between the cost of an acquired company and the sum of the fair values of tangible and identifiable intangible assets less liabilities.

In contrast, a business combination using "pooling of interests" is viewed as "the uniting of the ownership interests of two or more companies by exchange of equity securities. No acquisition is recognized because the combination is accomplished without disbursing resources of the constituents. Ownership interests continue and the former bases of accounting are retained."

Although use of either purchase or pooling (with pooling soon to be restricted or abolished by the Financial Accounting Standards Board) is not unique to the media industries, film and television program assets are, by nature, intangibles, and valuations are thus often highly subjective.[10]

As we have seen, accounting methods contain elements of both art and science. That will be further amplified as we next explore specific financial relationships between studios and creative participants.

4.3 Big-picture accounting

Financial overview

Preceding sections have described how financial statements appear from the corporate angle. But, as noted earlier, accounting statements for individual participants are properly viewed from a different perspective. This section illustrates the results for typical production, distribution, and exhibition contracts in terms of profit-and-loss statements for individual projects. For the producer, the legal heart of most such projects is the production-financing-distribution (PFD) agreement, which may broadly contain one or more of the following four sometimes overlapping attributes or elements.

1. *Step deals*, in which the financing proceeds in steps that allow the financing entity to advance additional funds or to terminate involvement depending upon whether various predetermined conditions (e.g., approvals of screenplay drafts and casting choices) are met.

2. *Packages/Negative Pick-ups*, in which a producer, or an agent, assembles the key elements of a project and then attempts to interest a studio in financing that project. A bank will lend against such a studio promise as long as the producer has obtained a completion guarantee bond. The studio will then "pick-up" the negative upon its completion.

3. *Presales*, in which the producer has financed all or part of a picture by selling off various exhibition or distribution rights to the completed picture prior to its being produced. Such sales of what are, in effect, licenses to distribute, normally involve home-video and foreign distribution entities that provide promissory notes discountable at banks. However, no more than 60% of the negative cost can usually be financed in this way.

4. *Private fundings*, in which the producer, usually of only a low-budget picture, taps into private sources of funds through arrangement of a limited partnership.

Each of these financing options provides the producer with different trade-offs in terms of creative controls and profits. In step deals, for instance, a relatively large degree of creative control and of potential share of producer profit may be relinquished in favor of speed and efficiency. At the opposite end of the spectrum, private financings may allow for unrestricted creative control, but may also severely limit the time and money available for actual production.

More generally, however, the production section of a PFD concerns the development process of making a feature (and, as such, does not normally apply to small-budget productions). It specifies the essential ingredients of a feature project – screenplay, director, producer, principle cast, and budget. And it then spells out who will be responsible for which steps in bringing the film to completion, who gets paid when, and under what conditions the studio-financier can place the project in "turnaround," that is, abandon the project and attempt to establish it elsewhere.

Also, of course, the financing section of a PFD provides financing-arrangement descriptions and stipulates completion-guarantee details and costs (which would normally average about 6% of total budget before rebates).[11]

Yet, ultimately, it is the distribution-agreement section that is of greatest importance. Included here are definitions of distribution fees (in effect, sales commissions or service charges for booking films and negotiating with other distribution outlets) and specifications concerning audit and ownership rights, accounting-statement preparations, and advertising and marketing commitments.

Table 4.3 provides an overview of revenue flows for a typical theatrical release. In looking at this, it helps to keep in mind that the exhibitor's objective is to minimize rentals, but the distributor's objective is to maximize them, and what participants see as their gross is the distributor's rental, not box-office gross as

Table 4.3. *Flowchart for theatrical motion-picture revenue: box-office receipts*

Distributor's gross receipts
   less:
     1. Distribution fees
     2. Distribution costs
     3. Third-party gross participations
          ↓
Producer's gross proceeds
   less:
     1. Negative cost
       (a) Direct cost
       (b) Overhead
       (c) Interest on loans
     2. Contingent deferments
First net profits
     ↓
Break-even
     ↓
Third-party net-profit participations (100% of net profits of picture)
     ↓
Producer's share of net profits of picture

Source: Breglio and Schwartz (1980). © John F. Breglio.

usually reported in the trade papers. For reasons previously discussed, the box-office gross can be much larger than the distributor's gross (i.e., rentals).

A convenient illustration of PFD concepts has been provided by Leedy (1980, p. 1), from which the following descriptions are drawn. Leedy's illustration (Table 4.4) for a major successful picture is particularly useful because it well illustrates the typical deferred payments to the writer and director, profit participations by the leading actors, and contingent compensations to the financier and producer. It further shows how a $14 million (negative cost) picture earning $100 million in distributor's rentals might generate $16 million of profit for financier and producer before participations and $8.1 million after adjustment for participations and deferments.

Although this model does not provide detailed revenue specifications for all new media sources, it nevertheless correctly portrays typical domestic theatrical-distribution fees (i.e., United States and Canadian) at about 30%, foreign distribution and television syndication fees at 40%, and other distribution fees at 15%.[12] Such distribution charges are, by long-standing industry practice, largely nonnegotiable. But because the charges are unrelated to actual costs, they will, on relatively rare occasions, be adjusted in order to retain the services of important producers. In those cases, a sliding-fee scale down to a predetermined minimum

Table 4.4. *Revenues and costs for a major theatrical release, circa 1992*

Gross revenue	
Subject to a 30% distribution fee:	
Theatrical film rental (U.S. and Canada)	$50,000,000
Nontheatrical film rental	1,000,000
Royalty on home video	5,000,000
U.S. network television	4,000,000
Total	60,000,000
Subject to a 40% distribution fee	
Foreign film rental	20,000,000
Foreign television license fees	5,000,000
Royalty on foreign home video	5,000,000
Television, pay & syndication	9,000,000
Total	39,000,000
Subject to a 15% distribution fee	
Merchandise royalties	950,000
Advertising sales	50,000
Total	1,000,000
Total gross revenue	$100,000,000
Distribution fee	
30% × $60,000,000	$18,000,000
40% × $39,000,000	15,600,000
15% × $1,000,000	150,000
Total distribution fee	$33,750,000
Balance	$66,250,000
Distribution expenses	
Cooperative advertising	$20,000,000
Other advertising and publicity	5,000,000
Release prints, etc.	3,000,000
Taxes	2,000,000
Trade-association fees and other	1,500,000
Bad debts	1,000,000
All other expenses	1,750,000
Total distribution expenses	$34,250,000
Balance	$32,000,000
Production cost $14,000,000	
Interest thereon 2,000,000	$16,000,000
Net profit before participations	$16,000,000
Deferments paid	125,000
Participations in gross and net	7,775,000
Total	7,900,000
Net profit to be split 50:50	$8,100,000

Source: Leedy (1980, pp. 1–3 and unpublished updates).

– with perhaps a 5% reduction for every $20 million of theatrical rentals generated – is used.

Table 4.4 can also provide an indication of how sensitive profits are to changes in the cost of capital. For example, an assumption of interest rates of 20% for this type of project brings interest cost on the production closer to $3 million than to the $2 million that is shown. If so, $1 million additional interest cost would reduce investors' profits by about 12% from $8.1 million to $7.1 million.[13]

Table 4.5 summarizes how other participants might have fared in Leedy's example of a picture bringing rentals of $100 million. Here it is important to remember that in contrast to the financiers and distributors, the potential profit participants, including the director and lead actors, are at no risk of loss. They generally do not have equity capital invested in a project, and their profit participations, if any, should thus be appropriately characterized as salary bonuses.

Participation deals

From a major studio's standpoint, risk is reduced if a production schedule contains a balanced mix of project source financings. For instance, a studio might plan to release 24 films a year, of which perhaps four might be fully financed and produced in-house, another 14 might be financed using PFD arrangements with affiliated production entities, and the remainder be financed with so-called "pickups."

However, no matter what the financing sources, revenue and profit participations are always the central issues. Participation arrangements are limited only by the imagination and bargaining abilities of the individuals who negotiate them. But, of course, only talents in great demand can command significant participations in addition to fees or salaries. In most situations, the filmmaker's trade-off for major studio funding includes ceding ownership of the film and control of the project to the studio, which then also shares substantially in the film's financial returns.

Pickups Of the several major variants of participation agreements, perhaps the simplest is a "pickup" – a completed or partially completed project presented to studio-financiers or distributors for further funding and support.[14] From the distributor's point of view, pickups are much less risky than are unfilmed projects in their early stages, which is when it may be especially difficult to evaluate how all in-process artistic elements fit together. For this reason, independent filmmakers often find that their best opportunity to distribute through a major is via such pickup agreements.[15] Indeed, assuming that the producer is able to fund prints and advertising (p & a) for the film through other sources and deliver a completed (or nearly completed) film, a so-called "rent-a-studio" deal can often be made in which access to a major's domestic theatrical distribution organization can be obtained for relatively low fees.

Coproduction-distribution Distributor-financiers often make coproduction deals with one or more parties for one or more territories in order that risks may be

Table 4.5. *Fee splits, deferments, and participations for a major motion-picture release: an example based on the results of Table 4.4*

Writer:		
Fee	$250,000	
Deferment	50,000	$300,000
Director:		
Fee	525,000	
Deferment	75,000	600,000
Major lead actor:		
Fee	2,000,000	
Participation[a]	6,875,000	8,875,000
Major lead actress:		
Fee	500,000	
Participation[b]	900,000	1,400,000
Producer:		
Fee	500,000	
Contingency comp.	4,050,000	4,550,000
Financier:		
Interest income	1,000,000	
Contingency comp.	4,050,000	5,050,000
Distributor:		
Fee		33,750,000

[a]Actor participation: Based on $2 million against a participation of 10% of gross revenue less cooperative advertising and taxes before break-even, and an additional 2.5% participation rate on this basis after break-even.

[b]Actress participation (based on 10% of net profits contractually defined as after the deferments and after the participation in gross):

Net profit before participations	$16,000,000
Deferments paid	125,000
Participation in gross	6,875,000
Total	7,000,000
Net profit after participations	$9,000,000
Participation rate	10%
Participation	$900,000

Source: Leedy (1980, p. 3 and unpublished updates).

shared. For instance, domestic and foreign distributors, in a "split-rights" arrangement, might each contribute half of a picture's production cost and each be entitled to distribution fees earned in their respective territories. Because distribution costs and box-office appeal often vary significantly in different markets, however, a picture might be profitable for one distributor and unprofitable for another. Also, the results for all distributors may be aggregated, with profits or losses split according to aggregate performance rather than territorial performance.

Talent participations and break-even Participations in net profits or in gross are contingent on a film making enough money to break even. Participations are thus a form of *contingent* compensation and, as such, may never be payable.

Writers, directors, or actors may become financial participants if their agents have been able to negotiate for gross "points" – which can be defined on a number of different grosses. Distributors' grosses are what have been called rentals, and participation points defined on this basis are obviously very valuable because a picture does not have to be profitable for such points to be earned. Accordingly, participations of this kind are rare and are assigned to only the very strongest box-office draws.

More usual, though, is a participation based on a designated actual or artificially set break-even level. For example, some talent participants might receive a percentage of distributor's gross after the first $30 million has been generated. In other instances, participations might begin after break-even – defined as distributor's gross minus distribution fees and distribution costs (including duties, licenses, and many other charges known as "off-the-tops"). Additional points might then be earned after, say, rentals reach 3.5 times the production cost. As can be imagined, the variations on these concepts are infinite, although such deals can be generally categorized into the three basic types: first-dollar, adjusted gross, or gross after break-even.

Of course, the more gross players attached to a project, the less the likelihood that a project will go into a net profit position.[16] Also, accounting for the costs of multiple-talent participations tremendously raises the level of complexity, and what usually begins as a simple agreement between an agent and a studio attorney or business-affairs representative often ends as a complicated financial-accounting document replete with the potential for widely divergent interpretations.

Is star *A*'s participation deducted before that of star *B*? Is participation based on only domestic rentals or on both foreign and domestic? Which distribution costs are subtracted before artificial break-even? Are both television advertising and national-magazine advertising included or excluded? And perhaps, more fundamentally, under what method are subdistributor and home-video revenues represented in "gross receipts?" Those are some of the subjects on which opinions may differ, especially within the context of the tens of thousands of transactions entries that are typically generated in the course of bringing a major feature to the screen. No wonder, then, that even in the best of circumstances, in which contract terms are sharply defined, it is time-consuming and expensive to follow an audit trail.

Nevertheless, still further complications may also be introduced with the concept of a *rolling break-even* – defined as the point at which revenues are equal to production costs plus distribution fees and expenses on a continuing basis. For instance, with a picture approaching profitability, a distributor's decision to spend more on advertising will delay or defer breaking even, thereby adversely affecting talent participants entitled to receive points in the picture's "net" profits.

As shown in the following formula, the amount of rentals required for a new break-even ("rolling break" in industry jargon) is found by dividing total expenses exclusive of the distribution fee (i.e., prints and ads plus negative costs) by 1 minus the distribution-fee percentage: Let a = required rentals, b = total expenses, and r = distribution-fee percentage. Then

$$a = b/(1 - r)$$

For instance, if r = 30% and b = $7 million, then a = $10 million. But if another $1 million is spent on advertising, then b = $8 million, and a = $11.43 million. In this situation, every $1 million of additional expenditure requires an additional $1.43 million of rentals to be generated in order to remain at break-even.

Break-even is also greatly affected by studio deductions for interest that are charged – normally at 125% of the bank prime rate – on the unrecouped cost of the picture: The studio views the cost of financing a film as a loan. In such calculations, studio overhead charges, usually in the range of 12.5% to 17.5% of the cost of the picture, are often included. In other words, there is interest charged on overhead – and sometimes, alternatively, overhead charged on interest.

Because of such complications, and also the aforementioned sequencing of deductions for fees and costs, potential profit participants often find that the ''net'' profits of a picture are elusive and subject to widely varying accounting definitions and interpretations (especially in relation to earlier upstream claims made by participants in the ''adjusted-gross'' receipts). Thus, as Baumgarten, Farber, and Fleischer (1992, p. 3) have noted, terms such as ''gross receipts'' or ''net profits'' ''have no intrinsic meaning. The words mean whatever the participants decide they mean.''[17]

Producers' participations and cross-collateralizations Producers are responsible for a film's production costs, and they often have contractual incentives to keep project expenses down. When costs exceed approved budgets by certain percentages, producers' shares may be penalized by several times the percentage overage. On the other hand, the share of profit, if any, that the producer will receive (in addition to earned production-services fees) can be structured so as to provide a floor or minimum payment that has priority over other (third-party) participations. Were it not for this floor, the presence of several third-party participations, each at perhaps 10% of 100% of net profit (equal to a 20% slice out of the producer's half of total net profit) would severely diminish the producer's potential income.

Producers are also affected if the financial fate of one picture is tied to that of another, or if the box-office performance of a single picture in one territory is linked to its performance in another. Such *cross-collateralizations* of producers' shares may imply that the profits of one picture must exceed the losses of another in order for there to be anything to share. It is especially frustrating for potential profit participants when profitable picture A is cross-collateralized with picture B that has perhaps yet to be produced, to be distributed, or to show a profit. In these situations, none of the profit on picture A will be credited to participants until picture B recovers most of its costs.

Home-video participations Because the system for distribution of home-video discs and cassettes has been developed from hybrid roots in the distribution of

Table 4.6. *Film rentals calculations: examples contrasting floor minimums versus percentages of net box-office receipts*

	Case 1	Case 2
Box-office receipts	$10,000	$8,000
Less deductions for second feature	2,500	2,000
Net box-office receipts	7,500	6,000
Minimum film rental at 70% of net	5,250	4,200
Contractual theater overhead (nut)	1,500	1,500
Net box-office receipts after nut	6,000	4,500
Maximum film rental at 90% of net after nut	5,400	4,050

recorded music (see Chapter 5) and book products, a different – and controversial – basis for participation accounting has evolved. Rather than subtracting distribution fees and expenses directly from defined gross receipts, as has already been described, home-video participants are instead entitled to royalties that are normally set (but subject to bargaining power) at 20% of the unit's wholesale price. As a result, studios will usually include only 20% of total home-video unit sales royalties in participant's gross receipt calculations and retain, except for residuals, the remaining 80% to cover the relatively modest costs of manufacturing, advertising, and duplication. The studio then still subjects the participant's home–video gross receipts to a distribution fee.[18]

Accordingly, with the bulk of home-video revenue thus shunted aside and taken out of the participants' calculus of a particular film's financial performance, the arithmetic for a studio's profitability on home-video distribution becomes quite compelling. It is therefore easy to see why home video has become such a boon for the filmed entertainment industry and such an acute question for the participants to negotiate. Indeed, from a corporate standpoint, it might be reasonably argued that home video has now become the primary source of profits.[19]

Distributor-exhibitor computations

As already indicated, rentals are that portion of box-office receipts owed the distributor. Table 4.6 shows an example in which the exhibitor's nut for fixed overhead is negotiated or set at $1,500, and there is a 90:10 split (90% for distributor, 10% for exhibitor) of box-office receipts after the nut (but not less than the previously agreed 70% of total box-office receipts to the distributor).

In case 1, the distributor will be owed $5,400, whereas in case 2 the distributor will be entitled to $4,200. In neither case will the distributor share in the theater's concession income from candy, beverages, popcorn, and video games (see section 3.4). And as can be inferred from Table 4.7, concession sales are a significant profit–swing factor for exhibitors.[20]

Rentals usually are accounted for on a cash basis when collected by the distributor, and expenses are recorded as incurred. In fact, this reporting method –

Table 4.7. *Exhibitor operating revenues and expenses: an example*

Box-office (BO) weekly gross	$3,000
Concession sales (at 15%)	450
Total weekly gross	3,450
Deduct:	
Distributor's share at 50% of BO	1,500
Advertising (10% of BO)	300
Payroll (10% of BO)	300
Food cost (23% of sales)	104
Rent and real-estate taxes at 15% of BO	450
Utilities at $150/week	150
Management fee at 10% of total weekly gross	345
Insurance and employee benefits	100
Repairs and maintenance	100
Miscellaneous (tickets, etc.)	100
Total average weekly expenses	3,449

Source: Lowe (1983, p. 346). From the book *The Movie Business Book* by Jason E. Squire, © 1983 by Jason E. Squire. New York: Simon & Schuster/Fireside.

reflecting the normally slow collection of cash and the delayed billing of period expenses such as co-op advertising – is reasonably equitable from the viewpoints of all participants.

Co-op advertising is normally calculated on gross receipts and allocated according to the distributor-exhibitor percentage revenue split in effect at the time the advertising appears. The following example indicates the true net percentage:

Box-office gross	$20,000
House expenses	4,000
Net	16,000

Ninety percent goes to the distributor: $14,400 (90:10 split); the true distributor co-op percentage here is 72% (14.4:20.0), not 90%.

In analyzing the corporate accounting statements of exhibition companies, it should also be noted that the mix of owned versus leased real estate, and the methods of accounting for real-estate transactions and leasehold improvements, can vary significantly from one company to another, thereby limiting financial comparability.[21]

Distributor deals and expenses

The previous hypothetical example of a film generating $100 million in rentals (Table 4.4) showed a distributor fee, or service charge for the sales organization, of $33.75 million. Although much of the fee may here be regarded as profit, it is

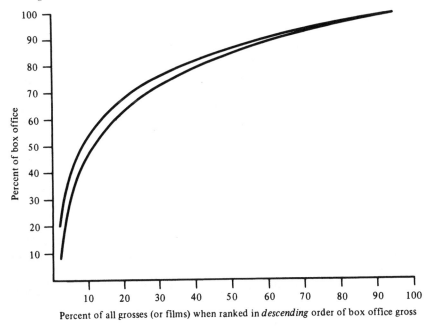

Figure 4.1. Ten % of films generate 50% of the box office. When film box-office figures are ranked (either by individual weekly grosses or by individual films in order of their box-office grosses), the results fall in the range shown by the plotted curves. *Source: Daily Variety,* July 31, 1984. Copyright 1984 by A. D. Murphy.

this very distribution profit on a hit that would be expected to more than offset losses sustained on other releases; 10% of the films released generate 50% of the total box-office receipts (Figure 4.1).

Simplistically, then, it is distribution profit – perhaps for a major distributor averaging over time a third or more of total distribution fees – that would normally provide the positive cash flow for investment in new films. And it is this very profit, derived by subtracting from distribution fees all office overhead costs, compensation for sales personnel, and various other publicity and promotion expenses *not* recouped through other charges (as described below), that keeps the distributor in business despite the high probability that many pictures will *in toto* lose money when *all* input factor costs and expenses are tallied.

As for the distribution fee itself, it is perhaps best conceptualized as being an access charge or a toll paid to a distribution organization for use of the established turnpikes and bridges that allow direct access to large audiences. As with all such major access routes or pipelines, there can only be a few, and the up-front capital investment required to establish them is sizable.[22] The tolls or rents charged by distributors for such access are thus not especially sensitive to bargaining pressures and are, by nature, quasi-monopolistic and unrelated to direct costs.

Within this structure, many, if not most, pictures operate under a ''net deal,'' in which the distributor charges a fixed or graduated percentage of rentals (e.g., 30% in domestic theatrical markets) as a distribution fee and then advances the funds for other distribution costs, including those for prints, trailers, and national advertising. In addition, there may be charges related to publicity and personal-appearance tours, co-op advertising with exhibitors, taxes (based on rentals) by countries and localities, trade-association and guild fees in the form of residuals (for exhibitions in ancillary markets), and bad debts. The distributor commonly recovers these expenses before making any payments to the producer and, as shown in Table 4.3, would normally, before arriving at a definition of "net profit," prioritize recoupment by taking distribution fees and expenses first, then interest on negative costs, then negative costs, and finally deferments and various participations.

Although the aforementioned net deal predominates, there is also a so-called "gross deal" wherein the distributor (usually of low-budget independently made pictures), is not separately reimbursed for distribution expenses, but instead retains a distribution fee (e.g., 50%–70%) that is considerably higher than normal. Distribution expenses are then recouped out of this higher fee, while the producer receives the remaining unencumbered portion of the gross rentals.[23]

For a picture performing poorly at the box office, the producer with a gross deal will have an advantage because overall distribution costs (which can be quite high on a percentage-of-revenue basis) are not chargeable. Contrarily, for a picture doing well at the box office, a producer might prefer a net deal, because marketing costs as a percentage of revenues then diminish rapidly and specific marketing charges become more bearable. It is also possible, to create a structure in which gross-deal and net-deal characteristics are combined as certain performance criteria are met.

In negotiating such formulations, the potential advantages to be derived from the control of ancillary-market revenues have inspired many independent producers to attempt to strip from domestic theatrical-distribution contracts, and to thus retain for themselves, the rights to exploit cable, home video, and other sources of income. Studios are, however, ordinarily reluctant to allow these rights to be taken away ("fractionalized") through so-called "split-rights" deals unless there is compensation through participations or through some other means. And, in all, it should be clear that the larger the total upfront studio fee, the less there is available for recoupment of production costs – and, ultimately, for profit of the independent filmmaker.

As we have seen, studio profits are centered on distribution activities, where fees range to over 30% of gross receipts, yet expenses might normally be covered by 8% to 15% of gross receipts. This cushion of profit is earned, in part, for taking the risk that a picture will not earn its releasing costs. But the cushion also, in effect, pays for maintenance and extension of the distribution pipeline. Of course, when a picture is doing well at the box office, distribution profits soar. Yet, on the other hand, as opposed to licensing to home-video, pay-cable, syndication, and network markets, *theatrical release is the only area where there is the possibility of a negative cash flow* – i.e., where releasing costs can exceed income.

Studio overhead and other production costs

The general characteristics of production-related costs were examined in Chapter 3. From the participants' view, large proportions of those costs are seen as studio overhead charges, which are calculated by applying a contract-stipulated rate to all direct production costs. Such overhead charges may or may not have any close relationship to the actual costs of, for example, renting sound stages or buying props and signs outside of the studio's shops and mills.

Indeed, because it would almost always be less expensive to buy or lease items on a direct-cost basis, participants may question what services and materials are actually covered by the studio rate. If agreements are not clearly written, and are thus open to different interpretations, disputes may arise with regard to contractual overhead charges for everything from cameras and sound equipment to secretarial services. But probably the most important question is whether or not full rates are applicable to location shooting. How these matters are resolved – before, during, or (hopefully not) after production – depends on relative bargaining positions.

Producers are motivated to obtain independent financing in order to avoid or reduce the effects of these charges, which can add between 15% and 25% to a picture's budget, and thereby significantly raise the break-even point required to activate net-profit participants' share payments.[24] Sometimes it is worthwhile and feasible for an independent producer with outside financing to minimize studio overhead charges by offering the film for pickup in an advanced stage of production. In other instances it is less time-consuming and, in the long run, less expensive to go with the studio.

In brief, although overhead rates generally are not negotiable, the things to which those rates apply (offices, vehicles, etc.) may be, so that it is important for producers to have a clear understanding of what their contracts specify. If a studio wants a project badly enough, the items excluded from the standard rule will be more numerous.

Once production begins, cost accounting follows a job-order cost procedure wherein time and materials are "charged against" a job or charge number. This is where careful control by the producer, who has final responsibility during the production phase, is essential. Costs can easily get out of hand because everyone from painters and electricians to cameramen and editors may have at least some authority to charge against the picture's number for materials and services.

Truth and consequences[25]

A synopsis of what usually happens to a dollar that flows from the box office will help clarify the processing thus far described. Assuming that house expenses are 10%, there remains 90 cents, to which (for an important release by a major) a 90:10 split for the first two weeks in favor of the distributor may be applied. That, in turn, leaves a distributor's gross ("rentals") of around 81 cents.

In the United States and Canada, a 30% distribution fee totaling 24 cents is then subtracted, leaving 57 cents. Advertising and publicity costs, which are gen-

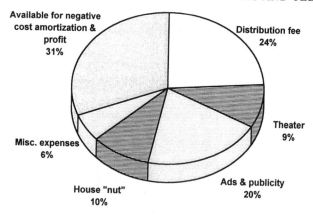

Figure 4.2. Splitting the box-office dollar for a major film.

erally at least 20%–25% of rentals, require deduction of another, say, 20 cents. The remainder is now 37 cents, out of which about 6 cents more is required for miscellaneous distribution expenses, including prints, taxes, MPAA seal, and transportation.

Thus, before considering the negative cost of the picture (which can be substantial), there is a residual pool of only 31 cents of the original dollar. Should there also be gross participations, say 10% (of rentals) to a major actor, there would then be 8 cents less with which to recoup the negative cost. And if the picture is studio-financed, half of any profit after recoupment would ordinarily be owed the studio, the other half split among other participants (Figure 4.2).[26] Small wonder, then, that so many firms have found production to be more difficult and less profitable than they had at first thought.[27]

The partial list of high-budget theatrical flops shown in Table 4.8 illustrates that box-office failure is usually congenital: No matter how large ancillary markets grow, they cannot a golden goose of a turkey make. And, there truly is little, if any, correlation between the cost of a picture and the returns it might generate (Table 4.9).

Still, despite the odds against profitability, many people find filmmaking financially attractive and worth taking a risk on. With a proper combination of luck and pluck, independent producers are sometimes able to arrange financing sufficient to own much or all of a possibly valuable negative at little or no direct cost to themselves.

4.4 Television-programming accounting

Television was initially thought to threaten the very survival of movies. The tube's mesmerizing influence and its presence in virtually all households indeed contributed to the reduction of annual theater admissions from the all-time peak of

Table 4.8. *Selected theatrical winners and losers*

Title	Distributor	Year of first release	Est. neg. cost ($ million)	Est. domestic rentals as of 1996 ($ million)
Winners (high and low budget)				
Jaws	Universal	1975	8	130
Star Wars	Lucasfilm/Fox	1977	11	225
Kramer vs. Kramer	Columbia	1979	7	60
Airplane	Paramount	1980	3	41
Raiders of the Lost Ark	Lucasfilm/Fox	1981	22	116
E.T. The Extra-terrestrial	Universal	1982	12	228
Return of the Jedi	Lucasfilm/Fox	1983	33	168
Beverly Hills Cop	Paramount	1984	14	80
Batman	Warner	1989	41	151
Home Alone	Fox	1990	18	140
Jurassic Park	Universal	1993	70	212
The Lion King	Disney	1994	65	173
Four Weddings & a Funeral	PolyGram	1994	7	25
Independence Day	Fox	1996	65	171
Losers (high budget)				
Raise the Titanic	ITC/AFD	1980	36	6
Heaven's Gate	UA	1980	44	2
Pennies from Heaven	MGM/UA	1981	22	4
Reds	Paramount	1981	52	21
Howard the Duck	Universal	1986	37	10
Ishtar	Columbia	1987	45	8
Hudson Hawk	TriStar	1991	55	6
Last Action Hero	Columbia	1993	75	28

Source: Variety, Anniversary and Cannes issues.

about 4 billion in 1946 to about 1 billion in the early 1960s. Yet, as it happened, television eventually became the film industry's first major ancillary market and, in the process, probably its savior. But it was a long time before the value of the television market was fully understood by moviemakers.

Today, studios engage in three distinct television-related activities: licensing of features to networks; syndication of features, series, and other programs to local stations; and production of made-for-television movies, series, and programs. Many small firms are also active in these areas. But easy this business is not. In comparison to the situation in feature films, the full earnings potential of a program or series is normally quite limited, while the uncertainty of sale or of eventual price in aftermarkets is at least as great.[28] Moreover, potential participant

Table 4.9. *Real reel numbers, selected examples, big and small*[a]

Title:	**Who Framed Roger Rabbit?**	**Commando**
Domestic release date:	June 1988	October 1985
Distributor:	Walt Disney Co.	20th Century Fox
Period end:	12/31/90	2/29/92

Gross receipts:			
Domestic theatrical	$80,763		$17,941
Foreign theatrical	80,102		24,022
Pay television	9,680		8,005
Home video	26,573		6,045
Non-theatrical	2,316		
Television			8,507
Consumer products &			
other	5,686		725
Total	$205,119		$65,245

minus
Distribution fees and costs:

Distribution fees		68,259	22,122
Advertising and publicity		48,333	11,529
Checking, collections,			
conversion, etc.		655	194
Other version		1,076	156
Residuals		3,415	3,135
Trade dues		843	371
Taxes, insurance		2,949	1,608
Prints		5,746	3,387
Transportation		951	431
Miscellaneous		166	140
Total		$132,394	$43,073

minus
Negative costs:

Production cost		50,579	15,946
Production overhead		7,587	
Interest		17,105	3,129
Gross participations &			
deferments		17,054	396
Total		$92,325	$19,471

Net profit (loss)	($19,600)		**$2,701**

[a]Data in $000s.

Source: Adapted from *The Hollywood Reporter*, with permission, August 17 and September 14, 1992.

accounting problems – delay and minimization of income recognition, and applications of numerous deductions – are often similar to those found in feature film accountings.

Feature licensing

The peak demand for network feature-film licenses appears to have been reached in the late 1970s, when pay-cable was still in a relatively early stage of development, and when the American Broadcasting Corporation, flush with ratings victories and cash, had the wherewithal to bid aggressively for rights to exhibit recent theatrical hits. Many of the major licenses at the time permitted up to five runs for fees that (with escalator clauses based on box-office performance) frequently were in the neighborhood of $20 million.

Bidding fervor cooled, however, when it became apparent that pay-cable was siphoning off the potential for high network ratings through early showings of uncut movies without commercial interruptions. The ratings of all but the biggest box-office hits also diminished relative to those of made-for-television movies. But, in spite of this, films making their first network appearance in the early 1980s could command an average of perhaps $5 million for two runs. That price reflected expected ratings for the film, the number of weekly hours allotted by the networks for feature-movie programming, and the cost of producing comparable programming in terms of running time and content.

Of course, out of any television-license fees, residual payments to participants have to be made and other distribution costs – including high-priced legal talent and, on a rainy day, taxi fare up New York's Sixth Avenue – must be deducted. A feature film licensed to network television might thus generate for the studio-distributor a profit margin in the range of 40%–65%.

An important accounting dilemma, nevertheless, appears in the situation in which a package of several features is licensed by a single vendor to one purchaser. According to trade-paper reports, for example, United Artists had followed an allocation formula that

divided the package price by the number of pictures in the package to determine average price per picture,
assigned a value of 1.5 times the average price to the feature with the highest theatrical rentals,
assigned a value of 0.5 times the average price to the feature with the lowest theatrical rentals,
ranked the remaining features by rentals earned and assigned a value in between the range of 1.5 and 0.5 times the average price.[29]

Similar formulas had been used by other distributors with the rationale that over the years "it has been determined that the ratings of the most successful pictures on television, in both domestic and foreign markets, receive no more than three times the rating of the least successful pictures."[30]

However, such formulas were legally challenged because they seemed to produce unfair results for some participants. Thus, under current practices, prices for features in a package are supposed to be negotiated separately for each title, even though questions concerning the basis for arriving at a specific price may still arise.

For outside participants, probably the easiest way to account for income from television-license fees is on a cash basis as of telecast date. Yet there can be many variations, to some extent configured by relative negotiating power. As already noted, for purposes of financial reporting, the studio-distributor will recognize revenues at the time the pictures are made available for exhibition. However, actual contract terms might stipulate cash payments of 20% on signing, 50% on availability, and 30% on subsequent runs, and with down payments on older features being even smaller.

Problems as to the timing of cash receipts, allocations, and different reporting requirements also frequently arise in situations involving licensing of syndication, pay-cable, and other ancillary-market rights (novelizations, games and toys, character merchandise, and music).

Program production and distribution

Development and financing processes Production of original programming for network television is generally in the form of made-for-television movies ("made-fors") or regularly scheduled series and miniseries such as *War and Remembrance* or *Roots*.[31] Each of these program forms may receive somewhat specialized cost-accounting treatment, with the procedures and methods applied to made-fors being similar to those used in making feature films.

Financing on made-fors and series, however, is provided by the networks on a piecemeal basis. About a year ahead of anticipated play dates, networks and program producers, including the television arms of the major film studios and many large television production independents, sift through hundreds of concepts to select those with the potential to become two-hour movies, miniseries (usually 8–12 hours in length), or one-hour or half-hour series. No more than two or three dozen of these concepts will then be provided with funding, and each will be developed into a "pilot" production that will introduce the major themes and characters.

Pilots allow network advertisers to sense how well the elements in a proposed program will work together on the screen. But pilots are often loaded with costly production values in an attempt to stimulate the buyers, who make their judgments based largely on first impressions.[32]

Of the 30 or so pilots ordered for the start of the television season, no more than 15 are likely to be accepted for regularly scheduled series programming by the three major networks combined. Acceptance by a network is usually accompanied by a funding commitment to produce 13 episodes initially and by an option contract for additional episodes (usually 9–11 more) if the program attracts relatively large audiences. For each episode, the network may pay one-third on commencement of filming or taping, another third on completion, and the last third on delivery and clearance (by network censors and others). However, the percentages at the various steps of a deal occasionally vary, and there may be an additional payment of 10% or so on rerun of an episode.

There are two reasons that producers do not generally profit immediately or directly from series or made-fors developed by the process just described. First, network funding via license fees (normally for two runs), does not typically cover all the out–of–pocket cash expenditures incurred by the program producer. In fact, on the average, such production costs may be only 80% to 85% recouped from the network license fee, with the remainder hopefully covered by revenues generated through licensing in foreign markets.[33] Under these circumstances, even a relatively efficient producer would have difficulty coming out ahead on a cash basis of accounting.[34]

But a financial deficit is also virtually assured using the accrual method of accounting, wherein noncash accruals for studio overhead expenses (at 10% or more of the budget) are included. It is thus common for program producers to "deficit finance" their series and made-fors while trusting that the network ratings will be strong enough to carry the show into the potentially more lucrative off-network syndication aftermarket at some future time.[35]

Network option clauses, however, are another reason that producers might not immediately profit from a successful series introduction. Option clauses for series usually allow the network to order programs for four to six additional broadcast seasons (with episode fees increasing at least 3%–5%, and more likely 7%–8%, each year), and also provide for first right of refusal beyond such a period. This means that even if another network or perhaps a cable channel were to offer the production company more money for a program, the offer could not be immediately accepted. Option clauses thus enable a network to retain a show at a cost below the current market rate in compensation for taking the original risk of placing the show in a crowded schedule before the willingness of an audience to watch it has been demonstrated.

Nevertheless, with a network contract in hand, a studio or, more likely, an independent producer can obtain additional financial support by borrowing from a bank, another lending institution, or investors' groups. Cash can also be obtained by selling in advance a program's anticipated syndication rights to distributors, who are generally in need of programs to fill their already established pipelines. Distributors will often obtain rights from a producer by guaranteeing a certain level of program sales, and they may also include cash advances as part of the guarantee. Such advances are then recouped by the distributor from the producer's initial share of program sales, with the distributor taking the risk that program sales will be sufficient to cover the outlay.

Still, after the initial run (and, presumably, rerun), the production company ends up owning the program and can do with it whatever it pleases. But the real payoff, if any, comes if the series can sustain competitive network ratings for at least three full seasons so that over 60 episodes (typically 22 per season) can be completed. The problem, of course, is that the probability of this occurring is relatively low; at best, about one in five new series survives the ratings wars that long.[36]

As for movies-of-the-week, first-run syndicated productions (i.e., programming designed for a non-network initial run), prime-time-access shows, and made-for-cable programs, financing is available from well-heeled television-program distribution companies (including, the television divisions of all major movie studios). For exclusive rights to such productions, a distributor will typically contribute part of the funding in return for profit participations and the opportunity to earn distribution fees.

Syndication agreements As already noted, should a series last three seasons on a network, it begins to have significant value for the syndication (used-film) market: Local television stations and cable systems can then obtain enough episodes to "strip" the program into scheduled daily runs over a period of at least several months.[37] Syndication-market licenses, which go to the highest local-station bidder, are conventionally for six consecutive runs of a series in a period of not more than five years and are now commonly for no longer than three years.[38]

A typical syndication agreement will provide that, out of the gross revenues collected, the syndication company will first deduct syndication fees, then deduct out-of-pocket expenses (including costs for shipping, advertising, and prints), and then recoup advances made to producers. Fees for syndication services (i.e., distribution fees) as a proportion of gross income are generally 15%–20% for net stripping sales, 30%–35% for domestic syndication, and 40%–50% for foreign syndication.

Table 4.10, based on syndications typical of a major movie studio, illustrates the profit potential for a distributor, and the similarity in structure to the aforementioned gross deal used in theatrical distribution of features. Operating margins for distributors of shows produced by others would normally average 30%, and for long-running self-produced programs around 40%.[39]

Television networks have historically relied on feature films and series to fill most of their prime-time hours. But since the early 1980s, *first-run* syndication has developed into an important means through which programming for independent (i.e., non-network affiliated) local television stations as well as network affiliates seeking to fill their prime-time access hours (i.e., the hours just before the network's evening schedule begins) can be obtained. First–run syndication, primarily of game, talk, or tabloid news shows, provides television stations with a relatively low-cost, disposable form of programming that is very immediate and that does not depend on or require a lengthy network run: The programming skips the network entirely and is syndicated to local stations onward from its first broadcast appearance.

Although an infinite number of variations can be devised to finance and distribute first-run programming, the primary requirement in launching a first-run program series is to have commitments from enough stations so that at least 65% to 70% of the national viewing audience can see the show. These commitments,

Table 4.10. *Network television program production and syndication: a structural example of successful program series, circa 1995*

Production

Network license fee covers 80%–85% of cash outlay.
Foreign sales may recoup remainder of cash outlay on 1-hour shows, but only half of remaining cash deficit on ½-hour shows.

Status on accrual basis including overhead and interest
  1-hour shows: 22 episodes/season
                      Cost per episode, $1.2 million
                      Accrued deficit per episode = $250,000
  ½-hour shows: 22 episodes/season
                      Cost per episode, $600,000
                      Accrued deficit per episode = $150,000

Syndication

Distribution fees: domestic 35%, foreign 50%

Assuming 100 episodes are available for syndication

1-hour shows:	Revenues per episode	
	Domestic	$325,000
	Foreign	250,000
		$575,000
	Minus:	
	Residuals, six runs	
	Domestic	65,000
	Foreign	25,000
	Production deficit	250,000
	Distribution costs[a]	65,000
	Studio profit[b]	$170,000
½-hour shows:	Revenues per episode	$1,000,000
	Minus:	
	Residuals, six runs	40,000
	Production deficit	150,000
	Distribution costs[a]	50,000
	Talent profit participations	200,000
	Studio profit[b]	$560,000

[a]Primarily promotion and distribution "bicycling."
[b]Profit would be split if show is independently produced, and does not take account of losses on shows that fail.

though, are normally made on the basis of pilots that are much less elaborately produced than are those for network series proposals. Also, unless a production is a proven ratings winner, it is unlikely that a station would make a syndication agreement that spans more than one year.[40]

Table 4.11. *Barter-syndication revenue estimate: an example*

Assume:	· 100 million tv households · average ratings of 5.0, i.e., 5 million homes viewing · percent of viewers in target demographic of 60% · a cost per thousand, or CPM of $9.00 for a 30-second spot

Then:	The estimated number of targeted viewers = 3 million
	  (i.e., 5 million times 0.60)
	the revenues per spot = $27,000
	  (i.e., 3,000 times $9.00)
	net revenues after deducting a 15% agency commission = $22,950
	barter revenue for 10 spots a week = $229,500
	cash license fee per week = $100,000
	total revenue per week = $329,500
	total syndicator revenues for 52-weeks = $17.65 millions*

Costs:	Production of 39-weeks at $125,000 a week = $4.9 million local marketing = $2.5 million distribution fees = 30% of revenues = $5.3 million
Profits:	$7.45 million*

*Available to be shared with producers and any other "back-end" participants.

Producers and distributors will generally, of course, prefer that stations pay cash for the rights to air the programs. But more often than not, the stations instead prefer to swap, or to barter, some of their advertising time-slots in return for broadcast rights. Such *barter syndication* arrangements, as discussed in more detail in Chapter 6, have grown rapidly into a $2 billion-a-year business that, on the margin, reduces revenues available to the networks.[41] Table 4.11 provides an example of how barter-syndication revenue for a particular program might be estimated. The sensitivity of the syndicator's profits to relatively small changes in ratings – and the degree of risk thus assumed by the syndicator – is notable.

The key accounting issue in barter syndication concerns the time at which barter revenues ought to be recognized. According to rulings by an FASB task force, such revenues should be recognized to the extent they are covered by noncancellable contracts (less an estimated value for "make-good" spots, i.e., adjustments for less-than-expected ratings), and at the point when a program is available for first telecast.[42]

Costs of production Networks attempt to keep their costs under control through tough negotiations on production contracts. The producer's problem is to then live within the budget constraints imposed by those contracts. That is often difficult, given the limited production time and the sharp union-mandated pay escalations for overtime work related to frequent rewriting and rehearsal.

As of the late 1990s, a prime-time one-hour network show required, on the average, up to seven days to shoot (several more to edit) and around $1.5 million to produce. But less popular shows with lower-paid performers might be made for perhaps 70% to 80% of that amount.[43]

For a long-running series, however, the fixed cost for sets, props, and general story concept decrease on a unit basis as more episodes are produced. Everything else then being equal, a series will, over time, become more profitable to make. But whether or not this is reflected in cost accounting depends on several additional factors.

First and foremost is the inclination of performers on a highly rated series to begin demanding much higher compensation per episode under threat of resignation. Per-episode compensation for stars can exceed $125,000 (e.g., up to $1 million in *Seinfeld*). And although most of the extra production cost can be passed on to the network through a higher license fee, there have been instances (e.g., *Three's Company*) in which performers' demands have been rejected.[44]

Another important determinant of reported profitability is the rate at which production costs are amortized. And this, to an extent, depends on the number of exhibition windows through which a program can be exploited.[45] Generally, as Owen and Wildman (1992, p. 48) have noted, the more windows, the higher the production budget that can be afforded.

Indeed, the theory plays out in practice whenever a producer-distributor begins to see series-syndication potential. At that point, the rate of cost amortization is reduced (i.e., amortization is stretched out over time), so that a portion of expenses can be charged against anticipated future syndication revenues. This treatment of amortization, of course, parallels that used in accounting for unamortized feature-film residuals as discussed in section 4.2.

In contrast, however, first-run production and syndication are relatively attractive to show producers and syndicators because the production costs of such shows are normally much below those of network series, and because the returns from syndication of a successful first-run series materialize much sooner than with syndicated off-network programs. Whereas it might cost well over half a million dollars to produce a typical half-hour network comedy series, a first-run half-hour might cost two-thirds as much. And a week's worth of half-hour game shows (five) can be produced for under a quarter million dollars.[46]

As for what are known as made-for-television movies ("made-fors"), or equivalently, movies-of-the-week (MOWs), the production cost considerations more resemble those of a standard filmed television series episode than those of a full-blown theatrical feature. As of the mid-1990s, for instance, most two-hour MOWs were being produced at a cost of approximately $3 million. With network license fees perhaps covering up to 85% of the cost, and with foreign sales and syndication bringing additional revenues, MOW productions can often turn an immediate yet modest profit.[47]

Costs and problems of distribution Distribution costs for television programming include sales-office overhead, travel, and the important variables of participant residual payments. Indeed, differences in residual payment schedules for broadcast as compared to cable network syndication often dictate syndication marketing

Table 4.12. *Program syndication expenditures estimates, 1984–96*

Year	Total station[a] syndication expenditures[a,c] ($ million)	Barter-syndication[b] revenues ($ millions)
1984	1,026	450
1985	1,168	550
1986	1,330	650
1987	1,515	775
1988	1,680	875
1989	1,785	1,050
1990	1,864	1,200
1991	1,850	1,275
1992	1,830	1,345
1993	1,925	1,500
1994	2,020	1,650
1995	2,120	1,800
1996	2,220	1,875

Source[a]: Association of Independent Television Stations (INTV), *Estimated TV Syndication Expenditures, 1975–1990,* December 1985, Wilkofsky Gruen Associates.
[b]Advertiser Syndicated Television Association.
[c]Affiliates normally account for one third, and independents two-thirds of the total.

decisions.[48] But, in addition, there may also be expenses for retitling episodes, for possible dubbing into other languages, and for printmaking – which taken together can become significant.[49]

As can be seen from Table 4.12, syndication expenditures have grown substantially, as both independent and network-affiliated stations have come to depend on programming provided by syndication companies through combinations of cash and time-barter arrangements. Inevitably, the same types of arrangements will also become quite common as European, Asian, and Latin American commercial television markets develop.

Still, in the 1990s, the greatest changes in program distribution relationships have come as a result of modifications to the government's so-called financial interest and syndication ("fin-syn") rules that had barred television networks from owning any syndication interests in shows that they broadcast and that had placed limits on the number of program hours that a network can self-produce.[50] These rules had originally been promulgated in the 1970s to open a way for many independent producers to flourish and to prevent program domination by the three major networks – who, up to that time, owned and produced many of the shows they aired.[51]

In fact, however, many independents have not flourished. And given the sizable risks and capital investments entailed in the development of television programs, production and distribution have become largely consolidated into the hands of the major movie studios and other media companies with deep pockets. The former dominance of the networks has, in the meantime, been eroded by collectively severe competition from cable, independent television stations, and other home-viewing options.

Relaxation of the restrictions on network participation in foreign syndication and ownership of financial interests was first approved by the FCC in April 1991. And removal of most other restrictions was indicated in 1993 – thus opening the way for networks to obtain a significant second source of income through sales of self-produced entertainment programming, and for studios and broadcast networks to be merged.[52]

Timing troubles Whenever a distributor owns a program series, revenues and earnings are recognized when the series is made available to stations – a practice identical with that established for feature-film licenses.[53] But for series in which only distribution services are being rendered, distribution fees would normally be recognized as being earned period-by-period as the episodes are played out and as cash payments are accordingly received.[54]

Producers, distributor-syndicators, and individual profit participants all have different claims on the television-license income stream, and individuals or corporations may simultaneously function in one or in several of these roles. Also, much as on the theatrical side, differences in perspective may often lead to great controversies and to audits. Disputes may occur because the timing of the disbursements and the profits recognized by one participant in a series project may be vastly different from the timing and profits received by another.

Illustrative cases, as discussed in a segment of the CBS show *60 Minutes* (December 7, 1980) and in a *TV Guide* story (Swertlow, 1982), have involved actors Fess Parker of the *Daniel Boone* series, produced by Twentieth Century Fox, and James Garner of the Universal series *Rockford Files*. These stars, who had contracted for deferred profit-participation points in addition to or in lieu of greater immediate salary, asserted that the distributors had earned substantial profits totaling many millions of dollars, whereas they had yet to receive any profit on participants' shares.

Parker sued Fox for $48 million, claiming that the one-hour series that ran in prime time for six years on NBC moved into successful syndication and grossed $40 million. Garner claimed that his long-running network series grossed over $52 million from both domestic and foreign sales. How, they asked, is it possible for these series to be reported as unprofitable?

The answer lies in the definition of ''profits'' used in the contracts. Just as in feature-film participations, a few rare talents may bargain for and be powerful enough to command high fees plus a percentage of gross revenues. Some others may bargain for a high salary and be entitled to only a small (or no) percentage of narrowly defined ''profits.'' And most others are not participants at all; they are fortunate simply to get a job at minimum scale.

Table 4.13. *Summary profit accounting for the television series participant; an example*

Studio's self-produced series (over five years)

Revenues ($ million):

Network payments for production	50.0
10% selling fee (program to network)	5.0
40% syndication distribution fee (125 episodes at $200,000 per)	10.0
40% foreign-sales distribution fee	5.0
Interest and other	3.0
Total	73.0

Expenses ($ million):

Production costs (including overhead)	65.0
Direct distribution costs	2.0
Residuals and other	6.0
Total	73.0
Studio profit before taxes	0.0

Take, for example, a hypothetical situation described by Robert Leeper, a former executive at Universal and Fox, in the *TV Guide* story:

A studio claims a production cost of $10 million for the first year of a one-hour series . . . 70 percent of those are hard, or actual costs for such items as sets, lights and film – but the remaining 30 percent includes studio charges for overhead such as the studio's parking lots and offices.

If the network carrying the $10 million show pays $8 million for the series the first year, then the series has lost $2 million for the year. If the series is a hit and runs for five years on that basis, it means that on the book, technically, the hit series has lost $10 million in production costs alone. There are other charges too. The studio also gives itself 10 percent as a commission for "selling" the series to the network. That's $800,000 a year – an additional $4 million in costs over five years, plunging the series $14 million in the hole on the books. The studio then charges the show interest on these losses. Say that, over the five years, with a fluctuating prime rate, the interest has amounted to $2.2 million. The series is now $16.2 million in the red.

. . . now, the 125 episodes produced over the five years are sold for a total of $100,000 per episode – a grand total of $12.5 million. The profit participant may think that the series' deficit has now been reduced to $3.7 million, and that he is on the verge of turning a profit. Wrong. Forty percent of the syndication revenue is lost to the distribution fee – the money the studio gives itself for selling the show to stations buying the reruns. In this case, that's $5 million. The remaining $7.5 million is then deducted, leaving the series $8.7 million in the red. The studio then charges the series what are called "actual costs" for distributing the series to syndication. They include costs for editing, making prints and negatives, costs for shipping the series to stations buying the reruns. These "actual costs" may amount to another $1.3 million. So our one-hour series is still $10 million in the red. (Reprinted with permission from *TV Guide* magazine, copyright 1982 by Triangle Publications, Inc., Radnor, Pennsylvania.)

Despite the deficit reported to participants, does the studio make a profit? The answer, in the case of a long-running series, is a qualified yes if it is indeed assumed that ''soft'' costs (which help to absorb the general overhead costs of running a studio) are embedded in the total production cost figure, if it is understood that the studio is in business to make a profit out of renting its distribution capability (and thus make a profit on the distribution fees charged), and if it is recognized that the studio tends to receive its cash payments a lot faster than do the participants – who might only see a summary accounting such as that shown in Table 4.13.[55]

Studios do not deny that production and distribution of series can be profitable for them even while the statements of individual participants indicate losses. But again, as in feature films, the difference is that the studio places some operating capital at risk with its investments in plant and equipment, sales offices, and other assets required to run the business over the long term. On the other hand, participants are normally paid handsome salaries for their services, and they do not incur such risks.

4.5 Weak links in the chain

Well-publicized financial-accounting disputes in movies and television support an impression that dishonesty and cheating are rampant in entertainment industries. And keen news-media coverage catering to the high level of public interest in industry affairs tends to magnify whatever problems exist. But just as in other segments of the economy, the great majority of individuals and companies in entertainment conduct their businesses ethically. Indeed, because creation of entertainment products is such a people-intensive process, success may depend as much on esteem and trust as on ability.

To guard against improper conduct, however, it is necessary to know where ''leakages'' in the revenue stream are most likely to occur. In this section we shall consider how and where people might cheat.[56]

Exhibitors: the beginning and the end

Customers' cash payments at the box office represent both the beginning of a chain of remittances and the end of a long creative manufacturing process – with a single, simple idea for a movie eventually generating hundreds of pounds of legal paperwork and hundreds of thousands of feet of processed film.

Because the precise terms of distributor-exhibitor contracts are rarely made known to anyone not party to the agreements, both exhibitors and distributors can, for publicity purposes, sometimes distort the true size of the box-office gross.[57] In this way, a small picture can for a brief while be made to look like a modest hit, and a modest hit may be proclaimed a virtual blockbuster.

On the next level of the cash stream's cascade, the exhibitor's house expense (nut) is a negotiated item that can be inflated to ensure a profit to the exhibitor.

In fact, a given theater may simultaneously have different house-expense understandings with different distributors. The degree of this inflation can be the result of long-standing tacit agreements, or it may be subject to momentary relative bargaining strength. Either way, though, the size of the nut ultimately affects the grosses (rentals) received by the distributor and thus the incomes of other parties downstream. The incomes of those parties would, of course, also be reduced if theater owners pay their bills slowly or if there are significant "adjustments" to the allowances for co-op advertising.

Ticket-pricing policies, however, would generally have the greatest effect on what the downstream participants might ultimately receive. Pricing is subject to local competitive conditions, moviegoer-demand schedules, and the exhibitor's interest in making as much as possible from concession sales. Exhibitors who attempt to promote concession sales by setting low admissions prices are in effect diverting and thereby diminishing monies available for downstream disbursements. To prevent abuses in this area, distributors occasionally write contracts specifying minimum per-capita ticket prices (see section 3.4).

Playing the "float" (i.e., the time value of money) is another endemic industry problem. This is somewhat surprising because box-office income is almost always in cash and, in theory, exhibitors should have absolutely no difficulty in paying rentals immediately due. Moreover, because theater owners normally have an interest in playing a distributor's next film, large distributors have important leverage to encourage prompt remittances. Nevertheless, in practice, playing the float appears at all levels of the industry, and at high interest rates it has a significant cumulative adverse effect on profit participants.[58]

Outright fraud occurs if exhibitors and distributors cooperate to falsely claim national advertising when the advertising is characteristically local. In such situations, national advertising is charged to the producer's share, leaving the exhibitor and distributor a larger profit. It is also sometimes possible for an unscrupulous exhibitor to obtain false invoices for more local advertising (paid on a co-op basis by the distributor) than is actually placed in local papers. Exhibitors might also conveniently forget to inform distributors that after a certain amount of newspaper lineage is placed, a quantity rebate is obtained.

Other unscrupulous practices that can be used to skim rentals properly belonging to the distributor include the following:

Bicycling (i.e., using a single print, without authorization by the exhibition contract, to generate "free" revenues by showing it at more than one location owned by the same management). In multiscreen theaters, for example, a picture that is not playing to capacity might, in violation of day and date (simultaneity) contract terms, be replaced in some showings by another feature that is unauthorized but more popular.

Running the film for an extra showing unauthorized by contract.

Palming tickets (i.e., leaving the ticket untorn and recycling it to the box office, where it can be resold without disturbing the number sequence of the ticket roll).

Changing the ticket roll after a few hundred tickets have been sold. Ticket sales on the substituted roll then go unreported.
Unauthorized reprinting of the negative. Nowadays this includes felonious reproduction of home videotape cassettes, which can result in significant loss of revenues.[59]
"Product-splitting" practices (discussed in section 3.4) that reduce bidding competitiveness and, in turn, the percentage of box office received by distributors.

In addition, distributors might also join with exhibitors in certain actions that further deprive producers and other participants of income that would otherwise be theirs. For instance, this might occur in the area of distributor-exhibitor *settlements* – renegotiations of terms for pictures that do not perform according to expectations.[60]

Distributor-producer problems

As we have seen, the income of profit participants is affected by charges for studio overhead, by publicity and other marketing fees charged for in-house departments, and by deductibles from producer's share that may include dubbing, editing, checking distributor receipts, copyrighting, screenings, censorship clearances, trailer preparation, insurance, tariffs, trade-association dues, print examinations, and print junking costs. If participant contracts are not carefully negotiated, the extent to which these charges are applied in any project is sometimes a source of dispute.

Major profit participants, such as leading performers, can also adversely affect the interests of other participants. For instance, this occurs when special antique furnishings, wardrobes, houses, or cars originally bought for a film are given to performers for personal use after production is completed.

Another version of this occurs when films are being shot in countries that have blocked currency remittances because of foreign-exchange controls. In these instances, it is not uncommon for family and friends of important actors to receive free trips to exotic film locales. Blocked currency earned within a country must be spent within the country of origin.[61]

As already indicated, there is inordinate potential for controversy in allocations of television-license fees, cross-collateralization deals, and studios' accounting for foreign taxes, which may be charged to a picture even though the parent company later receives a credit against U.S. taxes. Also, accounting for remittances from foreign-based sources may be especially difficult because auditing privileges may be contractually restricted to books based in the United States, foreign-exchange rates may be rounded off in favor of the distributor, and foreign collections may be unusually slow.

Producers may attempt to avoid entanglement in these issues by making their own arrangements for independent foreign distribution. This is often done most efficiently by contracting with experienced overseas foreign sales companies, whose service fees are generally in the range of 10%–15% of revenues collected and are subject to the right of recoupment of direct-sales costs if the film's gross is insufficient.[62]

4.6 Concluding remarks

The essential strength of the major film studios has been derived from their ability to control distribution from the early financing stages to the timing of theatrical release. But developments in technology are always presenting new challenges and growth opportunities for industry participants.

Such opportunities will allow many smaller companies to carve out profitable niches for themselves. Yet ultimately, the enormous amount of capital required to operate film and television program production and distribution facilities on a global basis presents a significant barrier to entry and reinforces the trend toward vertical integration of the industry. Moreover, because the costs of production are what financial economists call *"sunk costs"* – i.e., most of the expenditure to create a product is invested upfront, and incremental expenditures are thereafter relatively modest – it makes sense for a production to be exposed in as many windows of exhibition – from home video to pay cable to free television – as possible.

That is not necessarily to imply, however, that the emergence of new media markets has eliminated downside risk, or that a flood of eager new entrants will not drive down investment returns for the industry as a whole, or that product-appeal cycles have disappeared. These elements are a part of this business, just as they are for any other.

Although it is too soon to know whether recent industry consolidation trends will prove viable over the longer run, it is clear that the financial-economic structure of the movie and television production and distribution industry is fast becoming more complex and, as such, is providing a more interesting and potentially more profitable arena for investors.

Selected additional reading

Abelson, R. (1996). "The Shell Game of Hollywood 'Net Profits'," *New York Times,* March 4.

Abrams, B. (1984). "Why TV Producers Flock to New York to Just Sit and Fret," *Wall Street Journal,* May 7.

Barnes, P. W. (1987). "How King World Reaps Riches, Fame as a TV Syndicator," *Wall Street Journal,* June 9.

Chambers, E. (1986). *Producing TV Movies.* New York: Prentice–Hall.

"First-Run Syndicators Tune in on TV's Big Bucks," *Business Week* No. 2841 (May 7, 1984):78.

Gottschalk, E. C., Jr. (1972). "Film Makers Struggle with Major Studios for 'Creative' Control," *Wall Street Journal,* December 29.

(1978). "Feud in Filmdom: Movie Studios' System of Splitting Profits Divides Hollywood," *Wall Street Journal,* October 16.

Harris, K. (1991). "Feeding Frenzy," *Forbes* 147(7)(April 1):45.

Harmetz, A. (1987). "Now Lawyers Are Hollywood Superstars," *The New York Times*, January 11.

Harwood, J. (1985). "Hollywood Exposing More of Its Ledgers," *Variety*, March 13.

Kopelson, A. (1985). "Presales of Independently Produced Motion Pictures," *The Hollywood Reporter*, March 5.

Landro, L. (1985). "Overseas Distributor Takes on Big Studios by Doing Own Films," *Wall Street Journal*, April 16.

"Lenders Laughing All The Way to the Bank," *Daily Variety*, March 11, 1985.

Litwak, M. (1994). *Dealmaking in the Film & Television Industries*. Los Angeles: Silman-James.

Mariet, F. (1990). "La Télévision Américaine: Médias, Marketing et Publicité," Paris: Economica.

Mayer, J. (1991). "Hollywood Mystery: Woes at Orion Stayed Invisible for Years," *Wall Street Journal*, October 16.

Meyer, M., and Viera, J. D., eds. (1984). *1984 Entertainment, Publishing and the Arts Handbook*. New York: Clark Boardman.

Morgenstern, S., ed. (1979). *Inside the TV Business*. New York: Sterling.

Price Waterhouse & Co. (1974). *Accounting for the Motion Picture Industry*. New York: Price Waterhouse.

Rose, F. (1991). "The Case of the Ankling Agents," *Premiere* 4(12) (August).

——— (1995). *The Agency: The William Morris Agency and the Hidden History of Show Business*. New York:HarperBusiness.

Sansweet, S. J. (1983). "Even with a Hit Film, a Share of the Profits May Be Nothing at All," *Wall Street Journal*, July 21.

Scholl, J. (1986). "Bad Show: Picture Dims for Syndicators of TV Programs," *Barron's*, December 15.

Schuyten, P. (1976). "How MCA Rediscovered Movieland's Golden Lode," *Fortune* XCIV(5)(November):122.

Sherman, S. P. (1985). "Hollywood's Foxiest Financier," *Fortune* 111(1)(January 7):92.

Stevens, A. (1993). "Court Allows Movie Industry Big Tax Benefit," *Wall Street Journal*, July 20.

Trachtenberg, J. A. (1985). "The Other Green Revolution," *Forbes* 135(7)(April 8):101.

Turner, R. (1989). "For TV Comedy Writers, the Money Grows Serious," *Wall Street Journal*, August 2.

Turner, R. and King, T. R. (1994). "Movie Makers Find that Rights to Films Overseas Often Pay Off," *Wall Street Journal*, November 22.

Weinstein, M. (1998). "Profit Sharing Contracts in Hollywood: Evolution and Analysis," *Journal of Legal Studies*, (January).

5
Music

Life in the fast lane's no fun if you're running out of gas.

That is exactly what people in the music business discovered toward the end of the 1970s, when after three uninterrupted decades of expansion, recorded-music sales stopped growing. The 1980s, though, were another story.

Recorded music generates aggregate worldwide revenues of some $40 billion per year.[1] But because it is the most easily personalized and accessible form of entertainment, it readily pervades virtually every culture and every level of society. As such, it may be considered as the most fundamental of the entertainment businesses.

5.1 Feeling groovy

Experimentation with reproduction of moving images can be traced back into the early 1800s. But, apparently, there was little interest in the mechanical reproduction of sound until the venerable Thomas Edison in 1877 developed yet another of his novelty items – a tinfoil-wrapped cylinder that was rotated with a handle. While he cranked the handle and recited the nursery rhyme "Mary Had a Little Lamb" into a recording horn, Edison's voice vibrated a diaphragm to which a metal stylus was attached. The stylus then cut grooves on the surface of the tinfoil and – Voilà! When the procedure was reversed, the stylus caused the diaphragm to vibrate and the amplified recorded sounds to emanate.

Although early investors indeed tried to popularize the invention through demonstrations in concert halls, country fairs, and vaudeville theaters, the scratchy sound and limited number of times the foil could be used before it deteriorated discouraged enthusiasm for Edison's "phonograph." So it was not until other inventors (including Alexander Graham Bell) got into the act and improved the original phonograph by using a wax-coated cardboard tube over the cylinder, and until electric power was added, that the popularly called "talking machine" (and also forerunner of the jukebox) finally caught on.

At that stage, people would actually go to a parlor and pay a nickel to listen to these wax cylinders reproduce songs and comic monologues. And ludicrous as it now seems, "a brass band recording a two-minute march had to play that march over and over again, perfectly, to turn out hundreds of recordings."[2]

But already, by the 1890s, home phonographs had begun to appear. By then, a German immigrant, Emile Berliner, had developed a prototype that cut recording grooves onto discs – a modification that within 10 years led to the introduction of the gramophone or the "Victrola" by the Victor Talking Machine Company.

Technological development, this time of radio and of an electrical recording process, led to further sound reproduction improvements and also to conflicts among competing interest groups. Composers encountered tremendous resistance when they tried to collect royalties for performances of their music. And radio station owners insisted that once they had bought a recording, it was theirs to use without any further financial obligation to composers.[3] Indeed, throughout the 1920s, but especially in the early half of that decade, it was radio, not phonograph equipment, that experienced the greatest rise in demand.

The Great Depression triggered a collapse of record sales – from $75 million in 1929 to only $5 million in 1933 – and it was not until the late 1930s that recovery became evident. That recovery, however, was hindered by World War II and by a protracted musicians' union strike that prevented the manufacture of new records for over a year.[4] By 1945, industry sales were thus still only $109 million.

Postwar development of tape recordings, which replaced inefficient wax-blank masters, and introduction of the 12-inch long-playing (LP) vinyl record by Columbia Records in 1948 then initiated a tremendous wave of growth. But the new LPs, played at 33⅓ revolutions per minute (rpm), could hold only 23 minutes of music per side and did not clearly win out over older 45 rpm and 78 rpm configurations until the late 1950s – when industry sales first exceeded $500 million. Yet, the 1950s were also a time of innovation. New low-cost recording equipment made it possible for many small independent companies to spring up in competition with RCA, Columbia, and Decca – the long–established majors of the time.[5] The independents were the catalysts in bringing traditional jazz, Southern rhythm and blues, and gospel-based music styles into the American mainstream.

However, it was not until the mid-to-late 1960s that the business truly exploded, with the universal introduction of truer-to-life hi-fi stereo sound recordings at a

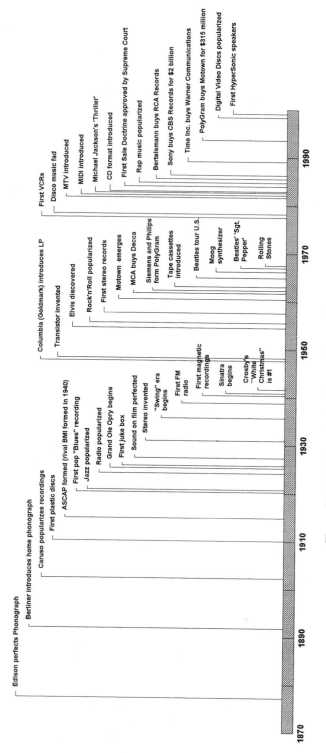

Figure 5.1. Milestones in the history of recorded music, 1870–2000.

time when the postwar baby boomers, then teenagers with lots of money to spend, were becoming ever more attracted to the expanding rock 'n' roll genre. The sixties were also a time in which the record business, paralleling the development of the film business some 30 years earlier, consolidated distribution (and the ownership of "independent" labels) into the hands of a few corporate giants that included RCA, CBS, Warner Communications, and PolyGram. This high-growth phase lasted through the 1970s and was given a powerful boost by the introduction of the standardized portable audiotape cassette configuration. By the late 1970s, industry sales at retail list prices hovered at the $4 billion level.

Yet, not all was well with the industry as it entered the 1980s in the fast lane and then promptly ran out of gas. A somewhat older population base with a diminished interest in the new recordings of the time, coupled with poor quality control of vinyl pressings, contributed to a noticeable decline in demand that was not to be reversed until the arrival of the compact (4.7-inch) disc (CD) configuration in 1983. Such digitally (computer) encoded and optically (laser beam) decoded discs provided consumers with distortion-free sound reproduction and with good reasons to again buy music. Indeed, by the early 1990s, CDs had become predominant and vinyl nearly extinct, while U.S. industry sales soared to $7 billion.

CDs, in standardized versions for use in audio, video, and personal computer applications are expected to be the main configuration until the early part of the twenty–first century, when the DVD (digital versatile disc) will likely become dominant.[6] Figure 5.1 displays key events in the history of the recorded music business.

5.2 Size and structure

Economic interplay

The American scene The United States has long accounted for a major portion of the world's recorded music business, both as a place of origination of new music trends and as a consumer of music products. Yet despite rapid growth of consumption in the rest of the world, and in developing countries in particular, the United States still absorbs (in dollar terms) about 30% of all the recorded music produced. Moreover, the structure of the business everywhere largely follows that which has been developed in North America and which is illustrated in Figure 5.2. This structure has evolved as a result of the need to efficiently compensate authors, composers, publishers, and performing artists for their work in creating the final product – be it a jingle, song, album, or opera.

First looking at the market in the United States, it can be seen from Figure 5.3 and Supplementary Table S5.2 that the demand for recorded music has tended to fluctuate cyclically and with some sensitivity to general economic trends. Although average annual growth in unit terms has averaged about 3.2% (and in dollar terms 7.6%) over the 23 years beginning in 1973, growth in recessionary periods has been notably below average. Typically, consumer spending on music

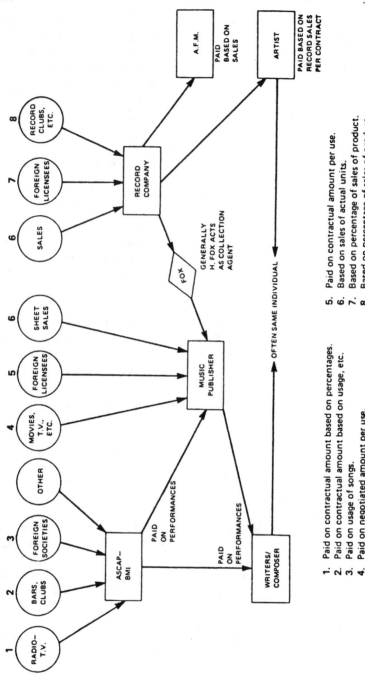

Figure 5.2. Music income flow in the entertainment field. *Source:* Arthur Young & Co. (prepared by E. Cook)

1. Paid on contractual amount based on percentages.
2. Paid on contractual amount based on usage, etc.
3. Paid on usage of songs.
4. Paid on negotiated amount per use.
5. Paid on contractual amount per use.
6. Based on sales of actual units.
7. Based on percentage of sales of product.
8. Based on percentage of sales of product.

appears to peak at, or just after, a peak of economic activity and to trough a few months after the overall economy does. Also, the secular influence of new sound carrier format introductions such as cassettes in 1973 and compact discs in 1983 can be clearly seen.

The experience in the United States and Canada since World War II suggests that development of a strong and rapidly growing market for recorded music requires the conjunction of several elements. First and foremost is an expanding teenage/young adult population within a thriving middle class. Then it is essential that there be national advertising media in which large and cost-efficient marketing campaigns can be placed. Of course, retail outlets ought to be plentiful and well stocked. And it also helps to have steady price and performance improvements in audio hardware and recording technologies.

All of these elements were present in the postwar period in North America and, not surprisingly, the recorded music business grew from $100 million to almost $6 billion in domestic (U.S.) retail sales in the space of 40 years. Because many of the same factors were present in other developed countries, sales of recorded music outside the United States have grown similarly.[7]

But changes in the system of distributing music products also had an important effect on the industry's sales. Until the late 1970s, records were essentially distributed on consignment – with unsold units returnable for full (or nearly full) credit against new albums. This meant that many stores could be opened on shoestring capitalizations and could pay their bills with ''plastic'' (i.e., returned records) instead of cash. Ultimately, however, as unit demand growth slowed and the major distributors sharply curtailed their returns policies, retailers were for the first time faced with a significant inventory risk. Retailers accordingly became much more cautious and selective in their purchases. And that, in turn, made manufacturers and distributors less willing to risk large sums on unproven new artists.

In addition, success up to the mid-1970s led to excess, as budgets and costs spiralled out of control, mostly in the areas of artists' royalty guarantees and marketing. Indeed, even the largest companies subsequently found that their stars could not consistently assure the ever-increasing ''megaton'' record shipments needed to underwrite large royalty advances.

Fortunately, by 1983, the advance of technology once again – as it had so often before – bailed the industry out of its funk. The catalyst this time was the development of low-cost, high-speed microprocessor and memory devices: In brief, the era of cheap computing power had arrived. And with this power came the ability to digitize sound – that is, to reduce sound to equivalent numerical data through frequent sampling and processing. As a result, undesired noises could be eliminated and a marked improvement in sound fidelity could be brought to the mass market in the form of inexpensively manufactured compact discs. Introduction of music synthesizers, computers capable of producing and mixing sounds in a manner not possible with traditional instruments, also followed quickly.[8]

The emergence of MTV, the new rock-music cable channel started in 1981 was significant as well in reversing the early 1980s downturn in demand for

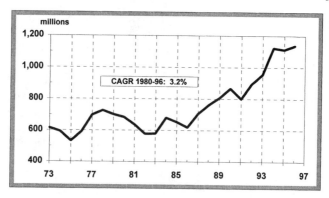

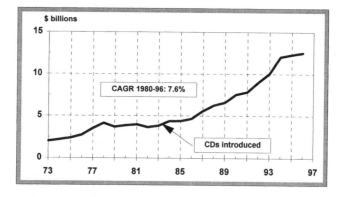

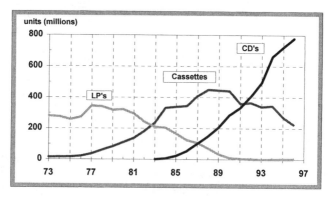

Figure 5.3. Trends in the American recorded music market, 1973–96. (a) Manufacturers' shipments in units; (b) shipments in dollars (at suggested list prices); (c) unit sales
by configuration. *Source:* RIAA.

recorded music. By 1984, MTV had gained wide distribution and influence as both a promotional platform for record labels and as a distinctive programming service.[9]

The global scene As nations emerge from under repressive or dysfunctional economic structures and then see discretionary incomes rise rapidly, one of the first areas to benefit is music – which is relatively low in cost to enjoy, yet highly personalizable. But although demand for music products is everywhere affected by the demographic, economic, and technological factors already discussed, development of local repertoire is now another important part of the international sales and marketing mix: Recordings of artists with a global following may account for only two-thirds of the total.

From Figure 5.4a it can also be seen that global sales as represented in dollar list prices at the retail level have grown at a compound average annual rate of over 13.5% since the mid-1980s, but that *unit* sales over the same span have grown at a rate of only 4.8%.[10] It would thus seem that price increases related to the migration of consumers toward higher-priced (but better-quality) sound-carrier formats has boosted total sales growth. However, per capita unit demand in the seven largest markets outside the U.S. (Figure 5.4b) had long been flat, which is possibly a consequence of the relatively older population skews in those countries.

Composing, publishing, and management

The process of creating a musical property and of then exploiting it is in many ways similar to property development and exploitation in movies. In both areas, relative bargaining power is a key element. An important difference, however, is that in music an enterprise can be launched with fewer people and with far smaller commitments of capital.

A new composer has several avenues through which work may begin to generate revenues, but the first step is usually publication. The composer can attempt to interest an existing publisher or can establish a new publishing firm. In any case, the normal arrangement is for publisher and composer to share evenly any income from their joint venture.

The publisher's role is to monitor and promote use of the music through sheet-music sales ("paper" houses specialize in this) and, more importantly, through live performances and recordings. At each step, royalty income, which may have to be further shared by subpublishers and coauthors, is derived. For a new artist-composer, contract terms are fairly well standardized, but for a recognized talent, many complex variations depending on tax, managerial, and other considerations are negotiated. There are tens of thousands of publishers and self-publishers in the United States, but the business is dominated by the publishing affiliates (Warner/Chappell, EMI, MCA, and BMG) of the major worldwide record distributors.

The services of lawyers and accountants are required in most stages of a com-

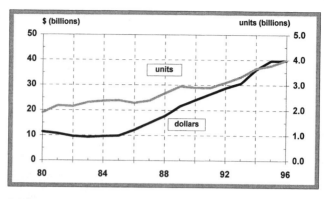

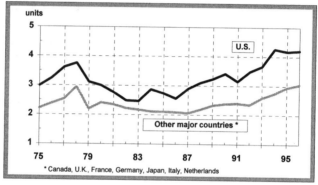

Figure 5.4. The global music market, (a) Worldwide recorded music sales in units and in retail dollars, 1980–96; (b) per capita unit sales in the eight largest markets, 1975–96. *Source:* IFPI.

poser's career, but if the composer is also a performing artist, as is increasingly common, any degree of success will entail the hiring of a manager and an agent to book concerts, television appearances, and recording schedules. Managers will generally take between 15% and 30% of a performer's income and talent agents 10%. For a new artist-composer, the functions of manager, legal advisor, and talent agent may be handled by a single individual.[11]

Royalty streams

Performances Assuming that a "demo" (demonstration) record or tape has attracted a publisher's interest, the next step is to work on a full-fledged recorded performance by the composer or to attract the interest of other performers in cutting a so-called cover record of the material. Publishers and performers are always on the lookout for good, fresh material, but only a small fraction of what is offered is accepted, and only a small fraction of what is accepted for publication succeeds in the marketplace. Of hundreds of new works introduced each week, on average not more than 5 to 10 seem to have any chance of receiving widespread recognition.

Whether the music is performed by orchestras, by college bands at football games, by radio stations, by nightclub singers, or by Muzak® speakers in elevators, it is entitled to performance royalties that are collected by two major agencies (and one smaller agency) in the United States. Of the two majors, the oldest and by far the largest in terms of billings is the American Society of Composers, Authors, and Publishers (ASCAP), but the larger, as measured by number of "affiliates," is Broadcast Music Incorporated (BMI). These two agencies combined collect over 95% of all U.S. performance royalties, with the Society of European Stage Authors and Composers (SESAC) receiving the remainder. All three organizations are protectors of composers' rights.

Because about 60% of performance royalties are derived from use in television, radio, and films, the major agencies have accordingly developed extensive computerized logging and sampling procedures to assure that composers receive proper remuneration for performances of their works anywhere in the world. To accomplish this, agencies in other countries cooperate with ASCAP, BMI, and SESAC.

The formulas used to determine royalty rates depend on the frequency of use and length of time the music is used, the estimated size of the listening audience, and other factors. For example, classical compositions are accorded more weight than popular jingles. Greater weighting compensates for the relatively greater expenditure of effort in classical composition and for the probable smaller size of audience and lesser frequency of play.

However, the sizes of royalties and the ways in which licenses should be granted to television and radio stations (i.e., blanket vs. specific performances) have often been subject to proposed legislative changes.[12]

Mechanical royalties Under so-called compulsory licenses, these royalties are derived from publication in sheet-music form (normally at a rate between 3% and 10% of retail price per copy in the United States) and from sales of recordings. But of the two sources, recordings are much more important. As of 1997, the rate for each recorded copy of a song was raised to the larger of 6.95 cents for a length of five minutes or less, with 1.3 cents charged for each additional minute or fraction thereof.

To keep pace with changing marketplace conditions, mechanicals are subject to upward revision overtime and are negotiated by the interested parties, or may go to arbitration by the Copyright Arbitration Royalty Panel (CARP).[13] Publishers generally split such royalties 50:50 with new writers and 25:75 (or 20:80) with more established composers. These royalties are taken after deduction of a 4½% collection charge by the Harry Fox Agency in the United States and the Canadian Mechanical Rights Reproduction Agency (CMRRA) in Canada, which charges 5%.

Synchronization fees In addition to paying a performance fee, anyone using music in films requires a synchronization license, which is a license to use music that is timed to the display of visual images. These royalties are individually negotiated by the various parties, but they are normally based on established standards for music length, potential audience, and frequency of use. In radio commercials, similar user fees are gathered from the granting of transcription licenses.

Publishers' synchronization and mechanical fees usually are collected from film and record companies by the Harry Fox Agency, which is a wholly owned subsidiary of the National Music Publishers Association. This agency licenses copyrights for commercial recordings, audits the books of record manufacturers, licenses music used in television and movie productions and commercials, and licenses background music used in public places.

Copyright The aforementioned royalty streams, including license fees from juke-box and other uses (e.g., wired music services such as Muzak®), were adjusted by Congress in a 1976 revision of the original, but technologically outdated, 1909 copyright law. The 1976 law grants copyright owners of a musical composition the exclusive right to be the first to record and distribute (or to assign to someone else) recordings embodying that composition.[14]

The Copyright Arbitration Royalty Panel meets to arbitrate disputes and to make adjustments for the effects of technological developments. Predictably, many such changes will, over time, alter allocation formulas for the industry's income.[15]

Another issue of particular importance in the rental of videocassettes involves the doctrine of "first-sale" rights – rights that allow the person or company initially purchasing a product to resell or rent that product to other parties without further obligation or compensation to the original seller.[16] Because of first-sale rights, producers do not receive compensation each time a videocassette is rented; they are compensated only on the first sale to the rental stores.[17]

In all, copyrights, and the protection of intellectual properties from counterfeiting and piracy, have played an important role in the growth of the music and home-video businesses. But royalty income losses remain substantial in many less-developed areas of the world.

Guilds and unions

The effects of labor-union contracts, primarily those of the American Federation of Television and Radio Artists (AFTRA) and the American Federation of Musicians (AFM), extend to every area of the music-making business. Singers, soloists, and choral ensembles are generally represented by AFTRA, whereas other musicians, including conductors, arrangers, copyists, and instrumentalists, are members of the AFM. However, opera, ballet, and classical concert and recital performances may be covered by the American Guild of Musical Artists (AGMA), and other representations may be made through the Actors Equity Association or the Screen Actors Guild. The New York Dramatists Guild is a trade association representing lyricists, composers, and writers for the Broadway musical theater (see also Chapter 12).

As in any other industry, labor unions help their employed membership by bargaining for higher wages and pension benefits. But it can also be argued that if it were not for the high production costs inherent in using union performers, there might be many more productions in which musicians could find work, albeit at lower average wages. It is not unusual for new artists and new record companies to attempt to circumvent the use of union labor, or for background-music recordings to be made in Europe, where labor costs are much lower.

Both AFTRA and AFM have tried to maintain strict union shops, but right-to-work laws in various states have reduced union influence, especially in the rock, country, and R&B segments. However, if a record master copy is transferred from a nonunion independent producer to a record company that is party to AFM agreements (which most record companies of any significance are), then union control over wages is reasserted. This control also appears in areas such as voice overdubbing, a situation in which a union contractor will charge a producer for an additional voice even though it is only electronically mixed.

Royalty artists, who are entitled to AFTRA scale plus royalties based on the number of records sold, must also conform to union-negotiated rules. And for musicians who participate in making broadcast commercial spots, there are, of course, extended repetitive payments. Whenever an AFTRA member performs on tape for one medium and that tape is used in another medium, the performer receives additional payments.

Concerts and theaters

Concerts by popular performers (in which an advance against a percentage of anticipated gate receipts may be obtained) may be profitable for their organizers if they are skillfully budgeted and planned. Most of the time, however, the purpose of a concert tour is to provide artists' exposure that can leverage sales of records and other licensed merchandise.[18]

Even less likely to turn a profit are theater presentations on Broadway, summer musical theater, classical music concerts, and opera. In fact, it has been estimated that, on average, performing-arts organizations, including symphonies, operas, and ballet companies, earn less than 40% of their costs of operation (Baumol and Bowen 1968). Yet, an increase in the number of performances, or in ticket and subscription prices, will not ordinarily reduce operating deficits (see Chapter 12). Instead, financial support from municipal and private sources is normally required to sustain these activities. Through creation in 1965 of the National Endowment for the Arts (NEA), Congress has provided support by allocating federal funds to match local contributions. Some 1,500 orchestras and 600 opera companies, plus individual artists, are eligible for grants. (The NEA's legislative mandate is limited to support for individuals and organizations that are tax-exempt.)

5.3 Making and marketing records

Deal maker's delight

Production agreements As seen in previous chapters, creativity is not limited to finished products; it also appears in financial and manufacturing arrangements. And if anything, the scope for deal making in records as compared to movies is greater because of the relatively smaller capital commitments and fewer people involved in making a recorded-music product. Still, most record companies are highly selective in signing talent, and fancy deal making is a privilege mostly reserved for already established artists.

Whereas in the early days of the business, the record companies simply signed an artist and had an in-house producer known as an artist-and-repertoire (A&R) man guide the project, today there is a tendency for artists to work with independent producers. Like record-company A&R people, these independents will help the artist select material and a music style, decide where and how the recording is to be made, and generally watch over budgets for studio recording and rehearsal times, mixing, and editing. Sometimes they also become involved with the design and artwork for CD-album liner notes.

Variations in financial arrangements usually develop as independent producers and independent ''labels'' (companies) work with the artist as subcontractors for the major record companies.[19] Yet, as Baskerville (1982, p. 300) notes, deals are typically structured in one of the following ways:

1. The label signs the artist and an in-house producer, compensated through salary plus perhaps some royalties, to handle the project.
2. Talent is already under contract with a label and the label retains an independent producer or company to deliver a master tape. The outside producer will intially receive a production fee and also negotiate a royalty of 1% to 5% based on retail sales. The record company will normally set the budget to which the independent will adhere.
3. Independent artists and producers make a master tape and then try to sell the master to a label. If the master is accepted, the label compensates the artist-producer team through royalties perhaps earned against an advance.
4. A label may form a joint venture with an independent producer or artist. Royalties will then be shared in proportion to the size of financial commitments.
5. An artist may form a production company to make and deliver a master tape to a label. A free-lance producer may then be hired by the artist's production company.
6. An artist may be employed by a corporation that then sells the artist's services to a label in return for royalty considerations.

Within this context, many ''independent'' labels emerge. But few are truly independent because the initial financing and manufacturing and distribution of the final product are much more efficiently handled by large record companies that are able to diversify their risks over many different labels while enjoying many other economies of scale. Independent labels and producers may also negotiate adjustments when, as is often the case, a given individual functions in several different capacities. The producer may be trained in both music and audio engineering; the performing artist may be a co-producer and fund-raiser. In the end, however, whether the producer or artist receives the most compensation depends on relative bargaining strengths. Important producers may receive from the label several percentage "points" in addition to production fees often between $25,000 and $125,000 (half paid on signing) that are nonrecoupable against royalties. In total, this may be more than what the artist receives.

Talent deals Talent royalty rates depend on the degree to which the artist is in demand. Major artists often can command over 15% of retail price, which would amount to well over $1.00 per album, but minor players will be signed at a rate of 10% or less of retail. A sliding scale may be used whereby the first 100,000 units sold are at 9%, and for every 100,000 units thereafter the royalty rate is scaled upward by one or two percentage points. In most cases, record companies will estimate the artist's annual royalties and then advance about one-half that amount. But for so-called "all-in" deals, the artist is also responsible for paying the producer "perhaps 3% of retail" out of the artist's share of royalties.

An important reason for the decline in record-industry profitability during the late 1970s was excessive royalty bidding by major companies for popular artists whose contracts were up for renegotiation. Significant losses ensued when large royalty advances were not covered by subsequent album sales. Hence, to at least partially protect themselves from such potential losses, companies may sign an artist to deliver several albums over a certain period of time and then, as in films, partially cross-collateralize royalty advances over those albums.

Production costs

Once the deal-making phase is completed, musicians and producers begin a long process that leads to delivery of a completed master. Decisions concerning the time and place of recording and the numbers of backup singers and musicians must be made. Rehearsals must be scheduled.

Production costs for a popular album are generally budgeted for at least $125,000, and if a lot of studio time is used, costs can soar well past $300,000. As production costs rise, it naturally becomes progressively more difficult for the record company to make a profit from the album (no matter what the sound-carrier medium).

Having delivered a master tape mixed down to two-channel stereo and formatted for an album, the producer will then typically be paid the remaining half of the production fee or an advance on royalties. But for the record company,

Table 5.1. *Manufacturing costs for typical*
compact discs, circa 1995[a]

Cost/unit	
Raw media	$0.10
Pressing/recording	0.30
Plastic case	0.10
Printed material	0.05
Other	0.05
Total	$0.60
Average selling price	$0.75

[a]Gross profit calculated for wholesale distributors of
final product would include writedowns of unsuccessful albums and also costs of marketing. Wholesale prices charged by the distributor might normally
be at least $8.00 for CDs and $6.00 for cassettes.

other expenses are just beginning: A marketing campaign must be planned, album
cover artwork must be commissioned, and a timetable for pressing and distribution must be established.[20]

Yet, unlike the period of the late 1970s, the costs of raw materials for cassettes
and compact disc composites, album covers and liners, and outer plastic shrink-
wrapping have been relatively well contained in recent years. The costs of manufacturing a typical CD album as of the mid 1990s are shown in Table 5.1. As
can be seen, the profitability of the CD configuration is most impressive (and is
further boosted by an artist(s) royalty rate often 80% to 85% of that paid on
cassette).

Marketing costs

Marketing campaigns for albums may frequently involve concert tours, cooperative advertising with local retailers, in-store merchandising aids (e.g., displays,
posters, and T-shirts), radio and television commercials, and "promo" press kits.
Also, free records may be sent to hundreds of radio stations. But none of this
comes cheap. And marketing costs can often reach $100,000 for a fairly standard
release and in excess of $500,000 for one by a major artist.

Of course, promotional efforts are generally aimed at the most influential reporting stations, that is, some 200 to 300 stations monitored by tip sheets and
trade papers such as *Billboard* and *Radio & Records*. Indirect spending for promotional purposes also used to include significant sums for bribery of station
managers and program directors until such so-called "payola" was publicized
and then outlawed in the 1960s. Nowadays, any station of importance is careful
to set policies limiting the size and frequency of gifts or favors that employees
are allowed to accept. Nevertheless, as documented by Dannen (1990), in the

1980s, payola again tainted the industry, this time through the hiring of independent promoters.[21]

In addition, record companies will also have their own staffs of "trackers," whose job it is to aid in promotional efforts by knowing which songs and albums radio stations around the country are adding or deleting to their play lists. With popular-music stations able to add at most three or four new cuts per week to their lists, competition for airplay is intense: Every year an estimated 2,600 albums, averaging some 10 cuts per album, are released.

Consequently, perhaps as little as 10% of new material must make a profit large enough to offset losses on the majority of releases – a situation that is even worse than in films, where, on average, 7 of 10 projects are losers. However, the most popular recordings – especially those by new artists starting at relatively low royalty bases – are immensely profitable. And again, as in other entertainment industry segments, a small part of the product line will generate a large part of the profits.

Distribution and pricing

With the rate of project failure so high, and with all but the most successful recorded music products having a relatively short life cycle, lasting at most a few months, there is no room for distribution inefficiency: It is essential that retailers located over a wide geographic swath have their inventories of hits quickly replenished. Thus, most records are distributed by large organizations with sufficient capital to stock and ship hundreds of thousands of units on a moment's notice.

The two major record distributors in the United States have long been Warner Music Group, the distribution arm for the Time Warner Inc. labels (including Warner Bros., Elektra, Atlantic, Asylum, Nonesuch, Reprise, Giant, Sire), and Sony (including the Columbia, Epic, and Masterworks labels, which were bought from CBS by the Sony Corporation of Japan in a 1987 transaction described by Boyer (1988)).[22] Together, these companies sometimes handle up to half the records sold in North America and about 35% of the total elsewhere.

Somewhat smaller in the United States, but still important distributors on a worldwide basis, are: (a) Dutch-owned PolyGram Group (Deutsche Grammophone, Decca, Mercury, Polydor, London, A&M, Island, Motown); (b) German-owned BMG or the Bertelsmann Group (RCA, Ariola, Arista); and (c) English-owned CEMA (Capitol, Angel, EMI, Chrysalis, Virgin, Manhattan, Blue Note). Also significant, but operating on a lesser international scale, is Canadian/American-owned Universal Music Group (MCA, Geffen). For the most part, the market shares of these major distributors tend to be fairly stable over long periods.[23]

Success in distribution depends on the size of capital commitment and on the ability to quickly sense where and how well new music is selling. To this end, distributors employ large staffs of sales and promotion people and rely extensively on outside intelligence-gathering sources. But whereas this structure works well in large regions, major distribution organizations are less efficient in servicing smaller stores and out-of-the-way territories. Thus, there exists a second tier of smaller independent distributors, known as one-stops, who handle all labels, including those of the majors. One-stops evolved in the 1940s to accommodate the needs of jukebox operators; today they also work with orders from small stores and from Internet-based promotional and marketing sites.

Another significant distribution channel for records is through clubs and *rack jobbers.* Sony (formerly CBS), in conjunction with Time Warner, owns the largest record club in the United States and RCA the second largest. Clubs account for an estimated 10%–12% of total dollar volume.

Rack jobbers have also substantially contributed to the growth of the music business since 1950 and, more recently, to the growth of the home video industry.[24] "Racks" may operate record departments in space leased from department stores. Or, for maintaining inventories and promotion displays in record departments owned and operated by other parties, they may earn fees based on a percentage of sales. Agreements with rack jobbers can take many different forms and may include such diverse retailing environments as drugstores and supermarkets. But the main attraction is always that the jobber can obtain quantity discounts and provide expertise in the rapid selection, display, and maintenance of inventories (i.e., warehousing) of products with a relatively short life cycle.

Rack jobbers, in effect, thus absorb the nonspecialized retailer's risk of purchasing too much of the wrong product or too little of the right product. In return, jobbers operate on the spread between large-quantity discount prices of major distributors and their own higher quasi-wholesale prices. Generally, the jobber's risk of guessing wrong on the order size for a particular item is reduced through diversification over many titles and also through some return privileges. The margin for error, though, is not too large, especially when changes in musical tastes become unusually volatile.

Last in the distribution chain is the cutout wholesaler, who buys, for prices at or below cost, records that have been returned to the distributor. *Cutouts,* which appear as secondary merchandise in discount stores, are the industry's errors in judgment as to production quantity and/or quality. They often provide real bargains for patient and knowledgeable consumers.

However, cutouts and overstocks have been an area of dispute and litigation between artists and record companies, because contracts are normally written in terms of royalties on the number of recordings *sold,* not the number manufactured. Such excess recordings may be used in barter for other goods and services or to raise cash for the record company. Only major artists have the bargaining power to negotiate that excess inventories be destroyed rather than sold as cutouts.

As might be expected, major-distributor pricing policies have an important effect on firms farther downstream in the distribution chain. There is, nevertheless, no easy method by which to analyze such policies because all major companies now have different scales for quantity discounts and return-privilege limits. However, the sizes of discounts are normally proportioned according to order quantities, which means that jobbers and one-stops operate in wholesaler price niches.

Although wholesale pricing is relatively straightforward, in retail pricing, there is also often an interesting economic anomaly in that the newest products in strongest demand may be priced lower than older items that are in lesser demand.[25]

For small music retailers forced by marketing considerations to add new video and audio product lines, rapid technological developments are at best a mixed blessing. Proliferation of different cassette and disc formats has substantially magnified capital requirements, and each format introduction multiplies the number of relatively high-value stockkeeping units (SKUs) that must be carried in inventory. All of this ultimately hastens the consolidation of music and home-video software retailing into stronger and larger specialty chain stores.

5.4 Financial accounting and valuation

As might be expected, the corporate financial-accounting perspective is different from that of the artist. From the corporate view, enough profit simultaneously must be generated to compensate shareholders with a competitive return on investment and to also underwrite development of as many new talents as possible. Individual artists, of course, are concerned primarily with their own financial statements.

Artists' perspective

Among the major issues that need to be negotiated between artists and record companies are the date of contract expiration, the number of albums committed, exclusivity, foreign-release intentions, and royalties and advances. For example, a contract may require that three master tapes be delivered within three years of signing and may further stipulate penalties to be paid if the albums are not released.

With the possible exception of contracts in the jazz field, labels generally require their artists to provide exclusive services, which may extend to music-video performances on cassettes and discs. And artist contracts may also delineate the foreign countries or territories for which album release is planned. This can be significant in that a major portion of sales may occur outside the United States (sometimes at royalty rates 75% of the domestic rate).

Greatest attention, however, is usually focused on negotiations for artist royalties and advances. Ten percent of retail price has historically been a normal starting point, and percentages are often scaled upward from this level in proportion to sales.[26] But royalties and advances may also be based on a published dealer (wholesale) price. Either way, though, payout increments are frequently contingent on attainment of an RIAA-certified (Recording Industry Association of America) gold-record (500,000 unit sales for albums and singles) or platinum-record (1 million albums and singles) sales level.[27]

Contract discussions may furthermore involve issues of creative control, ownership of masters, publishing-rights ownership, production-budget minimums,

Table 5.2. *Artist's financial perspective, first gold album*

Album units at $7.98 list price	$7.98
— 10% breakage	−0.80
— 10% packaging fee	−0.80
	$6.38
Royalties:	
10% on first 150,000 units	95,700
12% on next 350,000 units	267,960
15% on all additional units	
Gold-record-album royalties	$363,660
— advance	100,000
Royalties payable by label	263,660

conditions under which a contract can be assigned to another person or company, the artist's right to audit the firm's books, the label's minimum commitment to spend on promotion and tour support and music videos, and charge-back items such as production expenses that the record company has the right to recoup before paying royalties beyond the negotiated advance. Default and arbitration-procedure clauses are also included in many contracts in case of unforeseen disagreements or problems.

Such situations will readily arise if the label and artist do not have a clear understanding of the royalty base to which the aforementioned royalty rates are applied. The record company may limit the royalty base to 90% of actual sales to allow for "breakage" (damage) of records in shipment. There may be specifications for discounting royalties by up to 15% for free goods (i.e., promotional copies that are given away). Other discounts to royalties might include 10% for packaging (cover artwork), or 50% for record-club sales. And clauses involving merchandising, production costs for music videos, and cross-collateralizations (see section 4.3) may further affect the royalty base.

To fully recoup an advance against royalties and to begin to earn on incremental unit sales, artists will thus normally have to sell one album for every dollar spent on production and marketing. In other words, as Dannen (1990, p. 143) suggests, recoupment terms in standard industry contracts, in fact, imply that "most of the costs of making a record are to be repaid out of the artist's royalties rather than gross receipts."[28] Indeed, record companies will normally profit from a hefty mark-up on actual touring and other such expenses, thereby making it difficult for artists' advances to be fully recouped (and also making it advisable for artists to directly pay for some of these items). And sales approaching 1 million units might be needed to recoup an advance.

How a relatively new artist with a first gold album might fare financially can be seen from the hypothetical example of Table 5.2, in which the significant leverage for sales above 500,000 units is apparent.

Table 5.3. *Recorded-music industry composite of five companies, 1992–96 (in $ millions)*

	Revenues	Operating income	Operating[a] margin (%)	Assets	Operating cash flow
CAGR(%):[b]					
1992–96	8.8	8.9	N.M.[c]	N.A.	N.A.

[a]Average margin 1992–96 = 10.5%.
[b]Compound annual growth rate.
[c]Not meaningful.
Source: Company reports.

Company perspective

Record companies may earn a profit at many different levels of activity, ranging from production fees and breakage charges to distribution. But as previously indicated, large profits from a few winners (perhaps 10% of all releases) must more than offset losses on the many others. The corporate financial-accounting perspective, considerably different from that of the artists', can be understood through study of publicly owned recorded-music company reports.

Pretax operating profits and margins for distributors of major labels have historically fluctuated unpredictably (Table 5.3), and steady growth for even the largest organizations is far from assured. Although the basic financial operating structures are similar for all the major distributors, there are, nevertheless, differences in how interest and overhead expenses are charged to music divisions, and also differences in "return reserves." Such reserves are set aside as a fixed percentage of domestic sales (with much less need for them outside the U.S. and Canada) and are closely related to recent experiences with records returned by retailers. For example, during the late 1970s, when return privileges were still almost unlimited and the rate of returns accelerated, some distributor companies found their reserves inadequate. Losses, instead of profits, began to appear.

The following excerpt from the 1982 Warner Communications annual report illustrates return-reserves accounting policies:

Inventories other than motion picture inventories are stated at the lower of average cost or estimated realizable value. In accordance with industry practice, certain products are sold to customers with the right to return unsold items. Revenues from these sales represent gross sales less a provision for future returns. It is general policy to value returned goods included in inventory at estimated realizable value but not in excess of cost.

Industry practices in this area are delineated by Financial Accounting Standards Board (FASB) statement 48, which specifies how an enterprise should account for sales of its products when the buyer has a right to return the (nondefective) product. The key condition that must be met for applicability of this statement is that the amount of future returns must be reasonably estimable. In the case of music products, there is generally enough volume and historical experience with which to make such estimates.

Other corporate accounting issues are largely governed by FASB statement 50. In particular, under this statement, royalties earned by artists, as adjusted for anticipated returns, are charged to the expense of the period in which sale of the record occurs. But advance royalties paid to an artist are to be reported as assets (i.e., are capitalized) if the past performance and current popularity of that artist provide a sound basis for forecasting recoupment of the advance. Amortization of the asset would then, as in films, be related to the amount of net revenue expected to be realized over the estimated life of the recorded performance. Royalties and advances for new artists with unknown potential would thus normally be expensed in the period of payment.

In accounting for license agreements, minimum guarantees, and advance royalties, FASB statement 50 also specifies that licensors should initially report minimum guarantees as a liability and then recognize the guarantees as revenue as the license fee is earned under the agreement.

Valuation aspects

Valuation of music company assets must always begin with an assessment of the breadth and depth of the company's catalog of past releases: A catalog in recorded music – whether it be in the form of publishing rights or of ownership of master recordings – plays a role in valuation that is analogous to that of a film library in the motion picture business. The catalog, which is often nothing more than a bundle of rights, is usually the starting point for assessment.

Yet as in other areas, music-related assets will generally be evaluated on their ability to generate cash in future periods. A multiple of such projected cash flows – which are defined as operating income before amortization, interest, and taxes – is always a function of interest rate levels and the economic, political, and technological background at the time of assessment. But, of these factors, the interest rate is usually the most significant because it affects inversely the discounted present value of the future expected cash flows and also the ability of the purchaser of the asset to obtain or to service financing obligations.

In other words, the value of music company assets can generally be found by taking the going multiple of projected cash flow as determined from recent sales of similar properties and then subtracting net debt – a formula that is identical to the one shown in section 6.4 for evaluating broadcast properties. However, a variation on this is found in the evaluation of music publishers. Here, the key figure to which the multiple is applied is called the *net publisher's share* (NPS), which is equal to all the royalties the company takes in minus everthing it must pay out to writers and artists.[29]

Other assets of value might include record masters. But masters having a useful commercial life of more than a year from date of indicated release are rare.[30]

5.5 Concluding remarks

The music business never stops changing. And never has this been more evident than over the last 20 years. The takeovers of CBS and RCA by foreign interests have given the industry a truly global dimension, and systems of distribution and finance have been essentially consolidated into six giant companies.

But just as significantly, the late-twentieth-century years have been a time of major technological advances in the way music is produced, reproduced, and distributed. Until the computers of the 1980s, for example, sound was recorded and replayed using only embellishments of the processes discovered by Thomas Edison 100 years earlier. Yet thanks to new technology, we can be assured that the potential for creation, for enjoyment, and for use of music has never been greater.[31]

Selected additional reading

Baig, E. (1984). "The Can-Do Promotor of the Jacksons Tour," *Fortune* 110(4)(August 20):160.

Brabec, J., and Brabec, T. (1994). *Music, Money, and Success*. New York: Macmillan (Schirmer).

Brinkley, J. (1997). "After 15 Years, the Music CD Faces an Upscale Competitor," *New York Times,* July 28.

Brownstein, S. (1986). "Music Videos Hit a Sour Note," *New York Times,* July 6.

Burnett, R. (1996). *The Global Jukebox: The International Music Industry*. New York and London: Routledge.

Cieply, M. (1986). "A Few Promotors Dominate Record Business," *Wall Street Journal,* April 18.

Clarke, D. (1995). *The Rise and Fall of Popular Music*. New York: St. Martin's Press (London: Viking).

Cox, M. (1992). "As More Music Superstars Hit the Road, Summer Concert Season Sounds Strong," *Wall Street Journal,* May 20.

"Rock is Slowly Fading as Tastes in Music Go Off in Many Directions,"*Wall Street Journal,* August 26.

Dannen, F. (1994). "Showdown at the Hit Factory," *The New Yorker,* November 21.

Farr, J. (1991). "Turning Rock into Gold," *New York Times Magazine,* December 8.

Gottlieb, A. (1991). "The Music Business," *The Economist,* December 21.

Gubernick, L. (1993). *Get Hot or Go Home: Trish Yearwood, The Making of a Nashville Star*. New York: William Morrow.

Gubernick, L., and Newcomb, P. (1992). "The Wal-Mart School of Music," *Forbes* 149(5)(March 2).

Hamlen, W. A., Jr. (1991). "Superstardom in Popular Music: Empirical Evidence,*Review of Economics and Statistics,* 73(4)(November).

Kerr, P. (1984). "Music Video's Uncertain Payoff," *New York Times,* July 29.

Knoedelseder, W., Jr. (1985). "Cut Rate Albums Hit Sour Note," *Los Angeles Times,* May 18.

Kupfer, A. (1991). "The Next Wave in Cassette Tapes," *Fortune* 123(11)(June 3).

Landro, L. (1985). "Producers, Artists Push Music-Video Sales as Market for VCRs Expands and Changes," *Wall Street Journal*, March 20.

La Franco, R. (1995). "The Coolest Capitalists," *Forbes*, 156(7)(September 25).

Millard, A. (1995). *America on Record: A History of Recorded Sound*. New York: Cambridge University Press.

Miller, M. W. (1987). "High-Tech Alteration of Sights and Sounds Divides the Arts World," *Wall Street Journal*, September 1.

Newcomb, P., and Palmeri, C. (1991). "What's Not to Love?" *Forbes* 148(7)(September 30).

"Now Playing: The Sound of Money," *Business Week*, No. 3065 (August 15, 1988).

Passman, D. S. (1994). *All You Need to Know About the Music Business*. New York: Prentice-Hall.

Sancton, T. (1990). "Horns of Plenty," *Time* 136(17)(October 22).

Sanjek, R., and Sanjek, D. (1991). *American Popular Music Business in the 20th Century*. New York: Oxford University Press.

Sharpe, A. (1994). "Country Music Finds New Fans, and a Firm In Nashville Prospers," *Wall Street Journal*, January, 19.

Trachtenberg, J. A. (1995). "Clive Davis, Once Hit by Controversy, Is Back at Top of the Charts," *Wall Street Journal*, March 13.

Turner, R. (1991). "How MCA's Relations with Motown Records Went Sour So Fast," *Wall Street Journal*, September 25.

U.S. Congress, Office of Technology Assessment. (1989). Copyright and Home Copying: Technology Challenges the Law, OTA-CIT-422. Washington, D.C.: U.S. Government Printing Office.

Wade, D., and Picardie, J. (1990). *Music Man: Ahmet Ertegun, Atlantic Records, and the Triumph of Rock'n'Roll*. New York: W.W. Norton.

Zaslow, J. (1985). "New Rock Economics Make It Harder to Sing Your Way to Wealth," *Wall Street Journal*, May 21.

6

Broadcasting

Programs are scheduled interruptions of marketing bulletins.

Marketing bulletins, in fact, are the essence of commercial broadcasting in the United States.

This chapter is concerned with the economics of radio and television broadcasting – a topic that is closely tied to developments in the movie, recorded music, sports, and other entertainment-distribution businesses. By the end, it should be evident that maybe Marshall McLuhan (McLuhan, 1964) was onto something when he said, "the medium is the message."

6.1 Going on the air

Technology and history

Broadcasting began the twentieth century as a laboratory curiosity; it will end the century as a business generating over $50 billion per year. But monolithic the industry is not. In fact, many subsegments compete vigorously with each other.

Strictly speaking, commercial broadcasters sell time that is used for dissemination of advertising messages. In actuality, though, what is sold is access to the thoughts and emotions of people in the audience. Companies selling beer prefer

155

to buy time on sports-events programs, whereas toy and cereal manufacturers prefer time on children's shows.

To distribute commercial messages to audiences, or, conversely, to deliver audiences to advertisers, four basic broadcasting media have evolved over the last 75 years: AM (amplitude-modulation) and FM (frequency-modulation) radio and VHF (very-high-frequency) and UHF (ultra-high-frequency) television. All of these technologically defined media operate under identical macroeconomic conditions but different microeconomic conditions.

AM radio was the first medium to gain widespread popularity, during the 1920s. But as described by Barnouw (1990), television (VHF) was well into development at that time. Indeed, by the early 1930s the National Broadcasting Company (NBC) had begun transmitting experimental telecasts from the Empire State Building. Nevertheless, it was not until the 1939 World's Fair that NBC began regular program service to those few receivers then in existence. And, despite great consumer interest in this new medium, receivers did not begin to appear in significant numbers of households until the early 1950s: Economic restraints and contingencies related to World War II and to the Korean War, and the high initial prices of receiving equipment, bridled the industry's progress.

Also, in fact, neither FM radio, with its high-fidelity stereo-signal capability, nor UHF television could become financially viable until the late 1960s and early 1970s. FM radio achieved this through a shift to album-oriented popular music appealing to a rapidly expanding population of teens and young adults. And UHF television was helped along by the emergence of a third major network (American Broadcasting), more powerful UHF transmitters, and a congressional mandate for the manufacture of equipment with tuners able to receive UHF.

Indeed, throughout the history of broadcasting, portrayed by Figure 6.1, the economic values of television and radio properties have been closely related to the technological characteristics of the means of transmission.

Consider AM radio stations. AM signals bounce off the ionosphere at night-time, and can thereby cause interference with other stations operating on the same frequency hundreds or thousands of miles away. To prevent such interference, the Federal Communications Commission (FCC) does not permit many small stations to transmit, or to transmit at full power, once the sun sets. That obviously limits audience size and reduces a station's value. On the other hand, so-called clear-channel stations are permitted to transmit at a maximum of 50,000 watts (W), and can be heard at all times of the day and night over broad regions of North America.

FM radio, however, is essentially a local medium because signals can rarely be well received beyond a 60-mile radius from the transmitter. And VHF television signals, which have the same travel characteristics as FM, must be boosted by relay stations in order to reach beyond about 100 miles.[1]

Moreover, all other things being equal, UHF signals travel even less distance than VHF signals. UHF also requires significantly greater electric power for transmission, often more than 1 megawatt (MW). Not suprisingly, then, UHFs were the last to be commercially developed.

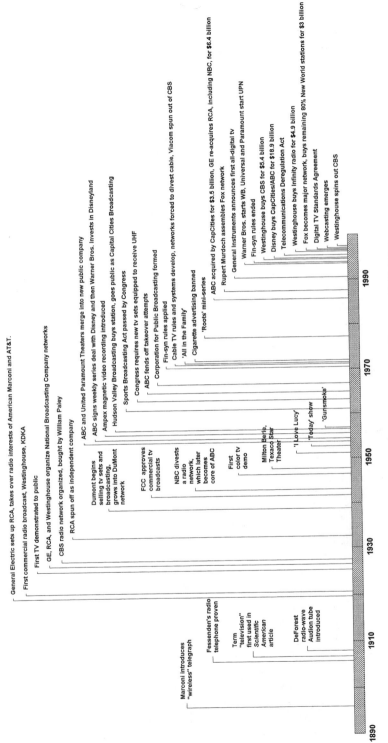

Figure 6.1. Broadcast industry milestones, 1890–2000.

Table 6.1. *U.S. broadcasting facilities, 1997*

Service	Total
Commercial AM	4,811
Commercial FM	5,477
Educational FM	1,889
Total radio	12,177
Commercial VHF TV	558
Commercial UHF TV	637
Educational VHF TV	124
Educational UHF TV	241
Total TV	1,560
VHF LPTV	555
UHF LPTV	1,446
Total LPTV	2,001
FM translators and boosters	2,800
VHF translators	2,270
UHF translators	2,721
Total translators	7,791

Source: Broadcasting & Cable, August 11, 1997.

Finally, as of the late 1980s, low-power VHF television stations (LPTV) were introduced. LPTV can meet many strictly local programming needs at minimal cost and can be established, complete with satellite earth station and origination equipment, for about half a million dollars. With a 1-kilowatt (1 kW) transmitter and a high-gain antenna, a signal can then extend as much as 18 miles from the transmission point.

As of August 1997, there were 4,811 authorized commercial AM radio stations, 5,477 commercial FM stations, and 1,195 commercial VHF and UHF television stations in the United States. In addition, there are hundreds more educational installations and television-signal translators (relay stations) (Table 6.1).

Basic operations

The success of a television or radio station in attracting an audience is measured by *ratings points* – the percentage of all TV or radio-owning households tuned to a show. If, for example, 100,000 households in a defined area own radios and 12,000 of these households are listening to a particular station, then that station's *rating* is 12.0.

A station's *share*, however, is measured as the percentage of all *switched on* sets tuned to a show. Assume that a signal area contains 100,000 households with televisions, that 60,000 of those sets are switched-on, and that 20,000 are watching channel 2. Then channel 2's share is 33.3.

Regular measurements of ratings and share figures have historically been offered by two major services: Nielsen (A.C. Nielsen Co.) and Arbitron (American Research Bureau). Arbitron discontinued its television services in 1993, but took its measurements over a signal's area of dominant influence (ADI), which essentially coincided with the U.S. Census Bureau's standard metropolitan statistical areas (SMSAs). Nielsen's equivalent is a designated market area (DMA).

In the so-called sweeps months (each November, February, May, and July), local-station advertising rates for upcoming periods are established with the assistance of the ratings measured by the ratings services. Although the May sweeps period is considered by stations and networks to be the most important of the year, programming battles remain particularly intense in the months of November and February, during which there is a strong seasonal tendency toward stay-at-home viewing and listening. Many appealing "specials" are aired in those months in attempts to boost audience levels.

The methods used by ratings services to sample homes using television (HUT) vary to a degree and are sometimes subject to dispute. But the methods will generally provide consistent trend results over time. Nielsen measurements for national network prime-time television shows, that is, programs broadcast in the period 8–11 PM for the East and West coasts (one hour earlier for Central Time and Mountain Time), are made through devices called People Meters that are connected to a scientifically selected sample of more than 4,000 homes. The Nielsen television index (NTI) that is so derived then provides advertisers with significant data on the audiences for various programs and thus forms the basis for how much a network can charge for the commercial time breaks within those programs. The Nielsen station index (NSI), derived from a combination of People Meters and viewers' diaries, provides similar information for local program and station evaluations.[2]

Of course, advertisers will want their messages to be delivered to the audiences most likely to be interested in purchasing their products or services. Advertising agencies accordingly attempt to find programs or stations attracting the best target audience, defined by demographic, income, and ethnic mix: Razor-blade commercials appear regularly on sports/action programs; ads for laundry products appear on the eponymic daytime soap operas.

Further distinctions are made between national (network) ads, national spot ads, and local ads. Large brand-name companies with national distribution often find that purchases of national-network time through agencies (which typically receive fees of 15% of their gross billings) are the most efficient – least expensive on a cost-per-viewer basis – means of communicating with potential customers.

However, for some nationally distributed products, a particular local audience can often be reached more effectively through so-called national spot purchases on local outlets, and as arranged with station representatives (reps). Rep firms funtion as extensions of a station's sales staff and are familiar with various rate cards (prices) and program research demographics. In return for such services, the firms charge commissions that range to an average of about 7% to 8%.[3]

On a local level, of course, smaller businesses buy time directly from local stations. Many of these transactions are at unpublished prices.

Broadcasters sell time to advertisers using the concepts of gross rating points

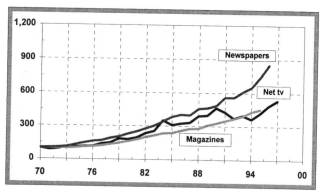

Figure 6.2. Cost per thousand index trends (1970–96) for network television (prime-time), magazines (four color), and newspapers, 1970–96. *Source:* McCann-Erikson data.

(GRP), reach, and frequency. Because a rating point is the estimated percentage of households or of target audience potentially exposed to a commercial, *gross rating points* are the sum of all the ratings figures. *Reach* is the percentage of households (or of target audience) exposed to a message at least once over a predetermined span. It is also called cume, short for cumulative audience. *Frequency* is simply the number of times an ad is used during a period of time. Thus, GRP is reach multiplied by frequency.

Advertisers generally assess the relative expense and efficiency of delivering a message via different media on the basis of cost per thousand households (CPM). Such data can be determined from a station's rate card or schedule, which, as posted with the Standard Rate and Data Service (SRDS), indicates how much half a minute will cost during a specific part of the day, day of the week, and season. Figure 6.2 illustrates CPM index trends for network television, magazines and newspapers since 1970. Over that span, CPM trends in network television have largely paralleled those for newspapers and magazines.

Another measure, most often used in radio, is the *power ratio,* which is defined as a station's percentage of revenue in a market divided by its total audience percentage (of adults over the age of 12). Ratios above 1.0 indicate that the station, or group of stations, is receiving a higher share of available market revenues than of available share of listening audience.

As in any other business, discounts for purchases in quantity are normally available. But because unsold time is lost forever, prices become increasingly negotiable as the broadcast date approaches. Advertisers, stations, and program producers also sometimes engage in *barter,* a practice in which time is swapped for goods and services or, more commonly, for programming. Barter-syndication deals, which amounted to about $1.9 billion in 1996, provide advertisers with time that is generally at least 15% less expensive than on the networks.[4]

The microeconomic considerations in commercial advertising, broadcasting operations, and government regulation have been formally investigated in a wide

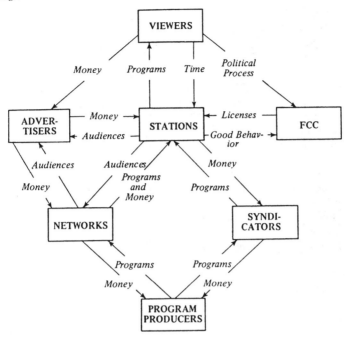

Figure 6.3. Organization of the television industry. *Source:* Owen et al. (1974). © 1974 Bruce M. Owen.

range of studies, several of which will be noted in section 6.2. The organization of the television industry is illustrated in Figure 6.3, and aggregate spending on various media since 1970 is presented in Table 6.2.

Regulation and technology

Broadcasting is one of the few entertainment sectors heavily regulated by the government. Such regulation is an outgrowth of the need, in the early years of this industry, to allocate scarce space in the broadcast frequency spectrum according to constraints imposed by technological factors and world political considerations.[5] Periodic meetings of the World Administrative Radio Conference (WARC) determine frequency allocations so that international frequency interference is minimized. Political and historical precedents have also been determinants as to which of several available television transmission systems a country has adopted.[6]

From the business-economics standpoint, knowledge of such issues is pertinent to decisions that television set manufacturers and broadcasters must make with regard to high-definition television (HDTV). HDTV signals, perhaps incorporating a nearly uniform standard throughout the world, will soon dominate as television sets become much more sophisticated in their digital signal-processing

Table 6.2. *Annual U.S. Advertising expenditures, 1970–95 (in $ billion)*

	1970	1975	1980	1985	1990	1995
Newspapers	5.704	8,234	14,794	25,170	32,281	36,317
Magazines	1,292	1,465	3,149	5,155	6,803	8,580
Farm publications	62	74	130	186	215	283
Television, total	3,596	5,263	11,469	21,022	28,405	37,828
Four networks[b]	1,658	2,306	5,130	8,060	9,863	11,600
Cable networks	—	—	45	594	1,860	3,535
Syndication	—	—	50	520	1,109	2,016
Spot (national)	1,234	1,653	3,269	6,004	7,788	9,119
Spot (local)	704	1,334	2,967	5,714	7,856	9,985
Radio, total	1,308	1,980	3,702	6,490	8,726	11,338
Network	56	83	183	365	482	480
Spot (national)	371	436	779	1,335	1,635	1,959
Spot (local)	881	1,461	2,740	4,790	6,609	8,899
Yellow pages	—	—	2,900	5,800	8,926	10,236
Direct mail	2,766	4,124	7,596	15,500	23,370	32,866
Business publications	740	919	1,674	2,375	2,875	3,559
Outdoor	234	335	578	945	1,084	1,263
Miscellaneous	3,848	5,506	7,558	12,107	16,237	20,660
Total[a]						
National	11,350	15,200	29,815	53,355	73,380	95,360
Local	8,200	12,700	23,735	41,395	56,210	67,570
Grand total	19,550	27,900	53,550	94,750	129,590	162,930

[a] Total is sum of major categories.
[b] Three networks prior to 1990.
Source: Robert J. Coen, McCann-Erickson, Inc., New York.

capabilities. New HDTV sets, essentially computers compatible with other computers, provide picture resolution quality nearly as fine as on film, and with aspect ratios approaching those of feature films (16:9).[7]

Organizational patterns and priorities

Networks and affiliates In the United States, the most obvious manifestations of government regulation are the granting of licenses and the promulgation of rules concerning how many stations a single business organization is allowed to own. To prevent concentration of ownership in too few hands, prior to 1985 the FCC had permitted one corporation to own a maximum of seven AM and seven FM radio stations, and a maximum of five VHF television stations (plus two UHFs). Since then, the limits have been lifted – originally to 12 stations each, so long as the total audience did not exceed 25% of the national television audience – and now, with passage of the Telecommunications Act of 1996, to 35%.[8]

As of the late 1990s, the three original major national television corporations (the networks) – Columbia Broadcasting (CBS), National Broadcasting (NBC), and American Broadcasting (ABC) – owned and operated (O&O) at least ten large-city television stations each, including local "flagships" in New York, Chicago, and Los Angeles. Meanwhile, Fox Broadcasting, with fourteen O&Os, has emerged as a full-fledged competitor to the three original majors.[9]

Television networks – in effect, programming and audience-delivery wholesalers – were established in the late 1940s and early 1950s (and radio networks in the 1920s) by attracting independently owned affiliates to carry regularly scheduled programming produced by the network itself or by outside contractors.[10] But except for news and sports programs, networks have not (in the modern era) until recently been able to participate to any notable degree in the ownership of productions.

Nevertheless, each of the original three major webs, as they are often called in the trade press, still have approximately 200 affiliates who normally receive cash compensation to carry the scheduled national programming that is provided gratis by the network. Networks, in effect, thus actually operate by leasing the advertising time and signal distribution capabilities of their affiliates. Affiliate compensation in the period 6–11 PM might generally be 30%–33% of the station's hourly rate and lower in other dayparts. But many factors, including area of coverage, number of competing UHFs and VHFs, and long-standing relationships, determine compensation rates.[11]

Notably, it was not until the early 1970s that ABC became financially viable. An important catalyst for this change was government regulation that allowed local affiliates access to prime time (7:00 to 11:00 PM EST) through the so-called *prime time access rule*. Such reversion of several hours per week (7:00 to 8:00 PM) to affiliates reduced the networks' inventories of evening time and drove prices up.[12]

But by the mid-1980s, general trends toward economic deregulation also began to affect the broadcasting industry: Capital Cities Communications, a group station owner, acquired ABC (and is now owned by The Walt Disney Company); NBC was acquired by General Electric; CBS became a target of several takeover attempts (which ended in 1995 with Westinghouse becoming the acquirer); and Twentieth Century Fox and Metromedia merged most of their operations to form the core of a viable fourth network.

By the 1990s – with Time Warner (WB) and Viacom (UPN) also starting networks, and with networks beginning to produce more of their prime-time productions and share advertising revenues with top-line talent – the traditional distinctions between network affiliates and independent stations and between studios and networks had begun to blur.

Outside the United States, the organization and regulation of broadcasting varies substantially from country to country, but the most common arrangement is to have a mixture of public and private enterprises placed under the supervision of a government agency.[13] However, as privately owned, advertiser-supported networks become significant, they typically begin to assume many of the operating features

Table 6.3. *Television outside the United States, selected countries, 1996*

	TV households (million)	Estimated TV advertising expenditures[a] (US$ billion)	Approximate penetration (%)		TV ad $s per HH
			VCR	Cable	
Australia	6.3	1.6	81	—	254
Canada	10.0	1.8	82	68	180
France	21.2	3.5	55	10	165
Germany	32.0	4.9	47	45	153
Italy	20.4	3.2	47	—	157
Japan	58.1	19.5	87	22	336
Mexico	17.0	2.7	50	16	159
Netherlands	6.1	0.7	62	90	115
Spain	11.7	1.9	53	10	162
Sweden	3.8	0.3	65	55	79
Switzerland	2.5	0.3	70	80	120
United Kingdom	22.2	5.3	71	10	239
Total	211.2	45.3	—		—
Average	—	—	64	32	177
United States	96.0	42.5	87	68	443

[a]For all forms of TV advertising including cable and satellite. See also Table S6.2.
Source: McCann-Erikson, Inc. Zenith Media, industry estimates.

that have characterized the American television system – with expenditures for programming tending to rise in line with total broadcast *industry* revenues.[14] Key comparative data concerning television in eleven major countries are provided in Table 6.3 (see, also, Supplementary Table S6.1). And the growth of advertising in all media in the U.S. and around the world is illustrated in Figure 6.4.

Ratings and audiences By definition, the network with the most popular shows attracts the largest audience. The ratings leader can command prices at higher-than-average CPMs because advertising time (spots) on the most popular programs is normally in short supply relative to advertiser demand. Advertisers are interested in shows with high ratings because of their reach, their consistency, and their potential for creation of numerous merchandising opportunities.

In addition, the ratings leader garners higher prices because advertising-campaign managers who buy large quantities of time well in advance of use – so-called "upfront" buyers – often bid aggressively in order to ensure that spots on programs attracting desired targeted audiences are obtained. Such large upfront buys, made by early summer, and just after new fall-season prime-time program schedules have been established, might command quantity discounts of 15%. Nevertheless, the remaining spots, available on a "scatter" basis, are sold closer to broadcast time and may not provide advertisers with optimal frequency or

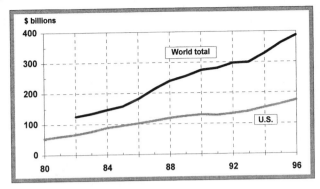

Figure 6.4. Total spending on advertising (all media) in the U.S. and around the world, 1980–96.

reach. Pricing exceptions may occur, however, with late-breaking campaigns or during periods of scarcity, when scatter prices can rise despite close proximity to the broadcast date.

Yet, except for programming-related outlays, which are the primary expense components, the costs of network operations remain relatively fixed regardless of ratings performance or numbers of affiliates.[15] Incremental revenues thus normally become almost pure operating profit for the ratings leader. Conversely, for the ratings laggard, weak ratings accentuate a decline in profitablility. A greater proportion of total expenses is incurred in ordering new shows and in then extensively promoting them on introduction. And advertisers disappointed by poor ratings performance often must be compensated with additional "free" time through so-called "make-goods" (more formally, they are audience-deficiency announcements).

In contrast to television, radio networks are much more varied and numerous, and they are more specifically targeted in terms of local-market demographic, ethnic, and other factors. But whether in television or in radio, significant leverage on profits accrues to the ratings leader. In network television, indeed, a prime-time ratings point won or lost may be worth at least $80 million in annual pretax profits.

The mechanics of all this might be sketched as follows:

Assume:
- 100 million households
- price of a 30-second network spot = $125,000
- eight spots per half-hour
- cost of programming = $600,000 per half-hour for *two* runs

Then:
- Network gross profit per half-hour = $700,000.

As might be expected, the tremendous importance of ratings performance to the profitability of a broadcast enterprise has led to much research into the kinds of programs certain demographically targeted audiences prefer to view. Only

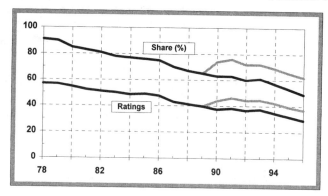

Figure 6.5. Combined ratings and shares for ABC, CBS, NBC, and Fox 1980–96.

recently, however, has there developed a substantial body of research that inves-
tigates the behavioral characteristics of television audiences in general. As noted
in a comprehensive review by Barwise and Ehrenberg (1988), two important
behavioral features have been observed: The *Duplication of Viewing Law,* and
the *Double Jeopardy Effect.*

In brief, the Duplication of Viewing Law states that "the percentage of the
audience of program B which also watches program A simply varies with the
rating of program A, with only small deviations." And, "for pairs of programs
on different days and different channels, the duplication of program B with A
generally equals the rating of A."[16]

The Double Jeopardy Effect is another interesting phenomenon that "occurs
when people have to choose between broadly similar items that differ in popularity. The less popular items are not only chosen by fewer people, but are liked
somewhat less by those who choose them."[17] In other words, viewers of programs
with low ratings are less loyal than viewers of programs with high ratings.

The Double Jeopardy Effect has probably been felt most acutely at the networks, where ratings have been significantly eroded by the increasing competition
from cable, independent stations, and videocassettes. As Figure 6.5 illustrates,
ratings and shares for the older three networks have been declining steadily. Yet,
as noted in Flax (1982) and as illustrated in Figure 6.6, there comes a point at
which a trade-off of profit for extra market share does not make economic sense.

Inventories Network prime-time inventories (of time allocated for commercial
messages) prior to 1981 used to be limited to six minutes per hour (seven minutes
during movies, sporting events, and specials) by voluntary adherence to unofficial
guidelines of the National Association of Broadcasters (NAB). But after such
adherence was found to be in violation of antitrust laws, the number of commercial minutes that a network sells during different times of day has been both
varied and increased.[18] Of course, all other things being equal, an increase in the
supply of time will cause prices to decline.

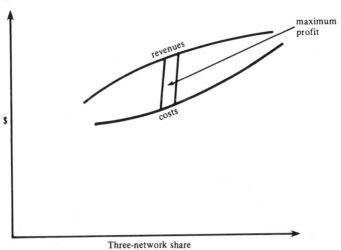

Figure 6.6. Curves for network profit-maximization strategy. *Source:* Flax (1982).

For network programs, of the usual 10 minutes per hour set aside for prime-time nonprogram material, and 16 minutes per hour in all other dayparts, affiliates might normally retain 2.5 minutes (60 seconds at the start and end, 30 seconds in the middle), with 30 seconds of this used for network and station promos, teasers, identification, and program titles and credits. This compares with 4 to 12 minutes that affiliates retain (at least 7 minutes on weekends) in daytime.

Affiliates, in turn, are motivated to provide broadcast clearances for network shows because network programs are generally the most profitable for them to run; network programming, with its inherently high production value, tends to attract the largest audiences. Moreover, the shows are provided to affiliates without expenditure of cash and without the headaches of production financing and creation.[19]

Independent and public broadcasting stations Television stations not affiliated with one of the four major networks are known as independents, and in recent years these stations have become serious competitors for network audiences. Independents try to counterprogram against network affiliates by offering news at times earlier or later than the networks, by providing viewers with more material of local interest, and by rerunning popular programs that were previously shown on networks. As such, these stations are the bulwark of the syndication market – into which shows canceled by the networks are sold if there are enough episodes to allow for *stripping,* which is continuous use of episodes over several days per week.

Although independent stations may purchase first-run programs, and to a limited extent self-produce programming, they normally rely on such syndicated products to fill prime-time schedules. Consequently, in cities with more than one independent station, there may be aggressive bidding to obtain rights to the most popular series coming off the networks. Because rights to a half-hour episode (the most efficient length) of a popular series may sell for upward of $75,000 in a major city, producers can often amass substantial sums from all markets (see section 4.4). In recent years, however, stations have been increasingly inclined to conserve cash through the use of barter-syndication arrangements such as those noted in Chapter 4. Such arrangements have also been used to good effect by independents, known as *superstations,* that send their signals via satellite to cable systems around the country.[20]

Syndicated (usually first-run) radio programs also generally follow a unified theme (e.g., "The History of Rock 'n Roll") or use a personality (e.g., Larry King). In payment for such programming, stations may make various arrangements, including combinations of cash, bartered goods and services, and time.

Considerably different in temper and means of funding, however, are the television and radio stations affiliated with the Public Broadcasting Service (PBS) – which is actually a confederation of nonprofit, independently owned stations or station groups. The distinguishing feature here is that programs are not interrupted by commercial announcements, but are instead usually "sponsored" (supported) by one or several corporate grants. Financing for public television programming is derived from viewers, from government subsidies, and from support of corporate contributors funneled through the nonprofit Corporation for Public Broadcasting, which was set up by act of Congress in 1967. Many programs on PBS stations are distributed by PBS, but others may be self-produced or purchased from other sources.[21]

6.2 Economic characteristics

Macroeconomic relationships

Broadcasting industry growth inevitably traces a path similar to that of the U.S. economy. Although factors such as presidential elections and Olympic Games (now every 2 years) noticeably affect supply and demand for the commercial-time inventory, macroeconomic trends are of overriding importance to the industry's secular financial performance.

Total corporate profits, though, are perhaps the most important influence on how much companies will spend on advertising through newspapers, magazines, billboards, direct mail, and commercial broadcasting services. During periods of economic duress, companies may find that advertising budgets are tempting and expedient targets for cost-cutting. But also, there are many firms, primarily those selling "soft" consumer products (e.g., soap, cosmetics, hamburgers), for which market-share and consumer-awareness considerations make it all but impossible to significantly trim advertising spending except under the most adverse circumstances. The variance of expenditures on advertising in relation to changes in corporate profits, and the share trends of broadcast media versus newspapers are illustrated in Figure 6.7.[22]

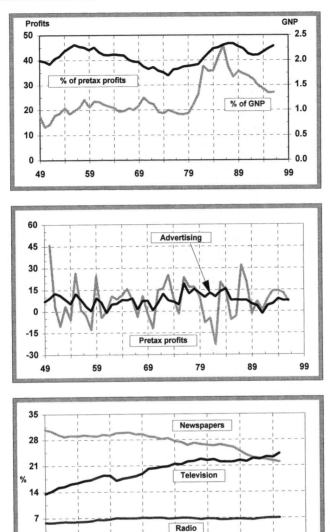

Figure 6.7. (a) Total U.S. advertising expenditures as a percentage of GNP and pretax corporate profits (excluding IVA adjustment), 1949–96, (b) Pretax corporate profits and spending for advertising, year-over-year percent changes, 1950–96, (c) Percent shares of total advertising: television, radio, and newspapers, 1960–96. *Source:* Based on data by Robert J. Coen, McCann-Erikson, Inc.

Still, when the economy weakens, some firms must inevitably reduce advertising budgets, and a decline (unevenly apportioned) in overall demand for broadcasting services ensues. Large, nationally known brands continue to be advertised on network television with approximately the same degree of intensity regardless of conditions. But prices for network time soften to the extent that major, highly cyclical consumer-products companies cut back.

Smaller local businesses, however, normally feel a recession much more immediately and would thus more sharply curtail advertising expenditures on local independent stations. In other words, in an economic downturn, network and *national spot* (regional/local ads for national brands shown on local-station time) advertising may hold up much better than local advertising. The one mitigating factor for stations is that, as their spot rates decrease relative to those charged for network time, some ads normally going to networks may instead be placed locally.

Since 1960, television revenues have, on the average, risen 14.2% in the contemporaneous presidential election/Olympics years, and 8.1% in the others. And over that span, advertising as a percentage of personal consumption expenditures has generally held to the range of 3.0% to 3.6%.

Microeconomics considerations

Broadcasting services, like national-defense services, are public goods: The cost of production is independent of the number of consumers who enjoy benefits, and one person's consumption does not reduce the quantity available to others.[23] Moreover, broadcasting is a highly regulated industry in which public-welfare and government-policy questions frequently arise. Economic theory has been helpful in analyzing the issues.

In fact, economic studies have been especially influential in setting the course of regulation in broadcasting and cable in the following areas: prime-time-access rules, network financial-interest and programming-syndication activities, funding for public broadcasting, distant-signal-importation guidelines for cable systems, and proposals for low-power VHF "drop-ins" (small stations that do not interfere with standard stations on the same frequency in other communities). But because of the public-good characteristics of broadcasting services, and the requirement that service providers sometimes be granted monopoly powers, in most studies it has been difficult to evaluate the relative efficiencies of alternative market structures.

Against this background, several microeconomic analyses, including theories of program choice and models of network behavior, have appeared (Noll, Peck, and McGowan 1973). As Owen, Beebe, and Manning (1974, p. 101) noted, in many of these models,

competition under advertiser support tends to produce less diversity and more "wasteful duplication" than is socially optimal. This is a direct parallel to Hotelling's [1929] famous spatial competition example of "excessive sameness." Such duplication occurs because there is a tendency for a decentralized system of broadcasting, with limited channel capacity, to produce rivalry for large blocks of the audience with programs that are, if not identical, at least close substitutes.[24]

In all, the economic literature on issues pertaining to broadcasting and advertising has come to include many studies attempting to describe industry-organizational and program diversity developments in an environment that includes numerous advertiser and viewer-supported program choices.[25]

6.3 Financial-performance characteristics

Variable cost elements

Because operating costs are relatively fixed, growth in broadcast revenue is the key variable behind changes in industry profitability. In other words, if demand for commercial time is high, prices for spots rise, but everything from the cost of powering the transmitter to the cost of programming does not vary much, at least over the short run.

That does not, however, imply that increases in operating costs may be ignored. In fact, profitability can be especially sensitive to changes in the general and administrative (G & A) and programming expense areas.

For networks, programming cost increases have been particularly steep, growing at a compound annual rate of 14.4% between 1971 and 1980 and at an estimated rate of 8.0% annually between 1980 and 1992. Although much of the more than $7 billion that the networks spend each year is for programs that are licensed from the television production divisions of movie studios, a considerable portion of their budgets is also allocated to self-produced programming in the form of news, sports, and daytime serials.

News, in fact, costs each network an average of around $300 million a year. But daytime drama serials (soap operas) can often be produced for about $100,000 per half hour ($125,000 for an hour), and game shows for one-third to one-half as much because of relatively low performers' salaries, fixed studio locations, and greater use of videotape. These production cost figures are, of course, well below those for regular prime-time network series, in which the production cost per hour is now generally above $1.2 million.[26]

For networks and some stations, daytime television is therefore the most profitable schedule segment. Program costs are lower and there are more commercial slots than in prime time: twelve network minutes per hour in daytime versus six minutes per hour in prime time, with local stations having at least three minutes of "adjacencies" plus three minutes of promos in each period. The availability of more minutes thus compensates for a smaller audience base. An hour-long soap, for example, will typically generate $1 million a day in revenue.

With such a significant portion of potential profits to be derived from daytime, networks have thus always had a strong incentive to increase, or to at least maintain, daytime ratings. In contrast, however, local news, accounting for 35% to 40% of the advertising base, provides the largest source of revenue for most affiliate stations.

Table 6.4. *Typical television station revenues (total time sales) and expenses in percent by major categories*

Total time sales (revenues)	%	Expenses	%
Network compensation	7.5	Engineering	11.5
National and regional	47.5	Program and production[a]	25.5
advertisements		News	13.5
Local advertisements	45.0	Sales	12.5
	100.0	Advertisements and promotion	4.0
		General and administrative	33.0
			100.0

[a]The typical independent station spends a far greater percentage (perhaps up to 50% of all expenses) on program acquisition, but much less (perhaps 6% of all expenses) on news. Because of such programming cost, the pretax margin of profit for independents is on average no more than one-half to two-thirds that of the typical affiliate.

Table 6.5. *Radio and television broadcasting industry operating performances: composite of 76 companies, 1992–96*

	Revenues	Operating income	Operating margin[a] (%)	Assets	Operating cash flow
CAGR(%):[b]	7.6	15.5	7.3	19.4	15.5

[a]Average margin 1992–96 = 17.2%.
[b]Compound annual growth rate.
Source: Communications Industry Report. New York: Veronis, Suhler & Associates, Inc.

Aggregate financial-performance numbers for television and radio stations as compiled by National Association of Broadcasters (NAB) annual surveys, and by the FCC prior to 1980, show that G & A is the largest expense category for affiliated television stations, but programming is the largest and probably most rapidly growing cost of operations for independents. Table 6.4 indicates revenue and expense category proportions for what might be a typical station.[27] Aggregate industry data are then presented in Table 6.5.

Financial-accounting practices

The timing of recognition of programming expense by a station and network is usually different from that for the producer-distributors discussed in section 4.4. Stations or networks will not charge the expense when the product becomes "available," but rather when it is broadcast. Using accrual accounting, about two-thirds of the total program expense of a continuing (old) series will usually be recognized on first run, and the remaining third on rerun. Cash payments, however, may vary in response to producer requirements and to relative beginning strengths.

As a percentage of operating costs at independent stations, amortization of syndicated television series cost has risen from 35% in the mid-1970s to over 45%–50% in the 1990s. This compares with levels of about 25% for affiliates, who regularly receive about 65% of their programming from the networks.

Prior to 1975, accounting practices for program materials varied widely. Some broadcasters recorded neither program rights nor related obligations on their balance sheets. In that year, however, an AICPA position paper on this subject brought greater uniformity to the industry's procedures, which were finally formalized in 1982 by issuance of Financial Accounting Standards Board statement 63 (Table 6.6).

According to this statement, a broadcaster (licensee) will account for a license agreement for program material as a purchase of a right or group of rights. The licensee will then report an asset and a liability for the rights acquired and the obligations incurred when the license period begins and the following conditions have been met:

1. The cost of each program is known or determinable.
2. The program material has been accepted by the licensee in accordance with the agreement.
3. The program is available for its first showing or telecast.

In addition, the asset will be segregated on the balance sheet between current and noncurrent based on estimated time of usage, and the liability segregation will be based on payment terms. The asset and liability are then reported either on a present-value basis in accordance with APB opinion 21 (which describes the general accounting treatment for discounting payables and receivables) or at the gross amount of the liability.

Capitalized costs of program-material rights are carried on the balance sheet at the lower of unamortized cost or estimated net realizable value on a program-by-program, series, package, or daypart basis, whereas network-affiliation agreements are presented as intangible assets.

Costs are then to be allocated to individual programs within a package on the basis of the relative value of each to the broadcaster. As determined earlier, capitalized costs are to be amortized on the basis of estimated number of future showings (or, when this is not possible, over the period of the agreement).

More specifically, feature programs are to be amortized on a program-by-program basis or approximation thereof for a package, whereas program series and other syndicated products are to be amortized as a series. Straight-line amortization may be used if all showings are expected to generate similar revenues (for example, as might be the case with "evergreen" programs such as *The Honeymooners*).

In all, FASB statement 63 provides broadcasters with considerable flexibility

Table 6.6. *Recognition of acquired-program material assets, liabilities, and expenses: an illustration*

Asset and liability recognition[a]

Film	License period		Year of asset and liability recognition		
	From	To	19X1	19X2	19X3
A	10/1/X1	9/30/X3	$8,000,000		
B	10/1/X1	9/30/X3	5,000,000		
C	9/1/X2	8/31/X4		$3,750,000	
D	9/1/X3	8/31/X5			$2,250,000

Expense recognition[a]

Film	Year of expense recognition[a]				
	19X1	19X2	19X3	19X4	19X5
A		$4,800,000[b]	$3,200,000[c]		
B		3,500,000[d]	1,500,000[e]		
C			2,813,000[f]	$ 937,000[g]	
D				1,463,000[h]	$787,000[i]
		$8,300,000	$7,513,000	$2,400,000	$787,000

[a]Under the gross approach, all costs under a license agreement are recorded as amortization of program cost.
[b]$8,000,000 × 60%.   [f]$3,750,000 × 75%.
[c]$8,000,000 × 40%.   [g]$3,750,000 × 25%.
[d]$5,000,000 × 70%.   [h]$2,250,000 × 65%.
[e]$5,000,000 × 30%.   [i]$2,250,000 × 35%.
Source: FASB statement 63. © Financial Accounting Standards Board, High Ridge Park, Stamford, CT 06905, USA. Reprinted with permission, Copies of the complete document are available from the FASB.

in terms of interest and program cost amortization alternatives. Such flexibility, however, makes it more difficult to directly compare the operating performance of companies using different accounting policies.[28]

6.4 Valuing broadcast properties

Although there are no absolute formulas for valuing broadcast properties, stations change hands often enough so that at any given time, the going rate in the market can be readily determined.[29] In addition to current profitability, other important variables to consider include the following:

Interest rates

Regional location (fast-growing states are preferable to economically-depressed areas)

Changes in regulatory stringency

Place on the channel selector/radio dial (in radio tuning, center is passed most frequently and is thus most desirable)

Allotted signal power and time of operation

Surrounding terrain (e.g., mountains and tall buildings may block signals)

Current program style and format relative to other local stations

Real estate value alternatives at transmitter and/or studio site

Amount of debt to be assumed

Short-term and intermediate-term potential effects of cable and other new local distribution services

The significance of interest rate levels is no different here than elsewhere. High real rates (i.e., as adjusted for the rate of inflation) not only undercut profits via macroeconomic effects on revenues, but also reduce the number of buyers who can obtain loans and service debt without strain. High rates also diminish the alternative-use value of any real estate that is included in a station transaction and, more noticeably, reduce the net present value of future expected cash flows.[30]

In determining station values, however, the second most important consideration after taking interest rates into account is often whether or not a significant improvement in profits can be effected through alterations in program content and style. In television this may entail changes in local news and sports personalities or changes in prime-time access programs. In radio, changing from ''top 40'' style to country and western, to all news or all talk, to adult/contemporary (A/C), to middle-of-the-road (MOR), to current hits (CHR), or to album-oriented rock (AOR) might be involved. Indeed, the rise of FM versus AM properties was initiated by format alterations that appealed to young, free-spending audiences.

Of course, all other things being equal, sales of stations with similar characteristics ought to command about the same multiple of *operating cash flow,* which is defined as operating income (earnings) before interest, taxes, and depreciation and amortization (EBITDA) – or of *broadcast cash flow,* which is EBITDA before corporate expenses.[31] Such cash-flow definitions are used because price and value comparisons may be more accurately determined prior to consideration of widely varying debt-financing arrangements and tax circumstances.[32]

In addition, comparisons using *net free cash flows,* (i.e., net income plus depreciation, amortization and deferred taxes, less capital expenditures) are often useful. And a *cash flow margin,* that is, operating cash flow taken as a percentage of revenue, will also normally be calculated. For healthy properties, margins generally average in the range of 25% to 45%. But the higher end of the range is typically seen only at larger stations.

So-called leveraged buy-outs – in which money is borrowed against a station's assets (in reality, cash flow) – have also been used to help finance purchases of broadcast properties.[33] But such leveraged transactions have not always worked according to plan. In the mid-1980s, cash flow multiples for some speculative properties rose to 14 or more in response to changes (in 1984) in an FCC rule that permitted corporations to own as many as 12 television, 12 AM, and 12 FM outlets (but in markets collectively containing no more than 25% of the nation's TV homes) instead of 7 each, the previous limit.[34]

Yet, by the late 1980s, bank credit available for broadcast and cable properties was severely circumscribed by the imposition of regulations against lending for highly leveraged transactions.[35] As a result, cash flow multiples for media properties declined steeply. And many properties bought earlier with relatively large amounts of debt as compared to equity capital became practically insolvent (i.e., they were unable to cover their operating and interest costs) once the economy turned down.[36]

To approximate the value of a broadcast (and, similarly, as in Table 7.6, a cable) property: Assign a multiple of cash flow – say in the range of 8 to 12 times, a higher or lower figure depending on prevailing interest rates and similar recent transaction prices. Then subtract from the product of the assumed multiple times the cash flow an amount representing "net debt," i.e., long-term debt minus net current assets. To then arrive at a per-share estimate, divide the resulting difference by the number of shares outstanding.

value = (assigned multiple $\times$ projected cash flow)

$-$ (long-term debt $-$ net current assets)

Such calculations focus attention on the difference in the value of broadcast and cable properties as measured by the going multiple of cash flow (i.e., the so-called private market value) and the value of the underlying publicly traded shares. A wide divergence will, of course, enhance takeover prospects.

Even so, however, it is not particularly easy to determine what a reasonable discount to private market value should be. Private market prices reflect the powers that derive from total control over an asset. Yet, from the standpoint of a potential seller, the taxes that will have to be paid on liquidation of the asset often loom large in the selling decision. In fact, because of normal uncertainties about the direction of interest rates and the course of economic growth, there is usually a significant speculative element involved, and public-share discounts to private market values are often 30% or more.

6.5 Concluding remarks

The potential for broadcast industry profitability in any one year depends more directly on the overall condition of the economy than on anything else. But over the long run, growth will most likely be affected by several new developments that will challenge the preeminence of television and radio broadcasting as evolved since the late 1940s. The major challenges have recently come from the growth of cable and cable-related services and from the introduction of video-cassette recorders and computerized entertainment devices such as video games.

Of these, cable is probably the most important because new or upgraded systems will be able to distribute up to 500 channels without interference from tall buildings and hilly terrain and without constraint in transmission power. In fact, cable has already significantly eroded network viewership from about 84% of homes in 1980 to an average share of approximately 55% in 1997. Network audience levels are being sustained only because of expansion in the number of television households to an estimated 100 million by the year 2000 from 79.9 million in 1980.

Although advertisers are just beginning to use it as a major medium, cable has the potential to significantly expand time inventories and therefore to mitigate price increases for commercial television spots. In addition, although most cable channels undoubtedly will be devoted to video programming, data-transmission and cable-radio services with no advertising may begin to supplant commercial FM radio.

Also competing with broadcast programming are Internet services, computerized-entertainment software (e.g., video games), and home-video playback devices (e.g., VCRs and DVDs) that divert audiences with alternative uses for the television's screen. Indeed, Internet broadcasting (see Chapter 8) is already evolving into a major distribution medium held back only by the rate at which bandwidth can be expanded.

All of these elements have reduced the growth potential for broadcasting profits. But the industry is nonetheless far from enervated; few businesses can regularly generate the high relative cash flows and pretax margins of over 20% that are common in broadcasting. And many advertisers will continue to be attracted to network television because of its great efficiency in reaching the mass of consumers at a relatively price-competitive cost-per-thousand.

In addition, many local businesses also still tend to underutilize local television services and may thus represent another source of secularly rising demand. Especially at the local level, it will be difficult to replace the strong news and sports-programming capability of commercial stations.

In summary, broadcasting is a multifaceted, regulated industry now entering a period of maturity in which expansion will be slower and the challenges greater. However, it remains a business in which profit margins are well above average and in which cash generation is unusually high. As such, broadcasting will, for a long time, continue to be a major source of entertainment.

Selected additional reading

Abrams, B. (1984). "CBS Program Chief Picks Entertainment for 85 Million Viewers," *Wall Street Journal,* September 28.

    (1985). "TV 'Sweeps' May Not Say Much, But for Now That's All There Is," *Wall Street Journal,* February 28.

Andrews, E. L., and Brinkley, J. (1995). "The Fight for Digital TV's Future," *New York Times,* January 25.

Berman, S., and Flack, S. (1986). "Will the Network Take It Out of Hollywood's Hide?" *Forbes* 138(4)(August 25).

Besen, S. M., Krattenmaker, T. G, Metzger, R. A. Jr., Woodbury, J. R. (1984). *Misregulating Television: Network Dominance and the FCC*. Chicago: University of Chicago.

Besen, S. M., and Soligo, R. (1973). "The Economics of the Network-Affiliate Relationship in the Television Broadcasting Industry," *American Economic Review*, June.

Block, A. B. (1990). *Out-Foxed: The Inside Story of America's Fourth Television Network*. New York: St. Martin's Press.

Botein, M., and Rice, D. M. (1980). *Network Television and the Public Interest*. Lexington, Mass.: Lexington Books, Heath.

Brown, P. B. (1983). "Where Else Can You Go?" *Forbes* 131(13)(June 20):48.

Bylinsky, G. (1984). "High Tech Hits the TV Set," *Fortune* 109(8)(April 16):70–81.

Carnegie Corporation (1979). *A Public Trust: The Landmark Reports of the Carnegie Commission on the Future of Public Broadcasting*. New York: Carnegie Corporation and Bantam Books.

Carter, B. (1997). "Where Did the Reliable Old TV Season Go?" *New York Times*, April 20.

Chakravarty, S. N. (1994). "We Bought, We Leveraged, We Improved," *Forbes* 154(11)(November 7).

Cherington, P., Hirsch, L., and Brandwein, R. (1971). *Television Station Ownership: A Case Study of Federal Agency Regulation*. New York: Hastings House.

Coase, R. H. (1966). "The Economics of Broadcasting and Government Policy," *American Economic Review* 56(May):440–66.

Colvin, G. (1984). "The Crowded New World of TV," *Fortune* 110(6)(September 17):156.

Day, J. (1996). *The Vanishing Vision: The Inside Story of Public Television*. Berkeley, (Calif.): University of California Press.

Dejesus, E. X. (1996). "How the Internet Will Replace Broadcasting," *Byte*, February 1996.

Donlan, T. G. (1983). "Clear Signal: Deregulation Touches off a Wave of Bids for TV Stations," *Barron's*, July 11.

Eastman, S. T., and Ferguson, D. A. (1997). *Broadcast/Cable Programming: Strategies and Practices*, 5th ed. Belmont, (Calif.): Wadsworth.

"Estimated U.S. Advertising Expenditures, 1935–1979," *Advertising Age*, April 30, 1980, p. 260; September 14, 1981; May 30, 1983; May 6, 1985.

"Feeling For the Future: A Survey of Television," *The Economist*, February 12, 1994.

Fabrikant, G. (1987). "Not Ready For Prime Time?" *New York Times*, April 12.

Foster, E. S. (1978). *Understanding Broadcasting*. Reading, Mass.: Addison-Wesley.

Gitlin, T. (1985). *Inside Prime Time*. New York: Pantheon (Random House).

Goldenson, L. and Wolf, M. J. (1991). *Beating the Odds: The Untold Story Behind the Rise of ABC*. New York: Charles Scribner's & Sons (Macmillan).

Greenberg, E., and Barnett, H. (1971). "TV Program Diversity – New Evidence and Old Theories," *American Economic Review* 61.

Gunther, M. (1997). "How GE Made NBC No. 1," *Fortune*, 135(2)(February 3).

Head, S. W. (1976). *Broadcasting in America: A Survey of Television and Radio*, 3d ed. Boston: Houghton Mifflin.

Hoynes, W. (1994). *Public Television For Sale*. Boulder, (Colo.): Westview Press.

Jensen, E. (1994). "Public TV Prepares For Image Transplant To Justify Existence," *Wall Street Journal*, January 13.

(1994). "Major TV Networks, Dinosaurs No More, Tune In to New Deals," *Wall Street Journal*, March 17.

(1994). "Many TV Stations Switch Networks, Confusing Viewers," *Wall Street Journal*, October 7.

(1995). "CBS's Tisch Is Faulted By Insiders, Affliliates For Network's Struggle," *Wall Street Journal*, May 22.

(1995). "Why Did ABC Prosper While CBS Blinked? A Tale of 2 Strategies," *Wall Street Journal*, August 2.

Kagan, P. (1983). "Broadcasting Bonanza: TV Stations Are Fetching Record Prices," *Barron's*, October 17.

Kneale, D. (1988). "'Zapping' of TV Ads Appears Pervasive," *Wall Street Journal*, April 25.

(1989). "Seeking Ratings Gains, CBS Pays Huge Sums for Sports Contracts," *Wall Street Journal*, October 10.

(1989). "CBS Frantically Woos Hollywood to Help It Win Back Viewers," *Wall Street Journal*, February 9.

(1990) "Duo at Capital Cities Scores a Hit but Can Network Be Part of It?" *Wall Street Journal*, February 2.

(1990). "TV's Nielsen Ratings, Long Unquestioned, Face Tough Challenges," *Wall Street Journal*, July 19.

Kupfer, A. (1991). "The U.S. Wins One in High-Tech TV," *Fortune* 123(7)(April 8).

Landro, L. (1984). "Independent TV Stations Assume Bigger Role in Broadcast Industry," *Wall Street Journal*, May 11.

(1984). "TV Networks Are Again Producing Films for Release in Movie Theaters," *Wall Street Journal*, December 5.

Larson, E. (1992). "Watching Americans Watch TV,"*The Atlantic Monthly*, (March)269 (3).

Leinster, C. (1985). "NBC's Peacock Struts Again," *Fortune* 112(3)(August 5).

Levin, H. J. (1980). *Fact and Fancy in Television Regulation: An Economic Study of Policy Alternatives*. New York: Russell Sage Foundation.

Levine, J. (1990). "The Last Gasp of Mass Media?" *Forbes*, 146(6) (September 17):176.

Mahar, M. (1993). "Life After Cable," *Barron's*, May 10.

Mathewson, G. F. (1972). "A Consumer Theory of Demand for the Media," *Journal of Business* (April)45(2):212–24.

Mayer, J. (1983). "Putting Ads on Public TV Angers Few," *Wall Street Journal*, March 24.

McTague, J. (1996). "Couch-Potato War," *Barron's* July 15.

Moore, T. (1986). "Culture Shock Rattles the TV Networks," *Fortune* 113(8)(April 14).

Neuman, W. R. (1991). *The Future of the Mass Audience*. New York: Cambridge University Press.

Newcomb, P. (1989). "Negative Ratings," *Forbes* 143(3)(February 6):138.

Noam, E. (1991). *Television in Europe*. New York and Oxford: Oxford University Press.

Peterman, J. L. (1979). "Differences Between the Levels of Spot and Network Television Advertising Rates," *Journal of Business* 52(4)(October):549.

Platt, C. (1997). "The Great HDTV Swindle," *Wired*, (February) 5.02.

Poltrack, D. F. (1983). *Television Marketing: Network/Local/Cable*. New York: McGraw-Hill.

Reitman, V. (1994). "Pittsburgh's WQED Failed to See Change in Public-TV Industry," *Wall Street Journal*, January 17.

Rothenberg, R. (1995). *Where the Suckers Moon: The Life and Death of an Advertising Campaign*. New York: Random House (Vintage).

Routt, E. (1972). *The Business of Radio Broadcasting*. Blue Ridge Summit, Pa.: TAB Books.

Rutherford, P. (1990). *When Television Was Young: Primetime Canada 1952-1967*. Toronto: University of Toronto.

Saddler, J. (1984). "Push to Deregulate Broadcasting Delights Industry, Angers Others," *Wall Street Journal*, April 16.

——— (1985). "Broadcast Takeovers Meet Less FCC Static, and Critics Are Upset," *Wall Street Journal*, June 11.

Saporito, B. (1990). "TV's Toughest Year Is Just a Preview," *Fortune* 122(13)(November 19):95.

Schmalensee, R. (1972). *The Economics of Advertising*. New York: North Holland Publishing Company (Elsevier).

Schmalensee, R., and Bojank, R. (1983). "The Impact of Scale and Media Mix on Advertising Agency Costs," *Journal of Business* 56(4)(October).

Sellers, P. (1988). "Lessons From TV's New Bosses," *Fortune* 117(6)(March 14):115.

Shames, L. (1989). "CBS Has Won the World Series . . . Now It Could Lose Its Shirt," *New York Times Magazine*, July 23.

Sharkey, B. (1994). "The Secret Rules of Ratings," *New York Times*, August 28.

Sherman, S. P. (1985). "Are Media Mergers Smart Business?" *Fortune* 111(13):98–103.

Simon, J. L. (1970). *Issues in the Economics of Advertising*. Urbana, (Ill.): University of Illinois Press.

Smith, S. B. (1990). *In All His Glory: The Life of William S. Paley*. New York: Simon and Schuster.

Spence, A. M., and Owen, B. M. (1977). "Television Programming, Monopolistic Competition and Welfare, " *Quarterly Journal of Economics* 91.

"The Fourth Network: Fox Is a Hit - But Can It Take on the Big Boys?" *Business Week*, No. 3178 (September 17, 1990):114.

"The Networks Produce Some Panic in Hollywood," *Business Week*, No. 2854 (August 6, 1984):90.

"Television Ratings: The British Are Coming," *Fortune* 111(7)(April 1, 1985):109.

"Television Turns 50," *Broadcasting*, May 1, 1989.

Telser, L. G. (1966). "Supply and Demand for Advertising Messages," *American Economic Review* 56(May):457.

Udelson, J. H. (1982). *The Great Television Race: A History of the American Television Industry, 1925-1941*. Tuscaloosa, Ala.: University of Alabama.

Weisman, J. (1987). "Public TV in Crisis," *TV Guide* (31, 32)(August 1, August 8).

"What Happened to Advertising?" *Business Week*, No. 3232 (September 23, 1991):66.

U.S. Congress, (1990). *The Big Picture: HDTV and High-Resolution Systems,*, Washington, D.C. Office of Technology Assessment, (OTA-BP-CIT-64), June.

Wirth, M. O., and Allen, B. T. (1980). "Crossmedia Ownership, Regulatory Scrutiny, and Pricing Behavior," *Journal of Economics and Business* 33(1)(fall):28–42.

7
Cable

You cannot plan the future by the past. – Edmund Burke

Though said some 200 years ago, this might well be a slogan for executives of fast-growing cable TV and other new video-media companies in which managements are in a never-ending scramble for franchises, funding, and subscribers. In this chapter, the historical and economic relationships among broadcasting, cable, and other new media are explored.

7.1 From faint signals

In the late 1940s, the technological marvel of wireless broadcasting was still in an early phase of development. But the first community-antenna television (CATV) systems were already being built in mountainous or rural regions where over-the-air television signals were difficult, if not impossible, to receive. CATV was an eminently logical idea, developed, according to legend, by a television set retailer who wanted to sell more sets: With a good antenna atop a nearby mountain, and a clear signal as retransmitted by wire (cable), a burgeoning number of new television households would be created.

Yet until the 1960s, with broadcasting expansively dominant, CATV remained a backwater of the video-communications business. Indeed, it took fifteen years,

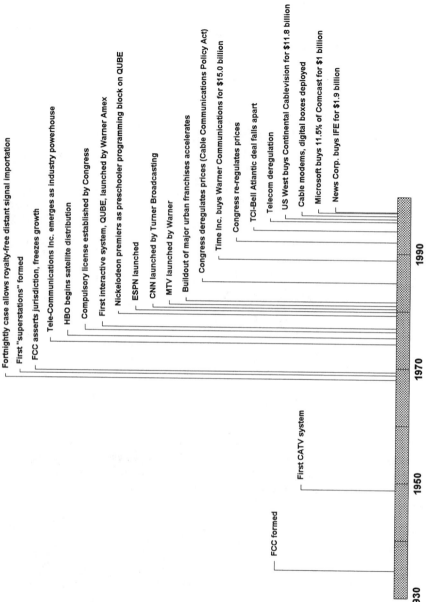

Figure 7.1. Cable Industry Milestones, 1930–2000

from 1948 to 1963, to connect the first million subscribers. Broadcasters' aggressive lobbying against competition from cable was manifest in arcane FCC regulations limiting the number of distant signals that could be imported into large markets and in prohibiting (in 1970) pay-cable systems from showing movies less than 10 years old and sporting events that had been on commercial television during the previous five years.

Pay services evolve

The dreams of pioneers notwithstanding, high and rising interest rates, inability to attract sufficient capital funding, and excessive rates of "churn" (i.e., household connects and then disconnects) plagued the industry well into the 1970s. By 1975, however, FCC restrictions on cable's distant-signal-importation and programming options began to ease. "Superstations" that programmed for a national cable audience sprung up. And, more significantly, Time Inc., the giant magazine publishing company with interests in electronic communications, started a pay-TV movie-distribution organization known as Home Box Office (HBO).[1] In contrast to over-the-air commercial-broadcast television services that provided viewers with ostensibly "free" signals, pay-TV required that a subscribing household make monthly cash payments for programming.

In and of itself, offering of a *premium pay cable* service as opposed to *basic cable* service – which simply brought a clearer signal from over-the-air broadcasts into the home – was not revolutionary. What made the difference was that pay-TV service was for the first time able to be nationally and simultaneously distributed to local franchises via earth-orbiting communications-satellite transponders. This technological advance made it possible to simultaneously provide households with several specially programmed movie and sports channels. Basic services thus became only the first of many pay "units" or tiers that the so-called *multiple system operators* (MSOs) – companies that operated more than one cable system – could offer viewers. In addition, it then also became possible to sell movie or sports events such as boxing matches on an á la carte, or *pay-per-view* basis.

Although it was largely unrecognized at the time (because of HBO's heavy start-up costs and losses), so was born not only a major new national television network, but also the first serious threat to the movie industry's strong grip on distribution and pricing of its product. Five years elapsed before the filmed-entertainment companies fully understood what had happened and before a subsequently ill-fated attempt was made at launching Premiere, a pay-channel service owned by four leading studio-distributor companies.[2]

Proliferation of pay services was by then well in progress, and by the late 1970s there were several major national film and special-entertainment-channel offerings in competition with HBO. The most important of these were Showtime, owned by the former Teleprompter and Viacom, and the Warner-Amex-sponsored The Movie Channel.[3] However, at least 50 other services catering to disparate groups of viewers had also been introduced.[4]

Nevertheless, the great eagerness with which new cable households embraced the plethora of pay-channel offerings misled many MSOs into bidding too aggressively for the then unbuilt large city franchises that had come up for proposal in the late 1970s and early 1980s. And many financially overextended MSOs had to later renege on their promises as construction and operating cost estimates soared well beyond the points at which reasonable returns could be expected.

Also, despite enormous industry growth, many services during this time continued to experience substantial losses because revenues from subscriptions and other sources were insufficient to cover operating expenses, including those for program production and acquisition, for marketing to system operators and consumers, and for leasing of time on satellites.[5]

Passage of the Cable Communications Policy Act of 1984, allowing deregulation (in 1987) of service pricing, clearly marked the industry's coming of age in terms of both political and economic power (Figure 7.1).[6] And with over half of all television homes subscribing to at least a minimal basic service, cable had, by the mid-1980s, become the dominant multi-channel program-delivery system in the United States and Canada (Figure 7.2). Cable viewing currently accounts for more than 30% of total television viewing spread over more than 130 cable networks (Table 7.1).

Going forward, development of video signal-compression methods along with the deployment of fiber and hybrid fiber/coax (HFC) network structures are expected to enable the industry to compete in emerging digital telecommunications markets.

7.2 Cable industry structure

Operational aspects

Coaxial (and/or fiber optic) cable has the capability of bringing into each home over 100 interactive channels of entertainment and other services. But construction projects are very capital- and politics-intensive, and years may elapse from the point of conceptualization to the stage of operational profitability. Such delays provide the more rapidly deployed and less expensive noncable alternative programming services with opportunities for expansion.

In the days when the business was primarily a CATV service, and cable companies were essentially construction enterprises, not much more than a well-located large antenna, a couple of signal amplifiers, and a few miles of wire were needed for operations to begin. But proliferation of pay services, rapid growth in the number of urban-based customers, demands for upgrading or rebuilding of older one-way systems, and requirements for subscriber addressability have substantially increased the complexity of equipment and the size of capital investment required to operate efficiently.

For instance, advances in electronics have made it possible for coaxial-cable channel capacity to increase: Systems now manage frequency bandwidths upward of 550 MHz (MegaHertz), versus 300 MHz or less in older systems. And new

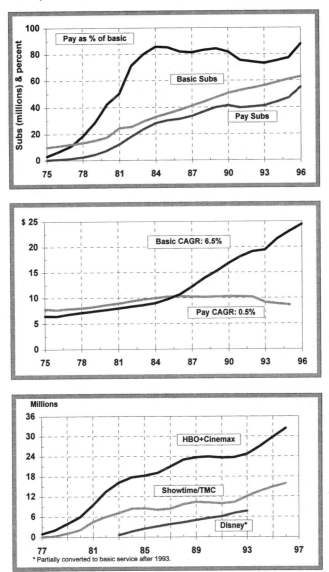

Figure 7.2. Cable industry trends, 1975–96. (a) Number of basic-cable and pay-cable subscribers, and pay-cable subscribers as a percentage of basic-cable subscribers; (b) Basic and pay cable estimated monthly rates; (c) Pay-channel service subscribers, major services, 1977–96. *Source data:* Company reports and Paul Kagan & Associates, Inc., Carmel, California.

Table 7.1. *Top 15 cable networks*[a]

Rank	Cable network	Start-up date	Systems	Subscribers (million)
1	Cable News Network	June 1980	11,411	65.8
2	ESPN	September 1979	12,017	71.0
3	TBS Superstation	December 1976	11,378	65.7
4	USA Network	April 1980	12,500	68.2
5	Discovery Channel	June 1985	10,683	69.4
6	TNT	October 1988	10,586	65.5
7	Nickelodeon	April 1979	11,788	66.8
8	C-Span	March 1979	6,114	62.4
9	The Family Channel	April 1977	13,213	59.0
10	Nashville Network	March 1983	13,932	69.0
11	MTV	August 1981	8,927	64.2
12	Lifetime	February 1984	6,556	62.7
13	Arts & Entertainment	February 1984	11,436	64.6
14	Weather Channel	May 1982	6,500	61.6
15	QVC Network	September 1986	6,202	61.2

[a]The subscriber number does not represent the actual viewing audience, but rather the total universe that can receive the network in question.
Source: Cablevision, June 30, 1997.

fiber optic systems readily provide further substantial performance improvements, leading to 1,000 Mhz (1 Ghz) widths that can transmit more than 150 channels, and propel data along at a rate of 1 billion bits a second – a rate at which the whole *Encyclopedia Britannica* could be sent in two seconds. Data compression algorithms also make systems with upward of 500 channels feasible. Yet many millions of previous-generation signal converters (which adapt cable-frequency transmissions so that they can be seen on ordinary television receivers) must still be replaced at considerable cost.

Computers and transportation vehicles are two other major capital items. At the head-end facilities, from where signals are sent to subscribing households, computers monitor the system's wires and amplifiers for any breakdowns that may occur and keep track of what each household is receiving. And computers are, of course, used to update records of connections, monthly billings, and program-guide shipments.

But in addition, field-service personnel (whose salaries are a major operating expense) also require extensive fleets of trucks and other mobile equipment in order to connect and disconnect homes, install converters, and repair and maintain wires. Especially in large cities, where installation is complicated by the density of population and the need to construct underground conduits (instead of renting the use of telephone utility poles as in rural regions), the problems of maintenance,

Table 7.2. *U.S. cable systems by subscriber size and channel capacity, 1996*

	Systems	% of total	Subscribers	% of total
Size by subscribers				
50,000 & over	263	2.40%	28,714,598	46.69%
20,000–49,999	446	4.07	13,557,866	22.04
10,000–19,999	507	4.63	7,258,235	11.64
5,000–9,999	666	6.08	4,788,959	7.62
3,500–4,999	401	3.66	1,676,587	2.72
1,000–3,499	1,968	17.97	3,730,537	6.07
500–999	1,457	13.31	1,045,512	1.70
250–499	1,494	13.65	536,941	0.87
249 & under	3,322	30.34	399,056	0.65
Not available	419	3.88	—	—
Total	10,943	100.00%	61,708,291	100.00%
Channel capacity				
54 & over	1,724	15.75%	33,582,395	54.420%
30–53	6,410	58.58	26,064,547	42.238
20–29	1,067	9.75	806,017	1.306
13–19	337	3.08	98,079	0.159
6–12	456	4.17	190,714	0.309
Not available	937	8.56	964,412	1.563
Total	10,943	100.00%	61,708,291	100.00%

Source: Television Factbook, No. 65. Washington D.C.: Warren Publishing Inc., 1997.

of customer service, and of signal piracy can be so severe as to noticeably reduce a system's profit potential. Table 7.2 shows a breakdown of U.S. cable systems by subscriber size and channel capacity as of 1996.

Franchising

Cable systems, by their very nature, operate in a way that is pretty close to what economists might define as being a natural monopoly – which is a market in which there is room for only one firm of efficient size. They also bundle the provision of transmission services along with the provision of program services. It is therefore not surprising that government regulation – more a political process than an effective antidote to monopolistic conditions – has become a prominent part of the industry's economic landscape.[7] Despite considerable easing of federal regulation since the early 1970s, the FCC retains authority even (as the Supreme Court ruled in 1984) to preempt city and state controls.[8]

Nowhere, however, have the regulatory features been historically more visible than at the local community level, from which franchises are originated and administered. Municipalities may receive up to 5% (normally 3% as a base) of system revenues and may negotiate strongly for other special benefits in return for granting a local monopoly.[9] And, until recently, they had governed increases on fees for basic services.[10]

Still, in order to bid successfully for a franchise that is yet to be constructed, cable companies must carefully forecast potential revenues and costs of operation over the typical 15-year franchise period. Franchise bidders will also often promise to contribute to the community fully equipped television studios, libraries, and "free" local-access channels.[11]

Construction proposals (so-called requests for proposals or RFPs) obviously involve large expenditures of time and money without any assurance that a bid will be successful. Furthermore, in the event of a successful bid, several years will elapse between the time the franchise is awarded and the time the new system becomes fully operational (is "energized") and profitable. In the interim, financing and construction expenses may rise substantially over the original estimates, and the cream of the market may be skimmed by other technologies (discussed in section 7.4) that can be implemented more rapidly.

Revenue relationships

As already noted, the introduction of pay-cable services on a nationally distributed basis was crucial in launching the industry on a high-growth path. Ultimately, though, the willingness of consumers to continue to subscribe to such services depends on the quantity and quality of the programming that is provided. For that reason alone it is important to understand the economic relationships between program suppliers, program wholesalers, and MSOs.

MSOs are, of course, perfectly capable of producing low-budget programs of local interest. But by and large, this is not what the paying customers want to see. And so a situation developed in which it became convenient for the MSO to purchase, from wholesalers like HBO or Showtime, the rights to play movies, or to obtain special-interest programming by joining with other MSOs in support of a specialized network like CNN (Cable News Network) or ESPN (Entertainment and Sports Network). In establishing such specialized cable networks, the costs of expensive productions could be covered by small charges to each subscriber and in the case of movies, there would be no need for each small MSO to deal inefficiently with the large Hollywood studios on a picture-by-picture basis.

Still, for the filmed-entertainment programming wholesalers – HBO and Showtime and The Disney Channel, for example – relationships with the MSOs on one side and the program suppliers on the other are rather complex. Since over 300 titles a year are normally required to fill out a channel's schedule, wholesalers will commit to spending hundreds of millions of dollars to license in advance a full (or nearly full) slate of a studio's output (sometimes exclusively) for a three- to five-year period.

Such arrangements provide studios with a solid base of production financing, while assuring wholesalers of a programming schedule that can retain the allegiance of their immediate customers, the MSOs. Yet the license fees thus negotiated with the studios will typically be calibrated to the theatrical box-office performances of the films in these packages. If averaged over all new titles in a package, the fees might generally work out to a cost of under 20 cents a channel-subscriber, but possibly more, depending on the popularity of the films included and the extent of exclusivity arrangements made.

However, in purchasing from the wholesaler, the MSO, in turn, abides by a rate card. This card sets a standard monthly minimum per household and also certain sliding-scale surcharges that are used by the wholesaler as an incentive for the MSO to sign up as many subscribers as possible.

A summary of a representative rate card prior to volume discounts, which can substantially lower the total cost to the MSO, might be as follows:

If the system charges over $12.00 a month, the wholesaler is to receive $6.25 + 50% of any amount over $12.00; systems at $11.00–$12.00 pay $6.50 flat, and those under are scaled down $0.25 for each dollar until a floor rate of $5.00 flat is reached for systems charging under $6.50.

Thus, the wholesaler will normally receive a little over half of what the retailer (the MSO) charges the average household for the pay-channel service. And then, on average, about one-half of what the wholesaler receives (or around 25% of the retail price) is used to pay the program suppliers, be they movie studios or other production and/or distribution entities.[12]

Fortunately, the revenue-sharing relationships for cable networks are considerably simpler to describe. Although the types of arrangements between MSOs and the specialized cable networks may vary considerably from one situation to another, it is common for each MSO to compensate a network for its programming on the basis of at least 5 or 10 cents, and sometimes as much as 25 cents, a month per subscriber.[13] The network may then also derive half or more of its total revenues from the sale of national or regional advertising.[14] Nevertheless, it is still an open question as to how much advertising on cable viewers will tolerate as the price of basic services, as shown in Figure 7.2 (b), rises.[15]

Figure 7.3 illustrates the growth of estimated advertising expenditures on cable services with data that are comparable to expenditures on network television advertising of $11.6 billion in 1995 and national spot and local spending of approximately $10 billion each. Whereas it remains to be seen how tolerant of commercials cable viewers will be, there is no doubt that commercial sponsorship of such programming will become increasingly attractive to advertisers as audiences for broadcast network television grow more slowly (if at all) and as demographic and income characteristics of cable audiences improve.

Hence, financial support for cable programmers, unlike over-the-air broadcasters, can come directly from viewers, from advertisers, from cable operators, or from a combination of all three sources. Clearly, by the early 1990s, the cable industry, then with aggregate revenues of more than $22 billion and operating cash flows in excess of $7 billion had reached and, in many respects, surpassed financial parity with the commercial broadcasting industry.

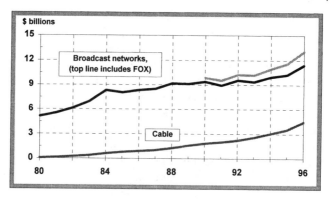

Figure 7.3. Cable advertising revenues, 1980–96. *Source data:* © Paul Kagan & Associates, Inc., Carmel California.

7.3 Financial characteristics

Capital concerns

The industry's tremendous thirst for capital to upgrade old systems and construct new ones ("new builds," in industry parlance) has led to concentration into fewer, but financially stronger, ownership entities. As can be seen from the data in Table 7.3, major publicly owned companies now control the largest subscriber groups.

Because capital costs for system expansions have been so large, it was not until the late 1980s that the industry could begin to show significant aggregate operating profits after deduction of interest expenses. Yet, just as in broadcasting, the more relevant (and also conventional) measure of financial performance for cable industry companies is not operating profit, but operating cash flow defined as earnings before interest, taxes, and depreciation and amortization expense (EBITDA). As in broadcasting, this definition of cash flow is used to avoid comparative distortions that may arise as a result of financing and tax variations.

Cable operating margins, calculated by taking operating cash flows as a percentage of revenues, also provide a handy means of comparison among different operating systems. Such margins would normally fall into the range of 35% to 50% for most financially strong companies.[16]

For many analytical purposes, however, the most convenient way to understand the profitability and cash-flow potential of a system is through use of population-density and penetration figures. Much of a system's operating cost is fixed and independent of subscriber numbers, and construction cost per mile may in some instances be essentially the same whether there is one subscriber or there are a thousand subscribers along that mile.[17] "Drop" charges (the cost of attaching a home to the main feeder cable) and the cost of installing converters (used to enable an ordinary 12-channel VHF TV tuner circuit to display more than 12 signals) are the only major variable expenses related to subscriber density.[18]

Table 7.3. *Top 10 multiple-system operators, data in millions, 1997*

Rank	System operator	Number of subscribers	Pay-cable units	Homes passed by cable
1	Tele-Communications Inc.	14.4	14.3	23.8
2	Time Warner Cable	12.3	8.2	19.0
3	US West Media Group	4.9	3.8	8.3
4	Comcast Cable Communications Inc.	4.3	3.7	6.9
5	Cox Communications Inc.	3.3	2.0	5.1
6	Cablevision Systems Corp.	2.9	4.8	4.4
7	Adelphia Communications Corp.	1.8	0.8	2.6
8	Jones Intercable Inc.	1.5	1.2	2.3
9	Century Communications Corp.	1.3	0.5	2.1
10	Marcus Cable	1.2	0.7	1.9

Source: TV Digest, May 12, 1997 by permission from Warren Publishing.

A simple exercise, with the following assumptions, will illustrate:

A new 1,000-mile system costs an average of $15,000 per mile, or $15 million, to build.

Both basic and pay monthly service charges are $10.00.

Penetration of the 10,000 homes along the 1,000-mile route is 50%, and the ratio of pay to basic subscribers is also 50%.

The cable operating margin is 40%.

Thus, annual revenues from basic service would be $600,000 ($10/month × 12 months × 5,000 subscribers), pay-service revenues would be $300,000 and total revenues $900,000. Applying a 40% operating margin, profits would then be $360,000, which is a 2.4% (360/15,000) return on total capital investment before accounting for depreciation, interest, and taxes.

The return on capital (ROC) in this example appears to be surprisingly inadequate for two reasons. First, the number of homes passed per mile of plant (that is, the density) is far too low to support a new build. The density of 10 homes per mile in this example compares with an average of about 80 homes per mile for all systems in the United States. Were this hypothetical system to contain the average homes per mile, and with all other things equal, the ROC would be 19.2%. (Also, in most instances, the returns to equity investors would be noticeably higher than in this example because most of the capital needed to build the system would be borrowed.)

But second, in a modern system, the ratio of pay to basic subscribers would almost certainly be well over 50%. And any incremental pay revenues (as well as higher penetration levels) would significantly boost returns; once a system is in place, the cost of adding subscribers or tiers of service beyond the basic service is minimal.

However, yet another interesting aspect is revealed by relating the total investment required per subscriber to the minimum average monthly charge that the system needs in order to stay in business over the long run. Assume, for example, that a 54-channel addressable system was to be built starting in 1995. Estimated investment per subscriber typical of the industry might then appear as in Table 7.4. If interest rates were around 10% per year, and the system were depreciated over the usual 15-year franchise period at 6% per year, then just to recover interest and depreciation the minimum average monthly charge to each subscriber household would have to be $17.33, that is, $[(0.10 + 0.06) \times \$1,300]/12$.

Typically, this industry is leveraged at six to seven times EBITDA. And, as of 1997, total borrowing by the industry was around $40 billion, which implies an average of about $625 of debt per basic subscriber, backed by perhaps another $300 or so (per sub) in equity. Still, with new builds costing at least $1,100 per subscriber, it is easy to see how billions of dollars more will probably have to be raised through issuance of stock, bonds, bank loans, and limited partnerships in order to maintain, upgrade, and expand systems into new fiber optic and digital-switching technologies. Recent industry operating data are shown in Table 7.5.

Accounting conventions

In the life-cycle development of a cable company, there are three distinct stages for which special accounting treatments have evolved and been codified – first by a March 1979 AICPA position paper and then by subsequent issuance in 1981 of Financial Accounting Standards Board (FASB) statement 51. The three distinct stages are as follows:

1. Start-up: the time between construction start and receipt of service by the first subscriber.
2. Prematurity: usually less than two years and coincident with construction completion; it is the time between first subscriber activation and maturation of the system.
3. Maturity: the system at maturity.

Before the AICPA guidelines, major cable franchises generally capitalized all start-up expenses until the system was profitable. But under FASB statement 51, construction, labor, interest, and other start-up expenses are normally capitalized only during the first phase. In effect, the prematurity period now bears a significant amount of cost, and installation-fee revenue accruals are not as high as they had been prior to implementation of FASB statement 51. More specifically (and paraphrasing the rules established by FASB statement 51):

In the second phase, most subscriber-related operating expenses are not capitalized, although plant costs may continue to be capitalized. Systemwide costs – such as for local programming, pole rentals, property taxes, and so forth – may be partially capitalized and partly expensed, the amounts depending on the

Table 7.4. *Typical investment per subscriber, circa 1995*

Fixed	
Plant (including labor)	$650
Head-end, vehicles, etc.	125
Origination, studios and equipment	75
Other	75
Total fixed	925
Variable	
Converters (set-top boxes)	300
Drops	75
Total variable	375
Total per subscriber	$1,300

Table 7.5. *Cable, system operators, operating industry performance: composite of 35 companies, 1992–96*

	Revenues	Operating income	Operating margin[a] (%)	Assets	Operating cash flow
CAGR(%):[b]	12.3	1.2	NM	16.6	8.4

[a] Average margin 1992–96 = 18.1%.
[b] Compound annual growth rate.
[c] Not meaningful.
Source: Communications Industry Report. New York: Veronis, Suhler & Associates, Inc.

ratio of the number of current subscribers to the expected number at the end of the prematurity phase. This formula is also used for depreciation and amortization, which must be over the same period and not longer than the life of the franchise.

In addition, the amount of interest cost to be capitalized during prematurity is determined in accordance with FASB statement 34, which indicates that the amount of interest cost capitalized shall not exceed the total amount of interest cost incurred by the system in that period.

The initial costs of subscriber installations, however, are capitalized and depreciated over the period used for the whole system. Similarly, the costs of successful franchise application are capitalized and amortized according to standards for intangible assets as delineated in APB (Accounting Principles Board) opinion 17.

Except for installation fees – which can be accrued as revenues only to the extent offset by direct selling costs incurred – revenues from monthly subscriptions are recorded as income. If installation fees exceed marketing costs, the difference is capitalized and recorded as income over the expected average period during which the subscriber is expected to be active.

Although accounting rules for system operations are obviously very precise, for cable systems that are being acquired, the excess price over book or fair value paid by the acquirer is now amortized over 15 years. Until the tax code was modified in 1993, there had been uncertainties as to whether such amortizations of goodwill (the excess price over book value) and intangible franchise rights would be tax-deductible, as they now are.[19]

7.4 Development directions

Pay-per-view

Were it not for the introduction of pay movie and sports channels beginning in the 1970s, the cable industry today would be far smaller than it is. But clearly, the next step, along with the replacement of coaxial cable by optical fibers and the introduction of high-definition pictures, is the burgeoning of pay-per-view (PPV) services. Throughout most of the 1980s, an average of less than 15% of all cable converters were capable of being directly addressed from a system's head-end, and subscription to pay *channels* rather than to specific program offerings was the only technologically practical means of sending several pay signals into the home.

But with the number of addressable households increasing rapidly, and with the cost of computing power decreasing, such PPV services are becoming a significant source of industry revenues. The degree to which these so-called video-on-demand (VOD) offerings eventually cannibalize subscriptions to the more traditional pay-channel services and also adversely affect videocassette rentals, is still, however, an open question.

That PPV has the potential to be an extremely profitable service for cable operators to provide, even if half or more of the MSO's revenues are remitted to program originators or distributors, can be seen from the following simple example. Assume:

A universe of 25 million addressable homes
A response rate ("buy rate") of 4%, or 1 million households
A PPV price of $10.00
That the movie company or other program supplier retains 40% of the PPV price
    to the viewer
That a program wholesaler/distributor retains 10% in return for setting up marketing and distribution and the MSO retains 50%.

Then, the program supplier will generate $4 million of revenue in one night, and the MSO $5 million.[20] For the movie company in this hypothetical situation, the amount could compare very favorably with what would ordinarily be obtained through licensing to a pay channel or through theatrical exhibition. And for the cable company, the potential exists for substantially enhanced profitability if the subscribing household makes more than one PPV selection a month or if the response rate is higher than 4%.[21]

Cable's competition

Cable has been, and will long continue to be, the major alternative distribution system to over-the-air broadcasts. Indeed, of all the broadcast-related media, cable's great advantage is that it is not at all constrained by electromagnetic spectrum availability. Cable, nonetheless, continues to be challenged by a veritable alphabet soup of competitors (or potential competitors) that include MMDS, SMATV, DBS, and a few smaller variants.

MMDS Multichannel multipoint distribution of signals via microwaves has the tremendous advantage of not requiring streets to be dug up or telephone poles to be rented. The line-of-sight amplitude-modulated signals for such "wireless" cable systems can be distributed locally to apartment or office clusters equipped with special antennae.[22]

SMATV Satellite master antenna television is an extension of this concept, except that the master community antenna is actually a receiving dish that can pull pay-channel signals from satellite transponders and distribute them locally to homes and apartments located nearby. In densely populated areas, SMATV can often circumvent the extensive and expensive politicking that usually accompanies cable-franchise bidding and can skim some of the cable franchise's cream years before a cable system is built.

DBS/DTH Direct broadcast satellites can send pay and basic channel signals to small receiving dishes owned or leased by viewers and thus bypass the need for a cable system's transmission services. With advances in technology, DBS has evolved into what is known as direct-to-home (DTH) digital service that provides an economic advantage over other video distribution systems in that costs do not rapidly increase with the number of subscribers receiving the transmissions. Also, DTH systems are not burdened by local regulation of prices, services, or payments of franchise fees. DTH has emerged as an important competitor to cable in the United States, and is already a strong challenger elsewhere.[23]

STV Subscription television using scrambled over-the-air UHF broadcast signals was an early competitor to cable in the United States but could not provide the programming and visual quality to compete over the long run.[24]

These alternatives to cable have not developed into major competitors and, altogether, they do not account for more than a small fraction (under 10%) of the total number of households that subscribe to a pay television service.[25]

Telephone companies

Until the early 1990s, the telephone and cable industries were arch enemies, and it was reasonable to assume that they would never want to do business with each other. But technological advances in the processing and distribution of digital signals have turned this all around. More computing power at ever-diminishing cost has made it financially feasible to send data, voice, and video signals down the same electronic/optical pipes. As a result, the distinctions between the two industries have blurred, and telephone service providers are now as likely to be competitive as cooperative with MSOs.

Indeed, convergence of the two industries is natural in view of their complementary strengths and changes arising from passage of the Telecommunications Act of 1996. Telephone networks have always been designed for two-way interaction from any point to any other point on the network – something that cable systems were not originally designed to do. Customer billing capabilities at the phone companies are also relatively sophisticated. And, as of the late 1990s, the regional Bell companies – with balance sheets relatively unencumbered by debt – were each year collectively accruing more than three times the revenues ($100 billion) and cash flows of the cable industry.[26]

Nevertheless, cable companies have audience-delivery expertise and access to programming that phone companies lack. And cable already provides video signal quality standards that phone companies would find difficult to match without spending enormously for new fiber optic installations.

7.5 Valuing cable-system properties

Although transfer prices are popularly and casually measured in terms of price per subscriber – with market prices in recent years averaging about $2,000 per subscriber – this measure can be misleading. Some factors that ought to be considered when making comparisons on the basis of per-subscriber averages are the following:

Long-term interest rates, which affect projected cash flows, construction costs, and perhaps consumers' willingness to take extra pay services.

New-household formation expectancy and demographic and income mix, which depend on the location of the system.

Franchise agreements, which may have widely differing terms.

The quality and quantity of off-the-air signals, which influence the willingness of consumers to pay for television programming.

The condition of a system's physical plant, which includes the number of miles of plant yet to be built, current channel capacity, and previous maintenance and repair policies.

Prospects for changes in government regulation, especially with regard to subscriber pricing policies.[27]

The probabilities that potential new competition from telephone companies or others might be permitted.

Table 7.6. *Public and private market valuation methods: Examples*

Public market values	
Price per share	$11.50
Shares outstanding	60
Total market value of equity*	690
plus	
Total long term debt	1,200
Total	1,890
less	
Cash	150
Other off-balance sheet assets	250
Enterprise value (EV)	1,490
EBITDA	165
Cash-flow multiple (EV/EBITDA):	9.0
Private market values	
EBITDA	165
times assumed multiple**	10
Unadjusted value	1,650
plus	
Cash	150
Other off-balance sheet assets	250
less	
Long-term debt	1,200
Net asset value	850
Shares outstanding	60
Net private market asset value per share	$14.17

*If preferred stock is in capitalization, its market value must also be included
**Derived by comparison with recent transfer-price multiples for similar assets.

A potential buyer of a system would then weigh all of the aforementioned factors and decide upon an appropriate valuation multiple of the system's EBITDA and asset base. Such a private market multiple would typically range between 8 and 15 times the cash flow that is *projected* for the next year (Table 7.6). The multiple would also be more precisely determined by comparing to cash-flow multiples on similar, recently traded, systems and to estimates of the potential for generating new revenue streams – economic value added (EVA) – on already invested capital. In such EVA models, share valuations key off of the difference between the weighted-average cost of debt and equity capital (WACC) and the returns in excess of the WACC.

WACC = debt/(debt + equity) × rd + equity/(debt + equity) × re where rd is the cost of debt expressed as an interest rate; and re is the cost of equity, as estimated using risk premiums and risk adjustment factors (known as betas).[28]

In all instances, cash flow is the critical element that enables system maintenance and expansion, pay-down of debt, and diversification. Accordingly, common measures of a cable company's financial strength would include ratios of cash flow to interest cost (EBITDA/net interest) and debt to cash flow (long-term debt/EBITDA).

Yet, just as with broadcasting properties, private market values, which include an implicit control premium, are normally much higher than are seen in public market trading of shares (see also section 6.4).

To estimate what the implied value per subscriber is for publicly traded shares, the number of shares outstanding for a company should be multiplied by the price of a share. Then the amount of debt should be added, and the result divided by the number of subscribers[29]:

$$\frac{\text{value per}}{\text{subscriber}} = \frac{[(\text{stock price} \times \text{shares outstanding}) + \text{debt}]}{\text{subscribers}}$$

Using the same concepts, it is also possible to derive an estimate of the value of whole cable (or broadcasting) industry segments.[30]

7.6 Concluding remarks

Significant advances in signal distribution technology combined with generous applications of capital, and also several doses of deregulation, have enabled the cable business to grow into a $30-billion-a-year giant in the space of 30 years. Now that cable reaches into more than 65% of U.S. households, however, it is showing signs of maturity: The thirst for capital to upgrade into fiber optics and to maintain plant is still present, but the growth rate as measured by the net addition of new subscribers and pay services has slowed. Moreover, significant capital investments will yet have to be made for the digital switches and other signal processing equipment that will be required to squeeze hundreds of new channels into presently available bandwidths.

As such, then, the great cash-flow and wealth-generating machine that is cable has inexorably attracted the attention of other major participants in the broadly defined telecommunications business – the telephone companies, or telcos as they are handily called. With fiber optics and the appropriate digital switching devices, telephone and cable services technologically resemble each other. And already the old walls of regulatory and political considerations that had long prevented telcos from providing cable services and cable systems from providing telephone services are crumbling.[31]

Although legislative and regulatory turf battles between the telcos and the cable industry are likely to extend over many years, it would appear that this epic political and economic power struggle will be ultimately resolved through technological developments that accelerate the blending of each industry's service capabilities into the other's. Clearly, television sets are no longer passive devices. As Chapter 9 explains, they can even play games with you.

Selected additional reading

Auletta, K. (1993). "Barry Diller's Search For the Future," *The New Yorker*, February 22.

Bibb, P. (1993). *It Ain't as Easy as It Looks: Ted Turner's Amazing Story*. New York: Crown.

Block, A. B. (1985). "Fat, Wired Cats," *Forbes* 135(4)(February 25):84–9.

Brauchli, M. W. (1993). "A Satellite TV System Is Quickly Moving Asia Into the Global Village," *Wall Street Journal*, May 10.

Button, G. (1991). "Stan Hubbard's Giant Footprint," *Forbes* 148(11)(November 11).

"Captain Comeback: Ted Turner Is Back from the Brink," *Business Week*, No. 3115 (July 17, 1989):98.

Carnevale, M. L. (1993). "Telephone Service Seems on the Brink of Huge Innovations," *Wall Street Journal*, February 10.

Cauley, L. (1995). "Phone Giants Discover The Interactive Path Is Full of Obstacles," *Wall Street Journal*, July 24.

Chippindale, P., and Franks, S. (1991). *Dished!:The Rise and Fall of British Satellite Broadcasting*. London: Simon & Schuster.

Cleaver, J. (1983). "The Medium Is Potent, If the Message Is Clear," *Advertising Age*, June 13.

Cooney, J. (1983). "Cable TV's Costly Trip to the Big Cities," *Fortune* 107(18)(April 18):82–8.

Cox, M. (1990). "Composers' Groups Try to Call the Tune in Battle over Cable-Television Payments," *Wall Street Journal*, September 5.

Crandall, R. W., and Waverman, L. (1995). *Talk Is Cheap: The Promise of Regulatory Reform in North American Telecommunications*. Washington, D. C.: The Brookings Institution.

Donlan, T. G. (1991). "Blurry Picture: Threat of Regulation, Competition Dims Outlook for Cable TV," *Barron's*, April 29.

Emshwiller, J. R. (1989). "Prying Open the Cable-TV Monopolies," *Wall Street Journal*, August 10.

Gilder, G. (1992). "Here Comes Cable," *Forbes*, 149(8)(April 13).

Gleick, J. (1993). "The Telephone Transformed – Into Almost Everything,"*New York Times*, May 16.

Gunther, M. (1996). "The Cable Guys' Big Bet on the Net,"*Fortune*, 134(10) (November 25).

Hazlett, T. W. (1993). "Why Your Cable Bill Is So High," *Wall Street Journal*, September 24.

"The HBO Story: 10 Years That Changed the World of Telecommunications," *Broadcasting*, November 15, 1982.

Holsendolph, E. (1982). "Tougher Times for Cable TV," *New York Times*, July 11.

Kupfer, A. (1993a). "Hughes Gambles on High-Tech TV," *Fortune* 128(4)(August 23).

(1993b). "The No. 1 in Cable TV Has Big Plans," *Fortune* 127(13)(June 28).

(1993c). "The Race to Rewire America," *Fortune* 127(8)(April 19).

(1994a). "The Future of the Phone Companies," *Fortune*,130(7)(October 3).

(1994b). "Set-Top Box Wars," *Fortune* 130(4)(August 22).

(1994c). "The Baby Bells Butt Heads," *Fortune* 129(6)(March 21).

(1995). "Can Cable Win Its Phone Bet?" *Fortune*, 132(6)(September 18).

Lee W. E. (1984). "A Regulatory Lock Box on Cable TV," *Wall Street Journal*, October 15.

Mahar, M. (1988). "Captain Courageous and the Albatross," *Barron's*, July 11 and "The Baby Bells vs. the Big Gorilla?" *Barron's*, August 1.

Mahon, G. (1984). "Fine-Tuning Cable TV," *Barron's*, July 16.

Marren, J. H. (1993). *Mergers & Acquisitions: A Valuation Handbook*. New York:Irwin.

O'Connor, J. J. (1984). "Where's That Promised New World of Cable?" *New York Times*, November 24.

O'Donnell, T., and Gissen, J. (1982). "A Vaster Wasteland," *Forbes* 129(11)(May 24).

O'Reilly, B. (1996). "First Blood in the Telecom Wars," *Fortune*, 133(4)(March 4).

Park, R. E. (1971). "The Growth of Cable TV and Its Probable Impact on Over-the-Air Broadcasting," *American Economic Review* 61(May):69.

"Pay-TV: Even HBO's Growth Is Slowing," *Business Week*, No. 2850 (July 9, 1984):40.

Roberts, J. L. (1992). "How Giant TCI Uses Self-Dealing, Hardball to Dominate Market," *Wall Street Journal*, January 27.

Robichaux, M. (1992). "Cable-TV Firms' Higher-Priced 'Tiers' Bring Cries of Outrage from Consumers," *Wall Street Journal*, January 15.

(1992). "Cable Firms Say They Welcome Competition but Behave Otherwise," *Wall Street Journal*, September 24.

(1993). "How Cable-TV Firms Raised Rates in Wake of Law to Curb Them," *Wall Street Journal*, September 28.

(1996). "As Satellite TV Soars, Big Firms Crowd the Skies," *Wall Street Journal*, March 11.

(1996). "Once a Laughingstock, Direct-Broadcast TV Gives Cable a Scare," *Wall Street Journal*, November 7.

(1997). "Malone Says TCI Push into Phones, Internet Isn't Working for Now," *Wall Street Journal*, January 2.

Robichaux, M., and Gruley, B. (1997). "Direct-Satellite TV Comes Under Attack By Networks, Affiliates," *Wall Street Journal*, January 30.

Seiden, M. H. (1972). *Cable Television U.S.A.: An Analysis of Government Policy*. New York: Praeger.

Sherman, S. (1994). "Will the Information Superhighway Be the Death of Retailing?" *Fortune* 129(5)(April 18).

Sloan Commission (1971). *On The Cable: The Television of Abundance*, Report of the Sloan Commission on Cable Communications. New York: McGraw-Hill.

Smith, R. L. (1972). *The Wired Nation*. New York: Harper & Row.

"Subscription Television," *Broadcasting*, August 16, 1982.

U.S. Department of Commerce (1988). *Video Program Distribution and Cable Television: Current Policy Issues and Recommendations*, NTIA Report 88–233, June 1988.

Waldman, P. (1990). "New Fees Alter 'Basic' Idea of Cable TV," *Wall Street Journal*, January 23.

Whittemore, H. (1990). *CNN: The Inside Story*. Boston: Little, Brown.

Williams, M. J. (1984). "Slow Liftoff for Satellite-to-Home TV," *Fortune* 109(5)(March 5):100.

Woodward, C. C., Jr. (1974). *Cable Television: Acquisition and Operation of CATV Systems*. New York: McGraw-Hill.

Yoder, S. K., and Zachary, G. P. (1993). "Digital Media Business Takes Form as a Battle of Complex Alliances," *Wall Street Journal,* July 14.

8
Publishing and New Media

Publish or perish

That's the guiding premise for university professors. And, broadly speaking, so is it also for the major media and entertainment companies, which – in this digital age of bits and bytes – might be accurately said to *publish* movies, television programs, recorded music, and games much as they might publish books or magazines. Nowadays, all information, or content, is reducible, copyable, and transportable into the same raw material of bits and bytes, no matter what the original form.

8.1 Gutenberg's gift

The first published work – one of great significance because of authorship, content, and form of delivery – was chiseled in stone and delivered from Mount Sinai by Moses. One might quip that, for the publishing industry, after delivery of the Ten Commandments, it's been downhill ever since.

Still, from the drawings of early cavemen, to the hieroglyphs of the ancient Egyptians, and then on to the first printed book, it is evident that people have always had a need to communicate with each other by publishing their thoughts, plans, and histories. Printing had already been developed in China in the sixth

Table 8.1. *Publishing Industry Segments, 1980–1995*

	1980	%	1985	%	1990	%	1995	%
Books & maps	$6.5	17.7	$10.6	18.4	$17.5	22.8	$20.9	23.9
Newspapers								
Personal consumption expenditures (PCE)	6.9	18.9	9.3	16.2	13.4	17.5	12.6	14.5
Advertising & Other	14.8	40.6	25.2	43.8	28.4	37.1	32.3	37.0
Magazines								
Personal consumption expenditures (PCE)	5.1	14.1	7.2	12.6	10.4	13.6	13.0	14.8
Advertising & Other	3.1	8.6	5.2	9.0	6.8	8.9	8.6	9.8
Total	$36.4	100.0	$57.5	100.0	$76.5	100.0	$87.4	100.0

*a*Dollars in billions. All figures are rounded.
Sources: U.S. Department of Commerce, McCann-Erickson.

century A.D. But it wasn't until the year 1455 – when a German pioneer by the name of Johann Gutenberg and his partner, Johann Fust, set up a movable metal-type press to print a Latin Bible – that the modern publishing era began. Today, world spending on books is estimated at $75 billion, of which approximately 35% is generated in the United States, where more than 50,000 titles a year are published.

Table 8.1 provides a segment overview of the publishing business in the U.S., and Figure 8.1 provides a timeline perspective. As the table illustrates, publishing industry revenues are now near $100 billion, or slightly over 1% of United States GDP. The largest component, almost half, is derived from newspapers. And the other half is split almost equally between magazines and books. However, it is also evident that books and magazines have taken, at the expense of newspapers, a rising share of total revenues.

8.2 Rules of the road

Laws of media

Media pioneer Marshall McLuhan (1964, p. 305) early on noted that "the content of any medium is always another medium." In other words, each medium, whether it be books, music, film, games, or theater borrows from the others and is interdependent: The content of the movie may be the novel, or the novel may create the movie or the song. *The Lion King* animated movie, for example, led to introduction of a children's game, while the video game, *Mortal Combat,* ended up being made into a movie.

This notion, however, forms the basis of only one of McLuhan's four immutable "laws" of media (McLuhan and McLuhan 1988, p.viii) which may be

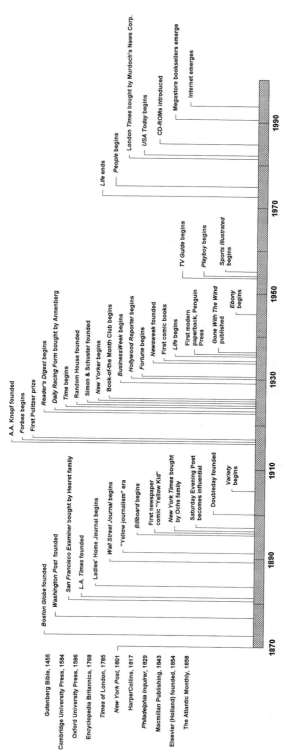

Figure 8.1. Milestones in publishing, 1870–2000.

directly verified by observation, applied to every product of human effort, and condensed as:

1. *Extension:* Every technology extends or amplifies some organ or faculty of the user – e.g., the wheel is an extension of the foot;
2. *Closure:* Equilibrium requires that when one area of experience is heightened or intensified, another is diminished or numbed;
3. *Reversal:* Every form, pushed to the limits of its potential, reverses its characteristics;[1]
4. *Retrieval:* The content of any medium is an older medium.

These laws apply as much to the Internet and other new information delivery systems as to any of the older ones such as radio, television, and movies. The laws also provide a platform for understanding the operational characteristics of what is, broadly, the business of publishing.

Operating characteristics

Many of the operating characteristics seen in the broadcasting, cable, and other mass communications and software segments are also seen in publishing. As in these other segments, the cost of creating the content is sunk at the start, and subsequent expenses of manufacturing and distribution are relatively small. The objective here, too, is to make demand more price-inelastic (as described in Chapter 1) and to stimulate unit volume sales since, on the margin, the contribution to profit of each additional unit sold is high.

Circulation – which is the term used to describe unit demand for newspapers and magazines from sales on newsstands or through postal subscriptions – is normally (except for most books) supplemented by sales of advertising space that is strategically interspersed with content. In this way, broadcast services, newspapers, magazines, telephone directories, CD-ROMS, and Internet web sites are all alike.

In fact, demand for advertising is central to the success of virtually all publishing enterprises. Profits are thus accordingly sensitive to changes in national and, sometimes, local economic conditions as reflected by changes in demand for advertising (Figure 8.2).[2] But raw material and distribution costs may also fluctuate cyclically and noticeably affect profitablilty, especially in the traditional publishing segments.

Still, it is the cost of creating the proprietary content to be published that is often the most difficult variable to predict and to control. As in other creative fields, the top people – the "star" writers of novels or magazine articles or syndicated newspaper columns or computer games – can all command considerable premiums for their services. And, occasionally, the cost is greater than a publisher can bear. Table 8.2 furnishes the financial operating characteristics for a sample of the major publishing companies.

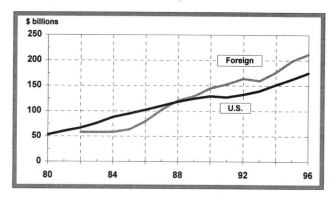

Figure 8.2. Total advertising expenditures, U.S. and foreign, 1980–96. *Source:* Based on data by Robert J. Coen, McCann-Erikson, Inc.

Table 8.2. *Publishing industry composite of 75 companies,*[a] *1992–96 (in $ millions)*

	Revenues	Operating income	Operating margin	Assets	Operating cash flow
CAGR (%)[b]					
Books	6.5%	6.9%	0.4%	12.9%	8.8%
Consumer magazines	3.9	5.6	1.7	2.2	4.3
Newspapers	5.1	7.1	2.0	6.5	4.6

[a]Average margin 1992–96, books 12.7%, magazines 10.6%, newspapers 15.0%.
[b]Compound annual growth rate

8.3 Segment specifics

Books

Book publishing, which accounts for about one-quarter of total publishing industry revenues, is composed of two major sectors: educational/professional and trade (otherwise known as general-interest). Each sector has a distinct consumer base and financial-economics profile. Revenue components by share are illustrated in Figure 8.3.

Educational/Professional Relatively high operating margins and significant barriers to entry are characteristic features in the educational/professional segment. In addition, revenues tend to be predictably tied to demographic trends, and content can often be easily repackaged for delivery by electronic media or through alternative distribution channels. This stands in contrast to trade/general publishing, which is hit-driven and thus inherently more volatile. On the educational

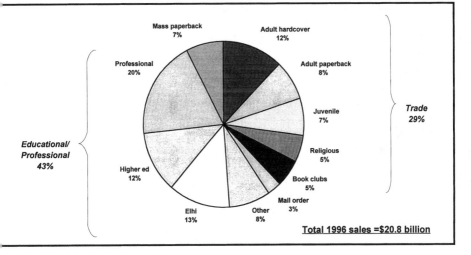

Figure 8.3. Book publisher sales by market segment, 1996.

side, sales to colleges amount to about half of revenues, while the elementary and high school components, the "ElHi" segment, makes up the other half.

Demographic changes affecting school enrollments can, of course, be reliably predicted for as much as ten years into the future and can provide a solid base from which to forecast demand for educational books and related materials. But, also, about half of the states, mostly in the South and West, purchase educational materials at the state level in a regular cycle of textbook adoption programs. In these procedures, state boards of education and adoption committees screen publishers' offerings and determine which books will be approved for purchase and which should be replaced.[3]

Last, it ought to be noted that demand in the ElHi sector is affected by the school funding environment at state and local levels – with the amount allocated to education somewhat dependent on local economic conditions and, occasionally, on political considerations at the federal level.

Although demographics are also destiny in measuring demand for college textbook and professional materials, rapid changes in technology and in subject emphasis tend to stimulate new sales. And, generally, pricing is not an important issue in either ElHi, college, or professional segments because the cost of textbooks is typically small when compared to tuition and other education-related costs.[4]

Trade The consumer area, however, presents a much different economic profile of demand and cost than that seen on the educational/professional side. Given that the cost of manufacturing a hardcover trade book in quantity is rarely more than $2 to $3 a unit (and for paperbound, $1), profitability will generally rise disproportionally to increasing unit sales. Also, as noted earlier, this segment is largely hit-driven and thus similar in character to the recorded music and video game businesses, where it often makes sense to pay significant advances and royalty rates to the top content creators and to then spur demand by spending aggressively on promotion.[5] As with all such businesses, margins are, from year-to-year, apt to be volatile and to be affected by the cost of competing for top authors.

Still, over the longer term, publishers' operating margins – normally ranging between 8% and 17% of sales, depending on category – have been trending down: The costs of marketing and of absorbing a rapidly increasing stock of slow-selling titles returned by retailers for credit have risen significantly in recent years. With chain bookstores in 1995 accounting for about 26% of consumer adult sales and book clubs 20% (versus 20% for independent stores), important retailers can now demand a larger cut of the cover price even as a rising proportion of returns – now commonly 35% or more of total shipments – gives credence to the industry adage of "Gone today, here tomorrow".[6]

Periodicals

Newspapers Among the earliest versions of what we today call newspapers were the handwritten notices that ancient Romans posted in public areas. Other fore-runners of modern papers appeared in Germany and other European countries in the sixteenth and seventeenth centuries and in colonial America by 1690. Today, in the United States, there are approximately 1,500 dailies with a combined cir-culation of 60 million readers and another 8,000 nondaily variants with combined circulation of over 5 million more. But only a dozen or so large companies dom-inate the business.[7]

Newspapers, like magazines, derive their revenues from advertising, subscrip-tion, and newsstand sales. As such, both newspaper and magazine revenues are normally sensitive to overall economic conditions – especially as affected by demand conditions for local advertising in the case of papers or highly targeted advertising in the case of magazines.

Yet newspapers also differ from magazines in that papers are often virtual monopolies in their markets and in that frequency of publication is much greater (usually daily). Accordingly, perishability of content and speed of delivery are of utmost concern. But in responding to these concerns, the relative distribution and manufacturing costs rise above those that would be proportionately incurred by publications with less frequency of issuance.

On the average, the apportionment of revenues and costs in operating a news-paper as opposed to a magazine would be approximately as shown in Table 8.3. A salient feature of the newspaper busines, however, is that advertising has con-sistently accounted for about 80% of revenues, with circulation, the remaining 20%.

Of total newspaper advertising, which late in the 1990s was running at an annual rate of approximately $40 billion, the largest and most troubling compo-

Table 8.3. *Newspapers versus magazines, estimated components of revenues and costs, 1997*

	Newspapers	Magazines
Sources of Revenue (%)		
Advertising		
Retail	40	9
Classified	32	12
National	8	35
Newsstand	17	10
Subscription	3	34
Total	100%	100%
Costs as % of revenue		
Advertising, selling & promotion	12	13
Editorial	14	12
Production	20	21
Distribution	13	6
Postage	1	5
Raw Materials (e.g., paper, ink, etc.)	18	25
Administrative & other	9	9
Total	87%	91%
Operating profit margin (% of revenue)	13%	9%

nent, accounting for half of the total, is retailing-related advertising. In recent years, retailers have shifted their promotional spending away from print and into electronic media at the same time that retail industry consolidation has been occurring. This has made it difficult for publishers to raise advertising prices enough to keep pace with their own raw material and distribution–cost inflation.

In contrast, classified advertising, which accounts for about 37% of total newspaper advertising, has been by far the most profitable component of ad revenues. Unfortunately, however, classified – which includes help-wanted, automotive, and real estate advertising – is also the most highly correlated to economic activity and to interest rates (inversely). Publisher profits thus tend to rise greatly when the economy is strong and fall noticeably when the economy is weak. In this respect, national advertising, which is primarily related to the travel and financial service sectors and accounts for around 13% of total newspaper advertising, cannot normally provide an offset to decline in local classified advertising.[8]

The most important traditional determinants of newspaper profits are the costs of labor and newsprint and the demand for help-wanted advertising. As Figure 8.4 illustrates, labor cost appears to have been tamed in recent years through increased capital investment and productivity, but newsprint costs and help-

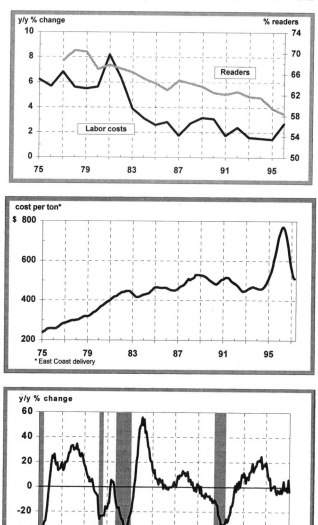

Figure 8.4. Newspaper profit determinants: (a) Average hourly wage changes in percent year-over-year and average percent of adults as weekly readers, (b) Newsprint costs per ton (East Coast delivery), six-month moving average, and (c) Year-over-year percent changes in help-wanted index (six-month moving average), 1975–96. Bars indicate periods of recession.

wanted demand have remained highly cyclical. Even small changes in the cost of newsprint become significant when applied to the approximately 20 billion units that the industry produces each year.

As for the longer term, gains in circulation and in classified advertising are likely to be increasingly difficult to achieve as households now derive an increasing share of their information from the electronic media. Already, household penetration of daily newspapers has fallen from around 100% in 1970 to approximately 60% today. Circulation for weekly papers has, meanwhile, been declining since the late 1980s, and for Sunday papers has plateaued (at around 62 million).[9]

Worse yet, the Internet is beginning to siphon off significant amounts of both classified advertising and consumers' time. As a result, publishers are applying their formidable information-gathering and cash-flow resources to development of electronically delivered products and services.

Magazines and other periodicals The first magazines–named from the French *magasin,* or "storehouse" – began to appear in Europe in the late 1600s. But it wasn't until the 1890s that mass market magazines, supported by the emergence of national advertisers, began to appear in the United States. Magazine publishing today is spread over more than 11,000 magazine and periodical titles and accounts for about one-fourth of all U.S. publishing revenues. Major categories include:

Consumer and general interest
Trade and technical
Farm
Noncommercial literary
Comics

Although magazine operating characteristics are in many ways similar to those of newspapers, revenues for consumer magazines and periodicals are much more dependent on circulation – about 55% of revenue comes from ads versus 80% for newspapers – and total distribution costs are thus much more closely related to the costs of postal delivery (Table 8.3). As Table 8.1 indicates, as of the mid-1990s, magazine advertising revenues of approximately $9 billion amounted to only one-fourth of the total ad spending in newspapers.

Although magazine publishers typically boast of the number of pages of advertising that are gained each year, appearances can be deceiving. In fact, it is impossible to gauge the financial health of a magazine without knowing how much is actually being charged for each page. More often than not, competition from a large and ever-proliferating number of magazines, targeting the same niche of readers, provides the advertiser with leverage to negotiate significant discounts to nominal rate card price schedules.[10] But, beyond price – and just as in other advertising-supported media – it is the cost of reaching a thousand readers (CPM) that is the industry's standard measure of efficiency.

In the United States, few pure magazine and periodical publishers of size remain independent. Most of the majors have been absorbed by larger media and entertainment companies.[11]

8.4 New media

Multimedia

Developer/publisher issues Multimedia products – combining digitized text, sound, and pictorial data that are generally carried in the form of CD-ROMs, DVDs, or cartridges – are an outgrowth of the same technology that has made home computers and compact discs common household items. However, the economics of developing and distributing multimedia products has evolved as a hybrid of business practices seen in the filmed-entertainment, music, book publishing, and video game industries.

As in the music business, a small number of titles generates the bulk of the profit and covers the often substantial losses on the majority of releases. Retailers also have full rights to return unsold units. But, as noted by Schuyler (1995, p. 88), most of the revenue stream, some 75% to 85% of the wholesale price, reverts to the publisher – who bears the risk of funding *both* development and marketing costs.

For developers, the costs of designing and externally funding a new title (to the gold master disk stage) will now generally range to over $1 million and be guided by work-made-for-hire publisher agreements that are customarily structured with elements taken from the following basic models:

1. The studio or publisher covers the direct costs of development of a gold master disk and an allocation of overhead, but retains ownership of the copyright and most of the revenues. In return, the developer is assured a profit margin of 10% to 12%.
2. The publisher provides the developer with an advance that is to be recouped against royalties and that may be scalable according to unit sales volume. Such royalties could range from 7% to 25% of net wholesale revenues (i.e., revenues less reserves for returns), but will normally average no more than 12% to 15%.[12]

Distribution issues Developers' choices for distribution would further include: (a) selling all rights to a studio and/or publisher for a lump sum, or, more commonly; (b) making an affiliate label deal in which the publisher arranges for manufacturing. In such deals, the affiliated company may receive up to 60% to 75% of the net wholesale price as a royalty, but with the royalty range dependent on which party pays for the cost of goods sold. Otherwise, it may be assumed that a distributor will typically receive 20% to 30% of the wholesale price and that the publisher will retain the rest, on which amount, 10% to 25% might then go to the developer.

Negotiations might also involve the deductibility of promotional units, exclusivity, co-op advertising, the rights of portability to different hardware platforms and media carriers (including online), the rights to ancillary revenues, and the allocation of territorial distribution rights. The issues are, in fact, similar to those seen in the music business, where reserves for returns, discounts, rebates, shipping charges, and stock-balancing costs are often adjustments that reduce earned royalties.

Internet

The underlying software linkages of the Internet began to develop in the 1960s, when the Pentagon's Defense Advanced Research Projects Agency scientists sought to build a computer communications network that could survive even if parts of it were destroyed.[13]

Fast-forward to the late 1990s, however, and the Internet has evolved into a low-cost mass communications medium that empowers anyone to instantly publish – anywhere around the world – words, moving pictures, music, computer software, and anything else that can be digitized. As such, the Internet has changed the means of distribution, production, and promotion of all entertainment products and services and has, in some instances, become – just as McLuhan's laws would suggest – the publishing and broadcasting medium of choice.[14]

Nevertheless, advertising on the Internet is still in an early stage of development, and baseline standards of effectiveness similar to those used in traditional broadcast and print media – for example, reach, frequency, gross ratings points, circulation, demographic spread, and cost per thousand – are only now being established. And the same may be said for the development of Internet distribution rights standards and for Webcasting, which uses software to automatically organize advertiser-supported content into channels selected by viewers.[15]

8.5 Accounting and valuation issues

Accounting

Accounting for publishing enterprises generally does not require unusual treatment. However, to the extent that the book industry in particular – with its investment in printing plates, in its licensing of rights from authors through royalty-related payments of advances and minimum guarantees, and in its return privileges – resembles the recorded music industry, tax and accounting methods similar to those in music would apply.

For instance, Financial Accounting Standards Board (FASB) statement 50 specifies that ''such minimum guarantees shall be reported as an asset by the licensee and subsequently charged to expense in accordance with the terms of the licensing agreement. If all or a portion of the minimum guarantee subsequently appears not to be recoverable through future use of the rights obtained under the license, the nonrecoverable portion shall be charged to expense.''

This principle applies to charging off the costs of printing plates and other such production elements and also to the treatment of royalties. Royalties earned by content creators are adjusted for returns – according to rules specified by FASB statement 48 – and are charged as an expense of the period in which sale of the item takes place.[16] Advance royalties paid are reported as an asset if the past performance and current popularity of the author suggest that the advance will be recoverable from expected future royalties. Otherwise, estimated unrecoverable royalties paid to the author would be charged as a period expense.

Sales of software products, however, are also governed by FASB statement 86, which specifies that internally incurred costs in creating computer software are to be expensed as research and development until technological feasibility is established. Thereafter, all software production costs are to be capitalized and then amortized based on current and future revenue forecasts for each product, with an annual minimum equal to the straight-line amortization over the remaining estimated life of the product.

Valuation

Publishing companies, like those in other media-related industries, are valued primarily on comparisons of cash-flow generation capabilities. As in broadcasting or cable, a multiple of projected cash-flow – often described by financial analysts in terms of earnings before interest, taxes, depreciation, and amortization (EBITDA) – is determined by taking into consideration the multiples of similar recently traded properties and also the following basic elements:

Interest rates and stage of economic cycle
Demographic, technological, social, and cost trend changes
Degree of local monopoly/franchise power
Potential for raising the price of advertising
Potential for increasing circulation and subscriptions and for raising the prices of
  each
Opportunities to decrease cost and/or to raise up standards of editorial inputs

The value that is thus derived would then (as described for cable in Chapter 7) be further adjusted for net debt and for the estimated worth of off-balance sheet items to arrive at the private market value of the property.[17] This is the price that a rational private investor might pay to take control of the property and its cash flows. But, in addition, this price estimate may also be used as a basis for measuring the relative investment attractiveness of publicly traded shares, which normally sell at a significant discount to the private market value estimate.[18] As a rule of thumb, book publisher asset transfers would be generally valued at one time sales.

8.6 Concluding remarks

In a broad sense, everything that we see and hear in entertainment is, in one form or another, published. New digital production and distribution technologies, however, already enable almost anyone – at relatively little cost – to publish anywhere, and to potentially reach everyone, wherever they may be. The effects on traditional publishing enterprises are thus likely to be as profound as they are disturbing.[19] With text, data, graphics, moving pictures, and sound now all being blended together into seamless webs of new "published" products and associated services, traditional publishing industry paradigms are being rapidly rendered obsolete.

Selected additional reading

Anderson, C. (1996). "The Software Industry," *The Economist,* May 25.

Bank, D. (1996). "How Net Is Becoming More Like Television to Draw Advertisers," *Wall Street Journal,*" December 13.

Book Industry Study Group, (1995). *Book Industry Trends 1995*. New York: Book Industry Study Group.

"Book Publishing," *The Economist,* April 7, 1990.

Carvajal, D. (1997). "Book Chains' New Role: Soothsayers for Publishers," *New York Times*, August 1.

Clark, D. (1997). "Facing Early Losses, Some Web Publishers Begin to Pull the Plug," *Wall Street Journal,* January 14.

Cortese, A. (1997). "A Way Out of the Web Maze," *Business Week,* No. 3515, February 24.

Cose, E. (1989). *The Press: Inside America's Most Powerful Newspaper Empires*. New York: William Morrow.

Cuozzo, S. (1996). *It's Alive! How America's Oldest Newspaper Cheated Death and Why It Matters*. New York: Times Books.

Dealy, F. X., Jr. (1993). *The Power and the Money: Inside the Wall Street Journal*. Secaucus, N.J.: Birch Lane (Carol Publishing).

Dejesus, E. X. (1996). "How the Internet Will Replace Broadcasting," *Byte,* February 1996.

Diamond, E. (1994). *Behind the Times: Inside the New York Times*. New York: Villard.

Geiser, E., and Dolin, A., eds. (1985), *The Business of Book Publishing*. New York: Westview.

Hafner, K., and Lyon, M. (1996). *Where Wizards Stay Up Late: The Origins of the Internet*. New York: Simon & Schuster.

Heidenry, J. (1993). *Theirs Was the Kingdom: Lila and DeWitt Wallace and the Story of the Reader's Digest*. New York: W. W. Norton.

Hutheesing, N. (1996). "CD-ROM Flopperoo," *Forbes,* 157(8)(April).

Klebnikov, P. (1995). "The Twain Shall Meet," *Forbes,*155(5)(February 27).

Knecht, G. B. (1997). "Book Superstores Bring Hollywood-Like Risks to Publishing Business, *Wall Street Journal,* May 29.

(1997). "Magazine Advertisers Demand Prior Notice of 'Offensive' Articles," *Wall Street Journal,* April 30.

(1996). "Microsoft Puts Newspapers in Highanxiety.com," *Wall Street Journal,* July 15.

"How Wall Street Whiz Found a Niche Selling Books on the Internet," *Wall Street Journal,* May 16.

Mahar, M. (1995). "Caught In the 'Net," *Barron's,* December 25.

McLuhan, E., and Zingrone, F., eds. (1995). *Essential McLuhan*. New York: Basic Books (HarperCollins).

McLuhan, M., and Powers, B. R. (1989). *The Global Village*. New York: Oxford University Press.

Peterson, I. (1996). "At Times Mirror, What's the Plan?," *New York Times,* June 26.

Pogrebin, R. (1996). "A Magazine Only a Mother Could Love? Reader's Digest Seeks to Change,"*New York Times,* July 22.

Reid, R. H. (1997). *Architects of the Web*. New York: John Wiley & Sons.

Reilly, P. M. (1996a). "Where Borders Group and Barnes & Noble Compete, It's a War," *Wall Street Journal,* September 3.

—— (1996b). "Guccione Sex Empire Falls From Penthouse Into the Basement," *Wall Street Journal,* March 22.

—— (1996c). "Newspaper Company Faces Succession Fight Despite Family Control," *Wall Street Journal,* January 22.

Shawcross, W. (1992). *Murdoch*. New York: Simon & Schuster.

Tebbel, J. W. (1987). *Between Covers: The Rise and Transformation of Book Publishing in America*. New York: Oxford University Press.

Tebbel, J. W., and Zuckerman, M. E. (1991). *The Magazine in America, 1741-1990*. New York and Oxford: Oxford University Press.

Wiggins, R. (1996). "How the Internet Works," *Internet World,* (October).

9
Toys and games

It's not whether you win or lose, but how you play the game.

In the age of computers, that statement takes on new meanings: Only a few people in the world can beat the best computerized chess-playing machines. And video games cannot ever really be defeated because, no matter how high the score, it is always the human who tires first or makes the fatal error.

This chapter, largely focusing on computerized toys and games, will show how microelectronic-chip technology has enabled game designers to conveniently and inexpensively transform plain television screens into playfields of extraordinary capability. And we shall see how, from a small kernel, there evolved in only 10 years, a business that at its short-lived peak in 1982 was larger in terms of domestic retail sales than either the movie or recorded-music industries.

First, however, we gain important perspective by examining the more traditional toy and game sectors.

9.1 Not just for kids

Toys are the quintessential entertainment products. Indeed, it is the very potential for entertainment – play aspect, if you will – that makes something a toy instead of a merely nondescript object composed of plastic or wood or fiber or metal.

217

The key additional ingredient, of course, is the imagination of the player. A toy, virtually by definition, alters a person's psychological state – diverting the attention in the same way that (as noted in Chapter 1) all entertainment products and services do. Thus the toy business is an integral part of the entertainment industry: It's not just for kids.

Financial flavors

Throughout the ages, toys have always reflected the technological capabilities and the cultural traditions of the societies in which they have been developed. Early primitive toys were made of clay or wood or cloth, for example. Yet the industry did not begin to take on a more modern cast until the early-twentieth-century, when rapidly improving mass-production and distribution methods were combined with the introduction of new plastics materials.

In fact, the toy industry has evolved into a rather sizable business that in the United States annually generates over $13 billion of sales at wholesale and about $18 billion at retail as of the mid-1990s. Moreover, on a worldwide basis, the amounts are probably two to three times as great, with thousands of companies involved in the manufacture and distribution of toy and game products of all types. Figure 9.1 provides an historical perspective.

Although the toy manufacturing industry remains highly fragmented, among the largest companies, significant consolidation has already occurred in order to take advantage of economies of scale in manufacturing, marketing, distribution, and advertising. Such consolidation has also occurred in recognition of the fact that much more capital is currently required to establish a base for competition on a global scale. It is therefore not surprising to see the toy industry following the patterns established in other entertainment subsegments. Nor, for that matter, is it surprising to see many of the major entertainment companies either owning manufacturing and (retail) distribution facilities or, more commonly, otherwise taking an interest in toys through licensing and merchandising ventures.

By the early 1990s, the industry in the United States had come to be dominated by three major manufacturer/distributor organizations that accounted for an estimated half of total sales. Those companies include Hasbro (Milton Bradley, Tonka, Kenner, Parker Bros.), Mattel (Fisher-Price, Tyco), and Nintendo. On the retail level, moreover, the business has come to be dominated by the Toys 'R' Us chain, which has an estimated 20% share of total retail toy sales in North America, and to a lesser extent by large discount chains such as Wal-Mart and K-mart.[1] Yet even so, nondurable toys have accounted for a gradually declining share of total U.S. personal consumption expenditures on recreation (Figure 9.2).

As can be seen from Table 9.1, toy manufacturers' revenues grew by 5.3% over the 1992–96 span, but with considerably greater variance of resulting earnings performance than in any of the other classified entertainment industry segments. Such variance also visible in Table 9.2 and in Figure 9.3, where the differing sales growth rates and dollar shipment volume changes of major product categories can be seen. Surely, the industry's volatility and great seasonality, with

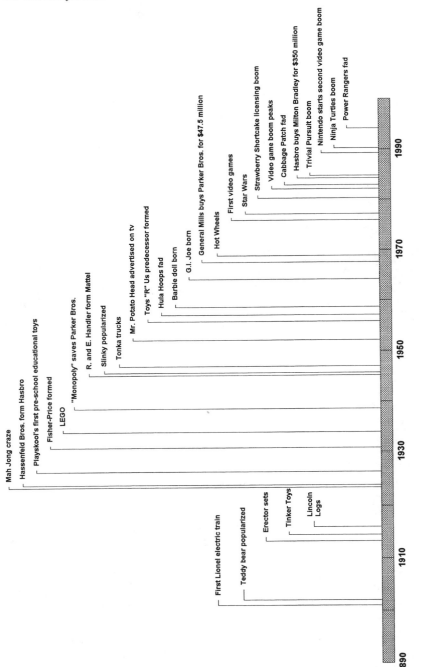

Figure 9.1. Toy industry milestones, 1890–2000.

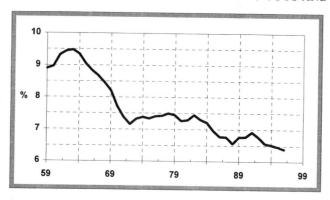

Figure 9.2. Toys (nondurable) as a percentage of total PCE on recreation, 1959–96.

Table 9.1. *Toy industry financial composite (8 companies),[a] 1982–96*

	Revenues	Operating income	Operating margin (%)	Assets	Operating cash flow
CAGR(%):[b]					
1992–96	5.3	3.8	−1.4	5.0	5.1
1982–91	8.7	11.6	2.7	10.5	11.7

[a]Average margin 1992–96 = 12.0%; 1982–91 = 8.1%.
[b]Compound annual growth rate.

two-thirds of annual sales always coming in the last twelve weeks of the year, is enough to make Santa dizzy.

Building blocks

As noted by Owen (1986), the roots of the giant American toy companies are humble indeed. Yet even today, with all the sophisticated market research that these companies can so readily command, the reasons for the success or failure of particular toy lines are often not well understood. Sometimes a toy line like the popular Strawberry Shortcake of the early 1980s can be successfully created out of thin air; at other times, all the preplanning and advertising in the world cannot move a product – movie and television show tie-ins notwithstanding.[2]

So-called trademarked *staple* products like the board game Monopoly, or like Lego blocks, or Mr. Potato Head, or the Barbie doll, however, seem to have an almost timeless appeal. As might be expected, such products produce unusually high profit margins for the companies that make them. But staples – though they are to the toy industry what film libraries are to the studios – are not normally a

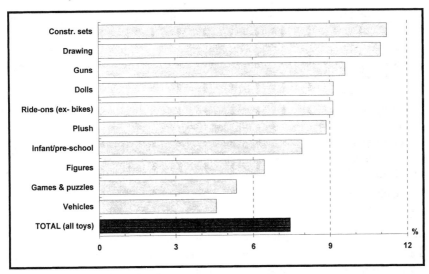

Figure 9.3. Comparative sales growth rates for major toy categories, 1983–96. *Source data:* Toy Manufacturers' Association.

Table 9.2. *Toy industry factory shipments of leading categories, 1985–95*[a]

Category	$ million		
	1985	1990	1995
Infant/preschool	824	992	1,329
Dolls	1,562	1,329	1,896
Plush	585	495	1,004
Figures	840	695	795
Vehicles	695	1,218	1,167
Ride-ons (excluding bikes)	283	414	797
Games and puzzles	642	947	1,263
Building/construction sets	189	198	345
Educational/scientific	58	44	57
Crayon/chalk/drawing	118	254	420
Model kits	86	74	148
Guns	68	67	175
Total[b]	5,882	6,660	9,221

[a]Shipment figures are for first U.S. billing in dollars.
[b]Total excludes TV video games and other miscellaneous toy categories.
Source: Toy Manufacturers of America.

sufficient fuel for growth. For that, toy companies require luck, pluck, and lots of spending on product development and television marketing. In this respect, the development process for new toys is similar to that in film and music. And as in film and music, it is often the singularly profitable hit that pays for the many new-product introductions that flop.

But the analogies between toys and other entertainment industries should not be stretched too far. The highly compressed seasonal pattern of retail demand combined with the enormous amount of physical inventory handling that is required to service this demand intensifies short-term delivery pressures on manufacturers and retailers.[3] More often than not, these pressures lead to inventory imbalances (of too many unsold products) that must be corrected before retailers are again ''open-to-buy'' (i.e., to order, in both a fiscal and physical sense) new toys for the next season.

Toy company valuation methods differ, too, in that brand names, which are of little consequence in filmed entertainment, count for a lot here. Beyond the standard techniques of analysis used to project cash flows and cash flow multiples (as in the media industries), stock market and corporate borrowing-power valuations must, in addition, make allowance for intangible brand name assets.[4]

Moreover, although demographic arguments are frequently invoked to favorably portray the industry's growth potential, most such generalized arguments must be tempered. For instance, it is usually more important in forecasting changes in industry demand to know the number of *first-births* than it is to know the projected total number of children in the population.[5] But in targeting a marketing campaign, it may be even more important to know the income level-distribution of couples expecting a first child.

9.2 Chips ahoy!

Toys may be differentiated from other entertainment industry segments, not so much because demand for them often tends to be so volatile and faddish, as because a relatively high percentage of their cost components (value added) is tied up in the manufacture and movement of physically bulky inventory. For most entertainment products and services, in contrast, the proportionally greatest amount of value added is to be found in the organized bits of information that we call programming, or software. Those bits are stored on inherently inert media such as compact discs or magnetic tapes, or relayed through cables, or broadcast over the air.

Because video games are again really no more than organized bits of information, storable on inert media, or capable of being electronically transmitted, they are indeed close technological cousins to many other entertainment-industry products. The only difference with video games, then, is that you need a computer to play them. As we shall see, both branches of the video game industry grow from the same roots and share a future governed by the rate of innovation in electronic-component and software design.[6]

Slots and pins

The history of coin-operated machines, which precedes that of home video by about 85 years, can be traced to the late 1880s, when the first nickel-in-the-slot machines in the gambling halls of San Francisco were introduced. The checkered and colorful saga of their development and use in the United States, documented in Fey (1989), follows closely the development trend of the gaming industry, which is the topic of the next chapter. For now it is sufficient to note that during the Great Depression of the 1930s there began to emerge amusement-only machines – the forerunners of today's sophisticated pinball and video gadgets.

One of the most important early pin models was the *Ballyhoo*, introduced by a struggling Chicago-based company, Lion Manufacturing. Lion was predecessor to the Bally Manufacturing Company, which, along with several other Chicago companies, including Gottlieb, Williams, and Stern, had by the early 1970s become the leading worldwide producers of such machines.[7]

But in the mid-1970s there were two critical events: Bally replaced electro-mechanical pinball components with new electronic circuitry, and large cities such as Los Angeles, Chicago, and New York legalized placement of pins in general public locations. The effects were to catapult Bally to a position of industry leadership and to dramatically expand the demand for state-of-the-art electronic models with enhanced features.

Pong: pre and après

As we now know, the market for coin-op machines was not limited to pinballs, and video games were already on the horizon by the end of the 1960s. In fact, their technological roots can be traced back to 1962, when an MIT graduate student demonstrated *Spacewar,* a science-fiction fantasy game played on a PDP-1 mainframe computer and a large-screen cathode-ray tube. That game attracted a wide cult following among computer buffs.

The next important step came in 1968, when a Sanders Associates engineer developed a console that could be used to display games on ordinary television sets. Sanders patented this idea and sold the rights to Magnavox, now a division of Philips, the large Dutch consumer electronics conglomerate.[8]

But it was not until the early 1970s that a young University of Utah engineering graduate, Nolan Bushnell, came to realize that the price of electronic computing power (integrated circuits) had declined to the point that adaptation of *Spacewar* from a large computer into coin-op form was becoming economically feasible. Bushnell and his associates began working on such a machine in a converted bedroom workshop. But what they ultimately developed instead was a simple tennis-like game that they named *Pong*.[9]

Pong took the industry by storm and quickly became the first coin-operated video game hit. And soon thereafter, commercial Pong-style home video games also appeared.[10] Yet despite early enthusiasm, consumer interest in this area proved much more fleeting and fickle than had been anticipated, and as price competition and losses mounted, most of the early manufacturers withdrew from the field.

Profits, moreover, proved to be just as elusive at Bushnell's company, Atari, where a rapidly growing market presence in coin-op and home video required greater infusions of capital and more professional management than the company could readily muster. By the end of 1976, the founders of Atari had sold their holdings to Warner Communications for about $28 million, a value approximating their sales in that year.[11]

At that point, coin-operated video games seemed just another passing fad. But introduction of *Space Invaders* – an arcade model produced by Japanese coin-op manufacturer Taito and sold through U.S. national distributor Bally-Midway – proved otherwise. With its more colorful graphics and quick-response shoot-'em-up play features, *Space Invaders* immediately captured the public's fancy, becoming the first popular machine to highlight the emerging capabilities of microelectronics and of software design.[12]

Quite naturally, then, there soon followed a flurry of popular videos that employed the same or better hardware and even more imaginative software.[13] Of these, *Pac-Man* (in 1980) was especially significant in that it was the first to attract female video game players in large numbers.

Yet the same software improvements and technological advances (faster microprocessors and larger memories) that permitted designers to produce spectacular aural and visual effects for coin-op machines were also being applied to home video units. And it was thus only a short while before the programmable consoles that had been languishing for lack of software suddenly began to sell in large numbers: Consumers had finally discovered that they could play a reasonable facsimile of their favorite arcade games at home. The impact on Atari was astounding. Unprofitable for the first three years under the aegis of parent Warner Communications, Atari had, by the end of 1979, hit its stride. By either self-designing or licensing the most popular arcade concepts for cartridge format, the company had captured some 80% of the worldwide market for home video games.[14]

Industry sales of consoles and cartridges rose from practically zero in 1977 to over $2 billion at wholesale ($3 billion at retail) in 1982.[15] By then, as Figure 9.4 shows, video game hardware and software sales accounted for nearly one-third of total U.S. toy manufacturers' shipments.

Pong had indeed pinged.

9.3 Structural statements

Home-video games

All of this, however, was too good to last. By late 1982, the public's fascination with arcade games had begun to wane and fewer hit concepts were becoming available for conversion to cartridges. At the same time, the market was flooded

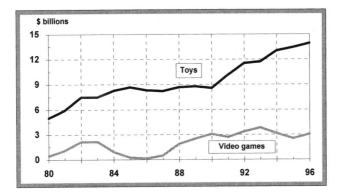

Figure 9.4. Home video game and toy sales, United States manufacturers' shipments in dollars, 1980–96. *Source data:* Nintendo of America Inc., and TMA.

with imitative software of all types.[16] It was thus not until the late 1980s that the industry's previously amorphous structure, at least on the software side, had stabilized and become, in many respects, rationalized along the lines of the recorded-music and book-publishing businesses.

Until 1986, when Japan-based Nintendo introduced a more technologically sophisticated and user-friendly game console, the hardware side was also in disarray.[17] But with tight control of software development and marketing, Nintendo was able to revive and to then capture up to 80% of a once-again booming market in which no significant competition appeared until the early 1990s.[18] Yet, by that point, the annual operating profits of Nintendo had already grown to over $1 billion – an amount exceeding the 1991 profits of all the major Hollywood studios *combined.*

With change the only constant, the game industry in the 1990s has rapidly moved toward standards that utilize computer platforms capable of processing in 32-bit and 64-bit formats and that are able to download game-play instructions delivered via wireless, cable, or telephone lines or inexpensive discs (CD-ROMs and DVDs). With 64-bit processing power at hand, games can readily incorporate full-motion video (FMV), which, in effect, turns them into interactive movies.

Coin-op

Coin-op has had a far more rigid industry structure than that seen in home video games. But fluctuations in demand have nevertheless been quite large (Figure 9.5). And the industry's dominant companies have, in response, become vertically integrated in performance of the four functions that define a presence in the coin-op business. Those functions include:

Game design, wherein designs may often cost up to $1 million per model.

Manufacturing and assembly, in which component producers of monitors,

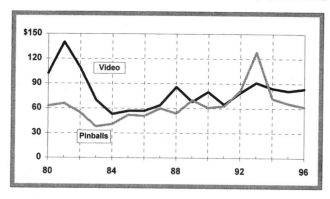

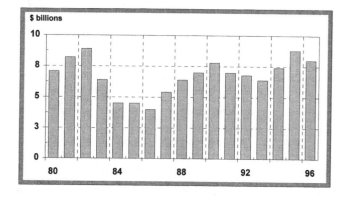

Figure 9.5. Coin-operated machines in the United States. (a) Average weekly gross collections by game type; (b) gross collections, 1980–96. *Source data: Play Meter.*

printed circuit boards, and memory and microprocessor chips participate. Both coin-op and home segments consume a significant portion of worldwide electronic-component production.[19]

Distribution, through which machines of various manufacturers are wholesaled, serviced, and sometimes exchanged. Distributors supply credit to smaller operators to finance purchase of machines and generally support new-model demand by accepting trade-ins of used equipment. Conversion kits, primarily new circuit boards that enable existing cabinets and monitors to be adapted for new games, may also be provided.

Operation or ownership of locations, either of arcades or of a string of smaller locations in which the machines are placed. Operators and location owners will normally split revenues on a 50:50 percentage or some similar ratio after a certain minimum payment or guarantee to the route operator has been assured.[20]

Profit dynamics

For the manufacturer, a hit game, like a hit movie or record, can generate extraordinary returns, particularly in home versions – where the profitability can far exceed that of the coin-ops'.[21] If, for example, the game is one like Nintendo's huge late 1980s success, *Super Mario Brothers 2* – at least one-third of Nintendo's 15 million console owners bought a copy – then direct gross profit can be estimated to have amounted to more than $45 million according to the following assumptions: Actual manufacturing and shipping costs were probably well under $5 a unit; the basic development and/or licensing cost was $1 million; advertising and promotion were $4 million; and the average wholesale price was about $15.

Of course, most games will not be nearly as profitable. And a large installed base of compatible consoles or computers is an essential precondition for achieving such impressive results.[22] Still, it is this kind of potential profitability – especially as ultimately projected on a global scale – that continues to attract consumer electronics companies and software developers to a business that thrives on technological improvements of game-playing multimedia machines for the home and for arcades and indoor theme park attractions.[23]

9.4 Concluding remarks

This chapter has told a story of boom and bust; of delight in transforming a television screen into a magnificent fantasyland, and of despair in discovering that losses can often come easier than gains. Toy and game demand can sometimes be as volatile as it is faddish.

Although the preceding structural descriptions will undoubtedly remain accurate for the near term, and also in poorer regions of the world, recent advances in telecommunications make it likely that the structure of both the home video and coin-op segments will, by the early years of the twenty-first century, be significantly altered. With fiber optic linkages to the Internet, highly compressed digital signal transmission capabilities, and substantially greater computing power available at relatively low cost, video games of both varieties will be deliverable to consoles with the same speed and efficiency as that of a telephone's dial tone. No longer will coin-op require the frequent physical movement of bulky cabinets and circuit boards. And no longer will the home player be limited in selection of titles or of playing partners.

Computerized games will, moreover, increasingly incorporate artificial intelligence and so-called virtual-reality capabilities and will evolve away from those requiring only simple hand-eye coordination skills to those in which thinking strategies and abstract reasoning are helpful factors. Thus will be provided challenging interactive role-playing "experiences."

Yet no matter what the technology or the format, the essence of a successful game will always be the same: It is simple to understand and to play on an elementary level, but it is compellingly, maddeningly, difficult – and forever impossible – to fully master.[24]

Surely, we will continue to be charmed in ways we can only begin to imagine. For as Frude (1983) has noted with regard to the eventual development of personal robots, another form of computerized entertainment:

> The scene is set for entirely new dimensions of human simulation. And the preposterous notion that a future "personal friend" might be purchased off the shelf now has to be seriously considered. . . . [But still,] getting a machine to laugh is easy. Getting it to laugh at a joke is very, very difficult.

Selected additional reading

Bylinsky, G. (1991). "The Marvels of 'Virtual Reality,' " *Fortune* 123(11)(June 3):138.

Carlton, J. (1995). "Nintendo, Gambling With Its Technology, Faces a Crucial Delay," *Wall Street Journal,* May 5.

Churbuck, D. (1990). "The Ultimate Computer Game," *Forbes* 145(3)(February 5):154.

Clark, D. (1995). "Multimedia's Hype Hides Virtual Reality: An Industry Shakeout," *Wall Street Journal,* March 1.

Cohen, S. (1984). *Zap: The Rise and Fall of Atari.* New York: McGraw-Hill.

Deutsch, C. H. (1989). "A Toy Company Finds Life After Pictionary," *New York Times,* July 9.

Diamond D. (1987). "Is the Toy Business Taking Over Kids' TV," *TV Guide* 35(14)(June 13).

Flax, S. (1983). "The Christmas Zing in Zapless Toys," *Fortune* 108(13)(December 26):98–108.

Hector, G. (1984). "The Big Shrink Is On at Atari," *Fortune* 110(1)(July 9):23–36.

Herz, J.C. (1997). *Joystick Nation.* Boston: Little, Brown.

Hubner, J., and Kistner, W. F., Jr. (1983). "What Went Wrong at Atari," *InfoWorld,* November 28 and December 5.

Losee, S. (1994). "Watch Out for the CD-ROM Hype," *Fortune* 130(6) September 19.

Markoff, J. (1994). "For 3DO, a Make-or-Break Season," *New York Times,* December 11.

Moffat, S. (1990). "Can Nintendo Keep Winning?" *Fortune* 122(12)(November 5).

Morris, B. (1996). "The Brand's the Thing," *Fortune,* 133(4) (March 4).

Nocera, J. (1984). "Death of a Computer: How Texas Instruments Botched the 99/4A," *InfoWorld,* June 4 and June 11; see also *Texas Monthly,* April.

Palmer, J. (1989). "'Joy Toy' Nintendo's Future Not All Fun and Games," *Barron's,* June 26.

Pereira, J. (1989). "As Ghosts of Yules Past Haunt the Toy Shelves, 'Gottahaves' Are Gone." *Wall Street Journal,* December 12.

(1991). "Nintendo Is Counting on New Super Game to Rescue U.S. Sales," *Wall Street Journal,* May 10.

(1993). "Toy Industry Finds It's Harder and Harder to Pick the Winners," *Wall Street Journal,* December 21.

(1994). "The Toy Industry, Too, Is Merging Like Crazy to Win Selling Power," *Wall Street Journal* October 28.

(1996a). ''Toy Business Focuses More on Marketing and Less on New Ideas,'' *Wall Street Journal*, February 29.

(1996b). ''If You Can't Locate that Special Plaything, Call, or Blame, a Scalper.'' *Wall Street Journal*, June 24.

Pereira, J., and Bannon, L. (1995). ''Toy Makers' Addiction To Hollywood Figures Reshapes Kids' Play,''*Wall Street Journal*, July 13.

Pollack, A. (1993). ''Sega Takes Aim at Disney's World,'' *New York Times*, July 4.

(1995). '' 'Morphing' Into the Toy World's Top Ranks,'' *New York Times*, March 12.

Ressner, J. (1982). ''Atari Celebrates First Decade of Record-Breaking Growth,'' *Cash Box*, November 20, p. 62.

Rheingold, H. (1991). *Virtual Reality: The Revolutionary Technology of Computer-Generated Artificial Worlds.* New York: Summit Books (Simon & Schuster).

''Sega!'' *Business Week*, no. 3359 (February 21, 1994).

Sella, M. (1994). ''Will a Flying Doll...Fly?'' *New York Times*, December 25.

Spiers, J. (1992). ''The Baby Boomlet Is for Real,'' *Fortune* 125(3)(February 10).

Tanzer, A. (1991). ''Heroes in a Half Shell,'' *Forbes* 148(10)(October 23).

Trachtenberg, J. A. (1996). ''How Philips Flubbed Its U.S. Introduction of Electronic Product,'' *Wall Street Journal*, June 28.

Turner, R. (1993). ''Video-Game Innovator Lures Corporate Giants to 'Interactive' Media,''*Wall Street Journal*, January 7.

U.S. International Trade Commission (1984), *A Competitive Assessment of the U.S. Video Game Industry*, Washington, D.C.: USITC Publication 1501.

''Virtual Reality,'' *Business Week*, No. 3286, October 5, 1992.

Wojahn, E. (1988). *Playing By Different Rules: The General Mills/Parker Brothers Merger.* New York: American Management Association.

Zachary, G. P. (1990). ''Computer Simulations One Day May Provide Surreal Experiences,'' *Wall Street Journal*, January 23.

Part III
Live entertainment

10
Gaming and wagering

It's better to be born lucky than to be born rich.

Perhaps nowhere is the preceding sentiment more appropriately expressed than in the gaming and wagering business – where kings and queens play amidst snake eyes and wild jokers, and horses run for the roses. The essential economic features of this fascinating business, in which consumers spend more in the aggregate than for any other forms of entertainment, are explored in this chapter.

10.1 From ancient history

At first

Interest in betting on the uncertain outcome of an event is not a recently acquired human trait. As noted by Berger and Bruning (1979, p. 10), "archaeologists believe that cave men not only beat their wives, they wagered them as well." Evidence of mankind's strong and continuing interest in gambling is found in the following historical examples:

In biblical times, the selection of Saul to govern the Hebrew kingdom was determined by lot.

In the tomb of Egyptian pharaoh Tutankhamen was found an ivory gaming board. Palamedes, according to Greek mythology, invented dice and taught soldiers how to play with them during the siege of Troy. Ancient Greek worshippers played dice games and bet on horse races.

The Romans invented the lottery, and they wagered on the outcomes of chariot races. The emperor Nero was said to be addicted to such racing.

The earliest playing cards were of Chinese origin and were derived from Korean playing sticks. Cards similar to those of today were used by the French in the fourteenth century and are descended from tarot decks used for fortune telling. France's Louis XV had a deck made of silver. And England's Henry VIII was a notorious gambler.

The sailing of the *Mayflower* to plant a colony in the New World was financed by a lottery. So were some great educational institutions, including Harvard, Yale, and Dartmouth. So was the colonial army that helped create the United States.

Gaming in America

Preliminaries Wagering already had a long and colorful history thousands of years before the United States came into being. But, as Findlay (1986) describes, in the process of its development, the United States added a few exciting chapters of its own – the often ambivalent American public attitudes toward legalization of such activities notwithstanding.

Even in colonial times there appears to have been some pretty fast action: Consider that four years after the *Mayflower* landed, the Virginia Assembly passed a law against gambling. And legislation passed in Boston in 1630 also decreed that ''all persons whatsoever that have cards, dice, or tables in their houses shall make away with them before the next court under pain of punishment''.[1]

Then there was the country's first lavish casino, referred to as a ''rug joint,'' that opened in New Orleans for 'round-the-clock operation in 1827. By 1832, a similar place – no doubt frequented by many of the fledgling nation's politicians – had been opened in Washington, D.C., on Pennsylvania Avenue.

The year 1850 saw San Francisco, with its gold-rush mentality and 1,000 assorted establishments, become the gambling capital of the West. The cowboy's midwestern equivalent was meanwhile to be found in Dodge City, Kansas. But all kinds of wagering and card playing were also common at that time on Mississippi riverboats, in the terminal port city of New Orleans, and in New York and Chicago. New York, for instance, had an estimated 6,000 gambling locations in the 1850s. And by the 1920s, Miami had become an important hub luring serious bettors.

Although gambling is certainly not unique to the American character, this country has contributed to the development of games such as poker and craps and toward rationalizing the marketing and operating procedures used in modern casinos and lotteries. Gaming and wagering activities are today a regular part of life for all income classes and ethnic groups. And gross industry revenues exceed $45 billion. (Table 10.1)

The Nevada experience Nevada's history as a center for betting goes back to the mid-1800s. There, as in San Francisco, a boom in precious metals mining attracted

Table 10.1. *Gross handle, revenues, and margins in the U.S., 1982–96*

Year	Total legal gross wager (Handle), $ billions	Gross revenues (Win), $ billions	Gross margin (Retention rate or win rate), %
1996	586.52	47.62	8.1
1995	557.48	44.39	8.0
1994	482.10	39.79	8.3
1993	394.11	34.70	8.8
1992	336.66	30.39	9.0
1991	304.30	26.68	8.8
1990	303.09	26.20	8.6
1989	251.20	23.52	9.4
1988	231.60	21.36	9.2
1987	185.85	18.38	9.9
1986	166.47	16.92	10.2
1985	159.16	15.34	9.6
1984	146.97	13.62	9.3
1983	132.14	11.84	9.0
1982	125.76	10.41	8.3
CAGR:[a] 1982–96	11.6	11.5	

[a]Compound annual growth rate, 1982–96 (%).
Source: Adapted from E. M. Christiansen data originally published in *Gaming Business* (April, May, June, and August 1984), and *Gaming & Wagering Business* (July and August) 1985–1997. See Table 10.3.

many rough-and-ready customers for gambling and affiliated services, including liquor sales and prostitution. Nevertheless, the territory's attitude toward legalization of gaming fluctuated – depending on the perceived degree of corruption and cheating – for over half a century before the state of Nevada finally legalized, in 1931, what could not in practice be stopped.

Yet curiously, before World War II, gaming activity in Reno was far more developed than in Las Vegas. "Founded" in 1905 by the sale of some Union Pacific Railway junction property to private interests, and incorporated in 1911, Las Vegas did not actually begin to come into its own until the 1930s. The major catalyst for change was construction of Hoover (alias Boulder) Dam, a major Bureau of Reclamation project located in Boulder City, about 30 miles away. Completion of the dam brought water and electric power to the region, and stimulated commercial growth. Also, many itinerant construction workers, who had bought their supplies and had spent their free time gambling in Las Vegas, eventually settled there permanently.

Las Vegas, however, only began to emerge as a world-famous entertainment capital just after the Second World War. The city's proximity to the burgeoning population of Los Angeles and the increasing availability of low-cost air travel contributed significantly to its success. But, in addition, there was Benjamin "Bugsy" Siegel. As Skolnick (1978, p. 111) indicates,

It had been Siegel's ambition to build a luxurious complex that would offer gambling, recreation, entertainment, and other services catering to the area's increasing tourist trade . . . Siegel had persuaded the crime syndicate that he could transform Las Vegas into a legal gambling oasis for organized crime, and he received their backing in 1943. With their support, he started to work on his initial venture – really the first of the major Strip hotels – the Flamingo.[2]

Nevada's decision (in 1946–7) to establish and to fund – through taxes on gross casino winnings[3] – regulation and enforcement agencies that would ensure fair and honest conduct of the games and of casino operations was of further importance. The irony, of course, was that at the start of legalized modern gaming in Nevada, often the only operators with enough expertise to run the games fairly were people previously affiliated with illegal organizations.

As might be expected, the "connections" of some of those operators created law-enforcement problems that surfaced most noticeably in the 1950s, as attempts at state licensing and gaming-control functions came into conflict with formidable mob interests in what was already a lucrative and rapidly growing business. Indeed, it was not until the mid-to-late 1960s that organized crime's grip on the industry's finances began to be loosened as a result of pressure from the Department of Justice and other federal government investigative agencies, and as a result of large-scale investments by billionaire Howard Hughes.

This process was further accelerated by passage in 1969 of the Corporate Gaming Act, which allowed companies with publicly traded shares to own and operate casinos in the state of Nevada. Ownership by large corporations provided an important means of financing casino-hotel expansions, of attracting middle-class and convention-related customers, and of developing an untainted corps of professional managers.

Enter New Jersey New Jersey's involvement in casino gaming, however, began much differently than Nevada's. New Jersey's Atlantic City had been a popular ocean resort in the early 1900s. But gradually, because of neglect and because of the increasing availability of low-cost air travel, it decayed into what was euphemistically called an economically depressed area. It was always clear, though, that with its proximity to dense population centers in Philadelphia and New York, the town would make an especially attractive location for casinos. And so – with the promise of stimulating urban renewal and providing extra funding for senior citizens' programs – began the efforts of developers to legalize gambling. Voters rejected the first referendum for statewide gambling in 1974, but in 1976 they approved a second one, limiting casinos to Atlantic City.

Public reaction to New Jersey's legalization was awesome. Immediately on opening the first Atlantic City casino in 1978, Resorts International was overwhelmed by enormous crowds betting huge stakes. And over the immediately following years the early momentum continued. Despite having only one-tenth as many first-class hotel rooms (5,000 as of 1984) as its Nevada counterpart, Atlantic City began to compete effectively with Las Vegas as a major center for entertainment and gaming (Figure 10.1 and Table 10.2). By 1984, for example, table-game and slot revenues in New Jersey had come to within 3% of the Las

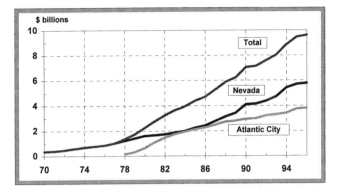

Figure 10.1. Annual casino revenues in Nevada and Atlantic City, 1970–96.

Vegas total of around $2 billion, and annual visitor arrivals in Atlantic City had reached 28.5 million as compared to 12.8 million in Las Vegas.[4]

Still, there remain considerable differences in the way the casino gaming business operates in Nevada as compared to Atlantic City. In Nevada, hundreds of locations scattered throughout the state are licensed to provide a wide variety of casino gaming services (from simple banks of slot machines to race and sports books). And the sixty largest casinos account for over 80% of total gross revenues. In contrast, as of the mid-1990s, there were only twelve large casino-hotels in operation in Atlantic City, and all of them located within five miles of each other. But because of earlier New Jersey regulations, these casinos are much less varied in the size and in the scope of their offerings than are their Nevada counterparts. Greater variation will, however, arrive with the debut of several new projects just after the year 2000.

Horse racing Casinos are nevertheless only part of the story of gaming and wagering in the United States. Horse racing has a particularly interesting history, with direct antecedents of the American experience traceable to England, where a public racecourse was opened in Smithfield, London, in 1174. By the eighteenth century, racing had developed into an important English sport (governed by the Jockey Club), and records of breeding and race results had begun to be published (in the *Racing Calendar*).

The first American racetrack with regularly scheduled meetings was founded in Hempstead (Long Island), New York, in 1665, and tracks soon appeared in several other colonies. It was not until 1821, however, that the first thoroughbred racecourse was built. And it was only after the Civil War that the sport began to achieve wide popularity because of the development of pari-mutuel (''between ourselves'') betting. Prior to that time, betting had been handled by bookmakers who had posted arbitrary odds: With a pari-mutuel system, bets could be pooled, and the odds determined by the opinions of bettors as measured by the amounts wagered on each horse.

Although the racing segment generates annual gross revenues of approximately

Table 10.2. *Gaming win in Atlantic City and Nevada*

Year	Atlantic City and Nevada casino revenues ($ billion)	Nevada total June fiscal year taxable gaming revenues ($ billion)	Las Vegas (Clark County)		Atlantic City	
			Gross winnings ($ billion)	Visitors (million)	Gross winnings ($ billion)	Visitors (million)
1973	0.804	0.804	0.588	8.5		
1974	0.937	0.937	0.685	8.7		
1975	1.066	1.066	0.770	9.2		
1976	1.188	1.188	0.846	9.8		
1977	1.380	1.380	1.015	10.1		
1978	1.805	1.671	1.236	11.2	0.134	7.0
1979	2.306	1.980	1.424	11.7	0.325	9.5
1980	2.917	2.274	1.617	11.9	0.643	13.8
1981	3.563	2.463	1.676	11.8	1.100	19.1
1982	4.093	2.600	1.751	11.6	1.493	23.0
1983	4.454	2.683	1.887	12.3	1.771	26.4
1984	4.943	2.991	2.008	12.8	1.952	28.5
1985	5.367	3.228	2.233	14.2	2.139	29.3
1986	5.647	3.366	2.393	15.2	2.281	29.9
1987	6.205	3.710	2.738	16.2	2.496	31.8
1988	6.809	4.074	3.003	17.2	2.735	33.1
1989	7.119	4.312	3.290	18.1	2.807	32.0
1990	7.864	4.912	3.870	21.0	2.952	31.8
1991	8.403	5.411	4.152	21.3	2.992	30.8
1992	8.913	5.697	4.378	21.9	3.216	30.7
1993	9.319	6.018	4.727	23.5	3.301	30.2
1994	10.069	6.647	5.431	28.2	3.423	31.3
1995	10.901	7.153	5.718	29.0	3.748	33.3
1996	11.340	7.522	5.784	29.6	3.817	34.0
CAGR:[a]						
1970-96	12.3	10.5	11.2	5.8		
1980-96	8.9	7.8	8.3	5.8	11.8	5.8

[a]Compound annual growth rate (%).
Source: Las Vegas Convention/Visitors Authority and Atlantic City Casino Association.

$3 billion, this total is now, as Table 10.3 indicates, considerably below revenues derived from casino table games. Yet even with minimal growth of interest in recent years, horse racing (including thoroughbred, quarter-horse, and harness varieties) has been legalized in over 40 states.[5]

Lotteries In contrast to racing, growth of interest in lotteries has been explosive. Lotteries, which began in Rome more than 2,000 years ago, have been common

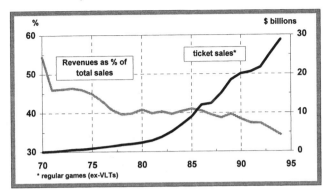

Figure 10.2. Lottery ticket sales and net government revenues as a percent of sales in the United States, 1970–96. *Source data*: *Gaming and Wagering Business.*

throughout the history of the United States. In fact, according to Scarne (1974, pp. 150–2), there were half a dozen of them operating in each of the 13 colonies before the American Revolution, and by 1831 there was an average of one major drawing per week in New York City alone. However, with many of the lotteries of that time privately owned and subject to little or no control, abuses and irregularities began to appear, and public opinion gradually turned against them. An act of Congress in 1890 finally forbade the sending of lottery tickets through the mails, and by 1894, the Louisiana Legislature had phased out the last of the legal lotteries of the nineteenth century.

Some 70 years would elapse before the state of New Hampshire (in 1964) revived the lottery as a fund-raising mechanism. The popularity of this approach to balancing state budgets was such that by 1995 lotteries had been legalized in 37 jurisdictions (and also in all Canadian provinces) and gross ticket sales had exceeded $25 billion, or almost $100 per capita (Supplementary Figure S10.1 and Figure 10.2).[6] By 1994, similar financing considerations even led England to reinstate a national lottery, which had been banned by Parliament since 1826.

Indian reservation, riverboats, and other wagering   The most significant developments of the early 1990s, however, came from the expansion of casino gaming activities onto Indian reservations and riverboats. The federal government's Indian Gaming Regulatory Act of 1988 opened the floodgates by allowing Indian tribes to operate on their reservations, and without restrictions, all forms of gambling previously approved by a state.[7]

Yet, as this was happening, the states themselves hard-pressed to find sources of tax revenues, also began to look more seriously at gaming as a potential new source of income. By the mid-1990s, many state legislatures (at least six) had already moved toward legalization of riverboat or other casino-type operations. Although most such riverboats are fairly small by comparison to Las Vegas casino

Table 10.3. *Gross handle, revenues, and margins in the U.S. by category, 1982–96.*[a]

Year	Casinos Slots	Casinos Table games	State lotteries	Pari-mutuels Horse racing (Track)	Horse racing (OTB)	Dog racing	Jai alai	Legal book-making	Card rooms (excl. Nevada)	Bingo	Charitable gambling (excl. bingo)	Indian reserv.	Non-casino gaming devices	Cruise ships	River-boats	Comm. other
Gross wager (handle); $ billion:																
1996	126.84	178.72	33.91	3.97	4.98	2.31	0.24	2.61	9.86	4.04	5.68	65.18	14.44	6.11	104.42	8.15
1995	121.30	185.58	32.52	4.63	4.53	2.73	0.30	2.60	9.44	4.13	5.65	57.67	12.86	5.757	88.08	7.74
1994	113.03	170.83	30.02	5.64	4.24	2.94	0.32	2.66	9.31	4.25	5.05	41.06	8.91	5.10	63.80	6.19
1993	102.56	150.91	30.87	8.86	4.89	3.28	0.38	2.26	8.45	4.23	4.89	28.96	7.41	4.49	27.12	4.89
1992	94.56	143.62	25.55	9.38	4.70	3.33	0.43	2.11	8.43	4.18	4.70	16.73	3.84	4.28	7.43	3.46
1991	84.40	149.74	20.99	9.86	4.07	3.50	0.49	2.26	8.40	4.23	4.61	5.44	0.36	4.08	1.10	0.77
1990	76.17	161.64	21.02	10.41	3.72	3.47	0.56	2.16	8.38	4.07	4.47	2.64	0.31	3.71		0.38
1989	65.79	127.77	19.49	10.51	3.42	3.21	0.55	1.84	7.56	3.79	4.22	1.00	0.25	1.76		0.02
1988	57.67	126.30	17.05	11.18	2.49	3.26	0.64	1.73	3.45	3.67	3.58	0.35	0.23			
1987	32.79	112.04	13.14	11.05	2.09	3.20	0.71	1.38	3.13	3.98	2.00	0.31				
1986	28.50	101.44	12.48	10.44	1.94	3.02	0.67	1.19	1.12	3.60	1.79	0.29				
1985	26.18	99.56	10.21	10.49	1.75	2.70	0.66	1.13	1.10	3.44	1.68	0.25				
1984	23.79	92.87	8.13	10.42	1.77	2.46	0.67	1.11	1.07	3.15	1.54	—				
1983[a]	18.80	87.20	5.17	9.93	1.72	2.33	0.62	0.85	1.05	3.07	1.40	—				
1982[a]	14.40	87.00	4.09	9.99	1.71	2.21	0.62	0.54	1.00	3.00	1.20	—				
CAGR[d](%):																
1982–96	16.8	5.3	16.3	-6.4	8.0	0.3	-6.6	11.9	17.8	2.2	11.7	n.m.				
Gross revenue, (win), $ billion:																
1996	7.29	3.78	15.34	0.82	1.06	0.50	0.05	0.09	0.68	0.95	1.48	5.36	1.48	0.43	5.54	0.61
1995	7.09	3.86	14.62	0.95	1.03	0.61	0.06	0.10	0.76	0.98	1.51	4.04	1.41	0.41	4.65	0.60
1994	6.61	3.57	13.67	1.12	0.91	0.63	0.07	0.16	0.73	0.99	1.39	3.42	1.08	0.36	3.26	0.49
1993	6.16	3.23	12.82	1.82	1.04	0.07	0.08	0.12	0.66	1.04	1.29	2.59	0.92	0.32	1.46	0.45
1992	5.83	3.12	11.43	1.92	1.01	0.69	0.08	0.10	0.66	1.03	1.24	1.63	0.57	0.31	0.42	0.35
1991	5.24	3.20	10.23	1.98	0.87	0.70	0.10	0.11	0.66	1.05	1.23	0.72	0.16	0.29	0.08	0.06
1990	4.89	3.41	10.29	2.09	0.81	0.69	0.11	0.13	0.66	1.02	1.19	0.49	0.13	0.26		0.03

Table (continued)

Year																
1989	4.35	3.10	9.63	2.21	0.61	0.63	0.11	0.11	0.30	0.91	1.12	0.12	0.12	0.12	0.12	0.20 · 0.00
1988	4.01	3.05	8.42	2.25	0.51	0.63	0.12	0.10	0.28	1.06	0.71	0.12	0.12	0.12	0.10	
1987	3.59	2.81	6.58	2.18	0.48	0.62	0.14	0.09	0.25	0.92	0.62	0.11	0.11	0.11		
1986	3.15	2.59	6.33	1.97	0.45	0.59	0.13	0.08	0.06	0.92	0.54	0.10	0.10	0.10		
1985	2.91	2.54	5.21	1.98	0.41	0.53	0.13	0.06	0.05	0.91	0.53	0.09	0.09			
1984	2.65	2.40	4.15	1.95	0.41	0.48	0.12	0.05	0.05	0.82	0.54	—	—			
1983[a]	2.36	2.25	3.04	1.86	0.40	0.45	0.11	0.04	0.05	0.80	0.46	—	—			
1982[a]	2.00	2.20	2.17	1.85	0.40	0.43	0.11	0.03	0.05	0.78	0.40					

CAGR[d] (%):

1982–96	9.7	3.9	15.0	−5.7	7.2	1.2	−5.1	9.0	20.5	1.4	9.8	n.m.	n.m.	n.m.	n.m.	n.m. · n.m.

Gross margin (retention rate or win rate), %:

Year																
1996	5.7	2.1	45.2	20.5	21.3	21.8	22.7	3.3	6.9	23.6	26.0	8.2	10.3	7.5	5.3	7.1
1995	5.8	2.1	45.0	20.5	21.4	21.7	22.4	3.9	7.9	23.7	26.6	8.2	10	7.7	5.3	7.1
1994	5.8	2.1	45.5	19.8	21.5	21.5	22.1	6.0	7.8	23.2	27.5	8.3	12.2	8.0	5.1	7.1
1993	6.0	2.1	41.5	20.5	21.4	21.2	22.0	5.1	7.8	24.5	26.4	9.0	12.4	9.3	5.4	7.1
1992[b]	6.2	2.2	44.8	20.5	21.5	20.8	19.3	4.6	7.8	24.7	26.4	9.8	14.8	10.0	5.6	7.1
1991	6.2	2.1	48.7	20.0	21.3	20.0	20.5	4.7	7.8	24.9	26.7	13.2	43.4	8.3	7.2	7.1
1990	6.4	2.1	49.0	20.1	21.7	20.0	20.4	5.8	7.8	25.0	26.7	18.5	43.2	8.3		7.0
1989	6.6	2.4	49.4	21.0	17.9	19.7	19.5	5.8	4.0	23.9	26.5	12.0	47.3	8.6		11.3
1988	6.9	2.4	49.4	20.1	20.5	19.3	19.4	6.0	8.0	28.7	19.9					
1987	10.9	2.5	50.1	19.8	22.9	19.5	19.5	6.2	8.0	23.1	30.8					
1986	11.1	2.6	50.8	18.9	23.3	19.5	19.5	6.8	5.0	25.6	30.4					
1985	11.1	2.6	51.0	18.9	23.3	19.5	19.5	5.4	5.0	26.5	31.2					
1984		2.6	51.0	18.7	23.2	18.3	18.3	4.7	5.0	25.9	35.0					
1983[b]	12.5	2.6	58.9	18.7	23.4	18.0	18.0	5.1	4.9	26.0	33.1					
1982[b]	13.9	2.5	53.1	18.5	23.4	18.0	18.0	4.8	5.0	26.0	33.0					

[a] Some figures may not be precise due to rounding

[b] Prior to 1984, sports books, horse books, and sports cards were combined into "other" category.

[c] The previous 1985 estimate of $582 million in gross revenues for charitable games has been subsequently reduced to $525 million.

[d] Compound annual growth rate.

Source: Adapted from E. M. Christiansen data originally published in *Gaming Business* (April, May, June, and August 1984), and *Gaming & Wagering Business* (July and August) 1985–1996. See Table 10.1.

Table 10.4. *Estimated U.S. casino gaming square footage by category, 1997.*

	Square feet (000s)
Atlantic City	925
Nevada	
Las Vegas	4,300
Laughlin	525
Reno/Sparks	925
Other	300
	6,975
Riverboats	1,600
Indian tribal lands	1,500
	3,100
Total	10,075

standards, they are collectively large enough to affect the growth of gaming in Nevada and Atlantic City (Table 10.4).

Legalization of video lottery terminals (VLTs) – in effect, slot machines tied into a lottery – spread rapidly in the early 1990s, but has since slowed. VLTs compete for revenues against established amusement video machines and on-line ticket lottery systems by essentially turning local restaurants and taverns (and also racetracks) into minicasinos.

Bingo, too, has developed into an important legalized activity that generates gross revenue of at least $1.1 billion in the 46 states where it is played.[8] Indeed, bingo attracts some 40 million participants and is the most widespread of all legalized wagering games.

Rapidly growing grosses are furthermore generated in public poker clubs, which have long been legal in certain counties in California. And casino games are also being operated in small former mining towns in states such as South Dakota and Colorado.[9]

Last, but not least, is gaming on the Internet, which has the potential to eventually become a major source of industry revenues if and when federal and state laws are changed and the security of transactions and the accountability of service vendors can be assured. In this regard, the U. S. Interstate Wire Act, which prohibits the taking of bets over a network that crosses state or international borders, is a prominent feature of the current legal landscape.

From all this it would thus appear that the gaming and wagering pie, while continuing to grow at above-average rates in comparison to the overall economy, will continue to be divided into more specialized slices. Moreover, similar patterns are also appearing outside the United States, especially in Canada, Western Europe, and Australia.[10] Major events in the industry's United States history are depicted in Figure 10.3.

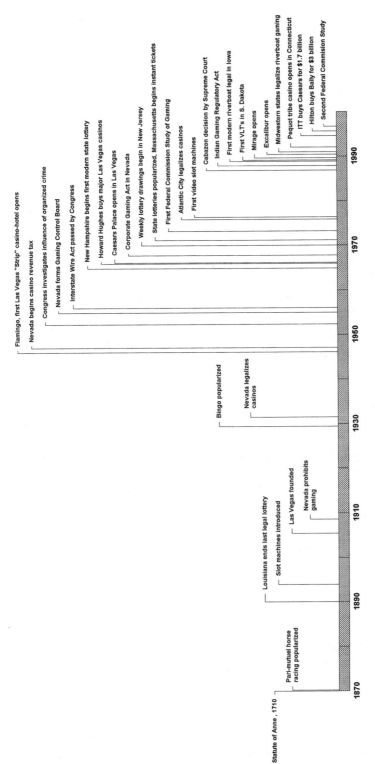

Figure 10.3. United States gaming industry milestones, 1870–2000.

10.2 Money talks

The $47 billion sum of gaming and wagering activity in the United States listed in Table 10.1 represents the total revenue (before expenses) that gaming operators have retained, or, in other words, won. But conversely, it also represents the *net* amount that players have *lost*. Of this total, lotteries (at around $15 billion) and casinos ($11 billion) have been the two fastest growing major components (Figure 10.4).[11] By comparison, domestic movie ticket sales in 1996 were only around $6 billion and recorded music sales about $13 billion.[12]

Macroeconomic matters

The rate of growth of legalized gambling, which comprises approximately 85% of the sums indicated, has been well above that of the aggregate economy for virtually the entire post World War II period. In part, gaming's compound annual growth rate, averaging above 10% during much of the last third of the century, has been a function of simply making the services more widely available and convenient for players to access. However, none of this could have happened if the public's perceptions of gaming and entertainment-spending preferences had not shifted. In 1960, net public spending (losses to operators of casinos, parimutuels, and bingo) on gaming and wagering accounted for around 0.2% of disposable income, while the current share has by now approximately doubled (Figure 1.13c).

Still, with game operators often leveraged financially as well as operationally, the industry's sensitivity to adverse business cycle fluctuations is potentially high. Indeed judging from spending patterns during the recessions of the early 1980s and 1990s, there is evidence that gaming revenues may be sensitive to both regional and national economic conditions.[13] In an economic downturn, for example, convention-trade travel to Atlantic City and Nevada would normally be curtailed as businesses attempt to pare expenses. And average spending per visitor might be reduced (Figure 10.5).

As it happens, many other factors, among which the following are most important, may also decisively affect revenue growth trends in a region:

Air fares and the cost and availability of gasoline
Recent number of room and square footage additions as a percentage of total
    industry capacity
Dollar-exchange rates against major Asian and European countries
Percentage of players coming from outside the region
Projected rates of inflation and factory employment

Funding functions

Gaming and wagering in the United States is governed by a hodgepodge of state and local laws that reflect the ambivalence of the population toward these activ-

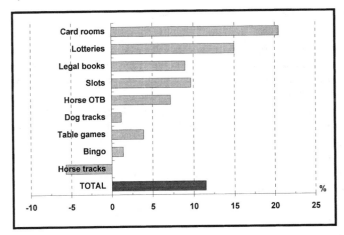

Figure 10.4. Compound annual growth rate comparisons of U.S. gaming revenues by category, 1982–96. *Source data: Gaming and Wagering Business.*

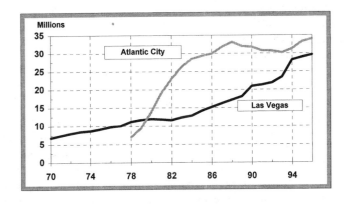

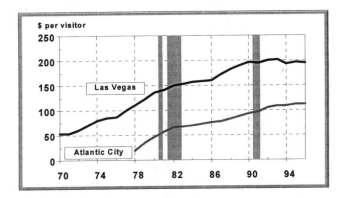

Figure 10.5. Las Vegas versus Atlantic City, 1970–96; (a) visitors and (b) spending per visitor. Bars indicate periods of economic recession.

ities. On the one hand, most jurisdictions have few if any qualms about permitting church or social bingo – a game that, as Cook (1979) notes, has a high cost to the player. Nor do people seem to object to lotteries – a game with even higher costs to the player than bingo. Yet people often rise up in moral indignation against casinos and race tracks, where the operators' percentage is much lower. As Rose (1986) discusses, other anomalies often appear: In communities such as those near Los Angeles, only card games of a precisely defined type are allowed to be played. And in Nevada, the acknowledged sports and race-book and gaming capital of the world, a state lottery is *illegal*.

The logic concerning when and where gaming establishments may advertise is also peculiar. The Federal Communications Commission, for example, follows a set of anti-lottery laws passed before the year 1900. However, states are exempted from the rules. And states thus regularly promote their lotteries on radio and television. But casinos can advertise only on cable: On regular television, they are only allowed to mention their noncasino attractions such as golf courses and restaurants.

It is not surprising, then, that all of this ambivalence and confusion spills over into the politics of regulation and legalization. Legalization in a state or city is always easier to achieve if, by reason of history and culture, the dominant population groups favor such activities. But what usually precipitates a move toward legal sanction is a need for more social-welfare funding than can be comfortably raised via direct taxation.

Thus, unfortunately, the public may sometimes be fooled into thinking that legalization is a costless way to raise net additional revenues. However, several studies – including those of Goodman (1994, 1995), Abt, Smith, and Christiansen (1986), Skolnick (1978, 1979), and Mahon (1980) – indicate that legalization of gaming is not a taxpayers' panacea. Gaming may, for instance, divert revenues needed to support other local retail business establishments. The net revenues raised from its legalization are often relatively small compared to budget gaps, especially if the additional costs of law enforcement and regulation and treatments for new player-addictions are also taken into account. And, as Sternlieb and Hughes (1983) and Goodman (1995, p. xi) have suggested, such legalizations tend to spawn huge, politically powerful bureaucracies that may ultimately operate against the public interest and that shift the role of government from being a watchdog of gambling to becoming its leading promoter.

Regulation

Government regulation is more visible in gaming than in any other entertainment-industry segment. It has developed from historical experience with a cash business that has often nourished the coffers of organized crime, deprived government of tax revenues, and plainly cheated ordinary players.

Regulative power usually rests in the state legislatures, which formally legalize gaming activities that include lotteries, tracks, and casinos. Legislators also establish agencies to oversee that all such activities are conducted honestly and competently, and with full accounting of tax revenues to the state. To achieve those ends, regulatory enforcement, investigative, and licensing agencies work in conjunction with local-community interests to promulgate specific standards and rules of conduct.

In racing, for example, there is the New York State Racing and Wagering Board, which institutes measures to safeguard the integrity of racing and compiles statistical and other information concerning New York Racing Association tracks and off-track betting (OTB) parlors. More widely known, however, are the Nevada and New Jersey gaming commissions, which oversee licensing and regulation of casino gaming and slot-machine operations in those states. New Jersey's regulatory bodies are to a great extent patterned on those earlier developed in Nevada, where there is a two-tier structure: The Gaming Control Board works at the staff level on investigation and audit, and the Gaming Commission acts as a quasi-judicial body that deliberates on licensing, revocations, and other related matters.

Agents and investigators representing the Federal Bureau of Investigation (FBI) and the Internal Revenue Service (IRS) have generally played a role ancillary to that of the state commissions. But should any of the state bodies prove ineffectual, it is likely that the federal government would immediately become more actively and visibly involved in industry affairs. The most direct influence would then probably be felt through augmentation of tax-reporting requirements.[14]

The difficulty of designing regulation that balances the needs of the business with that of the public's interest can be seen in the case of New Jersey, where, in its zeal to ensure that casinos would be impervious to influence by organized crime, the legislature in that state incorporated particularly detailed instructions in bills to legalize Atlantic City gaming. All employees – initially including restaurant busboys, hotel bellhops, and parking attendants far removed from gaming-transactions areas – had to submit detailed license applications.[15]

As Atlantic City gaming matured, many of these early regulations proved to be unnecessarily stringent, if not actually detrimental to industry growth and profitability. Those standards were then somewhat relaxed as the commission and its enforcement division began to concentrate on licensing of top executives and of people who directly oversee gaming activities and grant credit (dealers, pit bosses, shift managers, and cage personnel). Licensing of slot machines and of companies supplying the industry with goods and services (linen, liquor, food, etc.) also took priority.

Without close scrutiny at the financial-accounting and operational levels, there is a natural tendency for illegal activities to arise. And frauds and tax evasions are still occasionally discovered in lotteries (e.g., irregular printing of tickets), in horse racing (e.g., substitution by ''ringers,'' use of illegal drugs on animals, and fixing of races), and in casinos (e.g., skimming money before reporting to the state). Yet with a strong regulative mandate and ample funding for enforcement and licensing personnel, these problems can be largely prevented – with the public assured that games are being fairly conducted and with governments receiving full revenues due.

Table 10.5. *Gaming company revenues and earnings: composite of 39 companies, 1992–96*

Year	Revenues	Operating income	Operating margin[a] (%)	Assets	Operating cash flow
CAGR(%)[b]					
1992–96	11.3	9.2	−1.9	15.1	9.6

[a]Average margin 1992–96 = 15.6%.
[b]Compound annual growth rate.

Regulation is initiated and designed to support the commonweal. And segments of the legalized-gaming industry – even when not directly owned or operated by a state – will thus commonly have a close and lasting relationship with regulatory bodies established and controlled by elected officials. Accordingly, as Skolnick (1978) suggests, there is always the potential for gaming interests to become so politically powerful that they circumvent the spirit if not the actual letter of the law.

Financial performance and valuation

The variety of companies that derive some or all of their income from the operation of legalized gaming and wagering activities is surprisingly broad.[16] In addition to the relatively well-known casino-hotel companies, there are manufacturers of computer components and designers of software used in lottery systems management. There are producers of sophisticated slot and poker machines. Plastics and paper companies make dice and playing cards. And breeding and real-estate firms are involved in racing. However, of all these categories, the most readily definable and investable grouping is that of the casino-hotel operators.

Although casino returns on investment (ROI) have varied greatly from company to company, the casino industry has generally prospered in recent decades.[17] Moreover, as shown in Table 10.5, growth rates of revenues, assets, and operating income have mostly remained in balance, thereby enabling the industry to borrow heavily against a relatively small equity base.

Most investors or lenders would thus value a gaming enterprise by analyzing its potential in terms of earnings before taxes, interest, and depreciation and amortization (EBITDA). The multiple that would then be applied to such a projected cash flow figure would be a function of interest rates, local market growth and competitive considerations, the worth of underlying real estate for alternative uses, and general economic conditions.[18]

Similarly, enterprise value could be estimated as follows:
(number of shares × price) + net debt − off-balance-sheet assets
wherein net debt is defined as long-term debt minus cash.

Table 10.6. *Characteristics of casino games*

Games	Edge[a] (%)	Frequency of play (min.)
American roulette	2.7	0.75
French roulette	1.4–2.7	1.5–2
Blackjack	At least 0.6	2–3
Punto banco	1.25	2–3
Craps	1.4–5.6	1.5–2
Baccarat banque	0.9–1.5	2–3

[a]In a rational world it might be expected that the edge would be inversely proportional to the frequency with which the game is played, but this is clearly not so in the actual casino world. In any case, many players are under the illusion that the more often they can play, the more likely they are to win.

Source: Royal Commission on Gambling (1978, p. 451). Final Report, London, July 1978, Vol. 2, p. 451.

Of course, the concepts and methodology – and the existence of normally deep public market discounts to estimated private market values – are similar to those seen in valuations of media properties (sections 6.4 and 7.5).

10.3 Underlying profit principles and terminology

There are uncountable variations on the thousands of card, dice, and numbers games that have been invented over the millennia. But of these, only a few have been standardized for use in today's legalized-gaming environment. This section presents a framework for understanding how games generate profits on the transactions level.

Principles

It is easy to arrive at an impression that a casino's profits come only out of the collective hides of the losing bettors. But, surprisingly, a governing principle behind the conduct of every profit-making betting activity is to *pay less than true odds* to the winners. Indeed, it is the payment of less than true odds to winners (out of the losers' pool) that provides the casino with its "edge" (Table 10.6), the racetrack with its "take," and the lottery with its "cut." In other words, losers' money is used to compensate winners, but not as adequately as game mathematics would require. Hence, profits are, in a sense, derived from both losers and winners. Pari-mutuel betting, in which various taxes, track fees, and "breakage" charges (see Appendix B) are deducted from the pool of funds contributed by winners and losers, provides another example of this.

With a statistical advantage established, operating profitability is then affected by the number of decisions or completed betting events per unit time. A second governing principle is thus found in the steady pressure to raise or to maintain the rate of decision as high as possible so that statistical advantages are compounded as much as possible over time. If winners are shortchanged of true odds by even a small percentage often enough, then the aggregate amount kept by the game operator (the "house") can be substantial.[19]

A third governing principle in the operation of games of chance is applied when betting limits – the maximum amount permitted to be wagered on each decision – are imposed. Murphy (1976) notes that in a game with 50:50 odds – for example, tossing pennies or betting double or nothing – the usual assumption is that over a long period of time the outcome will be even. This, however, is untrue if one player has limited capital and the other has infinite capital: The expected outcome for the player with limited capital is total loss. The imposition of a betting limit (which, in effect, artificially constrains the player's capital relative to that of the game operator), in and of itself practically guarantees that over an extended period the operator will win all, even without benefit of a house edge.[20] In such cases, it is thus not the edge, but the limit, that defeats the gambler.

In practice, rather than dividing their stake into many smaller units and rebetting, players have the highest probability of winning if they make just one large bet; the house's edge here has minimal opportunity to grind down the player's capital. However, because most people would not enjoy going to a casino or track and making only one bet, people instead trade off the probability of winning for entertainment value derived through extended playing time. An excerpt from *Gambling Times* illustrates:[21]

In playing red or black on roulette with one $100 bet, the house edge is 5.26% (there are 18 reds, 18 blacks, and 2 greens – so odds are 20 to 18 against) and a bet may be expected to be won 47.37% of the time – almost an even chance. Now suppose $5 units are bet until $100 is either won or lost. Out of 1,000 trials, on average 873 times there would be a loss of $100, and only 127 times a win of $100. The average amount to bet to obtain a decision would be $1,451 compared to $100 with one large bet.

As for sports betting, an important principle noted by Moore (1996, p. 5) is that "it is the collective public perception that controls the odds." A bookmaker's proposed odds payoff schedule, his 'line,' thus does not express an opinion on how the two teams will fare. It instead represents the line-maker's expert opinion on what numbers will induce half the the public to bet on the underdog and the other half to bet on the favorite.

Terminology and performance standards

A positive expected return to the game operator is realized over many betting events – be they dice rolls, card flips, slot-machine pulls, races run, or lottery tickets sold. The total amount bet is called the *handle,* and the amount that remains for the game organizer after the betting-event result has been determined is the *win.*

In casino table games, cash or cash equivalents, such as credit slips called *markers,* are collected (dropped) into sealed boxes under the tables. The dollar-equivalent aggregates in the boxes have thus become known as the *drop* – a term that also applies to the coins (and/or tokens) fed into slot machines.[22] The *win rate*, expressed as a percentage, is then the total win (over time) divided by the total drop. This percentage is usually referred to as the *hold*.[23] In contrast, at tracks, states charge a fixed percentage of the handle as a "fee" for participation.

Although the operator's positive-expected-return percentage produced by trials over many betting events is generally small – ranging from almost nil at some points in a blackjack game to over 15% for some bets in craps, at the Big Six wheel, in lotteries, in bingo, and at the track – win rates normally range between 10% and 25% of the drop in casinos, 17% or more of the handle in racing, and ~50% of the handle in lotteries. In effect, then, the win percentage may be viewed as the average proportion of the bankroll of all players taken collectively that would be typically retained by the game operator. Note here, however, that the casino's "edge" – its expected value per unit bet, or, in casino jargon, the house p.c. – in table games is expressed as a percentage of the handle and not as a percentage of the drop (even though these might sometimes be the same).

Moreover, the similarity of conversion of cash at the track into tickets, and cash at the casino into chips, does not mean that the handle at tracks and lotteries can be compared to the drop in a casino. In casinos, handle is many times the drop because (a) it is unusual for all chips (cheques) purchased and counted in the drop to be immediately "invested" in the game, and (b) "reinvestment" of chips won or retained in the course of play may increase the handle without correspondingly increasing the drop through additional chip purchases. Such, though, is not the case with pari-mutuel tickets, where there is no fractional retention of the ticket's value. The full face amount of the ticket is bet in each race.

The following numerical example, assuming a one-roll-decision dice game in which the casino edge is 2%, should help clarify the terminology. Say there are five bettors, each betting $10 on a throw of the dice. The handle is then $50. Assume further that the players are not using cash, but instead chips issued by the casino and bought at the table for cash. The drop will then also be $50 at the start of the game. Theoretically, for each decision, the casino ought to expect to win 2%, or $1, of the total amount bet. Of course, this may or may not happen over the short run, but it will, on average, occur over the long run (i.e., over many betting decisions).

Now assume for a moment that on the first roll, the players as a group come out even, and that they then bet the second roll identically to the first. The handle at that table has now risen to $100, while the drop has remained $50; no player had to buy more chips.[24]

Another hypothetical situation can be examined to illustrate how the hold is over 10% even when the house's edge may be 1%. Suppose that a player beginning with a $100 stake, and buying $100 worth of chips, on each decision happens to experience the long-run average loss specific to that game of 1% per decision. On the first deal of the cards, the casino wins $1, and the player has $99 left over. On the second deal, the casino wins $0.99, and the player has $98.01 remaining.

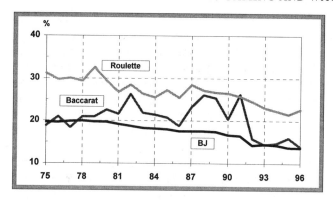

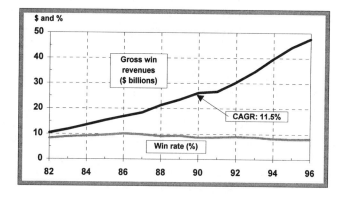

Figure 10.6. Win rate characteristics in Nevada by game, 1975–96: (a) by game, and
(b) overall U.S. industry average percentage.

Extrapolating, after 11 decisions the player has less than $90, and the casino more
than $10 – and at this stage, the win as percentage of the drop (the hold) is over
10% (with the handle over $1,000).

Most games have win rates that over time are characteristic, and are thus use-
able as statistical-norm benchmarks against which the performance of a specific
table (or of a casino with many tables) may be measured. Nevada's characteristic
win-rate averages, for example, are shown in Figure 10.6 and in Table 10.7. From
this it can be seen that baccarat is the most volatile (i.e., has the highest variance)
of all games in terms of gross win fluctuations. Indeed, the variance is so great
that casinos occasionally encounter losing months at their baccarat pits.[25]

Analysis of casino game performances may also be extended well beyond the
rudiments just presented. Detailed knowledge of the probability for each bet-
ting-decision result (and of the average number of events per final decision) is
required to calculate cost as a percentage of money bet (see, for example, Supplementary Table S10.3). And such knowledge may then be used to determine
the true cost to the casino of player junkets and comps. An interesting rule of

Table 10.7. *Hold (% win to drop) for Nevada, 1975–96[a]*

| | Major table games | | | | |
	Blackjack	Craps	Roulette	Baccarat	Total
Nevada (% total win by source)[b]					
Mean:	21.0	11.1	2.5	5.5	40.1
Hold (% win to drop)					
Mean:	17.5	17.1	26.9	20.4	20.5
Variance:	4.4	2.9	8.2	13.8	5.2

[a]Fiscal years ended June 30 beginning in 1984.
[b] Including slots.
Source: Nevada Gaming Control Board.

thumb mentioned by Kilbey (1985), for example, is that a casino has earnings potential of around one average bet per hour. That is, if the average bet is $25, then the casino can expect on average to win that amount in each hour of play.[26]

With slots often accounting for over half of a casino's activity, managers are also motivated to compare ROI performances of various machines. A model that can be used for such purposes is described by Johnson (1984, p. 62). As illustrated in the following, it includes variables for coin denomination, hold, average coins played, and cycle time:

Equations

1. denomination $\times$ hold $\times$ average coins played = win per game
2. average daily drop $\div$ win per game = games played
3. games played $\times$ cycle time $\div$ hours operated daily = utilization rate

Sample calculation

1. $0.05(denomination) $\times$ 0.15(percentage hold) $\times$ 2.2(average coins played) = $0.0165.
2. To win $25, this machine must be played 1,515 ($25/$0.0165) times.
3. Assuming an average cycle time of 10 seconds, it will take 15,152 seconds (4.21 hours) or a 17.5% utilization rate over 24 hours to reach these earnings.

10.4 Casino management and accounting policies

Marketing matters

One way to understand the business of a casino (or that of any other wagering establishment) is to visualize it as a retailer, ostensibly of betting opportunities, but in actuality, of experiences that are stimulating, exciting – *entertaining*. That

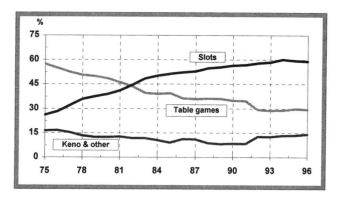

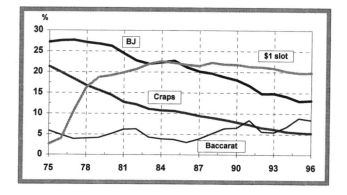

Figure 10.7. Nevada dollar volume market shares for table games versus slots, 1975–96. *Source:* Nevada Gaming Control Board.

such experiences have an inherent value to the customer is proven time and again by the fact that – although they receive nothing tangible on-balance in return for the money they spend – the customers tend to come back for another visit. The marketing challenge is to get customers into the store through advertising, marketing, and publicity, and to then keep them shopping for as long as possible under conditions in which "the customer sets the price ... decides when the show begins and how long it will last."[27]

Casinos in particular have found it necessary to create marketing images that most appeal to the core of players they are likeliest to attract. For example, Circus Circus casino-hotels have long and very profitably catered to low- and mid-budget players who do not require extensive credit-granting facilities or lavish meal and entertainment services. On the other hand, both Caesars World (ITT Corp.) and Mirage Resorts have profitably exploited – without sacrificing the important and vastly broader upper-middle-income player group – the so-called high-roller niche, in which practically any whim of the free-spending gamer is indulged.[28] And several casinos also still attract players by developing tour and travel discount packages and junkets.[29]

Even with all this, however, market shares for individual companies do not remain static and it is crucial for managements to accommodate the shifting demands of players by altering the mix of their games over time. In recent years, for instance, technological advances in the design of electronic slot machines (including video poker and blackjack) have made them so popular that they have come to account, at the expense of table games, for a steadily rising share of overall industry revenues (Figure 10.7). But the optimal mix of slots to table games may also, as Greenlees (1988, p. 12) has noted, vary considerably from one region to another. As has already been shown in Figure 10.5, the average amount of money and time spent by a visitor to Las Vegas differs greatly from that in Atlantic City.

Cash and credit

Large casinos will often have millions of dollars in cash and equivalents either in play or ready for play at the tables and slot machines. And in order to attract and to retain business, most casinos will also often extend credit and comps (free goods and services) to their better customers. The short-run management problem, then, is to oversee and control the flow of cash, credit, and comps – preventing the abuses by employees and by customers that can naturally be anticipated when there is regular and close contact with sizable amounts of money.

Achievement of such control requires implementation of highly detailed and regimented rules of conduct. But enforcement of the rules must also be accompanied by a strong commitment from upper management to subject any deviations and irregularities to close scrutiny. In practice, this means that operating procedures are broken into many small and well-defined steps: Many people must watch many people as credits and comps are granted and as the cash moves from the pockets of the players into the tables and slots, into the counting rooms, and then finally into a bank vault. The same applies with regard to chips, cash, and credits that are recycled back to tables and cashiers' windows as seed money to conduct the games.

Of all such activities, however, it is in the granting of credit that the casino establishes what is probably the most sensitive and important of relationships with its customers. Credit that is extended and then promptly repaid normally generates very profitable activity because the casino's edge is applied to a bigger volume of play than it would otherwise receive.[30]

But credit also has another, darker side. As Friedman (1974, 1982) has noted, casinos must win their money twice; first having to beat credit players at the tables and then having to collect the amounts they are owed. If a customer receives more credit than can be recycled in full over a reasonable time after play, casino margins will suffer from bad-debt write-offs. Accordingly, strict credit-granting procedures have been developed in both Nevada and New Jersey.[31] Using bank references and other information, managers can, for instance, certify with Central Credit Inc. in Nevada that the customer is in good standing at banks and at other hotel-casinos.

Credit policies usually also reflect casino marketing strategies – the effects of which can generally be seen on the balance sheet through bad-debt allowances as a percentage of accounts receivable. The Showboat hotel-casino in Las Vegas, for example, has a largely cash clientele and therefore virtually no need for bad-debt reserves. Conversely, Caesars Palace has largely positioned itself as a high-roller's mecca, and its allowances have been large, as measured in absolute dollars or as a percentage of receivables. Important deviations from prior reserve-percentage norms often signal changes in marketing policies – or in accounting procedures that may significantly influence reported earnings.

Moreover, rapid growth of receivables net of reserves as compared with the growth of gross win is often an early-warning indicator that current-period performance is perhaps being unsustainably boosted by "borrowing" from performance in future periods. In effect, players are being granted more credit than they can repay over a reasonably short time, and the likelihood is that they are being tapped out (or "burned" out).[32]

Procedural paradigms

Fill slips record the value of the bills, coins, and chips the cashier's cage issues to the gaming tables, and credit slips record the value of these items returned to the cage. Nevada Gaming Commission Regulations [number 6.040(5)] specify the method that must be used to transfer cash and equivalents between tables and the cage.[33]

According to the regulations [and following Friedman's (1974) presentation], "all fill slips and credit slips shall be serially numbered in forms prescribed by the board," and the serial numbers must include letters of the alphabet "so that no gaming establishment may ever utilize the same number and series . . . All series numbers that are received by the establishment must be accounted for. All void slips shall be marked 'VOID' and shall require the signatures of the 2 persons voiding the slip."

In addition, there are several detailed regulations as to how drop boxes are unlocked with two different keys – one issued by the cage and the other by the accounting department at the time the count is scheduled. Once the drop box is opened, regulations specify that the contents of each box or bag be counted and verified by three counting employees, and that the count be supported by all credit and fill slips taken from the box.

The count team notes shift win, shift currency drop, shift fill and credits, and shift IOUs to the cage, and typically sorts a box's contents into (a) currency, (b) chips, (c) fill slips, (d) chip credit slips, and (e) name credit slips. A table shift's records – its *stiff sheets* – will then include the table's opening chip bank (inventory) as a fill slip and the shift's closing chip bank as a chip credit. Calculations by shift can then be made as follows:

currency + chips + name credits + chip credits + closing bank
    = table income
opening bank + fills = table fills
table income − table fills = table win

More specifically, the win or loss at each table in each shift may, as illustrated in AICPA (1984, p. 7), be computed as in the following example:

Cash in the drop box		$6,000
Credit issued and outstanding		3,000
Total *drop*		9,000
Less: Beginning table inventory	$14,000	
Chip transfers		
Fills	5,000	
Credits	(1,000)	
	18,000	
Ending table inventory	(11,000)	7,000
Win		$2,000

Of course, all accounts, including cash, hold IOUs (a customer's check that a casino agrees not to process until some time in the future), and others are verified and balanced according to standard journal-entry procedures. But, in addition, table-game and slot results are regularly analyzed by shift, using statistical tests to signal possible significant deviations in win and drop figures from previously established averages. In this way, casino managers can detect where there might be any fraud by employees or customers.

Also, when aggregated over longer periods such as a week or a month, these statistics may be analyzed to indicate trends in win per square foot. Such data permit relative-efficiency comparisons to be made to experiences in prior periods and to the performances of other casinos and are similar to sales-per-square-foot calculations used in the retailing industry. Table 10.8, for example, shows Nevada revenues and average win per square foot data by game category.

10.5 Gambling and economics

The psychological roots of the desire to gamble are complex and not completely understood. In fact, some psychologists (e.g., Halliday and Fuller, 1974) view gambling as a neurosis rather than a form of entertainment.

Economists, however, deal with the demand for gaming services through utility-function models. In such models, consumers express their preferences by making purchases according to the utility they expect to derive from the goods or services bought.

To see how this line of thinking evolved, we have to go back over two hundred years. At that time, some mathematicians were concerned about resolving the so-called St. Petersburg paradox, which was presented in the form of a coin-tossing game. In theory, because the expected value (payoff, or return) of the game was infinite, players should have been willing to pay an infinite amount to participate. Yet no one was willing to do so.

Mathematicians Daniel Bernoulli and Gabriel Cramer solved the mystery by rejecting the principle of maximum expected return and by substituting instead the concept of expected utility. By recognizing the diminishing marginal utility

Table 10.8. *Nevada gaming revenue analysis, fiscal year 1996*

Category	Statewide	Las Vegas Strip
Revenue per square foot[a]		
Pit[b]	$1,909	$3,352
Coin-operated devices[c]	1,043	1,148
Poker and pan	2,422	4,561
Race and sports	566	698
Total casino	$1,218	$1,648
Casino department % of revenues from:		
Pit[b]	33.2%	44.2%
Coin-operated devices[c]	61.4	47.9
Poker and pan	2.7	4.6
Race book	1.4	1.9
Sports pool	1.3	1.5
Total revenue	100.0%	100.0%

[a]Statewide includes 229 locations, Las Vegas Strip 40 locations.
[b]Includes keno and bingo.
[c]Primarily slot machines.
Source: Nevada Gaming Abstract, State Gaming Control Board.

of money – the additional utility derived from additional units decreases as the money value of the prize increases – they could explain the paradox: Participants would determine the amount they were willing to play in a St. Petersburg type of game according to the game's expected utility and *not* its expected monetary returns.

Significant further work on the nature of utility functions was done in the 1930s, when it was demonstrated that unless the function is bounded, new paradoxes can be constructed. Yet it remained for von Neumann and Morgenstern (1944) to show, in their classic 1940s work on game theory, how the expected-utility hypothesis leads to optimal decisions under conditions of uncertainty.

Friedman and Savage (1948) then later published an important study discussing the application of the expected-utility concept to choices made by individuals. Why, they asked, would many people purchase insurance (pay a premium to avoid risk) and also gamble (undertake risk)? To answer, they postulated (as shown in Figure 10.8) that over some range, the marginal utility of wealth increases, which means that the utility functions of individuals contain both concave (risk-aversion curves graphically represented as outward-bending from the origin) and convex (risk-affinitive) segments. Also, as Yaari (1965) has suggested, players often substitute, for the objective or true probabilities of a game, their own subjective beliefs about those probabilities.

In contrast to the theoreticians just cited, however, other economists have ex-

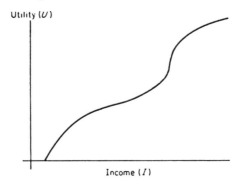

Figure 10.8. An individual's utility function. *Source:* Friedman and Savage (1948).

amined the gaming industry through a variety of standard econometric modeling approaches. Eadington (1976), for example, estimated for the Nevada economy the coefficients in a production function of the form $Q = f(K, L, M)$, where Q represents volume of finished product, K is capital equipment, L is labor, and M is quantity of raw materials. From this he was able to draw conclusions concerning economies of scale and the optimal mix and marginal productivities of various games and devices. Still others (e.g., Asch, Malkiel, and Quandt 1984) have, moreover, suggested that certain betting situations and the securities markets are behavioral analogs that can be studied through market-efficiency theories.

In all, the academic literature on gambling and economics has developed rapidly because gaming and wagering activities have so many quantifiable aspects, and because economic analysis can be readily applied to everything from game-playing to the determination of optimal casino comp and credit policies.

10.6 Concluding remarks

In total, more is spent on gaming and wagering activities than on movies and recorded music combined. This remarkable situation has, in part, since the early 1950s, reflected changes in American life-styles as well as advances in lottery, racing, communications, and slot-machine technologies.[34] As we have seen, however, the industry's growth potential depends on an unusually broad assortment of social, political, and economic factors.

Yet, as economists Ignatin and Smith (1976) have noted, the one constant throughout is that gambling possesses both consumption and investment characteristics; it provides direct utility with the hope of financial gain. In other words, people do not gamble only for money; they also gamble because it is entertaining.

Selected additional reading

Alchian, A. A. (1953). ''The Meaning of Utility Measurement,'' *American Economic Review*, March.

Auerbach, A. H. (1994). *Wild Ride: The Rise and Tragic Fall of Calumet Farm Inc.*, *America's Premier Racing Dynasty*. New York: Henry Holt.

Barron, J. (1989). "States Sell Chances for Gold as a Rush Turns to a Stampede," *New York Times*, May 28.

——— (1989). "Has the Growth of Legal Gambling Made Society the Loser in the Long Run?" *New York Times*, May 31.

Bass, T. A. (1985). *The Eudaemonic Pie*. Boston: Houghton Mifflin.

Bassett, G. W., Jr. (1981). "Point Spreads versus Odds," *Journal of Political Economy* 89(4):752–68.

Blum, H., and Gerth, J. (1978). "The Mob Gambles on Atlantic City," *New York Times*, February 5.

Brenner, R. and G. A. (1990). *Gambling and Speculation: A Theory, a History, and a Future of Human Decisions*. New York: Cambridge University Press.

Bulkeley, W. M. (1995). "Electronics Is Bringing Gambling Into Homes, Restaurants and Planes," *Wall Street Journal*, August 16.

Bulkeley, W. M., and Stecklow, S. (1996). "Long a Winner, Gtech Faces Resistance Based on Ethical Concerns," *Wall Street Journal*, January 16.

Calonius, E. (1991). "The Big Payoff From Lotteries" *Fortune* 123(6)(March 25).

Camerer, C. (1989). "Does the Basketball Market Believe in the Hot Hand?" *American Economic Review*, (December) 79, and comment by Brown, W. O. and Sauer, R. D. (1993). *Amercian Economic Review*, (December) 83.

Charlier, M. (1992). "Casino Gambling Saves Three Colorado Towns But the Price Is High," *Wall Street Journal*, September 23.

Clark, T. L. (1987). *The Dictionary of Gambling and Gaming*. Cold Spring, N.Y.: Lexik House.

Clotfelter, C. T., and Cook, P. J. (1989). *Selling Hope: State Lotteries in America*. Boston: Harvard University Press.

Cook, J. (1980). "The Most Abused, Misused Pension Fund in America," *Forbes* 126(10)(November 10):69–82.

Cook, J., and Carmichael, J. (1980). "Casino Gambling: Changing Character or Changing Fronts," *Forbes* 126(9)(October 27).

Cordtz, D. (1990). "Betting the Country," *Financial World* 159(4)(February 20).

Crist, S. (1989). "Race Tracks Step Lively to Keep up With Bettors," *New York Times*, May 29.

Curry, B. (1984). "State Lotteries: Roses and Thorns," *State Legislatures*, March.

Demaris, O. (1986). *The Boardwalk Jungle*. New York: Bantam.

Dombrink, J., and Thompson, W. N. (1990). *The Last Resort: Success and Failure in Campaigns For Casinos*. Reno and Las Vegas: University of Nevada Press.

Durso, J. (1991). "On Horse Farms, a Season of Distress Lingers," *New York Times*, April 23.

Elkind, P. (1996). "The Number Crunchers," *Fortune*, 134(9)(November 11).

Emshwiller, J. R. (1992). "California Card Casinos Are Suspected as Fronts for Rising Asian Mafia," *Wall Street Journal*, June 1.

Epstein, R. A. (1967). *The Theory of Gambling and Statistical Logic*. New York: Academic Press.

Hamer, T. P. (1982). "The Casino Industry in Atlantic City: What Has It Done for the Local Economy?" *Business Review*. Federal Reserve Bank of Philadelphia, January/February, pp. 3–16.

Harris, R. J., Jr. (1984). ''Circus Circus Succeeds in Pitching Las Vegas to People on Budgets,'' *Wall Street Journal*, July 31.

Hirshey, G. (1994). ''Gambling: America's Real National Pastime,'' *New York Times Magazine*, July 17.

Johnston, D. (1992). *Temples of Chance: How America Inc. Bought Out Murder Inc. to Win Control of the Casino Business*. New York: Doubleday.

Klein, F. C. (1983). ''Horse Racing Gives Bush-League Owner Thrills, Little Profit,'' *Wall Street Journal*, August 31.

Lancaster, H. (1980). ''Casino 'Hosts' Pamper High-Rolling Bettors to Keep Them Rolling,'' *Wall Street Journal*, September 3.

Lancaster, H. (1985). ''Investing in Horses Is a Lot Like Betting: Some Luck, Some Skill, Maybe a Payoff,'' *Wall Street Journal*, March 15.

Levine, L. (1995). ''Requiem for a Thoroughbred?,'' *Forbes*, 156(14)(December 18).

Liebau, J. (1983). ''Tearing Up the Turf,'' *Barron's*, August 8.

Longstreet, S. (1977). *Win or Lose: A Social History of Gambling in America*. Indianapolis: Bobbs-Merrill.

Meier, B. (1994). ''Behind the Glow of Jackpots, Scrutiny for a Lottery Giant,'' *New York Times*, December 19.

Messick, H., and Goldblatt, B. (1976). *The Only Game in Town: An Illustrated History of Gambling*. New York: Crowell.

Morehead, A. H., and Mott-Smith, G., eds. (1963). *Hoyle's Rules of Games*. New York: Signet Books, New American Library.

Myerson, A. R. (1996). ''A Big Casino Wager That Hasn't Paid Off,'' *New York Times*, June 2.

O'Donnell, J. R., and Rutherford, J. (1991). *Trumped! The Inside Story of the Real Donald Trump*. New York: Simon & Schuster.

Orwall, B. (1995). ''Casinos Aren't for Kids, Many Gambling Firms in Las Vegas Now Say,'' *Wall Street Journal*, December 7.

——— (1996). ''Gambling Industry Hopes to Hit Jackpot Through Consolidation,'' *Wall Street Journal*, June 10.

——— (1996). ''The Federal Regulator of Indian Gambling Is Also Part Advocate,'' *Wall Street Journal*, July 22.

Orwall, B., Rundle, R.L., and Rose, F. (1997). ''Hilton and ITT Took Two Different Paths to This Confrontation,'' *Wall Street Journal*, January 29.

Paher, S., ed. (1976). *Nevada Official Bicentennial Book*. Las Vegas: Nevada Publications.

Painton, P. (1989). ''Boardwalk of Broken Dreams,'' *Time* 134(13)(September 25).

Passell, P. (1994). ''The False Promise of Development by Casino,'' *New York Times*, June 12.

——— (1994). ''Foxwoods, a Casino Success Story,''*New York Times*, August 8.

Peterson, I. (1995). ''After 20 Years, Atlantic City Starts to Reap Casinos' Benefits,'' *New York Times*, December 26.

Pileggi, N. (1995). *Casino: Love and Honor in Las Vegas*. New York: Simon and Schuster.

Pollock, M. (1987). *Hostage to Fortune: Atlantic City and Casino Gambling*. Princeton, N.J.: Center for Analysis of Public Issues.

Reinhold, R. (1989). ''Las Vegas Transformation: From Sin City to Family City,'' *New York Times*, May 30.

Roemer, W. F., Jr. (1994). *The Enforcer: The Chicago Mob's Man Over Las Vegas*. New York: Ivy Books (Ballantine).

(1990). *War of the Godfathers: The Bloody Confrontation Between the Chicago and New York Families For Control of Las Vegas.* New York: Donald I. Fine.

Ross, I. (1984). "Corporate Winners in the Lottery Boom," *Fortune* 110(5)(September 3):20–5.

Sack, K. (1995). "Gambling Owners Spend Lavishly To Gain a Voice in Many States," *New York Times,* December 18.

Scheibla, S. H. (1984). "Good Horse Sense?" *Barron's,* December 31.

Schwartz, E. I. (1995). "Wanna Bet?" *Wired,* October.

Seligman, D. (1975). "A Thinking Man's Guide to Losing at the Track," *Fortune* XCII(3)(September):81

(1987). "Turmoil Time in the Casino Business," *Fortune* 115(5)(March 2).

Spanier, D. (1992). *Welcome to the Pleasuredome: Inside Las Vegas.* Reno: University of Nevada Press.

Swartz, S. (1985). "New Jersey Casino Commission Stirs Controversy with Rulings," *Wall Street Journal,* March 11.

Thorp, E. O. (1962). *Beat the Dealer.* New York: Random House (Vintage Books paperback, 1966).

Treaster, J. B. (1982). "Mob Alliance to Share Casino Riches Reported," *New York Times,* September 1.

Turnstall, J., and Turnstall, C. (1985). "Mare's Nest: The Market in Thoroughbreds Is a Mess," *Barron's,* July 15.

Vinson, B. (1986). *Las Vegas Behind the Tables!* Grand Rapids, Mich.: Gollehon.

Wartzman, P. (1995). "Gambling Is Proving To Be a Poor Wager For State of Louisiana," *Wall Street Journal,* September 11.

Wells, K. (1988). "Philip Anderson Has a Feeling He Knows What's in the Cards," *Wall Street Journal,* January 13.

Yoshihashi, P. (1990). "More States Like Odds on Sports Betting Despite Fierce Opposition to Legalization," *Wall Street Journal,* February 1.

Ziemba, W. T., and Hausch, D. B. (1984). *Beat the Racetrack.* New York: Harcourt Brace Jovanovich.

11
Sports

It ain't over 'til it's over. – Yogi Berra

In sports today, chances are the game's not over 'til there's another television commercial.

This chapter concentrates on sports – as much an entertainment business as any thus far discussed. The exposition underscores the importance of links to broadcasting, cable, and wagering segments, and illustrates how tax-law considerations are at the core of many sports business decisions. But it also indicates why professional sports may be the only business "where the owners want regulation, and labor – the players – want the free market."[1]

11.1 Spice is nice

Early innings

Trivia buffs might delight in learning that the first recorded Olympic running event occurred in Olympia, Greece, in the year 776 B.C.[2] Yet sporting activities had by then already been developing for thousands of years – from the earliest days of history and from a time when spears and clubs and bows and arrows were used in the provision of food and shelter.

Table 11.1. *Attendance at professional-sports exhibitions, 1960–95[a]*

Year	Attendance (millions)				
	Baseball	Basketball	Football[b]	Hockey[c]	Total
1995	51.3	19.9	15.8	17.1	104.1
1990	55.5	18.6	17.7	13.7	105.4
1985	47.7	11.5	14.1	12.8	86.1
1980	43.7	10.7	14.1	12.8	81.3
1975	30.4	7.6	10.8	10.3	59.0
1970	29.2	7.1	10.0	6.5	52.8
1960	20.3	2.0	4.2	2.6	29.0
CAGR[d]					
1980–95:	1.1	4.2	0.8	2.0	1.7

[a]Includes regular season, playoff, and championship attendance. The number of teams in 1997 was 28 in baseball, 29 in basketball, 30 in football, and 26 in hockey. Two new teams were added to basketball in 1988 and two more in 1989. In 1961, the number of teams was 16 in baseball, 9 in basketball, 14 in football, and 6 in hockey.
[b]National Football League.
[c]National Hockey League.
[d]Compound annual growth rate (%).
Source: Statistical Abstract of the United States, 1997, U.S. Department of Commerce, Bureau of the Census.

It has indeed been a long journey from those early primitive times to today's organized professional leagues, whose games are instantly televised to a global audience. But actually, it was not until the middle of the nineteenth century that the modern organizations first evolved. The catalyst was the Industrial Revolution, which expanded the middle class and, accordingly, the "leisure time" available. As roads and automobiles and other modern forms of communication and travel were invented and then perfected, rates of growth accelerated. Yet even so, over this time, the underlying principles of the games themselves have not been changed very much. Basketball dates from at least 1891. Predecessor concepts for baseball go back as far as 1744. And notions for games resembling football can be traced to 1609, and for hockey to 2000 B.C.

Since 1929, when the relevant economic data series were first defined, personal consumption expenditures on spectator sports have varied widely. As Figure 1.13 (p. 24) illustrates, spending in this area naturally declined during both World War II and the Korean War. And a peak of spending relative to personal consumption expenditures (PCE) on recreation services (at nearly 8%) then appeared in 1968. However, the sports-spending time-series does not suggest any discernible sensitivity to ordinary business-cycle fluctuations.

Trends in *admissions* to major professional sports contests also appear to have little correlation to the overall economic cycle. As indicated by Table 11.1, attendance at football (NFL), major-league baseball (NL and AL), basketball (NBA), and hockey (NHL) games expanded at an average annual rate of approx-

imately 3.7% from 1960 to 1995. Over this span, basketball has had the highest
compound annual growth rate (6.8%) and baseball the lowest (2.7%).

Yet, none of this has in any way impaired the values of team franchises, which
are essentially local monopolies created and controlled by the owners' associations.
These franchises benefit from tax-deductible amortizations of personal service contracts that are not available to other industries, and from *de facto* municipal subsidies that often appear in stadium financing agreements. As such, not even normal
short-run competitive pressures have an effect: Franchises can report operating
losses year after year and still maintain a high or rising valuation upon transfer.[3]

Nevertheless, there is an underlying sensitivity of franchise values to changes
in player contract standards, to changes in tax and antitrust laws, and perhaps
most importantly, to changes in the demand for broadcast and cable rights. Such
rights values have also been influenced by the events shown in Figure 11.1.

The broadcast and cable connection

The most striking feature of the modern sports business is how dependent it has
become on broadcasting and cable industry revenue growth. Indeed, in the absence of this electronic-media coverage and the fees so generated, many fewer
professional teams and probably many fewer fans would have been created: There
were 42 professional sports franchises, mostly in the Northeastern United States,
in 1960, and well over 100 franchises spread all over the country by 1995. Moreover, in the 1980s alone, the annual number of hours of sports programming aired
by the three major networks and cable systems rose from 4,600 to over 7,300.

All of this growth began with, and has been largely governed by, the Sports
Broadcasting Act, which Congress passed in 1961. This legislation gave sports
leagues the right to act as a cartel (free of any antitrust sanction) in bargaining
with television networks, and has had a beneficial effect on development of interest in all professional sports.

But although sales of transmission rights for sporting events are still heavily
weighted toward over-the-air broadcasters, as the cable subscriber base has grown
to two-thirds of television homes, cable has become much more important as a
source of team revenues. In fact, by the mid-1980s, major boxing events had
already become the province of pay-per-view cable, and other sports offerings
had become the mainstay for primarily advertiser-supported cable networks. It
thus seems that cable could eventually become a foremost licensee of rights to
major sporting events such as the World Series and the Super Bowl.

To a large degree, then, it is the expectation of steadily increasing aggregate
broadcast and cable rights prices in local, national, and international markets that
has made investments in professional sports so attractive for major media and
entertainment companies or for those wealthy private investors able to take advantage of favorable tax treatments.[4] In contrast, the appreciation potential of broadcast
rights for collegiate and other amateur sports events appears to be more limited.[5]

Table 11.2 illustrates the number of network hours allocated to sports events.
Network spending for broadcast rights to Olympics Games appears in Supplementary Table S11.1.

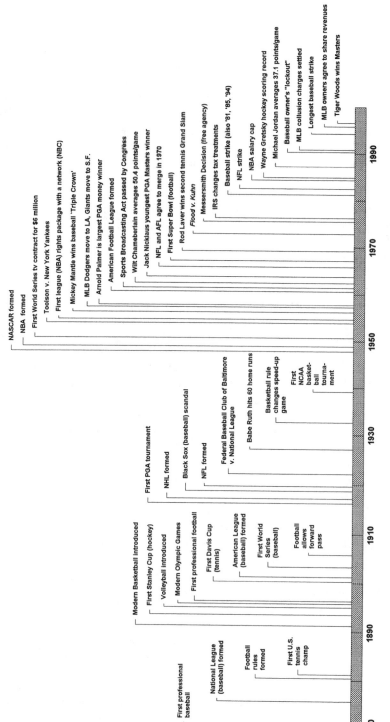

Figure 11.1. Milestone events in sports, 1870–2000.

Table 11.2. *Hours of broadcast network (1995) and cable network (1996) sports events*

Sport	Hours Broadcast	Percent of total	Hours Cable	Percent of total
Auto racing	63	3.6		
Baseball	117	6.7		
Major League			1,314	18.2
College			55	0.8
Other			59	0.8
Basketball	327	18.8		
NBA			374	5.2
NCAA-total			933	13.0
Football	462	26.5		
NFL			81	1.1
College			510	7.1
Other			428	5.9
Golf	307	17.6	807	11.2
Hockey	41	2.4		
Multi-sports	175	10.0	106	1.5
Tennis	115	6.6	516	7.2
Other	135	7.7	2,019	28.0
	1,742	100.0	7,202	100.0

Source: Nielsen Media Research.

The wagering connection

Wagering has always been an integral part of sports because a contest is always more exciting when spectators are personally involved in the outcome. Indeed, betting on virtually any type of match, from baseball through boxing, is legal and well developed in Nevada (and also in England). Everywhere else in the United States, however, legal sports betting is largely limited to racetracks (horses and dogs) or to jai alai (in Connecticut and Florida). Still, the absence of legal sanction has not stopped people from risking tens of billions of dollars each year on the results of football, baseball, basketball, hockey, boxing, and automobile racing.[6]

The spice that wagering adds to spectator sports is, moreover, also immediately reflected in increased demand for coverage by electronic and print media. The potential for high ratings leads sponsors to pay high prices for commercial time, and leads stations, networks, and cable systems to then bid aggressively for rights to distribute the programs. Because revenues generated from sales of these rights are essential to the operation of spectator-sports enterprises, wagering indirectly provides important financial underpinnings by creating demand for information that would otherwise be of narrow interest.

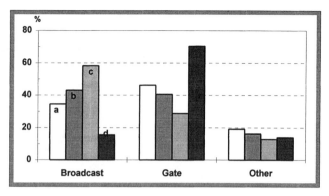

Figure 11.2. Sources of total revenues in percent by category for selected sports and teams: baseball, New York Mets, 1986; basketball, Boston Celtics, 1992; football, Greenbay Packers, 1989; hockey, Florida Panthers, 1996. See also Durs (1986).

11.2 Operating characteristics

Revenue sources and divisions

As Scully (1995, p. 19) notes, "all professional sports leagues restrict entry, assign exclusive franchise territory, and collude on a revenue-sharing formula." And although each professional sport or team may have its own special problems and circumstances, each shares concerns over: (a) the potential for tax-shelter, stadium-lease, and transfer pricing benefits for franchise owners, (b) the prices received for broadcast and cable rights, and (c) the cost of player salaries. Nevertheless, each of the three major sports (football, baseball, and basketball) has evolved differently with regard to these fundamentally common concerns.

Football, for example, has always been highly dependent on network-television money – a fact that became especially evident in the early 1980s when the National Football League (NFL) signed a $2 billion, five-year contract with the networks that was for the first time sufficiently large to provide each club with a profit before counting gate receipts.[7] A financial cushion on this order of magnitude clearly permits revenues to be shared among all teams – each gets an equal share of media and licensing revenues and 40% of gate receipts at away games – and furthermore insulates owners from the normal adverse financial consequences of prolonged mismanagement, incompetence, or competition.[8] As a result – despite considerable disparity in on-field performances – the richest NFL team has usually generated only about 20% more gross revenue than the poorest.

Moreover, until recently, football's allocation arrangements – which contained elements of immunity, or exemption from antitrust laws also seen in baseball – tended to reduce aggressive bidding for star athletes and to diminish the general usefulness of free-agency status for players.[9] This is in contrast to the traditional situation in baseball and basketball, where free-agency status has long been effective and has led to the signing of many multimillion-dollar-per-year contracts.

The operating structures of baseball and basketball have also differed markedly from that of football because a lesser percentage of total revenues in baseball and basketball has been shared by the teams, and because market size and gate receipts have historically been much more important determinants of profitability.[10] In both sports, as Figure 11.2 illustrates, ticket sales have typically accounted for approximately 40% of total revenues, with concession income from parking fees, advertising, and beer, peanut, and hot-dog sales accounting for only a small part of total income.[11]

Nevertheless, as of the late-1990s, salary-cost pressures and slower growth of media-rights prices appear to be gradually pushing revenue-sharing and salary-cap agreements of all the major sports into closer conformity.[12]

Labor issues

Player salary costs in professional sports have, in recent years, often accounted for as much as 60% of total team operating expenses. And it is thus not surprising to find that many conflicts between players and owners have involved player-compensation issues.

But, in fact, the stormy and well-publicized labor relationships that characterize modern professional sports can probably be best understood in the context of several landmark legal decisions, the most significant of which was *Federal Baseball Club of Baltimore* v. *National League,* argued in the U.S. Supreme Court in 1922. At the time, big league baseball was essentially operated as a cartel in which teams agreed not to hire away each others' players. Nevertheless, this case provided baseball clubs with continued immunity from antitrust laws and thus with the ability to hold on to young players as team property for the duration of their playing careers. Under these conditions, players had no choice but to accept whatever salaries the team owners decided was fair.

Toolson v. New York Yankees in 1953 presented the court with yet another opportunity to correct the obvious economic imbalances, but again the justices decided that baseball was entitled to a special status, and they passed the responsibility for any changes on to a reluctant Congress that, until recently, was satisfied with the status quo.[13]

However, legal challenges by players against the owners finally began to succeed in the 1970s. Although the Major League Baseball (MLB) reserve clause (that originated in 1887) held up under appeal in 1972 in the case of Curt Flood (*Curt Flood v. Bowie Kuhn* (1971)), free agency was approved in late 1975 in what came to be known as the Messersmith Decision.[14]

Prior to this decision, a team would sign a contract with a player for a brief period, usually one season and, under the so-called reserve system, could then hold on to the player for much longer by exercising options to extend contract terms. The system effectively eliminated competition and suppressed player salaries. It also created a valuable property right for the club owners. But after Messersmith, baseball players could, under much less restrictive conditions, become free agents and bargain with other clubs once their contracts expired.

Football and basketball, of course, were never granted the special antitrust immunity of baseball. Yet as Michener (1976, p. 482) has noted, both sports often

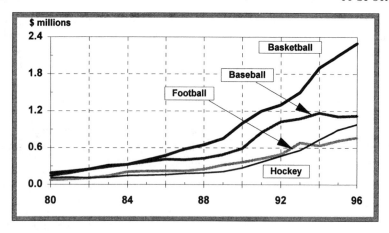

Figure 11.3. Player compensation in major sports, 1980–96.

acted as if they were immune.[15] Indeed, in both sports, although an athlete could in theory become a free agent after "playing out his option" on a reduced salary, an indemnity system (wherein the player's new team had to compensate his previous team) effectively reduced the player's value to a prospective new owner of his contract.[16]

The court decisions of the 1970s gave athletes the right to negotiate for higher compensation with teams other than their own, and contract terms are no longer necessarily extended beyond an initial period. As a result, in all major sports, but especially in baseball, the implementation of free-agency has significantly raised the level of player compensation (Figure 11.3) while also bolstering player-representation unions.[17]

Soccer, of course, has yet to attain the status of a major sport in the U.S., but is *the* major sport for the rest of the world. As might be expected, rapid growth of global private broadcast interests has led to a media, marketing, and player-compensation structure for professional soccer that is beginning to resemble that of the other major sports.[18]

11.3 Tax-accounting and valuation

Tax issues

From an economic point of view, the tax loopholes that provide benefits to professional team owners make little sense. As Zimbalist (1992, p. 35) has noted:

(a) The overwhelming share of the value of a franchise is derived not from players' contracts, but from the monopoly rent that is generated from belonging to a league that confers exclusive territorial rights. The value of these territorial rights does not diminish over time.

(b) The value of players does not depreciate over time. Most players reach peak performance beyond the midpoint of their careers.

Despite such economic advantages, however, in many cases it would be difficult for high-income owners to justify investments in professional-sports franchises if it were not for the tax benefits that may also accrue. It is thus worthwhile to at least outline the major tax concepts.[19]

Historical development Prior to 1954 there was a uniform practice of signing players to one-year contracts and of then expensing the acquisition costs of such player contracts during the year of play. In 1954, however, the IRS made a distinction between purchase of a single player's contract and purchase of substantially the entire roster of a baseball club's contracts acquired at one time. In the former case, expensing the cost over one year would remain appropriate; but in the latter, the aggregate amount assignable to players' contracts was to be capitalized and then expensed over the useful life of the assets.

These rulings remained in effect until 1967, when the IRS reconsidered treatment of individual player contracts in light of baseball's reserve clause, which effectively tied a player to a team for his entire career despite the one-year term of his contract. A team's effective long-term control over its athletes implied, according to the IRS, that the cost of individual players' contracts ought also to be capitalized and then expensed over the useful life of the asset.

Then, in the early 1970s, guidelines pertaining to professional-football expansion agreements provided favorable tax treatment to franchise owners. Of greatest importance was the IRS allowance that payments from new teams to established teams could be allocated between the franchise cost and the cost of player contracts for the veterans picked in the expansion draft. Because proceeds allocated to franchise cost were to be treated as capital gains, while proceeds allocable to player contracts were subject to recapture (of tax benefits by the IRS), owners were naturally provided with incentive to allocate as much as possible to franchise costs.[20]

Because most clubs were (and still are) owned by private individuals or by a small number of partners, owners' income from other sources could then be sheltered as long as the franchise was held as a sole proprietorship, partnership, or so-called subchapter-S corporation (or subsidiary of a profitable privately held corporation). All that needed to be done was to buy a franchise and to then allocate a large percentage (say 80%–90%) of the purchase price to player contracts. The resulting large write-downs and reported losses would provide substantial tax savings, and after a few years, the franchise could be sold at a gain (Table 11.3).

In effect, prior to the mid-1970s, player-contract depreciation deductions would be converted into capital gains because sellers would allocate most of the purchase price to the franchise asset and very little to player contracts, and buyers would allocate a large portion of the purchase price to depreciable player contracts.

Current treatments By 1976, concern about potential abuses of professional-franchise ownership had risen to the point that Congress felt it necessary to take corrective action against overstating the basis for depreciation, claiming large tax losses despite positive cash flows, and avoidance of depreciation recapture on players who had retired or were otherwise eliminated from the roster. The new

Table 11.3. *Franchise-cost example: rapid write-off and high purchase price attributed to player contracts prior to 1976*

Franchise cost:	$10,000,000
(10% cash, 90% long-term debt)	
Cost allocation:	
Player contracts: 80%, useful life 5 years	8,000,000
Depreciation: $8,000,000/5 = $1,600,000/year	
Franchise: 15%, nondepreciable	1,500,000
Equipment: 3%, useful life 10 years	300,000
Depreciation: $300,000/10 = $30,000/year	
Stadium lease: 2%, useful life 10 years	200,000
Depreciation: $200,000/10 = $20,000/year	
Income statement	
Revenues	
Gate receipts	$2,900,000
Television revenue	1,400,000
Parking concessions	345,000
Other income	80,000
Total revenue	$4,725,000
Expenses:	
Player salaries	$1,700,000
Coaching salaries	350,000
Administration	1,050,000
Training camp	175,000
Interest	900,000
Lease rental	100,000
Total expenses	$4,275,000
Net income	$450,000
Depreciation:	
Player contracts	$1,600,000
Equipment	30,000
Lease acquisition	20,000
	$1,650,000
Loss reportable for partners' tax filings	$1,200,000

Source: This table appeared originally in Horvitz and Hoffman (1976, p. 178), the March 1976 issue of *TAXES – The Tax Magazine,* published and copyrighted 1976 by Commerce Clearing House, Inc., in Chicago. It appears here with their permission.

law specified that franchise buyers and sellers would have to agree on an allocation formula, that no more than 50% of the purchase price of a franchise would be allocable to player contracts, and that there would be special recapture provisions designed to prevent the stocking of a team with new players possessing substantially undepreciated contracts just before sale of a franchise.

Since 1976, several important court decisions have further defined the tax and accounting ramifications in this area, but issues involving the tax deductiblity of television and cable rights amortizations have not until recently been settled.[21]

Asset valuation factors

The cash-flow valuation methods applied to media properties, described in Chapters 6 and 7, would also provide the basis for measuring asset values here. But at a minimum, the estimated worth of a professional-sports franchise would further require detailed knowledge of the following:

Demographic composition and potential size of the local market
Degree of competing professional-sports activity as a determinant of ticket pricing and local-broadcast/cable-revenue potential
Stadium ownership arrangements, and real-estate development potential, if any
Player-contract status and union-contract stipulations
Potential for network-broadcast, regional-cable, and international revenues
IRS treatments of deductions for player contracts and broadcast/cable rights
Current and forecasted interest rates
Cash flow volatility (the less volatility the higher the value)[22]

Of these elements, stadium ownership arrangements have recently taken on greater significance in view of the need for team owners faced with rapidly rising costs to capture and control as much of the ancillary revenues streams as possible.[23] In this regard, local and national political considerations have also become important.[24]

11.4 Sports economics

Franchise owners have argued that their cartel agreements to block competition are needed to uphold franchise values. Such arguments stand on weak legal ground, but make economic sense in that restriction on the number of clubs and maintenance of territorial exclusivity tends to support the relative and absolute quality of play. That is, professional sports contests would attract fewer fans if the quality of play were low and the uncertainty of the game results were to be reduced.

An interesting early mathematical model of a professional league was presented in Quirk and Hodiri (1974).[25] This model employed concepts such as a team's inventory of playing skills and cost per unit of playing skills acquired. Assuming that a league is in steady-state equilibrium (the stock of playing skills of each team remains fixed over time), and that franchise owners are motivated solely by profits from operations, the following conclusions were reached:

(a) Franchises located in areas with high drawing potential have stronger teams than franchises in low-drawing-potential areas.
(b) On balance, franchises in low-drawing-potential areas sell players to franchises in high-drawing-potential areas.

(c)   If local television revenues are ignored, the distribution of playing strengths among teams is independent of the gate-sharing arrangements.

(d)   The higher the share of television and radio revenues accruing to the home team, the higher the costs of players, and the smaller the chance of survival for low-drawing-potential franchises.[26]

In addition, many other studies of sports economics broadly suggest that:

A strong positive correlation between economic and athletic performance exists;

Restrictive labor market practices such as reserve clauses have been used by clubs to extract monopsony rents from player services;[27]

Under free-agency, player compensation rates generally reflect marginal revenue production expectations;

The earnings distribution in individual sports is more skewed than in team sports.

Athletes and teams respond to incentives as predicted by general economic theory.

11.5 Concluding remarks

Sports will continue to be a highly visible and important entertainment segment tightly linked to the broadcasting, cable, and wagering industries. As such, the tools and methods of economic analysis used in those sectors can be readily applied in the study of sports economics. The major trends currently include the following:

More sharing of network-broadcast and cable revenues by professional baseball, basketball, and hockey teams[28]

Emergence of large local and regional cable networks that support collegiate and individual athletic events

Greater emphasis on player mobility and player rights as reserve-clause control by owners is weakened

Significantly increased bargaining power of pay-cable networks and pay-per-view promoters relative to broadcast networks in obtaining distribution rights to major sporting events.

Selected additional reading

Abrams, B. (1984). "How Networks Vied in Grueling Bidding for '88 Winter Games," *Wall Street Journal*, February 22.

Alster, N. (1990). "Hoops Go Global," *Forbes* 146(8)(October 15).

    (1991). "Major League Socialism," *Forbes* 147(11)(May 27).

"Baseball Strike Issues," *New York Times*, August 1, 1981.

Behar, R. (1987). "Spreading the Wealth," *Forbes* 140(3)(August 10).

Blustein, P. (1983). "Are Baltimore Orioles Best Team in Baseball, Or Just the Best Run?" *Wall Street Journal*, October 5.

Bulkeley, W. M. (1985). "Sports Agents Help Athletes Win — And Keep Those Super Salaries," *Wall Street Journal*, March 25.

Byrne, J. (1986). *The $1 League: The Rise and Fall of the USFL*. New York: Prentice-Hall.

Chakravarty, S. N. (1983). "Character Is Destiny," *Forbes* 132(8)(October 10):114–23.

Chass, M. (1985). ''Baseball Strike Is Settled; Games to Resume Today,'' *New York Times,* August 8.

(1988). ''7 in Baseball Collusion Case Win Free Agency,'' *New York Times,* January 23.

Comte, E., and Chakravarty, S. N. (1993). ''How High Can David Stern Jump?,'' *Forbes* 151(12)(June 7).

Euchner, C. C. (1993). *Playing the Field.* Baltimore: Johns Hopkins University Press.

Fishof, D., and Shapiro, E. (1983). *Putting It on the Line: The Negotiating Secrets, Tactics & Techniques of a Top Sports and Entertainment Agent.* New York: William Morrow.

Friedman, R. (1984). ''Holmes-Coetzee Bout, A Promoter's Dream, Becomes a Nightmare,'' *Wall Street Journal,* May 22.

(1985). ''Playing Basketball in the Minors Offers Only Minor Rewards,'' *Wall Street Journal,* February 26.

(1985). ''They Get Little Ink. But 15 Other People Also Own Yankees,'' *Wall Street Journal,* April 16.

Galarza, P. (1995), ''The Mighty Bucks: Companies Are Learning How to Make Money with the Sports Teams They Own,'' *Financial World,* 164(25)(December 5).

Goff, B. L., and Tollison, R. D., eds. (1990). *Sportometrics.* College Station, Tex.: Texas A & M University Press.

Gorman, J. and Calhoun, K., (with Rozin, S.) (1994). *The Name of the Game: The Business of Sports..* New York: John Wiley & Sons.

Gorn, E. J., and Goldstein, W. (1993). *A Brief History of American Sports.* New York: Farrar, Straus & Giroux (Hill and Wang).

Gunther, M. (1997). ''They All Want to Be Like Mike,'' *Fortune* 136(2) (July 21).

Harris, D. (1986). ''New Troubles in the N.F.L.,'' *New York Times Magazine,* September 7.

Hart-Nibbrig, N., and Cottingham, C. (1986). *The Political Economy of College Sports.* Lexington, Mass.: D. C. Heath.

Harwood, S. J. (1983). ''Valuation of Player Contracts When Acquiring a Professional Baseball Team – An Analysis of *Selig v. United States,''* *Taxes* 61(10):670–7.

Helyar, J. (1984). ''More Cities Plan Domed Stadiums. But Returns May Prove to Be Small,'' *Wall Street Journal,* May 17.

(1984). ''Green Bay Packers Are Threatened by Football's Changing Economics,'' *Wall Street Journal,* December 14.

(1990). ''Lure of TV Loot Loosens Old College Ties,''*Wall Street Journal,* November 14.

(1990). ''Baseball's Expansion Is a High-Stakes Game of Money and Politics,'' *Wall Street Journal,* December 21.

(1991). ''Game? What Game? Arenas Emphasize Ambiance and Amenities to Entice Fans,''*Wall Street Journal,* March 20.

(1991). ''Play Ball! The Price Fans Pay Is Going, Going, Gone Up,'' *Wall Street Journal,* April 8.

(1991). ''How Peter Ueberroth Led the Major Leagues in the 'Collusion Era,' ''*Wall Street Journal,* May 20.

(1994). ''The Inflated Riches of NBA Are Pulling at the League's Seams,'' *Wall Street Journal,* February 11.

(1994). ''Baseball's Journeymen Face a New Challenge: The Low-Ball Salary,'' *Wall Street Journal,* April 4.

(1994). "NFL Story: New Man Takes Over the Eagles That Laid Golden Eggs," *Wall Street Journal*, August 18.

(1994). "How Fear and Loathing In Baseball Standoff Wrecked the Season," *Wall Street Journal*, Septemnber 15.

(1994). "Canadian Clubs Appear to Skate on Thin Ice Amid Hockey Lockout," *Wall Street Journal*, November 15.

(1995). "Baseball Players' Agent Offers Bargains on Stars In a Buyer's Market," *Wall Street Journal*, April 14.

(1995). "How Nashville Seeks, At High Cost, to Win Oilers From Houston," *Wall Street Journal*, November 21.

(1996). "A City's Self-Image Confronts Tax Revolt in Battle on Stadiums," *Wall Street Journal*, March 19.

(1996). "How Atlanta Went from Baseball Clowns to Kings of Diamond," *Wall Street Journal*, October 1.

(1997). "Free Agency Proves to Be the Cat's Meow for Jags and Panthers," *Wall Street Journal*, January 10.

Johnson, R. S. (1997). "Tiger! Now the Sky's the Limit for Golf - the Game and the Business," *Fortune*, 135(9)(May 12).

(1997). "Take Me Out to the Boardroom," *Fortune*, 136(2) (July 21).

Jordan, P. (1994). "Buddy's Boys and Their $100 Million Toys," *New York Times*, September 18.

Klatell, D. A., and Marcus, N. (1988). *Sports for Sale: Television, Money, and the Fans.* New York: Oxford University Press.

Klein, F. C. (1985). "Sports Teams Are Losing Their Bet That Fans Will Pay for TV Events," *Wall Street Journal*, February 19.

Krise, S. A. (1975). "Certain Tax Implications of Professional Sports," *CPA Journal*, April.

La Franco, R. (1997). "Profits on Ice," *Forbes*, 159(9)(May 5).

Lancaster, H. (1973). *The Business of Sports.* New York: H. W. Wilson.

(1985). "USFL Facing a Fourth-and-Long as It Staggers into Third Season," *Wall Street Journal*, February 26.

(1987). "Timeout: Despite Success of Celtics Sale, Doubts Remain about Sports Offerings," *Wall Street Journal*, May 8.

(1988). "Baseball Owners Found in Collusion in Free-Agent Case," *Wall Street Journal*, September 1.

Lane, R. (1995). "Pugilism's Lopsided Economics," *Forbes*, 156(14)(December 18).

Leifer, E. (1996). *Making the Majors: The Transformation of Team Sports in America.* Cambridge, Mass.: Harvard.

Linden, D. W. (1991). "Bases Loaded, Nobody Out," *Forbes* 147(7)(April 1).

Lueck, T. J. (1987). "Baseball Entrepreneurs Score in Bush Leagues," *New York Times*, August 24.

"The Man with the Golden Arm," *Newsweek*, CXIII(15), April 10, 1989.

Merwin, J. (1982). "The Most Valuable Executive in Either League," *Forbes* 129(8)(April 12):129–38.

(1983). "Big League Baseball's New Cash Lineup," *Forbes* 131(7)(March 28):168–9.

(1984). "It's Show Time," *Forbes* 133(4)(February 13).

Miller, J. E. (1990). *The Baseball Business: Pursuing Pennants and Profits in Baltimore.* Chapel Hill: University of North Carolina Press.

Moore, T. (1985). "Baseball's New Game Plan," *Fortune* 111(8)(April 15):16.

(1986). "It's 4ᵗʰ & 10 – The NFL Needs the Long Bomb," *Fortune* 114(3)(August 4):160.

Morgenson, G. (1992). "Where the Fans Still Come First," *Forbes* 149(10)(April 27).

"The NBA Is Paying Out Like There's No Tomorrow," *Business Week*, February 5, 1990, No. 3144.

Neale, W. C. (1964)."The Peculiar Economics of Professional Sports," *Quarterly Journal of Economics*, February.

Norton, E. (1993). "Football At Any Cost: One City's Mad Chase for an NFL Franchise," *Wall Street Journal*, October 13.

Oestreich, J. R. (1997). "Opera Enjoys Its Charmed Life," *New York Times*, April 28.

Phillips, M. M. (1997). "Top Sports Pros Find a New Way to Score: Getting Equity Stakes," *Wall Street Journal*, April 18.

"Professor Hardball," *Business Week*, no. 3098, April 3, 1989.

Queenan, J. (1991). "Squeeze Play: Plutocrat Players, Balky Payers May End Baseball's Big Boom," *Barron's*, April 29.

Rader, B. G. (1984). *In Its Own Image: How Television Has Transformed Sports*. New York: The Free Press.

Revzin, P., and Russell, M. (1985). "To Mark McCormack, Business Success Is Mostly Fun and Games," *Wall Street Journal*, June 27.

Robichaux, M. (1989). "Dallas Cowboys Face Financial Predicament Spreading in the NFL," *Wall Street Journal*, October 23.

(1990). "If Baseball Hurls Shutout, Many Will Be Losers," *Wall Street Journal*, January 23.

Robinson, E. (1997). "It's Where You Play That Counts," *Fortune*, 136(2) (July 21).

Rosen, S. (1981). "Economics of Superstars," *American Economic Review* 71(5)(December).

Rosentraub, M. S. (1997). *Major League Losers*. New York: Basic Books.

Rottenberg, S. (1956). "The Baseball Players' Labor Market," *Journal of Political Economy* 64(June).

Sandomir, R. (1996). "America's Small-Town Team," *New York Times*, January 13.

Saporito, B. (1987). "The Life of a $725,000 Scab," *Fortune* 116(9)(October 26):91.

(1991). "The Owners' New Game Is Managing," *Fortune*124(1)(July 1):86.

Scully, G. W. (1974). "Pay and Performance in Major League Baseball," *American Economic Review*, 64(December).

Sheehan, R. G. (1996). *Keeping Score: The Economics of Big-Time Sports*. South Bend, IN: Diamond Communications.

Shropshire, K. L. (1990). *Agents of Opportunity: Sports Agents and Corruption in Collegiate Sports*. Philadelphia: University of Pennsylvania Press.

Sims, C. (1993). "It's Not Just How Well You Play the Game ..." *New York Times*, January 31.

Spiers, J. (1996). "Are Pro Sports Teams Worth It?" *Fortune*, 133(1)(January 15).

Smith, T. K. (1992). "Players Charge NFL With Trying End Run on Disability Benefits," *Wall Street Journal*, December 7.

Smith, T. K., and Norton, E. (1993). "One Baseball Statistic Remains a Mystery: The Real Bottom Line," *Wall Street Journal*, April 2.

Sobel, R. (1985). "Baseball Rights Fees in 1985 to Remain at $275 Million," *Television/ Radio Age* 32(16)(February 18).

"The Sports Business: Faster, Higher, Richer," *The Economist,* July 25, 1992.

Staudohar, P. D. (1988). "The Football Strike of 1987: The Question of Free Agency," *Monthly Labor Review,* (August), U.S. Department of Labor.

———— (1990). "The Baseball Strike of 1990," *Monthly Labor Review* 113(10)(October). U.S. Department of Labor.

Stavro, B. (1985). "It's a Classic Turnaround Situation," *Forbes* 136(1)(July 1):66–70.

Stevenson, R. (1990). "Pony Up $95 Million? Sure, for a Baseball Team." *New York Times,* September 23.

Sullivan, N. J. (1992). *The Diamond Revolution: The Prospects For Baseball After the Collapse of Its Ruling Class.* New York: St. Martin's.

Thurow, R. (1997). "Women's NBA Pins Hopes on Clean Play and Hard Marketing," *Wall Street Journal,* June 12.

Thurow, R., and Helyar, J. (1995). "Jerry Jones Thinks NFL Revenue Sharing Is a Bit Socialistic,"*Wall Street Journal,* September 28.

Weber, B. (1986). "The Man Who Built the Mets," *New York Times Magazine,* August 3.

Wermiel, S. (1984). "NCAA Pacts to Televise College Football Violate Antitrust Law, High Court Rules," *Wall Street Journal,* June 28.

White, G.E. (1996). *Creating the National Pastime: Baseball Transforms Itself, 1903–1953.* Princeton, N.J.: Princeton University Press.

"Who Says Baseball Is Like Ballet?" *Forbes* 107(7)(April 1, 1971).

12
Performing arts and culture

Break a leg!

The performing arts traditionally generate more psychic than pecuniary income, and they operate under somewhat different economic assumptions than the other entertainment industries thus far discussed. In fact, many organizations in this segment are nonprofit – requiring for their very existence substantial subsidization from government and private-foundation grants and from contributions by individuals.

As we shall see, the fundamental creative processes in the performing arts have remained essentially unchanged for centuries, but technological developments have been important in mitigating the pernicious effects of inexorably rising costs. Fortunately, it still doesn't cost anything to wish performers well by telling them to "break a leg."

12.1 Audiences and offerings

The potential widespread appeal of live performances notwithstanding, there are severe time and financial constraints that limit audience size and scope. As Baumol and Bowen (1968) indicated in their seminal study, the audience for high culture is dominated by highly educated individuals in high income brackets, an observation supported by the more recent data presented in Figure 12.1.

Although education appears to have a somewhat stronger effect than income, another hypothesis as to why the audience for live performances seems to become ever more exclusive was offered by Linder (1970), who noted that as economic growth increases our incomes and the available array of consumption goods, there is a tendency toward more "goods intensity" at the expense of time spent on cultural activities. Time to consume goods does not increase commensurately with the number of goods available. Attendance at live performances, of course, normally requires a relatively large allocation of time and often entails substantial expenditures on tickets and on incidentals (Figure 12.2 on page 282).

Trends in demand for the major performing arts categories may be inferred from the selected data of Table 12.1, and a timeline representation of significant events is presented in Figure 12.3 on page 284.

Commercial theater

On and off-Broadway Professional drama became an important entertainment medium during colonial times, but it was not until the nineteenth century that theater organized into a stock system of local resident companies permanently engaged at a particular location. Yet, not long thereafter, accomplished performers began to form touring companies, which by the late 1800s, had mostly replaced resident stock companies.

By the early 1900s, syndicates owning chains of theaters and controlling bookings and fees had become dominant. The famous Shubert chain, for example, was formed in this period. But this was largely a transition phase, as commercial theater further evolved into the current structure, wherein producers select a play, raise funds, and hire a director and cast, while theater owners generally handle box-office personnel and stagehands, advertising and sales functions, and sometimes musicians. As Poggi (1968, p. xv) has noted:

> Like so many of our social and economic institutions, the commercial theater has become highly centralized . . . At the beginning of the century there were usually 250 to 300 productions touring the country at the height of each season; now there are about 20. In the late 1920s there were usually more than 250 productions opening on Broadway in a single season; now there would seldom be more than 60.

Still, however, it is Broadway – essentially the theater district in New York City – that attracts a significant portion of commercial theater receipts in the United States, that defines an industry, and that is of greatest historical significance.[1] Broadway attendance and ticket-price trends are illustrated in Figure 12.4(a), from which it can be seen that the number of tickets sold (demand) remains below the peak of the 1970s.[2] The line representing the number of play-weeks (plays times weeks of run) in each season, meanwhile, provides an approximation of the supply of performances available.[3] (Figure 12.4(b), and Supplementary Table S12.1.)

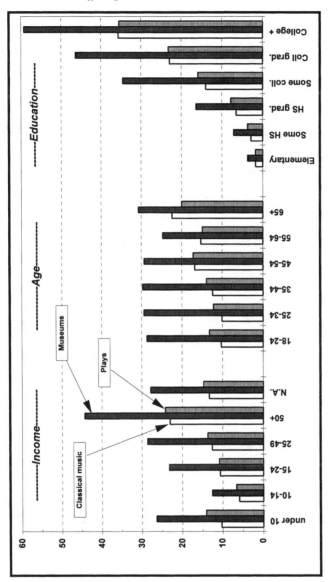

Figure 12.1. Characteristics of the culture audience by income distribution, educational attainment, and age in selected performance categories. Bars show the percentage of survey respondents participating. *Source:* U.S. NEA survey (1992).

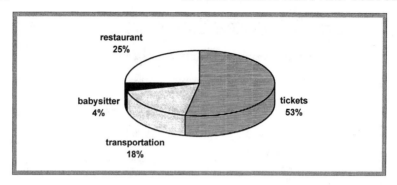

Figure 12.2. Cost of going out: ticket expense and associated costs of attendance at live performances. New York City (percentage distribution of total expenses by type). *Source:* William J. Baumol and William G. Bowen, *Performing Arts: the Economic Dilemma.* A. Twentieth Century Fund Study, © 1966, Twentieth Century Fund, New York.

In addition, it can be seen from Figure 12.4(c) that since 1990, gross receipts from commercial theater presentations on the road have overshadowed gross receipts on Broadway. This shift in economic balance has also led to the development of publicly owned companies that specialize in the production and staging of off-Broadway performances. As shown in Table 12.2, returns on investment in a major musical production can be relatively high and long-lasting, even in comparison to potential returns on popular films. In recent years, musical reproductions (touring versions of current or recent Broadway hits) or restorations (adaptations of past Broadway hits) have accounted for more than 80% of total commercial theater ticket sales.

The commercial theater segment also competes with, as well as benefits from, the existence of permanent nonprofit theaters (sometimes called regional or repertory theaters), which are resident in communities around the country. These resident theaters, supported by a combination of subscription fees, foundation grants, individual contributions, and ticket and merchandise sales, present a variety of plays – including the classics and those of Broadway and off-Broadway – and have sometimes been the source of new productions that later move on to commercial success and/or are adapted by Hollywood filmmakers. Such theaters attempt to preserve, develop, and extend the availability of performing arts productions.[4]

Circus According to Murray (1956, p. 26), elements of the circus that included performances by equilibrists and prestidigitators had already begun to emerge in Egypt as early as 2500 B.C. And circus has subsequently flourished in many different times and places, beginning the modern era in the circus ring of a horseback-trick rider in England in 1768 and America in 1785 (Culhane, 1990, p. 2).

Table 12.1. *Selected data for U.S. legitimate theater, opera companies, and symphony orchestras, 1980–95 (receipts and expenditures in millions of dollars; for season ending in year shown, except as indicated)*

Item	1980	1985	1990	1995
Legitimate theater:[a]				
Broadway shows:				
New productions	67	31	35	29
Playing weeks[b,c]	1,541	1,062	1,062	1,117
Number of tickets sold	9,380	7,156	8,039	9,045
(thousands)				
Gross box-office receipts	143.4	208.0	283.3	406.3
Road shows:				
Playing weeks[c]	1,351	993	944	1,312
Gross box-office receipts	181.2	225.9	367.1	694.6
Opera companies[d]	79	97	98	88
Number of companies				
Expenses[e]	122.4	216.4	321.2	435.0
Performances[f]	1,312	1,909	2,336	2,251
Total attendance	5.5	6.7	7.5	6.5
(millions)[g,h]				
Main season attendance	(NA)	3.3	4.1	3.9
(millions)[f,h]				
Symphony orchestras[i]				
Concerts	(NA)	19,513	18,931	18,543
Attendance (millions)	(NA)	24.0	24.7	23.2
Gross revenue	(NA)	252.4	377.5	458.7
Concert income	(NA)	168.6	253.3	316.5
Endowment income	(NA)	(NA)	52.1	64.5
Other earned income	(NA)	83.8	72.1	77.7

Note: NA, not available.

[a]*Source: Variety*, New York, NY, various June issues, copyright.

[b]All shows (new productions and holdovers from previous seasons).

[c]Eight performances constitute one playing week.

[d]*Source:* OPERA America, Washington, DC.

[e]United States companies.

[f]Prior to 1993, United States and Canadian companies; beginning 1993, US companies only.

[g]Includes educational performances, outreach, etc.

[h]For paid performances.

[i]*Source:* American Symphony Orchestra League, Inc., Washington, DC. For years ending Aug. 31. Data represent all United States orchestras, excluding college/university and youth orchestras.

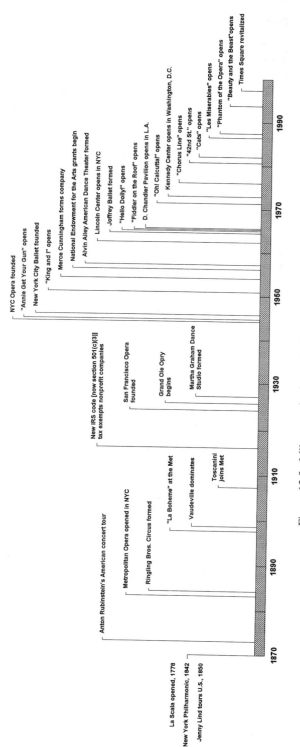

Figure 12.3. Milestones in the performing arts, 1870–2000.

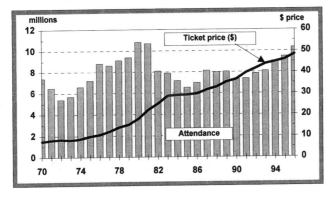

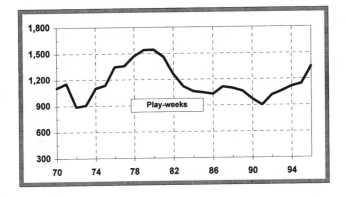

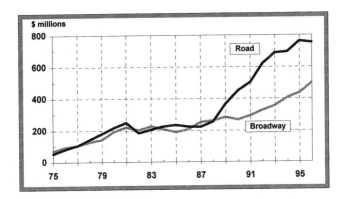

Figure 12.4. Broadway theater trends: (a) prices and ticket sales, (b) play-weeks, and (c)
gross sales on Broadway vs. the Road, 1970–96 seasons. *Source data: Variety* and
League of American Theatres and Producers.

Table 12.2. *Characteristics of a major hit musical versus a major hit movie.*

	Musical *Phantom of the Opera*	Motion Picture *Jurassic Park*
Global box office:	$2 billion	$913 million
Average production & pre-marketing cost:	$9 million	$70 million
Length of run:	10+ years	20 weeks

Today, though, circus is generally considered to be one of the major performing arts in Europe, but not in the United States – where companies are not government-subsidized and are instead operated by private for-profit organizations. As such, circus companies seem to be best categorized as a permanent traveling form of commercial theater, operating with a blend of the economic features seen in both theater and theme park operations.

Of the approximately 10 major domestic circuses, few are believed to be more than marginally profitable even though an estimated 20 million Americans, the largest audience in history, saw the circus in 1995. The problem in circus, as in several of the other performing arts, is that cost efficiencies are difficult to attain given the size and structure of the spectacle that must be assembled and then disassembled every few days or weeks.[5]

Orchestras

The history of orchestras also extends back to colonial times, but it was not until the founding of the New York Philharmonic in 1842 that formal organizations proliferated. In the early years, orchestras relied on a few wealthy patrons for support: J. P. Morgan, Andrew Carnegie, and Joseph Pulitzer were important contributors to the New York Philharmonic; Henry Higginson was guarantor of the Boston Symphony.

Today, the approximately 1,600 orchestras in the United States are categorized by the American Symphony Orchestra League according to the size of their budgets. Such major orchestras as those in Boston, Chicago, Cleveland, Los Angeles, New York, and Philadelphia would naturally attract the bulk of expenditures at concerts staged by professional groups.

Opera

Opera is drama set to music, and the development of opera has closely followed that of drama. The roots of opera can be traced to ancient Greek theater presentations and to the religious plays of the Middle Ages that illustrated biblical stories with action and music. However, it was not until the 1600s that opera evolved into a distinctive form using complicated plots and more varied orchestral arrangements. This form flourished in Europe over the next 200 years.

In the United States, opera seemingly came of age in 1883 with the organization in New York City of what was to become known as the Metropolitan Opera Company. However, as a reflection of the complexity and cost of staging grand opera, there are currently four major opera companies in the country: the Metropolitan (1996–97 budget, $118 million), the San Francisco Opera ($46 million), the Chicago Lyric Opera ($35 million), and the New York City Opera ($27 million). Also, companies in Los Angeles and Houston have recently become more prominent.

The economic problem is that when all lead and supporting singers, chorus, dancers, orchestra, conductor, and extras are included, there are 200 or more professionals on a payroll sustained by, at most, 4,000 seats per performance. It is thus understandable that even some fairly large cities do not have permanent grand-opera companies.

Dance

Little of professional ballet, a European art form, was seen in the United States before World War II. And not until the 1960s did significant philanthropic grants begin to support it. Major professional dance companies now include the New York City Ballet, the San Francisco Ballet, and the American Ballet Theater.

Modern dance, in contrast, has an essentially American flavor. There are now at least half a dozen important modern dance groups, most of which are dependent on a single choreographer and small groups of financial benefactors.

12.2 Funding sources and the economic dilemma

The core of the economic dilemma, as originally outlined by Baumol and Bowen (1968), is that it is virtually impossible to raise substantially the productivity of live performances. It takes as long to play a Brahms concerto today as it did 100 years ago, and a scene by Shakespeare requires the same acting time as it did over 350 years ago. Meanwhile, over the long run, productivity (output per person-hour) has steadily grown in virtually every other segment of the economy. As it happens, a live performance is unique in that it is itself an end product.

This economic dilemma – the productivity lag in the arts – becomes ever more pronounced as productivity in other sectors increases, as real-income growth makes society more goods-intensive, as operating costs rise in line with overall inflation, and as ticket prices rise relatively rapidly in an attempt to cover "income gaps."[6]

Empirical studies indeed suggest that ticket prices for live performances have risen at rates consistently higher than the consumer price index. And studies such as Baumol and Bowen's confirm that higher ticket prices reduce demand – especially from less well-to-do and younger segments of the population. Moreover, in periods of economic recession, even upper-income consumers may reduce spending in this area.

Yet there can be few educated people who would argue that live performing arts should be allowed to wither. From a purely practical viewpoint, traditional theater, opera, and dance forums provide a training ground for performers in the mass-entertainment media. Also, these training grounds undeniably enrich the surrounding society, making it more interesting, more spiritually invigorating – more "human." Still, in a world chronically mired in a crisis of budgets, a significant problem in the funding of a broadly diversified range of cultural activities remains. The solution to the problem, both in the United States and abroad, has been to fund through philanthropy and subsidy (Table 12.3).

As would be expected, the likelihood of regular contributions to the arts rises substantially with income, and contributions by individuals and estates are estimated to be the largest single source of voluntary funding; combined contributions from corporations and foundations account for only 10% or so of all private philanthropic support. Nevertheless, major orchestras and operas appear to receive proportionately more regular contributions than theater or dance.[7]

Performing and visual arts are further subsidized by government funding through state and local arts councils and through federal participation in matching-grant programs of the National Endowment for the Arts (Table 12.4). And federal tax exemption for nonprofit organizations under Internal Revenue Service code section 501(c)(3) also helps. Still, national-government support has a much longer and deeper tradition in Europe than in the United States – where emphasis has often been on construction of cultural centers tied to urban-renewal projects rather than on reduction of operating deficits. It is thus evident that the arts require support from a diverse set of benefactors.

Although it can be argued that, on purely economic grounds, taxpayers' financial support for money-losing arts programs enjoyed by an elite few is a waste of resources better spent elsewhere, justification of some government subsidy can be made:

Support for the arts opens opportunities for development of talented individuals from nonaffluent backgrounds.

Such support has educational benefit, exposing young people to cultural activities that they might not otherwise encounter.

Arts are public goods that, when provided to individuals, automatically become available to, and are of benefit to, other members of the community.

In this respect, arts are thus goods with both public and private characteristics and, like education, they can justifiably be supported by a combination of public and private contributions.

But there is more. For private corporations, support of cultural activities often stimulates local commercial activity and provides new business opportunities that have positive feedback effects on prospects for employment and for profits. For individuals, especially in North America, purely aesthetic pleasures are often further complemented by substantial tax benefits. And for the society as a whole,

Table 12.3. *Sources of funding for the performing arts, percentage distribution of total operating income by source, 1973–4*

Source of income	Theater companies 1973–4	Metropolitan Opera 1973–4	Other operas 1973–4	Symphonies 1973–4	Dance companies 1973–4	All, except Metropolitan Opera 1973–4
Government sources[a]	13	5	10	15	11	13
Ticket income	52	44	40	30	27	35
Services income, nongovernment	2	11	5	9	19	9
Recordings, radio, TV, films	—[b]	2	—[b]	2	2	2
Nonperformance earned income[c]	7	10	3	5	6	5
Other unearned income[d]	26	28	41	40	34	37
Number of organizations covered	31	1	28	78	15	152

Note: Because of rounding, detail may not add to 100%.

[a]Includes services income from government sources and government grants.
[b]Less than 0.5%.
[c]Income from performances of other groups, school income, and receipts from concessions, program advertising, facilities rentals, etc.
[d]Unearned income other than government grants, that is, individual, business, and foundation contributions and grants and endowment earnings.

Source: Netzer (1978, p. 101).

Table 12.4. *Financial support for the arts from the NEA, 1970–95*
($ million)[a]

Type of fund and program	1970	1980	1985	1990	1995
Funds available[b]	15.7	188.1	171.7	170.8	152.1
Program appropriation	6.3	97.0	118.7	124.3	109.0
Matching funds[c]	2.0	42.9	29.5	32.4	28.5
Grants awarded (number)	556	5,505	4,801	4,475	3,581
Funds obligated	12.9	166.4	149.4	157.6	147.9
Music	2.5	13.6	15.3	16.5	10.9
State programs	1.9	22.1	24.4	26.1	39.2
Museums	NA	11.2	11.9	12.1	9.0
Theater	2.8	8.4	10.6	10.6	7.3
Dance	1.7	8.0	9.0	9.6	7.1
Public media arts	0.2	8.4	9.9	13.9	8.9
Challenge[d]	—	50.8	20.7	19.7	21.1
Visual arts	1.0	7.2	6.2	5.9	4.4
Other	2.8	36.6	41.3	43.1	40.0

Note: NA, not available; dash indicates not applicable. *Source:* NEA.
[a]For years ending June 30 in 1970 and 1995; for years ending September 30 in later years.
[b]Includes other funds, not shown separately. Excludes administrative funds. Gifts are included through 1980 and excluded thereafter.
[c]Represents federal funds appropriated only on receipt or certification by endowment of matching nonfederal gifts.
[d]Program designed to stimulate new sources and higher levels of giving to institutions for the purpose of guaranteeing long-term stability and financial independence. Program requires a match of three private dollars to each federal dollar.

there are, as noted by Frey and Pommerehne (1989, p. 19) the following positive externalities:

An *option value* to having a supply of culture, even if an individual does not currently use the supply.

A *bequest value* for future generations unable to express preferences on currently existing markets.

An *existence value* such as for historic landmark buildings, which, once destroyed, cannot be rebuilt.

A *prestige value,* even for those who are not at all interested in art.

12.3 The play's the thing

Production financing and participations

Financial support for the arts, whether from public or private sources, is normally dedicated to the development of specific facilities or to the patronage of fixed dance, orchestral, and opera groups: Usually, no direct financial return on investment is expected. But when it comes to funding of theater, the motives for sponsorship are often much more speculative and entrepreneurial than in any of the other arts. In fact, the financing and development process for new commercial-theater productions most closely resembles that used for films.

To start, a producer normally acquires, through the signing of an option contract, the rights to a play or other literary property that is to be adapted for stage.[8] Such contracts will usually provide for an advance against future royalties and will apply to the interim period in which all the artistic and financial elements ultimately needed to mount a stage production are to be assembled.[9]

Once an option is acquired, a producer then sometimes seeks financing by approaching prospective individual investors known as *angels*. Angels must indeed love theater because tax sheltering is much more effective in oil, real estate, and professional sports franchises than on Broadway, where opportunities for depreciation are limited.[10] As such, then, an angel must also have enough income to afford a tax loss (write-off) because, historically, the odds against ever seeing a return on investment are well over 2 to 1.[11]

Indeed, given the high costs of today's productions, a run on Broadway is more likely to be funded by a large entertainment company than by a group of individual investors contributing relatively small amounts to the total. The large companies can more readily afford the risk, and will often use the Broadway run as a means of establishing a project for possible use in other media, or in other locations, without requiring that a show turn an immediate profit.[12]

Although financing is occasionally in the form of sale of stock in a corporation organized for production of a play, it may further be in the form of a large development investment that is granted by film studios in return for eventual, and perhaps strategically valuable, movie rights. Of course, Broadway's major theater owners – essentially the Shubert Organization, the Nederlander Organization, and Jujamcyn Theaters – might also take a piece of the action.[13] But, more typically, an offering prospectus describing anticipated running and start-up costs of a show is circulated to interested individual investors. Such investors are offered, in return for their capital, a share of potential profits (usually half of any profits earned by the production) through a limited partnership or, since 1994, a limited liability company (LLC) arrangement.[14]

Other investors might include the play's director, leading performer or performers, and individual theater owners (Table 12.5). Directors and lead performers will usually receive a small percentage (e.g., perhaps 5%) of the play's earnings in addition to salary or fee, whereas theater owners may (depending on season, theater quality, and the producer's reputation) receive 20%–30% of the box-office gross. However, as noted by Baumol and Bowen,

the locus of control of a production is sharply divided between the producer and the owner of the theater in which the play is performed.

While the producer selects the play, controls the artistic standards of the production, raises the funds invested in it, hires the director and the cast, sets wages, and decides on outlays on costumes and scenery, there are other matters which he normally does not

Table 12.5. *Typical financial participations in
theater productions*

Gross participation (%)	
Playwright	10
Lead performer	5
Director	2
Theater manager	25
Profit participation (%)	
Playwright	5–10
Director	5
Lead performer	5–10
Other performers and show manager	10
Producer	15
Investors	50–60

control completely. A powerful producer can obtain a contract providing a substantial voice in what may be termed the marketing of a play, but usually this is left largely in the hands of the theater owner, who often supplies, in addition to box office personnel and ushers, several stagehands and, where appropriate, several musicians. He bears part of the cost of advertising, consults in the setting of ticket prices, and supplies tickets to brokerage agencies. He has complete control of the box office, into which a producer may even be refused admittance . . .

The theater owner normally receives a percentage of the weekly gross of a play so that, aside from the advantages of length of run, it is in his interest to house a successful play. Since the contract usually provides that he can eject a play from the theater when the weekly gross falls below a prespecified figure, it is alleged that box-office personnel have sometimes been instructed to refuse to sell tickets to potential patrons, stating that all the seats were already sold (Baumol and Bowen, 1968, pp. 20–1).

Of course, as in movie deals, variations from fairly standardized percentages are based on the relative bargaining power of the participants. A major star in a small play can receive weekly guarantees plus increasing percentages of gross after receipts reach certain levels. Directors may receive fairly large upfront fees and smaller percentages of weekly grosses. Playwrights normally earn at least a minimum author's royalty of 10% weekly (but 5% of weekly receipts for non-musical productions off-Broadway).[15] And the show's general manager will receive a fee plus weekly salary and perhaps a small percentage of net profits, if any.[16]

Operational characteristics

A private placement memorandum will estimate the weekly break-even and weekly net profit at capacity for a show that is up and running. But even relatively modest productions require extensively detailed budgets and forecasts because of the many small items that will always collectively add up to significant amounts.

Table 12.6. *Budget estimates for a $950,000 Broadway stage production: an example, circa 1995*[a]

Scenery	$60,000
Props	17,000
Costumes	21,000
Electrics and sound	40,000
Fees	100,000
Rehearsals	69,000
Advertising	230,000
Other costs	100,000
Total production costs	$637,000
Pre-New York (rehearsals, hauling)	$108,000
Bonds (AEA, IATSE, ATPAM, theater)	70,000
Reserve for contingency and preview losses	135,000
Total capitalization	$950,000

[a]In the early 1980s, the cost of a similar production was approximately half of the cost in 1995.

The estimates in Table 12.6 are for a $950,000 Broadway production staged in 1995. As can be seen, advertising expenses constitute a major proportion of total running costs. In this example, the weekly break-even, including all royalties, was calculated at $204,000 per week, and at capacity, weekly receipts and net profits were estimated at $300,000 and $96,000, respectively.

The high fixed costs of operation naturally create a large leveraged effect on profits and, also, a tendency to have either a bona fide hit with substantial profit potential or an outright failure: Usually, there is little likelihood of anything in between the extremes.

The graph in Figure 12.5 illustrates the sensitivity of profits to changes in box-office receipts for a play with running costs of $100,000 per week, average ticket prices of $30, and seating of 500. Here it is assumed that the production does not garner additional revenues from cable-television or movie-rights sales, or from any other such ancillary sources, and that royalties and other payments are not scaled (usually they are).

Break-even example:
Running cost per week: $100,000
Seating: 500 persons
Average ticket price: $30
Performances per week: 8

Under these conditions, break-even requires an average capacity utilization of 83.3% (417 seats); figures consistently below that level will cause losses to mount rapidly.[17] Yet, as noted by Lawson (1983), levels of 70% or less are not uncommon.

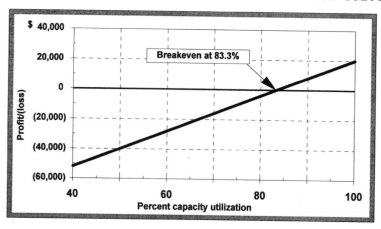

Figure 12.5. Break-even-capacity utilization: an illustration.

Last but not least in budgeting for a show, investors should have a solid grasp of labor union contract stipulations. Relationships with the Actors' Equity Association, the Dramatists' Guild (playwrights), the Society of Stage Directors and Choreographers, and the International Alliance of Theatrical Stage Employees may have important financial ramifications on performing-arts productions.[18]

12.4 Economist echoes

Studies of the economics of the performing arts are relatively recent, and the basic literature is still in development.[19] But an economic perspective may be gained through consideration of a few important concepts.

Elasticities As Heilbrun and Gray (1993, p. 94) have noted, "most studies have shown the demand for attendance at the live performing arts to be price inelastic." What this means is that consumers of such services are not especially sensitive to changes in price: A rise in price does not cause a proportionate decline in demand as might be measured by number of tickets sold per unit time.[20]

But empirical studies suggest that *income* elasticities with regard to the demand for performing arts cluster around 1.0.[21] It seems that as incomes rise, the greater opportunity cost of time spent on cultural activities may offset the pure positive income effect that derives from higher purchasing power. Over the longer term, this further implies that overall demand for the performing arts and for cultural events will probably grow at about the same rate as that of the domestic economy.

Price-discrimination However, existing differences in elasticity of demand among potential members of an audience might still be exploited by a discrimi-

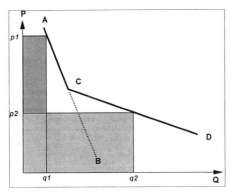

Figure 12.6. Price discrimination and the consumer surplus.

nating monopolist – which would be an economist's way of describing the producer of a specific performance or event. In such instances, a price-discrimination strategy, wherein different parts of the audience can be charged different prices (see Chapter 1), might be implemented so as to maximize the monopolist's income. The producer would then thereby extract what is known as the consumer surplus – the price difference between what consumers actually pay and what they would be willing to pay.

This is illustrated in Figure 12.6 (and in Figure 1.8c), where the quantities of theater seats sold to business guests is q1 and to tourists with discount tickets is q2. The theater's total revenue is p2q2 + (p1-p2)q1. Selling all seats at the lower price of p2 would provide revenues of p2q2, and all at p1 would make p1q1. But price discrimination raises the total above what would likely be received by setting a single selling price.

Externalities According to economic theory, and as noted by Hendon, Shanahan, and MacDonald (1980, p. 21), "art goods themselves are not public goods . . . [A] necessary but not sufficient condition for a pure public good is that it can be jointly consumed perfectly. The exclusion principle says that a product, though jointly consumed, can be provided in separable units to various consumers. Because admission to an artistic event (or right to use) can be provided in separable units, the exclusion principle is operable in the arts." But in addition, "the more definitive externalities generated by the arts usually flow to special-interest groups."[22]

12.5 Concluding remarks

Performing arts organizations seem always to live on a financial precipice. This condition is, of course, a function of live-audience size limitations, the great expense of coordinating an effective production, and the perpetually high cost of money for risky ventures. Live performances are also economically inefficient because, unlike manufactured goods, performances are "consumed" at the point of production.

From an economist's view, however, the most important and ineluctable element is that productivity cannot be raised significantly in the performing arts. On the programming-cost side, an hour of performance still takes an hour, whether it is done before a camera for distribution on television or cable or in front of a live audience.[23]

Of course, advances in technology enable much larger audiences to enjoy performances. And revenues thus derived from the new media are becoming significant considerations in financing of the arts. For instance, backers of commercial-theater productions may look increasingly to cable-television license fees or home-video presentation formats to enhance profits and to reduce the risk of loss. Indeed, it seems likely that the convenience and relatively low cost of home-viewing options will encourage more frequent sampling by people who would not otherwise have an interest in seeing such events.

Cultural achievements reflect not only the discipline, devotion, and intelligence of individuals, but also the most basic values of the society. That is why, for example, the free expression inherent in two distinctly American art forms, jazz and modern dance, could not develop or thrive in an authoritarian environment.

Yet no matter what the politics, the economic dilemma for performing arts cannot be circumvented. In a free society, some manner of subsidy – usually a combination of government support and tax incentives for private individuals and corporations – is normally required to sustain or to expand high-culture activities.

Selected additional reading

Albrecht, E. (1995). *The New American Circus*. Gainesville, Fla.: University Press of Florida.

Andresky, J. (1983). "So You Want to Be an Angel?" *Forbes* 131(3)(January 31):92–7.

Atkinson, B. (1990). *Broadway*, rev. ed. New York: Limelight Editions (reprint), and (1974) Macmillan.

Baumol, H., and Baumol, W. J., eds. (1984). *Inflation and the Performing Arts*. New York: New York University Press.

Benedict, S., ed. (1991). *Public Money and the Muse: Essays on Government Funding for the Arts*. New York: The American Assembly (Columbia University).

Biddle, L. (1988). *Our Government and the Arts: A Perspective from the Inside*. New York: American Council for the Arts.

Blau, J. R. (1989). *The Shape of Culture: A Study of Contemporary Cultural Patterns in the United States*. New York: Cambridge University Press.

Blumenthal, R. (1997). "On Broadway, Serious Plays Are Headed for Serious Trouble," *New York Times*, January 9.

Brockett, O. G. (1979). *The Theater: An Introduction*, 4th ed. New York: Holt, Rinehart and Winston.

Clark, L. H., Jr. (1985). "Why Can't the Arts Be More Businesslike?" *Wall Street Journal*, June 11.

Cornes, R. and Sandler, T. (1996). *The Theory of Externalities, Public Goods and Club Goods,* 2nd ed. New York: Cambridge University Press.

Cox, M. (1984). "Orchestra Thrives by Playing the Music People Didn't Want," *Wall Street Journal,* July 19.

Duka, J. (1982). "Cable TV Turns Hungrily to the Theater," *New York Times,* June 27.

Dunning, J. (1986). "Dance as Big Business May Pose a Threat to Dance as Art," *New York Times,* March 30.

Farber, D. C. (1981). *Producing Theatre: A Comprehensive Legal and Business Guide.* New York: Drama Book Specialists.

Feld, A., O'Hare, J., and Schuster, J. M. D. (1983). *Patrons Despite Themselves. Taxpayers and Arts Policy. A Twentieth Century Fund Report.* New York: New York University Press.

Gapinski, J. H. (1986). "The Lively Arts as Substitutes for the Lively Arts," *American Economic Review* 76(2)(May).

Godley, W. (1977). "The Economics of the Arts," *Economic Journal 87* (September).

Goldstein, M. (1995). "Re-Inventing Broadway," *New York,* May 29.

Goodman, W. (1984). "Scholars Debate Need to Aid Arts," *New York Times,* May 2.

Gubernick, L. (1995). "A Hundred Broadways Now," *Forbes,*156(12)(November 20).

Haithman, D. (1997). "Opera to Die For," *Los Angeles Times,* February 2.

Hoelterhoff, M. (1987). "New York City (Opera) on $112,452 a Day," *Wall Street Journal,* August 18.

Honan, W. H. (1989). "Arts Dollars: Pinched as Never Before," *New York Times,* May 28.

Hummler, R. (1990). "Expenses Take Off for Off-Broadway Shows," *Variety,* September 24.

Kleinfield, N.R. (1994). "How Shubert Fund Produces and Directs," *New York Times,* July 10.

Kozinn, A. (1993). "City Opera Turns 50, But Who's Counting?" *New York Times,* July 25.

Kroeger, B. (1987). "Raising a Million for 'Les Mis.'" *New York Times,* July 19.

La Franco, R. (1996). "Popera," *Forbes,* 158(1)(July 1).

Langley, S. (1990). *Theatre Management and Production in America.* New York: Drama Book Publishers.

Larson, G. O. (1983). *The Reluctant Patron.* Philadelphia: University of Pennsylvania Press.

"London's West End Fights Off an Attack of the Glums," *The Economist Magazine,* May 17, 1986.

Lowry, W. M., ed. (1978). *The Performing Arts and American Society.* New York: The American Assembly (Columbia University).

Lyman, R. (1997). "Two Powerhouses of the Theater Meld Broadway and the Road," *New York Times,* June 9.

Lynes, R. (1985). *The Lively Audience: A Social History of the Visual and Performing Arts in America, 1890–1950.* New York: Harper & Row.

Malitz, N. (1995). "A Hardy Survivor Rides the Wave of the Future," *New York Times,* March 19.

Marks, P. (1996). "Broadway's Producers: A Struggling, Changing, Breed," *New York Times,* April 7.

Marsh, B. (1992). "Bunting & Red Tape: The Modern Circus Walks a High Wire," *Wall Street Journal,* August 31.

Mayer, M. (1983). "The Big Business of Grand Opera," *Fortune* 108(8)(October 17):146–60.

Miller, J. (1996). "As Patrons Age, Future of Arts Is Uncertain," *New York Times,* February 12.

Moore, T. G. (1966). "The Demand for Broadway Theatre Tickets," *Review of Economics and Statistics* 48(1)(February):79–87.

Mulcahy, K. V., and Swain, C. R., eds. (1982). *Public Policy and the Arts.* Boulder, Colo.: Westview Press.

Murray, M. (1956). *Circus!* New York: Appleton-Century-Crofts.

National Endowment for the Arts (1981). *Conditions and Needs of the Professional American Theater.* Washington, D.C.: NEA.

Osborne, C. L. (1991). "Opera's Fabulous Vanishing Act,"*New York Times,* February 17.

Oestreich, J. R. (1997). "Opera Enjoys Its Charmed Life," *New York Times,* April 28.

Pedersen, L. (1996). "The Risks of Buying Into Broadway," *New York Times,* December 8.

Pope, K., and King, T. R. (1995). "Andrew Lloyd Webber Is Planning an Empire Built on His Musicals," *Wall Street Journal,* May 4.

Revzin, P., and Patner, A. (1989). "Conductor Barenboim Survives Tough World of Orchestral Music," *Wall Street Journal,* May 2.

Rose-Ackerman, S., ed. (1986). *The Economics of Nonprofit Institutions.* New York: Oxford University Press.

Rosen, S. (1981). "The Economics of Superstars," *American Economic Review* 71(5)(December).

Ross, A. (1994). "Easy Does It: The Met Edges Into the Future," *New York Times,* May 15.

Silk, L. (1978). "The Metropolitan Opera – The High Price of Being Best: The Books Reveal the Cost Squeeze," *New York Times,* February 12.

Snyder, L. (1977). "How to Lose Less on Broadway," *Fortune* XCV(5)(May):147.

Taylor, F., and Barresi, A. L. (1984). *The Arts at a New Frontier: The National Endowment for the Arts.* New York: Plenum.

Trachtenberg, J. A. (1996). "How to Turn $4,000 Into Many Millions: The Story of 'Rent'," *Wall Street Journal,* May 23.

Wickham, G. (1985). *A History of the Theatre.* New York and Cambridge: Cambridge University Press.

13
Amusement/theme parks

Mickey is the mouse that roared.

The American themed amusement park industry – begun in July 1955 by Mickey Mouse, the famous Disney character – has evolved into a multibillion-dollar entertainment segment that draws visitors from around the world and has spawned many imitations. In this chapter, the economic outlines of amusement/theme park operations are sketched.

13.1 Flower power

Gardens and groves

The roots of this business extend back to medieval church-sponsored fairs and to seventeenth-century France, whose concept of pleasure gardens with fountains and flowers gradually spread throughout Europe. London's Vauxhall Gardens, for example, were established in 1661.[1] And by the eighteenth century, as Kyriazi (1976) has noted, entertainment and circus acts, including trapeze and tightrope, and ascension balloons and music were added. In England, meanwhile, affiliations with nearby taverns or inns also became common.

Yet it was not until the 1873 Vienna World's Fair, held at The Prater, that mechanical rides and fun houses were introduced. As Mangels (1952, p. 4) describes it,

for more than three hundred years, elaborate outdoor amusement centers have existed in several European countries. Known usually as "pleasure gardens" they were remarkably similar to those of today in their general layout and variety of entertainment. Some of the larger parks provided events and devices which thrilled their visitors as keenly as present-day attractions. Queens of the slack wire and daredevils of the flying rings brought gasps of fascinated terror, much as they do beneath the Big Top today . . . free balloon ascensions, and parachute jumps held crowds spellbound as far back as the seventeen-nineties.

In the United States, however, amusement areas did not begin to appear until the late 1800s, when streetcar companies began to build picnic groves to attract weekend riders. But still, as Adams (1991, p. 19) notes, it was the World's Columbian Exposition, held in Chicago in 1893, that "introduced most of the essential elements of American amusement parks." Soon thereafter, food and rides came to be emphasized, and major facilities such as New York's Coney Island sprang into national prominence.[2] Although, by the 1920s, some 1,500 such parks existed in the United States, the Great Depression, the development of movies, television, and automobiles, and the decay of inner cities eventually led to the demise of most.

Modern times

Walt Disney, at first a struggling cartoonist and later a successful filmmaker, liked spending time with his children. Trouble was that there were few bright, clean parks where all members of the family could have fun. So being an extraordinarily imaginative and entrepreneurial fellow, he envisioned creation of such a park modeled in part after the famous Tivoli Gardens that he had seen in Copenhagen (Thomas, 1976, Chapter 20).[3]

As the legend goes, Disney brought his plans for an amusement park containing themed areas before a rather skeptical and reluctant group of bankers. Yet, with perseverance, bank loans supplemented by borrowing on his life insurance policies, and the sale of concession rights and a 34% equity stake to the young American Broadcasting Company, he nevertheless managed in 1955 to open Disneyland amidst the Anaheim, California, orange groves.[4] The rest, as they say, is history.

Disneyland's immediate success led to numerous expansions. But it was not until the late 1960s that other large public companies began to invest heavily in this business.[5] And the Disney company itself did not until 1971 extend into the swamps of Florida to construct, for an estimated $300 million, the core of Disney World.[6]

More recently, the concept of *location-based entertainment* (LBE) has come into vogue as a convenient way to describe technologically sophisticated away-from-home attractions – the largest examples of which are the major theme parks.[7]

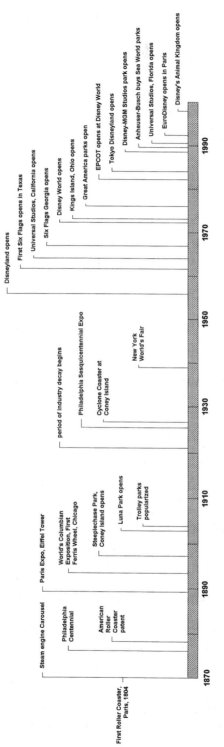

Figure 13.1. Amusement/theme park industry milestones, 1870–2000.

Table 13.1. *Estimated attendance (millions) at major theme park facilities in the United States, 1975–96[a]*

Year	Total	Year	Total
1996	135.7	1984	86.9
1995	131.3	1983	93.6
1994	122.5	1982	80.
1993	124.4	1981	82.7
1992	122.7	1980	81.7
1991	112.5	1979	80.5
1990	114.9	1978	80.5
1989	112.5	1977	73.2
1988	106.4	1976	68.3
1987	104.9	1975	60.9
1986	97.6	CAGR[b]	
1985	91.4	1980–96	3.2

[a]Fiscal years.
[b]Compound annual growth rate, (%).

As of the late-1990s, theme parks in the United States – including about 30 majors and a host of smaller ones – generated over $7 billion a year from more than 150 million visitors (Table 13.1).[8] It is also not surprising – in view of advances in technology, design and marketing – that American-style LBE concepts of the late twentieth century are being exported back to Europe and elsewhere around the globe.[9] A compilation of such major theme parks and annual visitor estimates appears in Table 13.2. And a history of developments is displayed in Figure 13.1.

13.2 Financial operating characteristics

Operating a theme park is very much like operating a small city: The streets should be frequently swept clean and occasionally repaved; sewer and sanitation systems should be efficient yet invisible; and police, fire, and health departments should be trained and available at a moment's notice. Those elements alone are difficult for most cities to handle well. But, in addition, a park also issues its own currency in the form of ticket books, and it provides visitor-transportation systems, live-entertainment services, and sometimes extensive shopping, hotel, and car-care facilities.

Furthermore, parks – subject as they are to seasonal and circadian rhythms of attendance and to rapidly changing weather patterns – usually depend on a largely unskilled seasonal workforce that turns over at inherently high rates. In all, it is not easy to juggle these elements and to further generate a stream of consistently rising profits (Table 13.3). For a specific park, operating-margin performance may

Table 13.2. *Selected major theme park facilities*

Facility	Year opened	Approximate number of annual visitors, 1996 (millions)
North America		
Disney World, Florida	1971	35.0
Disneyland, California	1955	15.0
Universal Studios Tour, Florida	1990	8.4
Universal Studios Tour, California	1964	5.4
Sea World, Florida	1973	5.1
Busch Gardens, Florida	1959	4.2
Six Flags Great Adventure, New Jersey	1973	4.0
Sea World, California	1963	3.9
Six Flags/Magic Mountain, California	1971	3.9
Knotts Berry Farm, California	1940	3.6
Kings Island, Ohio	1972	3.6
Cedar Point, Ohio	1870	3.5
Six Flags/Texas	1961	3.1
Six Flags/Great America, Illinois	1976	3.0
Canada's Wonderland, Toronto	1981	2.8
Great America, California	1975	2.5
AstroWorld, Texas	1968	2.4
Kings Dominion, Virginia	1975	2.4
Six Flags/Georgia	1967	2.2
Busch Gardens, Virginia	1975	2.2
Hersheypark, Pennsylvania	1907	2.1
Opryland, Tennessee	1972	2.0
Six Flags/Mid-America, Missouri	1971	1.8
Europe		
EuroDisney	1992	11.7
Tivoli Gardens, Denmark	1843	3.1
De Efteling, Netherlands	1951	3.0
Alton Towers, U.K.	1924	2.7
Tibigardens, Spain	1995	2.7
Europa Park, W. Germany	1975	2.5
Liseberg Park, Sweden	1923	2.4
Thorpe Park, U.K.	1979	1.3
Duinrell, Netherlands	1935	1.2
Asterix, France	1989	1.1
Grona Lund, Sweden	1883	1.0
Bellewaerde, Belgium	1969	0.6
Other		
Tokyo Disneyland, Japan	1983	17.0
Lotle World, S. Korea	1989	5.2

Source: Amusement Business.

Table 13.3. *Theme parks, industry operating performance: composite of five companies,[a] 1982–96[b]*

Year	Revenues	Operating income	Operating margin (%)	Assets	Operating cash flow
CAGR:(%)					
1992–96	6.2	8.4	2.0	7.0	8.0
1982–91	10.5	11.1	0.6	8.2	8.4

[a]Industry data are heavily weighted by Disney's parks.
[b]Average margin 1982–91 = 20.8%; 1992–96 = 19.5%.
[c]Compound annual growth rate.

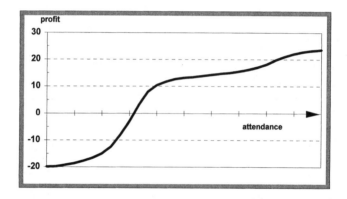

Figure 13.2. Profit as a function of attendance: an illustration.

thus be uneven and volatile: One year the problem may be high fuel prices; the next it may be abnormally hot summer temperatures, rainy spring weekends, or competition from other events.

No matter what the uncertainties, however, operating leverage – familiar in the airline and hotel businesses – is a constant feature. The costs of labor, electricity, insurance, and so forth remain relatively fixed, and once the break-even point is reached, every additional admission ticket sold produces a high marginal profit.[10]

Such is the case until the park becomes crowded. At that point, long lines at popular attractions reduce opportunities for impulse spending, crimp the initial good mood of the visitors, and entail additional labor and materials costs. Most parks will find that in analyzing daily results, marginal-profit curves as a function of attendance would probably be similar to the one shown in Figure 13.2.

On the other hand, Table 13.4 demonstrates how sensitive operating profits are

Table 13.4. Theme park operating leverage: an example

	A	B	C	D
Visitors, avg./day	25,000	30,000	25,000	30,000
Visitor-days (att.)	2,500,000	3,000,000	2,500,000	3,000,000
Per-cap. spending ($)	20.00	20.00	24.00	24.00
Total annual revs. ($)	50,000,000	60,000,000	60,000,000	72,000,000
Operating expenses	30,000,000	30,000,000	30,000,000	30,000,000
Operating profits ($)	20,000,000	30,000,000	30,000,000	42,000,000

to changes in two key variables: visitor-days (attendance equivalent to the number of separate visitors times the number of days of operation) and average per-capita spending. In this example, it is assumed that because of climatic factors, a park has an effective operating season of 100 days per year, that on an average day there are 25,000 visitors, and that average per-capita spending on admissions, rides, foods, beverages, and trinkets is $20. With a relatively stable operating expense of $30 million, operating earnings, as shown in column A, will be $20 million.

Assuming, however, that the number of visitors increases by 20% to 30,000 per day, and that expenses remain largely unchanged, operating profit will increase by 50% to $30 million (column B). And the same 50% increase in operating profit will naturally appear if attendance holds constant and per-capita spending rises by 20% (column C). But finally, assume that per-capita spending and attendance each rise by 20% (column D). Then operating profit will increase to $42 million – a gain of 110% over that shown in column A.

Of course, in the real world, operating expenses will rise along with attendance, per-capita spending will tend to decrease as attendance rises to near capacity (if only because the crowds are immobilized), and the gains in profit will not be as large as indicated in this simplistic example. But substantial operating leverage, both up and down, will nonetheless still be visible in actual results.

Because the compounding of changes in both attendance and spending has such a great impact on profits, park managers devote much of their time to figuring how each input factor can be increased without adversely affecting any of the others. Toward this end, many fancy mathematical modeling techniques (linear programming, production-function, and queuing-system estimators, etc.) can be used to improve the efficiency of park operations. Norms for average daily attendance conditioned on weather, queuing times, and price elasticities may then be established and tested much as though parks were production-line factories.

Yet, because there really is no such thing as a typical theme park – operations depend so much on region, weather patterns, number of season days, local demographic and income characteristics, and age and amount of capital invested –

Table 13.5. *Financial ratio averages for theme parks, foreign and domestic,*
1993.[a]

	U.S.	Foreign
Percent of average per capita revenue		
Admissions	51.3	47.9
Retail	16.5	8.0
Food & beverage	22.8	29.1
Average operating expenses as a % of total revenues		
Salaries, wages, and benefits	35.8	24.7
Advertising & promotions	7.0	4.4
EBITDA[b]	22.2	20.1

[a] Selected Non-Disney parks with > 1 million admissions
[b] Earnings before interest, taxes, depreciation and amortization.
Source: International Association of Amusement Parks & Attractions, 1994 survey.

it is difficult to establish a representative statistical composite. Each facility must
develop its own set of standards. Table 13.5 provides some recent industry sample
ratios.

13.3 Economic sensitivities

A sense of how this industry's operating performance compares with those of
other economic segments is not easily derived. But evidence from the U.S. *Census
of Selected Service Industries* suggests that parks have not, in the aggregate, been
particularly good at mitigating the inherent labor intensity of operations.

Unfortunately, there are also difficulties in correlating theme park admissions
trends with important economic time series such as those for GDP or real disposable income. Although an economic recession could be expected to adversely
affect admissions growth trends at high-profile themed resort parks, other parks
more dependent on day-trip and regional visitors might conceivably do better in
such an environment.

As might be anticipated, however, aggregate theme park admissions do seem
to be positively correlated with respect to consumer credit as a percent of personal
income, and negatively with respect to the unemployment rate. But the lags, as
suggested by Figure 13.3, are not well defined. Some additional variables to
consider would, of course, include changes in real admission-ticket and fuel
prices, changes in airline fares, and demographic shifts over time. Yet, as is the
case for performing arts, it is likely that the demand for theme park services is
more sensitive to the overall cost of travel rather than any of its specific
components.

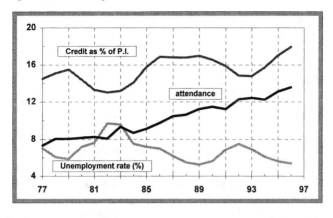

Figure 13.3. Theme park attendance (including Disney's) in the United States in tens of thousands versus the unemployment rate (%) and consumer credit as a percentage of personal income, 1977–96.

13.4 Valuing theme park properties

Real estate – the key asset of any park – normally has the potential to provide the extraordinary long-term returns on investment that are plainly not obtainable from day-to-day operations. But for this to occur, a park must be located in the path of population expansion, where it will ultimately be worth more dead than alive. In such instances, the land is a true hedge against inflation, and operation of a park may be seen as merely an interim holding action in anticipation of the maturation of higher-value alternative uses.

Assuming, nevertheless, that a park will continue to be operated, the usual established methods for valuing other entertainment properties may also be applied here. As in the broadcasting and cable industries, for example, theme park asset values are taken as a multiple of projected operating earnings before taxes, interest, and depreciation and amortization (EBITDA). Such multiples would, of course, normally be expected to vary inversely to interest rates. And other factors also affecting the multiple applied to this definition of cash flow would further include:

Age and condition of the park's rides and attractions
Demographic and income trends in the surrounding region
Potential for expanding ride and admissions capacity
Potential for raising prices and/or per capita spending
Prospects for development of nearby transportation facilities
Proximity of other similar attractions

Again, as in other entertainment segments, public market valuations are often only one-half to two-thirds of what private market valuations based on a multiple of cash flow might be. Well-situated theme parks with proven operating characteristics are thus often attractive candidates for leveraged buy-outs, in which large institutions will lend a major percentage of the required funding for the buy-out based on the security of the park's cash flow.[11]

13.5 Concluding remarks

In the United States, admissions growth trends have, over long periods, held consistently above the growth trends of real GDP – a fact that has not escaped the attention of investors. The potentially high operating margins and significant free cash flows that are regularly generated by established major park facilities have also been widely recognized.

However, in recent years, the amount of capital investment and technological sophistication required to maintain a leadership position has grown enormously. New motion simulator rides and other computer-controlled "experiences" such as those developed in the framework of "artificial reality" and interactive video games are the new frontiers in the evolution of theme park concepts. No wonder, then, that major filmed entertainment and video game companies now view theme park investments as a natural fit.

The industry seems to be rather mature in North America, where it has developed into an entertainment form dominated by a few large companies that have the marketing expertise and capital to continually upgrade and expand their facilities. But the industry also seems to be on the verge of substantial growth in other parts of the world. Regardless of location, though, the degree of success will have as much to do with intangible elements – quality of design, efficiency of service, and public fancy – as with anything else.

Selected additional reading

Bannon, L. (1996). "Universal Studios' Plan to Expand in Florida Moves Disney to Battle," *Wall Street Journal*, October 2.

Berck, J. (1994). "When Broadway Meets the Midway, It's Big Business," *New York Times*, August 28.

Braithwaite, D. (1967). *Fairground Architecture: The World of Amusement Parks, Carnivals, & Fairs*. New York: Praeger.

Eliot, M. (1993). *Walt Disney, Hollywood's Dark Prince: A Biography*. New York: Carol Publishing (Birch Lane).

Finch, C. (1975). *The Art of Walt Disney: From Mickey Mouse to the Magic Kingdoms*. New York: Harry N. Abrams.

Flower, J. (1991). *"Prince of the Magic Kingdom: Michael Eisner and the Re-making of Disney*. New York: John Wiley & Sons.

Grover, R. (1997). *The Disney Touch*, rev. ed. Chicago: Irwin.

Gumbel, P., and Turner, R. (1994). "Fans Like Euro Disney but Its Parent's Goofs Weigh the Park Down," *Wall Street Journal*, March 10.

Hannon, K. (1987). "All Aboard!" *Forbes* 140(3)(August 10).

Mosley, L. (1987). *Disney's World: A Biography*. Briarcliff Manor, N.Y.: Stein and Day.

Mrowca, M. (1983). "Amusement Park in Ohio Has Its Ups and Downs but Continues to Draw Crowds after 114 Years." *Wall Street Journal*, July 8.

Ono, Y. (1990). ''Theme Parks Boom in Japan as Investors and Consumers Rush to Get on the Ride,'' *Wall Street Journal,* August 8.

Rayl, A. J. S. (1990). ''Making Fun: Theme Parks of the Future,'' *Omni* 13(2) November.

Ross, I. (1982). ''Disney Gambles on Tomorrow,'' *Fortune,* 106(October 4).

Schickel, R. (1968). *The Disney Version: The Life, Times, Art and Commerce of Walt Disney.* New York: Simon & Schuster.

Tagliabue, J. (1995). ''Step Right Up, Monsieur!: Growing Disneyfication of Europe's Theme Parks,'' *New York Times,* August 23.

Part IV
Roundup

14
Epilogue

Time flies when you're having fun.

Entertainment is a big and rapidly changing international business, and the study of its economic characteristics is still at an early stage. As a platform for such studies, this book has attempted to convey a sense of the industry's dynamics in relation to the financial and economic features that enduringly characterize entertainment enterprises. This closing chapter provides a review and summary of those features.

14.1 Common elements

As seen in Chapter 1, leisure time – broadly defined as time not spent at work – has been expanding very slowly, if at all, in recent years. Indeed, over the long run, the potential to expand leisure time depends on the rate of gain in economic productivity, which is in turn affected by the rate of technological development.

Yet after deducting life-sustenance activities from nonwork time, we have what is known in the vernacular as free time. But time is never really free in an economic sense because there are always alternative-opportunity costs. Entertainment, defined as that which has the effect of pleasurably diverting the psyche,

thus competes for – and is ultimately limited by – the amount of free time available.
Beyond these generalities are several frequently observed industry characteristics.

Many are called, but few are chosen:

Perhaps the most noticeable tendency of entertainment businesses is that in the steady-state growth phase (i.e., after a segment has attained a size at which long-run domination by several large companies has been established), *profits from a very few highly popular products are generally required to offset losses from many mediocrities.* This is evident in movies, of network television production, toys and video games, and recorded music. But this tendency appears to a much lesser extent in the performing arts category; there even a few occasional hits cannot counterbalance chronic operating deficits.

Marketing expenditures per unit are proportionally large:

Many entertainment products or services have unique features that must continuously be brought to the attention of potential consumers. In addition, the life cycle of an entertainment product may be very brief. Therefore, be it casinos in Las Vegas, theme parks in Florida, or a new video game, *per-unit marketing expenditures tend to be large relative to total unit costs of operation or production.* For instance, it may be recalled that marketing typically adds at least 50% to the cost of the average major feature film release. In economic terms, such spending on marketing attempts to shift the demand schedule to the right and to make demand less sensitive to price (i.e., more price-inelastic).

Ancillary markets provide disproportionately large returns:

Indeed, as a result of *sunk-cost characteristics* – wherein almost every dollar of revenue goes first toward recoupment of direct costs – *entertainment products often derive a large proportion of their returns from ancillary or secondary markets.* This also means that *price-discrimination opportunities between classes of consumers having different demand elasticities can be exploited.* Films, for instance, on the average now derive over half their revenues from exposures on cable and home video rather than from initial theatrical release. And spin-offs of character licenses into popular TV series or movie sequels and novelizations may often be sources of significant additional income. Price-discrimination effects are readily observed in the pricing of tickets to cultural events and in the sequencing of a movie through various exhibition windows.

Capital costs are relatively high; oligopolist tendencies are prevalent:

As happens in many other industries, once beyond the very early stages of a segment's development, *the cost of capital and the amount of it required for operations becomes a formidable barrier to entry by new competitors.* Most entertainment industry segments thus come to be ruled by large companies with relatively easy access to large pools of capital. Such oligopolistic tendencies can, for example, be seen in distribution of recorded music and movies, and in the gaming, theme park, cable, video game, and broadcasting industries.

Entertainment products and services often have strong public-good characteristics:
With pure public goods, the cost of production is independent of the number of consumers; that is, consumption by one person does not reduce the amount available for consumption by another. Although delivered to consumers in the form of private goods, *many entertainment products and services, including movies, records, television programs, and sports contests, have public-good characteristics.*

Many products and services are not standardized (which is good for entrepreneurs and bad for relative-productivity gains):
There are four important consequences of such nonstandardization:

1. Despite the oligopolistic framework, *there is considerable freedom for the entrepreneurial spirit to thrive.* That is, operas, plays, movies, ballets, songs, and video games are uniquely produced and are normally originated by individuals working alone or in small groups and not by giant corporate committees. One can become rich and famous as a direct result of one's own creative efforts.

2. *The entrepreneurial spirit, and thus the importance of the individual to the productive process, is accommodated by means of widely varying, uniquely tailored financing arrangements.* This is especially evident in movies, recorded music, and sports.

3. *Where the production is the product itself* (e.g., live performance of music or dance), *it is difficult to enhance productivity.* To some extent this feature also appears in areas as diverse as filmmaking, sports, and casino gaming.

4. Under the aforementioned conditions, *the costs of creating and marketing entertainment products such as movies and television programs tend to rise at above-average rates.*

Technological advances provide the saving grace:
Fortunately, ongoing *technological development makes it ever easier and less expensive to manufacture, distribute, and receive entertainment products and services.* Over the long run, this leads to more varied and more affordable mass-market entertainment.

Entertainment products and services have universal appeal:
Demand for entertainment cuts across all cultural and national boundaries, and many cravings (for laughter, for music, or for gambling) have deep-seated psychological roots. This means that many entertainment products have worldwide market appeal and that incremental revenues from international sources can have an important effect on profitability.

14.2 Guidelines for evaluating entertainment securities

The preceding chapters provide a background for analysis of entertainment industry investments. But many factors not explicitly treated here – Federal Reserve Bank policy, overall economic trends, and investor psychology – also influence investment performance (Figure 14.1). Happily, it is not necessary to delve into those subjects to extract a few basic investment-decision guidelines.

Cash flows and private market values:
Most entertainment companies are first analyzed in terms of what a private buyer might be willing to pay for the right to obtain access to the cash flow (earnings before deduction of interest, depreciation and amortization, and taxes) of the enterprise. Public market valuations are often in the range of one-half to two-thirds of the private values, which are derived as multiples of projected cash flow (minus debt).

Debt-equity ratios:
The ability to service debt varies widely among entertainment companies, but it is always a function of the volatility of projected cash flows. The less volatile the cash flow, the higher is the debt level relative to equity that can be comfortably accommodated on the balance sheet. Casino-industry companies, for instance, would generally be expected to experience far less cash flow volatility than companies in the toy and game industries. And by and large, the major movie and record companies, relying on libraries and catalogs as they do, would usually fall somewhere in the middle of the volatility range.

Price/earnings ratios:
For entertainment stocks, the price/earnings ratio seems to have lost a great deal of its usefulness as a tool in comparative investment analysis. In movies and television, for example, earnings trends can be easily distorted because of accounting conventions that require management forecasts of anticipated revenues and recognition of syndication earnings when a series is made available. Furthermore, in the United States (as opposed to Britain and elsewhere), accounting for acquisitions has a major effect on reported earnings because of requirements to write down goodwill (over a period of 40 years). If price/earnings ratios are nevertheless used to compare entertainment stocks to alternative investments, then adjustments for such differences in the accounting practices must obviously be made.

Price/sales ratios:
Because price-to-sales ratios do not suffer from the accounting distortions that are frequently present in the calculation of earnings, such ratios have become increasingly popular in the evaluation of common stocks. For entertainment securities, however, the price/sales ratio (price per share divided by revenues per

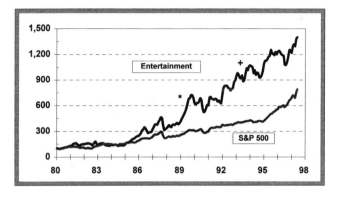

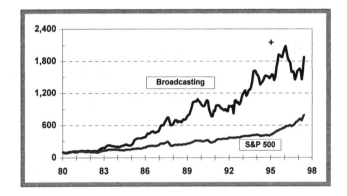

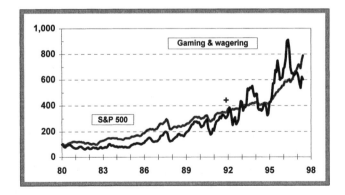

Figure 14.1. Standard & Poor's stock price indices for (a) entertainment, (b) broadcasting, (c) gaming and wagering, (d) toys, (e) publishing, and (f) newspapers versus the S&P 500 stock composite index, 1980–96, based on month-end prices.

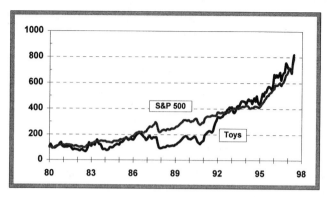

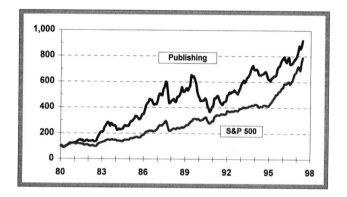

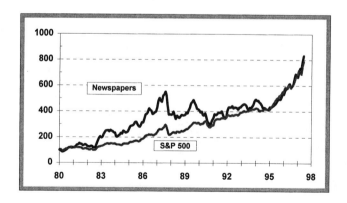

Figure 14.1. *(cont.)*

share) is perhaps most useful as a "reality-check" – especially if adjustments that smooth or normalize sales over several periods are made to take into account any evidence that current period sales may be far above or below trend. Sales may be temporarily boosted far above trend, for example, with release of an unusually popular movie, or toy, or recording, or be temporarily depressed far below trend because of an economic recession.

Book value:

This traditional yardstick for financial analysis normally has little relevance in the evaluation of entertainment company stock prices because the key earnings power may reside – as in the case of film libraries or song catalogs – in assets that have already been largely or completely written down. Moreover, in the case of real estate assets – studio backlots, theme park facilities, transmission tower sites – the historical cost basis is usually far below what a property might currently be worth. Brand names and relative market positions may also have considerable value, yet not be reflected in the stated book numbers.

14.3 Final remarks

Entertainment has proven to be one of life's essentials – perhaps just behind food, shelter, and clothing in its importance to many people. Indeed, once a society develops to the point that there is what economists call discretionary income, a substantial portion of such discretionary income can be expected to be spent on entertainment products and services.

As we have also seen, technological development has been the driving force behind the growth of the entertainment industries. Development of technology leads indirectly to an increase in leisure time availability through economic productivity enhancements, and leads directly to qualitative improvements and cost reductions in manufacturing and distribution.

Current trends suggest that the entertainment industries will, in the aggregate, continue to grow at faster than average rates and that they will continue in the process of integrating vertically and globally. But no matter how large or widespread the corporate entities become, entertainment industries will remain dependent on the vitality and creativity of individuals. In this respect, they will not have changed at all.

Notes

Chapter 1

1. Similarly, the concept of *play* has been studied under the disciplines of sociology and psychology. The Dutch anthropologist, Johan Huizinga, in his book, *Homo Ludens* (Man the Player, 1938, 1955), advanced the notion that play might be its own end. Huizinga (1955, p. 8) notes that the first main characteristic of play is "that it is free, it is freedom. A second characteristic . . . is that play is not 'ordinary' or 'real' life." It also demands order, casts a spell over us, and contains elements of tension and solution, such as in gambling. See, also, Roberts (1995).

2. Also, as De Grazia (1962, p. 13) notes, it is obvious that "time on one's hands is not enough to make leisure," and free time accompanied by fear and anxiety is not leisure.

3. As Smith (1986, p. 8) has further noted, such surveys indicate that for full-time, day-shift plant workers, the average workweek decreased by 0.8 hour between 1973 and 1985, but that over the same period, "the schedule of full-time office workers in the private sector rose by 0.2 hour, with the result that the workweek of these two large groups converged markedly."

Also, Hedges and Taylor (1980) show that hours for full-time service workers declined faster than for white-collar and blue-collar employees between 1968 and 1979.

And the BLS estimated that the percentage of nonagricultural salaried jobs in which the work week exceeded 49 hrs rose to 18.5% in 1993 as compared to 14.2% in 1973.

4. The Harris nationwide cross-section sample survey of 1,501 adults found that the estimated hours available for leisure have been steadily decreasing from 26.2 hours per week in 1973 to 16.6 hours per week in 1987. Harris argues that an apparent combination of economic necessities and choices by women who want to work has increased the number of families in which both husbands and wives hold jobs. Also see Gibbs (1989).

5. In more detail, Schor's data indicate that the annual hours of paid employment of labor force participants in 1969 and 1987 changed as follows:

	1969	1987	Change
All participants	1,786	1,949	163
Men	2,054	2,152	98
Women	1,406	1,711	305

These estimated changes in hours worked appear strikingly high. It seems that while the analysis has probably been correct in catching the direction of change, it may not have correctly estimated its magnitude. Schor's book is so politically imbued with an anti–capitalist theme that the methodology and the objectivity of its findings are accordingly suspect. See also, *The Economist*, December 23, 1995, p 12.

6. Robinson (1989, p. 35) found, for example, that "people aged 51 to 64 have gained the most free time since 1965, mainly because they are working less. Among people in this age group, the proportion of men opting for early retirement increased considerably between 1965 and 1985." Also, Robinson and Godbey (1997) suggest that Americans, in the aggregate, have more time for leisure because of broad trends toward younger retirements and smaller families. Except for parents of very young children, or those with more than four children under 18, everyone else, they say, has gained at least one hour per week since 1965.

7. Roberts and Rupert (1995) state that the presumption of declining leisure is a fallacy. "Previous studies purporting to have uncovered such a fact have not adequately disentangled time spent in home production-activities . . . from time spent enjoying leisure activities. [W]hile hours of market work and home work have remained fairly constant for men since the mid-1970s, market hours have been rising and home production hours have been declining for women . . . Possible reasons include an increase in market versus nonmarket productivity or labor-saving technological advancements in the home."

8. Rybczynski (1991) provides a detailed history of the evolution of the weekend. And Spring (1993) provides a study of the popularity of spare-time activities classified by day of the week. Television viewing, consuming one-third of free time on weekdays and one-fourth on weekends, leads the list by far on every day of the week.

9. Also, studies comparing time allocation in different countries can be found in Juster and Stafford (1991), where, for example, it can be seen that both men and women allocate more time for leisure in the U.S. than in Japan or Sweden. Also, data from government reports of various countries (as shown in *The Wall Street Journal* of October 2, 1992) suggest that the average working hours per year as of the early 1990s were as follows:

Japan	2,120
Britain	1,950
U.S.	1,940
France	1,680
Germany	1,590

10. According to Curran (1984), on a "multifactor" basis, including capital and labor, productivity growth averaged 2% per year from 1948 to 1973 and 0.2% in the subsequent eight years.

11. There are many fine texts providing full description of these tools; see, for example, Henderson and Quandt (1971).

12. In most mathematical presentations, the independent variable or "cause" of change is presented along the horizontal x-axis and the dependent variable on the vertical y-axis. Economists, however, have generally found it more convenient to depict prices (the independent variable) and quantities by switching the axes. Thus, prices are usually seen on the vertical and quantities on the horizontal.

13. In Linder (1970), standard indifference-curve-budget-line analysis is used to show how the supply of labor is a function of income and substitution effects. The standard consumers' utility function is $V = f(Q, T_c)$, where Q is the number of units of consumption goods, and T_c is the number of hours devoted to consumption purposes. Two constraints are $Q = pT_w$, and $T = T_w + T_c$, where p is a productivity index measuring the number of consumption goods earned per hour of work (T_w), and T is the total number of hours available per time period.

To maximize utility, V now takes the Lagrange multiplier function

$$L = f(Q, T_c) + \lambda[Q - p(T - T_c)]$$

which is then differentiated with respect to Q, T_c, and multiplier λ.

14. See Trost (1986) and *Monthly Labor Review,* U.S. Department of Commerce, Bureau of Labor Statistics, November 1986, No. 11.

15. Owen's (1970) exhaustive study of these issues leads to a model supporting the hypothesis of a backward-bending labor-supply curve and suggesting that demand for leisure activity has positive income and negative price elasticities consistent with economic theory.

16. Utility can often be visualized in the form of a mathematical curve or function. For instance, the utility a person derives from purchase of good x might vary with the square root of the amount of x; i.e., $U(x)$ = square root of x. Also see section 10.5 and Levy and Sarnat (1972).

17. A dependency ratio is the number of people who are net consumers (children and senior citizens) divided by the number of net producers; see, for example, Burton and Toth (1974).

18. The table, however, does not do justice to the cable television and lottery spending categories, which are the largest and fastest growing segments, but are unfortunately lumped into the "other" section.

19. Both Figure 1.10 and Supplementary Table S1.1 are based on NIPA data series.

20. However, the entertainment services series as a percentage of total recreation spending has demonstrated considerable volatility since 1929. This series hit a peak of nearly 50% in the early 1940s, when there were relatively few consumer durables available. Then, for a dozen or so years ending in the late 1970s, the percentage had been confined to a fairly narrow band of 33% to 36%.

21. To make the distinction, GNP measures output belonging to U.S. citizens and corporations wherever that output is created, but GDP measures the value of all goods and services produced in a country no matter whether that output belongs to natives or foreigners. In actuality, in the U.S., the differences between the values of the two series have been slight.

However, critics of National Income Accounting, for example, Cobb, Halstead, and Row (1995), argue that GDP measurements allow activities in the household and volunteer sectors to go entirely unreckoned. As a result, GDP measurements mask the breakdown of the social structure and are grossly misleading. "GDP does not distinguish between costs and benefits, between productive and destructive activities, or between sustainable and unsustainable ones. The nation's central measure of well-being works like a calculating machine that adds but cannot subtract . . . The GDP treats leisure time and time with family the way it treats air and water: as having no value at all." (pp. 64–67)

22. Another interesting aspect revealed in the data from Table 1.5 is that rapid expansion of the cable industry – highest in measures of revenue and earnings growth – did not translate into substantial pretax income growth acceleration for filmed entertainment programmers and distributors.

23. Official data on entertainment industry exports is sketchy, but as noted in U.S. Department of Commerce (1993, p. 20), net exports (using country-based rather than firm-based measurements) of motion picture and television programming amounted to $2.122 billion in 1991. And for the same year, net exports of records, tapes, and other media amounted to $283 million. Other areas may have generated the following amounts: theme parks, $0.5 billion; casinos, $0.5 billion. Bernstein (1990) discusses the implications of global acceptance of American entertainment products and services. See also *Variety,* January 9, 1991.

Chapter 2

1. This argument has especially been advanced by Gilder (1995), who makes the case that because bandwidth (or signal-carrying capacity) of fiber optic cable is tremendously larger than that of ordinary electronic computers and switches, fiber optic networks will quickly begin to supplant the current electronics-based communications infrastructure.

2. This and other aspects of the industry's long and colorful history are recounted in books such as those by Stanley (1978), Knight (1978), and Balio (1976).

3. The industry continues to consolidate, but at a somewhat slower rate than before the 1986 Tax Reform Act took effect.

Values in this business, as in the others related to entertainment, are calculated in terms of cash flow multiples (pretax, preinterest, and predepreciation). At the height of the bidding, most of the multiples for properties in large cities were in the range of 10 to 14 times, based on projected cash flows for the following year. But many properties in smaller cities are priced at five or six times. Also, although many big-city purchase prices averaged well over $1 million per screen, including big and small cities together, transfer prices per screen averaged just below $500,000 during the 1980s.

4. Tri-Star Pictures was a new studio formed in 1982 by Columbia (Coca-Cola), CBS, and Home Box Office (see Sansweet, 1983), with equal initial capital contributions totaling

$50 million. Prior to a public stock and debt offering in 1985, the principal shareholders contributed another $50 million. CBS soon thereafter, however, sold its interest, while Coca-Cola increased its share of ownership. Nonetheless, in late 1987, Coca-Cola merged the former Embassy Pictures and Merv Griffin Enterprises television properties into TriStar, and renamed the whole package Columbia Pictures, while retaining a 49% interest in the total entity. All of Columbia was then bought by Sony, the Japanese electronics giant in November 1989.

5.   As of the mid-1990s, the six majors could, like investment banking firms, be further classified. The mega-distributors such as Disney and Warner are now capable of handling between forty and sixty titles a year, while the next layer, including Fox, Paramount, Sony, and Universal, could handle twenty to thirty. The mini-majors would now include MGM/UA, and New Line, a division of Time Warner Inc.

6.   Two large companies that made feature films, CBS and ABC, reentered production (but not distribution) in the early 1980s after a hiatus of about 10 years. Both companies had produced movies in the late 1960s and early 1970s, but after sustaining substantial losses had withdrawn from the field. CBS originally distributed its Cinema Center Films (e.g., *My Fair Lady*) through National General Corp., and American Broadcasting's ABC Pictures used a now-defunct subsidiary of Cinerama (Cinerama Releasing). By 1984, however, both companies again withdrew from theatrical production.

7.   So-named at the time, prior to national distribution networks becoming fully operational.

8.   Contracyclicity of ticket demand was studied by Albert Kapusinski (see Nardone, 1982), who matched 42 economic measures of the motion-picture industry for the 1928–75 span against similar variables used to assess the performance of the whole economy. The variables were then subjected to five tests of cyclical movement and led to the results cited.

   Preliminary experiments using spectral-analysis techniques hint at the possibility of a 4-year cycle and a 10-year cycle in movie admissions, but, as noted, the statistical evidence in this regard is inconclusive. A more heuristic approach based on unit ticket sales and general operating conditions also seems to suggest the existence of a 25-year cycle, which would be confirmed if ticket sales peak within a year or two of the recent 1996 high. Spectral analysis is a statistical technique often used in signal-processing applications (in this case, economic time series) to determine whether or not cyclical patterns exist. References include Bloomfield (1977), Koopmans (1974), and Gottman (1981).

9.   Such seasonal relationships remain consistent over long periods. For instance, between 1983 and 1992, the summer box office as a percent of the year's total ranged between 35% and 41% and averaged 37.8%.

10.   Regression models attempt to explain, via statistical testing based on probabilistic assumptions, the extent to which some variables affect others. For example, a first naive attempt at constructing such a mathematical relationship might be in the form of an equation indicating that aggregate industry profit (the dependent variable) is a function of the number of admissions and the number of releases (the independent variables).

11.   The number of films rated by MPAA is published each year in *Variety*.

12.   These comparisons would suggest that significant marketing opportunities may be available in foreign markets. However, it is not enough for a country to have a large population base. For example, even with the large population bases in Russia and China, theater ticket prices are so low – under five cents – that a large number of admissions would hardly generate an important amount of income for the major studios or exhibitors.

13.   However, the former United Artists subsidiary of Transamerica, which did not en-

gage in series production activities, reported operating income on sales to both theatrical and television markets. Supplementary Table S2.2 illustrates the performance of United Artists in each of those markets during the 1970s.

14. Home viewing options did not multiply rapidly until the mid-1980s. In many large cities, it was not until 1983 and 1984 that cable systems began to be constructed or to be activated. And it was not until 1985 that video recording or playback-only machines were present in over 20% of U.S. television households. When videocassette recorders (VCRs) reached into more than 20% of households in Germany and Australia, theatrical admissions in those countries declined noticeably, and pretty much the same effect was seen in the United States by 1986.

15. Also, presales impair industry profitability because projects financed in this way – about one of every six involves presales of foreign rights – increase the supply of films and heighten the demand for, and thus the cost of, various input factors (screenplays, actors, sound stages, etc.).

16. Case histories from the mid-1980s include Cannon Group and DeLaurentiis Entertainment as examples of presales-strategy companies that ultimately ran into such fatal financing problems.

17. For example, in pay-cable, Time Warner, Inc.'s cable program wholesaler, Home Box Office (HBO), emerged in the 1970s as a powerful, almost monopsonistic (a market with one buyer and many sellers) intermediary for Hollywood's products. In its position as dominant gatekeeper to the nation's wired homes, HBO was able to bargain effectively for retention of an important part of the revenue stream derived from sale of pay cable services (also see Chapter 7). And by 1981, HBO had already surpassed the large theater chains to become Hollywood's single largest customer, licensing in excess of $130 million in that year (and around $500 million by the early 1990s). But it was not until the alternative Movie Channel and Showtime pay-cable services merged, and until videocassette recorder (VCR) penetration rates reached over 20% of television households (in 1984), that HBO experienced significant competition. Prior to merging, Showtime was owned by Viacom and the Movie Channel was jointly owned by Warner Communications and American Express. Ownership of Showtime/TMC was split 50% Viacom, 40.5% Warner, and 9.5% American Express until 1985, when Viacom bought it all. In 1989, half of Showtime was then sold to Tele-Communications Inc.

The preceding history is that around 1980, the major studios finally recognized that they had lost control of unit pricing and distribution in the important new medium of pay-cable, and they accordingly attempted to reassert themselves by launching their own pay channel called Premiere. The studio consortium participants, however, encountered great difficulty in arriving at consensus decisions – especially under threat of antitrust litigation aimed at preventing films from being shown exclusively on Premiere. Showtime was meanwhile able to formulate exclusive five-year license agreements with Paramount. This $500 million agreement, signed in 1983, has subsequently been followed by other exclusive arrangements between cable wholesalers and film producers. The history of HBO and its competitors is covered in Mair (1988).

18. To see this, note that consumers' out-of-pocket costs per hour of entertainment generally range from approximately 50 cents to $2, with pay-per-view events occasionally at $3 or more. On average, a typical household may buy about 100 hours of such entertainment in a year.

Still, that same average household spends about 2,500 hours per year (almost seven hours per day) with free advertiser-supported television. Sponsors reach this audience at a cost of around 12.6 cents per hour per household ($30 billion divided by 2,500 hours divided by 95 million households). If it were possible to sell another 100 hours or so per household per year at 50 cents rather than at 10 cents, all other things being equal (and they never are), entertainment industry revenues would be enhanced by about $3.7 billion. However, this is easier said than done in view of the time and income constraints discussed in the previous chapter.

As of 1996, consumers spent approximately $48 billion on such direct purchases ($6 billion in tickets, $27 billion on cable, and $15 billion for home video), whereas advertisers spent about $36 billion to sponsor programming.

19. See Brown (1984).

20. Advances in technology have also made it easier to slow or prevent chemical and physical decay of important film masters. Many libraries literally fade in the vault as color dyes decompose over time. Although chronically inadequate funding of preservation efforts permits a part of the industry's heritage to fade into oblivion every year, the costs of restoration have declined along with the cost of computing power. Indeed, several companies now colorize films and television shows originally produced in black and white. Although such colorizations (of materials largely in the public domain from a copyright standpoint) have often been denounced by filmmakers concerned about detracting from the artistic integrity of the originals, they have been rather well received by a public now accustomed to seeing entertainment in color. As Linfield (1987) notes, colorization does not destroy the original black and white negatives or prints, which remain available for viewing by future generations. As of 1996, the cost of colorizing a full-length black-and-white feature had declined to $75,000 – one-third the cost of ten years prior. See *Variety,* March 11, 1996.

21. The most important transfer of the early 1980s was MGM's 1981 purchase of the United Artists subsidiary of Transamerica for $380 million (including UA's worldwide distribution organization and library of over 2,200 titles, many of Academy-Award-winning best-picture stature). However, a subsequent (1985) transaction then again split MGM/UA Entertainment into separate pieces. The whole company, including MGM/UA's distribution arm and a combined total of about 4,600 features, was sold to Turner Broadcasting for $1.5 billion, which was only the first of numerous transactions of great complexity. In 1989, United Artists' 1,000-feature library, distribution arm, and television business again came up for sale, and by 1992 the MGM remnants were acquired by the French bank Credit Lyonnais.

In 1981 and 1982 there were two other notable transfers involving more than just film libraries and distributing organizations. The 1981 takeover of Twentieth Century Fox for $722 million included extensive real-estate properties and several profitable divisions (a soft-drink-bottling franchise, an international theater chain, Aspen Ski Corporation, five television stations, and Deluxe Film Laboratories). Likewise, the 1982 purchase of Columbia Pictures (for about $750 million) by the Coca-Cola Company included some broadcasting properties, part of the Burbank Studios real estate, and an arcade-game manufacturing subsidiary.

Also of historical interest, Warner Bros. sold 850 features and 1,500 shorts to PRM, an investment firm, and Associated Artists Productions, a television distributor, in March 1956. Through its purchase of Associated Artists Productions in late 1957, United Artists, for about $30 million, then gained control of some 700 pre-1948 Warner films and several hundred other features, short subjects, and cartoons. In addition, as Stanley (1978, p. 152) notes, in 1958 MCA paid approximately $50 million ($10 million cash) to acquire Paramount's pre-1948 library of 750 features.

22. Significant changes in studio real estate included the early 1970s combination of the

Columbia Pictures and Warner Bros. lots (at a time when Columbia was in great financial distress) and MGM's decision in 1973 to reduce production and to thus sell 130 out of 175 acres in Culver City. Eighteen acres of the Columbia studio were sold in 1977 for $6.1 million, while MGM's early 1970s sale of the Culver City assets brought $12 million. More recently, the former MGM Culver City property was bought by Lorimar, which was subsequently merged into Warner Communications (now Time Warner Inc.). In 1989, Columbia (Sony) then swapped its Burbank holdings for the Culver City property held by Warner. Lorimar's 1987 purchase from Turner Broadcasting of the remaining Culver City property was for over $50 million, but it is impossible to attribute an exact price because other assets were included in the transaction.

23. In fact, the demand for production space had become so strong that other parts of the country were able to compete effectively against Hollywood with so-called runaway studios by promising more accommodating shooting schedules or lower overall costs. See Bagamery (1984) and also Harris (1981).

Chapter 3

1. Root (1979) and Nash and Oakey (1974), for example, explain the screenplay development process.

2. Other box office hits such as *Driving Miss Daisy, Gandhi,* and *Teenage Mutant Ninja Turtles,* also encountered difficulties in finding distributors. The *Turtles* story is, for example, described in Brown (1991) and the *Gandhi* experience in Eberts and Ilott (1990). More recently, *Independence Day* was rejected by Sony, and Fox lost faith in *The English Patient,* which Miramax (Disney) distributed.

3. In order to preclude excessive charges (''double-dipping'') on the talent packages put together for television, agencies have devised alternative compensation approaches for themselves. The alternative, in its simplest form, and as described by Davis (1989), is to receive ''the equivalent of 5 percent of the money paid the show's production company by the network, 5 percent of half the profit, if any, the production company gets from the network, and 15 percent of the adjusted gross – basically, syndication sales less the costs not picked up by the network. . . . An agency like [William] Morris can expect to make anywhere from $21,000 to $100,000 from every episode of a network show, and the eventual take from the syndication of a hit can be staggering. The Cosby show, a Morris package, is expected to give the agency an income of $50 million from reruns alone.'' In consideration for negotiating and structuring television deals, many powerful agencies will charge 5% of revenues (including those derived from syndication). Others may charge a 3% packaging fee plus 10 percent of the ''backend''revenues.

A so-called 3%-3%-10% package had been the most common in the late 1980s, but more aggressive agents have extracted 5%-5%-10% formulas. The first figure is a percentage of the per episode license fee that is paid to the agent, which the agent receives for the life of the show. The second figure, also based on the license fee, is tied to the profitability of the series and is deferred until net profit is achieved. The third figure, however, is the one that is most lucrative to the agencies and is tied to the ''backend'' or syndication revenues.

See also *Variety,* March 25, 1991, and *Broadcasting,* September 23, 1991.

4. ICM was a subsidiary of Josephson International, which had been publicly traded. With the exception of the years in which Josephson was public, financial statements are not available. However, estimated revenues (in $ millions) and the number of agents in 1995 were as follows:

	Revenues	Agents
Creative Artists	$175	120
William Morris	125	105
International Creative Management	110	150
United Talent Agency	40	50

The number of clients represented by each agency ranges from 1,200 at CAA to 2,200 at ICM. See Lippman (1995).

CAA was formed by former William Morris agents in 1975 and over the next twenty years went on to become the most powerful movie packager in Hollywood, as well as the most broadly influential agency across all entertainment industry segments. In the movie business, package deals essentially turn studios into banks that finance film ideas generated outside the studio. See Akst and Landro (1988), Gubernick (1989b), and especially Davis (1989).

5. As of 1987, domestic rentals, according to *Variety,* were $6.7 million.

6. Arguably, an exception in 1993 was the flotation of the Australian *Lightning Jack* Film Trust of 36 million units to solely finance the $26 million Paul Hogan production. Still, nearly $3 million and three months were spent putting the deal together. Also, Australian tax laws helped by allowing investors to deduct 90% of their investment over two years. See *Hollywood Reporter,* 1993 Independent Producers Issue.

7. This, despite the fact that presales for domestic home video may be payable 25% upon commencement of principal photography, 25% upon delivery of an answer print, 25% three months after initial theatrical release, and the remainder on availability in home video markets.

8. Until the Tax Reform Act of 1986, which caused the gradual withdrawal of investment tax credits (ITCs) for the entertainment industry, such credits had been one of the most important sources of cash for movie and television-series producers. Feature films – recognized in the tax code as capital assets having useful lives of over three years – had been eligible for ITC treatment. Such qualification had resulted from the industry's lobbying efforts directed at Congress, and from precedents set in tax litigation involving Disney and MCA. In the 1970s, both companies won ITC benefits in appeals-court rulings. Dekom (1984, p. 194) discussed the ITC options available to filmmakers under Section 48K of the pre-1986 IRS code.

9. For illustrative purposes, though, it is nevertheless of interest to examine more closely several of the widely distributed pre-1986 limited partnerships. Good examples are to be found in the 1981 SLM Entertainment Ltd. offerings of participations in a package of MGM's films, and in the 1982, 1983, and 1984 Delphi-series packages of Columbia Pictures films that Merrill Lynch originated.

The SLM limited partnership was sold in units valued at $5,000, with a general partners' contribution of 1%. Investors shared up to 50% ownership with MGM of some 15 films (5 films were initially specified), and were entitled to 99% of capital-contribution recoupment and a sliding percentage of profits generated by those productions.

Similarly, in Delphi II (1983), the partnership retained all distribution rights, and until the limited partners received cash equal to their investment they were entitled to 99% of all cash distributions and equal allocation of all income, loss, or credits. After cash payments to limited partners equaled the proceeds of the offering (less selling commissions and marketing and sales management fees), the general partners were to receive 20% of all cash distributions. Any partnership losses were thus compensated out of distribution fees due the studio.

Delphi III (1984), also offered in units of $5,000 (for a total of $60 million), was even more favorable to investors because all distribution fees were to be deferred until the partnership recouped 100% of its share of a film's negative (production) costs. Only after that condition had been satisfied was the distributor entitled to recoup its deferred distribution fee of 17.5% of gross receipts from the film. In addition, Delphi III partners were entitled to 25% of net proceeds earned by a film (after deducting a 17.5% distribution fee), or 8% of gross receipts, whichever was greater. This ensured some payment to the partnership even if the film was unsuccessful.

10.   From the investors' perspective, the interest-free loan contains a not-so-obvious cost of inflation; i.e., the guaranteed return of capital is in absolute dollars, not inflation-adjusted dollars. Moreover, because HBO retains pay and syndication rights, major theatrical distributors would normally be reluctant to distribute Silver Screen features – perhaps unless offered a juicier-than-average distribution fee.

11.   As may be inferred, this type of partnership arrangement, and HBO's other participations (e.g., in TriStar Productions and in Orion Pictures), have made HBO a major force in feature-film production, as well as in distribution on pay-cable systems. HBO's interest in filmmaking stems from a simple economic fact: With such a large subscriber base, it often costs less (some $3 million to $6 million) to produce a feature directly for cable than to buy rights on a per-subscriber basis from the other studios. Also see Mair (1988).

12.   According to Securities Exchange Commission 10-K filings, as reported in *Variety* of May 10, 1989, Silver Screen Partners (SSP) I through IV were all profitable in 1988. SSP IV ended 1988 with net income of $16.15 per unit. Each unit was sold for $500 in June of 1988. In the same year, SSP III, which raised $300 million and invested in 19 pictures – including *Good Morning Vietnam, Three Men and a Baby,* and *Who Framed Roger Rabbit* – netted $61.63 per unit. Roughly, that would suggest that the return for the year, including these three extraordinarily popular films, was 12.3% on the base of $500 a unit. A discussion of film partnership financial performance through the 1980s appears in *Variety* November 5, 1990.

13.   Under Regulation D, accredited individual investors (as of 1986) are those with at least $1 million of liquid net worth and $200,000 of annual income in each of the two most recent years. Rules for a Regulation D offering are differentiated for issues of over and under $5 million. Offerings of under $1.5 million fall under Regulation A. See also Muller (1991). Perhaps the most noteworthy of such partnerships was FilmDallas, originally established in 1984 as a private limited partnership with an initial capital contribution of $2.4 million. This company subsequently produced the well-regarded low-budget pictures *Kiss of the Spider Woman* and *The Trip to Bountiful.*

14.   As in modern portfolio theory applied to stocks and bonds, diversification over many projects reduces overall risk. However, systemic risk, i.e., risk inherent to investment in the movie industry as a whole, cannot be diversified away. See, for example, Hagin (1979).

15.   In the mid-1990s, new financing structures, not all fully tested against tax and accounting challenges, began to emerge. The goal is to finance with off-balance sheet debt through, say, a bank joint venture that can defer and smooth some of the risks through pooling (cross-collateralization) of potential profits while still allowing the distribution company to earn its fees. See *Daily Variety,* February 21, 1997.

16.   For the lender, many other differences in structure and risk are also evident. The lender, for example, would be exposed to loss if, for whatever reason, a licensee failed to accept delivery of a completed picture. This would most likely occur in foreign jurisdictions, where remedies may be difficult to obtain. In contrast to most commercial loans, moreover, a motion picture loan will often be made for a term of more than three years because it will usually require more than three years for full syndication, network television, and other downstream revenues to be realized. The longer the term, of course, the greater the risk that the underlying credit conditions will become substantially changed. Also, interest payments and commitment fees would be larger. For all these reasons and more, a bank will advance less than the total value (usually less than 75%) of the presales advances.

17. This could arguably be compared to the average production cost of a major feature of $300,000 in 1940 and of $100,000 during the depths of the Depression in 1932.

18. But there were other inflationary influences too. Well-heeled people from outside the Hollywood establishment decided to apply to the movie business their fortunes earned in shopping centers, real estate, oil and gas exploration, and other diverse endeavors. Their infusive and intrusive effect on the industry's internally generated cash-flow and financing rhythms and processes added visibly to the aggressive bidding for scarce talent resources. Such neophyte investors may have been led astray by extrapolating the then record-breaking box-office performances of *Jaws* and *Star Wars* and by enthusiasm for the "new media" revolution.

19. Easy credit conditions in Japan during the late 1980s enabled Japanese companies to borrow at tax-adjusted rates of as low as 1% and boosted Japanese real estate and equity values to incredible heights. As a result, Japanese industrial companies such as Sony and Matsushita could bid for American movie studios (Matsushita bought MCA in 1990) at prices that no one else could come close to matching.

20. There are still a few instances, however, where feature films have been produced by small studios for modest sums. For example, Troma Inc., based in New York City, has specialized in the production and theatrical distribution of raunchy comedies that are also of interest to pay-cable networks. In addition, several other independent filmmakers now specialize in the production of low-budget features. EO Corporation (Earl Owensby) was another company (in North Carolina) that, in the early 1980s, specialized in films that appeal primarily to working-class and rural audiences.

Troma was featured in the work of Schumer (1982) and Trachtenberg (1984). See also Cox (1989b). EO Corporation was described in *Variety,* July 23, 1980, in *Esquire,* November 1980, and on the CBS *60 Minutes* program of August 8, 1982. Rosen and Hamilton (1987) also describe low-budget independent feature marketing and financing in more detail.

21. It is estimated that labor fringe benefits add 20%–30% to above-the-line costs and 30%–40% to below-the-line costs. Such costs have, on average, approximately doubled to $200,000 a day (for an "A" title) in the early 1990s as compared to the cost 10 years prior, while average shooting schedules have expanded from around 40 days to 60 days over the same time.

22. Therefore, to prevent major financial losses in case of natural or other catastrophe, and to secure the positions of major lenders on a picture (be they studios or banks), completion-bond guarantees must normally be obtained from specialty insurers. Such contracts were historically priced at about 6% of a film's budget, and with a 50% rebate in the event there were no claims. However, there is some variation depending on the riskiness of the location, on the previous experience of the director and producer, and on the size of the production budget. As a practical matter, lending institutions do not provide interim financing for projects whose completion is not assured. In order to activate loan agreements, independent producers must thus always obtain completion bonds in conjunction with signed distribution contracts from creditworthy organizations.

The worldwide completion bond business is about $300 million in size, and as Angeli (1991) notes, two companies, Film Finances, and The Completion Bond Company (a part of Transamerica Insurance since 1990) dominated the business in the early 1990s. Each of these companies had been guaranteeing over 100 pictures a year. By 1993, however, price competition, with rates often as low as 1% of budget, forced The Completion Bond Company to discontinue operations. As a result, a third company, International Film Guarantors, has become more important. And in late 1994, a new company, Cinema Completions International, a joint venture between insurance companies CNA and AON, was formed. Also see Scholl (1992) and *Variety,* April 12, 1993, and June 7, 1993.

23. The accounting classifications for below-the-line costs are thus normally broken into three components: production, post-production, and other.

24. It may be argued that the unions' featherbedding and work-restriction rules have also contributed to unemployment. Hollywood unemployment rates, as estimated from industry pension-plan contributions that depend on person-hours worked, are chronically high; they vary cyclically with changes in production starts and, to a lesser extent, secularly with growth of new entertainment media. Perhaps as a result, negotiations between the AMPTP and the guilds have not normally been cordial.

Relations became especially bitter during bargaining sessions in 1980 and 1981, when SAG and the Writers Guild demanded significant participation rights in license fees from new media sources such as pay-cable, discs, and cassettes. Then again, in 1988, the Writers Guild and the AMPTP sustained a lengthy strike centered on the issue of television residual payments. A settlement was ultimately reached on a formula with elements similar to those used for television-license residuals – originally negotiated in the early days of television by SAG's then-president, Ronald Reagan.

In outline, the writers agreed to 2% of producers' revenues after the producer had recouped $1 million per hour of taped programming and $1.2 million per hour of filmed programming from any combination of sales to pay-television systems, videodiscs, and cassettes. Actors received residuals for original programming made for pay-television and received 4.5% of a distributor's gross after a program had played for 10 days within a year on each pay-television system.

In the 1983 SAG-AFTRA settlement with the AMPTP, there was an increase from 4.5% to 6% of distributors' gross (4.95% to 6.66% counting pension and welfare contributions), and no change in the terms requiring sales of 100,000 videocassettes before compensation begins.

In 1984, the Directors Guild won an increase in the share of residuals from films distributed on videocassettes. Directors had been entitled to 1.2% of producers' revenues on cassette sales, but under the 1984 contract this rose to 1.5% of the first $1 million and 1.8% thereafter. The directors had initially sought to link home-video royalties to the much larger base of distributors' revenues. Also, under the previous agreement, directors are entitled to receive a fraction of a cent for each subscriber to pay-television systems until a production has recouped $2 million per hour of programming. They are then entitled to 2% of gross receipts.

25. Seligman (1982) supports the notion that in the absence of union featherbedding and other work-restriction rules, the available capital resources for production could be spread over more film starts, capital costs would be lower, and moviemakers would not be as eager to shift production to foreign locations, where wages are lower. Also, labor inefficiencies raise the cost of capital by inordinately increasing investors' risk of loss. Over the long run, such higher capital costs would tend to reduce employment growth opportunities by decreasing the number of film starts.

26. Article 20 is controversial because studios can cut costs by developing a film concept, farming it out to a nonunion independent, and then take it back for distribution as a negative pickup while claiming to have no creative control. See Cones (1995, p. 56) and *Variety* September 14, 1992.

27. With widespread availability of pay-per-view cable, for instance, studios will have the potential to generate millions of dollars by one-night showings of their most important films. This would, in effect, raise viewing prices per person well beyond those traditionally received from subscription-television channels (see Chapter 7).

However, total revenues might be adversely affected by diminishing contributions from markets pushed farther downstream in the distribution sequence: For example, now that films are first widely exposed to large pay-cable audiences, broadcast networks are, with only a few exceptions, no longer as interested in bidding aggressively for licenses to run theatrical features. Networks seem more interested in first-run made-for-television productions, which are less expensive and often more effective in generating high ratings.

Windowing strategies, as Owen and Wildman (1992, p. 30) have noted, must therefore account for many factors, among which they list:

(a) differences in per-viewer prices earned in different channels of distribution;

(b) incremental differences in each channel's contribution to a program's total audience;

(c) interest rates as a measure of opportunity costs of money;

(d) the extent to which viewers of one channel are eliminated as viewers of another;

(e) the vulnerability of each channel to unauthorized copying;

(f) the rate at which viewing interest declines after initial release.

28. Indeed, there are indications that major pay-per-view film events might, in the future, become scheduled just ahead of theatrical release. In 1995, Carolco and Tele-Communications Inc. planned to make the first attempts at this, but with no follow-through. However, an old example of rearranged sequencing occured in 1980, when Twentieth Century Fox showed *Breaking Away* on network television before showing on pay-cable. Fox even contemplated simultaneous release in theaters and on videocassettes. But the market was not, and is probably still not, quite ready for this idea because, for most pictures, the greatest marginal revenue per unit time remains to be derived from theatrical issue. Moreover, most pictures require theatrical release in order to generate interest from sources further down the line. Thus, for the foreseeable future, theatrical release will come first for the great majority of films. Also see section 2.4.

29. A pure public good is defined by economists as one for which the cost of production is independent of the number of people who consume it. This would apply, for example, to television programs or to other performances as discussed in section 12.4. See also Glossary.

30. Such bid letters would always include a schedule of admissions prices, the number of showings on weekends and weekdays, the number of seats in the auditorium in which the film is expected to play, and other conditions that the distributor might find desirable. Some studios prefer to bid their pictures, and some don't, or they will bid their pictures only in some cities or under special circumstances. The process itself, however, is often in the nature of a public auction. As already noted, the majority of exhibition licenses are negotiated. Whether bid or negotiated, under a gross-receipts formula, first-run film rental usually begins at 70% of box office admissions receipts and gradually declines to as low as 30% over a period of four to seven weeks. And second-run rentals begin at 35% of box office admissions and often decline to 30% after the first week. For instance, in the 1995 release of *Batman Forever,* the admissions revenue sharing formula terms were 90/10 (after house expenses) for the first three weeks and 80/20 for the next three weeks; or, under the gross receipts formula, theaters paid 65% of the aggregate box office for the run, whichever formula was higher.

Although there has been little formal economic analysis of bidding behavior in the movie business, game theory provides many economic bidding models that could be readily adapted; for example, see Davis (1973).

31. Use of "clearance" rights became an issue with Sony's June 1996 release of *Cable Guy,* in which Sony attempted to open the picture as wide as possible in metropolitan areas by asking national theater owners for a waiver on clearances. Some theater owners agreed to honor Sony's request. See *The Hollywood Reporter,* June 13, 1996.

32. More details on this can be found in section 4.3, where a sample calculation illustrating split percentages and minimum conditions can be found.

33. In mid-1983, a U.S. District Court ruled that splits are a form of price fixing and an illegal market allocation in violation of the Sherman Antitrust Act. According to the court's ruling, split agreements entered into by Milwaukee exhibitors caused the amounts paid to distributors to be reduced by 92% from $1.8 million in 1977 to $140,000 in 1981. The ruling had been appealed by the defendant exhibitors (see *Hollywood Reporter,* June 22, 1983, *Variety,* March 23, 1988, and other legal transcriptions regarding the Kerasotes Theater cases). The practice of product splitting was brought to the attention of the Department of Justice by distributors, who responded to exhibitors' charges that distributors had been illegally engaged in the practice of block booking.

34. Real-estate value is the key determinant as to whether or not existing theater sites can be used more profitability for office buildings, parking lots, or other purposes. Standard-discounted-cash-flow and internal-rate-of-return modeling, as explained by Van Horne (1968), can be applied.

To illustrate, consider a theater generating an average annual net income of $100,000 over its expected 10-year life. The internal rate of return on an original $500,000 investment will be just over 15%. However, if the required rate of return is 18%, then, using the net-present-value (NPV) method, the net present value of this theater is about $450,000.

35. If each household pays $4, if one-third of that is remitted as rental to the distributor (the remainder to cable operators and program wholesalers), and if there are 15 million households, then $20 million will be generated. There is an additional benefit to the distributor because of the much faster cash return than from theaters.

36. Pressure to do well on opening weekends has been significantly intensified in recent years. It all began with *Jaws* in 1975, which was the first major film nationally advertised and widely released, day and date, on over 700 screens. Nowadays, pictures that do less than $10 million in domestic box office on an opening weekend are likely to be pulled rather quickly. Conversely, a film that declines by 20% or less on its *second* weekend is considered to be a potentially large winner.

It also occasionally happens that one strong film will block another. Such a situation arose when the long-running *Star Wars* blocked the timely exhibition of a previously booked run of *Close Encounters of the Third Kind,* thereby starting a round of lawsuits and countersuits involving distributors and an exhibitor. Details on this particular situation can be found in *Variety,* December 21, 1977. But note also, that to get around this problem, exhibitors occasionally "piggyback" one film with another in violation of their contracts.

37. Moreover, in theory, an even better measure of how one film has performed as compared with another can be derived by calculating the percentages of potential total weekly exhibitor capacity that the films have utilized. It would, for instance, be interesting to see how opening-week receipts from *Indiana Jones* compared with opening-week receipts from *Superman*, by deriving for each picture a capacity-utilization percentage – profiled first across the whole industry's capacity and then across the capacity of theaters that played both pictures in their initial weeks of release. Unfortunately, data of this kind are rarely available.

Opening weekend gross receipts for important releases are, however, carefully analyzed and compared to those of previous important releases. As of May 1997, *The Lost World: Jurassic Park* had generated the largest three-day opening weekend, with receipts of $72.4 million, and a four-day total of $92.7 million. The prior four-day record, was set by *Mission: Impossible,* with a total of $56.8 million in May 1996. In 1995, *Batman Forever* generated a three-day opening weekend with receipts of $52.8 million. And in 1993, *Jurassic Park* generated $50.2 million in three days. *Lost World* also holds the record for the highest single-day grosses for Friday ($22 million), Saturday ($24.8 million), and Sunday ($25.6 million). Opening weeks for an average picture accounted for 32% of a film's total theatrical gross in 1996 versus 24% in 1990.

38. The correlation between number of releases and rentals percentage is about −0.4.

39. At first, of course, it was not at all clear how the home video market would evolve. As described in detail by Lardner (1987), the videocassette recorder (VCR) was introduced by the Sony Corporation in 1975, yet it was not then at all evident that it would prevail. The machine was not perceived as something for which plentiful software in the form of movies would be available: at the time, there was no prerecorded software. And the machine, known as the Betamax, could only record on one-hour magnetic tape cassettes. Worse still, it soon faced competition from a noncompatible but similar two-hour video-cassette format, the VHS system (Video Home System), that was quickly introduced by Sony's manufacturing rival, Matsushita. This battle of the formats caused great confusion and hampered the initial growth of the market for VCRs, following as it did close on the heels of earlier home-video technologies that had notoriously failed. Those technologies included the so-called Electronic Video Recording (EVR) system, developed by Dr. Peter Goldmark at CBS Laboratories in the late 1960s, and Cartrivision. See Lessing (1971) for a description of Cartrivision and Donnelly (1986) for a quick overview of the development of EVR.

Note also, that by the late 1970s, consumers were being introduced to so-called videodisc players that did not have a recording capability and were therefore useless for "time-shifting," i.e., recording a program for delayed viewing. These videodisc machines were developed in two versions: a laser/optical system (closely related to the now standardized system in compact disc players) that used a laser beam to read encoded video and audio signals, and a capacitance system that used a stylus to skim a recording and measure changes in electrical capacitance. Both versions fared poorly and were eventually withdrawn by their respective corporate sponsors. The optical video disc was at the time promoted by MCA and Pioneer, while RCA spent hundreds of millions of dollars before scrapping the capacitance system in 1984.

Although early optical videodiscs obviously did not gain wide acceptance, modern formats that are compatible with compact disc players for music (see also Chapter 5) are likely to coexist with magnetic tape technologies for the foreseeable future. And indeed, as of the mid-1990s, erasable/recordable optical disc media seem poised to take a significant market share.

40. This despite the fact that the studios initially fought hard against the introduction of VCRs into the home. See the Chapter 5 discussion of the First Sale Doctrine.

41. It seems likely that the proportion of feature films to other home video software categories (e.g., exercise, instructional, etc.) will in the foreseeable future, remain fairly close to the two-to-one ratio that has thus far prevailed.

42. As described by Blumenthal and Goodenough (1991), for example, the cost of manufacturing a cassette is under $4.50 a unit, including $1.00 for packaging, $1.00 for raw materials and duplication, and $1.50 for royalties and copyrights.

43. Estimates by New York video consulting firm Alexander & Associates further indicate that in 1996 there were:

Total video rentals	4.23 billion
Average price paid	$2.71
Total rental revenue	$11.45 billion
Total purchases	735.1 million
Average price paid	$14.12
Total purchase revenue	$10.38 billion

Accordingly, total consumer spending of $21.83 billion ($11.45 plus $10.38) here compares to $14.0 billion estimated by the *Video Store* data illustrated in Figure 3.5. *Video Store* data are believed to include mostly larger retailers and may thus understate the industry's size.

Also, from the retailer's perspective, at an average per rental price of $3.00 and an average cost per tape of $66, it takes at least 22 turns over a period of 4–6 weeks to reach break even. The early weeks usually generate 40% of the total expected for the first 6 months after release.

44. As of the early 1990s, film company distributors, in effect, the ''publishers'' of home video titles, generally sold units designated for the rental market at a 37% discount to the suggested retail price. As noted by R. Childs in Squire (1992), this figure is derived from a ''30 plus 10'' formula, in which the retailer buys at 30% discount, and 10% of the balance (7%) goes to wholesalers. This then leaves the film distribution company (the publisher) with 63% of the suggested retail price.

45. This is because of the First Sale Doctrine. However, if special arrangements known as pay-per-transaction were agreed upon in advance, there is no theoretical reason for the distributor not to participate in subsequent rental income. Several companies have, with varying degrees of success, established such pay-per-transaction operations.

46. As of the mid-1990s, the indicated crossover point was around 1.6 million sell-through units, or about four times what could be expected from the rental market. But in consideration of higher marketing costs, most distributors would want to be assured of a ratio of six to ten times the number of rental units before deciding on a sell-through strategy.

As of 1992, for example, the priced-for-rental best-seller of all time was *Ghost*, which shipped about 645,000 units. This, in effect, implies that currently a realistic ceiling in the rental unit market is on average around one-half million units. If so, the marketing decision becomes relatively easy since the for-rental revenues under these conditions peak at roughly $32 million ($100 a unit times 0.63 times 500,000). Assuming a $13.50 wholesale sell-through price, for–rental market revenues would be exceeded with sell-through shipments of 2.4 million units – which, as the following commentary indicates, has been readily exceeded by many ''A''titles.

On *Top Gun,* for example, Paramount decided to promote a sell-through by going with a suggested retail price of around $25 (but with the tape including a brief Pepsi-Cola advertisement). Paramount ended up selling almost three million units, thereby generating over $40 million in revenues. Given that the cost of manufacturing the physical product was (and is still) so low, Paramount probably netted over $30 million in profits from this one home video release. In this situation, Paramount almost surely generated more profit in targeting the sell-through rather than rental market.

Disney, however, was able to exceed Paramount's *Top Gun* numbers with its Christmas 1987 release of *Lady and the Tramp* (3 million units), its 1990 releases of *Pretty Woman* (6 million), and *The Little Mermaid* (9.8 million) at a $20 retail price. Also, the Christmas 1988 release of *Cinderella* sold 7.2 million units, and the spring 1992 release of *101 Dalmatians* sold 11 million. Disney holds the sell-through record with its 1995 release of *Lion King* (30 million), which exceeded the 1994 release of *Snow White* (27 million units), the 1993 release of *Aladdin* (24 million units), *Beauty and the Beast* (21 million domestic units in 1992), and *Fantasia* (nearly 14.2 million copies in the U.S. and Canada during a 50-day period in 1991). The previous record was MCA's 1988 issue of *E.T.*, which sold 12.5 million units at a retail price (after a $5 rebate) of around $20. Warner's *Batman* in 1989 generated unit sales of 9.5 million, also at a $20 retail price point. And MCA's *Jurassic Park* sold 21 million units in 1994. Only 13 titles went as sell-through in 1992, but there were 19 in 1994, 27 in 1995, and 32 in 1996.

47. Interestingly, video revenues often turn out to be the same percentage of production costs, as are the costs of prints and advertising (p & a). Thus, a convenient rule-of-thumb is to look for video revenue to approximate p & a.

48. ''Fractured-rights'' deals – in which producers could package a film idea, presell domestic and international video rights, and then arrange for a major studio to distribute (for a fee) in domestic theatrical markets – flourished during the first days of the home video business in the early to mid-1980s. Such presales typically covered all of the production and most, if not all, of the domestic releasing costs – leaving the producer's share of theatrical revenues and television rights as potential sources of profit. Such deals worked until the studios developed strong video distribution facilities of their own, and as long as banks were willing to fund such production costs. Once the value of home video and international rights failed to keep pace with the rise of production and releasing costs, the viability of such deals fell apart. However, by the early 1990s, so-called ''split-rights'' deals in which a studio took *all* domestic rights, while a producer retained international rights, came into greater use. Studios today will rarely split domestic rights.

49. Note also that in return for making a commitment to finance (or partially finance) a picture, an independent home-video distributor would normally insist that the picture receive a predetermined amount of support in initial theatrical release through spending on prints and advertising, or p & a as it is known. Such p & a commitments are important because they, in effect, ''legitimize'' the picture by bringing name recognition to what is hoped will be a broad audience for the home-video product. Home-video distribution rights contracts with independent filmmakers will typically extend over seven years. And the producer might normally receive an advance against a royalty base of between 20% to 40% – i.e., the producer of a $20 million picture could expect an advance of between $4 million and $8 million for domestic home-video rights.

Perhaps the best-known home-video independent of the mid-1980s was Vestron, which went public in 1985 in the hopes of becoming an important video alternative to the releasing arms of the majors. However, the company ultimately failed once the majors took full control of their video rights and after Vestron attempted to develop its own library of feature films.

50. Interest in this area was heightened with Disney's 1994 direct-to-video release of the *Aladdin* sequel *Return of Jafar,* which at a production cost of $5 million generated estimated wholesale revenues of $120 million on unit sales of 11 million. See Hofmeister (1994).

51. Already, for example, there is evidence that the frequency of home-video rental – which had averaged almost one tape a week for the typical VCR-owning household of the late 1980s – is declining in the 1990s even though the cost of an overnight rental (averaging around $2.50 per night in 1997) is low.

In recent years, however, large video superstores such as Blockbuster Entertainment have emerged and have indeed become one of Hollywood's major customers – buying $1.3 billion of tapes a year as of 1997. Such stores compete on service by carrying many thousands of titles and by having great depth-of-copy (i.e., lots of copies) of the most popular films. Because of this, they may be somewhat resistant to the inroads being made by PPV cable.

Video rental store profits are derived from fast turnover of a title in the first six months after release in videocassette format. With overhead and other costs included, the normal retailer would probably require at least 30 turns in order to break even. And in 1992, the typical cassette was rented an average of some 50 times.

Note also that video stores are able to measure gross profits by multiplying the number of times a copy is rented by the average rental price, adding salvage-value revenues, and then subtracting the cost of the tape. For each title, the average weekly turns per copy thus becomes the critical variable.

52. Many published products are designed for purposes of entertainment. Although comic and children's books are among the most obvious categories, most, if not all, fiction and some nonfiction also qualifies. Moreover, newspapers and magazines often have entertainment motives in mind when they publish about personalities or develop "lighter" subjects or "style" or "leisure" sections. Indeed, as Table 1.4 illustrates, sales of newspapers, books, and magazines are included in National Income Accounting data as a part of recreation expenditures.

More recently, the publishing industry has become involved in what is generally called multimedia – products and services blending digitalized images, sounds, and text that can be used with personal computers and distributed over cable, telephone, or wireless networks. See Chapter 8.

53. North American retail sales of entertainment-based licensed merchandise were estimated by the *Licensing Letter,* a trade publication, to have been $16.2 billion in 1995.

Most royalties would be in the area of 5% to 6% of the value of wholesale shipments, but the percentages can reach higher, and terms might also include advances and guarantees against royalties. Of such revenues, producers might, depending on contractual details, be entitled to perhaps a 25% to 50% share. And, on products using an actor's visage, the percentage can range from 2.5% to 8.0% of the studio's net.

An example of how lucrative merchandising can be is provided by the 1989 release of *Batman,* in which the distributor, Warner Bros., received licensing fees ranging from $2,000 to $50,000 plus royalties of 8% to 10% on revenues estimated to be $250 million in the first year of release. See Lipman (1990). Also, Lane (1994) further illustrates the merchandise potential from *Jurassic Park.*

54. Independent producers in particular also incur additional costs in attempting to market their pictures directly at various international marketing conventions, the most important of which are the American Film Market (AFM) based in Los Angeles in March, the Cannes Film Festival held in Cannes, France, in early May, and MIFED, a somewhat similar event held in Milan, Italy, each October. Negotiations between foreign sales agents and foreign distributors' representatives form the core of these conventions.

Television producers and distributors also have several marketing conventions, including the midwinter National Association of Television Program Executives (NATPE), held in the United States, and the March Internationale des Programmes de Television (MIP), held each spring in France.

55. In fact, the study by De Vany and Walls (1996) delves deeply into the dynamics of demand for movies, suggesting that the industry's structure is well-suited to adapt sequentially to changes in supply and to provide reliable signals of demand given relatively fixed admissions prices and real time reporting of box office revenues. This important study also indicated that: (a) weekly revenues are autocorrelated; (b) audiences select or ignore films largely through an informational cascade in which individuals follow the behavior of preceding individuals or "opinion-makers" without regard to their own information; (c) widely released films show more variance in revenues and, on average, shorter run lives; (d) distribution of box office revenue is not log normal; (e) revenues in the industry follow a Bose-Einstein distribution in which outcomes differing "in the extreme are equally likely and similar outcomes are extremely unlikely" – "the quintessential characteristic of the movie business." Informational cascades are analyzed in Bikhchandani, Hirshleifer, and Welch (1992).

56. But generally, as Kagan (1995) illustrates, the following rule-of-thumb relationships derived over a large sample of major studio releases between the years 1989 to 1993 would seem to apply:

* To reach cash-on-cash breakeven, *domestic box-office receipts should approximate the negative cost* (or, comparably, half of the negative cost should be recovered from domestic theatrical rentals)

* Worldwide rentals (including all theatrical, home video, cable, tv receipts, etc.) tend to be twice the domestic box-office receipts.

57. Although it is not usually practicable to calculate precisely the return on investment (ROI) for a specific production, such a figure could be approximated by taking the total profit (if any) of all participants, adding the cost of capital, and then dividing by the total amount invested.

A simple ROI estimate for a purely hypothetical distributor-financed project that ignores the effects of typical cash-flow delays, compounding of interest, and taxes might then be made as follows: The assumed distributors' gross from all sources is $30 million.

(*a*) Distributor profit from distribution fee, overhead charge, and other sources: $5 million

(*b*) Distributor share of net profit: $3 million

(*c*) Producer share of net profit: $3 million

(*d*) Cost of capital: $2 million

(*e*) Total investment including negative and marketing (prints and ads): $30 million

The return on investment (over two years) is

$$\text{ROI} = 100 \ (a + b + c + d)/e = 43.3\%$$

or 21.7% per annum.

To be placed in proper perspective, this rate should always be annualized and compared with the risk-free rate of return available on government securities during the period the

film project went through its life cycle (from production start to ancillary-market release).
58. Even with the aforementioned advantages, however, it is not always easy for a studio
to be profitable. Assuming, for example, a full production slate of 20 pictures per year
made at an average cost of $25 million (which includes overhead and operating expenses),
and prints and advertising at an average of $10 million per movie, there is a total investment
of $700 million to be amortized over the releasing cycle. Further assuming that 40% of
this cost is to be amortized against theatrical revenues (see Chapter 4), the minimum
theatrical distributors' gross in order to reach break-even would have to be $280 million.
Using an approximate industry rentals percentage of 42%, this is equivalent to $667 million
(in retail terms) at the box office. With total domestic box-office figures in 1993 having been around $5 billion, such a studio would require a minimum market share of over
13% in order to break even. Yet, as of the early 1990s, with the equivalent of some eight
major studios in operation, a share of that size has become much more difficult to obtain
regularly. As shown in Supplementary Table S2.4, there have been many years when
– in a less crowded field than today – various studios have achieved much less than
10% share.

Chapter 4

1. Copyright 1951 and 1952 by Paramount–Roy Rogers Music Co., Inc. Copyright renewed 1979 and 1980 and assigned to Paramount–Roy Rogers Music Co., Inc.
2. Rosen (1981) was the first to provide rigorous economic analysis to the ''superstar''
phenomenon. Subsequent papers on the same subject include Adler (1985), MacDonald
(1988), and Hamlen (1991). See also, Frank and Cook (1995).
3. Litigation concerning *Bad News Bears,* which was licensed to ABC by Paramount for
$6.75 million as part of an $18.5 million package, helped set legal precedent in a 1979
lawsuit. Details are in *Variety,* January 21, 1981, and July 2, 1980.
4. Companies using amortization tables periodically tested their continuing validity
based on actual experience, with most tables amortizing total production costs allocated
to theatrical exhibition over a 104-week period by charges to income equal to about 65%
of such costs in the first 26 weeks of release and 90% in 52 weeks.

MCA Inc., for example, had amortized according to tables prior to FASB statement 53,
but found that such estimates were not consistent with those on an individual-picture basis.
In order to restore consistency, in 1981 the company adjusted its inventories on films
already released by taking a ''write-down'' of about $50 million against previous years'
retained earnings.
5. There were also some 16mm screenings at educational and penal institutions.
6. Growth in television revenues is illustrated by the following: In 1956, MGM received
about $250,000 for a network showing of *Gone with the Wind;* in 1979, based on a $35-
million face-value 20-year contract with CBS, the average per run was over $1 million.
More recently, networks have been paying record amounts for top films. For example, in
a 1994 agreement, NBC paid MCA $50 million for pre-cable rights (four runs) of *Jurassic
Park.* And, in 1996, ABC acquired the rights to two runs (after pay-per-view and pay
cable) to *Mission: Impossible* for $18 million to $22 million, depending on box office
performance. Also, the Fox network agreed in 1997 to pay $80 million for early broadcast
rights to *Lost World.*

7. In 1995, the FASB and the AICPA began work on new rules that would look at Hollywood's accounting for advertising costs, on the discrepancy between reporting a profit for the studio and a loss for participants, and the possibility that filmmakers might continue to declare profits even up to the point of bankruptcy.

8. To illustrate, when Lorimar-Telepictures was acquired by Warner Communications in early 1989, over $450 million of its equity was eliminated through adoption of Warner's more conservative accounting practices.

The sensitivity of reported earnings to relatively small changes in early period revenue estimates is also substantial. As a rule-of-thumb, a 10% increase in total estimated revenues could normally be expected to at least double profit margins in such early periods.

Also, companies with high inventory-to-sales ratios will generally correlate with optimistic projections of income ultimates, and vice versa.

9. Leedy (1980, p. 9) expresses the view that accrual accounting would be to the detriment of outside participants.

10. The quasi-reorganization of Filmways Corporation in 1982 illustrates this point well. A spate of expensive box-office failures had led Filmways into financial difficulties. It was only through injection of fresh capital and reorganization that the company was saved from probable bankruptcy.

As applied here, the ''quasi'' is a form of purchase accounting in which the film library is assessed on a picture-by-picture basis, with some written up and some written down. New amortization rates are then established for recent releases and in-process productions, and a fair market valuation of the company's distribution system is made. In the case of Filmways, an immediate cash infusion of $26 million (in exchange for issuance of debt and equity securities) combined with sale of assets and various accounting adjustments gave the company a new lease on life under the name of Orion Pictures. Although according to the rules, tax credits previously accumulated from the Filmways net operating losses had to be abandoned, the film library (composed of over 600 theatrical and television motion pictures) was written up by $18.2 million. In addition, the distribution system, which had not been on the balance sheet as such, was assigned an estimated fair-market value of $14 million (out of the eliminated $22.2 million in goodwill carried on the prior company's books).

Welles (1983) discusses Orion's quasi-reorganization and overhead-amortization accounting policies in a generally critical vein. Management, however, notes that a quasi is not all that uncommon and that the reorganization was done in consultation with various regulatory agencies and under the guidance of auditors from Arthur Young & Co. Filmways' auditor had been Arthur Andersen & Co.

MGM's acquisition in 1981 of United Artists Corporation from Transamerica Corporation provides another example of applied purchase-method accounting. The $380 million purchase price was allocated to the assets and liabilities of United Artists based on independent appraisals of such assets and liabilities. That portion of the acquisition cost not allocated to specific assets – in other words, goodwill – and the appraised value of the worldwide distribution organization acquired in the purchase of United Artists were to be amortized on a straight-line basis, over a 40-year period. The interesting contrast here, though, is that MGM's assigned distribution-system value of $190 million is being amortized over 40 years, whereas Orion's distribution system is being amortized on a straight-line basis over only 25 years. A faster amortization rate, of course, places a greater burden on current reported income.

11. If a picture is completed on time, and is within 10% of budget, as much as half the premium may be refunded. See also Chapter 3, note 22.

12. A notable exception to the standard 30% theatrical rate existed in the 1970s when United Artists distributed MGM's products for 22.5% of gross. Also, limited financing partnerships such as those discussed in Chapter 3 have more recently been able to obtain agreements for below-average rates.

13. Return on investment in this example is, simplistically, 54% (i.e., $8.1 million/$15 million). However, many other factors, including length of time needed to make the movie, taxes, and so forth, would need to be known in order to make useful comparisons.

14. However, as Cones (1995, p. 46) notes, "when a film is independently financed and presented to a distributor for pickup, that transaction is more accurately referred to as an *acquisition*. The term *negative pickup* should be more properly reserved to describe lender-financed transactions.

15. After seeing what is in most cases the equivalent of a rough draft of the movie, an interested distributor will attempt to forecast a minimum rentals expectation and then offer an advance toward further production and postproduction costs based on the forecast. Knowing, for example, that distribution expenses for release in, say, the 450 theaters sought by the producer will be $6 million, and taking a standard distribution fee of 30%, the distributor will break even on film rentals of $20 million.

Minimum distribution expense/fee = distributor's break-even
$6,000,000/30% = $20,000,000

Given these circumstances the distributor could extend a maximum advance of $14 million to the producer or promoter.

However, the amount of advance actually offered by the distributor may be only half of that indicated because: (a) The distributor requires a cushion against the risk that the rentals forecast may turn out to be too optimistic; (b) The distributor is in business to do better than break even; (c) Not all distribution expenses are included in the minimum figure; (d) This variable-cost example does not reflect the large fixed costs of maintaining a major distribution organization, nor does it reflect studio operating expenses; (e) Studio distribution slot availabilities are time-perishable.

See also, Curran (1986) and Baumgarten, Farber, and Fleischer (1992).

16. Essentially, the bigger the budget, the more costly the advertising campaign, and the more gross players, the less the likelihood that the net profits point will be reached. Gross participants payments, for example, are cycled back into the negative cost. As a rough approximation, net profits are achieved when the studio's revenues are about 1.5 times the studio's costs of production and promotion, including the salaries of the stars. According to Robb (1992), net profits of $155 million were paid to 94 participants on Paramount releases between the years 1974 and 1987.

17. Current studio agreements tend to use phrases such as "defined proceeds" instead of "net profits." This comes in the wake of a well-publicized dispute over the definition of "profits" developed in a 1990 case in which writer Art Buchwald won credit in a state court for developing the concept behind Paramount's *Coming to America*, one of the highest-grossing films of 1988. The issue then fought in Los Angeles Superior Court concerned the definition of such profits. Studios would generally argue that they deserve to take a large part of their profits up front in order to compensate for the risk of investing their money in flops that never show any return on investment. Buchwald, however, argued that such up-front studio profits should not come at the expense of net profit participants and that such net profit contracts are unfairly manipulated by the studios. Good overviews of this case are presented in Stevenson (1990), Weinstein (1998), and especially by Robb (1990a) and (1990b), with the Buchwald side fully described in O'Donnell and McDougal

(1992). The accountings for this picture (in $ millions) by Paramount and by Buchwald's attorney were as follows:

Paramount

Gross receipts	$125
−distribution fee	−42
	$83
−distribution expenses	−36
	$47
−Murphy, Landis gross participations	−11
	$36
− interest	−5 to 6
	$30 to 31
− negative costs including direct production costs, and studio overhead	$48
net deficit	$17 to 18

Buchwald's Interpretation

Income	$151
− distribution fee	53
	$98
− distribution expenses	40
	$58
− negative costs including direct production costs studio overhead, and gross participations	$63
deficit	$5
− interest	$6.2
net deficit	$11.2

The accounting for one of Warner Bros.'s largest box-office hits, *Batman*, has also been revealed, and it suggests that net–profit participants will probably not be compensated. McDougal (1991) shows that as of 1991, the film had grossed $253.4 million from all sources, but from that amount the distribution fee of 35% or $80 million was first, as usual, taken out. Then, expenses included:

Advertising and publicity	$62.4
Prints	9.0
Editing & dubbing	1.1
Taxes, duties, & customs	4.7
Trade association fees	2.1
Freight, handling, insurance	1.4
Checking, collection, etc.	1.6
Guild & union residuals	1.6

These expenses, however, do not include the film's actual production cost, at $53.5 million, interest charges, and gross-profit participations. Through September 1990, interest on the entire production cost was $10.8 million. Yet it was gross-participations, especially that of star actor Jack Nicholson (who played The Joker), that truly rolled the break-even point upward. In addition to an "up-front" fee advance of $6 million, the actor also reportedly negotiated to receive 15% of the gross, with an escalator clause that ultimately brought his total percentage of the gross close to 20%. Other participants had similar advances-against-gross embedded in the film's production cost, but at much smaller "adjusted gross" levels. In all, the gross-profit participants took about $60 million of the film's income and left net-profit participants with nothing.

Several other examples of profit participation statements, for example, *Who Framed Roger Rabbit, Three Men and a Baby*, and *Beverly Hills Cop* are shown in Robb (1992). And the effect of gross participations can also be seen in the case of *Last Action Hero*, wherein production, overhead, and p & a costs of $150 million were almost fully recouped from all markets until gross participation talent and interest costs ate up another $15 million. See *Variety*, September 13, 1993 and also *Daily Variety* November 20, 1995. As of early 1997, a suit concerning net profits contracts for the film *JFK* was moving through the courts.

18. Breimer (1995, p. 76) notes that studios also receive benefit from any nonreturnable advances for sale of cable or home-video rights and that such advances are not included in calculation of participants' grosses until they are *earned*. Here, again, there is a different definition for the studio and for the participant.

19. A simple example makes the point. If, for instance, half a million cassettes are sold at $50 a unit, $5 million might be credited to gross receipts of the participant, out of which a distribution fee is taken. But the studio, in this illustration, retains $20 million out of total revenues. And after deduction of expenses of perhaps $6 a unit for manu-facturing, sales, and advertising, and perhaps another $2 a unit to cover overhead, the studio-distributor still has a gross profit of $16 million ($20 million minus $8 times 500,000) before adding back the distribution fee earned out of the participant's gross receipts.

Moreover, from the industry's viewpoint, a fix on the order of magnitude can be obtained by assuming, say, that each studio on average releases about 20 titles a year (less than two a month), that each title sells a domestic average of 200,000 units, and that the gross profit per unit, blending both sell-through and rental titles, is $10. Then with the equivalent of seven studios, total gross profits from domestic shipments would be $280 million. Further assuming that foreign home video profits are at least as much would imply that aggregate studio profits from home video may be in the area of $600 million, or about half of what total industry profits had been in the early 1990s.

20. A study sponsored by the National Association of Concessionaires and Coca-Cola indicated that in dollar terms about 40% of refreshment-stand sales come from pop-corn, 40% from soft drinks, and 20% from food items and candy. A 1990 study further indicated that at some theaters, concession sales may account for 90% of profits. The reason: A soft drink priced at $2.50 may cost the owner less than 25 cents. As of 1990, the national average spent on snack bar items was $1.20, with urban area averages around $1.60.

21. For instance, in its 1988 annual report, Cineplex Odeon shows a significant operating income figure, yet if profits from real estate transactions are excluded, it can be seen that the company's basic theater business operated at a loss. See also Wechsler (1989).

22. The cost of operating a major domestic-distribution organization is estimated to be $30 million annually as of the mid-1990s. Assuming an average fee of 33%, this $30 million "nut," which covers sales expenses, is earned after the first $100 million of theatrical rentals. But as A. D. Murphy notes in Squire (1992, p. 286), earnings in excess of that figure should not be called profits "in the sense of free-and-clear money available for dividends and such." The excess is instead first largely used to recover other out-of-pocket unrecouped marketing and production costs and is also recycled into new film productions. See also Wechsler (1990).

23. Donahue (1987, p. 183) provides a good example: ". . . a picture earns $10 million in film rental while the marketing costs amount to $5 million. In the distribution fee deal, the distributor takes $3 million and costs are recouped out of the $7 million, with $2 million left for the producer. In the gross percentage deal, the independent producer receives $3 million, costs are recouped out of the $7 million, leaving $2 million for the distributor."

24. Major studios, however, no longer include overhead in the budgets of their own productions.

25. This example follows Garey (1983, p. 104).

26. The old rule of thumb is that the box-office gross must be two or three times the negative cost to reach break-even. However, for major-event pictures, this ratio might actually be nearer to two times.

27. The following is a partial list of companies that, since the early 1970s, have attempted to enter production and either have failed totally or have substantially withdrawn from the field: ABC Pictures (ABC's first venture distributed by Cinerama in the early 1970s), Associated Communications, Avco-Embassy, Cannon Group, Cinema Center Films (CBS's first venture distributed by National General in the early 1970s), De Laurentiis Entertainment Group, Filmways (reconstituted as Orion), General Cinema Corp., and Time-Life Films. Some of these production entities had considerable financial backing and experience and yet (the new-media revolution notwithstanding) couldn't buck the odds.

28. A good real-world example of this is discussed in Eberts & Ilott (1990, p. 109).

29. See *Daily Variety,* October 24, 1979.

30. Quoted from *Daily Variety,* October 24, 1979. Litman in Kindem (1982) discusses pricing of series and movies from the perspective of the 1970s.

31. "War and Remembrance" was noted for its high-quality production values, but also for its huge cost and the over $20 million in losses that the ABC network sustained on its original broadcast of the 32-episode, $110 million miniseries that was shown in the fall of 1988 and the spring of 1989. See Kneale (1988).

32. The high costs and generally unrepresentative nature of pilots, and the great probability that most will not be extended into full series, have led many in the television industry to question the wisdom of using this massive and wasteful spending system for program-development purposes. Unfortunately, satisfactory alternatives have yet to be discovered.

33. Prior to the phasing out of investment tax credits in 1986, $6\frac{2}{3}\%$ of production costs had qualified as tax credits – a factor that had considerably eased the production deficit problem.

34. Indeed, because it is so difficult to generate positive cash flows in the start-up phase of production, many production companies have encountered financial difficulties and have been forced to co-venture or to merge with larger organizations or studios.

35. The issue of deficit financing is at the heart of the financial interest and syndication rule debate that had raged since the early 1980s. In return for paying higher license fees for original programming, the networks have long felt entitled to participation in some of the so-called "back-end" syndication profits, which, at least through 1990, they had been barred from sharing. Deficits had risen from an average of around $64,000 a half-hour show in 1982–83 to over $170,000 by 1986–87. For hour-long shows, the deficits are estimated to have risen from $198,000 to over $370,000 in the same period. And in the 1989–90 season, the Alliance of Motion Picture & Television Producers indicated that deficits on one-hour series averaged $300,000 and for half-hour filmed series, $258,000.

36. As indicated in Owen and Wildman (1992, p. 184), the probability of renewal increases markedly for series that have been renewed at least once. According to Lorimar Research, for example, the longest-running TV series through the 1992–3 season were *Gunsmoke* with 402 episodes, *Dallas* with 356, *Knots Landing* with 344, *Bonanza* with 318, and *The Love Boat* with 255. Through 1997, the longest running prime-time series have been *60 Minutes* (30 years beginning in 1968), *The Ed Sullivan Show* (24 years, 1948–71), *Gunsmoke* (21 years, 1955–75), and *The Red Skelton Show (21 years, 1951–71)*.

37. In the late 1960s and early 1970s, the probability of making a syndicatable, highly profitable series was greater than in the late 1970s and early 1980s. By the 1980s, viewers had become increasingly discriminating in their choices. Because of disruptions by strikes and other factors, the start of the TV season had become irregular, and cable, videocassette, and movie-of-the-week viewing alternatives had become more numerous.

38. The increasing competitive influence of pay-TV implies that producers now may be less willing to tie up their best properties for long periods whereas networks will seek longer option periods. The relative values of syndicated half-hour and hour series episodes, as well as typical contract terms, are thus in a state of flux. Also, networks may have a strategic interest in "warehousing" best-drawing feature films in order to delay appearance on competing pay-cable networks.

Moreover, as noted in *Variety* of January 13, 1997, the Katz TV Group has formulated three criteria for predicting the syndication success of an off-network sitcom: (a) At least 18% of viewers of a comedy during its primetime network run should be men 18 to 49 years old; (b) If a show substantially benefits from a network hit-comedy lead-in, its syndication performance will probably be disappointing; and (c) Throughout its four-year network primetime run, a comedy series should have a Nielsen rating 20% above the average sitcom rating for adults 25 to 54 years old.

39. For a show with the potential to last three years or more on a network, program-distribution companies may be willing to guarantee, in installments, say, at least $50,000 per episode against a percentage of anticipated syndication profits. Here producers may sacrifice some percentage of ownership in return for immediate cash, and distributors may obtain long-term project commitments on which they can rely to keep pipelines filled. The risk to the distributor is that the program will be canceled or that the show will, over time, lose its audience appeal. Should the producer enter into such an agreement, an important issue for negotiation is which party will pay what percentage of talent residuals and royalties. As in features, however, residuals would normally be expected to come out of the producers' side. For top producers, the percentage of the so-called "back-end" can be quite high. Witt Thomas Harris, producers of *The Golden Girls*, which is distributed by Disney and is estimated to have earned about $1.5 million for each of its 150 episodes, might have received as much as a 25% cut out of the back-end profits. The milestone Carsey-Werner deal for *The Cosby Show* is believed to have been for a 33% cut. See also note 40 below.

40. An important recent exception has been the distributor King World, which has been able to sign stations to three-year contracts on the basis of the ratings strength of its shows *Wheel of Fortune, Oprah Winfrey,* and *Jeopardy!*

41. Barter prices naturally ride on the back of network cost per thousand (CPM) prices and are usually 80% of what a network might charge. Barter, however, clearly shifts the financial burden from the station to the syndicator, who must arrange to aggregate and sell the time to national advertisers.

42. Note that because barter contracts are not negotiated until fairly close to actual time of telecast, the carrying value of such bartered shows cannot be accurately assessed and therefore be subsumed as a part of a production/distribution company's long-term license-fee "backlog." The effect is that barter-program licenses tend to generate earnings that, for the distributor, are much more dispersed over time and that are of smaller relative magnitude than is the case with cash-licensed, off-network program syndication fees (which are recognized in large clusters at the time of first availability).

43. The costs of network prime-time productions are estimated to have risen at a 14.4% compound annual rate during the 1970s. Although comparable data are not available for the 1980s, it seems fair to assume that the cost of production probably continued to rise by an average of 10% a year between 1980 and 1990, and by at least 5% a year in the 1990s.

44. The squeeze from higher star salaries comes mostly out of network profits. For instance, in *Seinfeld* – the most expensive regular series in television history, costing $4 million per ninth-season episode – NBC sells nine 30-second spots for about $500,000 each, or $4.5 million. With a rerun, the gross is $9.0 million, and less agency commissions, the total for the year might approach $8 million per episode. Assuming 25 episodes per season, NBC would take in $200 million in revenues. But with the series stars receiving as much as $1 million each under proposed new contracts, the cost of the show might rise to $5 million an episode, up from perhaps $2 million in the early years of the program. The $3 million difference would thus reduce NBC profits from $150 million to $75 million. See also, *Business Week,* June 2, 1997.

45. In the case of a popular series coming off-network, such syndication window revenues can be substantial. For instance, a record total of $200 million ($1.5 million per episode) was initially received in the mid-1980s by MCA for the one-hour series *Magnum, P.I.* But many series, especially hour-longs, have not until recently even come close to the positive results shown in Table 4.10. *Walker, Texas Ranger* was sold in 1996 for $750,000 per episode to the USA Network, and is looking to take in about the same from weekend runs on broadcast stations.

Soon after the record price for *Magnum* (which ultimately averaged $1.7 million per episode) was obtained, television industry demand for hour-long series plummeted and through the second half of the 1980s, most off-network hour-long series could not command more than $300,000 to $400,000 per episode – scarcely enough to cover the costs of marketing and of residual payments. For example, eight of the top-10 programs in the 1983–84 season were one-hour dramas, but the number had fallen to virtually zero by the end of the decade before a revival, led by the Fox network, ensued in the early 1990s. Licensing to cable networks has thus developed as an attractive alternative to syndicating to local TV stations, especially in that Hollywood guilds take 10% of the cash license fees in cable sales, which is half the cost of broadcast-deal residuals. Hour-long series sold to such networks for prices up to $250,000 an episode include *Murder She Wrote, Cagney and Lacey,* and *Miami Vice.* And hour-long dramas such as *ER* have later been sold to cable for $1.2 million an episode. In 1996, Lifetime, owned jointly by Disney and Hearst, bought rights to 112 episodes of the sitcom *Ellen* for more than $600,000, a record for a cable network purchase. See also Goldman (1992).

46. As of the late 1990s, most magazine-style shows had weekly production budgets upwards of $400,000 a week (double the cost of the early 1990s), whereas most new game and talk shows cost in the range of $150,000 to $225,000 a week to produce. Most such shows would need to attract at least $80,000 a week in national barter advertising in order to reach break-even. The theme and content of a program like *Entertainment Tonight,* however, brings production costs up to more than $500,000 a week. Such magazine shows would have to maintain a minimum household rating of 4.5 to be profitable.

But not all first-run series are necessarily low-budget productions: *Star-Trek . . . The Next Generation,* with an initial per-episode budget of $1.3 million plus $75,000 for special effects, had been among the costliest first-run series produced in the early 1990s. And not all network productions are high-budget; for example, as of 1997 it had cost about $400,000 an hour – one-third as much as drama – to produce network newsmagazine programs such as *60 Minutes* (CBS), *20/20* (ABC), *PrimeTime Live* (ABC), and *Dateline* (NBC). The relative popularity and low cost of such programming has led to more frequent appearance of these shows on prime-time network schedules.

47. As of the mid-1990s, U.S. distributors took in an estimated $225 million in foreign sales of two-hour movies. Titles generally gross between $400,000 to $1.4 million overseas, with producers of major telefilms able to get a $400,000 to $900,000 advance from a distributor for foreign sales rights. This often amounts to one-third of the financing of a network TV movie. In all, some 250 such films are made each year.

48. For example, in syndicated television, talent unions have negotiated a sliding scale of residuals that calls for 75% of original pay for the first and second replay, 50% for the third through fifth, 10% for the sixth, and 5% for every run beyond that. However, for cable network syndication, there is only a one-time flat 10% of the gross that is divided among writers, actors, and directors. Thus, syndication of an off-network series to one of the national cable networks for, say, $150,000 an episode would cost the distributor only $15,000, whereas broadcast syndication of six runs of the same series to broadcast stations could cost anywhere from $120,000 to $150,000 an episode in residuals (because the charge per episode is fixed no matter what the license fee). In addition, selling to broadcast incurs more expense in that the series must be sold market-by-market instead of to just one buyer. This means that for the distributor to profit from a broadcast syndication of an off-network series, gross revenues generally must well exceed $300,000 an episode – which is nowadays difficult to amass.

49. The number of prints needed for national syndication can be reduced by "bicycling," the swapping of episodes from one station to the next, only when the sequencing of episodes does not matter. In theory, however, increased use of low-cost distribution by satellite technology promises that ultimately only one print will be required.

Also, prior to the advent of "superstations"– local television stations that send their signals via satellite to cable systems around the country – syndicated programs in a local market had been protected from competition through contract exclusivity clauses. Such protection was only restored in 1990, when the FCC reinstated such exclusivity with so-called "syndex" rules.

50. Constraints on self-production were the result of a 1980 consent decree that limited each network to in-house production of 2½ hours on average per week until the fall of 1985, when the cap began to gradually rise toward 5 hours per week in 1988. In actuality, however, networks have to date not proven to be particularly efficient in production. An episode of the once-popular one-hour ABC-network–produced series *Moonlighting* reportedly set a record at a cost of $3 million.

In recent years, though, changes in the fin-syn rules have made it more likely for a network to own a stake in new series productions. As an example, in late 1992, ABC made an agreement with Wind Dancer Productions to fund the entire cost of producing a new series rather than paying a flat license fee, which typically compensates the producer for only 80% to 85% of the full cost of production. By owning such a stake, ABC would participate in potential syndication revenues should the shows succeed in the ratings comparisons. Also, in late 1994, the new DreamWorks SKG studio arranged to coventure with ABC and be compensated with a share in ABC's *advertising* revenues. Although this appears on the surface to be a revolutionary development, in financial impact, it isn't much different than what happens when a studio significantly raises the license fee for option renewal on a hit show.

51. Both the Syndication and Financial Interest and the Prime Time Access rules were adopted by the FCC in 1970 in response to conditions that had existed in the 1960s, when the networks had been at the peak of their relative competitive strength. The disallowance of network financial interest went into effect on August 1, 1972, and of network syndication on June 1, 1973.

In 1980, the three national networks also entered into consent decrees in connection with antitrust suits brought against each of them by the Department of Justice in the early 1970s. These consent decrees contain provisions that parallel but are not identical to the original Syndication and Financial Interest Rules.

In 1983, movement toward deregulation encouraged networks to challenge some of the restrictions and there ensued a bitter political battle between the networks on one side and independent producers, independent television stations, and movie studios on the other. The independents feared that the networks would stifle their creative and financial well-being, while the networks contrarily argued that they were no longer oligopolistic because of the inroads made by strongly competitive cable and home-video industries. See section 6.1 and also Crandall (1972), Landro and Saddler (1983), Colvin (1983), Owen and Wildman (1992), and *Variety,* August 10, 1983.

As of 1992, rule modifications had allowed a network to distribute, or to have an interest in the proceeds from distributing its own product. And in prime time, the networks were allowed to produce or coproduce up to 40% of their schedules. Then, by early 1993, almost all restrictions on financial interest were dropped, and all restrictions expired in late 1995. The Prime Time Access Rules, restricting affiliates in the top-50 markets from running syndicated off-network series in the hour before primetime, were allowed to expire in 1996.

52. The Fox network evolved in the late 1980s. Yet, because it did not program a full week's schedule and because it thus did not fall under the FCC's definition of a network, it was free to own syndication interests in its self-developed shows. Under the modified fin-syn rules of 1991, Fox was allowed to broadcast no more than an average of 15 hours of programming per week in prime time during any six-month period (and an unlimited number of hours of non–prime time programming). Thus, News Corp., the parent company, owned a movie studio, a quasi-network, and a television syndication arm prior to the 1993 relaxation of the rules. By 1994, however, other network-studio combinations had begun to form, with United/Paramount and Warner Bros. becoming the fifth and sixth networks.

53. However, the cash-flow sequence may begin with up to a 10% down payment on signing or on first availability date and be followed by three annual installments of 30% of total revenues due. Following standard accounting procedures, the future cash receivables are then discounted, using an appropriate interest rate, to a present-value receivable that appears on the balance sheet.

54. Foreign receipts would also normally be booked on an episode-by-episode cash basis, but unlike the domestic situation, without regard as to whether a show is self-produced and/or owned.

55. Mr. Garner's *Rockford Files* (NBC, 1974–80) agreement with Universal had entitled him to 37.5% of the net profits of the show in return for taking a smaller upfront fee. By 1988, receipts from the show had reached $119.3 million according to Universal's own accounting. Nevertheless, Universal claimed that the show would have to earn another $1.6 million before it would realize net profits as described in Garner's contract.

According to the accounting statement, as described by Scholl (1989a), subtracted from the $119.3 was $32.6 million for distribution fees. Then another $14.6 million was deducted for distribution expenses including the cost of prints and storage. Then another $57.8 million was taken off for production costs, which left only $14.2 million. That $14.2 million, however, by Universal's accounting was insufficient to cover the $15.8 million in interest expenses that the company (and most other studios) charges on the theory that the money spent on production could have been invested at risk-free rates.

However, according to Garner's auditors, Universal overstated costs and/or underestimated receipts by at least $10.9 million. For example, the auditors claimed that Universal failed to pass along quantity discounts (of $443,000) received on development of extra print copies.

Another issue involved whether to count print and dubbing costs as gross receipts or as expense reimbursements. If counted as the former, Universal would take a 50% fee off the top, whereas in the latter case, it is a direct expense reduction that leads to faster profitability for the participant. An even larger amount ($7.9 million), and one that is at the crux of the interest payments charges issue, involved Universal's alleged practice of immediately recording expenses while deferring the recording of revenues and profits until cash was in hand.

However, as Scholl (1989b) indicates, the Garner suit, initiated in 1983, was settled in 1989 for approximately $10 million.

56. This topic is also treated in Salemson and Zolotow (1978).

57. This is especially seen in preliminary distributor weekend box-office estimates, which are made by (sometimes aggressively) extrapolating Entertainment Data Inc. (EDI) Friday and Saturday tallies through Sunday, and by estimating uncounted results from small and rural theaters in order to gain position in early weekend rankings.

58. During periods of high interest rates and economic duress, playing the float is obviously not unique to entertainment businesses.

59. Piracy is estimated to cost the industry at least $500 million per year. A bill signed by President Reagan in 1982 made piracy a felony punishable by five years in prison.

60. The practice of settlements is sometimes pushed to the ethical borderline and, interestingly, does not seem to apply in reverse. That is, if a picture performs better than expected, distributors do not ordinarily extract stiffer terms from exhibitors. Settlements are much less likely to be found in exhibitor contracts that are bid rather than negotiated. Universal, Fox, Sony, and DreamWorks apparently negotiate on the basis of "firm terms," which are terms supposedly not reviewable after a movie closes. But many studios and exhibitors favor "settling" terms 60 to 90 days after a picture opens, and even studios with firm terms often compensate exhibitors for box office losers with lower rates on future releases. See *Variety*, March 17, 1997.

61. Blocked currency funds have occasionally served as a source of new film production financing. Normally, such funds are accumulated by different companies or industries operating in a country, and as long as the funds are used within that country, it does not matter that the funds were generated in selling automobiles or textiles. See also *Variety*, August 20, 1986.

62.   There are several foreign sales organizations, but most are relatively small. The most famous of these, mentioned in Paris (1984) and Salamon (1984), was Producers Sales Organization, which eventually went out of business.

Chapter 5

1.   According to the International Federation of Phonogram and Videogram Producers (IFPI), an international industry trade organization, direct world sales of records and cassettes were approximately $40 billion in 1996. See Figure 5.4.

2.   As noted by Eliot (1989, p. 15). For a detailed history of recorded sound, also see Gelatt (1977), Read and Welch (1976), Walch and Burt (1994), and White (1988).

3.   It was not until 1941 that the originally formed ASCAP (American Society of Composers, Authors and Publishers) settled on the same royalty formula (based on 2¾% of radio stations' annual advertising revenues) as had been standardized by BMI (Broadcast Music Inc.) – the organization that had been formed in 1939 to compete with ASCAP.

4.   The musicians' union (American Federation of Musicians) sought compensation from the record companies for income lost as demand for live performances declined as a result of the increasing use of recorded performances.

5.   New majors of the latter half of the 1950s included Capitol, MGM, and Mercury, for a total of six dominant companies in all.

6.   After a prolonged battle, the computer and movie industries finally agreed on a DVD standard that enabled introduction of DVDs in 1998. An ordinary DVD holds 4.7 gigabytes (GB) of information, or about seven times the 650 megabytes of a CD. With a dual layer (one opaque, one shiny), storage can be almost doubled again to 8.56 GB. And a second side can be further added. Using MPEG-2 compression, the ordinary DVD can thus store, on one side, a 133-minute movie along with Dolby AC-3 audio tracks.

7.   In the United States, unit shipments of albums increased at a compound annual rate of 3.9% between 1971 and 1980 (Supplementary Table S5.1). But in the early 1980s, the combination of economic recession, higher prices, more off-the-air taping, and other factors caused shipments to decline. Over this period, however, the prerecorded-cassette format gained steadily against the vinyl disk, eight-track, and open-reel tape configurations, and by 1984, cassettes accounted for over half of total album units.

   Moreover, according to surveys (see Table S5.2), the largest group of record buyers in the early 1980s were not teenagers, but young adults. Teens of the 1950s and 1960s thus apparently carried an interest in music well into their twenties and thirties, thereby significantly broadening the market's demographic boundaries. In addition, there was a substantial increase in the number of new households as the relatively large post–World War II population cohorts matured. And major improvements in semiconductor technology had, by this time, also brought down the prices of stereo components for home and car. Accordingly, the emergence of FM stereo radio as the popular music medium of choice was of considerable importance.

   Note, too, that because of the much higher costs of petroleum-based products such as vinyl, record prices in the late 1970s were sharply increased, while the quality of vinyl pressings decreased. Indeed, for a while it was not uncommon for consumers with top-of-the-line stereo receivers located in strong-signal areas to make off-the-air recordings whose quality matched or surpassed that of some store-bought records.

8.   After the 1982 introduction of a so-called musical-instrument digital interface (MIDI), which converts musical control information into a uniform computer code, the productivity of recording studios, musicians, and composers increased substantially. MIDI standardization was introduced through the efforts of Yamaha Corp., Kawai Instrument Manufacturing Co., Roland Corp., and Sequential Circuits Inc.

9. Music Television (MTV) is a 24-hour network that bases its programming on a mixture of rock-music videos, music news, and specials. Owned by Viacom Inc., MTV now attracts a global audience measured in the tens of millions. MTV's development was, of course, also accompanied in the early 1980s by introduction of low-cost videocassette machines, which enabled a whole subindustry of music video recordings to spring up. MTV's history is discussed in Banks (1996).

10. Better reporting of data, as well as more stringent policies against bootleggers, may also account for the apparently higher growth rates of demand reported in the less-developed countries.

11. The role of managers is comprehensively covered in Frascogna and Hetherington (1978).

12. Disputes in this area have mostly concerned music rights in syndicated television programming and commercials. Stations generally do not receive music rights along with the other rights conveyed in consideration of their broadcast license fees. Instead, they normally operate under blanket music licenses – by definition nonspecific as to the music used in the show – for which they are charged by ASCAP and BMI about 2% of adjusted station gross receipts, and which entitle stations to use any of the approximately 4 million titles in the ASCAP and BMI catalogs.

A *blanket license,* however, is only one of four ways in which to license music for a show: (a) a blanket license that covers any music used in the composers' rights catalogs; (b) through each composer; (c) on a per-program basis; and (d) through the producer, who has already obtained a license. See Boucher (1986), *Broadcasting,* February 1, 1988, p. 44, and especially Flick (1988), who provides a cogent description of the situation, and Zollo (1989). As described in *Broadcasting & Cable,* May 17, 1993, SESAC is now also offering Hispanic broadcasters a niche blanket license or per-program license.

13. The Copyright Royalty Tribunal, created by the 1976 Copyright Act, was abolished in December 1993, when its functions were transferred to the Library of Congress and the Copyright Office. Between January 1, 1988, and January 1, 1996, this rate had been adjusted every two years in proportion to changes in the Consumer Price Index. See *Billboard,* October 1, 1994.

14. This compulsory license system, in which the copyright owners have the opportunity to be the first to record and distribute their works, is intended to provide such owners with fair remuneration while preventing the owners from retaining a monopoly over all future uses of a particular musical composition. But according to the 1976 copyright law, which largely parallels those in other countries, an author retains a copyright for life plus 50 years.

15. The Copyright Royalty Tribunal had also collected and distributed license fees from cable-television operators. Of the $161 million-pool in 1990, 60% went to the MPAA and 24% to sports. See Carlson (1984).

16. As Lardner (1987) describes, legal and marketing battles fought over the introduction of home videocassette recorders were intense until the U.S. Supreme Court ruled in January 1984 that off-the-air taping of movies for noncommercial purposes is legal.

Yet the issue of home taping and the degree to which such taping harms the video and music industries is one of great importance and complexity. Of the many studies that have been conducted in order to determine the net effects, the most comprehensive has been the 1989 Survey of Home Taping and Copying conducted by the Office of Technology Assessment, an advisory agency to the U.S. Congress. According to the study (U.S. Congress, 1989), the net effects on the entertainment industries may not be as severe as had originally been feared. Economic models that explain why some consumers copy are discussed in Johnson (1985).

Also, passage of the Audio Home Recording Act of 1992 by the U.S. Congress for the first time provides compensatory royalties to record companies, publishers, and songwriters by imposing a 2% surcharge on digital audio tape recorders (with a $1 minimum fee and an $8 cap for single recorders), and a 3% surcharge on blank digital tapes. However, no royalties will be paid for analog hardware or blank analog tapes. Royalties are paid by manufacturing companies to the Copyright Office. In the United States, unlike in other countries such as Germany, there had not until 1992 been any tax placed on blank tape or on taping machines to compensate composers and authors for purported royalty losses from home duplication of audio-visual materials created by others.

17.   However, several pay-per-transaction schemes have been developed that would allow producers and distributors to participate directly in the revenues from each and every rental transaction. For example, Rentrak Corporation offers pay-per-transaction services. Video suppliers such as movie studios receive a cut of every rental transaction, and in return, participating stores buy tapes at very low prices, which allows them to stock more hit titles. See also section 3.4.

18.   The financial dynamics of a concert tour are discussed by Kronholz (1984) and Newcomb (1989).

19.   It is estimated that there are 1,200 record companies and over 2,600 labels in the United States. However, most of the recording activity is concentrated with the largest dozen firms.

20.   Release strategies have occasionally been hampered by production or distribution bottlenecks. At CBS and Capitol Records, the major domestic pressing companies of the late 1970s, short-run demand outstripped production capacity when release of the (until then) all-time best-selling (20 million plus) *Saturday Night Fever* album and the deaths of Elvis Presley and Bing Crosby occurred within an 18-month span. As of the late 1980s, Time Warner had a major CD pressing facility, and in 1991 PolyGram also bought two plants. The industry has since experienced no problems in servicing demand, as can be seen when Bertelsmann's Arista label soundtrack album to the film *The Bodyguard* sold over 20 million units (and made an estimated $60 million in worldwide profits) in 1993. Although Michael Jackson's 41 million plus *Thriller,* issued in 1982, is generally considered to be the all-time top selling album, the official RIAA domestic unit-sale certifications as of 1997 are as follows:

Michael Jackson *Thriller* (Epic, 1982)	24-million
Eagles *Greatest Hits, 1971–75* (Asylum, 1976)	24-million
Fleetwood Mac *Rumours* (Warner Bros., 1977)	17-million
Bodyguard soundtrack, (Arista, 1992)	16-million
Boston (Epic, 1976)	16-million
Led Zeppelin IV (Atlantic, 1971)	16-million

Hootie & the Blowfish *Cracked Rear View* (Atlantic, 1994), Bruce Springsteen, *Born in the U.S.A.* (Columbia, 1984) and Alanis Morissette's *Jagged Little Pill* (Maverick/Reprise/Warner, 1995) are all tied at 15-million units.

21.   The laxity of enforcement of laws against payola, and the tremendous pressures on artists and their managers to obtain broadcast exposure of their songs, led the largest record distribution companies to come to depend on the services of independent promoters, some of whom had alleged ties to organized crime families. As Dannen (1990, p. 9) said, ''promotion, the art and science of getting songs on the air, drove the record business. Not marketing, because no amount of advertising or even good reviews and publicity were enough to sell millions of albums. Not sales, because record stores only reacted to demand and did not create it. Even the best A & R – artist and repertoire – staff in the world couldn't save you if radio gave you the cold shoulder.''

Yet, as Dannen (1990, p. 15) further notes, ''For all its power, the Network (of independent promoters) could not make a hit record. No one could do that except the marketplace. You could saturate the airwaves with an uncommercial song and have some moderate success, but in the end you could not force people to buy a record they did not like.'' This ''new payola'' as it has come to be known, and which involves large fees paid to promoters for getting songs added to station play lists is also described by Goldberg (1988). Knoedelseder (1993, p. 305) indeed notes that the ''payola law was poorly written, taking into account primarily money . . . [B]ut record promotion practices had become increasingly sophisticated in the years since the law was passed.''

Another form of payola may also occur when stations (and sometimes also record stores) overstate a song's popularity to the chart services in return for record-company advertising. Because such overstatements are not based on actual sales, but just on inflated figures put down on paper, they are known in the industry as ''paper adds'' (Hull, 1984). However, today's computer-scanned retail sales reports make this more difficult to do (Sorkin, 1997).

22. As with most other entertainment company assets, including film libraries and broadcast stations, music-related assets are generally evaluated on the basis of projected pretax, preinterest cash-flow multiples.

Although there have been several significant corporate asset transfers in recent years, which include the sale of CBS Records to Sony, of RCA Records to Bertelsmann, and of Chappell Music Publishing to Warner Communications, financial information as to the precise cash-flow multiples used in these transactions has been difficult to obtain. A rough estimate of the Sony/CBS deal is that the transfer price was probably at around nine times projected cash flow. Another valuation angle is provided by measuring transfer prices as a multiple of revenues. In 1992, for example, Thorn EMI paid approximately $960 million to acquire Virgin Music. This was 1.6 times Virgin's 1991 sales. By comparison, PolyGram paid about 2.1 times sales for A & M Records in 1989, and 2.3 times Motown's (prior year) sales in 1993, while MCA paid about 2.6 times sales when it bought Geffen Records in 1990. The aforementioned sale of CBS Records to Sony in 1987 was at 1.3 times sales.

23. Kronemyer and Sidak (1986) analyzed the industry for the years 1970–84 and provided the most comprehensive market share data available for that span. Unfortunately, however, it is generally not possible to easily update the market share data.

As for PolyGram, it was almost merged with Warner Communications in 1984, but the merger was blocked by the Federal Trade Commission because of antitrust considerations. At the time, PolyGram had sales of around $700 million. PolyGram, with 1989 sales of over $1.5 billion, sold 20% of its shares to the public in December 1989.

24. In the 1970s, Pickwick International was the largest rack jobber in the United States. It was acquired by American Can Co., which in 1984 sold most of the Pickwick assets to Handleman. Handleman, long the dominant rack jobber, acquired the second largest jobber, Lieberman Enterprises, in 1991.

25. Although suggested retail list prices are used to compile industry sales figures, these numbers are misleading because record stores normally do not charge suggested list.

26. The highest royalty rate ever paid by the industry to a single artist was apparently established by Sony in 1991, when Michael Jackson reportedly commanded 22% of retail, or $1.90 an album, on 100% of units sold. Other top acts have only been able to receive royalty rates approaching this level on a standard 85% of unit sales. See *Rolling Stone,* May 4, 1991. However, the largest *advance* was reportedly the $10 million per album for six albums (*if* the albums sell over 5 million units each) on the deal that the artist formerly known as Prince signed with Warner Bros. Records in 1992. By comparison, Michael Jackson and Madonna are believed to get unconditionally about $5 million an album, and the Rolling Stones $8 million. See *Hollywood Reporter,* September 4, 1992.

27.   As the importance of singles has diminished, the RIAA has reduced the unit sales requirements for gold and platinum certification of singles by half since 1990.

28.   Similarly, Wadhams (1990, p. 109) says, ''The record industry is the only one, even among the entertainment industries, in which the creative artist is ultimately charged for the entire cost of producing the work.''

29.   As described by Flack (1989), the multiple of NPS rose from the area of 5 or 6 times to around 10 times in the 1989 SBK/EMI deal.

On the average, and using another rough rule-of-thumb, song publisher catalogs seem in recent years to have been transferred at a going rate of around $1,000 per title. In August 1990, for example, Thorn EMI bought the rights to 90,000 titles held by independent British music publisher Filmtrax Copyright Holdings for $115 million. Filmtrax, formed in 1984 to acquire the music assets of Columbia Pictures Entertainment, owned rights to songs such as ''Stormy Weather'' and ''Ain't Misbehavin'. '' See also Gubernick (1989a), *Variety,* August 15, 1990, and Krasilovsky and Shemel (1994, chapter 12).

30.   Shemel and Krasilovsky (1985, p. 362) note that in terms of tax treatment, ''the costs incurred in preparing master recordings, used for substantially more than one year to produce records for sale, are required to be depreciated over the period that the master recordings are utilized for that purpose.''

Also, prior to the 1976 tax-code revisions, recording costs could be treated as totally current expenses deductible from current income, or they could be capitalized and subject to regular depreciation deductions. As of the 1976 revisions, however, for noncorporate producers, the costs attributable to the production of a sound recording, film, or book are deductible – on a ''flow-of-income'' basis – pro rata over the period in which the property generates income. This ''flow of income'' method of cost amortization for noncorporate producers also applies to record master costs and uses the same approach as in the film business, where estimates as to the total amount of income to be received over the economic life of the asset must also be made. But corporate producers may have the option to treat recording costs as current expenses deductible in the year incurred.

In other words, producers must capitalize costs incurred in the production of record masters, and then deduct the costs over time using the income forecast method of depreciation. However, costs incurred to produce demo records are not capitalized or recovered through depreciation deductions. Producers may instead elect to treat such demo costs as research and developmental expenses to be amortized over a period of 60 or more months. See also *Billboard* April 9, 1994.

31.   Although an estimated 40 million Americans play musical instruments, aggregate industry sales have not grown in real terms since the early 1970s – when unfavorable demographic, economic, and social trends first appeared. Indeed, the percentage of personal-consumption expenditures going to this segment (including sheet music and accessories) has declined noticeably (from 0.21% in 1974 to 0.11% in 1996) as interest in learning to play has declined and as the availability of equipment and instruction in schools has been significantly reduced.

According to the American Music Conference (San Diego, Ca.) annual survey, musical instrument retail sales rose to $5.6 billion in 1996 up from a recent low of $2.2 billion in 1980. Aggregate figures, however, mask the variation in popularity of different instruments. For instance, in the 1960s and 1970s, unit shipments of guitars gained rapidly, while shipments of pianos leveled off.

Shrinking school enrollments – a trend that will reverse in the 1990s – as well as municipal and state funding problems, have had the greatest effects in retarding sales growth. But young people's fascination with video games and computers has also diverted spending that might otherwise have been directed to this area.

Although prior to 1985 there had been several major publicly held instrument manufacturing companies, many of the brand-name divisions of those companies have been restructured into smaller privately owned firms, and financial operating data on the industry is rather limited.

Chapter 6

1. FM frequencies are between channels 6 and 7 on the VHF television spectrum; that is, channels 2 through 6 operate at 54 to 88 megahertz (MHz) and channels 7 through 13 operate at 174 to 216 MHz. Harmonic distortions prevent the use of channel 1 in VHF television transmissions. Also, to prevent interference, VHF-band stations are separated by one empty channel, while UHF stations are usually separated by eight channels.

2. Despite technological improvements, measurement of audiences has become more difficult and subject to controversy as channels, networks, and sets have proliferated. Nielsen had long relied on "audimeters" (audience meters) in the largest markets (and diaries in the smaller ones), but sampling has been enlarged and now depends on People Meters that require viewers to log in their presence on a console attached to the television set. As Berry (1984) describes, Britain's AGB Research had accelerated a movement toward using more sophisticated audience sampling methods than had previously been used by Nielsen and Arbitron, and efforts continue toward development of "passive" people meters. Also see Couzens (1986), and Jensen (1996).

Both Arbitron and The Birch Scarborough Research companies are perhaps better known for radio audience measurements.

3. As of the late 1990s, commissionable spot billings for the three leading national TV rep firms (Cox, Petry, and Katz) were over $6 billion. National sales average about 40%–50% of a station's total revenue, but are a larger part of the mix in more major markets. At an average commission rate of 7% to 8%, estimated rep firm revenues were thus around $500 million.

4. Barter syndication is discussed in section 4.4. The growth of the business is shown in Table 4.12.

5. In theory, allocation of scarce frequency space would normally be more efficient if free-market auction bidding, as in the 1994 example of the FCC's auctions of personal communication systems telephone frequencies, were permitted.

6. Government regulation of all aspects of broadcasting is generally much more stringent in foreign countries. However, the United States was the first country to develop television into a mass medium, and in the process, the United States standardized the earliest (now technologically inferior) system, known as NTSC (National Television Systems Committee), with a 525-line scan. The same system is used in Canada, Mexico, Japan, and 23 other countries. But elsewhere around the world, there are different standards, with 625-

line scans. The SECAM (sequential color and memory) system originated in France and is used in more than 20 nations. And the PAL (phase-alternation line) system is used in 37 others. Picture resolution with SECAM and PAL is superior to that with NTSC because of more scanning lines per frame, but their use of alternating current of 50 Hz (vs. 60 Hz in the United States) leads to more flickering.

Also, in the old NTSC system, the electron beam produces 30 different pictures, or frames, per second, and each frame is made up of 525 scanning lines. By contrast, movies show 24 different frames a second interrupted by a shutter in the projector that reduces flicker by showing each frame twice.

To reduce flicker in the TV picture, however, each frame is separated in two, and each half-frame (field) is shown separately, which means that each field composed of either odd or even scan lines is on the screen for one-sixtieth of a second. The process is known as interlacing.

7.   In the United States, a fully digital HDTV standard was established in late 1996, although the basic elements were in place by 1993. The standard, similar to that used in computer monitors, includes a 1,080-line progressive-scan image. See Brinkley (1997, 1996), Andrews (1993), and *Broadcasting & Cable,* May 31, 1993. As of the early 1990s, an HDTV (1,250-line, 60 MHz) system known as MUSE (Multiple Sub-Nyquist Sampling and Encoding) was just beginning to be implemented in Japan, even though it had not yet been determined which of several competing systems would prevail in the United States and Europe. In Europe, the plans for HDTV had been to use 1,250-line 50-Hz signals based on a MAC (multiplexed analog component) signal standard for direct broadcast satellite distribution.

8.   Note that only half of UHF viewers are counted in determining audience percentage figures. Also, other significant rules pertaining to cross-media ownership and foreign ownership are less likely to be eased: Newspaper and cable concerns are forbidden to own television and radio stations in the same communities; a single company is prohibited from holding two broadcast properties in a market; and foreigners are limited to ownership positions of less than 25% of a holding company with broadcast licenses or 20% of a license directly.

9.   Fox's collection of twenty-two O&O's covering 34.83% of FCC-defined households in every one of the top-ten markets except San Francisco was significantly enlarged through the $3 billion acquisition of the remaining 80% of New World Communications Group stations in 1996 that it did not yet control. The contrast is to the position as of 1989, when Fox operated a full schedule of prime-time programming on three nights of the week (Saturday, Sunday, and Monday), and owned and operated stations in the three major markets but, according to strictly interpreted FCC definitions, was not a network because it then provided less than 15 hours a week of programming. By FCC definition, a network also has to provide interconnected program service to at least 25 affiliated licensees in 10 or more states. At the time, this had significance with regard to the financial interest and syndication rules (discussed in Chapter 4) because, as a ''non-network,'' Fox had been permitted to have a financial interest in the programming that it developed and distributed.

10.   As Auletta (1991, p. 4) notes, ''A network is an office building, where executives package programs they do not own and sell them to advertisers and local stations they do not control.''

11.   In the late 1980s, long-standing affiliate compensation relationships began to shift as the networks sought to lower their expense ratios in recognition of their diminished shares of audience. New affiliate compensation contracts appear to be evolving toward payments related to local market ratings performance. Nevertheless, there have been in-

stances in which stations actually pay the networks for the privilege of affiliation. As of the early 1990s, annual compensation to affiliates by each of the networks was averaging approximately $125 million. By then, moreover, the greatly increased availability of first-run programming alternatives was making affiliate preemptions of network fare more frequent, and was further pressuring the traditional network/affiliate "partnership" and compensation arrangements. See *Broadcasting,* August 8, 1983, and September 3, 1988. Also see Cox (1989a) for a complete review.

12. As it happens, ABC's ratings also began to improve, and by the late 1970s ABC finally ended the dominance CBS had held for over 20 years. There immediately ensued considerable switching of the affiliates of other networks to ABC. Another bout of affiliate switching occurred in 1994 and involved Fox and CBS.

13. In Canada, for example, the Canadian Radio-Television and Telecommunications Commission (CRTC) is charged with the authority to license, regulate, and supervise all aspects of the Canadian broadcasting industry, which includes five major television networks. Two of the five are operated by the Canadian Broadcasting Corporation (a federal crown corporation with a budget of over C$1 billion) and provide basic national services in both English and French. The CTV Television Network Limited (CTV) operates a national, privately owned English-language network, and Les Télé-Diffuseurs Associes (TVA) and Quatre Saisons do the same in French-speaking areas.

In many countries, one significant difference from the American system, however, is the use of programming quotas, which are not of regulatory concern in the United States. As of 1989, for example, the CRTC required that Canadian television stations devote 60% of their programming throughout the day and 50% of it in prime time to Canadian material. However, sports and news programming can be counted against these limits.

A major advertiser-supported network company outside the U.S. would, for example, be Grupo Televisa of Mexico.

14. For instance, between 1980 and 1993, total television industry revenues, including broadcast and cable segments, rose by 160% (8% annually) in real terms, while program expenditures rose by 165%. Throughout this period, *the expenditure/revenue ratio remained fairly constant* at around 32%. But for the networks, the share of total industry revenues (in 1993 prices) declined from 37% ($6.8 billion) in 1980 to 21.6% ($10.4 billion). And program expenditures as a proportion of network revenues rose from 52% in 1980 to 60% in 1993 as competition for audiences intensified.

15. But, as seen in the case of ABC, the network that leads the ratings has the potential to attract new affiliates. The addition of affiliates further boosts total network revenue because the percentage of the national population reached by an advertising message is thereby increased.

16. From Barwise and Ehrenberg (1988, p. 36).

17. Barwise and Ehrenberg (1988, p. 44) cite sociologist William McPhee as having recognized and named the "double jeopardy" effect. In the same discussion, they also note that the percentage of audience in one week that watches another episode of the following week is only about 40% in the United States and probably no more than 50% in Britain. Even among the most popular series, only a small percentage of the audience, perhaps under 2% or so, may see every episode of the season.

18. In 1982, a federal district court judge ruled that the NAB's code, which placed certain restrictions on the number of commercials and their scheduling, violated antitrust regulations. And shortly thereafter, ABC and CBS began to expand commercial availability, with ABC adding one minute per evening. By 1991 (according to a *Wall Street Journal* report of March 30, 1992), CBS ran an average of 11 minutes and 6 seconds of ads per hour, NBC ran 11 minutes, and ABC aired 10 minutes and 16 seconds. On the whole, the average is 9 minutes of commercial advertising at each network, not including promos for coming shows, public service ads, and other nonprogram material. Thus, all three older networks currently exceed the previous National Association of Broadcasters nonprogram material standards of 10 minutes per hour in prime time and 16 minutes per hour in all other dayparts.

An *Advertising Age* survey of July 2, 1990, also confirms that all four networks (including Fox), as of 1989, provided significantly more nonprogram material than in earlier years. In prime time, ABC and CBS reached record highs of 10 minutes, 42 seconds, and 11 minutes, 40 seconds, respectively, while NBC averaged 10 minutes, 58 seconds, and Fox averaged 13 minutes, 23 seconds.

Note, however, that at the behest of Congress, in 1991, limitations of 10.5 minutes per hour on weekends and 12.5 minutes on weekdays were placed on commercials in children's programming.

19. To wit: 2.5 minutes per hour on a popular network show will often generate substantially greater revenue for the affiliate than will a full 9 minutes accompanying a program that the local station has either self-produced or acquired elsewhere for cash or barter of time.

20. One of the best known of these had been Turner Broadcasting's Atlanta-based WTBS, which transmited Atlanta Braves baseball games as far away as Alaska and which was transformed into a basic-cable channel as a result of the 1996 purchase by Time Warner. Reimposition of syndication exclusivity rules in the late 1980s limited the growth potential for superstations. And by 1997, high fees charged to MSOs (e.g., 10 cents a month per sub, plus up to 12 cents a month per sub for distribution, plus no commercial time for local advertising) made MSOs reluctant to carry superstations. Most basic-cable networks set aside two minutes per hour for such advertising. As of 1997, Chicago's WGN is the last of the nationally distributed superstations. See *Broadcasting,* November 30, 1987, and *Variety,* January 6, 1997, for a complete discussion and history.

21. PBS television stations have from time to time considered the possibility of carrying a limited amount of commercial advertising in order to supplement their income. This idea was discussed in "PBS May Get a Few More Words from Its Sponsors," *Business Week,* No. 2811 [(October 10, 1983):70]. Tucker (1982) also discusses the costs of operating public television. And *Broadcasting,* May 11, 1987, p. 60, provides a thorough review of the 20 years of CPB history. As of 1990, the CPB had total income of $1.581 billion, of which federal appropriations accounted for 14.5% and total private contributions 53.1%.

22. The correlation between advertising expenditures and corporate profits for the post–World War II period is approximately 0.97.

23. Movies and books have characteristics of both public and private goods: Content here is a public good, but delivery is in the manner of a private good, in which consumption by one person makes the product or service unavailable for someone else (Owen, Beebe, and Manning 1974, p. 15).

24. Hence, it shouldn't be surprising to see that even in a 500-channel universe, programs tend to look alike. Programs that are radically different are apt to fail. See also Rothenberg (1996).

25. A thorough review of such recent studies appears in Owen and Wildman (1992), where, for example, it is noted (p. 148) that biases "against programs that cater to minority-interest tastes, against expensive programs, and in favor of programs that produce large audiences . . . are less pronounced for pay television [than for broadcast television] because the intensity of viewers' preferences is reflected in the prices they pay."

Several other examples: Peterman and Carney (1978) found evidence that "larger buyers of network TV advertising do not purchase time at prices significantly below those charged smaller buyers." Fisher, McGowan, and Evans (1980) studied the audience-revenue relationship for local television stations. Wyche and Wirth (1984) described a mathematical model that can be used to project future financial performance for a station. And Crandall (1972) analyzed the implications of FCC rules barring network investments in ancillary program rights.

Also, a most important article on the economics of advertising is by Stigler and Becker (1977). A follow-up on this, which suggests a net positive relationship between a firm's advertising and product output, is by Hochman and Luski (1988).

26. As suggested in Chapter 4, prime-time program producers may directly recover only 80% to 85% of the total production cost through the network license fees. Also, as noted, the proportion of self-produced versus licensed programming had been stable up to 1995 and since the 1970s, when antitrust cases against the three networks were settled by consent-decree agreements that had limited networks to producing no more than 2.5 hours per week of entertainment prime-time programming.

27. As a percentage of operating costs at independent stations, film amortization of syndicated television series has risen from 35% in the mid-1970s to over 45% in the late 1980s. This compares with levels of about 25% for affiliates, who regularly receive about 65% of their programming from the networks.

28. Frankenfield (1994) notes, for example, that a licensee using the gross method of accounting for program costs would incur no interest expense; those using the net of imputed interest method would show an interest cost below the operating line, and thus a higher gross margin. Also, FASB statement 63 provides considerable flexibility in selection of a program cost amortization schedule. Six methods prevail in the industry:

(1) income forecast;
(2) arbitrary acceleration;
(3) sum-of-the-runs digit;
(4) sum-of-the-years digit;
(5) straight-line-per-year;
(6) straight-line-per-episode.

In addition, FASB statement 63 indicates that capitalized costs of program rights be recorded at the lower of unamortized cost or net realizable value using the following bases:

(1) program-by-program;
(2) series;
(3) package;
(4) daypart.

The daypart aspect is the most controversial because, arguably, writedowns might not be needed if a program can be shifted into a better daypart.

29. The FCC had a rule against "trafficking" that prevented turnover of a broadcast property more frequently than every three years. Under deregulation, this rule was abolished in November 1982, and the rate of station trading has increased. In 1995, there were $8.3 billion of radio and television station transactions and over $6.0 billion of cable-system transactions (versus $3.5 billion and $1 billion, respectively, in 1988). In 1995, the average price for an AM radio station was $547,500, and an FM $2.1 million. The average price for a television facility was $42.3 million in 1995.

30. Buyers often pay 30% down and receive a loan from sellers for up to 70% of the station's value. The loan is usually repaid in 10 annual installments. These terms appear to have evolved in response to capital-gains-tax treatments that were in effect during the 1960s and 1970s. Also, note that in the late 1970s, with real interest rates low and credit readily available, the prices of television and FM radio properties rose steeply. As inflationary psychology took hold, transfer prices for television stations began to be affected by the asumption that there would be high inflation of both land and time prices well into the future.

31. The term "broadcast cash flow" is also used as a measure of operating performance, but it is defined as operating income before depreciation and amortization, write-down of franchise costs, and corporate expenses.

32. Depreciation and amortization policies may vary from one company to another, but treatments of these items tend toward uniformity. Also, an important aspect of station trading prior to the Tax Reform Act of 1986 was the ability of station owners to cash in on a station's increased market value at capital-gains tax rates. The tax code had allowed owners to trade up to more expensive properties without paying any capital-gains taxes at all through the use of tax-deferral certificates. The certificates had been granted for like-type exchanges or upgrades that produced the effect of deconcentrating local-media ownership. Such exchanges were very appealing to owners, who, after depreciation had been exhausted, faced the prospect of paying taxes on a rising stream of earnings.

Tax certificates are discussed in *Broadcasting,* May 28, 1990. The certificates, which can be applied to sales of both broadcasting and cable properties, allow sellers to defer taxes and to thus also reduce the selling price of qualified properties.

Another important tax-related issue for the broadcasting and cable industries involves amortization of intangible assets. Amortizable intangible assets may include leasehold interests, broadcast rights, and program licenses. Nonamortizable intangibles may include FCC licenses and network affiliation agreements. This whole area is significant in considerations of a station's asset value, but had been in a state of flux vis-à-vis the Internal Revenue Service. See also note 19 of Chapter 7 and *Broadcasting,* September 1, 1986, and August 7, 1989.

33. See "Limited Partnerships and Leveraged Buyouts: Growing Means to Broadcast Ownership," *Broadcasting,* November 14, 1983.

34. In an attempt to boost the prospects of the troubled radio industry, the FCC in 1992 voted to allow, by 1994, a licensee to own as many as 20 AM and 20 FM stations nationwide. But the Telecommunications Act passed in early 1996 eliminates national ownership limits. In markets with 45 or more commercial radio stations, a broadcaster may own eight stations, but no more than five of a kind (AM or FM) in markets with 30 to 44 stations. See *Broadcasting & Cable,* February 5, 1996.

35. Highly leveraged transactions, or HLTs, were officially defined as recapitalizations in excess of $20 million and that: (a) double liabilities and result in a leverage ratio above 50%; (b) result in total liabilities in excess of 75% of total assets; and (c) are so designated by a bank. Such HLT restrictions were phased out by the Federal Reserve Board in mid-1992. See *Cablevision,* May 7, 1990.

36. As an example, take a hypothetical property that was financed at 10 times projected cash flow of $1 million. The total value is then $10 million, and in the late 1980s, banks would have typically financed 60% (or 6 times c.f.) of the total value. The remaining $4 million would have been funded through equity and subordinated debt. However, by the early 1990s, the same station might have been valued at 8 times *trailing* cash flow of perhaps $800,000. Thus, with a value of $6.4 million – a loss of $3.6 million – the senior lender would be able to recoup the original $6 million in principal, but the remaining subdebt and equity positions would be worth only $400,000, or 10% of the original amount. Also, any new lenders would likely finance only $4 million, or about 60% of the station's new value. Under such conditions, the only way for a potential purchaser to finance the station might be for the seller to extend a loan to the buyer. See, for example, *Broadcasting,* July 9, 1990.

Chapter 7

1. A more detailed historical review of the cable industry's development is found in Whiteside (1985). A key decision that also helped launch HBO came in 1977, when the Washington D.C. Circuit Court of Appeals struck down the FCC's restrictions on pay television.

2. This is also discussed in the notes to section 2.4.

3. In 1983, The Movie Channel and Showtime were merged in order to compete with HBO, which in terms of subscribers (12 million) was substantially larger than the other two services combined.

4. The jointly owned Mattel/General Instruments Playcable channel, for example, provided properly equipped households with cable-interactive games and was one of the first unconventional experimental channels. The experiment was discontinued in 1984.

5. In fact, competitive and cost pressures were so great that CBS, for example, discontinued its advertiser-supported cable venture in 1982 with a write-down of about $30 million and a year later RCA discontinued its Entertainment Channel at a cost of over $60 million.

6. The Cable Act of 1992, which reregulated rates, showed that the industry had lost political influence – in part due to arrogance and lack of focus on consumer satisfaction. As Crandall and Furchtgott-Roth (1996, p. 37) note, the act also addressed issues such as retransmission consent and consumer protection and service, and placed restrictions on MSO ownership of other forms of video distribution. Rate relief (by 1999) for all but basic tier services was again, however, gained in the Telecommunications Act of 1996.

7. A survey of regulation effects in a wide range of industries appears in Winston (1993).

8. See *Broadcasting,* June 25, 1984.

9. In an important 1985 decision involving a suit by Preferred Communications, Inc. against Los Angeles, it was decided that a city may not create an artificial monopoly (Kelley, 1985).

10. In 1983 and 1984, bills were proposed in Congress to limit cities' power vis-à-vis operators. Passage of such legislation would have made it difficult for cities to refuse franchise renewals, would have allowed companies to modify onerous contracts under a significant change of circumstances, and would have limited municipal fees to 5% of gross annual revenues (Cohen, 1983). In 1985, a compromise agreement included essentially all of these elements, but most significantly terminated (by 1987) a municipality's right to regulate the price of basic cable services. As of 1985, cable systems were also no longer required to carry local broadcast signals, although legal battles on this issue have dragged on for several years. See also note 27.

11. In the early 1980s, the bidding procedure for a franchise was fraught with political considerations. In practice, that often meant that bidders would have to employ so-called ''rent-a-citizen'' schemes whereby local prominents would be offered shares of stock in the cable company at below market prices in return for supporting the company's bid. The issue, as seen from the perspective of the late 1980s, is discussed in *CableVision,* May 22, 1989.

12. The 25% figure may be approximated by assuming that the average major-film rental is 25 cents per subscriber and that there is an average of 10 such films per month, for a total of $2.50. This is around 25% of the total monthly retail charge.

13. In an unusual twist, however, News Corp. sought, in 1996, to rapidly build up to the required 15 million to 20 million subscribers for its fledgling 24-hour news channel by *offering* MSOs $10 a subscriber to carry the service. In actuality, a two–tier structure has recently evolved wherein the older major–brand cable networks such as CNN/Headline News can command 35 cents a subscriber (with volume discounts off the rate card), while newer networks must begin by providing programming for free or for a few cents per subscriber.

14. Of course, should commercial advertising begin to appear more regularly, cable offerings are likely to more closely resemble those found on commercial television, where the theory of least objectionable programming – programs appealing to the largest mass audience – has held sway.

15. Presumably, the higher the price of the service, the less advertising will be tolerated. In the limiting case of "free" over-the-air broadcasts, people would be expected to tolerate the most advertising.

A 1983 Benton & Bowles (ad agency) survey indicated that 17% of all current or previous cable subscribers canceled at least one pay service for reasons other than changing residence: 51% said shows were repeated too often; 42% said it was not worth the money. Only 10% of subscribers bought three pay channels at once, and 7% bought four or more (Landro, 1983). It has been estimated that on the average, pay tiers are discontinued (disconnected) by about 3.5% of system subscribers each month (sometimes rates are as high as 8%). This is at least double the rate for other utilities (telephone, gas, etc.) that are disconnected when households move.

16. In terms of total operating costs, a typical system might have payroll accounting for about one-third of the total expenses and programming costs (for pay-cable programs) about 40% of the same. Franchise fees may amount to around 4% of basic-service revenues.

17. In practice, of course, it may cost $15,000 per mile to build a rural or suburban system and $125,000 per mile or more to build an urban franchise.

18. In general, the early 12-channel systems might currently provide the highest margin of profit (up to 65% per subscriber) because they are not burdened by the costs of investment in modern equipment. However, the growth potential of such an old system is likely to be very limited. On newer systems, some with more than 55 channels, revenues per subscriber may be twice as high as on 12-channel systems. Yet because labor expenses for administration and maintenance rise sharply with an increase in the number of pay-programming options, margins on the newer systems may average 40% or less. See *Broadcasting,* December 19, 1983.

19. Franchise rights are generally amortizable under Internal Revenue Code Section 1253, enacted by the Tax Reform Act of 1969. However, the Internal Revenue Service argued (in a 1978 cable system acquisition case involving Tele-Communications, Inc.) that a cable franchise is not covered by Sec. 1253. This was resolved in favor of the cable companies through a court decision in 1990 and by 1993 changes in the tax code (i.e., section 197 intangibles). Thus, cable companies are now able to amortize franchise rights and goodwill. However, sports franchises are *not* considered to be section 197 intangibles. See also note 32 of Chapter 6.

20. The first notable PPV movie experiment was done in early 1983. With about 2 million addressable converters in place, MCA offered its *Pirates of Penzance* first-run feature film to MSOs for a minimum of $6 per household. In charging viewers an average of $10 for the privilege of seeing the movie, MSOs are believed to have profited by about $4 million that night. But it wasn't until 1993 that Tele-Communications Inc., after investing $90 million in a nearly insolvent Carolco, indicated that it would attempt to release high-budget movies on PPV prior to release in theaters.

21. To date, response rates to PPV offerings have generally fallen into the 2% to 5% range of addressable homes with access to PPV services. Request Television (then co-owned by Reiss Media and Group W Satellite Communications) and Viewer's Choice (owned by eight MSOs including Fox Cable, Viacom, Times Mirror, The Walt Disney Company, and Warner Brothers) became the leading PPV wholesaler/distributors with access to over 10 million addressable households as of 1992. Reiss began operations in November 1985 by effectively employing with each of its studio-suppliers a "time-shared condominium" concept. Each program year was divided into 10 units, each of which entitled holders to 10% of the program exhibition time on a channel.

The separately contracted unit holders were originally 10 movie studios and/or suppliers for which Reiss provided transmission services, entered into affiliation agreements with cable systems, and billed and collected payments for a fixed fee plus a variable fee that is based on revenues generated. The first Request Channel provided between two and four new movies each week, augmented by special sporting and concert events. In effect, the studios thus each owned an equal share of the available PPV time, and they had the flexibility to swap or sell channel time among themselves while retaining approximately half of the PPV revenues generated at retail. An automatic number identification (ANI) system technology made it possible for one-way addressable cable households to order virtually on impulse.

With Request, the studios negotiate fees directly and separately with each MSO. Viewer's Choice, however, is a more hands-on intermediary service that negotiates all deals with movie studios and event distributors to place their programs on MSOs. Viewer's Choice thus takes a larger percentage of each transaction than does Request. In April 1992, Twentieth Century Fox and Tele-Communications Inc. each bought a 40% interest in Request Television, which had become the largest PPV distributor. Reiss Media Enter-prises remained the third partner in the venture. TCI bought out the other partners in 1996. See also *Variety*, July 22, 1991, and April 6, 1992.

22. Local Multipoint Distribution (LMDS) is a close cousin to MMDS. Instead of the 33-channel AM signal in MMDS, LMDS can carry 49 channels and uses an FM signal that can be received on a smaller dish antenna. For a description of "wireless" cable see *Broadcasting*, December 4, 1989, p. 86.

23. DBS signals, transmitted via high-power satellites, are receivable from rooftop or window-mounted antenna dishes (or flat surfaces) that, as of early 1997, cost about $200 at retail. In Europe, Rupert Murdoch's Astra and British Satellite Broadcasting were two of the early entrants. In the United States, however, DBS service applications to the FCC in the early 1980s were originally sponsored by several major communications companies, including Comsat, RCA, and General Instruments. After several false starts and substantial losses, most of the early entrants withdrew from this field.

Indeed, it wasn't until 1994 that DBS finally made a start in the United States with the launch of a GM Hughes digital-TV satellite. The satellite signal, with break-even potential at fewer than 3 million subscribers, can carry 175 channels of pay TV that are fed by two services, DirecTv and United States Satellite Broadcasting. PrimeStar, a service operated by a competing consortium of six cable company partners that include Tele-Communications Inc. (22%) and Time Warner, Inc., got off to a slower start in 1990 using analog signals. And News Corp. joined in 1997. Originally, the services were thought to be most likely to prosper in rural areas where it would be uneconomical to provide regular cable. See *Broadcasting,* March 13, 1989, for a full historical discussion, *Broadcasting,* December 6, 1993, and *Business Week,* March 13, 1995.

24. In Los Angeles, for example, in the early 1980s, ON-TV and SelecTV services were quite popular. And nationwide, STV subscribers numbered 2 million at the peak. STV has, however, fared much better in France, where Canal Plus has, since 1984, signed up more than 3 million subscribers and has proven to be a great financial success.

25. Many other signal-distribution schemes have been either proposed or tested, but none of them flourished. American Broadcasting, for example, initially implemented and then withdrew (in 1984) an addressable system in which a scrambled VHF signal was sent during unused network overnight hours to homes equipped with a descrambler and a VCR. The system was intended to allow subscribers to play back relatively recent full-length feature films at their own convenience. Also, in late 1977, Warner Communications was the first company to attempt two-way cable service in Columbus, Ohio, under the trade name QUBE, but the financial performance of the system was disappointing.

26. In 1994, revenues for the Baby Bells were approximately $75 billion, and operating profits $16 billion. For major long-distance companies, 1994 service revenues were $62 billion and operating profits $8 billion.

27. For example, in response to consumer complaints about pricing and service, Congress decided in the early 1990s, to revise the previous 1984 Cable Communications Policy Act that had deregulated basic cable service pricing if "effective competition" in a city was provided by the existence of at least three over-the-air broadcast signals. At the time the specter of price regulation adversely affected valuations of MSO properties.

Also, reregulation in the form of the 1992 Cable Act included a section requiring that during 1993 broadcasters negotiate with MSOs in regard to payments for signal retransmission or elect to be automatically carried by MSOs. Many small broadcast stations, having no leverage with the MSOs, immediately opted for must-carry. However, important independent broadcasters and network affiliates opted to request signal retransmission payments from MSOs by arguing that without such signals the value of an MSO's service would be much diminished. In turn, the major MSOs, among them Tele-Communications Inc. and Time-Warner postured against the idea of paying anything.

The cable industry has historically fought legislative and regulatory battles with broadcasting interests. Moreover, the industry found "must-carry" rules to be cumbersome because of the limited channel capacity of many older systems and sought to have the rules changed (the Washington, D.C., Court of Appeals repealed must-carry rules in 1985).

Also, the political spotlight has fallen on so-called compulsory license issues. In 1976, Congress passed a new copyright act that extended to cable television systems a compulsory license to retransmit broadcast signals and especially the right to carry all local broadcast signals without payment to owners of the programs being broadcast. Changing economic power vis-à-vis broadcast television suggests that in the future, some cable systems may have to pay (i.e., obtain retransmission consent) for the right to broadcast popular programs (which, by definition, attract subscribers).

28. The Stern Stewart consulting firm in New York City is known for its development of EVA and market-value added (MVA) theory and practice. Methods involving estimation of the WACC, beta, and the cost of equity capital are described in standard finance texts such as *Principles of Corporate Finance*, 4th ed., Brealey, R. A. and Myers, S. C. (1991). New York: McGraw-Hill.

29. See "Heard on the Street," *Wall Street Journal*, May 20, 1983.

30. Similarly, cable *networks* generate a cash-flow margin of around 20%, and thus with 1990 estimated revenues at $2.1 billion the total cash flow would be $420 million. At 10 times cash flow, the valuation of cable networks would be $4.2 billion minus any long-term debt. See *Broadcasting,* August 12, 1991, for more details.

31. As of July 1992, for example, the Federal Communications Commission proceeded with plans to allow telephone companies to transmit a broad menu of television programming, including movie channels and home shopping, over their phone lines (i.e., to provide a "video dial tone"). However, the FCC stopped short of allowing telcos to produce programming, although a phone company would be permitted to acquire up to 5% of a programmer. But even more significant was the August 24, 1993, watershed ruling by a federal (Virginia) district court (in a Bell Atlantic suit) that struck down as unconstitutional the section of the 1984 Cable Act that restricts telcos from creating, owning, or packaging video programming distributed inside their telephone service regions. The Fourth Circuit Court of Appeals upheld the decision in November 1994. Also, by late 1994, US West and BellSouth had won this right in the federal courts. And by March 1995, Judge Greene of the Federal District Court in Washington ruled that Bell Atlantic could compete directly with cable operators and broadcasters by transmitting programs anywhere in the country. See *New York Times,* March 18, 1995.

Chapter 8

1. An example of *Reversal* given by McLuhan and McLuhan (1988, pp. 107–109) includes the change of the country, which used to be the center of all work, into a place of leisure and recreation, and vice versa for cities. More recently, we can see that cable companies are turning into telephone companies, while telephone companies are interested in providing cable. Also, the network (Internet) has become a computer, and computers, the network.

2. Critics note that much of today's advertising wastes money. For instance, competitors' expenditures cancel each other out if two companies producing similar soft drinks spend greatly to increase brand awareness and market share and neither gains. Because the money must be spent in order to maintain share, the extra expense will be passed on to consumers even though consumers do not derive the benefit of additional information.

3. In open states, local school districts decide how to spend their textbook money. But in adoption states, materials have to be "adopted" in order to qualify for state funding. When adoption cycles in major disciplines such as reading, math, or science coincide in several populous states, profits of the winning publishers are, of course, significantly enhanced.

4. With prices relatively insensitive to changes in demand, an educational publisher's profits will be determined by how successfully the company competes for adoption programs. It might take three years and an investment of perhaps $30 million to create a new math program, and perhaps twice as much for reading. The barrier to entry is that these upfront costs must be carried for several years before any revenues are generated. Products generally stay in the market for five years, over which time capitalized development costs are amortized against revenues. The largest public companies in the business include Viacom (with an estimated 20% share of the $5 billion U.S. market), Harcourt General, Houghton Mifflin, and the U.K.-based Pearson.

5. Large commercial publishers will often allocate $1 per book printed for marketing. To project the profit potential for a book, it is, of course, also necessary to: (a) estimate the average unit costs of paper, printing, and binding (PPB); (b) provide an allowance for publishers' overhead, say, 25% of gross sales on a trade book; (c) account for the publisher's discount to booksellers and other distributors, usually 52%; and (d) deduct as cost the author's advance. See Stewart (1994), and Greco (1997, p. 160).

6. As Carvajal (1996) notes, "Returns are the most significant barometer of the financial success of a book, a measurement more critical than a ranking on a best-seller list because rejects cut directly into profits." Most returns are shipped back within three to nine months. Independent stores generally sell 80% of the books ordered, superstores sell less than 70%, and discounters such as Wal-Mart sell about 60% – a situation that has led to a rising rate of returns and the Hollywood-style emphasis on obtaining wide distribution for a few, heavily-promoted, titles. However, large wholesale distributors such as Ingram or Baker & Taylor act as buffers between publishers and retail outlets.

7. The large public companies include Gannett, New York Times, Tribune, Dow Jones, and Times Mirror.

8. Nevertheless, as noted in Peterson (1997), the *New York Times* has found that "national advertising is not only more profitable than classified or local advertising, it also spreads the sources of revenue across the country, better insulating the paper from local economic slumps." This paper's situation may, however, be unique in that it derives approximately 44% of total column inches in all editions from national advertising at premium prices. National ads thus account for 53% of all ad revenues. By contrast, in the *Los Angeles Times* national only amounted to 15% of total column inches in 1996.

9. Note that a Sunday paper may account for up to half of a daily paper's revenues and earnings.

10. Such discounts may be as much as 50% off, and may take the form of bonus pages or subsidies of various sales efforts or a sharing of data bases. See Pogrebin (1996).

11. For instance, Time Warner is the largest magazine publisher in the world (e.g., *Time, Fortune, Sports Illustrated, Money*). Meredith Publishing, Reader's Digest, and Hachette (France) are other majors. *TV Guide,* a magazine with the second-largest circulation in the U.S. is owned by News Corp.

12. Normally, as a percent of net revenues, the cost of goods sold for a multimedia publisher of consumer-oriented software will amount to 30% to 40%, for sales and marketing 15% to 30%, and for product development, 15%.

13. The first "node" in the network was installed by Bolt, Beranek, & Newman (now BBN Corp.) at UCLA in 1969. By 1975, about 100 such nodes linking research centers and government facilities had been established around the world. In 1985, the National Science Foundation then created a high-speed, long-distance artery – the network's "backbone" – which by 1990 supplanted the original military network. The World Wide Web, developed by British scientist Tim Berners-Lee in 1991, then allowed researchers to readily swap images instead of just messages. Despite an early ban on them, commercial Internet services quickly emerged once effective "browser" software, the Mosaic program, developed by the University of Illinois, became available. By 1995, the NSF backbone was replaced by services operated primarily by seven companies. See also Ziegler (1996).

14. Underlying technological concepts driving the Internet's growth might be summarized as: (a) the network is the computer, (b) computing power doubles every 18 months

(Moore's Law), (c) bandwidth, a measure of how many bits per second can be transmitted, is doubling every year, (d) the bandwidth capacity of fiber approaches infinity.

15. Advertisers would, of course, pay more for an ad on a World Wide Web (i.e., graphical/multimedia) Internet site that must be "clicked-through" than for one which only appears as a banner on a page that is merely "hit." Hutheesing (1996), for example, suggests that the cost for a website banner ad in 1996 was about 3 cents a "hit," but that for an advertising page that must be clicked-through in order to say, play a game, the cost might be 25 cents. Also, audits by third-party firms such as Internet Profiles Corporation (I/PRO) and PC Meter enable advertisers to analyze reach, website visits per month, visit length, visits by day or week or time of day, etc. – information essential to building advertising activity. Moreover, with Webcasting, advertisers are provided with much more accountability than in print or tv.

16. As noted in Chapter 5, the key element of FASB statement 48 is that the amount of future returns can be reasonably estimated. If so, then sales revenue and cost of sales reported in the income statement are reduced to reflect estimated returns.

17. As in other industries, enterprise value (EV) is determined by taking shares outstanding times price per share and then adding net debt and subtracting off-balance sheet assets. EV is then divided by EBITDA to obtain a multiple that allows value comparisons to be made.

18. Discounts to private value might be as much as 40%, and EBITDA multiples will, in publishing, typically range from six to ten times projections – with the long-run historical average ratio of total market value to EBITDA for newspaper publishers at approximately 8.2. Also, other corroborating valuation measures might include estimates of earnings-per-share growth and multiples of projected sales. Such measures are often more appropriate for young companies in new industries, e.g., Internet companies.

19. For example, print and broadcast media advertising availabilities, which are already largely standardized, will likely come to be traded in markets similar to those for stocks or bonds.

Chapter 9

1. Relationships between toy manufacturers and retailers, like those between movie distributors and exhibitors, are sometimes strained. Yet it is a rare toy manufacturer who will refuse to help an important retailer out of an inventory problem. The manufacturer will usually provide the costly incentives (so-called "mark-down money"), sometimes in the form of rebates or price cuts that are required to clear the shelves. Toy industry investors would thus do well to regard manufacturers' receivables more as inventories held in storage by the retailer than as final sales in the strictest sense of financial accounting. As has been proven time and again, harsh post-Christmas earnings surprises may await investors who are unaware that receivables from retailers are not solid until the toys actually sell-through to consumers.

2. See, for example, Watkins (1986) and especially Stern and Schoenhaus (1990) for discussions of the toy development process.

3. For example, it is usually easy enough to make more prints so that a popular movie can be shown in more theaters; it is next to impossible to make and deliver more copies of a popular toy the week before Christmas.

4. In determining the value of a brand name, most methods would take total brand sales and then subtract cost of goods sold, selling, general and administrative expenses, and depreciation in order to arrive at an operating profits figure. From this, an amount equal to what could be earned on a basic or generic version of the product is deducted. A tax rate is then applied to this adjusted amount to estimate what net brand profit might be. Finally, a multiple, depending on how strong the brand is in terms of consumer recognition, stability, leadership, internationality, support, and protection would be used to make a final assessment of the brand's value. *Financial World,* in its issue of September 1, 1992, describes these methods, estimating that Mattel's Barbie brand of dolls was worth $2.2 billion and that the Fisher-Price toy brand was worth $582 million. *Financial World* updates appear every year, and as of the July 8, 1996 edition, the Barbie and Fisher-Price values had grown to $2.5 billion and $1.1 billion, respectively.

5. Parents tend to buy more toys for a first child than for any other.

6. Software is the instruction set that controls a machine's functions.

7. By that time the worldwide market had become fairly mature and predictable, with Gottlieb (eventually renamed Mylstar) later discontinued by its owner (Coca-Cola) and Williams holding dominant market positions. In the late 1980s, Bally sold its pin and video business to a successor company of Williams, WMS Industries.

8. The Sanders engineer was Ralph Baer, and the Sanders patents were eventually licensed to all major home video game manufacturers. The name of the aforementioned MIT graduate student was Steve Russell.

9. Bushnell and his associates produced a version of *Spacewar* called *Computer Space.* But with sales of only 1,500 units, *Computer Space* was not a commercial success, and the rights to it were sold to Nutting Associates, the small firm that had originally agreed to produce it.

Still, following this, Bushnell wanted his design company, Syzygy, to develop a driving game. Yet, for a tiny outfit with limited resources and experience, that was a rather ambitious goal. And so, to gain the necessary skills, Bushnell had the company start by building a prototype that could simulate the simplest game he could think of: tennis. Much to the surprise of its designers, the game was fun to play. But because manufacturers were not interested in producing it, Syzygy had no choice but to assemble the product itself. *Pong,* as it was known, became an instant rage in bars and restaurants where pinball was popular.

In all, Syzygy – by early 1973 renamed Atari after a term (meaning prepare to be engulfed) from the Japanese game of go – sold about 10,000 units, and 90,000 or so copies or adaptations from other manufacturers flooded the market.

Bushnell subsequently bought controlling interest in the company from his associates and then sold the renamed Syzygy (Atari) to Warner Communications. See also Owen (1983) and Kubey (1982).

10. Consoles dedicated to playing only a few variations of one or two games were introduced in 1972 under the Magnavox Odyssey label. And Magnavox was at once joined by several other companies. Besides Atari, the other manufacturers included Coleco, Fairchild Instrument, National Semiconductor, and RCA.

11. Losses at Fairchild and at Warner's new Atari division continued into 1977, when both companies introduced new cartridge-loaded programmable consoles that they hoped would turn the tide. But although these models were a distinct improvement over the previous generation of dedicated machines, they did little to excite the average consumer. Game-design capabilities were at a primitive stage, and the semiconductor chips used in consoles and cartridges had very small and relatively expensive memories. There was no software.

Around this time, Bally Manufacturing and RCA also made major efforts to enter the programmable market, but both companies soon found their participation unrewarding. Bally sold its loss-plagued division to Astrocade, a private company that eventually folded, and RCA discontinued its line. Long-suffering Fairchild also gave up on the business.

12. *Space Invaders* was also instrumental in raising coin-op-industry unit-volume expectations well beyond the 20,000 or so that was considered exceptional in the heyday of pinball.

13. The hit parade included *Asteroids* and *Missile Command,* developed by Atari, *Defender* from Williams Electronics, and the ubiquitous *Pac-Man* and its variants, designed by the private Japanese company Namco and distributed in coin-op version by Bally and in cartridges by Atari.

14. Atari's revenues, which had been $28 million in 1976, expanded to over $2 billion in 1982, while annual operating income went from a loss of several million dollars to profits of more than $320 million.

Also, by 1980, the industry's potential looked good enough for Mattel, then the largest toy company in the United States, to introduce its Intellivision® brand of consoles. And this helped to further boost growth rates. Intellivision's key selling point was pictorial resolution (graphics) superior to that of Atari's 1977-vintage Video Computer System® (VCS), and to the older Odyssey® line. In short order, Mattel garnered about a 16% share of market – second only to Atari's.

Nevertheless, Intellivision was vulnerable in two areas: Its price was relatively high compared with that of the VCS (at retail over $200 versus about $150 for Atari), and it was largely dependent on a software library of generic sports-related games instead of arcade hits. This provided Coleco, a late (1982) entrant, with the opportunity to surpass Mattel's unit volume with ColecoVision® – a lower-priced product that successfully combined high-resolution graphics with top-licensed arcade titles.

Although Atari and Mattel initially had complete control of titles for their own cartridge formats, by late 1981 growth of console shipments had attracted several other plug-compatible software designers and manufacturers, including Activision, Parker Bros. (a division of General Mills), Coleco, CBS, and Imagic.

15. Unit sales in that year climaxed at an estimated 8.3 million consoles and 77 million cartridges.

16. Also at that time, the first inexpensive home computers began to come to market. These home computers included the Texas Instruments (TI) model 99/4A and the Commodore model VIC-20. Both machines were marketed with the promise of combining education and game entertainment.

17. During this time, as saturation became more evident to all participants, price cutting and wholesale dumping of excess hardware and software inventories accelerated – thereby producing aggregate industry losses that amounted to an astounding $1.5 billion in 1983 alone. The bulk of these aggregate net industry losses were generated by Atari ($539 million), Mattel ($361 million), and Texas Instruments ($660 million).

18. Nintendo was joined in this revival by a much shrunken Atari and by another Japanese-based company, Sega Enterprises Ltd. However, Nintendo's software, particularly titles such as *Super Mario Bros. 2*™ and *The Legend of Zelda*™, which each sold over 3 million copies, were especially important in maintaining the company's leading share of market. (*Super Mario Bros.*®, introduced in 1987, sold 9.1 million units.) In fact, the company delivered 7 million hardware units and 32.5 million software units in 1988, and in 1990, nearly 9 million game sets and 60 million software units were sold (with a title such as *Super Mario Bros. 3*™ selling 8 million units).

From the fall of 1986 through year-end 1989, the company estimated that 19 million Nintendo hardware units and 101.5 million Nintendo and Nintendo-licensed software units had been sold. Industry totals for the same period were estimated at 24.5 million hardware units and 125 million software units. Although another potentially serious challenger to Nintendo's primacy was also launched in 1990 by NEC, a large Japanese electronics company, Sega, ultimately proved to be the more important competitor. See also Pollack (1986) and especially Sheff (1993) for a detailed history.

19.   At the peak in 1982, for example, it is estimated that video games absorbed about 25% of all 16K ROMs (read-only memories) and up to 50% of all 32K ROMs produced by the then economically depressed semiconductor manufacturers.

20.   Servicing is the responsibility of the operator, who is often indirectly supported for parts, labor, and financing by local wholesaler/distributor branches. Note also that operators and location owners exercise control over the pricing and frequency of play, and may have obvious opportunities to divert cash if strict accounting is not enforced. All estimates as to the annual coin-drop are thus approximations based on number of units in use and average play per machine.

21.   Manufacturers need a production run of at least 5,000 units in order to cover development and fixed costs, but rarely would there be a demand for more than 30,000 units. And on locations, receipts per square foot are important. At the height of the *Pac-Man* or *Asteroids* frenzy of the early 1980s, for example, some locations were taking in $400 or more per week on a machine that cost $2,400. However, under more normal conditions, collections will average significantly below $100 a week on machines that have been out for a while.

Street operators will, of course, try to extend the useful life of a machine by "rotating" it to a different location. And arcade operators will use variable pricing on tokens in order to be able to collect more during times of peak demand and to encourage greater use at slower times of the day. But the income per week and resale value for a typical machine usually declines rapidly during the first year. And once a machine's drawing power begins to decline noticeably, the owner has to make a financial decision based on projected cash flows, taxes, and salvage values. To provide perspective, according to a 1982 survey by *Play Meter,* a video machine required an average of $117 per week over a 10.5-month period to break even after considering operating costs for rent, taxes, and license fees.

22.   In the early 1980s, the Atari VCS (Video Computer System) had an installed base of over 10 million, and hits such as *Asteroids, Space Invaders,* and *Pac-Man* were bought by at least 50% and perhaps up to 75% of console owners.

23.   The profit dynamics of games are obviously quite similar to those of other entertainment industry segments. On a game cartridge that sells for $40, the wholesale price would normally be about $24 as of the 1990s. A software manufacturer's sales rep would also receive a commission of about 5% for marketing services provided to toy stores. Royalties might amount to $1 or $2 per unit and manufacturing costs up to $10, depending on the media material used. Also, software royalties paid by publishers to game developers might normally range between $1.00 and $1.50 a unit. Developers might also receive advances against royalties, just as in the music business. Chace (1983) discusses such arrangements as they appeared in the early 1980s.

However, software development deals in Silicon Valley are structured differently from those in Hollywood, where about 65% of a project's revenues (total revenues minus the standard 35% distribution fees) would be generally available for recoupment of costs and potential payouts to participants. In game development a typically far lower percentage –

perhaps 15% – is available for such cost recoupments and participant payouts, which are, by definition, related to sales rather than profitability (the Hollywood model).

24. When a new game is introduced, players' skills specific to that game obviously are not well honed, and many coins per unit time are dropped. But as familiarity with the machine's features increases, players are able to endure longer on a single coin, thereby reducing the operator's return. In recognition of this, operators sometimes use "speed-up" kits that make the game more challenging to skilled players.

Chapter 10

1. Berger and Bruning (1979, p. 17).

2. The Flamingo Hotel was designed by Siegel to attract the rich and famous to the middle of the desert. The hotel started a building boom that was not to slow until the early 1980s, when more than 50,000 hotel rooms were available to host some of the largest business conventions in the world. Also see Puzo (1976).

3. Taxes are currently at a rate of 5¾% of gross winnings in Nevada and 8% in New Jersey, where a surcharge of 1¼% of gross revenues to be invested in urban development over 25 years also exists.

4. However, the average length of stay of Atlantic City visitors is probably a little less than a day, and for many visitors just a few hours. In Las Vegas, the average length of stay is about 3.8 days.

5. According to *Gaming Business,* in 1983 there were 92 thoroughbred racing associations, which attracted 51.1 million patrons and handled about $7.2 billion, and 62 standardbred (harness) racing associations that reported a total annual handle of $2.81 billion and a total attendance of 23.3 million. In more recent years, these figures have not changed appreciably.

6. Net revenues retained by the states would normally be about half as much. The rest, after deduction of administrative and selling expenses, is returned to the public as prizes.

7. As Harden and Swardson (1996) note, Indian gaming began in 1975, when the Oneidas of New York began to use bingo as a fund-raising mechanism to pay for a fire department. The Oneidas argued that because they are an Indian nation, their sovereignty entitled them to run their own game. The Seminoles of Florida quickly began their own high-stakes bingo game, and were challenged in *Seminole Tribe v. Butterworth,* a landmark 1981 case.

The Indian Gaming Regulatory Act (IGRA) of 1988 had its roots in two U.S. Supreme Court decisions. In *McClanahan v. Arizona Tax Commission* (1973), the Court pronounced that Indian tribes "have a right to make their own laws and be governed by them," which essentially recognized certain tribes as sovereign nations. And in *Bryan v. Itasca County, Minnesota* (1976), the Court said that states lack civil regulatory jurisdiction over Indian tribes and members on their reservations or trust lands.

In a later decision, *California v. Cabazon Band of Mission Indians* (1987), the Court decided that if a state didn't have a public policy against gaming activities and allowed various forms of gambling, the state could neither prohibit nor regulate gaming activities on tribal lands. Congress, then recognizing the sovereignty of Indian tribes, passed the IGRA. This act established an independent federal regulatory body (the National Indian Gaming Commission) and federal standards governing the operation of gaming on reservations.

Three categories of gaming activities have been defined:

Class I: Traditional social gaming activities for prizes of minimal value, the regulation of which is the responsibility of the tribal government.

Class II: Primarily bingo, but also lotto, pull-tabs, and card games. Such games are regulated by the National Indian Gaming Commission (NIGC).

Class III: All other games not otherwise classified – which means casino-type gaming. Such games must be approved by tribal ordinance and be conducted in conformity with a tribal-state compact entered into by the tribes and the states. The compact must be approved by the NIGC.

As of 1996, over 200 Native American tribes had set up 126 casinos in twenty-four states. Goodman (1995, pp. 111–113) describes background for the *Cabazon* decision in more detail.

8.   From surveys, Scarne (1974) estimated a bingo handle of about $3 billion. However, Abt, Smith, and Christiansen (1985) estimated that same handle for 1982; also see Christiansen (1989) and Cook (1979).

9.   In North Dakota, where low-stakes charity games are legal, the state receives 5%, the charity 65%, and the location owner 30% of the casino's gross win. Similar charity-designated games are also conducted in Canadian provinces. In Alberta, for instance, charities split 10% of their gaming profits with the provincial government, and the operator is entitled to 40%. See also note 10 below.

10.   In Canada, for example, casino gaming has been legal since 1969, when the Canadian federal government's criminal code allowed provinces or charities to establish casinos using the games of roulette or blackjack. And more recently, video lottery terminals and slot machines have been approved. But no gaming licenses are permitted to be held by commercial businesses. Instead, the licenses are held either by provincial governments or by nonprofit organizations. Also, just as in the U.S., Indian tribes (or bands, in Canada) have been in the process of developing a special legalistic framework for the provision of gaming services on their reservations. See also *Gaming & Wagering Business,* April 1993. One of Canada's largest casinos opened in Windsor, Ontario, in May 1994.

11.   These numbers are also not to be confused with the gross amounts bet, or the handle, which is estimated in 1997 to be around $600 billion. Scarne (1974) conducted surveys that indicated much larger numbers – numbers that most observers believe to be highly exaggerated. As of the early 1970s, Scarne estimated that the total U.S. gambling handle (defined as the money handled, the total amount wagered, or the annual gambling exchange) amounted to an astonishing $500 billion. Of this, he estimated that the actual cost to the betting public was about 10% of $500 billion, or $50 billion. See Scarne (1978).

12.   There is evidence to suggest that the majority of players consider gaming to be a form of entertainment. As the survey in the U.S. Congress (1976) indicates, 81% of respondents said that one of the reasons they bet at a casino is to have a good time. See Supplementary Table S10.1.

13.   Judging by history, the industry has experienced only two important setbacks in the postwar period – in 1981 and in 1991 – and both episodes coincided with an economic recession. It seems likely, however, that new competition will probably heighten the industry's future sensitivity to changes in the overall economy.

14.   As of 1985, for example, cash transactions above $10,000 have had to be reported to the Treasury Department.

15.   Acting on the wishes of the legislature, the commission specified the following:

minimum size of table bets

numbers of tables and slots of different denominations and type allowed in each casino

hours of operation

number of square feet of public space relative to number of rooms

numbers of security guards required

number of days per week that live entertainment had to be provided (in the first off-peak seasons there were days when there were more performers on stage than people in the audience)

various other aspects of hotel-casino operations, including limitations on marketing that are normally considered in the province of management

16. For example, as of 1996 the major public companies include Aztar, Circus Circus Enterprises, Grand Casinos, Hilton, ITT, MGM Grand, Mirage Resorts, Harrah's, Sahara Resorts, and Showboat. Racing includes Hollywood Park, San Juan Racing, Santa Anita Consolidated, and United Tote. Bingo includes Stuart Entertainment (formerly Bingo King). And lotteries, especially video lottery terminals, include International Game Technology, Video Lottery Technology, Gtech, and WMS Industries.

17. Yet, in May 1989, the Atlantis (originally Playboy) hotel-casino next to the convention center in Atlantic City closed. Long operating under bankruptcy laws, it failed for a number of reasons, but mostly because it was never able to overcome its initial design handicap of having a casino on three levels.

18. Multiples have generally ranged between five and nine in recent years. Also, in evaluating individual casino properties for the purposes of merger or acquisition, "casino" cash flow, which is EBITDA before corporate expenses, might be considered a more appropriate measure against which to apply a multiple than against EBITDA itself.

19. For this reason, when a management attempts to assess the profitability of, for example, "junkets" – in which travel, hotel, and other expenses are paid by the casino-hotel in return for a promise to gamble a certain minimum over a few days' time – it should use a formula including an estimate of the house edge, the average number of decisions per hour, and the average size of betting units. Similar criteria should be used in determining whether or not a bettor qualifies for "comps" (complimentaries), which may include any, or all, of free drinks and meals, shows, rooms, and transportation.

20. However, Binion's Horseshoe in downtown Las Vegas has a unique policy whereby the player's limit is as high as his first bet. Also, a group of very high-stakes players can "pool" their play.

21. *Gambling Times,* August 1983, p. 16. Also note that this example is a variation on the "Gambler's Ruin" formula. Assume that payoff odds are 1 to 1, that each bet is of one unit, and that the player keeps gambling until a certain goal is reached or the player goes broke. Then the chance that the goal is reached is represented as follows:

Let: p = chance of winning one bet

$q = 1 - p$

i = initial betting units

N = goal (where $N > i$)

Then, if p is less than 0.5, the probability of reaching the goal before going broke equals:

$$1 - (q/p)^i / 1 - (q/p)^N$$

and if $p = 0.5$, the probability of reaching the goal before going broke = i/N.

For instance, in craps, the win probability on the Pass Line bet is 0.493. If the goal is to turn $100 into $250, and the unit bet is $50, then p = 0.493, q = 0.507, i = 2 (initial two betting units), N = 5, and the probability, after applying the formula, is 0.383. If the goal was to reach $500 before going broke, the probability would be only 0.18. See *Win,* January–February 1993, p. 51.

22. Note that for slot machines, the coins-in, or slot handle, is obviously a known quantity and is reasonably well correlated with the slot drop, i.e, what falls into a slot machine's bucket after winners have been paid out. However, as explained later in the text, in table games, the handle is, under actual playing conditions, very difficult to calculate and may be quite different from the drop.

23. Interestingly, the definitions of hold percentage are somewhat different in Nevada and in New Jersey. New Jersey's definition includes all cash and markers, but Nevada's definition does not include markers that may be redeemed at the table where the credit slip originated. All other things being equal, New Jersey hold figures are normally lower by 3% to 4% than those of Nevada. The hold percentage, or the hold p.c. as it is also known, of course, should not be confused with percentages used to express casino advantages (expected values) for table games. Such casino advantages are stated as percentages of handle and not as percentages of drop.

24. If, however, as is more likely, players initially buy many more chips than they bet on each decision (some lose and some tend to walk away from a table without betting all the chips initially bought), then the ratio of handle to drop does not grow as rapidly as in this example.

25. Win rates, of course, also depend on game rules, which may vary (especially in Nevada) according to the discretion of management.

26. Another illustration: In craps, on the pass line, the average cost per roll as a percentage of money bet is 0.42%. This is determined by taking the house advantage of 1.41% and dividing by the average number of rolls per decision, which is 3.38. The average cost per roll of the dice to the player, or conversely win per roll for the casino, can then be used to determine how long on the average it would take for the casino to generate a certain amount of revenue, or what minimum average pass bet at the table might be required to win a certain amount. If in one hour of play, for example, there are an average of 60 rolls, then 60 rolls per hour times 0.0042 cost per roll equals 0.252. For the casino to win $500 in that hour from just the pass line bets, the average pass line bet for the whole table would have to be $500/0.252 or $1,984.13.

27. Provost (1994, p. 59).

28. It is estimated that perhaps 20% of players may account for 80% of the upper-end business.

29. Junkets, in which rooms, meals, and travel costs may be picked up, i.e., "comped" by the casino, have diminished in popularity as the casinos have found that junkets are not as profitable as they had been thought to be. For instance, a casino wanting to earn at least $100 should know that if it costs $400 to bring a junket player in the door, it must – assuming a 20% hold (win/drop) – realize a minimum drop that averages $2,500. As noted in Stefanelli and Nazarechuk (1996, p. 135), a casino is generally "willing to comp guests up to one-half of the amount it expects to win from them." Players are rated by: (a) buy–in amount to the game; (b) average bet; (c) largest bet; and (d) duration of play.

30. The volume increase is a direct function of the credit extension itself and may also be indirectly affected by the exciting atmosphere that surrounds high-stakes tables, where smaller noncredit bettors may feel that they should become less conservative with their funds.

31. Credit play is, however, much less significant on most riverboat and Indian reservation casinos. Also note that prior to June 1983, gaming debts were not legally enforceable in Nevada. See Rose (1986).

32. For instance, in 1983, receivables in Atlantic City casinos rose at about twice the rate of win and foreshadowed the potential for a noticeably slower growth of revenues (win) in 1984.

33. The cage, as noted in (Eade, 1996, p. 157), is the casino's operational nerve center, which is responsible for the custodianship of and accountability for the casino's bankroll, provides a vital link to the casino pit areas, deals with customer transactions, interfaces with every casino department, and is responsible for the preparation and maintenance of internal control forms.

34. Indeed, if it weren't for the Interstate Wire Act of 1956, which makes transmission of bets using phone lines a felony, wagering on the Internet would already probably be huge.

Chapter 11

1. See Ozanian and Taub (1992).

2. See Durant (1969).

3. Indeed, Quirk and Fort (1992, p. 62) indicate that "on average, over their league histories, baseball franchise prices have been increasing at a rate of about 8% per year, NBA basketball franchises at about 16% per year, and NFL franchises at about 20% per year... There is insufficient information about prices of NHL franchises." Estimates in Sheehan (1996, p. 45) are even higher for MLB.

4. For instance, as La Pointe (1989) indicates, in 1989, a sports bidding war erupted among the cable and broadcast networks. CBS paid $1.1 billion for four years of major league baseball and NBC paid $600 million for four years of NBA games. Yet even with such hefty aggregate payments, in the average year perhaps one-third of league teams may report losses. However, without more details concerning the methods of accounting, it is difficult for outsiders to know how much credence to place in such profit and loss statements. Deferred player salaries, an important potential liability for professional teams, might, for example, be an area of differences in accounting treatments.

5. Whereas a degree of immunity from application of antitrust laws exists for professional teams, a 1984 Supreme Court decision found that the National Collegiate Athletic Association's (NCAA) exclusive agreements with three television networks violated federal antitrust statutes. That decision left NCAA colleges free to negotiate individual contracts with commercial broadcast and cable networks and nullified the NCAA's traditional role as sole exclusive negotiator for broadcast rights to college football games.

Although the Supreme Court decision increases opportunities for cable and regional sports networks and independent broadcasters to bid for licenses to show games of local interest, the amounts being paid by these new bidders had for a while in the aggregate proved to be below the amounts that had regularly been obtained in contracts negotiated by the NCAA. In 1994, however, CBS extended its coverage of NCAA games through 2002 in a $1.73 billion rights package – which averages out to $216 million a year, or a 50% gain over the $143 million CBS paid for annual rights in the previous deal negotiated in 1989.

6. According to Christiansen (1989), for instance, the illegal gross handle for such activities in 1988 was probably greater than $26 billion, with the largest portion wagered on football.

7. Gate receipts are shared 65:35 between home and visiting teams. In 1980, the net profit margin for NFL teams was 5.2%, and net income was $694,000. This compares with total television payments of only $926,000 for the NFL title game in 1963 (Michener, 1976, p. 360). Under the 1982 television contract, teams derived an average of $14.2 million per year from television. See note 12 below.

8. See, for example, the discussion by Frank (1984) of the United States Football League.

9. As Moldea (1989, p. 82) notes, the U.S. Supreme Court ruled in 1957 that, "unlike major-league baseball, the NFL was subject to federal antitrust laws." But relaxation of antitrust-law restraints has enabled leagues to bargain with networks as a unit. In this respect, the sports business has an advantage not available to other entertainment segments. Also see Rivkin (1974) and note 12 below.

10. Indeed, in baseball and basketball, the size of the local market and the degree of competence demonstrated are much more highly correlated to the total amount of television, cable, and stadium-admission revenues that can be attracted than is the case in football. Also, in the NBA and NHL, gate receipts are not shared with the visiting team; the home team takes 100%. In baseball, there is limited sharing of gate receipts, but not nearly to the extent of that in the NFL. As Helyar (1995) notes, "The economic underpinning of the league has long been its generous revenue-sharing arrangements: equal sharing of network television money and a 60-40 home-visitor gate split." See also Waggoner (1982).

However, as Lubove (1995) notes, Major League Soccer uses a co-op organizational model in which approximately half of all revenues from ticket sales, local television, and sponsorships are shared equally among all teams. All national television rights and commercial tie-ins are also split evenly.

11. Local broadcast/cable license fees, which have averaged 25% of a team's total revenues, may become proportionally more important as a source of income if national network payments grow less rapidly. The team income disparities that might then arise could put more pressure on baseball and basketball owners to share more of the locally generated revenues than they now do. In fact, large-market teams already take in far more from sale of local rights than do their small-market counterparts. For example, in 1990, the New York Yankees received $55.6 million from local broadcast revenues, while the Seattle Mariners took in only $3 million. Note that cable and pay-TV revenues are split 75% home club, 25% visitors.

Of course, license fees from sales of network television rights, which *are* shared, remain significant. As of the mid-1980s, baseball franchises began splitting the income from network broadcasts, with each major league team deriving about $7 million annually (before other possible deductions) from this source. By 1990, this amount had doubled to $14 million per team. For historical perspective, it might be noted that radio, television, and cable-rights fees paid to baseball's major-league teams rose from a mere $44.5 million in 1975 to almost $268 million in 1984.

As for hockey, the NHL agreed (in 1994) to have a number of its games televised by Fox Sports and ESPN. In this five-year deal ending in the 1998–99 season, the NHL is guaranteed to receive about $150 million in either advertising sales or rights fees.

12. As of 1993, for instance, the NBA and the NBC network announced a new four-year $750 million rights deal that may be a template for others in the future. The parties here agreed to share advertising revenues once NBC reaches a certain sales level (about $1.06 billion) over the four years. Annual payments are escalated in the first three years of the deal.

Under baseball's 1993 agreement, MLB would receive no rights fee for its games, but instead would retain 87.5% of the revenues derived from the deal, with the ABC and NBC networks splitting the rest until the joint venture investment is recovered. After that, the split goes to 80-10-10. See *Broadcasting & Cable,* May 31, 1993.

Also, in 1995, MLB made a $1.7 billion contract to air games between 1996 and 2000 on a combination of Fox, NBC, ESPN, and the Fox Sports/Liberty cable networks. See *Daily Variety,* November 7, 1995.

The NFL's last three rights deals (in $ billions) were as follows: 1990–93 $3.65; 1987–89 $1.43; 1982–86 $2.07.

Moreover, at the end of 1993, the Fox network won the rights to four years of National Football Conference games with a bid of $1.58 billion. NBC also paid $880 million for other NFL games, including two Super Bowls, while ABC retained its package of Monday night games plus one Super Bowl for $950 million. Rights fees for regular network broadcasts for 1994–97 thus totaled $3.41 billion.

Note, however, that in 1990, CBS wrote off $115 million of its $1.06 billion baseball contract because of a World Series sweep and the effects of a spring lockout, and wrote off $282 million more a year later. And in 1995, Fox took a $350 million write-off to reflect future losses on its $1.58 billion NFL contract.

13. As Bradsher (1994) notes, "The antitrust exemption – which no other major league sport shares – allows baseball owners to impose industry-wide salary limits, while remaining partially shielded from any lawsuits that the players may file. The exemption also allows a majority of the owners to block other owners who may want to move their franchises to new cities, and to reserve players' freedom to move up to a certain level of service." As of early 1997, the owners committed to negotiate a partial end to antitrust exemption.

14. The case of *Flood v. Kuhn* served to advance some of the issues that ultimately led to free-agency – wherein veteran players became eligible free agents after six seasons, and those with three seasons of experience could seek arbitration. The original reserve system was secretly adopted in 1879 and first implemented by the National League in 1880. It was designed to minimize players' bargaining power and to prevent a few wealthy owners from destroying a league's competitive balance by buying all the best talent. See also Demmert (1973), who, from the perspective of the early 1970s, argues that competitive balance has generally not been attainable: The richest teams in the most lucrative markets, regardless of new-talent draft policies, have over the long term tended to field clubs with the highest overall athletic quality.

Prior to free-agency, baseball's so-called waiver rules had restricted the sale of a player's contract to a team outside the league, and an owner wishing to make such a sale had to first secure agreement from each team owner in the league to relinquish the right to purchase the player's contract at a fixed price. Union contracts still generally require a player testing free-agency to give his old club an opportunity to match a new team's offer. Also, teams losing valuable players may be entitled to receive some compensation. These issues are thoroughly discussed in Miller (1991). Charges of collusion by Major League Baseball owners against players were settled in December 1990 at a total cost to the league of $280 million. See also, note 17, below.

15. Several times during the 1960s and 1970s, the National Football League attempted to obtain immunity from the Sherman Antitrust Act of 1890, which declared "every contract, combination . . . or conspiracy in restraint of trade or commerce to be illegal." One of the key cases was *John Mackey et al. v. National Football League,* which was filed in 1972 by the players' union to fight against the so-called Roselle Rule. As Harris (1986,

p. 71) notes, this rule, named after the League's commissioner, suggested that "any franchise whose contract with a player expired had the right to compensation from the player's new employer should that player subsequently work for another franchise. The compensation was to be a player of equal caliber, selected by the commissioner." The effect of this, Mackey argued, was to suppress player salaries by reducing competition between franchises. Mackey won the original case, but an appeals court decision in October of 1976 said, in effect, that the labor issues should be settled by collective bargaining. Both sides agreed on a 76-page contract in February of 1977.

Public-policy implications deriving from baseball's immunity to antitrust laws and the previously severe restrictions on the economic mobility of players enmeshed in the reserve system are extensively reviewed in Markham and Teplitz (1981).

16. In the NBA, owners and players settled on free agency after four years' experience in 1988. In the NFL, a free agency agreement for players with five years experience and with expired contracts was reached in 1993. However, under the so-called Rooney Rule, the top clubs are not allowed to go into the free-agent market unless they have lost a free agent. Also, if salary costs reach 67% of designated NFL revenues, eligibility for free-agency drops to four years. Player mobility is still most restrictive in hockey. See Scully (1995, pp. 37–40) for details.

17. Note that the effectiveness of free-agency was challenged in 1987 as team owners apparently stopped aggressively bidding against each other (i.e., colluded). See, for example, Spitz (1987) and Miller (1991).

Also, there have been numerous strikes or threats of strikes in professional sports. Baseball players went on strike in 1972 (13 days), 1981 (50 days), 1985 (two days), and 1994 (34 days), and football players in 1982 and 1987. Baseball team owners' lockouts occurred in 1976 and 1990 (during spring training). And hockey players struck for 10 days in the 1992 postseason playoffs, and didn't work for half of the 1994–95 season.

The 1982 National Football League Players Association strike was based on an attempt to gear compensation to a fixed percentage of gross revenues and to create a salary scale based on seniority and performance. The players did not achieve their initial primary objective of sharing a percentage of gross revenues from network television and therefore did not significantly alter the balance of power of owners over athletes. But their collective salary pool totaling $1.6 billion over five years amounted to just under 50% of gross revenues, as compared with 35%–44% before the strike. In addition, a modest salary scale – and the right to bargain for income above minimums that started at $30,000 per year for rookies and went up to $200,000 per year for veterans – was established.

An important decision was reached by a Minneapolis jury in September of 1992. In a suit challenging the National Football League's system of limited free agency, the jury ruled that the NFL's Plan B free-agency system (introduced in 1989) violated the federal antitrust laws. Still, professional baseball and basketball, as of 1992, had more liberal free-agency than football. See, for example, *New York Times,* September 12, 1992.

The outcome in football, however, is similar to the situation in the 1981 Major League Baseball Players Association strike, in which the primary issue was compensation to clubs losing players through free-agency transfers. The complicated settlement delineates rules for player rankings and performances under which such transfers are conducted.

The Basketball Players Association in the NBA and the National Hockey League Players Association negotiated with team owners on issues similar to those in football and baseball. But a new revenue-sharing agreement was developed in the NBA in 1983. The agreement was designed to prevent richer franchises from dominating the game, to create more consistent competition between teams, and to stop cost escalation caused by free agency. Beginning in the 1984–5 season, the NBA guaranteed players 53% of the league's gross revenue – which included money from rapidly growing sales of regional pay-cable rights. The 53% was distributed among 23 teams, with a "cap" for the richest teams, and a "floating minimum" for the poorest. See "The NBA's Ingenious Move to Cap Players' Salaries," *Business Week,* October 31, 1983, and Barra (1995), who illustrates how the NFL's 49ers were able to beat salary caps.

Reluctant MLB owners also approved an agreement with the players in November 1996 that applied for at least five years, beginning in 1996, called for a "luxury" tax of 35 percent on the proportion of 1997 payroll over $51 million, and provided for the 13 clubs with the highest revenues to contribute to a pool to be divided by the 13 teams with the lowest revenues. See *New York Times,* November 27, 1996.

18. Until a 1995 landmark ruling in the European Court of Justice broke the cartel arrangements, teams could field only three nonlocal players. European Union players, however, are now no longer counted as foreigners; at the end of a contract, a player becomes a free agent. Soccer clubs used to be able to block player trades or insist on big fees for allowing them. In the U.S., Major League Soccer (MLS) is the professional organization that controls the sport. See also note 10 above, Lubove (1995), and *Business Week,* September 23, 1996.

19. In recent years, tax-law revisions and court interpretations have made this an exceedingly complicated subject, the discussion of which is largely beyond the scope of this book. More detail is presented in Horvitz and Hoffman (1976), Raabe (1977), Ambrose (1981), and Harmelink and Vignes (1981).

20. Other IRS rulings further indicated that the "option clause" in football-player contracts would be regarded as similar to baseball's "reserve clause," that television revenue did not constitute "passive investment income" (and would therefore not adversely affect election of subchapter S treatments), and that franchise proceeds received in return for relinquishment of exclusive territorial rights would be granted favorable capital-gains treatment.

In 1974, two additional regulations concerning amortization of intangibles and the distinction between nonamortizable goodwill and amortizable intangibles also helped set the stage for employing sports-franchise ownership as a tax shelter.

21. Important cases included: *Laird v. United States; First Northwest Industries of America, Inc., Houston Chronicle Publishing Co. v. United States*; *KFOX Inc. v. United States.* However, tax deductibility of intangible asset amortizations would now, in most instances, follow the 1993 tax code revisions, which provide a write-down period of 15 years for so-called section 197 intangible assets. Professional sports franchises, however, are specifically excluded from this category.

Scully (1995, p. 137) notes that sports team owners, unlike those holding franchises in other industries, cannot amortize the goodwill of the business. Also, "broadcast rights (*Laird; McCarthy v. United States,* (1986)), exclusive territorial rights, and parking and concessions are considered part of the franchise value and are not depreciable." This implies that as the value of broadcast rights rises, the depreciable component of the franchise price at the time of sale declines.

22. Professional team valuations as of 1991 appear in Baldo (1991), where the rule of thumb is to use 2.5 times revenues for football and basketball teams, 2 times revenues for baseball, and 1.8 times revenues for hockey. Baseball's multiple is lower than football's because the revenue stream, more dependent on gate receipts, is less predictable. Hockey's multiple is even lower, because hockey, without a national TV contract, is most dependent on gate receipts. The most valuable team in this study was the New York Yankees, with an estimated franchise value of $225 million. The average NFL team was estimated to be worth $132 million, MLB team $121 million, NBA team $70 million, and NHL team $44 million. This study has been extended in Ozanian and Taub (1992 and 1993) and appears annually in *Financial World* surveys.

Note also that several MLB teams changed hands in 1992: The Houston Astros and the Astrodome lease for $115 million, the Detroit Tigers for approximately $85 million, the Seattle Mariners for $125 million, and the San Francisco Giants to an investor group for $100 million. Both the Florida Marlins and the Colorado Rockies also paid $95 million to join the National League beginning with the 1993 season. And in 1993, an investors' group agreed to a price of $174 million for the Baltimore Orioles. Moreover, the 1994–95 strike did not stop the expansion of MLB to 30 teams. Each new team – the Arizona Diamondbacks and the Tampa Bay Devil Rays – was charged $130 million (up 42% from 1990's expansion) to join the industry.

Moreover, as of 1993, the NFL set the cost of an incoming franchise at $140 million. This compares to $16 million in 1974, when Seattle and Tampa Bay joined the NFL. But in 1994, the Philadelphia Eagles were sold for $185 million. And, in 1995, the Tampa Bay Buccaneers (valued at $16 million in 1974) were bought for $192 million – the highest price ever for an NFL team.

In hockey, the bankrupt Los Angeles Kings were bought for more than $100 million in 1995. In 1996, Comcast bought a controlling interest in the Philadelphia Flyers (along with basketball's 76ers) for $430 million. And, in 1997, News Corp. acquired baseball's Los Angeles Dodgers for $350 million.

23. Baade (1994) analyzed 48 U.S. cities between 1958 and 1987, including cities that hosted professional teams, and found that professional sports stadiums and teams generally have no significant impact on a region's economic growth. ''. . . sports spending simply substitutes for other forms of leisure spending.'' See also Forsyth (1995).

24. For example, see Wayne (1996) and Laing (1996), who notes that in the 1990s, 30 professional sports facilities have been built in the U.S. at a total cost of $4 billion.

25. This is also more recently explored in Quirk and Fort (1992) and in Scully (1989).

26. Another early inquiry by Noll (1974) concerned demand for sports contests. Among the factors that, a priori, can be expected to influence demand are ratios of skillful to unskillful players, a winning as opposed to a losing home team, population size and characteristics of the city in which a game is played, amount of competing entertainment available, and ticket prices (e.g., average price per seat). Noll's regression results for baseball attendance in the 1970 and 1971 seasons, for example, indicated that:

(a) A negative correlation between attendance and income gives the impression that baseball is a working-class sport.

(b) There is a strong positive effect on attendance from winning a pennant.

(c) The drawing power of baseball is substantially enhanced if a team has star players.

(d) The demand for baseball appears relatively price-inelastic, which means that teams could raise ticket prices without significant loss of paid attendance.

27. As Demmert (1973, p. 96) has noted, ''institutional restrictions on the economic mobility of professional athletes . . . serve as a rent transfer mechanism, assuring the economic viability of the league at the expense of the players.'' And as Scully (1989, p. 191) has noted, ''equalization of playing strengths within a league occurs only through the equalization of revenue among the clubs, or, lacking that development, through a system of player reservation, reverse order drafting, and a ban on the cash sale of player contracts.''

28. Despite this, however, publicly traded shares of professional sports teams have generally not proven to be good investments because opportunities to expand are usually minimal, and there is considerable upward pressure on wages, frequent labor strife, and dependence on the performance of a few key employees. Shares of the Boston Celtics and the Florida Panthers are now publicly traded, but the Cleveland Cavaliers, the Milwaukee Bucks, the New England Patriots, and the Baltimore Orioles were all public in the 1970s.

Chapter 12

1. As Figure 12.4(c) shows, until 1989, stage productions garnered most of their dollars on Broadway – legally defined as a production in the Broadway District of New York City in a theater seating more than 499 persons. In contrast, ''Off-Broadway'' is defined as a New York City production in a theater seating no more than 499 and no fewer than 99.

2. In looking at this, Baumol and Baumol (1984) noted that over the 50 years following the Great Depression, top Broadway prices rose about 14-fold, while movie-ticket prices rose 35-fold. Admission trends for less expensive off-Broadway performances are probably quite similar, but data on this are not reliable. See also Disch (1991).

3. The total ''supply'' today would also include performances within a nonprofit network of more than 200 resident or regional theaters. The Theatre Communications Group publishes an annual survey of a sample of theaters in *American Theatre*. In 1995, for example, the box office covered 62.6% of expenses in a large private sub-sample group of 66 theatres. And for all 215 theatres covered in the survey, 18.6 million people attended 56,600 performances of some 2,600 productions that generated $281 million of earned income.

4. As indicated in the previous note, The Theatre Communications Group, Inc. regularly tracks the finances of such resident theaters. Typically, at least 35% of all income is unearned, i.e., is from contributions. See also Reich (1996).

5. According to Hirsch (1987), Ringling played, in 1987, before 11 million people in 89 cities at ticket prices ranging from $6.00 to $11.50. Revenues in 1987 were $250 million, but according to Gilpin (1993) revenues were probably twice as much by 1993. Labor costs are 50% of budget; ads and promotion consume another 25%; and the remainder of the budget is absorbed by train costs, arena rentals, props, and equipment and insurance expenses. Even when owned by Mattel, which purchased the company for $47 million in December 1970, the huge Ringling Bros. and Barnum & Bailey units (Red and Blue, each with 350 employees) were not financially impressive.

Most circuses cover their costs at the gate and make profits with concessions. RB&BB's yearly advertising and promotion budget is between $10 million and $12 million, with half of this total going to TV and 25% to newspapers, according to *Advertising Age,* December 12, 1983. A review of the RB&BB history at age 100 appears in *Variety,* January 11, 1984, with a follow-up appearing in *Variety,* July 24, 1995. See also *Time,* May 4, 1970, and *Amusement Business,* August 15, 1970. Other recent touring groups include: The Big Apple Circus, The Carson & Barnes Circus, the Clyde Beatty–Cole Bros. Circus, the Pickle Family Circus, the Culpepper & Merriweather Great Combined Circus, the Royal Hanneford Circus, and the Canadian Cirque du Soleil.

6. However, as Heilbrun and Gray (1993, p. 133) note, the rising real incomes that are derived from rising productivity in the overall economy make higher ticket prices more affordable for more people, thus mitigating some of the adverse productivity-lag effects.

7. However, some private-institution grants (from foundations, corporations, and labor unions) are regularly directed toward specific support of other organizations and projects, including those in museums, music, architecture, and literature. Note also that in recent years, symphony orchestras and theater, opera, and dance companies have steadily derived approximately 55% to 60% of total revenues from earned income, while private support and public funding have accounted for roughly 35% to 40% and 5% to 10%, respectively, of revenues.

8. In practice, copyright considerations are often illegally ignored in small off-off-Broadway or regional productions. Copyrights would, of course, be enforced in any important commercial production.

9. In acquiring rights to a play, the producer adheres to Dramatists' Guild option-contract stipulations that provide the playwright with a nonrefundable deposit, to be forfeited if the play is not produced within a year or some shorter period. In addition, the dramatist is entitled to royalties on a sliding scale, between 5% and 10% of the box-office gross, and to the bulk of receipts from ancillary rights, including film, cable-television, and foreign productions.

A prominent example is the Rodgers & Hammerstein musical *Oklahoma!*. The fees for rights for a major performance of this show are customarily in the area of 8% of box-office gross, with an advance against royalties of $18,000 or more. See *Variety*, March 29, 1993.

10. Yet, as Frey and Pommerehne (1989, p. 35) have noted, theatrical productions *can* be profitable if the audience size is large, the fixed costs are small, there is price discrimination (e.g., seats with a better view are priced higher), and there are subsidiary sources of income (e.g., video, films, etc.).

11. The New York State Attorney General's office had at one time compiled statistics on offering prospectuses for Broadway and off-Broadway shows. Over the 11 seasons between 1972–3 and 1982–3, for example, some 948 shows in this sample (which included shows that never opened, but excluded some very prominently successful shows in which funding was privately raised) lost a grand total of $66.6 million on capitalizations of $267.5 million. There was not a single season in which these shows, in the aggregate, generated profits.

Rosenberg and Harburg (1993, p.14) illustrate that the percentage of Broadway musicals (including revivals) that failed to return investors' funds, the "flops," consistently averaged 76% of the projects launched between 1945 and 1990. The figure is close to the flop average between 1925 and 1935. Rothstein (1988) also notes that in the 17 months after *Starlight Express* opened (in March 1987), this show took in $35 million and was seen by more than 925,000 people – and it had not yet recouped its investment. As of 1995, the most expensive nonmusical flop in Broadway history was "On the Waterfront," which lost its entire $2.6 million capitalization after eight performances.

12. Despite the odds against success, angels, as well as large entertainment companies, continue to be attracted to Broadway: Every so often a show will provide spectacular returns on investment, especially when sales of cable–television, movie, recording, and other rights, as well as profits from road-show productions are included.

That is because, when shows are successful, they are incredibly so. *Cats,* according to *Variety* of February 15, 1989, has become the most profitable (in absolute dollars) theatrical production to date, earning net profit in North America (United States and Canada) of approximately $44 million (and another $14.5 million from the London and other foreign editions). The base investment made by the Shubert Organization, ABC Entertainment, Metromedia Corp., and Geffen Records in 1982 was $3.9 million, and the Andrew Lloyd Webber production thus returned over 11 times the investment in North America alone. Because Webber, as author, and the other royalty participants receive about 25% as a license fee plus royalties, the actual gross profit was $58 million. As of June 1997, when it became the longest-running show in Broadway history, *Cats* was still grossing more than $350,000 a week and had generated revenues of more than $329 million on Broadway and $2.2 billion worldwide. See Grimes (1997).

Other big winners have included *Hello, Dolly,* which netted $9 million on a $420,000 investment (a 21-to-1 return, with investors splitting the profit equally with the producer David Merrick) and *Fiddler on the Roof,* which earned $12.4 million on a $375,000 investment. And, Disney's *Beauty and the Beast,* with an initial investment believed to be $11.9 million, was also a huge success despite its cost. See Witchel (1994), and Lyman (1997).

Reibstein (1986) suggests that, in order to succeed, straight plays should generally have weekly production costs that are half or less of the theater's box-office capacity, although musicals will usually range higher. And in Weber (1993), it is suggested that a musical should now be able to pay back within a year. Also see Passell (1989).

13. Rosenberg and Harburg (1993, p. 8) note that, as of 1991, the Shubert Organization owned or operated seventeen theaters, the Nederlander, ten theaters, and Jujamcyn five, with the proportion of the Broadway gross taken by each organization split approximately 53%, 28%, and 19%, respectively.

14. The New York Limited Liability Company Law became effective in October 1994, and has stirred debate as to whether an LLC structure offers significant advantages over traditional limited partnerships. See Farber (1995) and Wasser (1995).

Also, until 1990, New York State theatrical law did not permit a pool of capital to be raised for the financing of more than one show. Andrew Lloyd Webber's Really Useful Group (RUG) was the first company to attempt, in 1990, to solicit investment capital for more than one show and for shows that are not specifically identified. RUG had hoped to raise $20 million from a private placement offering to finance *Aspects of Love* and a touring company of *Phantom of the Opera.* However, the offering, for various reasons, was not as large as had been planned. See *Variety,* October 1, 1990.

15. For off-Broadway productions, Farber (1993, p. 6) notes that if the author is not well-known, the usual royalty payment is a rate of 5% of the gross weekly box office for nonmusicals and a rate of 6% for musicals. But the rate for famous authors would scale up to 10%. Off-Broadway producer's fees are usually between 1% or 2% of gross weekly box-office receipts, with the higher amount sometimes only after recoupment of costs. Also, investors in a show's limited liability partnership would normally receive 50% of the producing company's profits.

16. Box-office cash flows may also be diverted from the production or be collected in ways that are disadvantageous for the producer. For example, as Collins (1992) notes, ticket brokers sometimes offer box-office workers payments, known as "ice," for a block of seats to a hit show. The brokers then resell the tickets at a premium. The practice reduces the number of good seats available to the public and potentially caps the producer's total receipts at a point below which they would otherwise be.

17. If x = utilization percentage, then the formula is x = $100,000/(500 seats × $30 ticket price × 8 performances).

18. Although all Broadway productions follow contract-specified minimum-scale guidelines, the percentage of unemployed members of performing-arts unions is chronically high, and for smaller productions, union specifications are often ignored or waived. For instance, in order to encourage low-budget productions that will provide good experience for new performers, Equity waives many of its minimums in theaters with seating of under 100.

19. Several important works, including those of Baumol and Bowen (1968), Blaug (1976), Netzer (1978), and Throsby and Withers (1979), can be cited. Topics of potential interest to economists, all treated in the volume edited by Hendon, Shanahan, and Mac-Donald (1980), include a mathematical model for support of the arts (Seaman, 1980), an analysis of artistic innovation using information theory (Owen and Owen, 1980), development of a composer supply function (Felton, 1980), and estimation of a demand function for Broadway theater tickets (Kelejian and Lawrence, 1980). In addition, Moore (1968) developed a model of demand for theater as a function of income, the supply of shows, and the real price of tickets. The *Journal of Cultural Economics* is also an important source for the most recent studies in this field.

20. Such price elasticity estimates appear to range from 0.4 to 0.9.

21. The empirical work is compared in Heilbrun and Gray (1993).

22. Frey and Pommerehne (1989, p. 46) note that ''theaters, operas, ballet and orchestras behave differently with respect to output, inputs and the production process depending on whether they are co-operatively run, profit-oriented and private, or non–profit-oriented and public.'' And in this vein, Hansmann (1981) explores the reasons for the preponderance of nonprofit-institution involvement in the high-culture performing arts and notes that high fixed production costs relative to marginal costs and overall demand force performing-arts groups to engage in price discrimination if they are to survive without subsidy. But because opportunities for effective ticket-price discrimination are limited, the nonprofit-organization structure seems best suited for encouraging voluntary donations. Also, in examining the nonprofit aspects, DiMaggio (1984, p. 57) suggests that, ''because nonprofit organizations need not maximize net income, public policy assumes that they will maximize something else . . . a combination of services and aesthetic quality.''

23. In reference to the network television business, for example, it has been noted by Baumol and Baumol (1984, p. 36) that there will be ''an initial period of decline in total costs (in constant dollars) followed by a period in which . . . costs begin to behave in a manner more and more similar to the live performing arts. The reason is that the cost of the highly technological component (transmission cost) will decline, or at least not rise as fast as the economy's inflation rate. At the same time, the cost of programming increases at a rate surpassing the rate of inflation.

''If each year transmission costs decrease and over-the-line or programming expenses increase, eventually programming cost will begin to dominate the overall budget . . . One of the major networks reports . . . that while over-the-line costs comprised 30% to 35% of a dramatic presentation 10 years ago, they now constitute 50% of the budget.''

Chapter 13

1. Actually, the oldest amusement park is Bakken, just north of Copenhagen, which began attracting visitors in 1583. See *Amusement Business,* March 3, 1996.

2. Indeed, the first true amusement park was Steeplechase Park at Coney Island, which was opened in 1897 by George Tilyou. Also, as Nasaw (1993, p. 85) notes, Luna Park, in competition with Steeplechase and Dreamland, in 1904 attracted 4 million people – a remarkable number for that time.

3. As Adams (1991, pp. 43–5) notes, the underlying concepts had also been proven in Tilyou's Steeplechase Park.

4. The 160-acre site for Disneyland was selected by the Stanford Research Institute.

5. In attempts to emulate Disney's concepts on a smaller scale, the Marriott Corporation, Taft Broadcasting, Six Flags, and others began a construction boom that lasted throughout most of the 1970s. A total of at least $500 million was spent in the construction of parks such as Busch Gardens Old Country, Great Adventure, Kings Dominion, Great America, and Canada's Wonderland. As of 1997, the largest corporate park operators after Disney in terms of total admissions were Anheuser-Busch (Sea World, Busch Gardens Tampa, Fla., and Williamsburg, Va.), Six Flags (partly owned by Time Warner), Paramount (Kings Island, Kings Dominion, Canada's Wonderland), and Seagram (Universal Studios, Orlando and Los Angeles).

6. That was, of course, followed by another initial investment of $1.1 billion to open the EPCOT Center in 1981 as well as $500 million for the Studio Tour that opened in 1989.

7. Location-based entertainment is a recent nomenclature that has been generally used to describe ride-simulator theaters and advanced video-game arcades built in urban or suburban shopping centers. However, LBE is a term that could as well be used to describe theme parks, movie theaters, themed restaurants, sports stadiums, or casinos. LBE companies generate revenues by selling and/or leasing systems and production equipment, by licensing film software to operators, or by owning and operating attractions.

8. A subset of the themed amusement business involves regularly scheduled state fairs and regional expositions. These fairs are, in essence, movable, impermanent theme parks that have operating characteristics similar to those of permanent facilities. According to compilations by *Amusement Business,* the industry trade journal, in 1996 the top 50 fairs attracted combined attendance of 46 million. But because only about 60% of all admissions are paid, the industry generates less than $200 million at the gate. Several times this amount, however, is derived from activities conducted within the fairs.

Waterparks, another subset, have also become popular in recent years. In 1996, an estimated 55 million people visited the nation's approximately 100 waterparks, according to *Amusement Business* estimates.

See also Lyon (1987).

9. A number of major European parks date to the early 1900s. As shown in Brown and Church (1987), Alton Towers in the United Kingdom was opened in 1924 and Kantoor (Duinrell) in the Netherlands in 1935.

Also, Asian parks are becoming important, especially in Japan, Indonesia, and Korea.

10. Both traditional carnival-type games and electronic video games also generate high marginal profits.

11. Significant transactions in the 1980s included:

The sale of Six Flags to Wesray Capital Corp. by Bally Mfg. in 1987 for approximately $350 million plus assumption of $250 million of debt, a price of about 15 times estimated operating cash flow.

Marriott's sale of its 195-acre Santa Clara property to the city of Santa Clara for $101 million, and the 325-acre Gurnee, Illinois, park to Bally Mfg. for about $114.5 million in 1984. Gurnee attracted some 2.6 million visitors and generated revenues of over $50 million.

The purchase by Gaylord Broadcasting, in 1983, of Opryland, which included a 120-acre park, a theater, the Opryland Hotel (1,068 rooms), two radio stations, and the Nashville Network (cable), for an estimated $270 million.

Taft Broadcasting Company sold to Kings Entertainment Company, theme parks that included Kings Island, Kings Dominion, Carowinds, and Hanna Barbera Land for $167.5 million in 1983. Together these parks earned $10.7 million on revenues of $97.2 million.

The purchase, in 1982, of the Six Flags parks (six facilities with 1982 attendance of approximately 12.6 million) for $147 million plus assumption of about $100 million in debt, by Bally Mfg. Operating income in 1982 was $36 million on revenues of $259 million. Six Flags was subsequently again transferred in 1994 by Time Warner Inc. to an investment consortium at a value of approximately $1.1 billion.

Appendix A
Sources of information

The most convenient sources of macroeconomic data for use in entertainment-industry studies include the following regular U.S. Department of Commerce publications:

Survey of Current Business, containing personal-consumption expenditure figures for the preceding four years.
Business Conditions Digest, especially for detailed industrial price data.
U.S. Labor Department, *Monthly Review* and *Handbook of Labor Statistics,* for articles and data on labor and employment issues.
U.S. Census of Manufactures and, especially, *Census of Selected Services,* which contains regional data on revenues, employment, and productivity.
U.S. Statistical Abstract for historical series.
U.S. Industrial Outlook, published every year with forecasts for the next five years.

Information on specific entertainment-business topics is also widely available in the following regularly published non–government–sponsored magazines and newspapers:

Advertising Age
Amusement Business
Billboard
Broadcasting & Cable
CableVision
Cable World
Cash Box
Editor & Publisher
Electronic Media

Gaming & Wagering Business
Hollywood Reporter
Play Meter
Public Gaming
Publisher's Weekly
Replay
Television Digest
Variety (daily and weekly)

Appendix B
Major games of chance

In studying the financial economics of gaming, it is essential to have at least a cursory knowledge of how the major games are played. This appendix is designed to provide such knowledge, but it is by no means intended as a complete guide. Many other widely available books contain far greater detail concerning the finer points of play strategy and money management (i.e., the number of units wagered at each betting decision).[1] Tax consequences may also have some relevance.[2]

Blackjack

In blackjack, alternatively known as twenty-one or vingt-et-un, the player's goal is to receive cards totaling more than those of the dealer, but not exceeding 21 – and to do this before the dealer has to show his or her hand. An ace card can be counted as either 1 or 11, other numbers count as their actual values, and picture cards count as 10. Suits do not matter. The payoff to a winning player is equivalent to the amount bet, that is, even money – except in the case of ''blackjack'' (a ''natural'' 21 on the first two cards), when the payoff is three units to two.

The player is initially dealt two cards that must compare against the dealer's two cards – positioned in front of the dealer, one face down and one face up. Although casino rules vary, the dealer generally must "stand" (i.e., cannot draw another card) on the total of 17. Players have an option to request another card (called getting "hit") whenever they want, as long as the cards they already hold total less than 21.

Depending on casino rules, players may also "double down" on certain totals (usually, with a 9, 10, or 11), which means the initial bet can be doubled while drawing one, and only one, more card. Also, if the first two cards are of the same number, a split into two betting hands is permitted, but not always advisable.

The player or dealer exceeding 21 is said to go "bust," and tie hands, in which no money is exchanged, are a "push." (Technically, however, if both player and dealer bust, that kind of tie is won by the dealer, because sequencing requires that players show their hands and relinquish the bets first.)

After seeing that the dealer's face-up card is an ace, a player can also take "insurance," which allows protection against losing in case of a dealer's blackjack (an ace and a 10 card). Insurance is a side bet, at most equal to one-half the amount of the original bet. If the dealer indeed has a natural, the insurance is paid at 2 to 1; otherwise it is lost. The original bet is then settled in the usual way regardless of the decision on the side bet.

Strategies on whether to stand (not request an additional card) or to hit, on how to evaluate a "soft" total (composed with an ace), and on when to double down or to split have been devised by experts in probability theory and computer-simulation techniques. By assigning point values to cards already dealt and by playing proper strategy in response, a "card counter" can obtain information as to the shifting probabilities in the remaining deck. A remaining deck rich in 10-value cards would, for example, make it relatively easier than otherwise for the player to attain a two-card hand close to 21.

The game operator's advantage in blackjack is difficult to compute at any point of play. However, from the top of a deck, blackjack ordinarily provides the house with an edge of a little over 2%.[3] As the game progresses, however, the house edge (which depends importantly on the fact that the dealer turns over his cards *after* the player has gone bust) may disappear, and a skilled card counter can take advantage of such moments by increasing the size of the bet at that time. Blackjack is thus the only casino game that can be beaten by players, and it is this well-advertised fact that has made blackjack the most popular of casino table games.

To win consistently, however, skills in card counting, in play strategy, and in money management must be employed simultaneously in the typical high-speed, pressurized casino environment. But because attainment of such skills requires innate ability in mathematics and extensive study and practice (the patience for which is not apt to be found in most players), the threat to casino profits from self–proclaimed card counters is usually more imagined than real.

The presence of card counters has nonetheless tended to unnerve managements, and rather than simply foiling recognized counters by setting low betting limits, casinos have devised a multitude of card-cutting and multi-deck variations – the effect of which is to slow the rate of play and to probably reduce profitability.

Craps

Craps (Figure B.1) has long been a favorite in American casinos and, along with poker, is a quintessential American game. It evolved from the English game, hazard, and was adopted and refined by American blacks in New Orleans in the early 1800s. Thereafter it spread to immigrant neighborhoods on the East Coast. In contrast to 21, in which probability calculations are especially complicated, the house edge in bank craps as regularly conducted in casinos can be readily computed.

Two cubes (dice) – each die's surfaces marked one through six with embedded dots – are thrown by the player (''shooter'') against a backboard on the opposite side of the table. Betting decisions are dependent on the sum of dots on the top surfaces of the dice after they come to rest.

There are 36 possible outcomes (6 × 6), and the probabilities of a number being thrown are measured against those outcomes. With two cubes there are more ways (six) to make a seven (i.e., 1:6, 2:5, 3:4, 4:3, 5:2, 6:1) than to make any other number [Table B.1(a)], and craps uses this as a central theme for decision making.

The game focuses on what number the shooter makes on the first roll, the ''comeout'' throw. A 7 or 11, also known as a natural, provides an even-money win for players betting with the shooter on the ''pass line'' and a loss for those betting against the shooter on ''don't pass.'' If the outcome is a 2, 3, or 12 (known as craps), the converse is true. However, either the 2 or the 12 is selected by local custom to be used as a ''push'' or standoff number. Thus, there are no winners or losers if the sum on the top faces of the dice agrees with the designated standoff number that is indicated by diagram on the table's felt-cloth layout. Probabilities and game strategies remain the same whichever number is designated for this purpose.

If the comeout throw was neither a natural (7, 11) nor a craps (2, 3, 12), then one of the other possible numbers (4, 5, 6, 8, 9, 10) was thrown. One of those numbers then becomes the ''point.'' Players on the pass line are betting that the point number will appear again before a 7 appears. Don't-line bettors are hoping that 7 appears before the point. Winners are paid even money.

Although there are many additional bets that can be made at any stage in the game, of particular importance is the opportunity to ''take the odds'' or ''lay the

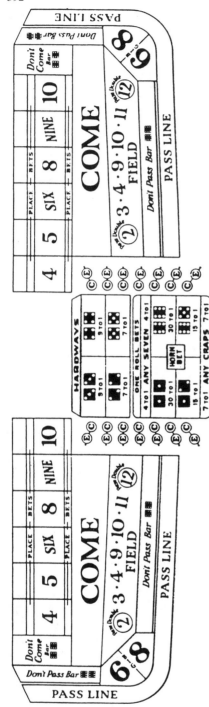

Figure B.1. Craps-table layout. *Source:* Reprinted by permission of the Putnam Publishing Group from *Playboy's Guide to Casino Gambling* by Edwin Silberstang. Copyright © 1981 by Edwin Silberstang.

Table B.1. *(a) Number of ways to throw a given number with two dice, and (b) point numbers and odds that 7 appears first*

(a)		(b)	
Roll	Ways	Number	Odds
2	1	4	2 to 1
3	2	5	3 to 2
4	3	6	6 to 5
5	4	8	6 to 5
6	5	9	3 to 2
7	6	10	2 to 1
8	5		
9	4		
10	3		
11	2		
12	1		
Total	36		

odds.'' From Table B.1(a) it can be seen that there are three ways to make a 4 and six ways to make a 7. Thus, over the long run, 7 is twice as likely to appear as 4, and the correct odds are 2:1 in favor of the number 7 [Table B.1(b)]. On some bets (e.g., those involving ''taking'' or ''laying'' the odds behind the ''line''), casinos will pay off the correct odds, thereby lowering the house edge. As previously noted, however, casinos make their profits by generally *not* paying off correct odds to winners (Table B.2).

So-called front-line bets in craps generate a house edge of 1.41%, calculated by the following method:

Assume a perfect dice shooter on each new comeout roll throws each of the 11 numbers exactly as often as predicted for the long run by probability theory.

To avoid complicated arithmetic with fractions and to derive a lowest common multiple, multiply 36 possible outcomes by 55, which is 1,980.

Then, out of 1,980 throws, a 7 will appear 6/36 of the time (i.e., 330 times). Similarly, a 4 will be made 3/36 of the time (or 165 times), and so forth.

After adding all the winning figures as shown in Table B.3, it can be seen that there will be 976 winning rolls and 1,004 losing rolls, the house edge being the difference of 28 rolls out of 1,980, or 1.41%.

Roulette

Historians disagree on the origin of roulette. Some say it was invented by the French mathematician Blaise Pascal in 1655; others support more arcane theories.

Table B.2. *Craps payout odds*

Bet	Payout odds	Bet	Payout odds
Pass line bet	1 to 1	Don't pass line bet	1 to 1
Come bet	1 to 1	Don't come bet	1 to 1
Pass line odds, come bet odds and buy bets		Don't pass line lay odds: don't come lay odds and lay bets:	
Points of 4 or 10	2 to 1	Points of 4 or 10	1 to 2
Points of 5 or 9	3 to 2	Points of 5 or 9	2 to 3
Points of 6 or 8	6 to 5	Points of 6 or 8	5 to 6
Place bet to win:		Big six or eight:	
Points of 4 or 10	9 to 5	Bets of $6 or multiples thereof	7 to 6
Points of 5 or 9	7 to 5	Bets of less than $6 or odd multiples	1 to 1
Points of 6 or 8	7 to 6		
Field bets:		Hard ways:	
3, 4, 9, 10, or 11	1 to 1	Hard 6 or 8	9 to 1
2 or 12	2 to 1	Hard 4 or 10	7 to 1
Proposition bets:			
Any 7	4 to 1		
Any craps	7 to 1		
Two craps or twelve craps	30 to 1		
Three craps or eleven	15 to 1		

Horn high bets: payout based on 2 craps, 3 craps, 12 craps, and 11 payout odds shown above

Table B.3. *Front-line bets*

Number	Times thrown	Winning rolls
Natural 7	330	330
Natural 11	110	110
Craps 2, 3, 12	220	—
Point 4	165	55
Point 10	165	55
Point 5	220	88
Point 9	220	88
Point 6	275	125
Point 8	275	125
Totals	1,980	976

Source: Scarne's Guide to Casino Gambling. Copyright © 1978 by John Scarne Games, Inc. Reprinted by permission of Simon and Schuster, Inc.

In any event, the game has evolved into European and American versions – the European wheel with a single zero, the American with zero and double zero (Figure B.2).

Mixed in standardized format around the roulette wheel are the numbers 1 through 36 and, in addition, depending on the version, either zero or both zero and double zero. The numbers on the wheel have adjacent background colors that alternate red and black and are arranged so that alternate low and high, odd and even, and red and black numbers are as mathematically balanced as possible. A perfect balance cannot be achieved, because the sum of the numbers 1 through 36 is 666, but the odd numbers sum to 324, and the even numbers sum to 342.

By placing one or more chips on a number, color, or odd or even, the player is betting that a ball spinning near the rim of the wheel will stop on that number, color, or number type. Payoffs on winning odd-even or black-red bets are 1:1, but for a specific number the payoff is 35:1. With an American double-zero wheel, there is a total of 38 positions, with the correct odds being 37:1. Thus, the casino keeps 2/38, or 5.26% in the American game, or 1/37 (2.70%) in the European game.

Other betting variations that are often offered by casinos normally do not significantly affect the casino's percentages. For instance, the *en prison* option reduces the house advantage by half on even-money bets (i.e., color, high-low number, or odd-even). On such bets, when zero or double zero is the outcome of the last spin of the wheel, players may settle for half the original wager or let the original amount ride (imprison the wager). If the choice is to let it ride and the following spin is a winner, the original bet is returned intact. Roulette bets and odds are given in Table B.4.

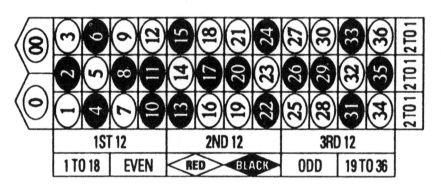

Figure B.2. Roulette wheel and table layout. *Source:* Reprinted by permission of the Putnam Publishing Group from *Playboy's Guide to Casino Gambling* by Edwin Silberstang. Copyright © 1981 by Edwin Silberstang.

Baccarat

Baccarat (Figure B.3) and its close cousins, Punto Banco, Chemin de Fer, and Baccarat-en-Banque are popular high-stakes games in casinos all over the world. All current versions are derived from the Italian *baccara,* first introduced into France circa 1490 and later adopted as a favorite game of the nobility. But it was not until the late 1950s that modern baccarat was taken seriously by Las Vegas casinos.

The earlier chemin de fer is played the same way as baccarat, except that in

Table B.4. *Roulette bets and odds*

Position	Description	Payout odds
Straight bets		
Straight up	All numbers, zero & double zero	35 to 1
Column bet	Pays off if any of the 12 numbers in the column bet is spun	2 to 1
Dozen	Pays off if 1 through 12, 13 through 24, or 25 through 36 is spun depending on the dozen bet	2 to 1
Red or black	Pays off if the color on the number spun corresponds to color bet	1 to 1
Odd or even	Pays off if number spun corresponds to the bet made	1 to 1
1 to 18 or 19 to 36	Pays off if number spun falls within the range indicated	1 to 1
Combination bets		
Split	Pays off if either of two numbers split is spun	17 to 1
Row	Pays off if any of the three numbers in the row bet is spun	11 to 1
Corner	Pays off if any of the four numbers forming the corner is spun	8 to 1
Five numbers	Pays off if 0, 00, 1, 2, or 3 is spun	6 to 1
Six numbers	Pays off if any of the six numbers in the two rows bet is spun	5 to 1

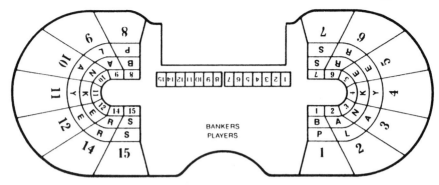

Figure B.3. Baccarat-table layout. *Source:* Reprinted by permission of the Putnam Publishing Group from *Playboy's Guide to Casino Gambling* by Edwin Silberstang. Copyright © by Edwin Silberstang.

chemin, the casino takes no risk because players bet against each other – the house merely acts as a "cutter" for a standard 5% charge taken from the player-banker's winning bet (coup).

In American baccarat, eight standard 52-card decks are shuffled and placed in a "shoe." There may be as many as 12 people seated at the table, and each makes a bet by placing chips for the *Player,* for the *Banker,* or for a tie hand. Winning bets (subject to commissions, as discussed below) are paid even money, and ties usually are paid at 8 to 1.

A bettor and the dealer are each dealt two cards, with picture cards and 10 counting as zero and number cards counting their actual face values. Should the two-card sum be in double digits (i.e., 10 or more), then the right-hand digit is considered the card count. A two-card sum of 14 would thus be counted a 4.

Normally, the gamer's goal is for the side he or she is betting on – either Player or Banker – to have a two-card count of 9. However, if either side has less than 8 or 9, a "natural," there are fairly standardized rules (Table B.5) that specify when additional cards may be drawn. A count of zero is "baccarat."

Through complicated arithmetic it has been determined, according to Scarne (1978, p. 266), that the chance of the Player's side winning is about 49.33%, and for the Banker's side, 50.67%. The Player's disadvantage, or cost to participate, is thus about 1.34%. However, in order to even out the sides (and save time on making change), the casino retains a 5% "commission" out of the Banker's winnings (it actually recaptures 5% of excess payoff). [Because the Banker's side, on average, wins 50.67% of the hands dealt, the actual charge is 2.53% (0.5067 times 5%).] In so reducing the aforementioned Banker's advantage of 1.34% by 2.53%, the Banker's cost of play after commission then nets to about 1.19% (1.34 minus 2.53). Thus, the casino's edge is somewhere between 1.19% and 1.34%.[4] But on bets that Banker and Player have tie hands, casinos usually pay 8 to 1 and have an edge of 14.36%. Bets on ties may thus typically account for only 3% of the total money wagered, but perhaps 10% of the total won by the house.

Table B.5. *Baccarat rules*

Player having		
1–2–3–4–5–10		Draws a card
6–7		Stands[a]
8–9		Natural. Banker cannot draw.

Banker having	Draws when giving	Does not draw when giving
3	1–2–3–4–5–6–7–9–10	8
4	2–3–4–5–6–7	1–8–9–10
5	4–5–6–7	1–2–3–8–9–10
6[a]	6–7	1–2–3–4–5–8–9–10
7	Stands	
8–9	Natural. Player cannot draw.	

Note: Pictures and tens do not count.
[a]If player takes no card, banker stands on 6.

Because most of the play, at a rate of about seventy hands an hour, is concentrated on Player or Banker – where the margins are thin – the casino win results for baccarat are generally far more volatile than for any of the other games.

Slots

Slot machines have steadily evolved since Charles Fey first introduced them in San Francisco in 1887 and, for most casinos, they now draw over 40% of revenues and an even larger share of profits.

In recent years, slots and their video game relatives discussed in Chapter 8 have all been greatly enhanced by the development of sophisticated electronic microprocessors. Nonetheless, the basic concept of slot play remains the same as always: to line up certain randomly generated symbols on a window or video screen. In return for so doing, players are rewarded with various levels of monetary prizes determined proportionally by the probability of occurrence.

For example, in a mechanical three-reel model with 20 different symbols per reel, and with each reel spinning independently, the probability of three of the same figures lining up is $1/20 \times 1/20 \times 1/20$, or 0.000125, which is 1 in 8,000. Of course, as in other games, the casino will profit by setting the actual payout to be less than 7,999 to 1. Yet in new microprocessor-controlled machines, "virtual" reels, wherein each reel may represent 256 different numbers, can be created with a much wider range of payouts and probabilities. In New Jersey, by law, slot machines cannot pay out less than 83% of the drop, but there is no such rule in Nevada.

Slot machines today come in many different versions, including "progressives'' (which are linked to the coin-drop in other machines), color-action (non-reel) videos, and multi-line-payoff models. But whatever the type, the chief advantages to casinos are the low operating costs and relatively high hold percentages of slots as compared with table games. Indeed, because of the low operating costs, coin-operated machine adaptations of blackjack and poker have also been emphasized by casinos.

Other casino games

Poker

America's all-time favorite private card game, poker, is believed to have evolved from an ancient Persian card game, *As-Nas.* Variations of the game eventually appeared in Europe, and by the early 1800s it had been brought to Louisiana by French settlers. *Poque,* as it was initially known, was refined by active use on the Mississippi riverboats of the 1800s and then spread rapidly through the North after the Civil War.

The principal concept in the game's many variations is to arrange the dealt cards in sequence of value and in suits, and to determine the relative ranking of each player's final hand to establish a winner of the money pool (pot) generated during the course of play. Players bet according to the actual and perceived strengths of the various hands, with bluffing a normal part of strategy.

Despite poker's popularity in private settings, it has not been an important contributor to the earnings of publicly owned casino companies. Most licensed poker-club operators (in California and Nevada) charge an hourly fee for playing based on the minimum-size bet. The operators who host the game and insure its integrity, have no stake in the outcome of any game, but will more generally charge a commission, or so-called rake-off, that equals 5% of the pot.

Low-denomination electronic video-poker machines are, however, expected to represent an increasing proportion of casino coin-operated devices. Payout percentages on these machines usually are set by management.

Keno

Keno, which is normally a more important profit maker for Nevada casinos than is poker, will also benefit from conversion to electronic video units. Keno is played by marking several numbers (spots) out of a total of 80 with a crayon (in the manual version) or with a light pen (in the electronic version). Winning spots are then determined by a random-number generator, and payoffs are made to winners in proportion to how many spots match the preselected choices of the bettor. According to calculations by Scarne (1974, p. 499), the house percentage on a keno ticket varies between approximately 20% and 25% and depends on the number of spots on the ticket.

Big Six wheel

The Big Six wheel is fairly popular in Atlantic City and it has been a staple in Nevada for a long time. In older versions, the wheel's rim is divided into 54 spaces, in each of which are representations of the faces of three dice bearing different combinations of the numbers 1 through 6. Bets are placed on a layout containing those numbers. After the wheel is spun and its ratchet peg comes to rest, for every bet that corresponds to a number in the section where the peg stops, there is a winner who is paid even money. If the player bets $1 on the number 2, and the section on the wheel where the peg stops shows dice with faces 1, 2, and 2, the bettor will thus receive $2 (a dollar for each 2) plus return of his original bet. Similarly, if the number is 5, and the stop is at 5-5-5, the payback will be $3 plus the original dollar. The Atlantic City version, however, merely has the numbers 1, 2, 5, 10, 20, and two jokers distributed over the 54 spaces. There are 24 ones, 15 twos, 7 fives, 4 tens, 2 twenties, and 2 jokers. A bet on 1 pays 1:1, on 2 pays 2:1, and so forth, except for jokers, which pay 45:1. The Big Six operator normally has a favorable advantage ranging to over 22%, which makes this game one of the most profitable for casinos. As can be seen from Atlantic City monthly statistics, casino hold percentages often approach 50% on the Big Six.

Bingo

Bingo, an offspring of the Italian lotto game, has been historically prominent in the development of Indian gaming ventures. It emerged after World War I and spread rapidly during the Great Depression years as a back-room attraction at vaudeville shows and carnivals. It remains as one of the most popular and widely legalized of wagering activities, and is normally very profitable for operators.

The traditional game is played to fill a card's row, column, or diagonal containing numbers between 1 and 75 under the word "bingo." A random-number selector or caller picks the numbers that qualify to fill the card, and the first card so filled is declared prize winner. The house edge for bingo is calculated to be around 22%.

Pai Gow, Fan Tan, Sic Bo

Players from the Orient have a long history of interest in gambling, and this is reflected in marketing studies of Nevada and Atlantic City casinos indicating that such players are among the most avid. To accommodate these good customers, Nevada casinos have introduced three favorite Chinese games, Pai Gow, Fan Tan, and Sic Bo, the first of which is the most important.

Originated in ancient China, *Pai Gow* (Figure B.4) is played with 32 specially designed dominoes that are scrambled and then placed in eight stacks of four. The dealer and as many as seven players are each dealt one stack of four specially

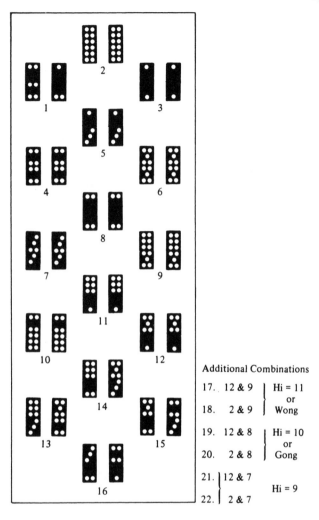

Additional Combinations

17.	12 & 9	Hi = 11
		or
18.	2 & 9	Wong
19.	12 & 8	Hi = 10
		or
20.	2 & 8	Gong
21.	12 & 7	
		Hi = 9
22.	2 & 7	

Figure B.4. Pai Gow: The chart lists 16 pairs and 4 combinations that compose the top-ranking 20 hands. Hand number 1 is called the king pair; each subsequent pair or hand is one value lower than the hand preceding it. The rank of each lesser hand is determined by the numerical value of the hand after discarding 10s from the total. Examples: Two dominoes 12 and 7 = 19, which becomes a 9 after the 10 is discarded; 8 and 7 = 15, which likewise becomes a 5. The higher number is the winning hand. *Source: Gambling Times,* November 1982.

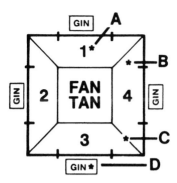

Figure B.5. Table layout for Fan Tan; bets A–D are explained in the text. *Source: Gambling Times,* February 1983.

marked dominoes (or cards), with the player to receive the first stack determined by rolling three dice.

The objective is to make two hands of the highest possible value from four dominoes – with both of the player's hands of higher value than the banker's corresponding hands. The player loses if both hands are lower, but if one hand is higher and the other lower, no one wins or loses. The house retains a 5% commission on all winning bets.

Fan Tan (Figure B.5), in contrast, is basically a game of guessing the number of beans in a cup. (A card game has taken the same name, but it is not similar.) A pile of beans is "cut" with a long, thin wand, four at a time, until 4, 3, 2, or 1 is the winning number or section. Figure B.5 illustrates the possibilities: (a) straight up on a number pays 3 to 1; (b) the corner inside the hash mark of a side pays 2 to 1 if the side hits; (c) a split of any two sides pays even money; (d) a gin bet pays even money if the closest side hits and is a standoff if adjacent sides hit. The house retains 5% of all winning bets as commission.

Sic Bo (Figure B.6) was first brought into the United States by migrant Chinese in the mid-1800s. Three dice are placed in a sealed shaker, and bettors select individual numbers or combinations of numbers that will appear on the dice after shaking. Winning payoffs are made according to the game layout in Figure B.6.

Pan

Pan, short for *panguingue,* is sometimes found in Nevada casinos or is played in commercial clubs. It is a card game related to rummy. The standard 52-card deck is modified by eliminating all eights, nines, and tens. The sevens are in sequence with jacks, and aces rank low, below deuces. Eight decks are generally used, and to each hand, 10 cards are dealt, 5 at a time.

By discarding and drawing, a meld or grouping of three cards of the same rank, or a sequence of three in the same suit, is composed. Several rules govern the game, in which the object is to be the first to meld exactly 11 cards.

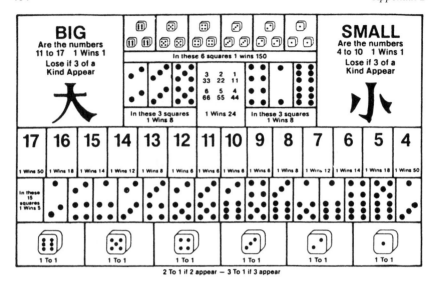

Figure B.6. Sic Bo. *Source: Gambling Times,* January 1983.

As in poker or the Chinese games, the house will normally take a percentage of the pot (5%) for conducting the game.

Trente-et-quarante (Rouge et Noir)

This card game is rarely found in U.S. casinos, but is quite popular in Europe. In *trente-et-quarante* (literally, thirty-and-forty) (Figure B.7), a dealer and croupier cut and shuffle a six-deck shoe in which cards are dealt face up in two rows: The first and farthest away is the black row, and the nearest is the red row. Dealing continues until the sum of points on the cards exceeds 30 but never 40.

The black row is dealt until the critical value of 40 or less is reached; then the red row is similarly presented. Suits have no value; face cards count ten, aces one, and others their pip value.

Players can bet on four even-money propositions: red versus black and color versus inverse. The color row whose total is closer to 30 is the winner. When the color of the first card dealt in the black row is the same as the color of the winning row, then color wins; otherwise inverse wins. The bank makes its money when – on an average of once every 47 hands – the total for each row is 31 (called the *refait* or *un après*). The bank then collects half of each player's stake, which provides an advantage of 1.25%.[5] All other ties are disregarded, and as in roulette, an *en prison* option may be available.

Mathematical studies of this game have indicated that, as in blackjack, there may be times during the course of play in which the house may have little or no edge. However, it is not clear that effective card-counting strategies exist.

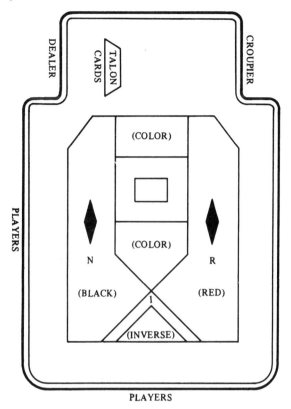

Figure B.7. Table layout for *trente-et-quarante. Source: Gambling Times,* December 1983.

Lotteries

Lotteries have been around a long time and have been used for many purposes. For instance, the concept appeared in classical Greek mythology, and Roman emperors entertained dinner guests with door-prize drawings. But the first recorded money lottery designed to raise funds for government appeared in Italy in the year 1530. A British defense lottery also was held in 1566. Yet it was the Virginia Company, which colonized Virginia, that provided the prototype for other early American colonial lottery financings. Indeed, founding fathers Benjamin Franklin and George Washington both sponsored lotteries, and many public-works programs and educational institutions, including Harvard, Yale, Columbia, and Princeton, were in part financed through this means.

Although lottery drawings were very popular in the early 1800s, several large swindles cooled the fervor and, by midcentury, most states had banned sales of lottery tickets. Of course, illegal lottery sales then flourished, and these became especially common in the 1920s and 1930s.

But it was not until 1964, when the state of New Hampshire introduced a sweepstakes game, that lotteries were legally renewed. And by the end of the 1980s, a majority of the states, the District of Columbia, and all Canadian provinces had legalized lotteries as a means of raising funds for welfare and public-works grants.

As a percentage of sales, states typically net about 36%–38%: Administrative expenses absorb up to 6%, system operators and designers receive 2%–3%, retail vendors receive a commission of 5%, and winning players receive an average of about 50%. However, payouts of 50% to players appear to be relatively generous only until comparison is made against casino-game payouts, which exceed 85%. Moreover, states may pick up extra income from interest earned on funds escrowed in the time between prize drawings and payments to winners (out of annuities).

Modern lotteries have evolved in several distinct stages. The original New Hampshire–style lotteries employed a sweepstakes concept that had limited appeal because of relatively small payoffs and a long time between ticket purchase and event decision. However, that was remedied in a second stage of development in which many more "instant-winner" scratch-off-type tickets and on-line three-digit daily number games were introduced, with significant increases in sizes of cash prizes and in numbers of retail outlets handling sales.

By the late 1970s, a third phase of expansion was initiated as greater sophistication of on-line computer systems made it possible to introduce games of the so-called lotto variety. These games select winners on almost a daily basis and allow for buildup of substantial prize money over several drawings: If the major prize is not won, the money spills over into the pool used for subsequent drawings.

In the state of New York, for example, the player selects 6 out of 54 numbers on two "boards" – panels with boxes labeled 1 to 54. The cost to play two boards is $1, and there are 10 boards on a card. Prizes are paid on a pari-mutuel basis, wherein for each draw (twice a week), 40% of that draw's sales revenue (less 2% prize fund reserve) is allocated as the winning pool for payment of the prizes under the conditions and odds indicated in Table B.6. Of course, many variations on this scheme are possible.

However, as of the mid-1980s, the industry entered a fourth phase featuring the placement of microprocessor-controlled lottery machines – video lottery terminals (VLTs) – that may use bingo, keno, or other similar random-number-generator-based concepts. Such machines are essentially hybrid slot and video game units.

Tracks

Horse races were popular during the reign of England's Henry II (1154–89), and they were regularly scheduled by New York's first English governor in 1665. But to this day, horse and dog racing is where direct government participation in legalized betting is greatest.

Table B.6. *New York State Lotto-game payout*

===

First prize: 50% of the winning pool plus any first-prize money carried forward from previous draws. Six winning numbers in one game panel, with odds on a $1 bet (two panels) 1:12,913,583.

Second prize: 11.0% of the winning pool for that draw. Any five winning numbers in one game panel. Odds on a $1 bet, 1:44,839.

Third prize: 28% of the winning pool for that draw. Any four winning numbers in one game panel. Odds on a $1 bet, 1:763.

Fourth prize: 11.0% of the winning pool for that draw. Any three winning numbers plus the supplementary number in one game panel. Odds on a $1 bet, 1:597.

Overall odds of winning a prize are 1:332 for a $1 bet.

===

Source: New York State Lottery.

There are many betting variations now allowed at tracks specializing in thoroughbred racing, harness racing, or greyhound racing. In addition to standard wagering on *win* (bettor collects if the selection bet to win finishes first), *place* (collects on first or second finish), and *show* (collects on first, second, or third finish), more exotic bets such as the quinella, exacta, and daily-double have been designed to heighten public interest.

The variations, however, have not changed the operational economics whereby the state may take up to 20% of pari-mutuel sales, and so-called breakage (actually a rounding of winners' payout to the last nickel or dime) further adds to the state's advantage. The following example, paraphrasing Scarne (1974, p. 51), well illustrates how pari-mutuel betting pools are shared by the state.

Supposing that a race is conducted "where the combined mutuel take of state and track is 15%" and breakage is to a nickel. "Assume that $129,400 was bet on all horses in the win (straight) pool, and the red-hot favorite and eventual winner was backed to the amount of $100,000." The combined state and track deduction of 15% of $129,400 is $19,410, leaving $109,990 in the win pool. The $100,000 wagered on the winner is then deducted from the net $109,990, leaving $9,990 to be divided among holders of winning tickets. "The $100,000 bet on the winning animal is set aside so that it may be returned to the winners."

Dollar odds, meaning earnings on each $1 unit bet on the winner, are then calculated by dividing $9,990 by $100,000 to give "a dollar-odds figure of $9\frac{99}{100}$ cents." Breakage to the last nickel is then performed, which leaves an additional 4.99 cents on each dollar to the track and the state. That is, the winners give up an additional $4,990, the state and track total becomes $24,400, and the winning wagerers' earnings on each dollar are reduced from 9.99 cents to 5 cents per dollar. As reported in newspapers, the standard $2 win bet in this example would have returned $2.10.

To calculate the return on place bets, "the total amount of money (gross place pool) bet on all the horses to place (run first or second)" is used as the base on which to apply state and track percentages. After subtracting the appropriate percentages from the gross place pool, the amount bet on first and second finish is then deducted to arrive at the net place pool. This is then divided by 2 because half the pool goes to holders of place tickets on the horse that finished first, the other half to the holders of place tickets on the horse that finished second. The resulting "(half net place pool) is divided by the amount bet to place wagers on the horse whose place payoff is being calculated." Breakage is then deducted.

"The method . . . to compute show mutuels [is] the same as . . . for place mutuels except that three horses who finished first, second, and third share in the show pool."

Depending on the betting variations used and the aggressiveness with which winners reinvest their gains in other races, the player's disadvantage at the track generally ranges upward of 17%. Another disadvantage as compared to sports book betting is that the price of the bet is not fixed, but changes right up to the moment before the race begins. Astute sports bettors, however, can often use time to their benefit.

Sports book

Wagering on sports events is probably the most common type of gaming, and it is certainly among the most widespread of illegal activities in the United States. Legal sports betting based on the same principles used by neighborhood bookies is sanctioned and available only in Nevada gaming establishments or at betting shops in England.

Beginning in the late 1930s, the concept most frequently used in both the legal and illegal varieties is that of a *point spread* which, in theory, mathematically compensates for the different abilities of competing teams. As calculated by expert handicappers, the spread is how many points the winning team's score must exceed the losing team's score in order for wagers on the winning team to be paid. For example, if team *A* is favored to beat team *B* by 4 points, and it does so by only 3 points, wagers on the underdog win.

Sports-book operators generally attempt to equalize the total *amounts* bet on both sides of the book and to avoid a "push" (making the exact point spread) by adjusting the spread, or *line,* that is offered to bettors. In football and basketball, for example, wagers (based on a point spread) are normally made at odds of 11:10 – which means that whether betting favorite or underdog, in effect you wager $11 to win $10. The bookie thus retains a $1 commission known in the vernacular as vigorish or "vig."

In practice, however, this implies a return to the bookmaker of 4.5%, because the bookmaker receives $11 from each side (a total of $22), and, no matter which team wins, retains $1 out of the $22 in total wagered. The bookmaker will obviously attempt to move the point spread (or line) so that an equal number of dollars are wagered on both teams. But if the line has been moved, as it often is, so that the number of dollars on each side are uneven, then the operator might make more or less than the theoretical 4.5% or might actually lose. As Moore (1996, p. 100) shows, the *theoretical keep percentage,* equals (true odds minus payoff odds)/true odds. Yet, in fact, for all of Nevada, the sports book hold percentage in recent years has averaged around 2.8%, compared to an average race book hold of approximately 15%.

Moreover, as Gollehon (1986) explains, baseball betting differs in that it uses a "money-line" rather than point-spread system. This is because baseball teams are rated in terms of probability of winning rather than of team point scoring potential. Yet, unlike most other wagering situations, where odds of winning are quoted, in baseball it is the odds *against* winning that are quoted. Thus, in baseball, odds on a favored team may be quoted at 7 to 5, for example, with the first number representing the number of times (out of 12 contests) that a team will typically be expected *not* to win.

The next step is to convert these odds figures into dollar amounts bet. To convert to the bookmaker's $100 betting units requires, for instance, that odds of 7 to 5 be converted to wagers of $140 and $100, respectively. Accordingly, the money-line quoted says −140, with the minus sign in front of the quote to indicate that the team is favored to win. To go with the favored team, a bettor must then put up $1.40 to win each $1.00 and, using the same line, put up $1.00 to win $1.30 on the underdog (which would be quoted as +130). In this case, known as a "dime-line," there is a 10-cent difference between what the favorite takes from the bettor and what the underdog gives.

Theoretically, then, the bookmaker breaks even when the favored team wins and wins when the underdog wins. This works out to about a 2% return to the operator: Of the total of $240 bet on a −140 and +130 line, the operator keeps $10 of the $240 it holds if the underdog wins, which should be half the time if the line is correct. The larger the difference (e.g., there are 20-cent lines), the more profit potential there is for the operator.

Because of the nature of the games and the different ways in which they are bet, football especially attracts far more action (about 40% of all Nevada sports wagering according to Manteris and Talley (1991)) than baseball. But the spread of sophisticated electronic terminals and computers − able to automatically and instantaneously equalize the book by adjusting the spread − will eventually make sports betting technically, if not legally, playable almost anywhere.

Notes

1. Economists familiar with the efficient-market hypothesis will recognize many of the concepts (a martingale, for instance) that are involved in money management. A martingale is any system of trying to make up losses in previous bets by doubling or otherwise increasing the amount bet. The pyramid or D'Alembert system is also popular.

2. Players should also be aware that the IRS requires bingo and slot-machine winners of over $1,200, and keno winners of over $1,500, to file form W-2G. In the case of lotteries and racetrack winners, witholding of 20% for federal taxes may begin at $1,000.

3. Estimates are approximate and assume application of basic strategy.

4. Silberstang (1980, p. 388) has slightly different figures of -1.36% for Player and -1.17% for Banker. Also see Thorp (1984).

5. Numbers are from Barnhart (1983) and differ from those of Scarne (1978).

Appendix C
Supplementary data

Entertainment industry data of interest to economists and investors are volumi-nous, and the material most significant to the flow of discussion has been placed in the text. The following additional data of historical interest has been organized according to chapter topics.

($ billion)

Year	Disposable income	Personal consumption expenditures	PCE on recreation	Recreation as % of disp. income	PCE on total recreation services	Recreation services as % of rec. PCE
1929	81.8	77.48	4.40	5.38	1.72	39.11
1930	73.2	70.17	4.00	5.46	1.68	41.88
1931	63.0	60.69	3.30	5.24	1.56	47.18
1932	48.0	48.72	2.50	5.21	1.21	48.32
1933	44.8	45.91	2.20	4.91	1.09	49.55
1934	51.5	51.43	2.50	4.85	1.12	44.76
1935	57.9	55.89	2.60	4.49	1.28	49.19
1936	65.8	62.16	3.00	4.56	1.43	47.80
1937	70.5	66.83	3.40	4.82	1.59	46.71
1938	64.9	64.24	3.30	5.08	1.53	46.39
1939	69.7	67.17	3.50	5.02	1.57	44.71
1940	75.0	71.21	3.80	5.07	1.70	44.74
1941	91.9	81.02	4.30	4.68	1.85	43.12
1942	116.6	88.87	4.70	4.03	2.12	45.02
1943	133.1	99.70	5.00	3.76	2.43	48.68
1944	145.8	108.48	5.40	3.70	2.69	49.83
1945	149.4	119.85	6.20	4.15	3.00	48.37
1946	159.3	144.28	8.60	5.40	3.71	43.09
1947	169.1	162.35	9.30	5.50	3.80	40.83
1948	188.4	175.43	9.70	5.15	3.83	39.52
1949	188.1	178.88	10.00	5.32	3.83	38.32
1950	207.7	192.70	11.20	5.39	3.87	34.57
1951	228.1	208.69	11.70	5.13	4.04	34.55
1952	240.2	219.67	12.30	5.12	4.25	34.59
1953	255.5	233.47	13.10	5.13	4.50	34.34
1954	261.2	240.75	13.60	5.21	4.79	35.22
1955	279.9	259.11	14.60	5.22	5.18	35.47
1956	298.8	271.94	15.50	5.19	5.59	36.09
1957	315.2	286.69	15.90	5.04	5.65	35.50
1958	326.3	296.31	16.30	5.00	5.83	35.79
1959	346.7	318.11	17.65	5.09	6.34	35.94
1960	360.5	332.16	18.48	5.13	6.92	37.46
1961	376.2	342.65	19.24	5.11	7.43	38.61

412

Year	6.5	6.5	7.1	0.5	7.2	0.09
1963	418.4	383.00	22.43	5.36	8.51	37.92
1964	454.7	411.44	24.56	5.40	9.10	37.06
1965	491.0	444.27	26.84	5.47	9.60	35.77
1966	530.7	481.88	30.85	5.81	10.40	33.72
1967	568.6	509.47	33.11	5.82	11.06	33.40
1968	617.8	559.81	36.70	5.94	12.44	33.90
1969	663.8	604.65	39.94	6.02	13.76	34.45
1970	722.0	648.11	43.08	5.97	15.03	34.89
1971	784.9	702.52	46.00	5.86	16.30	35.43
1972	848.5	770.69	51.44	6.06	17.57	34.15
1973	958.1	851.55	57.68	6.02	19.70	34.15
1974	1,046.5	931.17	63.58	6.08	22.49	35.37
1975	1,150.9	1,029.11	70.90	6.16	25.36	35.77
1976	1,264.0	1,148.79	78.77	6.23	28.34	35.98
1977	1,391.3	1,277.06	86.38	6.21	31.42	36.37
1978	1,567.8	1,428.76	96.98	6.19	34.74	35.82
1979	1,753.0	1,593.53	109.71	6.26	38.55	35.14
1980	1,952.9	1,760.42	117.60	6.02	43.08	36.63
1981	2,174.5	1,941.29	130.50	6.00	49.66	38.05
1982	2,319.6	2,076.81	139.97	6.03	55.27	39.49
1983	2,493.7	2,283.41	154.04	6.18	62.12	40.33
1984	2,759.5	2,492.29	171.62	6.22	68.36	39.83
1985	2,943.0	2,704.78	185.89	6.32	76.08	40.93
1986	3,131.5	2,892.68	202.70	6.47	82.06	40.48
1987	3,289.5	3,094.49	222.02	6.75	88.21	39.73
1988	3,548.2	3,349.71	246.34	6.94	98.90	40.15
1989	3,787.0	3,594.78	264.88	6.99	107.62	40.63
1990	4,166.8	3,839.31	281.61	6.76	117.42	41.70
1991	4,343.7	3,975.09	292.03	6.72	122.45	41.93
1992	4,613.7	4,219.80	310.75	6.74	134.02	43.13
1993	4,790.2	4,454.13	339.03	7.08	146.78	43.29
1994	5,021.7	4,700.91	374.84	7.46	157.60	42.04
1995	5,320.8	4,924.87	401.74	7.55	166.39	41.42
1996	5,588.5	5,151.42	430.31	7.70	179.18	41.64
[a]CAGR(%) 1929-96:	6.5	6.5	7.1	0.5	7.2	0.09

[a]Compound annual growth rate.

Source: Department of Commerce.

Table S1.1. (*cont.*)

Year	Books/Maps	Commercial theater	Movies	Cable	Pari-mutuel betting	Lotteries	Spectator sports	Casinos	Consumer price index (1983=100)
1929		0.127	0.720		0.008		0.066		0.17
1930		0.095	0.732		0.007		0.065		0.17
1931		0.078	0.719		0.006		0.057		0.15
1932		0.057	0.527		0.004		0.047		0.14
1933		0.041	0.482		0.006		0.050		0.13
1934		0.042	0.518		0.019		0.065		0.14
1935		0.044	0.556		0.026		0.072		0.14
1936		0.050	0.626		0.029		0.083		0.14
1937		0.053	0.676		0.038		0.089		0.14
1938		0.058	0.663		0.044		0.095		0.14
1939		0.064	0.659		0.041		0.098		0.14
1940		0.071	0.735		0.055		0.098		0.14
1941		0.079	0.809		0.065		0.107		0.15
1942		0.092	1.022		0.069		0.090		0.16
1943		0.118	1.275		0.079		0.062		0.17
1944		0.142	1.341		0.131		0.080		0.18
1945		0.148	1.450		0.153		0.116		0.18
1946		0.174	1.692		0.241		0.200		0.20
1947		0.187	1.594		0.255		0.222		0.23
1948		0.180	1.506		0.257		0.232		0.24
1949		0.182	1.451		0.247		0.239		0.24
1950		0.183	1.376		0.239		0.222		0.24
1951		0.186	1.349		0.255		0.221		0.26
1952		0.190	1.319		0.327		0.222		0.27
1953		0.198	1.292		0.372		0.225		0.27
1954		0.222	1.373		0.368		0.229		0.27
1955		0.248	1.474		0.381		0.237		0.27
1956		0.272	1.541		0.414		0.245		0.27
1957		0.293	1.238		0.438		0.252		0.28
1958		0.304	1.085		0.454		0.261		0.29
1959	1.091	0.324	1.043	0.009	0.503	0.001	0.311	0.139	0.29
1960	1.141	0.349	1.045	0.020	0.539	0.001	0.364	0.160	0.30
1961	1.213	0.333	1.044	0.029	0.569	0.001	0.412	0.180	0.30

Year									
1963	1.413	0.361	1.029	0.057	0.694	0.001	0.527	0.255	0.31
1964	1.614	0.390	1.038	0.067	0.769	0.004	0.587	0.272	0.31
1965	1.652	0.397	1.163	0.080	0.814	0.003	0.660	0.284	0.32
1966	1.846	0.444	1.219	0.102	0.848	0.002	0.744	0.326	0.33
1967	1.855	0.489	1.227	0.139	0.881	0.019	0.780	0.368	0.34
1968	2.016	0.491	1.400	0.185	0.947	0.036	0.959	0.396	0.35
1969	2.309	0.506	1.507	0.245	1.035	0.035	1.053	0.448	0.37
1970	2.922	0.531	1.629	0.295	1.096	0.061	1.136	0.510	0.39
1971	2.976	0.530	1.733	0.340	1.195	0.104	1.222	0.570	0.41
1972	2.944	0.571	1.744	0.410	1.263	0.223	1.198	0.691	0.42
1973	3.053	0.624	1.647	0.512	1.449	0.351	1.207	0.854	0.45
1974	3.192	0.702	2.022	0.643	1.559	0.428	1.249	1.050	0.50
1975	3.570	0.787	2.197	0.783	1.662	0.531	1.333	1.254	0.54
1976	3.576	0.943	2.074	0.951	1.802	0.634	1.423	1.494	0.57
1977	4.074	1.083	2.368	1.237	1.883	0.803	1.582	1.725	0.61
1978	4.984	1.328	2.752	1.554	1.988	0.967	1.842	2.227	0.66
1979	5.719	1.529	2.823	1.878	2.121	1.104	2.070	2.640	0.73
1980	6.450	1.792	2.578	2.458	2.291	1.240	2.292	3.171	0.83
1981	7.332	2.057	2.721	3.596	2.508	1.465	2.361	4.454	0.91
1982	8.025	2.152	3.134	4.655	2.590	1.964	2.692	5.124	0.97
1983	9.004	2.464	3.188	6.070	2.639	2.648	3.062	5.766	1.00
1984	9.974	2.832	3.421	7.279	2.834	3.462	3.472	6.268	1.03
1985	10.584	3.221	3.244	8.292	2.844	4.608	3.279	6.801	1.07
1986	11.418	3.940	3.338	9.433	2.927	5.403	3.283	7.186	1.09
1987	13.003	4.087	3.443	10.711	3.000	6.007	3.365	7.931	1.12
1988	14.303	4.534	3.892	12.450	3.334	7.274	3.556	8.839	1.17
1989	15.228	4.667	4.591	13.216	3.259	8.323	4.060	9.293	1.23
1990	16.458	5.603	5.168	14.777	3.361	8.722	4.367	11.048	1.29
1991	16.852	5.988	5.274	15.904	3.304	9.078	4.486	11.776	1.34
1992	17.674	6.796	4.991	17.662	3.326	9.783	4.772	14.207	1.38
1993	18.981	7.930	5.195	19.414	3.279	10.805	5.096	17.854	1.42
1994	20.052	8.747	5.524	19.294	3.252	11.760	5.251	20.355	1.46
1995	20.888	8.952	5.604	20.079	3.345	12.474	5.306	21.732	1.50
1996	22.095	9.154	6.019	22.298	3.473	13.214	6.260	24.438	1.54
CAGR(%)[a]									
1929-96:									
1959-96:	8.5	6.6	3.2	23.5	9.5	29.2	7.0	15.0	3.3

[a]Compound annual growth rate.

Table S1.2. *Average hours and earnings for production or nonsupervisory workers, selected industry categories, 1965–96*

Year	Total private[a]			Manufacturing			Services		
	Weekly hours	Hourly earnings	Weekly earnings	Weekly hours	Hourly earnings	Weekly earnings	Weekly hours	Hourly earnings	Weekly earnings
1965	38.8	$2.46	$ 95.45	41.2	$ 2.61	$107.53	35.9	$ 2.05	$ 73.60
1970	37.1	3.23	119.83	39.8	3.35	133.33	34.4	2.81	96.66
1975	36.1	4.53	163.53	39.5	4.83	190.79	33.5	4.02	134.67
1976	36.1	4.86	175.45	40.1	5.22	209.32	33.3	4.31	143.52
1977	36.0	5.25	189.00	40.3	5.68	228.90	33.0	4.65	153.45
1978	35.8	5.69	203.70	40.4	6.17	249.27	32.8	4.99	163.67
1979	35.7	6.16	219.91	40.2	6.70	269.34	32.7	5.36	175.27
1980	35.3	6.66	235.10	39.7	7.27	288.62	32.6	5.85	190.71
1981	35.2	7.25	255.20	39.8	7.99	318.00	32.6	6.41	208.97
1982	34.8	7.68	267.26	38.9	8.49	330.26	32.6	6.92	225.59
1983	35.0	8.02	280.70	40.1	8.83	354.08	32.7	7.31	239.04
1984	35.2	8.32	292.86	40.7	9.19	374.03	32.6	7.59	247.43
1985	34.9	8.57	299.09	40.5	9.54	386.37	32.5	7.90	256.75
1986	34.8	8.76	304.85	40.7	9.73	396.01	32.5	8.18	265.85
1987	34.8	8.98	312.50	41.0	9.91	406.31	32.5	8.49	275.93
1988	34.7	9.28	322.02	41.1	10.19	418.81	32.6	8.88	289.49
1989	34.6	9.66	334.24	41.0	10.48	429.68	32.6	9.38	305.79
1990	34.5	10.01	345.35	40.8	10.83	441.86	32.5	9.83	319.48
1991	34.3	10.32	353.98	40.7	11.18	455.03	32.4	10.23	331.45
1992	34.4	10.57	363.61	41.0	11.46	469.86	32.5	10.54	342.55
1993	34.5	10.83	373.64	41.4	11.74	486.04	32.5	10.78	350.35
1994	34.7	11.12	385.86	42.0	12.07	506.94	32.5	11.04	358.80
1995	34.5	11.43	394.34	41.6	12.37	514.59	32.4	11.39	369.04
1996	34.4	11.81	406.26	41.6	12.78	531.65	32.4	11.79	382.00

[a] Data relate to production workers in mining and manufacturing, construction workers in construction, and nonsupervisory workers in transportation and public utilities, wholesale and retail trade, finance, insurance, real estate, and services.

Table S1.3. *Top 20 favorite American free and leisure-time activities, 1996[a]*

Type of activity	Percentage
Reading	33.5
Watching TV	20.7
Time with family and friends	19.1
Movies	11.7
Traveling	11.0
Shopping	10.5
Fishing	10.4
Walking	9.4
Gardening	7.5
Listen to radio	7.3
Sewing and knitting	7.3
Cycling	6.3
Golf	6.0
Exercising	5.8
Hunting/shooting	5.7
Swimming	5.2
Spectator sports	5.0
Sports—general	4.6
Camping	4.5
Arts and crafts	4.3
Eating out	4.3

[a]Based on surveys conducted by Leisure Trends Group, Boulder, Co. Reprinted by permission.

Year	No. establishments	Receipts ($ thousands)	Payroll ($ thousands)	Paid employees	Receipts per establish. ($)	Receipts per employee ($)	Payroll/ receipts (%)	Employees/ establish.
Selected service industries, total								
1987	1,624,622	752,474,203	283,224,996	15,688,243	463,169	47,964	37.6	9.7
1982	1,339,229	426,981,971	158,624,502	11,106,144	318,827	38,446	37.1	8.3
1977	725,096	164,219,449	56,054,955	6,337,275	226,480	25,913	34.1	8.7
1972	683,614	95,675,519	33,424,040	5,305,181	139,955	18,034	34.9	7.8
1967	521,410	55,527,000	17,524,045	3,841,174	106,494	14,456	31.6	7.4
1963	504,356	41,023,378	12,192,105	3,261,541	81,338	12,578	29.7	6.5
Motion-picture prod./dist. services								
1987	11,242	19,916,629	4,973,497	171,328	1,771,627	116,249	25.0	15.2
1982	8,347	10,117,034	2,451,083	127,209	1,212,056	79,531	24.2	15.2
1977	5,473	5,314,465	1,376,657	88,372	971,033	60,137	25.9	16.1
1972	4,704	2,856,799	795,490	64,660	607,313	44,182	27.8	13.7
1967	3,375	2,169,424	699,072	64,581	642,792	33,592	32.2	19.1
1963	2,829	1,510,315	479,207	48,806	533,869	30,945	31.7	17.3
Motion-picture theaters								
1987	7,776	3,977,078	584,337	94,086	511,455	42,271	14.7	12.1
1982	10,020	3,575,737	566,647	103,461	356,860	34,561	15.8	10.3
1977	10,696	2,570,309	461,950	112,210	240,306	22,906	18.0	10.5
1972	11,670	1,815,916	381,065	127,435	155,605	14,250	21.0	10.9
1967	11,478	1,283,003	281,126	112,109	11,779	11,444	21.9	9.8
1963	12,040	1,058,224	249,999	112,521	87,892	9,405	23.6	9.3
Dance groups and artists								
1987	104	32,981	11,477	717	317,125	45,999	34.8	6.9
1982	142	27,125	10,246	980	191,021	27,679	37.8	6.9
1977	425	20,660	8,249	1,776	48,612	11,633	39.9	4.2
Symphony orchestras, opera companies, chamber-music groups								
1987	56	26,474	9,639	989	472,750	26,768	36.4	17.6
1982	61	17,911	5,958	730	293,623	24,536	33.3	12.0
1977	87	10,302	5,281	785	118,414	13,124	51.3	9.0
Producers of legitimate theater								
1987	940	809,222	201,536	11,199	860,874	72,258	24.9	11.9
1982	873	750,487	203,423	13,449	859,664	55,802	27.1	15.4
1977	750	304,100	98,626	9,113	405,467	33,370	32.4	12.2

Professional sports clubs, managers, and promoters

Year								
1987	807	1,904,388	1,354,231	26,566	2,359,836	71,685	71.7	32.9
1982	498	1,128,428	684,139	19,430	2,265,920	58,077	60.6	39.0
1977	526	937,148	366,131	14,693	1,781,650	63,782	39.1	27.9
1972	537	512,904	207,019	14,515	955,128	35,336	40.4	27.0
1967	455	226,067	116,648	10,321	496,851	21,904	51.6	22.7
1963	445	158,804	70,862	8,663	356,863	18,331	44.6	19.5

Racing, including track operation

Year								
1987	2,377	3,118,806	692,922	48,957	1,312,077	63,705	22.2	20.6
1982	1,862	2,290,039	485,879	43,017	1,229,881	53,236	21.2	23.1
1977	2,133	1,551,660	351,511	38,804	727,454	39,987	22.7	18.2
1972	2,196	1,007,375	226,431	33,793	458,732	29,810	22.5	15.4
1967	1,946	700,534	158,928	29,010	359,987	24,148	22.7	14.9
1963	1,647	537,444	177,662	21,374	326,317	25,145	33.1	13.0

Coin-operated amusement devices

Year								
1987	4,450	1,396,312	296,688	24,924	313,778	56,023	21.2	5.6
1982	5,434	1,422,726	285,438	26,886	261,819	52,917	20.1	4.9
1977	2,665	486,892	115,955	14,525	182,699	33,521	23.8	5.5
1972	2,061	297,406	72,027	10,165	144,302	29,258	24.2	4.9
1967	2,400	257,514	57,252	10,641	107,298	24,200	22.2	4.4
1963	3,074	260,640	50,175	11,142	84,789	23,393	19.3	3.6

Amusement parks

Year								
1987	744	3,469,836	819,552	60,414	4,663,758	57,434	23.6	81.2
1982	491	1,823,728	603,104	46,464	3,714,313	39,250	33.1	99.7
1977	663	1,172,419	352,645	37,014	1,768,354	31,675	30.1	55.8
1972	682	467,718	159,043	20,399	685,804	22,928	34.0	29.9
1967	786	174,105	56,000	8,339	221,508	20,878	32.2	10.6
1963	997	115,939	41,846	4,733	116,288	24,496	36.1	4.7

Carnivals and circuses

Year								
1987	351	266,952	39,648	3,572	760,547	74,735	14.9	10.2
1982	298	196,271	32,992	3,851	658,628	50,966	16.8	12.9
1977	368	155,404	28,522	3,175	422,293	48,946	18.4	8.6
1972	337	97,565	19,726	3,205	289,510	30,441	20.2	9.5
1967	548	62,857	13,844	2,229	114,703	28,200	22.0	4.1
1963	363	46,536	11,250	1,730	128,198	26,899	24.2	4.8

*a*Because of changes in classifications and in scope of data collected, data from one year often are only roughly comparable to those of another.

Table S2.1. *Percent of total yearly movie admissions by age category, 1984-96*

Age group	12–15	16–20	21–24	25–29	30–39	40–49	50–59	60+
1984	13	23	18	13	18	8	4	3
1985	14	21	18	14	18	7	4	4
1986	14	21	17	14	20	8	3	3
1987	11	21	15	15	18	10	5	5
1988	12	20	12	13	20	11	5	7
1989	11	19	14	16	18	12	4	7
1990	11	20	11	14	20	12	5	7
1991	12	19	12	12	19	13	5	8
1992	13	16	11	11	19	15	7	8
1993	9	17	10	13	19	15	7	11
1994	10	14	11	10	18	16	8	12
1995	9	16	11	12	20	16	7	10
1996	11	16	11	11	18	16	8	8

Frequency of attendance (%)

Frequency	Total public (ages 12+)		Adult public (ages 18+)		Teenagers (ages 12–17)	
	1996	1981	1996	1981	1996	1981
Frequent[a]	28	25	26	22	48	50
Occasional[b]	32	29	31	30	37	32
Infrequent[c]	11	10	11	10	10	5
Never	28	36	31	38	4	12
Unreported	1	<1	2	<1	1	1

[a]Attend movies at least once a month.
[b]Attend movies once in 2–6 months.
[c]Attend movies less than once in 6 months.
Source: MPAA study conducted by Opinion Research Corp.

Table S2.2. *United Artists' revenues and operating income by division, 1972–9*

Year	Revenues ($ thousand)		Operating income ($ million)		Margin (%)	
	Theatrical	Television	Theatrical	Television	Theatrical	Television
1979	380,997	57,000	23.2	18.9	6.1	33.2
1978	294,490	76,010	31.8	19.1	10.8	25.1
1977	318,483	59,691	38.7	16.8	12.1	28.1
1976	229,482	55,543	16.6	10.9	7.2	19.6
1975	187,399	29,626	14.2	4.8	7.6	16.2
1974	142,667	40,606	8.0	8.7	5.6	21.4
1973	163,843	51,725	14.8	14.1	9.0	23.3
1972	152,749	50,620	9.1	11.0	6.0	21.7

Source: UA-Transamerica corporate reports.

Table S2.3. *Average price of a movie ticket in America, 1933–62*[a]

Year	Admission price	Year	Admission price
1933	23¢	1948	40.1¢
1934	23¢	1949	46¢
1935	24¢	1950	52.8¢
1936	25¢	1951	52.8¢
1937	23¢	1952	60¢
1938	23¢	1953	60¢
1939	23¢	1954	44.7¢
1940	24.1¢	1955	49.8¢
1941	25.2¢	1956	49.7¢
1942	27.3¢	1957	50.5¢
1943	29.4¢	1958	50.5¢
1944	31.7¢	1959	51¢
1945	35.2¢	1960	69¢
1946	40.3¢	1961	69¢
1947	40.4¢	1962	70¢

[a]Between 1942 and 1953, there was an amusement tax on movie tickets. In 1942 the tax was 2.7 cents; in 1953, 10 cents. The figures given for those years include the tax.
Source: Real Facts, © Random House, Inc. Through 1962 these statistics were compiled by *Film Daily Yearbook.* The Research Department of the Motion Picture Association of America is the source for data beginning in 1963.

Table S2.4. *Major-distributor North American theatrical rental market shares in percent, 1970–96*[a]

Year	Sony/Columbia[b]	Disney	Fox	MGM/UA[c]	Orion[d]	Paramount	Tri-Star[b]	Warner[e]	Universal	Total
1996	10	21	13	5	1	13	—	16	8	86
1995	13	19	8	6	0	10	—	17	13	86
1994	5	20	9	3	0	14	5	16	13	85
1993	11	17	11	2	1	10	7	19	14	91
1992	13	19	14	1	—	10	7	20	12	96
1991	9	14	12	2	9	12	11	14	11	94
1990	5	16	13	3	6	15	9	13	13	92
1989	8	14	6	6	4	14	7	19	17	95
1988	3	20	11	10	7	16	6	11	10	94
1987	4	14	9	4	10	20	5	13	8	87
1986	9	10	8	4	7	22	7	12	9	88
1985[f]	10	3	11	9	5	10	10	18	16	92
1984	16	4	10	7	5	21	5	19	8	95
1983	14	3	21	10	4	14	—	17	13	96
1982	10	4	14	11	3	14	—	10	30	96
1981	13	3	13	9	1	15	—	18	14	86
1980	14	4	16	7	2	16	—	14	20	93
1979	11	4	9	15	5	15	—	20	15	94
1978	11	5	13	11	4	24	—	13	17	98
1977	12	6	20	18	4	10	—	14	12	96
1976	8	7	13	16	5	10	—	18	13	90
1975	13	6	14	11	5	11	—	9	25	94

1974[g]	7	7	11	9	4	10	—	23	19	90
1973[h,i]	7	7	19	11	3	9	—	16	10	82
1972	9	5	9	15	3	22	—	18	5	86
1971	10	8	12	7	3	17	—	9	5	71
1970	14	9	19	9	4	12	—	5	13	84
Mean	10	10	13	8	4	14	7	15	13	90

[a] Feature film rentals from U.S. and Canadian theaters, expressed in percentages of total industry rentals (including those of minor distributors) except after 1993, when figures are based on box-office estimates (which track rentals closely). Percentages do not add to 100% in any year; the residual amount is accounted for by smaller and/or defunct distributors.

[b] Tri-Star Pictures began operations in April 1984, absorbed Columbia Pictures late 1987; corporate name changed to Columbia Pictures Entertainment. Columbia and Tri-Star retain separate marketing controls, but certain administrative functions are performed by Triumph Releasing, an entity which has no operational significance. Metro-Goldwyn-Mayer, Inc. acquired Orion in 1997.

[c] MGM/UA means the present distribution company as well as the ''old'' UA, which took over domestic distribution of MGM product late in 1973.

[d] Includes old American International Pictures (1970–9), and Filmways Pictures (1980–1). Name changed to Orion in 1981.

[e] Allied Artists Pictures had a 4% market share in 1974. Insignificant in other years. Lorimar acquired assets in 1981. Lorimar began domestic distribution operations in August 1987. Warner Bros. acquired Lorimar in late 1988.

[f] Embassy Pictures market shares as follows: 3% in 1980, 5% in 1981, 1% in 1983 and 1985, nil in 1984, insignificant in other years. Company bought by Columbia Pictures in 1985. Dino De Laurentiis acquired Embassy's theatrical production–distribution operations from Columbia later in 1985. Name changed to De Laurentiis Entertainment Group, distribution operations resumed June 1986. Market share for 1986 just over 2%; for 1987, just over 1%.

[g] Pre-'74, the ''old'' MGM market shares as follows: 4% in 1970, 9% in 1971, 6% in 1972, and 5% in 1973. Company exited distribution late in 1973.

[h] National General Pictures (most of its release schedule being CBS-Cinema Center Films) market shares as follows: 7% in 1970, 8% in 1971, 3% in 1972, and 8% in 1973. NGP also released First Artists product under a commitment transferred to Warner Bros. in 1974 when NGP folded.

[i] Cinerama Releasing Corp. (most of its releases being ABC Pictures product) market shares as follows: 3% over 1970–3 period. CRC folded thereafter.

Source: Variety, January 18, 1989. © A. D. Murphy, now at The Hollywood Reporter.

Table S2.5. *Approximate movie theater admissions[a] in eight major developed countries, 1970–95*

Year	Total	England	France	Germany	Italy	Japan	Netherlands	Spain	Sweden
1995	715.5	116.1	129.7	124.5	91.4	127.0	17.2	94.0	15.6
1994	725.2	125.1	124.4	132.8	98.2	123.0	16.0	89.1	16.6
1993	719.0	114.4	132.7	130.5	92.2	130.7	15.9	87.7	14.9
1992	647.0	102.5	116.7	105.9	83.6	125.6	13.7	83.3	15.7
1991	674.3	101.5	117.5	119.9	88.6	138.3	14.9	79.1	15.1
1990	665.8	96.4	121.9	102.5	90.7	145.5	14.6	78.5	15.7
1989	664.8	91.6	120.9	101.0	94.8	143.6	15.6	78.1	19.2
1988	657.0	83.5	124.8	108.9	93.1	144.8	14.8	69.6	17.5
1987	694.6	78.4	136.7	108.1	108.8	143.9	15.5	85.7	17.5
1986	751.3	74.0	167.8	105.2	124.9	160.8	14.9	87.3	16.4
1985	761.9	70.2	175.0	104.2	123.1	155.1	15.3	101.1	17.9
1984	791.0	53.8	190.8	112.1	131.6	150.5	16.5	118.6	17.1
1983	902.5	65.7	198.8	125.3	162.0	170.4	20.2	141.0	19.0
1982	938.6	64.0	201.9	124.5	195.4	155.2	22.0	155.9	19.7
1981	1,002.9	86.0	189.2	141.3	215.2	149.5	26.7	173.0	22.1
1980	1,053.8	101.0	174.8	143.8	241.9	164.4	27.9	176.0	24.0
1979	1,128.2	111.9	178.1	142.0	276.3	165.1	28.4	200.5	25.9
1978	1,199.9	126.1	178.5	135.5	318.6	166.0	30.5	220.1	24.5
1977	1,230.7	103.5	170.3	124.2	373.9	165.2	26.3	244.9	22.5
1976	1,321.3	103.9	177.3	115.1	454.5	171.0	26.5	249.3	23.7
1975	1,423.3	116.3	181.7	128.1	513.7	174.0	28.3	255.8	25.4
1974	1,497.3	138.5	179.4	136.2	544.4	185.7	28.1	262.9	22.1
1973	1,512.3	134.2	176.0	144.3	544.8	185.3	26.5	278.3	22.9
1972	1,578.7	156.6	184.4	149.8	553.7	187.4	25.0	295.2	26.7
1971	1,616.9	176.0	177.0	161.4	535.7	216.8	28.7	295.3	26.0
1970	1,707.8	193.0	184.4	167.4	525.0	254.8	24.1	330.9	28.2

[a] In millions.

424

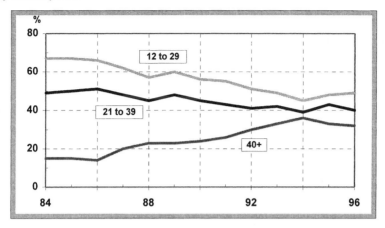

Figure S3.1 Percent of total yearly movie admissions by age category, 1984–96.

Table S4.1. *Average rental-flow table: an example (as average percentage of estimated ultimate rentals realized)*

Source	Number of quarters after initial release								Subsequent	Total estimated theatrical rentals
	1	2	3	4	5	6	7	8		
Domestic	71	19	5	2	1	1	$-^a$	–	1	100
Foreign	4	33	24	14	7	5	3	2	8	100
Total	47	24	12	6	3	2	1	1	4	100

Note: Data are based on films released during fiscal years 1976–8. TV, pay-TV, and other nontheatrical revenues are excluded from these statistics.
[a]Less than 1%.
Source: Columbia Pictures Industries (1982), p. 39.

Table S5.1. *Music industry shipments in millions of units and dollars, 1976–96*

Year	LPs/EPs	Cassettes	CDs	Singles	Other (incl. 8-track)	Total
Units Shipped (net after returns)						
1996	3	225	779	10	120	1,137
1995	2	273	723	10	105	1,113
1994	2	345	662	12	102	1,123
1993	1	340	495	15	104	956
1992	2	366	408	20	100	896
1991	5	360	333	22	81	801
1990	12	442	287	28	98	866
1989	35	446	207	37	82	807
1988	72	450	150	66	24	762
1987	107	410	102	82	6	707
1986	125	345	53	94	2	618
1985	167	339	23	121	4	653
1984	205	332	6	132	6	680
1983	210	237	1	125	6	578
1982	244	182		137	14	578
1981	295	137		155	49	635
1980	323	110		164	86	684
1979	318	83		196	105	701
1978	341	61		190	134	726
1977	344	37		190	127	698
1976	273	22		190	106	591
Dollar Value						
1996	37	1,905	9,935	48	610	12,534
1995	25	2,304	9,377	47	568	12,320
1994	18	2,976	8,465	47	562	12,068
1993	11	2,916	6,511	51	558	10,047
1992	14	3,116	5,327	66	501	9,024
1991	29	3,020	4,338	64	384	7,834
1990	87	3,472	3,452	94	436	7,541
1989	220	3,346	2,588	116	309	6,580
1988	532	3,385	2,090	180	67	6,255
1987	793	2,960	1,594	203	18	5,568
1986	983	2,500	930	228	10	4,651
1985	1,281	2,412	390	281	25	4,388
1984	1,549	2,384	103	299	36	4,370
1983	1,689	1,811	17	269	28	3,814
1982	1,925	1,385		283	49	3,642
1981	2,342	1,063		256	309	3,970
1980	2,290	776		269	526	3,862
1979	2,136	605		275	669	3,685
1978	2,473	450		260	948	4,131
1977	2,195	250		245	811	3,501
1976	1,663	146		245	678	2,732

Source: Recording Industry Association of America.

Table S5.2. Music consumer profile by genre and age group, in percent of dollars spent 1987–96

Genre	Rock	Country	R&B	Pop	Rap	Gospel	Classical	Jazz	Other
1987	45.5	10.6	9.0	13.5	3.8	2.9	3.9	3.8	7.0
1988	46.2	7.4	9.1	15.2	4.2	2.5	3.5	4.7	7.2
1989	41.7	7.3	9.5	15.0	6.4	3.1	3.6	4.9	8.5
1990	36.1	9.6	11.6	13.7	8.5	2.5	3.1	4.8	10.1
1991	34.8	12.8	9.9	12.1	10.0	3.8	3.2	4.0	9.4
1992	31.6	17.4	9.8	11.5	8.6	2.8	3.7	3.8	10.8
1993	30.2	18.7	10.6	11.9	9.2	3.2	3.3	3.1	9.8
1994	35.1	16.3	9.6	10.3	7.9	3.3	3.7	3.0	10.8
1995	33.5	16.7	11.3	10.1	6.7	3.1	2.9	3.0	12.7
1996	32.8	14.7	12.1	9.3	8.9	4.3	3.4	3.3	11.2

Age group	1987	1996
10–14	7.3	7.9
15–19	24.2	17.2
20–24	19.1	15.1
25–29	14.5	12.5
30–34	10.8	11.4
35–39	8.2	11.1
40–44	4.8	9.1
45+	10.7	15.1

Source: Recording Industry Association of America (RIAA).

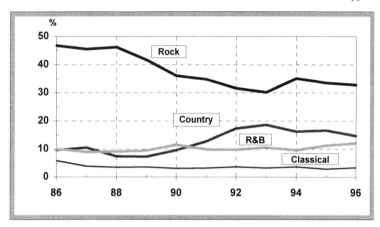

Figure S5.1. Music consumer profile by genre, in percent, 1986 and 1996. *Source:* Recording Industry Association of America.

Table S5.3. *Costs for vinyl LPs^a*

A. Financial commitment also called "investment" or "risk" of record company
  1. Recording costs of LP: $125,000 to $250,000
  2. Promotion, advertising, initial pressing: $100,000 to $300,000, plus video – formidable costs for no return
  3. Advance to artists
B. Profit structure: the following structure is based on a wholesale selling price of records, about $4.30 on an $8.98 suggested retail list price
  1. Costs
     (a) Pressing and jacket: $.75 to $.80
     (b) Royalties to artists and producers: $0.82 (12% royalty, all-in, beginning artist – all records shipped); each 1% increases rate by about 6.8 cents
     (c) Copyright royalties: 35 cents (average)
     (d) AFM: $0.08 to $0.09
     (e) Freight: $0.10 or more
     (f) Costs of distribution: $0.60, some costs not readily available on a per-unit basis.
     (g) Approximately $1.60 to $1.65 profit on these figures before the following (varies widely with structure):
         (i) Promotion advertising: Uncertain figure per unit, e.g., $100,000 over 200,000, LPs = $0.50 per unit
         (ii) Overhead
         (iii) Returns, obsolescence, write-offs

^{a}*Source:* L. Lee Phillips, Esq. of Manatt, Phelps, Rothenberg, and Tunney (Los Angeles). From Biederman and Phillips (1980); data updated to 1984.

Table S6.1. *TV homes, major countries, 1996 estimates*

Country	Number of homes (million)	Country	Number of homes (million)
United States	96.9	Asia	
Canada	11.6	China PDR	300.8
Europe		China (Taiwan)	5.8
Austria	3.1	Hong Kong	1.7
Belgium	4.0	India	69.5
Denmark	2.3	Indonesia	25.0
France	22.0	Japan	42.7
Greece	4.0	S. Korea	11.7
Germany	36.7	Philippines	5.9
Italy	21.9	Singapore	0.8
Netherlands	6.5	Thailand	6.7
Spain	12.1	Total	470.4
Sweden	3.9		
Switzerland	2.9	Oceana	
United Kingdom	23.1	Australia	7.2
Total	142.5	New Zealand	1.1
		Total	8.3
Africa			
Algeria	2.0	Central &	
Egypt	5.5	South America	
S. Africa	3.7	Argentina	8.7
Nigeria	4.5	Brazil	46.0
Total	15.6	Chile	4.0
		Colombia	7.5
Middle East		Mexico	15.1*
Israel	0.8	Venezuela	4.6
Jordan	0.3	Total	85.8
Kuwait	0.5		
Lebanon	0.6	Approximate number	
Saudi Arabia	4.5	of TV homes	
Turkey	8.1	outside of U.S. and	
Total	14.8	Canada	737.4

*From different source.

Source: Screen Digest International, March 1993 and industry estimates.

Table S6.2. *Radio and Television Broadcasting Services–Operating Revenue and Expenses:[a] 1994*

Item	Total Broadcasting	Radio	Television
Operating revenue, total	31,064	7,980	23,084
Station time sales	21,352	7,397	13,955
Network compensation	455	95	360
National/regional advertising	7,794	1,646	6,148
Local advertising	13,103	5,656	7,447
Network time sales	8,702	338	8,364
Other operating revenue	1,010	245	765
Operating expenses, total	25,038	6,769	18,269
Annual payroll	7,178	2,709	4,469
Employer contributions to Social Security and other supplemental benefits	1,197	362	835
Broadcast rights	7,396	236	7,160
Music license fees	347	181	166
Depreciation	1,192	441	751
Lease and rental	487	228	259
Purchased repairs	257	83	174
Insurance	168	73	95
Telephone and other purchased communication services	251	122	129
Purchased utilities	269	106	163
Purchased advertising	942	367	575
Taxes	200	72	128
Other operating expenses	5,154	1,789	3,365

[a]In millions of dollars. Based on the *1987 Standard Industrial Classification Manual.*

*Source:*U.S. Bureau of the Census, *1994 Annual Survey of Communication Services.*

Table S7.1. *Cable and Other Pay TV Services–Operating Revenue and Expenses: 1994*

Item	Total (mil. dol.)	Percent of total
Operating revenue, total[b]	30,563	100.0
Advertising	3,353	11.0
Program revenue	5,626	18.4
Basic service	14,477	47.3
Pay-per-view and other premium service	5,346	17.5
Installation fees	469	1.6
Other cable and pay television revenue	1,292	4.2
Operating expenses, total	23,915	100.0
Annual payroll	4,011	16.8
Employer contributions to Social Security and other supplemental benefits	957	4.0
Program and production costs	7,926	33.1
Depreciation	4,087	17.1
Lease and rental payments	652	2.7
Purchased repairs	399	1.7
Insurance	167	0.7
Telephone and other purchased communications	200	0.8
Purchased utilities	255	1.1
Purchased advertising	683	2.9
Taxes	454	1.9
Other operating expenses	4,124	17.2

[a] Based on the *1987 Standard Industrial Classification Manual.*

[b] Includes other amounts not shown separately.

*Source:*U.S. Bureau of the Census, *1994 Annual Survey of Communication Services.*

Table S8.1. *Number of U.S. Daily Newspapers, 1946–1996*

Number of Daily Newspapers		Dailies Over 50,000 Circulation	
Year	Total	Number	Percentage of total
1946	1,763	199	11.3
1950	1,772	201	11.3
1955	1,760	212	12.1
1960	1,763	223	12.7
1965	1,751	241	13.8
1970	1,748	257	14.7
1975	1,756	252	14.3
1980	1,745	266	15.2
1985	1,676	258	15.4
1988	1,642	265	16.1
1989	1,626	264	16.2
1990	1,611	268	16.6
1991	1,586	250	15.8
1992	1,570	247	15.7
1993	1,556	239	15.3
1994	1,548	240	15.5
1995	1,533	233	15.1
1996[a]	1,520	231	15.1

[a] Preliminary data.
Source: Editor & Publisher.

Table S8.2. *Newspaper advertising by major category, 1970–96*

Year	National advertising (millions)	Retail advertising (millions)	Classified advertising (millions)	Total newspaper advertising (millions)
1970	891	3,292	1,521	5,704
1975	1,109	4,966	2,159	8,234
1980	1,963	8,609	4,222	14,794
1985	3,352	13,443	8,375	25,170
1986	3,376	14,311	9,303	26,990
1987	3,494	15,227	10,691	29,412
1988[a]	3,821	15,790	11,586	31,197
1989	3,948	16,504	11,916	32,368
1990	4,122	16,652	11,506	32,280
1991	3,924	15,839	10,587	30,349
1992	3,834	16,041	10,764	30,639
1993	3,853	16,859	11,157	31,869
1994	4,149	17,496	12,464	34,109
1995	4,251	18,099	13,742	36,092
1996[b]	4,679	18,394	15,106	38,179

[a]Data for 1988 not directly comparable due to a change in methodology.
[b]Preliminary.
Source: Newspaper Association of America.

Table S8.3. *Book unit sales in the United States in millions, 1982–95*

	Adult trade	Juvenile trade	Mass paperbacks	Professional	Educational
1982	315.2	144.0	382.1	121.0	348.3
1983	340.2	166.1	377.6	128.3	340.0
1984	340.6	179.1	388.9	120.5	343.3
1985	359.9	192.6	381.5	125.7	343.8
1986	352.3	210.3	381.1	132.6	338.9
1987	357.3	219.5	391.0	135.9	325.7
1988	365.3	244.4	418.9	142.0	332.0
1989	403.7	281.2	441.0	145.3	349.2
1990	403.1	301.4	432.9	148.6	346.2
1991	412.1	325.6	442.6	147.0	339.2
1992	441.6	318.7	438.7	152.9	344.9
1993	462.7	299.1	451.9	155.9	360.1
1994	489.0	317.3	461.0	161.7	346.9
1995	463.0	341.0	432.2	165.4	378.2
CAGR[a] 1982–95(%):	3.0	6.9	1.0	2.4	0.6

[a]Compound annual growth rate.
Source: Book Industry Study Group, Inc., Veronis, Suhler & Associates.

Table S8.4. *Unit circulation of consumer magazines in millions of copies, 1980–95*

	Single-copy	% of total	Subscription	% of total	Total
1980	90.9	32.4	189.8	67.6	280.7
1981	86.8	30.0	202.8	70.0	289.6
1982	85.4	28.7	211.8	71.3	297.2
1983	83.8	27.5	221.3	72.5	305.1
1984	81.8	26.1	231.8	73.9	313.6
1985	81.1	25.0	242.8	75.0	323.9
1986	77.7	23.6	250.9	76.4	328.6
1987	80.1	23.5	260.4	76.5	340.5
1988	80.1	22.7	272.4	77.3	352.5
1989	78.8	21.5	287.3	78.5	366.1
1990	73.7	20.1	292.4	79.9	366.1
1991	71.9	19.7	292.9	80.3	364.8
1992	70.7	19.5	291.6	80.5	362.3
1993	69.4	19.1	294.9	80.9	364.3
1994	67.9	18.7	295.6	81.3	363.5
1995	65.8	18.0	.299.1	82.0	364.9
CAGR[a] 1980–95(%):	−2.1		3.1		1.8

[a]Compound annual growth rate.
Source: Magazine Publishers of America, Veronis, Suhler & Associates.

Table S10.1. *Reasons for gambling*

Reasons for betting[a]	%	Reasons for not betting[a]	%
To have a good time	81	Not available	48
For excitement	47	Don't know about it	27
Challenge	35	Not interested	26
To make money	35	Other things to do	23
To pass the time	23	Don't think about it	22
Something to look forward to	21	Odds against you	22
Chance to get rich	11	Don't want to lose money	16
Net activity reasons	94	Don't have the money	16
Net money reasons	43	Waste of money	14
		Illegal	10
		Not lucky	8
		Net money reasons	53
		Net activity reasons	55
		Net moral reasons	8
		Net legal reasons	12

[a]Respondents chose one, two, or three reasons from a list of 11 reasons provided for betting and 18 reasons provided for not betting.
Source: U.S. Congress (1976).

Table S10.2. *Nevada and New Jersey casino industry statistics, 1996*

	Las Vegas			Atlantic City	
	Total hotel/motel rooms	Hotel occ rate %	Casino sq. ft.	Total hotel rooms	Casino Sq. ft. (000s)
1970	25,430	70.0			
1971	26,044	82.5			
1972	26,619	86.5			
1973	20,198	88.3			
1974	32,826	86.0			
1975	35,190	84.2			
1976	36,245	85.9			
1977	39,350	85.3			
1978	42,620	86.9		724	55.0
1979	45,035	86.8		1,572	115.0
1980	45,815	82.8		3,257	270.0
1981	49,614	80.5		4,781	412.1
1982	50,270	76.1		4,770	425.8
1983	52,529	77.4		4,779	422.7
1984	54,129	78.1		5,494	510.1
1985	53,067	84.7		6,342	577.7
1986	56,494	86.3		6,351	593.6
1987	56,474	87.0		6,835	664.5
1988	61,394	89.3	1,206.6	7,314	696.2
1989	67,391	89.8	1,261.8	7,584	648.6
1990	73,730	89.1	1,557.9	8,828	770.5
1991	76,879	85.2	1,570.2	9,419	775.2
1992	76,523	88.8	1,584.5	8,961	777.7
1993	86,053	92.6	1,539.0	8,946	797.2
1994	88,560	92.6	1,954.0	9,227	839.9
1995	90,046	91.4	2,013.3	9,398	875.2
1996	99,072	93.2	2,203.0	10,531	987.3
CAGR[a] 1970–96 (%):	5.4		7.8	16.0	17.4

[a]CAGR = compound annual growth rate.

Source: Nevada Gaming Abstract and New Jersey Casino Control Commission.

Table S10.3. *Comparison of individual bets at craps*

Bet	House advantage (%)	Average no. of rolls for decision	Cost per roll[a]
Pass line or come odds	0.00		0
Pass line or come	1.41	3.38	0.0042
Place 6 or 8	1.51	3.27	0.0046
Place 5 or 9	4.00	3.60	0.0111
Place 4 or 10	6.67	4.00	0.0167
Buy of 10 (5% vigorish)	4.76	4.00	0.0119
Hard-way 4 or 10	11.11	4.00	0.0278
Hard-way 6 or 8	9.09	3.27	0.0278
Any craps (7-to-1 odds)	11.11	1	0.1111
2 or 12 (30-to-1)	13.90	1	0.1390
2 or 12 (30 for 1)	16.67	1	0.1667
3 or 11 (15-to-1)	11.11	1	0.1111
3 or 11 (15 for 1)	16.67	1	0.1667
Big 6 or 8 (even money)	9.09	1	0.0909
Any 7	16.67	1	0.1667
Field bets			
2–3–4–9–10–11–12 (2 & 12 pay double)	5.26	1	0.0523
2–3–4–9–10–11–12	11.11	1	0.1111

[a]As a percentage of money bet.
Source: Rouge et Noir Newsletter, March 1984, p. 16.

	Charitable bingo	Charitable games	Card-rooms	Casinos	Gaming devices	Sports wagering	Lottery Games: Video lottery terminals	Lottery Games: Keno	Lottery Games: Instant (& pulltab) games	Lottery Games: Lotto
Alabama	♣	♣								
Alaska	♣	♣								
Arizona	♣	♣		♣	♣				♣	♣
Arkansas										
California	♣	♣	♣					•	♣	♣
Colorado	♣	♣	♣	♣	♣			♣	♣	♣
Connecticut	♣	♣		♣	♣				♣	♣
Delaware	♣	♣				♦	♥		♣	♣
Florida	♣	♣	♠						♣	♣
Georgia	♣								♣	♣
Hawaii										
Idaho	♣	♣		♣					♣	♣
Illinois	♣	♣	♣	♣	♣			♦	♣	♣
Indiana	♣	♣		♥	♥				♣	♣
Iowa	♣	♣	♣	♣	♣				♣	♣
Kansas	♣	♣						♣	♣	♣
Kentucky	♣	♣							♣	♣
Louisiana	♣	♣		♣	♣				♣	♣
Maine	♣	♣							♣	♣
Maryland	♣	♣	♣		♣			♣	♣	♣
Massachusetts	♣	♣						♣	♣	♣
Michigan	♣	♣		♣	♣			♣	♣	♣
Minnesota	♣	♣	♣	♣	♣				♣	♣
Mississippi	♣	♣		♣	♣					
Missouri	♣	♣		♣	♣				♣	♣
Montana	♣	♣	♣	♣	♣	♣		♣	♣	♣
Nebraska	♣	♣						♣	♣	♣
Nevada	♣		♣	♣	♣	♣		♣		
New Hampshire	♣	♣							♣	♣
New Jersey	♣	♣	♣	♣	♣				♣	♣
New Mexico	♣	♣		♣	♣				♥	
New York	♣	♣		♣				♣	♣	♣
North Carolina	♣									
North Dakota	♣	♣	♣	♣	♣	♣				
Ohio	♣	♣							♣	♣
Oklahoma	♣	♣								
Oregon	♣	♣	♣	♣	♣	♣	♣	♣	♣	♣
Pennsylvania	♣	♣						♣	♣	♣
Rhode Island	♣	♣					♣	♣	♣	♣
South Carolina	♣				♣					
South Dakota	♣	♣	♣	♣	♣		♣		♣	♣
Tennessee										
Texas	♣	♣							♣	♣
Utah										
Vermont	♣	♣							♣	♣
Virginia	♣	♣							♣	♣
Washington	♣	♣	♣	♣				♣	♣	♣
Wash., D.C.	♣	♣							♣	♣
West Virginia	♣	♣					♣	♣	♣	♣
Wisconsin	♣	♣		♣	♣				♣	♣
Wyoming	♣	♣								
Puerto Rico	♣			♣	♣					♣
Virgin Islands		♣							♣	

Legend: ♠ Authorized but not yet implemented
♦ Permitted by law and previously operative

Figure S10.1. Legalized gambling in the United States by state, 1996.
Source: Gaming and Wagering Business, 1996.

		Parimutuel Wagering								
Numbers	Passives	Greyhound	Jai alai	Harness	Quarter horse	Thoroughbred	Interstate Inter-track wagering	Intrastate inter-track wagering	Off-track betting	Telephone betting
		♣		♣	♦	♦	♣			
		♣			♣	♣	♣	♣	♣	
		♣			♣	♣	♣			
♣	♦			♣	♣	♣	♣	♣	♣	
	♦	♣			♣	♣	♣	♣	♣	
♣	♦	♣	♣	♣	♣	♣	♣	♣	♣	♦
♣	♦			♣		♣	♣			
♣		♣	♣	♣	♦	♣		♣		
♣										
		♦			♣	♣	♣	♣		
♣	♦			♣	♣	♣	♣	♣	♣	
♣				♣	♣	♣	♣	♣	♣	
		♣		♣	♣	♣	♣	♣		
♣		♣		♦	♣	♣	♣	♣		
♣				♣	♣	♣	♣	♣	♣	♦
♣				♦	♣	♣	♣	♣	♣	
♣	♦			♣		♦	♣		♣	
♣	♦			♣		♣	♣	♣	♣	♦
♣	♦	♣		♣	♦	♣	♣	♣		
♣	♦	♣		♣	♣	♣	♣			
♣	♦			♣	♣	♣	♣	♣		
♣				♦	♦	♦	♦	♣	♣	
				♣	♣	♣	♣	♣	♣	
					♣	♣	♣	♣		
		♦	♦	♦	♣	♣			♣	♦
♣	♦	♣		♣		♣	♣	♣		
♣	♦			♣		♣	♣	♣	♣	
					♣	♣	♣	♣		
♣	♦			♣	♦	♣	♣	♣	♣	♦
				♣	♣	♣	♣	♣	♣	
♣	♦			♣	♣	♣	♣	♣	♥	
♣		♣			♣	♣	♣	♣	♣	
♣	♦	♣		♣	♦	♣	♣	♣		♦
♣	♦	♣	♣	♦		♣	♣			
		♦			♣	♣	♣	♣	♣	
				♣	♣	♣	♣	♣		
♣		♣			♣	♣	♣	♣		
					■					
♣	♦	♦		♣		♦	♣			
♣				♣	♦	♦	♣	♣	♥	
♣				♦	♣	♣	♣	♣	♣	
♣										
♣	♦	♣		♣	♣	♣	♣			
♣		♣		♣	♣	♣	♣	♣		
				♦	♣	♣	♣	♣	♣	
♣	♦					♣	♣		♣	
	♦									

♣ Legal and operative   **■** Operative but no parimutuel wagering

♥ Implemented since June 1995   **•** Previously operative but now not permitted

Figure S10.1. (*cont.*)

Table S10.5. *Financial data for major Nevada hotel-casinos, fiscal 1996*
(amounts represent 30 locations)

Casino Department

Revenue		Dollars	Pct
Pit revenue (includes keno and bingo)		1.837	42.4
Coin operated devices		2.184	50.5
Poker and pan		0.176	4.1
Race book		0.067	1.5
Sports pool		0.065	1.5
Total revenue		4.329	100.0

Rooms department

Revenue		Dollars	Pct
Room sales		1.214	84.3
Complimentary rooms		0.226	15.7
Total revenue		1.439	100.0

Ratios

	Pct
Total current assets to total current liabilities	108.6
Total capital to total liabilities	142.1
Total complimentary expense to gaming revenue	15.8
Total revenue to average total assets	86.3
Return on invested capital[a]	17.8
Return on average assets[b]	14.8

Statistical averages

Average pit revenue per room per day	$97.01	Average beverage sales per room per day	$19.33
Average slot revenue per room per day	115.36	Average rooms department payroll per room per day	20.10
Average food sales per room per day	45.83	Average room rate per day	76.10

Gaming revenue per square foot of floor space

Area	No. of casinos operating	Average area in square feet	Gaming revenue per square foot
Pit (includes bingo and keno)	30	17,889	3,422
Coin operated devices	30	55,533	1,311
Poker and pan	20	2,007	4,346
Race and sports	30	6,439	686
Total casino	30	81,199	1,777

[a]Equals total of net income (before federal income taxes and extraordinary items) and interest expense divided by the total of average total assets less average current liabilities.
[b] Equals total of net income (before federal income taxes and extraordinary items) and interest expense divided by the average total assets.
Source: Nevada Gaming Control Board.

Table S11.1. *Network-television-rights fees for Olympic Games, 1960–2004*

Year	Summer location	Network	Amount paid ($ million)	Winter location	Network	Amount paid ($ million)
1960	Rome	CBS	0.4	Squaw Valley	CBS	0.1
1964	Tokyo	NBC	1.5	Innsbruck	ABC	0.6
1968	Mexico City	ABC	4.5	Grenoble	ABC	2.5
1972	Munich	ABC	7.5	Sapporo	NBC	6.4
1976	Montreal	ABC	25.0	Innsbruck	ABC	10.0
1980	Moscow	NBC	87.0	Lake Placid	ABC	15.5
1984	Los Angeles	ABC	225.0	Sarajevo	ABC	91.5
1988	Seoul	NBC	300.0	Calgary	ABC	309.0
1992	Barcelona	NBC	401.0	Albertville	CBS	243.0
1994				Lillehammer	CBS	295.0
1996	Atlanta	NBC	465.0			
1998				Nagano	CBS	375.0
2000	Sydney	NBC	715.0			
2002				Salt Lake City	NBC	555.0
2004	Athens	NBC	793.0			
2006					NBC	613.0
2008		NBC	894.0			

Season beginning:[a]	Show attendance (millions)	Average price per ticket ($)	Play-weeks	Plays New	Plays Revivals	Musicals New	Musicals Revivals	Grosses ($ millions) B'way	Grosses ($ millions) Road
1970	7.4	7	1,107						
1971	6.5	8	1,157						
1972	5.4	8	889	22	14	18	3		
1973	5.7	8	907	21	12	12	3		
1974	6.6	9	1,101	25	17	11	3		
1975	7.182	10	1,136	18	21	16	5	70.8	52.6
1976	8.815	11	1,348	24	9	10	8	93.4	82.6
1977	8.621	12	1,360	20	7	7	5	103.8	106.0
1978	9.116	14	1,472	22	5	17	3	128.1	143.9
1979	3.381	15	1,541	29	7	20	5	143.4	181.2
1980	10.822	18	1,545	25	7	19	7	194.5	218.9
1981	10.694	22	1,461	24	4	12	4	221.2	249.5
1982	8.102	25	1,259	24	9	13	4	203.1	184.3
1983	7.899	29	1,119	14	7	11	4	226.5	206.2
1984	7.157	29	1,062	14	9	5	2	208.0	226.0
1985	6.527	30	1,049	12	9	11	1	190.6	235.6
1986	6.968	32	1,031	15	11	11	2	207.2	224.3
1987	8.143	33	1,114	11	3	14	3	253.5	223.0
1988	7.968	35	1,097	13	7	7	1	262.1	255.5
1989	8.039	37	1,062	15	5	9	5	283.4	367.1
1990	7.314	40	970	14	1	9	3	267.2	450.2
1991	7.366	42	901	15	10	7	3	292.4	502.7
1992	7.857	44	1,018	8	10	9	0	327.7	620.6
1993	8.116	45	1,062	12	10	9	7	356.0	687.7
1994	9.045	46	1,117	8	11	6	3	406.3	694.6
1995	9.468	48	1,146	8	13	2	4	436.1	762.3
1996	10.318		1,346	10	11	7	4	499.4	752.9

Table S12.2. *Top 20 Broadway long runs*[a]

Show	Designation	Opening season	No. of performances
A Chorus Line	M	1975–76	6,137
Cats*[b]	M	1982–83	6,117
Oh, Calcutta!	R	1976–77	5,852
Les Miserables*	M	1986–87	4,225
Phantom of the Opera*	M	1987–88	3,925
42nd Street	M	1980–81	3,486
Grease	M	1972–73	3,388
Fiddler On The Roof	M	1964–65	3,242
Life With Father	P	1939–40	3,224
Tobacco Road	P	1933–34	3,182
Hello, Dolly!	M	1963–64	2,844
My Fair Lady	M	1955–56	2,717
Miss Saigon*	M	1990–91	2,558
Annie	M	1976–77	2,377
Man of LaMancha	M	1965–66	2,328
Abie's Irish Rose	M	1921–22	2,327
Oklahoma!	P	1942–43	2,212
Pippin	M	1972–73	1,944
South Pacific	M	1948–49	1,925
Magic Show	M	1973–74	1,920

[a]Broadway shows that have played at least 1,000 performances, not including previews. Excluded are multiple productions, but an exception is "Oh, Calcutta!," in which both original and revival played more than 1,000. Designations are as follows: (P) is for play, (M) denotes musical and (R) means revival. An asterisk means the show is continuing. Figures are as of June 1, 1997, the final day of the 1996–97 season.
[b]"Cats" became the longest running show in June 1997.
Source: Variety, June 9, 1997.

Glossary

This abbreviated glossary has been mainly compiled with help (and permission) from two sources: *Dictionary of Marketing and Related Terms in the Motion Picture Industry,* by Donn Delson, Bradson Press, Thousand Oaks, California, 1979 (a lexicon of motion picture terminology); *The McGraw-Hill Dictionary of Economics,* McGraw-Hill, New York, 1974. The *Dictionary of Economic and Statistical Terms,* U.S. Department of Commerce was supplementary. Additional references include Oakey (1983), Konigsberg (1987), and Cones (1992).

Above-the-line costs: Those production-period costs related to acquiring the story rights and screenplay and signing the producer, director, and major members of the cast.

ADI (area of dominant influence): An Arbitron (ARB) audience-market classification designating a certain market area in which local stations have partial or complete signal dominance over stations from other market areas. Commonly referred to as a television broadcast area. Similar to Nielsen DMA (designated market area).

Advance: Monies paid by an exhibitor to a distributor prior to the opening of a film in a market as an "advance" against film rentals due. Advances, unlike guarantees, are refundable if the film does not generate enough box-office revenue at the exhibitor's theater to justify the advance film-rental monies paid out. The portion not earned by the distributor in film rental will be returned to the exhibitor.

Affiliate: Generally, an independently owned broadcast station that contracts with a network to show that network's programming in certain time periods. Each of the three older major U.S. networks (ABC, NBC, and CBS) has approximately 200 affiliated stations. Fox now also has over 160 affiliates.

Aggregate: The familiar type of summary series shown in most statistical reports. Generally, it is a total, such as the gross national product or retail sales, but sometimes it is an average, such as the index of industrial production or the index of wholesale prices.

AM (amplitude modulation): Technically, the variation of the amplitude of a radio wave in accordance with the sound being broadcast. AM radio broadcasting is from 535 to 1,705 kilohertz. Signal reception occurs in two ways: Either via ground waves that follow the curvature of the Earth or via bounced sky waves that are reflected off the ionosphere back to Earth. AM signals are subject to atmospheric or local interference, but generally are unimpeded by topographic or physical obstructions.

Amortization of debt: A gradual reduction of a debt through periodic payments covering the interest and part of the principal. Generally, amortization is used when the credit period is longer than a year. Common examples of amortization of debt are mortgage payments on homes, which extend over a period of 20 years or more.

Amortization of negative costs: Accounting procedure by which negative cost is charged against film revenue.

Answer print: A positive print made from the original negative that is balanced for color and sound. "Answers" the question affirmatively that a viable working negative exists from which prints can be made for commercial presentation.

ARB (American Research Bureau): One of the major companies involved in national research for television and radio. ARB publishes numerous audience-market surveys throughout the year, rating the comparative audience viewing and listening habits for each medium both locally and nationally.

Aspect ratio: A ratio of the horizontal to the vertical dimensions of a movie or television screen.

Asset: A physical property or intangible right, owned by a business or an individual, that has a value. An asset is useful to its owner either because it is a source of future services or because it can be used to secure future benefits. Business assets are usually divided into two categories: current and fixed.

Asset values: The implied price buyers might be willing to pay in order to obtain control of an asset's profit- and/or cash-generating potential. Asset values fluctuate according to changes in general economic conditions, interest rates, and expected returns.

Audience, primary or target: A particular audience composition or demographic to which a message is believed to have the most appeal and is therefore primarily directed.

Availability: 1. The date when a motion picture is able to be shown commercially in a market as offered by the distributor to the exhibitor. 2. Commercial-broadcast time periods available for purchase, including radio time periods (such as Drive Time, Housewife Time, etc.) and television programming.

Bandwidth: A measure of the capacity of a communications channel in terms of the range of frequencies that can be contained or transmitted within defined upper and lower limits. A television channel, for example, normally occupies a bandwidth of approximately 6 MHz (6 million cycles per second).

Basic service: Initial cable-television service that usually consists of 12 to 20 channels available off-the-air and satellite channels supported by advertising.

Below-the-line costs: All costs, charges, and expenses incurred in the production of a motion picture other than the above-the-line costs, including such items as extras, art and set costs, camera, electrical, wardrobe, transportation, raw film stock, etc.

Bicycling (print): The use of one print in two theaters for staggered showings. Originated with the transporting by bicycle of consecutive reels of film from one theater to another and back again.

Bid: A written notification from a theater-exhibition company in response to a bid solicitation from a distribution company, competing for the right to license a motion picture for showing in a given market beginning on or about a specific date. This notification usually includes commitments, if applicable, for minimum playing time, clearances, guarantees, advance, film-rental terms, advertising terms, etc.

Bid request: A written notification from a distributor to all motion-picture exhibitors who own or operate theaters in a market area, informing them that a specific motion picture is available for showing in that area on or about a certain date and inviting them to submit a bid to license that picture. This request may contain suggestions such as length of playing time, guarantees, advances, film-rental terms, advertising terms, deadlines for submission, etc. Such a bid request usually specifies that bid offers must be received by a certain time and date, usually no later than 10 days subsequent to its issuance.

Blind bidding: The practice by which film-distribution companies, through a bid-request letter and without having previously screened the film, request that interested exhibition companies submit bids to license a motion picture for showing in a market.

Block booking: Governed by the Paramount consent decree of 1948, major distributors were forbidden to employ the practice of tying together one or more motion pictures for licensing within a market. The basic premise of this decree is that motion pictures must be licensed picture by picture, theater by theater, so as to give all exhibitors equal opportunities to show a given film.

Bond: 1. A written promise to pay a specified sum of money (principal) at a certain date in the future or periodically over the course of a loan, during which time interest is paid at a fixed rate on specified dates. Bonds are issued by corporations, states, localities (municipal bonds), foreign governments, and the U.S. government, usually for long terms (more than 10 years), although any security issued by the U.S. government for more than five years is defined as a bond. 2. In movies, *completion bonds* are insurance policies that assure distributors and/or financiers that their investments in the movie will not be lost due to incompletion.

Booker: The person responsible for all aspects of monitoring and trafficking the actual motion-picture prints throughout the markets over which the branch office has jurisdiction.

Book value: The value of a corporation according to its accounting records. It is computed by subtracting all debts from assets; the remainder represents total book value. Total book value is also referred to as net assets. If a corporation has assets of $300,000 and debts of $100,000, its total book value is $200,000. In reports of corporations, the book value is usually represented on a per-share basis. This is done by dividing the total book value by the number of shares. In the example given above, if the corporation had 10,000 shares outstanding, its book value would be $20 per share. The book value differs from the par value of the shares and also from the market value.

Box-office receipts: The money that has been paid by the public for admission (tickets) to see a specific motion picture.

Branch: The office located in a given city, staffed by employees of a film-distribution company, responsible for bidding out (licensing) the film company's products, servicing prints to legitimate customers, and collecting on film rentals due. Business is generally conducted with exhibitors within certain geographic regional boundaries of relative proximity to the branch. The major distribution companies will have individual branches in 25 to 30 major U.S. cities. Branch staffs consist of the branch manager, sales representatives, bookers, cashiers, clerical personnel, etc.

Break: 1. Each stage of the release of a motion picture within a market (first-run break, second-run break, etc.) consisting of a distinct array of theaters playing a motion picture in a given "availability." 2. The commercial time available for sale either within a particular show or between two shows on television or radio. 3. A short hiatus in production activity for meals, personal needs, etc.

Break-even point: The specific volume of sales at which a firm neither makes nor loses money. Above this point, a firm begins to show a profit; below it, a loss. Break-even-point analysis is used to compute the approximate profit or loss that will be experienced at various levels of production. In carrying out this analysis, each expense item is classified as either fixed (constant at any reasonable level of output) or variable (increasing as output increases and decreasing as output declines).

Business cycles: Alternate expansion and contraction in overall business activity, evidenced by fluctuations in measures of aggregate economic activity, such as the gross national product, the index of industrial production, and employment and income. A business cycle may be divided into four phases: expansion, during which business activity is successively reaching new high points; leveling out, during which business activity reaches a high point and remains at that level for a short period of time; contraction, during which business volume recedes from the peak level for a sustained period until the bottom is reached; recovery, during which business activity resumes after the low point has been reached and continues to rise to the previous high mark.

Cable TV: Transmission of a television signal for home viewing by wire (cable) as opposed to airwave broadcast. A fee or monthly subscription charge is assessed. Often used in remote or isolated viewing areas, many cable systems offer subscribers an opportunity to see movies, sporting events, and other special programming not available on free TV.

Capitalized value: The terms applied to a technique used to determine the present value of an asset that promises to produce income in the future. To calculate the present value, the total future income expected must be discounted, that is, offset against the cost (as measured by the current interest rate) of carrying the asset until the income has actually been realized. If the asset promises a stream of income, its capitalized value is calculated by adding together the present discounted value of the income in each year. The general formula for this calculation is $I/(1 + r)^t$, where I is the annual income, r is the current rate of interest, and t is the number of years involved. In this manner, an investor confronted with a choice of properties can determine which alternative is the most remunerative, though the formula tells nothing about the relative risks involved.

Cash flow: The sum of profits and depreciation allowances. (Instead of profits, many economists use retained earnings, which are profits after taxes and after deductions for dividend payments.) Gross cash flow is composed of total profits plus depreciation; net cash flow of retained earnings plus depreciation. Thus, cash flow represents the total funds that corporations generate internally for investment in modernization and expansion of plants and equipment and for working capital. The growth of depreciation allowances over the years has made them a much more important part of cash flow than retained earnings. To facilitate comparisons of property values, however, entertainment businesses often take cash flow to be profits prior to deductions of interest, depreciation and amortization, and taxes.

Clearance: The relative exclusivity a theater specifies as a condition to licensing a motion picture within a market. A theater may request an exclusive run within an entire market or may request exclusivity for exhibition of a motion picture only over those theaters that are in geographic proximity and may be considered competitive.

Commercial: An advertisement broadcast on a television or radio station for which the station receives some form of compensation (also called spot announcement).

Common stock: The capital stock of a corporation that gives the holder an unlimited interest in the corporation's earnings and assets after prior claims have been met. Common stock represents the holder's equity or ownership in the corporation. Holders of common stock have certain fundamental legal rights, including the following: preemptive rights; the right, in most cases, to vote for the board of directors, who actually manage the company; the right to transfer any or all shares of stock owned; the right to receive dividends when they are declared by the board of directors.

Competition: The condition prevailing in a market in which rival sellers try to increase their profits at one another's expense. In economic theory, the varieties of competition range from perfect competition, in which numerous firms produce or sell identical goods or services, to oligopoly, in which a few large sellers with substantial influence in the market vie with one another for the available business. Early economists envisioned perfect competition as the most effective assurance that consumers would be provided with goods and services at the lowest possible prices.

Compulsory license: A rule, legislated by the U.S. Congress, that permits cable systems to carry all TV station signals in their geographic area without having to pay any money for the rights.

Contract: The mutually binding licensing agreement between a distribution company and an exhibition company for the showing of a motion picture at a particular theater on or about a given date. Included are the terms for computing payment for film rental, playing time, clearance, advertising sharing, etc.

Convertible debenture: A certificate issued by a corporation as evidence of debt that can be converted at the option of the holder into other securities (usually common stock, but sometimes preferred stock) of the same corporation. Each debenture can be converted into a specified number of shares of stock at a stipulated price for a certain period. There are two advantages to convertible debentures for the issuing corporation: (a) The conversion privilege makes the debentures more attractive to investors and tends to reduce interest costs. (b) The debentures facilitate the extinction of debt, because debt declines and equity (stock) increases as holders convert their debentures. The major disadvantage is discrimination against the company's stockholders, whose equity is diluted as the holders of debentures convert them. At all times during the conversion period, there is a price relationship between the debenture and the stock. It is based on the conversion price, the number of shares into which each debenture can be converted, and the value that the market puts on the conversion privilege. For example, a $1,000 debenture that can be converted into 50 shares of common stock at $20 per share will normally trade in the market at a price higher than $1,000 because of the conversion privilege.

Correlation: The statistical technique that relates a dependent economic variable to one or more independent variables over a period of time in order to determine how close the relationship between the variables is. This technique can be used for business forecasting. When more than one independent variable is used, the relationship is called a multiple correlation.

Cost per thousand (CPM): Determined by dividing the cost of a print or broadcast advertisement or of a total advertising campaign by the total estimated audience, computing the total audience on a base of thousands.

Cost recovery: Accounting method of amortization in which all costs are charged against earned revenue and no profit is recognized until cumulative revenue equals cumulative costs. This method is not acceptable for financial-statement reporting under generally accepted accounting principles.

Cross-collateralization: The practice in film and music distribution of offsetting profits in one territory or nation or category of earnings by losses in others. It is a practice that obviously favors the distributor.

Current assets: Cash or other items that will normally be turned into cash within one year and assets that will be used up in the operation of a firm within one year. Current assets include cash on hand and in the bank, accounts receivable, materials, supplies, inventories, marketable securities, and prepaid expenses.

Current liabilities: Amounts owed that will ordinarily be paid by a firm within one year. The most common types of current liabilities are accounts payable, wages payable, taxes payable, and interest and dividends payable.

Day and date release: Simultaneous (same day, same date) release of a motion picture in two or more theaters in a given market. Also used to indicate simultaneous opening in two or more markets (e.g., "L.A. and New York, day and date openings," or "opening 50 markets in the United States day and date").

Debenture: A bond that is not protected by a specific lien or mortgage on property. Debentures (debts), which are issued by corporations, are promises to pay a specific amount of money (principal) at a specified date or periodically over the course of the loan, during which time interest is paid at a fixed rate on specified dates. The distinction between a debenture and a note of a corporation is that the debenture, like a bond, is issued under an indenture or deed of trust.

Demand: The desire, ability, and willingness of an individual to purchase a good or service. Desire by itself is not equivalent to demand: The consumer must also have the funds or the ability to obtain funds in order to convert the desire into demand. The demand of a buyer for a certain good is a schedule of the quantities of that good that the individual would buy at possible alternative prices at a given moment in time. The demand schedule, or the listing of quantities that would be bought at different prices, can be shown graphically by means of the demand curve. The term *demand* refers to the entire schedule of possibilities, not only to one point on the schedule. It is an instantaneous concept, expressing the relationship of price and the quantity that is desired to be bought, all other factors being constant.

Depreciation: A reduction in the value of fixed assets. The most important causes of depreciation are wear and tear (loss of value caused by the use of an asset), the effects of the elements (i.e., decay or corrosion), and gradual obsolescence, which makes it unprofitable to continue using some assets until they have been fully exhausted. The annual amount of depreciation of an asset depends on its original purchase price, its estimated useful life, and its estimated salvage value. A number of different methods of figuring the amount of depreciation have been developed. Using the simple straight-line method, which considers depreciation a function of time, the annual depreciation cost is calculated by dividing the cost of the asset (original minus salvage cost) equally over its entire life.

Designated market area: Nielsen audience-market classification that designates a certain market area in which local stations have partial or complete dominance over stations from other market areas. Similar to Arbitron ADI.

Direct-distribution expense: Expense incurred in relation to the distribution of a specific picture: The two largest items relating to the release of any picture are prints and advertising and publicity costs. Other direct expenses include such things as checking costs, freight, guild payments, trade-association fees and assessments, market research, and certain taxes.

Discounted-cash-flow method: A method of measuring the return on capital invested. The value of a project is expressed as an interest rate at which the project's total future earnings, discounted from the time that they accrue to the present, equal the original investment. It is more precise than most of the other methods used to measure return on capital invested because it recognizes the effect of the time value of money. It can be used to determine whether a given project is acceptable or unacceptable by comparing each project's rate of return with the company's standard.

Discount rate: 1. Interest rate charged member banks by the Federal Reserve for the opportunity to borrow added reserves. 2. Percentage by which a bank will discount the financing value of a filmmaker's distribution contract.

Discretionary spending: A measure, developed by the National Industrial Conference Board, that reflects the extent of consumer spending as the result of a decision relatively free of prior commitment, pressure of necessity, or force of habit. It includes all personal expenditures not accounted for specifically or in equivalent form in imputed income, fixed commitments, or essential outlays. The series measures the growth and ability of American consumers to exercise some degree of discretion over the direction and manner of their spending and saving.

Distribution fee: Contractual rate assessed by a distributor on the gross film revenue. Used in computation of contingent compensation (i.e., profit participation).

Drop: A term used in the gaming industry to indicate the total monetary-equivalent value of cash, IOUs ("markers"), and other items that are physically deposited or dropped into a cash box of a gaming table or slot machine.

Econometrics: The branch of economics that expresses economic theories in mathematical terms in order to verify them by statistical methods. It is concerned with empirical measurements of economic relations that are expressible in mathematical form. Econometrics seeks to measure the impact of one economic variable on another in order to be able to predict future events or advise on economic-policy choices to produce desired results. Economic theory can supply qualitative information concerning an economic problem, but it is the task of econometrics to provide the quantitative content for these qualitative statements.

Economic growth: An increase in a nation's or an area's capacity to produce goods and services coupled with an increase in production of these goods and services. Usually, economic growth is measured by the annual rate of increase in a nation's gross national product (GNP) as adjusted for price changes.

Economic model: A mathematical statement of economic theory. Use of an economic model is a method of analysis that presents an oversimplified picture of the real world.

Economics: The social study of production, distribution, and consumption of wealth.

Elastic demand: The percentage change induced in one factor of demand divided by a given percentage change in the factor that caused the change. For example, if the price of a commodity is raised, purchasers tend to reduce their buying rate. The relationship between price and purchasing rate, which is known as the elasticity of demand, expresses the percentage change in the buying rate divided by the percentage change in price.

Elasticity: The relative response of one variable to a small percentage change in another variable.

Equilibrium: The state of an economic system in which all forces for change are balanced, so that the net tendency to change is zero. An economic system is considered to be in equilibrium when all the significant variables show no change over a period of time.

Equity: 1. Amount of capital invested in an enterprise. It represents a participative share of ownership, and in an accounting sense is calculated by subtracting the liabilities (obligations) of an enterprise from its assets. 2. The shorthand name for the Actors Equity labor union.

Excess reserves: The surplus of cash and deposits owned by commercial member banks of the Federal Reserve System over what they are legally required to hold at Reserve Banks or in their own vaults. The excess-reserve position of a bank is an indication of its ability to invest in government bonds or to make loans to customers. Therefore, if the Federal Reserve System is trying to stimulate business in periods of economic sluggishness, it buys government bonds from private sellers, thus increasing bank reserves; and vice versa.

Film rental: The monies paid by the exhibitor to the distributor as rental fees for the right to license a film for public showing. Generally computed weekly on a consecutive seven-day basis (Wednesday through Tuesday or Friday through Thursday, depending on the day on which the film first opens in the market). Film rental may be determined by several different methods, including a 90:10 basis, sliding scale, fixed percentage, minimums (floors) that relate specifically to the gross box-office receipts, or a flat-fee basis that is a predetermined, unchanging amount. The film rental earned usually changes from week to week, with the distributor's relative share generally decreasing and the exhibitor's share increasing from the first through subsequent weeks.

FM (frequency modulation): Technically, the variation of the frequency of a radio wave in accordance with the sound being broadcast. Radio (audio) transmission from 88 to 108 megahertz. Signal is unaffected by atmospheric interference, but it is a high-fidelity, line-of-sight beam impeded by topographic or physical obstructions.

Foreign exchange: All monetary instruments that give residents of one country a financial claim on another country. The use of foreign exchange is a country's principal means of settling its transactions with other countries.

Fourier analysis: A technique for analyzing periodic movement in composite time series – hence, a form of harmonic analysis. It treats the variable under study as the sum of a series of sine and cosine terms in which the unknown periods of component series are not necessarily identical. Variances of deviations from a fitted Fourier series provide estimates of the variance of the error term.

Four-wall: A technique used by some distribution companies in which theaters are offered a flat weekly rental fee that is guaranteed to the exhibitor regardless of the film's revenue intake at the box office. The distributor pays all advertising expenses and usually hires personnel to be at each theater for supervision and nightly collection of all monies taken in at the box office. The exhibitor has virtually no risk in that rental income is guaranteed. The distributor incurs a greater risk, but is also in the position, should the film be successful, of reaping the benefits of 100% of the monies taken in at the box office, less advertising, administrative, and rental costs.

Franchise: 1. A contractual agreement between a cable operator and a government body that defines the rights and responsibilities of each party in the construction and operation of a cable system within a specified geographic area. 2. A territorial agreement between a league and team owners.

Free reserves: The margin by which excess reserves exceed borrowings at Federal Reserve Banks. They are a better indicator of the banking system's ability to expand loans and investments than excess reserves. Manipulation of the net free-reserve position of member banks is an indication of the monetary policy that the Federal Reserve wishes to pursue.

Gross domestic product (GDP): GDP measures the value of all goods and services produced in a country no matter whether that output belongs to natives or foreigners, whereas GNP measures output belonging to U.S. citizens and corporations wherever that output is created. In actuality, in the U.S., the differences between the values of the two series have been slight. *See* Gross national product.

Gross national product (GNP): The most comprehensive measure of a nation's total output of goods and services. In the United States, the GNP represents the dollar value at current prices of all goods and services produced for sale plus the estimated value of certain imputed outputs, that is, goods and services that are neither bought nor sold. The rental value of owner-occupied dwellings and the value of farm products consumed on the farm are the most important imputed outputs included; the services of housewives are among the most important non-market values included. The GNP includes only final goods and services; for example, a pair of shoes that costs the manufacturer $2.50, the retailer $4.50, and the consumer $6.00 adds to the GNP only $6.00, the amount of the final sale, not $13.00, the sum of all the transactions. The GNP can be calculated by adding either all expenditures on currently produced goods and services or all incomes earned in producing these goods and services.

GRP (gross rating point): A rating basis for determining the estimated percentage of households or target audience exposed to a broadcast commercial or magazine advertisement (newspaper GRP data generally are not readily available). GRPs are the sums of all rating points and an indication of potential exposure. One rating point is equal to 1% of the population of the total universe in which the advertising campaign is being run. However, this does not mean that 100 GRPs provide advertising exposure to 100% of the population; this measurement does not eliminate audience duplication from its number totals. GRPs can be computed on the basis of reach multiplied by average frequency.

Gross rentals: The total of the distributor's share of the money taken in at the box office computed on the basis of negotiated agreements between the distributor and the exhibitor (also called gross proceeds).

Gross win: For a casino, gross win is equivalent to revenues or sales in other businesses. It is from the win that operating expenses must be deducted.

Handle: In the gaming industry, the handle is the total dollar amount bet on the outcome of an event.

Head end: The electronic-origination center of a cable system and the site of signal-processing equipment.

Hold: A term used in the gaming industry to indicate how much of the drop is retained (won) by the game operator through the course of play. Hold can be expressed as a percentage of the drop, in which case it is known as the hold percentage, often in a shorthand way called "win."

Holdover figure: A minimum weekly dollar figure for monies taken in at the theater box office that a film must reach in order to be held over for another week. This figure is mutually agreed on by the exhibitor and distributor when the terms under which the film will be played are originally established. It is an objective means by which either the exhibitor or the distributor may insist that the picture continue if the figure was achieved or, if not, cease to be shown in a specific theater.

Homes passed: The number of households in a market that a cable system has the ability to serve. This does not mean that these homes have elected to utilize the cable system.

Homes using television: The estimated percentage of the homes in which people are viewing television at any given time. The result of extrapolations made on the basis of audience-measurement techniques.

Income effect: A term used in demand analysis to indicate the increase or decrease in the amount of a good that is purchased because of a price-induced change in the purchasing power of a fixed income. When the price of a commodity declines, the income effect enables a person to buy more of this or other commodities with a given income. The opposite occurs when the price rises. By using indifference curves, it is possible to separate the income effect from the so-called substitution effect, in which the demand for a price-reduced good rises as it is substituted for other goods whose prices have remained constant.

Indifference curve: A graphic curve that represents the various combinations of two goods that will yield the consumer the same total satisfaction. For example, a household may receive the same satisfaction from consuming four pounds of steak or one pound of chicken. By assuming that the two commodities can be substituted for each other, it is possible to draw an indifference schedule that contains all of the possible combinations of the commodities that will yield the same satisfaction. When the schedule is plotted on a graph, with one commodity along the vertical axis and another along the horizontal axis, the curve that connects the points is called an indifference curve.

Inelastic demand (inelasticity): A term used to describe a proportionally smaller change in the purchase rate of a good than the proportional change in price that caused the change in amount bought. When the demand for a product is inelastic, a relatively large price change is necessary to cause a relatively small increase in purchase. To calculate the elasticity of demand, the percentage change in buying rate (the quantity bought per period of time) is divided by the percentage change in price.

Inflation: A persistent upward movement in the general price level. It results in a decline in purchasing power.

Interest: The price paid for the use of money over a period of time. Individuals, businesses, and governments buy the use of money. Businesses pay interest for the use of money to purchase capital goods because they can increase production and productivity through the introduction of new plants and new machines.

Inventory: The supply of various goods kept on hand by a firm in order to meet needs promptly as they arise and thus assure uninterrupted operation of the business. In manufacturing, for example, inventory includes not only finished products awaiting shipment to selling outlets, but also raw materials and countless other items required for the production and distribution of the product.

Labor force: According to the concept of the U.S. Department of Labor and the U.S. Bureau of the Census, the noninstitutionalized population, 16 years of age or older, who either are employed or are looking for work.

Lead–lag relationship: The timing of changes in one statistical series in relation to changes in another series. The term is frequently used in sales forecasting, which makes use of the timing pattern between a company's sales and a particular economic indicator.

Legs: In the movie business the term indicates a film that attracts strong audience interest and that will therefore run (play) in theaters for a relatively long time.

Liabilities: The debts or amounts of money owed by an individual, partnership, or corporation to others. Considered from another point of view, liabilities are the claims or rights, expressed in monetary terms, of an individual's or a corporation's creditors. In accounting, liabilities are classified as either short-term or long-term liabilities or as secured or unsecured liabilities. Short-term liabilities are those that will be satisfied, or paid, within one year.

Local Marketing Agreement: In the broadcasting industry, an LMA is a time-brokerage arrangement between two separately owned stations in the same geographic area that allows one station to exchange programming for the right to sell advertising time on the other station. LMAs are designed so as to save costs by combining the marketing efforts of at least two local broadcast stations.

Macroeconomics: Modern economic analysis concerned with data in aggregate as opposed to individual form. It concerns itself with an overall view of economic life, considering the total size, shape, and functioning of economic experience rather than the workings of individual parts. More specifically, macroeconomics involves the analysis of the general price level rather than the prices of individual commodities, national output or income rather than the income of the individual firm, and total employment rather than employment in an individual firm.

Make-good: An offer by a medium to rerun, at no additional charge, an advertisement or commercial. Generally of equal or greater value than the original placement and used to compensate advertisers for unanticipated shortfalls.

Marginal cost: The additional cost that a producer incurs by making one additional unit of output. If, for example, total costs were $13,000 when a firm was producing two machine tools per day and $18,000 when it was producing three machine tools per day, the marginal cost of producing one machine tool was $5,000. The marginal cost may be the same or higher or lower in moving from three to four machine tools. The concept of marginal cost plays a key role in determining the quantity of goods that a firm chooses to produce. The purely competitive firm, which faces a given price set in the market, increases its output until marginal cost equals price. That point is the firm's best-profit output point. The imperfectly competitive firm equates marginal cost to marginal revenue (additional revenue) to obtain the highest profits. For most firms, marginal costs decline for a while and then begin to rise. The pattern of the marginal-cost graph depends on the nature of the firm's production function and the prices of the goods that it buys.

Marginal revenue: The additional revenue that a seller receives from putting one more unit of output on the market.

Margins: *See* Profit margin.

Market share: The ratio of a company's sales, in units or dollars, to total industry sales, in units or dollars, on either an actual basis or a potential basis for a specific time period.

Mechanical rights (royalties): The rights to reproduce and to distribute to the public copyrighted materials. So-called mechanical royalties, usually on a per-copy basis, are paid to obtain such rights.

Microeconomics: Modern economic analysis concerned with data in individual form as opposed to aggregate form. It is concerned with the study of the individual firm rather than aggregates of firms, the individual consuming unit rather than the total population, and the individual commodity rather than total output. Microeconomics deals with the division of total output among industries, products, and firms and the allocation of resources among competing uses. It is concerned with the relative prices of particular goods and the problem of income distribution.

Model: In econometrics, an equation or set of equations depicting the causal relationships that are believed to generate observed data. Also, the expression of a theory by means of mathematical symbols or diagrams.

Modern portfolio theory: A theory that enables investment managers to classify, estimate, and control the sources of investment risk and return.

Monopoly: A market structure with only one seller of a commodity. In pure monopoly, the single seller exercises absolute control over the market price because there is no competitive supply of goods on the market. The seller can choose the most profitable price and does so by raising the price and restricting the ouput below what would be achieved if there were competition.

Monopsony: A market structure with a single buyer of a commodity. Pure monopsony, or buyer's monopoly, is characterized by the ability of the single buyer to set the buying price. In the case of a monopsonist who maximizes profits, both the buying price and the quantity bought are lower than they would be in a competitive situation.

MPEG (motion picture experts group): Pertains to two video standards that had been developed as of the early 1990s. MPEG-1, which provides VCR-quality video, was originally developed for CD-ROM systems and operates at 1.5 Mbps (million bits per second), whereas MPEG-2 was first initiated by broadcasters for live video services that can be transmitted at 6 Mbps.

MSO (multiple-system operator): A company that owns and operates more than one cable-television system.

Multimedia: A term broadly used to describe the convergence of digitalized computer, telephone, and cable technologies in the development of new entertainment software applications that mix text, audio, and video.

National income: The total compensation of the elements used in production (land, labor, capital, and entrepreneurship) that comes from the current production of goods and services by the national economy. It is the income earned (but not necessarily received) by all persons in the country in a specified period.

Negative cost: All of the various costs, charges, and expenses incurred in the acquisition and production of a motion picture. These include such items as facilities (sound stage, film lab, editing room, etc.) and raw material (set construction, raw film stock, etc.). Typically segregated as above-the-line production-period costs and post-production-period costs.

Negotiated deal: If the film-distribution company rejects all bid offers submitted by exhibitors for the right to license a film for exhibition within a market, the branch office will in turn either rebid the picture, suggesting different terms, or send out a notice to all exhibitors by which it offers to negotiate openly in an effort to award the film to the theater that offers the most attractive deal.

Net profits (contractual): Generally, the amount of gross receipts remaining after deducting distribution fees, distribution expenses, negative cost (including interest), certain deferments, and gross participations.

Nielsen station index (NSI): A service provided by the A. C. Nielsen Company for rating television viewing habits, audience profiles, etc., on a local basis or within a given broadcast area.

Nonborrowed reserves: A reserve aggregate consisting of total bank reserves (deposits of the Federal Reserve and vault cash) minus borrowings by member banks from the Federal Reserve.

Oligopoly: A type of market structure in which a small number of firms supplies the major portion of an industry's output. The best-known example in the U.S. economy is the automobile industry, in which three firms account for 65% of the output of passenger cars. Although oligopolies are most likely to develop in industries whose production methods require large capital investments, they also cover such diverse items as cigarettes, light bulbs, chewing gum, detergents, and razor blades. In economic theory, the term *oligopoly* means a mixture of competition and monopoly. The benefit or harm to the economy at large by oligopolies remains in dispute.

Operating cash flow: In the cable and broadcasting industries, earnings before depreciation and amortization, interest, other income, and taxes.

Operating income: Earnings before interest, other income, and taxes.

Opportunity costs: The value of the productive resources used in producing one good, such as an automobile, instead of another good, such as a machine tool. With relatively fixed supplies of labor and capital at any given time, the economy cannot produce all it wants of everything.

Overage: In movies and music, generally any dollar amount beyond which advances and guarantees have been earned or, in industry parlance, have been recouped. The term is also applied to extensions of payments for work rendered beyond that stipulated in original contracts.

Paretian optimum: A situation that exists when no one (say person *A*) in a society can move into a position that *A* prefers without causing someone else (person *B*) to move into a position that *B* prefers less. In other words, a situation is not a paretian or social optimum if it is possible, by changing the way in which commodities are produced or exchanged, to make one person better off without making another person (or persons) worse off. *See* Second-best theory.

Partnership: A type of business organization in which two or more persons agree on the amounts of their contribution (capital and effort) and on the distribution of profits, if any. Partnerships are common in retail trade, accounting, and law.

Pay-per-view: A cable service that makes available to a subscriber an individual movie, sporting event, or concert on payment of a fee for that single event.

Pay-TV: A generic term used to indicate subscriber-paid-for television, presented in an uncut and uncensored format.

Periodic-table computation method: An accounting method of amortization in which cost is related to gross revenue recorded during a period; may be based on an average table established from experience with previously released films.

Personal-consumption expenditures: Expenditures that reflect the market value of goods and services purchased by individuals and nonprofit institutions or acquired by them as income in kind. The rental value of owner-occupied dwellings is included, but not the purchases of dwellings. Purchases are recorded at cost to consumers, including excise or sales taxes, and in full at the time of purchase whether made with cash or on credit.

Personal income: According to the concept of the U.S. Department of Commerce, the amount of current income received by persons from all sources, including transfer payments from government and business, but excluding transfer payments from other sources. Personal income also includes the net incomes of unincorporated businesses and nonprofit institutions and nonmonetary income, such as the estimated value of food consumed on farms and the estimated rental value of homes occupied by their owners.

Price/earnings ratio: The current market price per share of a company's stock expressed as a multiple of the company's per-share earnings.

Print: 1. A copy made from the master for the purpose of motion-picture presentation. For all intents and purposes, the print is the specific motion-picture release, because the master is preserved for additional duplication. A distribution company may make only a few copies or more than 1,500 prints, depending on the expected or experienced success with a particular motion picture. 2. Advertising placed in newspapers as part of an advertising campaign.

Production function: The various combinations of land, labor, materials, and equipment that are needed to produce a given quantity of output. The production function expresses the maximum possible output that can be produced with any specified quantities of the various necessary inputs. Every production function assumes a given level of technology; once technological innovations have been introduced, the production function changes.

Production overhead: Those costs and expenses incurred for the production of motion pictures in general that cannot be directly charged to specific pictures. They include such things as salaries of production-department executives and their related expenses, story–abandonment costs, certain studio-facility costs, and general and administrative costs relating to the production area.

Productivity: The goods and services produced per unit of labor or capital or both; for example, the output of automobiles per person-hour. The ratio of output to all labor and capital is a total productivity measure; the ratio of output to either labor or capital is a partial measure. Anything that raises output in relation to labor and capital leads to an increase in productivity.

Profit margin: The percentage that net profit from operations is of net sales. This percentage measures the efficiency of a company or an industry. Nevertheless, profit margins vary widely among industries and among companies within a given industry. *See* Returns.

Profits: The amount left over after a business enterprise has paid all its bills.

Prospectus: Any communication, either written or broadcast by radio or television, that offers a security for sale. The prospectus contains the most important parts of the registration statement, which must give all information relevant to the issue.

Public good: A good for which the costs of production are independent of the number of people who consume it. National defense is an example where one person's consumption does not diminish the quantity available to others. TV programs are almost pure public goods because the program, no matter how it is recorded, remains unchanged regardless of how many people view it. In contrast, pure *private goods*, once consumed by an individual, are no longer available for someone else. For *private goods*, say a slice of bread, the costs of production *are* related to the number of people who consume it.

Reach: The number of households or the target audience exposed to an advertising message at least one time over a predetermined period of time (also called *cume*).

Reach and frequency: Criteria for evaluating the level of cumulative audience exposure for an advertising campaign on the basis of a percentage of all persons or households who are exposed to the advertising (reach) and the average number of exposures (frequency) over a given period of time: reach × frequency = gross rating points.

Regression line: A statistical term that indicates a relationship between two or more variables. The regression line was first used by Sir Francis Galton to indicate certain relationships in his theory of heredity, but it is now employed to describe many functional relationships. A regression, or least-squares, line is derived from a mathematical equation relating one economic variable or another. The use of regression lines is important in determining the effect of one variable on another.

Required reserves: The percentages of their deposits that U.S. commercial banks are required to set aside as reserves at their regional Federal Reserve Bank or as cash in their vaults. Reserve requirements vary according to the category of the bank.

Returns: 1. The earnings or profit compensations received for owning assets or equity positions. Also, returns on sales are equivalent to profit margins. 2. The term used in the record business in regard to goods sent back to the manufacturer or distributor for credit.

Risk: The exposure of an investor to the possibility of gain or loss of money. Profit is the investor's reward for assuming the risk of economic uncertainty, such as changes in consumer tastes or changes in technology. The financial risk is based on natural, human, and economic uncertainties.

Scatter market: In network television, the remnants of unsold commercial time that remain after preseason up-front buying has been completed.

Second-best theory: A theory that analyzes alternative suboptimal positions to determine the second best when some constraint prevents an economy from reaching a paretian optimum. *See* Paretian optimum.

Secular trend: A statistical term denoting the regular, long-term movement of a series of economic data. The secular trend of most economic series is positive, or upward, indicating growth, the angle of the trend depending on how fast or how slow the growth rate is.

Share of audience: The percentage of total households or population (either local or national depending on survey criteria) that are using television or radio during a specific time and that are also tuned into a particular program.

Sherman Antitrust Act: A U.S. federal statute, enacted in 1890, that forbids all contracts in restraint of trade and all attempts at monopolization. The main purposes of the act were to prevent the exercise and growth of monopoly and to restore free enterprise and price competition.

Spectral analysis: In statistics and econometrics, a technique for isolating and estimating the duration and amplitudes of the cyclical components of time series. It results in separating the random from the systematic components of time series.

Spot TV: Local TV commercial time purchased on a given TV station within a specific market through a local salesperson within that market or through a national representative of the station.

Stripping: Generally applied to the use of off-network syndicated series episodes several times a week, as in a continuous strip.

Superstation: Independent TV stations (in Atlanta, Boston, Chicago, Dallas, Los Angeles, and New York) that broadcast their programming nationally via satellite to cable systems. The systems pay for copyrights and also an average of 10 cents a subscriber every month to the satellite companies (common carriers) that distribute the signals.

Supply: The ability and willingness of a firm to sell a good or service. The firm's supply of a good or service is a schedule of the quantities of that good or service that the firm would offer for sale at alternative prices at a given moment in time. The supply schedule, or the listing of quantities that would be sold at different prices, can be shown graphically by means of a supply curve. The term *supply* refers to the entire schedule of possibilities, not to one point on the schedule. It is an instantaneous concept expressing the relationship of price and the quantity that would be willingly sold, all other factors being constant.

Syndication: A term usually applied to the process whereby previously exhibited or recorded material is reused by (licensed to) a collection of buyers such as independent television and radio stations.

Tax credit: A legal provision permitting U.S. taxpayers to deduct specified sums from their tax liabilities.

Tax deduction: A legal provision permitting U.S. taxpayers to deduct specified expenditures from their taxable income.

Terms: The conditions under which the distributor agrees to allow the exhibitor to show its product in a given theater and the exhibitor agrees to show the product. Relates to such items as the basis on which film rental will be paid (as a percentage of weekly gross box-office receipts or flat fee), the playing time (number of weeks), choice of theater, dollar participation in cooperative advertising expenditure, clearance over other theaters, etc.

Time series: A set of ordered observations of a particular economic variable, such as prices, production, investment, and consumption, taken at different points in time. Most economic series consist of monthly, quarterly, or annual observations. Monthly and quarterly economic series are used in short-term business forecasting.

UHF (ultrahigh frequency): Television signals in the range 300 to 3,000 megahertz. Television channels 14 through 83.

Underwriter: Any person, group, or firm that assumes a risk in return for a fee, usually called a premium or commission.

Unemployment rate: The number of jobless persons expressed as a percentage of the total labor force. The U.S. counts as unemployed anyone 16 years of age or over who is out of work and would like a job (even if that person is doing little about finding one).

Up-front buying: In network television, the preseason purchasing of commercial time in selected program blocks.

Utility: The ability of a good or a service to satisfy human wants. It is the property possessed by a particular good or service that affords an individual pleasure or prevents pain during the time of its consumption or the period of anticipation of its consumption. The degree of utility of a good varies constantly. Thus, utility is not proportional to the quantity or type of the good or service consumed.

VHF (very high frequency): Television signals in the range of 30 to 300 megahertz. Television channels 2 through 13.

Warrant: An option that gives the holder the privilege of purchasing a certain amount of stock at a specified price for a stipulated period. There are two types of warrants: *stock-purchase warrants* and *subscription warrants*. Stock-purchase warrants (also called option warrants) are sometimes issued with or attached to bonds, preferred stock, and, infrequently, common stock. They entitle the holder to buy common stock in the same corporation at a certain price. Some of these warrants limit the right to buy to a specified period; others are perpetual. Stock-purchase warrants are sometimes attached to the underlying issue and cannot be detached; their value is a part of the bond or preferred stock. Others are detachable, sometimes after a waiting period, and frequently have inherent value that depends on the current price of the common stock.

Win: *See* Gross win.

Window: In films and television, the period of time during which contracts permit exclusive exhibition of a product. For example, a film's initial domestic theatrical window would normally be followed, four to six months later, by a home-video market release window. Six months later, a pay-television window lasting two years will open.

Working capital, net: The excess of current assets over current liabilities. These excess current assets are available to carry on business operations. As demand increases in prosperous times, a large volume of working capital is needed to expand production.

Workweek: The number of weekly hours per factory worker for which pay has been received, including paid holidays, vacations, and sick leaves. In the United States, workweek figures cover full-time and part-time production and related workers who receive payment for any part of the pay period ending nearest the fifteenth of the month. Because of increasing amounts of paid holidays, vacations, and sick leave, the paid workweek exceeds the number of hours actually worked per week. The average-workweek series compiled from payroll data by the U.S. Bureau of Labor Statistics differs from the series of weekly hours actually worked that is compiled from household surveys by the U.S. Bureau of the Census. It also differs from the standard or scheduled workweek, because such factors as absenteeism, part-time work, and stoppages make the average workweek lower than the standard workweek.

Write-off: The act of removing an asset from the books of a company. The term *write-off* is related to *write-down,* but the latter is more closely associated with partial reduction of the book value of the asset rather than with removing the asset from the books entirely.

Yield: The percentage that is derived from dividing the annual return from any investment by the amount of the investment.

References

Abt, V., Smith, J. F., and Christiansen, E. M. (1985). *The Business of Risk: Commercial Gambling in Mainstream America.* Lawrence: University of Kansas Press.

Adams, J. A. (1991). *The American Amusement Park Industry: A History of Technology and Thrills.* Boston: Twayne Publishers (G. K. Hall & Co.).

Adler, M. (1985). "Stardom and Talent," *American Economic Review,* (75)(March).

AICPA (1984). *Audits of Casinos.* New York: American Institute of Certified Public Accountants.

Akst, D., and Landro, L. (1988). "In Hollywood's Jungle the Predators Are Out and Feasting on Stars," *Wall Street Journal,* June 20.

Ambrose, J. F. (1981). "Recent Tax Developments Regarding Purchases of Sports Franchises – The Game Isn't Over Yet," *Taxes* (Chicago: Commerce Clearing House) 59(11)(November):739–61.

Andrews, E. L. (1993). "Top Rivals Agree on Unified System For Advanced TV," *New York Times,* May 25.

Angeli, M. (1991). "My Name Is Bond. Completion Bond," *New York Times,* August 11.

Asch, P., Malkiel, B. G., and Quandt, R. E. (1984). "Market Efficiency in Racetrack Betting," *Journal of Business* 57(2)(April):165–75.

Auletta, K. (1991). *Three Blind Mice: How the TV Networks Lost Their Way.* New York: Random House.

Baade, R. A. (1994). "Stadiums, Professional Sports, and Economic Development: Assessing the Reality," Heartland Policy Study No. 62 (April 4). Detroit: The Heartland Institute.

Bagamery, A. (1984). "We Sell Space, Not Fantasy," *Forbes* 133(3)(January 30):60–4.

Baldo, A. (1991). "Secrets of the Front Office," *Financial World* 160(14)(July 9).

Balio, T., ed. (1976). *The American Film Industry.* Madison: University of Wisconsin Press, rev. ed. 1985.

Banks, J. (1996). *Monopoly Television: MTV's Quest to Control the Music.* Boulder, Colo.: Westview Press.

Barnhart, R. T. (1983), "Can Trente-et-Quarante Be Beaten?" *Gambling Times* 3(8)(December):74–7.

Barnouw, E. (1990). *Tube of Plenty: The Evolution of American Television.* New York: Oxford University Press, rev. 2nd ed.

Barra, A. (1995). "How the 49ers Beat the Salary Cap," *New York Times,* January 8.

Barrett, N. S. (1974). *The Theory of Microeconomics Policy.* Lexington, Mass.: Heath.

Barwise, P., and Ehrenberg, A. (1988). *Television and Its Audience.* London: Sage.

Baskerville, D. (1982). *Music Business Handbook,* 3rd ed. Denver, Colo.: Sherwood.

Baumgarten, P. A., Farber, D. C., and Fleischer, M. (1992). *Producing, Financing, and Distributing Film,* 2nd ed. New York: Limelight Editions. (First edition by Drama Book Specialists, New York, in 1973.)

Baumol, W., and Baumol, H. (1984). "In Culture, the Cost Disease Is Contagious," *New York Times,* June 3, section 2, p. 1.

Baumol, W. J., and Bowen, W. G. (1968). *Performing Arts – The Economic Dilemma.* New York: Twentieth Century Fund; Cambridge, Mass.: M.I.T. Press.

Becker, G. S. (1965). "A Theory of the Allocation of Time," *Economic Journal* LXXV(299)(September):493–517.

Berger, A. J., and Bruning, N. (1979). *Lady Luck's Companion.* New York: Harper & Row.

Bernstein, C. (1990). "The Leisure Empire," *Time* 136(27)(December 24).

Berry, E. J. (1984). "Nielsen May Face U.K. Rival in Researching TV Audiences," *Wall Street Journal,* February 2.

Biederman, D., and Phillips, L. (1980). "Negotiating the Recording Agreement," in *Counseling Clients in the Entertainment Industry,* edited by M. Silfen. New York: Practising Law Institute.

Bikhchandani, S., Hirshleifer, D., and Welch, I. (1992). "A Theory of Fads, Fashion, Custom, and Cultural Change as Informational Cascades," *Journal of Political Economy,* 100(5).

Blaug, M., ed. (1976). *The Economics of the Arts.* Boulder, Colo.: Westview Press; London: Martin Robertson.

Bloomfield, P. (1977). *Fourier Analysis of Time Series: An Introduction.* New York: Wiley.

Bluem, A. W., and Squire, J. E., eds. (1972). *The Movie Business: American Film Industry Practice.* New York: Hastings House.

Blumenthal, H. J., and Goodenough, O. R. (1991). *This Business of Television.* New York: Billboard/Watson-Guptill.

Boucher, F. C. (1986). "Performing Music Licensing Procedures," *Billboard,* November 24.

Boyer, P. J. (1988). "Sony and CBS Records: What a Romance," *The New York Times Magazine,* September 18.

Bradsher, K. (1994). ''Congressmen Pledge to Revoke Baseball's Antitrust Exemption,'' *New York Times,* December 24.

Breglio, J. F., and Schwartz, S. (1980). ''Introduction to Motion Picture Production and Distribution and Motion Picture Financing,'' in *Counseling Clients in the Entertainment Industry,* edited by M. Silfen. New York: Practising Law Institute.

Breimer, S. F. (1995). *Clause By Clause: The Screenwriter's Legal Guide.* New York: Dell Trade Paperback.

Brinkley, J. (1996). ''Defining TV's and Computers for a Future of High Definition,'' *New York Times,* December 2.

(1997). *Defining Vision: The Battle for the Future of Television.* New York: Harcourt Brace & Co.

Brown, A. C. (1984). ''Europe Braces for Free-Market TV,'' *Fortune* 109(4)(February 20):74–82.

Brown, C. (1991). ''Who Lost the Turtles?'' *Premiere* 4(6)(February).

Brown, J., and Church, A. (1987). ''Theme Parks in Europe,'' *Travel & Tourism Analyst,* London: The Economist, February.

Browne, Bortz & Coddington (1983). *An Analysis of the Television Programming Market.* Denver, Colo.: Browne, Bortz & Coddington (prepared for ABC).

Burck, C. G. (1977). ''Why the Sports Business Ain't What It Used to Be,'' *Fortune* XCV(5)(May):295.

Burton, J. S., and Toth, J. R. (1974). ''Forecasting Long-Term Interest Rates,'' *Financial Analysis Journal* 30(5)(September/October):73–87.

Carlson, M. B. (1984). ''Where MGM, the NCAA, and Jerry Falwell Fight for Cash,'' *Fortune* 109(2)(January 23):169–71.

Carvajal, D. (1996). ''Many, Many Unhappy Returns,'' *New York Times,* August 1.

Chace, S. (1983). ''Computer Game: Key Software Writers Double as Media Stars in a Promotional Push,'' *Wall Street Journal,* December 12.

Christiansen, E. M. (1989). ''1988 U.S. Gross Annual Wager,'' *Gaming and Wagering Business* 10(7)(July):7, and 10(8)(August):1.

Cobb, C., Halstead, T, and Rowe, J. (1995). ''If the GDP Is Up, Why Is America Down?'' *The Atlantic Monthly* 276(4)(October).

Cohen, L. (1983). ''Cable-Television Firms and Cities Haggle Over Franchises That Trail Expectations,'' *Wall Street Journal,* December 28.

Collins, G. (1992). ''The Daunting Task of Preventing Theft at Theater Box Offices,'' *New York Times,* March 25.

Columbia Pictures Industries (1982). *Columbia Pictures Industries Financial Factbook, 1981.* New York: Columbia Pictures Industries.

Colvin, G. (1983). ''The Battle for TV's Rerun Dollars,'' *Fortune* 107(7)(May 2):116–20.

Cones, J. W. (1992). *Film Finance & Distribution: A Dictionary of Terms.* Los Angeles: Silman-James.

(1995). *43 Ways to Finance Your Feature Film: A Comprehensive Analysis of Film Finance.* Carbondale, Ill.: Southern Illinois University Press.

Cook, J. (1979). ''Bingo!'' *Forbes* 124(3)(August 6):37–45.

Couzens, M. (1986). ''Invasion of the People Meters,'' *Channels* (June):40.

Cox, M. (1989a). ''Networks Overhaul Payouts for Affiliates,'' *Wall Street Journal,* May 31.

(1989b). ''The 'Toxic Avenger' May Not Win Any Prizes, But Fans Don't Care,'' *Wall Street Journal,* August 18.

Crandall, R. W. (1972). "FCC Regulation, Monopsony, and Network Television Program Costs," *Bell Journal of Economics* 3(2)(autumn):483–508.

Crandall, R. W., and Furchtgott-Roth, H. (1996). *Cable TV: Regulation or Competition*. Washington, D.C.: The Brookings Institution.

Culhane, J. (1990). *The American Circus: An Illustrated History*. New York: Henry Holt and Company.

Curran, J. J. (1984). "How High the Bull?" *Fortune* 109(3)(February 6):44–9.

Curran, T. (1986). *Financing Your Film: A Guide for Independent Filmmakers and Producers*. New York: Praeger.

Dannen, F. (1990). *Hit Men: Power Brokers and Fast Money Inside the Music Business*. New York: Times Books/Random House.

Davis, L. J. (1989). "Hollywood's Most Secret Agent," *New York Times Magazine*, July 9.

Davis, M. D. (1973). *Game Theory: A Nontechnical Approach*. New York: Basic Books.

De Grazia, S. (1962). *Of Time, Work and Leisure*. New York: Twentieth Century Fund.

De Vany, A., and Walls, W. D. (1996). "Bose-Einstein Dynamics and Adaptive Contracting in the Motion Picture Industry," *The Economic Journal*, November.

Dekom, P. J. (1984). "Transition in the Motion Picture Industry – Financing and Distribution, 1984," in *Counseling Clients in the Entertainment Industry*, edited by M. Silfen, pp. 189–203. New York: Practising Law Institute.

Demmert, H. G. (1973). *The Economics of Professional Team Sports*. Lexington, Mass.: Heath.

DeSerpa, A. C. (1971). "A Theory of the Economics of Time," *Economic Journal* (December):828–46.

DiMaggio, P. J. (1984). "The Nonprofit Instrument and the Influence of the Marketplace on Policies in the Arts," in *The Arts and Public Policy in the United States*, W. M. Lowry, ed. New York: The American Assembly (Columbia University).

Disch, T. M. (1991). "The Death of Broadway," *The Atlantic Monthly* 267(3)(March).

Donahue, S. M. (1987). *American Film Distribution: The Changing Marketplace*. Ann Arbor, Mich.: UMI Research Press.

Donnelly, W. J. (1986). *The Confetti Generation*. New York: Henry Holt.

Durant, J. (1969). *Highlights of the Olympics: From Ancient Times to the Present*, 3rd ed. New York: Hastings House.

Durso, J. (1986). "Mets a Baseball 'Jewel' in Attendance, Revenue," *New York Times*, August 22.

Eade, R. H. (1996). "Casino Cage Operations," *The Gaming Industry: Introduction and Perspectives*, Las Vegas: University of Nevada; New York: John Wiley & Sons.

Eadington, W. R., ed. (1976). *Gambling and Society*. Springfield, Ill.: Thomas.

Eberts, J., and Ilott, T. (1990). *My Indecision Is Final: The Rise and Fall of Goldcrest Films*. London: Faber and Faber (paperback 1992).

Eliot, M. (1989). *Rockonomics: The Money Behind the Music*. New York: Franklin Watts.

Farber, D. C. (1993). *From Option to Opening: A Guide to Producing Plays Off-Broadway*, 4th rev. ed. New York: Limelight Editions.

(1995). "Theater Lawyers Seem to Be Avoiding LLCs," *New York Law Journal*, January 20.

Felton, M. (1980). "Policy Implications of a Composer Labor Supply," in *Economic Policy for the Arts*, edited by W. S. Hendon, J. L. Shanahan, and A. J. MacDonald, pp. 186–98. Cambridge, Mass.: Abt Books.

Fey, M. (1989). *Slot Machines.* Reno, Nev.: Liberty Belle Books.

Fielding, R., ed. (1967). *A Technological History of Motion Pictures and Television: An Anthology from the Journal of the Society of Motion Picture and Television Engineers.* Los Angeles: University of California Press.

Financial Accounting Standards Board (1983). *Accounting Standards: Original Pronouncements.* Stamford, Conn.: FASB.

Findlay, J. M. (1986). *People of Chance: Gambling in American Society from Jamestown to Las Vegas.* New York and Oxford: Oxford University Press.

Fisher, F. M., McGowan, J. J., and Evans, D. S. (1980). "The Audience-Revenue Relationship for Local Television Stations," *Bell Journal of Economics* 11(2)(autumn):694–708.

Flack, S. (1989). "The Real Music in Music Publishing," *Corporate Finance,* March.

Flax, S. (1982). "Why Cable TV Is a High-Risk Investment," *Forbes* 130(6)(September 13):36–7.

Flick, R. (1983). "Squeeze on the Networks," *Fortune* 108(5)(September 5):84.

(1988). "ASCAPS's Out of Tune with Composers," *Wall Street Journal,* May 27.

Forsyth, R. W. (1995). "Stadiums Built With Taxpayer Funds Don't Pay Their Way," *Barron's,* November 13.

Frank, A. D. (1984). "The USFL Meets the Sophomore Jinx," *Forbes* 133(4)(February 13):41–2.

Frank, R. H., and Cook, P. J. (1995). *The Winner-Take-All Society.* New York: Simon & Schuster (The Free Press).

Frankenfield, W. C. (1994). "What Are the Generally Accepted Accounting Principles in the Broadcasting Industry?" *Broadcast Cable Financial Journal,* June-July.

Frascogna, X. M., and Hetherington, H. L. (1978). *Successful Artist Management.* New York: Billboard/Watson-Guptill.

Frey, B. S., and Pommerehne, W. W. (1989). *Muses & Markets: Explorations in the Economics of the Arts.* London: Basil Blackwell.

Friedman, B. (1982). *Casino Management, rev. and enlarged edition.* Secaucus, N.J.: Lyle Stuart.

Friedman, M., and Savage, L. J. (1948). "The Utility Analysis of Choices Involving Risk," *Journal of Political Economy* 56(4)(August):279–304.

Frude, N. (1983). *The Intimate Machine: Close Encounters with Computers and Robots.* New York: New American Library.

Garey, N. H. (1983). "Elements of Feature Financing," in *The Movie Business Book,* J. E. Squire, ed. New York: Simon & Schuster/Fireside.

Gelatt, R. (1977). *The Fabulous Phonograph, 1877–1977,* 2nd rev. ed. New York: Macmillan.

Ghez, G. R., and Becker, G. S. (1975). *The Allocation of Time and Goods Over the Life Cycle.* New York: National Bureau of Economic Research.

Gibbs, N. (1989). "How America Has Run Out of Time," *Time* 133(17)(April 24):58.

Gilder, G. (1995). *Telecosm.* Internet address: www.forbes.com.

Gilpin, K. (1993). "The Circus Is Just One of His Acts," *New York Times,* March 24.

Goldberg, M. (1988). "Inside the Payola Scandal," *Rolling Stone,* January 14.

Goldman, K. (1992). "The One-Hour Drama Stages a Comeback on TV After Being Preempted by Sitcoms," *Wall Street Journal,* September 1.

Gollehon, J. (1986). *All about Sports Betting.* Grand Rapids, Mich.: Gollehon.

Goodman, R. (1994). *Legalized Gambling As a Strategy for Economic Development.* Northampton, Mass.: Broadside Books.

(1995). *The Luck Business: The Devastating Consequences and Broken Promises of America's Gambling Explosion.* New York: The Free Press (Simon & Schuster).

Gottman, J. M. (1981). *Time Series Analysis: A Comprehensive Introduction for Social Scientists.* New York: Cambridge University Press.

Greco, A. N. (1997). *The Book Publishing Industry.* Boston: Allyn and Bacon.

Greenlees, E. M. (1988). *Casino Accounting and Financial Management.* Reno and Las Vegas: University of Nevada Press.

Grimes, W. (1997). "With 6,138 Lives, 'Cats' Sets Broadway Mark," *New York Times,* June 19.

Gubernick, L. (1989a). "Last Laugh," *Forbes* 143(4)(May 15):56.

(1989b). "Living Off the Past," *Forbes* 143(12)(June 12):48.

Hagin, R. (1979). *Modern Portfolio Theory.* Homewood, Ill.: Dow Jones-Irwin.

Halliday, J., and Fuller, P., eds. (1974). *The Psychology of Gambling.* New York: Harper & Row.

Hamlen, W. A., Jr. (1991). "Superstardom in Popular Music: Empirical Evidence," *Review of Economics and Statistics,* LXXIII(4) (November).

Hansmann, H. (1981). "Nonprofit Enterprise in the Performing Arts," *Bell Journal of Economics* 12(2)(autumn):341–61.

Harden, B., and Swardson, A. (1996). "America's Gamble," *Washington Post,* March 3–6.

Harmelink, P. J., and Vignes, D. W. (1981). "Tax Aspects of Baseball Player Contracts and Planning Opportunities," *Taxes.* (Chicago: Commerce Clearing House) 59(8)(August):535–46.

Harris, D. (1986). *The League: The Rise and Decline of the NFL.* New York: Bantam.

Harris, L. (1995). *The Harris Poll 1995, #68.* New York: Louis Harris & Associates, Inc.

Harris, W. (1981). "Someday They'll Build a Town Here, Kate," *Forbes* 128 (October 26):135–9.

Hedges, J. N., and Taylor, D. E. (1980). "Recent Trends in Worktime: Hours Edge Downward," *Monthly Labor Review* (U.S. Department of Labor) 103(3)(March):3–11.

Heilbrun, J., and Gray, C. M. (1993). *The Economics of Art and Culture.* New York and Cambridge (U.K.): Cambridge University Press.

Helyar (1995). "Losers on the Field,, L.A. Rams Win Big in Move to Missouri," *Wall Street Journal,"* January 27.

Henderson, J. M., and Quandt, R. E. (1971). *Microeconomic Theory: A Mathematical Approach,* 2nd ed. New York: McGraw-Hill.

Hendon, W. S., Shanahan, J. L., and MacDonald, A. J., eds. (1980). *Economic Policy for the Arts.* Cambridge, Mass.: Abt Books.

Hirsch, J. (1987). "Big Business Under the Big Top," *New York Times,* October 4.

Hochman, O., and Luski, I. (1988). "Advertising and Economic Welfare: Comment," *American Economic Review,* 78(1)(March).

Hofmeister, S. (1994). "Appeal of 'Direct-to-Video' Grows Among Film Studios," *New York Times,* November 8.

Horvitz, J. S., and Hoffman, T. E. (1976). "New Tax Developments in the Syndication of Sports Franchises," *Taxes* (Chicago: Commerce Clearing House) 54(3)(March):175–84.

Hotelling, H. (1929). "Stability in Competition," *Economic Journal,* March.

Huizinga, J. (1955). *Homo Ludens: A Study of the Play-Element in Culture.* Boston: Beacon Press.

Hull, J. B. (1984). "Music Charts Move Against False 'Hits'," *Wall Street Journal*, February 16.

Hutheesing, N. (1996). "An On-Line Gamble," *Forbes*, 157(10)(May 20).

Ignatin, G., and Smith, R. (1976). "The Economics of Gambling," in *Gambling and Society*, W. R. Eadington, ed., pp. 69–91. Springfield, Ill.: Thomas.

Jensen, E. (1996). "Networks Blast Nielsen, Blame Faulty Ratings for Drop in Viewership," *Wall Street Journal*, November 22.

Johnson, R. (1984)."Applying the Utilization Theory to Slot Decisions," *Gaming Business*, April.

Johnson, W. (1985). "The Economics of Copying," *Journal of Political Economy*, vol. 93, no. 11.

Juster, F. T., and Stafford, F. P. (1991). "The Allocation of Time: Empirical Findings, Behavioral Models, and Problems of Measurement," *Journal of Economic Literature*, June, vol. 29.

Kagan, P. (1995). *Motion Picture Investor*, No. 145 (January).

Kelejian, H., and Lawrence, W. (1980). "Estimating the Demand for Broadway Theater: A Preliminary Inquiry," in *Economic Policy for the Arts*, W. S. Hendon, J. L. Shanahan, and A. J. MacDonald, eds., pp. 333–46. Cambridge, Mass.: Abt Books.

Kelley, D. (1985). "Cable Television Unshackled? The Courts Have Just Struck a Blow for Freedom of Speech," *Barron's*, April 22.

Kilbey, J. (1985). "Estimating Revenue Through Bet Criteria," *Gaming and Wagering Business* 6(3)(March):57.

Kindem, G., ed. (1982). *The American Movie Industry: The Business of Motion Pictures*. Carbondale: Southern Illinois University Press.

Klein, H. J. (1982). "Gaming's Growing Slice of the American Leisure Pie," *Gaming Business* 3(9).

Kneale, D. (1988). "How Wouk Epic Became a Sure Loser," *Wall Street Journal*, November 11.

Knight, A. (1978). *The Liveliest Art: A Panoramic History of the Movies*. New York: Macmillan.

Knoedelseder, W. (1993). *Stiffed: A True Story of MCA, The Music Business, and The Mafia*. New York: HarperCollins.

Konigsberg, I. (1987). *The Complete Film Dictionary*. New York: New American Library.

Koopmans, L. H. (1974). *The Spectral Analysis of Time Series*. New York: Academic Press.

Krasilovsky, M. W., and Shemel, S. (1994). *More About This Business of Music*. New York: Billboard (Watson-Guptill).

Kraus, R. (1978). *Recreation and Leisure in Modern Society*, 2nd ed. Santa Monica, Calif.: Goodyear Publishing.

Kronemyer, D. E., and Sidak, J. G. (1986). "The Structure and Performance of the U.S. Record Industry," *1986 Entertainment and the Arts Handbook*. New York: Clark Boardman.

Kronholz, J. (1984). "Pop and Rock Tours Like Michael Jackson's Grow More Complex," *Wall Street Journal*, July 9.

Kubey, C. (1982). *The Winners' Book of Video Games*. New York: Warner Books.

Kyriazi, G. (1976). *The Great American Amusement Parks: A Pictorial History*. Secaucus, N.J.: Citadel Press.

Laing, J. R. (1996). "Foul Play?" *Barron's*, August 19, 1996.

Landro, L. (1983). "Pay-TV Industry Facing Problems After Misjudging Market Demand," *Wall Street Journal,* June 29.

——— (1984). "Merger of Warner Unit, Polygram Angers Troubled Record Industry,"*Wall Street Journal,* April 12.

Landro, L., and Saddler, J. (1983). "Network, Film Moguls Blitz Capital in Battle for TV Rerun Profits," *Wall Street Journal,* November 8.

Lane, R. (1994). "I Want Gross," *Forbes,* 154(7)(September 26).

La Pointe, J. (1989). "Television Lavishes Money on Sports, But Does It Pay?" *New York Times,* December 3.

Lardner, J. (1987). *Fast Forward: Hollywood, The Japanese, and the VCR Wars.* New York: W. W. Norton.

Lawson, C. (1983). "Broadway Is in Its Worst Slump in a Decade," *New York Times,* January 3.

Leedy, D. J. (1980). *Motion Picture Distribution: An Accountant's Perspective.* Los Angeles: David Leedy, C.P.A., P.O. Box 27845.

Lessing, L. (1971). "Stand By for the Cartridge TV Explosion," *Fortune,* April, LXXXIII(4).

Levy, H., and Sarnat, M. (1972). *Investment and Portfolio Analysis.* New York: Wiley.

Linder, S. B. (1970). *The Harried Leisure Class.* New York: Columbia University Press.

Linfield, S. (1987). "The Color of Money," *American Film,* vol. 12, no. 4.

Lipman, J. (1990). "Movie Merchandising Takes Off, Bat-Style," *Wall Street Journal,* January 5.

Lippman, J. (1995). "Talent Agents Now Often Share Billing," *Wall Street Journal,* August 17.

Lowe, P. M. (1983). "Refreshment Sales and Theater Profits," in *The Movie Business Book,* 1st ed. J. E. Squire, ed., pp. 344–9. New York: Simon & Schuster/Fireside.

Lubove, S. (1995). "Major League Soccer: Can It Work?" *Forbes,* 156(14)(December 18).

Lyman, R. (1997). "An Endangered Species: The Angels of Broadway," *New York Times,* May 27.

Lyon, R. (1987). "Theme Parks in the USA," *Travel & Tourism Analyst,* London: The Economist Publications, January.

MacDonald, G. (1988). "The Economics of Rising Stars," *American Economic Review,* (78)(March).

Mahon, G. (1980). *The Company That Bought the Boardwalk.* New York: Random House.

Mair, G. (1988). *Inside HBO: The Billion Dollar War Between HBO, Hollywood and the Home Video Revolution.* New York: Dodd, Mead.

Mangels, W. F. (1952). *The Outdoor Amusement Industry: From Earliest Times to the Present.* New York: Vantage Press.

Manteris, A., and Talley, R. (1991). *SuperBookie: Inside Las Vegas Sports Gambling.* Chicago: Contemporary Books.

Margolies, J., and Gwathmey, E. (1991). *Tickets to Paradise: American Movie Theaters and How We Had Fun.* Boston: Little, Brown and Company (Bulfinch Press).

Markham, J. W., and Teplitz, P. V. (1981). *Baseball Economics and Public Policy.* Lexington, Mass.: Heath.

Marx, S. (1975). *Mayer and Thalberg: The Make-Believe Saints.* New York: Random House; Los Angeles: Samuel French (1988).

McDougal, D. (1991). "A Blockbuster Deficit; 'Batman' Accounts Show a $35.8-Million Deficit: The Film May Never Show Profit." *Los Angeles Times*, March 21.

McLuhan, M. (1964). *Understanding Media: The Extension of Man*. New York: McGraw-Hill and Cambridge, Mass. (MIT Press, 1994).

McLuhan, M., and McLuhan, E. (1988). *Laws of Media: The New Science*. Toronto: University of Toronto Press.

Michener, J. A. (1976). *Sports in America*. New York: Random House (paperback, Fawcett Crest/Ballantine Books, 1983).

Miller, M. (1991). *A Whole Different Ball Game: The Sport and Business of Baseball*. New York: Birch Lane Press (Carol Publishing Co.), and in paperback (Fireside) Simon & Schuster (1992).

Moldea, D. E. (1989). *Interference: How Organized Crime Influences Professional Football*. New York: Morrow.

Moore, J. (1996). *The Complete Book of Sports Betting*. New York: Carol Publishing (Lyle Stuart).

Moore, T. G. (1968). *The Economics of the American Theater*. Durham, N.C.: Duke University Press.

Muller, P. (1991). *Show Business Law: Motion Pictures, Television, Video*. Westport, Conn: Quorum.

Murphy, A. D. (1982). "21 Fundamental Aspects of U.S. Theatrical Film Biz," *Daily Variety*, October 26.

(1983). "Distribution and Exhibition: An Overview," in *The Movie Business Book*, J. E. Squire, ed. New York: Simon & Schuster/Fireside.

Murphy, J. M. (1976). "Why You Can't Win," *Journal of Portfolio Management* (fall):45–9.

Murray, M. (1956). *Circus! From Rome to Ringling*. New York: Appleton-Century-Crofts.

Nardone, J. M. (1982). "Is the Movie Industry Contracyclical," *Cycles* 33(3)(April):77.

Nasaw, D. (1993). *Going Out: The Rise and Fall of Public Amusements*. New York: HarperCollins (Basic Books).

Nash, C., and Oakey, V. (1974). *The Screenwriter's Handbook*. New York: Barnes & Noble (Harper & Row).

Netzer, D. (1978). *The Subsidized Muse: Public Support for the Arts in the United States*. New York: Cambridge University Press.

Neulinger, J. (1981). *To Leisure: An Introduction*. Boston: Allyn and Bacon.

Newcomb, P. (1989). "Welcome Back, Grace Slick," *Forbes* 143(10)(May 15):56.

Noll, R., ed. (1974). *Government and the Sports Business*. Washington D.C.: Brookings Institution.

Noll, R. G., Peck, M. J., and McGowan, J. J. (1973). *Economic Aspects of Television Regulation*. Washington, D.C.: Brookings Institution.

Oakey, V. (1983). *Dictionary of Film and Television Terms*. New York: Barnes & Noble.

O'Donnell, P., and McDougal, D. (1992). *Fatal Subtraction: The Inside Story of Buchwald v. Paramount*. New York: Doubleday.

Owen, B. M., Beebe, J. H., and Manning, W. G., Jr. (1974). *Television Economics*. Lexington, Mass.: Heath.

Owen, B. M., and Wildman, S. S. (1992). *Video Economics*. Cambridge, Mass.: Harvard University Press.

Owen, D. (1983). "The Second Coming of Nolan Bushnell," *Playboy* 30(6)(June):128.

(1986). "Where Toys Come From," *The Atlantic Monthly*, October.

Owen, J. D. (1970). *The Price of Leisure*. Montreal: McGill-Queen's University Press.

(1976). "Workweeks and Leisure: An Analysis of Trends, 1948–75," *Monthly Labor Review* (U.S. Department of Labor) 99(8)(August):3–8.

(1988). "Work–Time Reduction in the U.S. and Western Europe," *Monthly Labor Review* 111(12)(December).

Owen, V., and Owen, P. (1980). "An Economic Approach to Art Innovations," in *Economic Policy for the Arts*, W. S. Hendon, J. L. Shanahan, and A. J. MacDonald, eds., pp. 102–11. Cambridge, Mass.: Abt Books.

Ozanian, M. K., and Taub, S. (1992). "Big Leagues, Bad Business," *Financial World* 161(14)(July 7).

(1993). "Foul Ball," *Financial World* 162(11)(May 25).

Paris, E. (1984). "Ronald Reagan Is Not the Only Actor Who Made Good," *Forbes* 133(5)(February 27):154–6.

Passell, P. (1989). "Broadway and the Bottom Line," *New York Times*, December 10.

Peterman, J. L., and Carney, M. (1978). "A Comment on Television Network Price Discrimination," *Journal of Business* 51(2)(April):343–52.

Peterson, I. (1997). "Times Expanding Nationwide Distribution," *New York Times*, January 22.

Poggi, J. (1968). *Theater in America: The Impact of Economic Forces, 1870–1967*. Ithaca, N.Y.: Cornell University Press.

Pogrebin, R. (1996). "The Number of Ad Pages Does Not Make the Magazine," *New York Times*, August 26.

Pollack, A. (1986). "Video Games, Once Zapped, in Comeback," *New York Times*, September 27.

Provost, G. (1994). *High Stakes: Inside the New Las Vegas*. New York: Dutton (Truman Talley).

Puzo, M. (1976). *Inside Las Vegas*. New York: Grosset & Dunlap.

Quirk, J., and Fort, R. D. (1992). *Pay Dirt: The Business of Professional Team Sports*. Princeton, N. J.: Princeton University Press.

Quirk, J., and Hodiri, M. (1974). "The Economic Theory of a Professional Sports League," in *Government and the Sports Business*, R. Noll, ed., pp. 33–80. Washington, D.C.: Brookings Institution.

Raabe, W. (1977). "Professional Sports Franchises and the Treatment of League Expansion Proceeds," *Taxes*, (Chicago: Commerce Clearing House), July.

Read, O., and Welch, W. L. (1976). *From Tin Foil to Stereo: Evolution of the Phonograph*. Indianapolis: Bobbs-Merrill and Howard W. Sams.

Reibstein, L. (1986). "Broadway 'Angels' Often Settle for Glitz, but the Prospects for Profit Are Improving," *Wall Street Journal*, January 28.

Reich, H. (1996). "Why Can't the Arts Survive on their Own?" *Chicago Tribune*, August 26.

Rivkin, S. (1974). "Sports Leagues and the Federal Antitrust Laws," in *Government and the Sports Business*, R. Noll, ed., pp. 387–410. Washington, D.C.: Brookings Institution.

Robb, D. (1990a). "Paramount Says 'America' $17–18 Mil Below Break–Even,"*Daily Variety*, March 21.

(1990b). "Buchwald, Par Experts Wrestle in Profits Bout,"*Variety*, June 27.

(1992). "Net Profits No Myth, But Hard to Get Hands On," *The Hollywood Reporter*, August 17, August 24, and August 31.

Roberts, K., and Rupert, P. (1995). "The Myth of the Overworked American,"*Economic Commentary*. Cleveland: Federal Reserve Bank of Cleveland, January 15.

Roberts, P. (1995). "The Art of Goofing Off," *Psychology Today*, 28(4)(July/August).

Robinson, J. P. (1989). "Time's Up," *American Demographics* 11(7)(July):33.

Robinson, J. P., and Godbey, G. (1997). *Time for Life: The Surprising Ways Americans Use Their Time*. University Park, Penn.: Penn State Press.

Root, W. (1979). *Writing the Script: A Practical Guide for Films and Television*. New York: Holt, Rinehart & Winston.

Rose, I. N. (1986). *Gambling and the Law*. Los Angeles: Gambling Times.

Rosen, D., and Hamilton, P. (1987). *Off-Hollywood: The Making and Marketing of American Specialty Films*. New York and Colorado: The Independent Feature Project and The Sundance Institute.

Rosen, S. (1981). "The Economics of Superstars," *American Economic Review*, (71) (December).

Rosenberg, B., and Harburg, E. (1993). *The Broadway Musical: Collaboration in Commerce and Art*. New York: New York University Press.

Rothenberg, R. (1996). "Planet of the Apers," *Esquire*, 126 (1)(July).

Rothstein, M. (1988). "'Starlight Express' Out of the Tunnel?" *New York Times*, August 20.

Royal Commission on Gambling (1978). *Final Report*. London (July), Vol. 2.

Rybczynski, W. (1991). "Waiting for the Weekend," *The Atlantic Monthly*, 268(2)(August), and *Waiting for the Weekend*. New York: Viking.

Salamon, J. (1984). "Blue Dots: Selling U.S. Films Abroad," *Wall Street Journal*, May 22.

Salemson, H. J., and Zolotow, M. (1978). "It Didn't Begin With Begelman: A Concise History of Film Business Finagling," *Action* (Los Angeles: Directors Guild of America) 11(7)(July/August):40–9.

Sansweet, S. (1983). "As New Studio Starts Work, It Seeks Credibility," *Wall Street Journal*, May 23.

Scarne, J. (1978). *Scarne's Guide to Casino Gambling*. New York: Simon & Schuster.

(1989a). "The Rockford File," *Barron's*, February 6.

Scholl, J. (1974). *Scarne's New Complete Guide to Gambling*. New York: Simon & Schuster.

(1989b). "No Rockford Trials," *Barron's*, April 3.

(1992). "Lights! Camera! Money! Hollywood's Bonding Companies Are Feeling the Pinch,"*Barron's*, June 8.

Schor, J. B. (1991). *The Overworked American: The Unexpected Decline of Leisure*. New York: Basic Books.

Schumer, F. R. (1982). "More Than Merely Colossal," *Barron's*, June 21.

Schuyler, N. (1995). *The Business of Multimedia*. New York: Allworth Press.

Scully, G. W. (1989). *The Business of Major League Baseball*. Chicago: University of Chicago Press.

(1995). *The Market Structure of Sports*. Chicago: University of Chicago Press.

Seaman, B. (1980). "Economic Models and Support for the Arts," in *Economic Policy for the Arts*, W. S. Hendon, J. L. Shanahan, and A. J. MacDonald, eds., pp. 80–95, Cambridge, Mass.: Abt Books.

Seligman, D. (1982). "Who Needs Unions?" *Fortune* 106(1)(July 12):54–66.

Sharp, C. H. (1981). *The Economics of Time*. Oxford: Martin Robertson.

Sheehan, R. G. (1996). *Keeping Score: The Economics of Big-Time Sports.* South Bend (Ind.) Diamond Communications.

Sheff, D. (1993). *Game Over: How Nintendo Zapped an American Industry.* New York: Random House.

Shemel, S., and Krasilovsky, M. W. (1985). *This Business of Music,* 5th rev. ed., 1988. New York: Billboard.

Silberstang, E. (1980). *Playboy's Guide to Casino Gambling.* New York, Playboy Press.

Skolnick, J. H. (1978). *House of Cards.* Boston: Little, Brown.

(1979). "The Social Risks of Casino Gambling," *Psychology Today* 13(2)(July).

Smith, S. J. (1986). "The Growing Diversity of Work Schedules," *Monthly Labor Review,* U.S. Department of Commerce, BLS, November, vol. 109, no. 11.

Sorkin, A. R. (1997). "Soundscan Makes Business of Counting Hits," *New York Times,* August 11.

Spitz, B. (1987). "Is Collusion the Name of the Game?" *New York Times Magazine,* July 12.

Spring, J. (1993). "Seven Days of Play," *American Demographics* 15(3) March.

Squire, J. E., ed. (1983, 1992 2nd ed.). *The Movie Business Book.* New York: Simon & Schuster/Fireside.

Stanley, R. (1978). *The Celluloid Empire: A History of the American Motion Picture Industry.* New York: Hastings House.

Stefanelli, J.M., and Nazarechuk, A. (1996). "Hotel/Casino Food and Beverage Operations," *The Gaming Industry: Introduction and Perspectives,* Las Vegas, University of Nevada. New York: John Wiley & Sons.

Stern, S., and Schoenhaus, T. (1990). *Toyland: The High–Stakes Game of the Toy Industry.* Chicago: Contemporary Books.

Sternlieb, G., and Hughes, J. W. (1983). *The Atlantic City Gamble.* New York: Twentieth Century Fund; Cambridge, Mass.: Harvard University Press.

Stevenson, R. W. (1990). "The Magic of Hollywood's Math," *New York Times,* April 13.

Stewart, J. B. (1994). "Moby Dick in Manhattan," *The New Yorker,* June 27 and July 4.

Stigler, G. J., and Becker, G. S. (1977). "De Gustibus Non Est Disputandum," *American Economic Review* 67(March):76–90.

Swertlow, F. (1982). "How Hollywood Studios Flimflam Their Stars," *TV Guide* 30(18)(May 1):6–14.

Thomas, B. (1976). *Walt Disney: An American Original.* New York: Simon & Schuster (Pocket Books, 1980).

Thorp, E. O. (1984). *The Mathematics of Gambling.* Secaucus, N.J.: Lyle Stuart.

Throsby, C. D., and Withers, G. A. (1979). *The Economics of the Performing Arts.* New York: St. Martin's Press.

Trachtenberg, J. A. (1984). "Low Budget," *Forbes* 133(7)(March 26):116.

Trost, C. (1986). "All Work and No Play? New Study Shows How Americans View Jobs," *Wall Street Journal,* December 30.

Tucker, W. (1982). "Public Radio Comes to Market," *Fortune* 106(8)(October 18):205–10.

U.S. Congress (1976). *Gambling in America.* Washington, D.C.: Commission on the Review of the National Policy Toward Gambling.

(1989). *Copyright and Home Copying: Technology Challenges the Law.* Washington D.C.: Office of Technology Assessment, OTA-CIT-422, U.S. Government Printing Office.

(1989). *Survey of Home Taping and Copying*. Washington, D.C.: Office of Technology Assessment.

U. S. Department of Commerce (1993). *Globalization of the Mass Media*. Washington, D. C.: National Telecommunications and Information Administration, NTIA Special Publication 93-290.

U.S. National Endowment for the Arts (1992). *Survey of Public Participation in the Arts*.

Van Horne, J. C. (1968). *Financial Management and Policy*. Englewood Cliffs, N.J.: Prentice-Hall.

Veblen, T. (1899). *The Theory of the Leisure Class*. New York: Macmillan (paperback, New American Library, 1953).

Vecsey, G. (1981). "In Sports, Money Is the Main Issue," *New York Times*, March 16.

von Neumann, J., and Morgenstern, O. (1944). *Theory of Games and Economic Behavior*. New York: Wiley.

Wadhams, W. (1990). *Sound Advice: The Musician's Guide to the Recording Industry*. New York: Schirmer Books (Macmillan).

Waggoner, G. (1982). "Money Games," *Esquire* 97(6)(June):49–60.

Wasser, D. M. (1995). "Theater: Limited Partnerships Preferred Over LLC," *New York Law Journal*, September 8.

Watkins, L. M. (1986). "A Look at Hasbro's 'Moondreamer' Dolls Shows Creating a Toy Isn't Child's Play," *Wall Street Journal*, December 29.

Wayne, L. (1996). "Picking Up the Tab for Fields of Dreams," *New York Times*, July 27.

Weber, B. (1993). "Make Money on Broadway? Break a Leg," *New York Times*, June 3.

Wechsler, D. (1989). "Every Trick in the Books," *Forbes* 143(11)(May 29):46.

(1990). "Profits? What Profits?" *Forbes* 145(4)(February 19):38.

Welch, W., Burt, L. B. S. (1994). *From Tin Foil to Stereo: The Acoustic Years of the Recording Industry, 1877–1929*. Gainsville, FL: University Press of Florida.

Welles, C. (1983). "How Accountants Helped Orion Pictures Launch Its Financial Comeback," *Los Angeles Times*, May 15.

White, A., ed. (1988). *Inside the Recording Industry: An Introduction to America's Music Business*. Washington, D.C.: Recording Industry Association of America.

Whiteside, T. (1985). "Onward and Upward with the Arts, Cable Television," *New Yorker* 61(13)(May 20):45–87; 61(14)(May 27):43–73; 61(15)(June 3):82–105.

Winston, C. (1993). "Economic Deregulation: Days of Reckoning for Microeconomists," *Journal of Economic Literature*, (September).

Witchel, A. (1994). "Is Disney the Newest Broadway Baby?" *New York Times*, April 17.

Wyche, M. C., and Wirth, M. O. (1984). "How Economic and Competitive Factors Affect Station Results," *Television/Radio Age*, January 9.

Yaari, M. E. (1965). "Convexity in the Theory of Choice Under Risk," *Quarterly Journal of Economics*, May.

Ziegler, B. (1996). "Slow Crawl on the Internet," *Wall Street Journal*, August 23.

Zeisel, J. S. (1958). "The Workweek in American Industry 1850–1956," in *Mass Leisure*, E. Larrabee and R. Meyerson, eds. Glencoe, Ill.: The Free Press.

Zimbalist, A. (1992). *Baseball and Billions*. New York: Basic Books.

Zollo, P. (1989). "The Per-Program License: Broadcaster's New Cost-Cutting Initiative," *Hollywood Reporter*, August 29.

Index